ON THE ROAD TO QUALITY
www.pnsqc.org
36th Annual Pacific Northwest Software Quality Conference
October 8 - 10, 2018
Portland, Oregon

36th Annual Pacific Northwest Software Quality Conference 2018

On the Road to Quality

October 8-10, 2018

Printed from e-media with permission by:

Curran Associates, Inc.
57 Morehouse Lane
Red Hook, NY 12571

Some format issues inherent in the e-media version may also appear in this print version.

ISBN: 978-5108-7042-0

Printed by Curran Associates, Inc. (2018)
For permission requests, please contact PNSQC/Pacific Agenda at the address below.

PNSQC/Pacific Agenda PO Box 10733
Portland, OR 97296-0733 USA

Phone: 503 223-4630

www.pnsqc.org

Additional copies of this publication are available from:

Curran Associates, Inc.
57 Morehouse Lane
Red Hook, NY 12571 USA Phone: 845-758-0400
Fax: 845-758-2633
Email: curran@proceedings.com
Web: www.proceedings.com

Monday, October 8, 2018 Schedule

7:00-10:00 AM	**Registration and Wake Up with Coffee & Tea** Level 3 Skybridge Terrace			
8:00-8:15 AM	**Welcome and Highlights for the Day** Level 3 Auditorium			
8:15-9:30 AM	**Keynote** (Auditorium Level 3) Taking the SAFe 4.0 Road to Hyper Speed and Quality: How High Performance Teams Disrupt Their Marketplace and Drive Change Michael Mah, QSM Associates Inc.			
9:30-9:50 AM	**Break in Exhibit Hall** Level 2 Mezzanine			
	Level 3 Auditorium	**Level 1 Plaza Room**	**Level 2 Mezzanine Room**	**Level 3 Skybridge Room**
	Invited Speaker	***Automation***	***Security & Performance***	***People & Management***
9:50-10:35 AM	**INVITED SPEAKER** Testers and Teams on the Agile Fluency™ Path Diana Larsen FutureWorks Consulting	**Mobile Testing Beyond Physical Reach** Juan de Dios Delgado Bernal Mobica	**Influence of Architecture Validation on Performance Engineering** Krithika Hedge Amith Shetty McAfee	**Growing Engagement – How to Shape And Grow Your Team or Organization** Levi Siebens Ascentis
		How to Automate Testing for Next Generation Interfaces (BOTs, Alexa, Mobile) Andrew Morgan Sanjil Pillai Anu Raturi Infostretch	**Enhancing Product Security Design Through Product Performance Testing, a New Dimension in Testing** Vittalkumar Mirajkar Snenha Mirajkar Narayan Naik McAfee India	**Quality & Risk Management Challenges When Acquiring Enterprise Software Systems** Ying Ki Kwong State of Oregon Philip Lew, XBOSoft

11:30- 12:45 AM	**Grab & Go Luncheon, Quality Panel & Presentation SkyBridge Terrace, Dessert in Exhibit Hall, & Mezzazine Lobby**			
11:30- 12:45 AM		**Game On! Quality Mind Challenges** Oregon Room	**On the Road with PDX Bike Share** Level 2 Mezzanine Room	**Panel on Defining & Measuring Quality** Level 3 Skybridge Room
	Level 3 Auditorium	**Level 1 Plaza Room**	**Level 2 Mezzanine Room**	**Level 3 Skybridge Room**
	Invited Speaker	***Automation***	***Security & Performance***	***People & Management***
12:20- 1:00 PM	**INVITED SPEAKER** Future Proofing Your Software: Design Inclusively Michael Larsen Socialtext	**Automated Visual Regression Testing with BackstopJS** Angela Riggs	**Eliciting Application Security Requirements – It's a Complex Undertaking!** Bhushan Gupta Gupta Consulting LLC	**Why is Communication So Difficult?** Peter Hartauer QualityMinds GmbH
		Structure, Design, Extensible and User Experience – Foundations for an Automation Framework Hemant Prasad Abhishek Sharma McAfee	**Security Tsunami! SDL Fundamentals and Where to Start** SAFEcode.org Tania Skinner John Martin Intel Corp & Boeing	**How to Get There from Here: REI's Journey Toward the Right Data and Environments for Their Enterprise Testing Ecosystem** Bob Stuart James Wilson REI

2:40-3:00 PM	**Break in Exhibit Hall** Level 2 Mezzanine			
	Level 3 Auditorium	**Level 1 Plaza Room**	**Level 2 Mezzanine Room**	**Level 3 Skybridge Room**
	Invited Speaker	***Automation***	***Security & Performance***	***People & Management***
3:00-3:45 PM	**INVITED SPEAKER** The Dark Side of Test Automation Jan Jaap Cannegieter Squerist B.V.	**Effective CI Using Automated Quality Checker** Ruchir Garg Red Hat	**$, $$, $$$ Which QA Tools Are Worth it at Their Respective Pricepoints** Victor La Parametric Portfolio Associates	**Collaborating with Students to Produce High-Quality Production Software** Sean Murthy Andrew Figueroa Steven Rollo Western Connecticut State University
3:55-4:40 PM		**How to Fix "Test Automation" For Faster and More Valuable Quality Knowledge** Matt Griscom MetaAutomation	**On the Road to Reliability for Android Robots in a Physical World** Krishna Saxena Torin Perkins Catherine Lee James Menezes Bo Li Jesuit High School Portland, Oregon & Intel	**Diverse Teams are Essential for Quality Software** Rebecca Long Future Ada

4:50-5:35 PM	Speed Networking Room TBD	**High Maturity, But Yet You're Late?** Emanuel Baker Betsy Clark Angela Tuffley Adrian Pitman Software Eng'g Consultants, Software Metrics, CASG, Australian Department of Defence & RedBay Consulting	**Chaos Engineering And Testing for Availability and Resiliency in Cloud** Amith Shetty Krithika Hedge McAfee	**From a Controlled Chaos to a Well-Oiled Machine: Agile Develops Complement Each Other** Rajasree Talla New Relic Inc.
5:35-6:35 PM	**Networking Happy Hour with Poster Papers** Mezzanine Level 2			
6:35 PM	**Portland Dine Around Dinner**			

Tuesday, October 9, 2018 Schedule

8:00-8:15 AM	**Highlights for the Day** Auditorium Level 3			
8:15-9:30 AM	**Keynote** (Auditorium Level 3) Rise of the Machines: Can Artificial Intelligence Terminate Manual Testing? Tariq King, Ultimate Software			
9:30-9:50 AM	**Break** Level 2 Mezzanine			
	Level 3 Auditorium	**Level 1 Plaza Room**	**Level 2 Mezzanine Room**	**Level 3 Skybridge Room**
	Invited Speaker	***Testing***	***Technologies & Tools***	***Processes, Practices and Methods***
9:50-10:35 AM	**INVITED SPEAKER** Adventures in Modern Testing Alan Page Unity Technologies	**Is the Testing Role Relevant?** Sriratna Josyula Jonathan Li On Wing ZIllow	**Addition by Abstraction: A Conversation About Adding Value to an Automated Test Suite Through Dynamic Coding and Abstraction Concepts** Jerren Every Hunington National Bank	**A Case Study in Improving Cross Functional Collaboration** Dain Peter Charbonneau Parametric
10:45-11:30 AM		**Better Testing Through Process Automation** Rick Tracy Hapalion Consulting	**The Path Beyond Cucumber 3.0.** Thomas Haver Huntington National Bank	**Quality Assurance in an Agile Development Team** Michelle Wu Parametric Portfolio Associates

11:30-12:30 PM		**Risk Based Testing: Communicating Why You Can't Test EVERYTHING** Jenny Bramble WillowTree Apps	**Hardening Your Development Process** Nicolas Guini Andres More McAfee	**Automated Detection of Individual Anomalies and General Behavioural Changes in Timeseries Metrics** Tifany Yung Renato Martins Groupon Inc
12:30-1:45 PM	**Grab & Go Luncheon, Quality Panel & Presentation** **SkyBridge Terrace, Dessert in Exhibit Hall, & Mezzazine Lobby**			
11:30-12:45 AM		**Game On! Quality Mind Challenges** Oregon Room	**On the Road with TBD** Level 2 Mezzanine Room	**Panel on Driving Change, Agile Fluency, Transformation and Improvement** Level 3 Skybridge Room

	Level 3 Auditorium	Level 1 Plaza Room	Level 2 Mezzanine Room	Level 3 Skybridge Room
	Invited Speaker	***Automation***	***Security & Performance***	***People & Management***
1:30-2:15 PM	**INVITED SPEAKER** Software Test Architectures and Advanced Support Environments for IOT Jon Hagar Grand Software Testing LLC	**AI-Driven Test Generation: Machine Learning from Human Testers** Dionny Santiago Tariq King Peter Clarke Ultimate Software	**Gating Code Commits, Approaches Taken by Two Large Scale Open Source Projects** Jack Morgan Clark Boylan Intel Open Stack	**Talking About Quality: How to Define Quality Targets in an Agile World** Kathleen Iberle Iberle Consulting Group Inc.
2:20-2:40 PM		**The "Do Nots" of Software Testing** Melissa Tondi Rainforest QA	**Finding and Fixing Your Agile Organizational Potholes** Les Grove Catalyte	**Virtual Platforms Driving Software Quality in Pre-Silicon** Amith Pulla Intel Corp
2:50-3:30 PM		**Testing All the World's Apps** Jason Arbon Test.ai	**Using Open Source MEAN Stack Tools to Develop Web Applications and Maintain Big Data** Kavitha Naveen Rishikanta Mohanty Tektronix	**Changing Engineering Culture with SDETS** Sheetal Hulloli Santosh Sahu Mayur Premi McAfee
3:10-3:45 PM	**Break** Level 2 Mezzanine			

3:45- 4:45 PM	**CLOSING KEYNOTE** (Auditorium Level 3) The Lost Art of Live Communication, Get Connected to Your Customers Jennifer Bonine, TapQA
5:00- 6:00 PM	**Social & Networking – Skybridge Terrace Level 3**

Wednesday, October 10, 2018 Schedule

7:30- 8:30 AM	**Workshop Registration Opens**
Breaks 10:00 AM and 2:45 PM, Level 2 Mezzanine Lobby	
Lunch 12:30-1:30 PM, Level 3 Skybridge Terrace Plated service on the covered terrace, please dress for the weather	

	8:30AM-12:30PM	**8:30AM-12:30PM**	**8:30AM-12:30PM**	**8:30AM-12:30PM**	**8:30AM-12:30PM**	**8:30AM-5:30PM**
8:30 AM - 5:30 PM	**W01: Use Mind Maps to Increase Team Velocity and Commun-ication to Customers** Jennifer Bonine Tap QA	**W02: Unit Testing: What Every Developer and Tester Should Know** Tariq King Ultimate Software	**W03: Quality and Productivity Bench-marking, Estimating and Release Planning** Michael Mah QSM Associates Inc.	**W04: Software Testing for Mobile Embedded and IOT Devices Using Data Analytics** Jon Hagar Grand Software Testing	**W05: CMD+CTRL Hackerthon** Joe Basirico Security Innovation	**W11: Hands-on-Selenium** Alan Ark Duo Security

8:30 AM - 5:30 PM	8:30AM-12:30PM	8:30AM-12:30PM	8:30AM-12:30PM	8:30AM-12:30PM	8:30AM-12:30PM	8:30AM-5:30PM
	W06: Quality and Risk Manage-ment in the Acquisition of Enterprise Software Systems Ying Ki Kwong Office of the State CIO	**W07: Building a Testing Framework from Stratch** Tariq King Ultimate Software	**W08: Under-standing and Imple-menting Accessibility** Amelia Abreu UX Night School	**W09: Test Mobs in Theory and Practice** Jan Jaap Cannegieter Squerist B.V.	**W10: Testing Today's Web Appli-cations: Tools You Can Use** Alan Page Unity Techno-logies	**W11: Hands-on-Selenium** Alan Ark Duo Security

Table of Contents

Influence of Architecture Validation on Performance Engineering

Authors

Krithika Hedge (krithika_hedge@mcafee.com)
Amith Shetty (amith_shetty@mcafee.com)

Abstract

It's common for humans to err, so goes with software makers. We don't just come across performance issues they generally are designed into the product. We make reasonable assumptions when we design and write the code and that's where we stumble. With the increasing adoption of virtualization and the transition towards Cloud Computing platforms, modern business information systems are becoming increasingly complex and dynamic. This raises the challenge of guaranteeing system performance and scalability while at the same time ensuring efficient resource usage.

This paper exhibits an approach for analyzing the performance of layered, service-based enterprise architecture models, which comprises of two phases- analysis of workload parameters with 'top-down' propagation, and a 'bottom-up' propagation of performance or cost measures. It also aims at detecting and predicting performance problems at the early stages of development process by evaluating the software design or deployment using simulation, modeling or measurement. Considering the tradeoffs that come with security parameters and their impact on performance. People use terms "performance" and "scalability" as synonyms, this paper concludes with few highlights on how the two are quite different problems having the same symptoms.

Biography

Krithika Hegde is a Senior Software Development Engineer at McAfee, with over 8 years of experience in product development and Integration Activities. She has participated in various product life cycles and been a key contributor to various releases within McAfee. She is passionate about leveraging technology to build innovative and effective software security solutions.

Amith Shetty is a Technical Lead, at McAfee, based in Bangalore, India. He has over 10 years of experience in building applications in Microsoft .NET technology stack. He is experienced working on highly scalable, fault tolerant cloud applications with Amazon Web Services

1. Introduction

Nowadays, performance and scalability requirements have drastically increased to cater modern business information systems. It is often seen that the performance validation is pushed to the end of the release cycle this could result in uncovering problems that can jeopardize the original project goals and deadlines. Hence, it is essential to focus on performance at the early stages of development.

We often see that it is a dedicated (Quality Assurance) QA team's responsibility to execute performance testing. On the contrary, if everyone responsible for the development lifecycle contributes their bit to improve the performance then we can surely ensure that when the output gets to the dedicated performance analysis team it is already in an optimized state.

When it comes to the overall performance of a system these are few questions that cross our mind:

1. How well an application handles the incoming demand?
   a. How can we estimate the average response time?
   b. How large should buffers be?
2. Given a maximum acceptable response time, what is the highest demand the web site can handle?
3. How will you handle unexpected load?
   a. Do you drop additional request or downgrade response time for a higher throughput?
   b. What are parameters do you decide on the elasticity?
4. Which component is the bottleneck?
   a. Should it be upgraded or replicated?
   b. How does the transmission rate of the data affect performance?

2. Differentiating Performance from Scalability

It is very important to understand the subtle difference between performance and scalability. In an everyday scenario we often hear people saying, "the performance of the application is bad", but does this mean that response times are too high or that the application cannot scale up to more than some large number of concurrent users? The symptoms might be the same, but these are two quite different problems that describe different characteristics of an application.

Performance refers to the speed and effectiveness of system under a given workload within a given timeframe. We consider several factors when talking about performance efficiency (ISO 25000 Standards 2018):

- **Time-Behavior:** degree to which the response and processing times and throughput rates of an application, when performing its functions, meet requirements.

- **Resource Utilization:** degree to which the amounts and types of resources used by an application, when performing its functions, meet requirements.
- **Capacity Degree:** to which the maximum limits of the application, parameter meet requirements.

Scalability on the other hand, is the ability of an application to handle a sudden increase in workload. The increase could come from a surge in simultaneous users, a rising amount of data being processed, or it could also arise from large number of individual requests for access. The increase could be from anything that places higher demand on available resources. Scalability requires applications and platforms to be designed with scaling in mind, such that adding resources results in improving the performance. In case redundancy is introduced, the system performance should not have an adverse effect.

3. Use Case

It is very important to understand the subtle difference between performance and scalability. In an everyday scenario we often hear people saying, "the performance of the application is bad", but does this mean that response times are too high or that the application cannot scale up to more than some large number of concurrent users? The symptoms might be the same, but these are two quite different problems that describe different characteristics of an application.

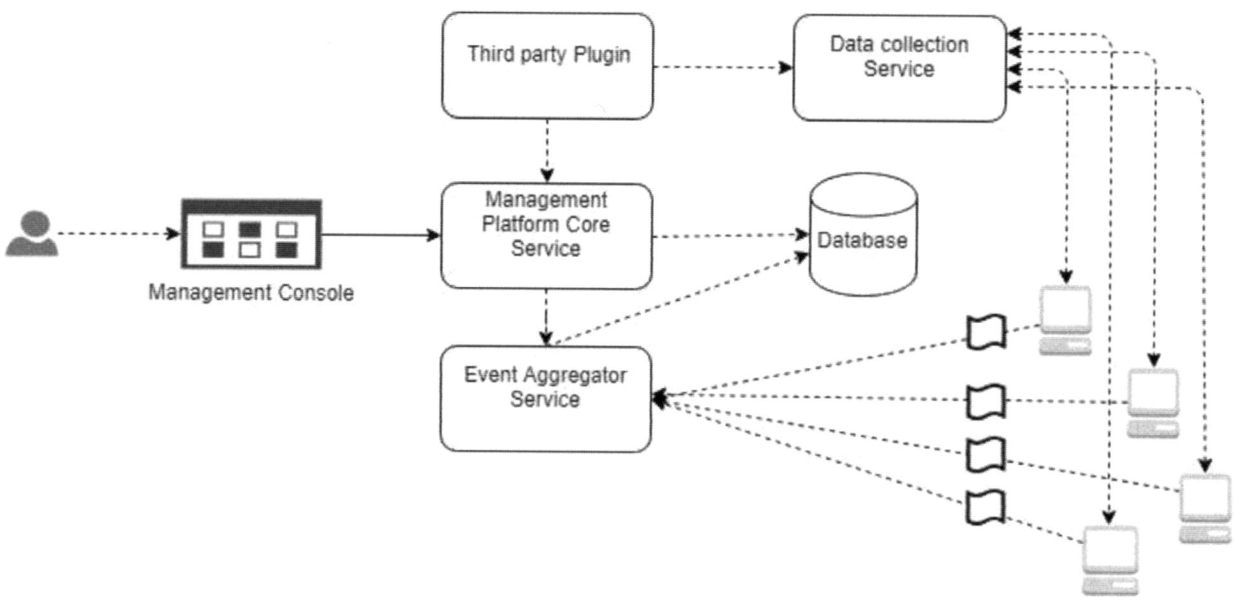

Figure 1: Management platform plugin workflow

Before we dive into the details of the above system it is important to understand performance expectation from the perspectives of different stakeholders.

4. Perspective on Performance Architecture

The views on architecture are aimed at different stakeholders that have an interest in the modelled system. Also, for the performance aspects of a system, many perspectives can be discerned, resulting in different (but related) performance measures

End User perspective: The user of the system would be interested in response time, which is the time between issuing a request and receiving the result. The response time is the sum of the processing time and waiting times taking into consideration the synchronization loses. In our workflow this refers to the time required to retrieve search results from each of the end node.

Process perspective: the performance consideration that need to be taken from the process perspective. It refers to the time required to complete one instance of a process which could involve multiple products, services etc., as opposed to the response time, which is defined as the time to complete one request. This perspective takes into consideration the entire process of input events arriving at the system, aggregation of these events made by other plugins and the think time the user puts in before triggering the search operation.

Product perspective: As the above example consists of platform management system with several plugins/products we would need to consider the processing time for a product for a given workflow, the amount of time that actual work is performed for a certain product or outcome. In this scenario the response time is considered without waiting times. Hence it can be orders of magnitude lower than the response time.

System perspective: This perspective focuses on the performance consideration for a given system in the workflow. It can be considered as the throughput, the number of transactions/requests that are completed per time unit.

Resource perspective: It is very critical to understand how well resources can be utilized, this refers to the percentage of the operational time that a resource is busy. In terms of performance utilization can be considered a measure for the effectiveness with which a resource is used. On the other hand, a high utilization can also be an indication of the fact that the resource is a potential bottleneck.

5. Analysis of Architecture Components

Now that we have a good understanding of the workflow and performance expectations, we can take a deeper look at service layers and implementation layers. By identifying common architectural implementation errors, many potential performance issues can be caught and fixed early in the development process, including excessive remote service calls or making too many database retrievals, which can introduce architectural problems like latency bottlenecks.

5.1. Detecting Performance Problems at Design Phase

Let's have closer look at the layers present in the current workflow. A service layer exposes external functionality that can be used by other layers, while an implementation layer models the implementation of services in a service layer. Thus, we can separate the externally observable behavior (expressed as services) from the complex internal organization (contained within the implementation layers). The implementation layer further relies on the infrastructure layer for serving the request that comes from the Service layers, like connections for database or network related operation between plugins.

In a layered view, analysis across layers is possible by propagating quantities through the layers. Which is nothing but the arrival frequency of the requests that come from the user. To analyze the load propagation between layers we need to first characterize our workload. This characterization can be done based on whether the load propagated through the layers is rhythmic and regular, whether it varies seasonally or by time of day, whether it is growing over time, and whether it is inherently subject to potentially disruptive bursts of activity. These workload characteristics must be understood for performance requirements to be properly formulated and for the system to be architected in a cost-effective manner to meet performance and functional needs (Andre 2008). The main components of the workload are identified by the amount of traffic that arrives at the system from an external source. Examples include HTTP requests, Web service invocations, database transactions, and batch jobs.

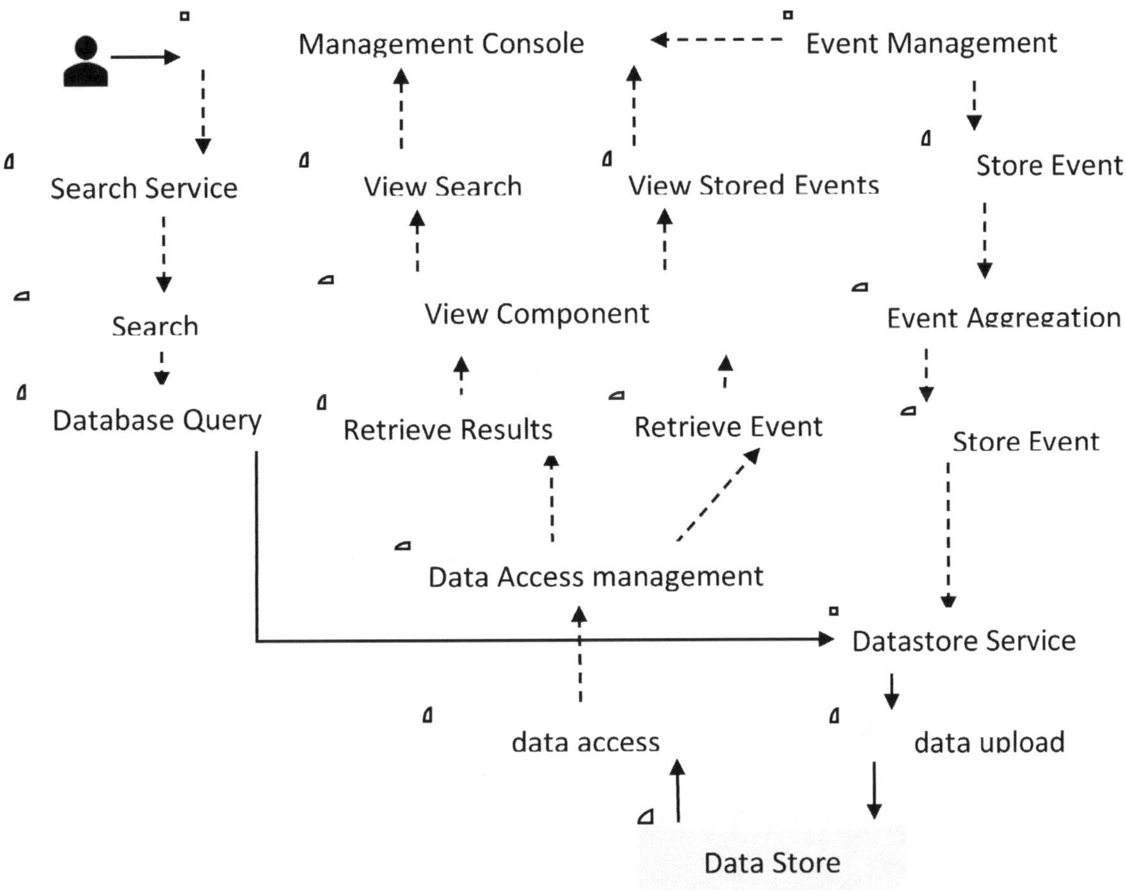

Figure 2: Layered software architecture

In our flow we can consider the arrival frequency of requests as the "demand" from the topmost layer which consists of the admin/ users. These requests are propagated towards the deeper layers of the architecture, yielding the demands of each of the model elements. Once the workloads have been determined, we can determine the effort these workloads require from the system resources. This effort can be expressed in terms of performance indicators: Throughput, System response time, Queue time for events, and Queue length for components. The throughput and the system response time indicate the overall performance of the system, while the other two metrics provide information about the internal behavior of the system, e.g., contention, possible performance bottlenecks, and starvation.

From the 'deepest' layers of the models, these measures are propagated to the higher layers. In general terms we can assess the performance of a system by the degree to which the system meets its objectives for timeliness and the efficiency with which it achieves this. We can measure timeliness in terms of meeting certain response time and/or throughput requirements, response time referring to the time required to respond to a user request (e.g., a Web service call or a database transaction), and throughput referring to the number of requests or jobs processed per unit of time.

We can use the throughput and response time values to create a performance profile for top down flow and bottom up flow of workload. Using this we can figure out how queueing times from the lower layers of the architecture accumulate in the higher layers, which results in response times that are orders of magnitude greater than the expected results which are derived during the profiling.

In the workflow mentioned above Events are analyzed by the user and the query to search for similar behavior on other end nodes is triggered by the user. As the system needs to trigger this search on all the systems in the environment, this search task will be queued to be executed on the end nodes. If the queuing time from the search task goes over the permissible utilization threshold then the response time to retrieve search result task is going increase drastically.

Below is the formula derived from Little's Law (Simchi and Trick. 2013) for application in Performance analysis scenarios.

Arrival rate or Throughput(λ):

$$\lambda = L/R \tag{1}$$

L- no of requests/users in the system R- Response time

Another useful relationship is the Utilization Law, which states that utilization is throughput times service time. We can derive **Utilization(ρ)**

$$\rho = \lambda S \tag{2}$$

If you have M number of servers,

$$\rho = \lambda S / M \tag{3}$$

λ- Arrival Rate S- service time

We also consider the response time which consist of the wait time and the service time can be donated as

Response time(R)

$$R = W_q + S \tag{4}$$

The response time in an M/M/1 queuing system:

$$R = S/1 - \rho \tag{5}$$

W_q-Wait Time S - Service time

Analysis of workload from top layers to the bottom layers:

We have taken a small subset of values from our experiment to depict performance evaluation on the model depicted in Figure 1. Below table shows the workload for services 's' in the Figure

1 in terms of arrival rate λ. The arrival rate depends on the frequency of requests coming from the administrators/users. We have scaled the arrival rates as arrivals per second.

Analysis of performance from the bottom layers to the top layers:

This shows the performance results i.e., the processing and response times for services and utilizations for resources at the implementation and infrastructure layer. For simplicity we have assumed Poisson arrivals (This means that the requests arrive randomly and independently of each other, with average rate λ) and the time between arrivals is exponentially distributed, with mean 1/λ.

Resource(r)	Service(s)	λ (sec^{-1})	S (sec)	R (sec)	U
Data Store	Data access	0.0382	6.0	7.8	0.229
Data Store	Data upload	0.0278	0.2	0.2	0.006
Data access Component	Retrieve results	0.0313	12.8	25.0	0.488
Data access Component	Store events	0.0069	12.8	25.0	0.488
Datastore Component	DB query	0.0278	0.7	0.7	0.019
Datastore Component	DB update	0.0069	0.7	0.7	0.019
Search Component	Search results	0.0278	1.2	1.2	0.025
View component	View result	0.0313	27.0	172	0.813
Event aggregator	Event aggr.	0.0069	33.7	44.0	0.234

Table 1

The results show that the queuing times from the lower layers accumulate in the higher layers. The 'view' component of the platform management application has a utilization of over 81%, which results in a response time of the 'view search result' service of almost 3 minutes.

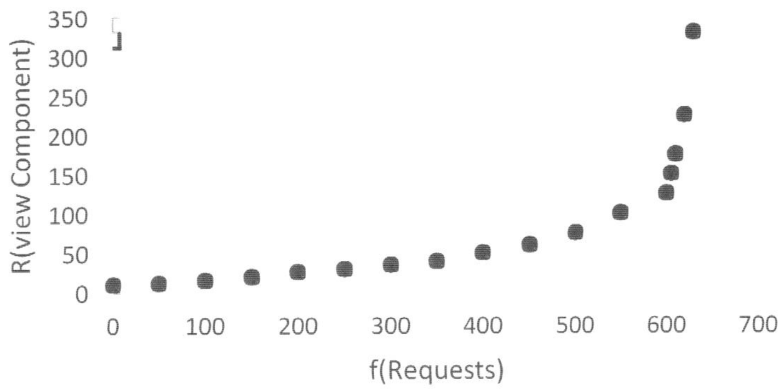

Figure 3: Arrival rate vs. response time

In the design stage these results help us decide the number of components required during the actual development phase.

There has been a lot of research in creating automated models and calculating performance at early stage of development (Balsamo, Marco, Inveradi and Simeoni. 2004, 295-310)

- Model-based software performance analysis introduces performance concerns in the scope of software modeling, thus allowing the developer to carry on performance analysis throughout the software lifecycle. (Cortellessa, Marco and Inverardi 2011)
- Evaluation of non-functional properties of a design (such as performance, dependability, security, etc.) can be enabled by design annotations specific to the property to be evaluated. Performance properties, for instance, can be annotated on UML designs by using the "UML Profile for Schedulability, Performance and Time (SPT)" (Bernardi, Donatelli and Merseguer. 2002,35-45). However, the communication between the design description in UML and the tools used for non-functional properties evaluation requires support, particularly for performance where there are many alternative performance analysis tools that might be applied. (Woodside,Petriu, Shen ,Israr and Merseguer. 2005)

As a good performance engineering process, we recommend predicting (at early phases of the life cycle) and evaluating (at the end) performance of an application, based on performance models, whether the software system satisfies the user performance goals.

5.2. Detecting Performance Problems at Design Phase

In section 5.1 of this paper we saw how we could analyze performance of an application at design phase. We would like to talk about an automated solution to evaluate performance that can be deployed in our development cycles, which could help accelerate the overall product performance. As part of this automated solution we add checkpoints that we consider are crucial in creating a feedback loop based on the inputs obtained during the runtime monitoring of system performance. We are all familiar with concept design patterns which defines good practices to design software. Conversely, the concept of antipatterns has been defined for characterizing bad design patterns. In this context, Smith and Williams introduced performance antipatterns (Smith and Williams 2002), which are bad design practices that may lead to performance degrade. We would like to state some common performance design flaws and how adding a rule check for each these performance antipatterns helps in creating a feedback loop to the software architectural models.

5.2.1. Scattered Information

The information required by an object is scattered in several different places. The processing required to retrieve this information from different sources results in application suffering from performance problems.

In our work flow as depicted in figure-1 the user retrieves information from the events table and the aggregation plugin then uses those results to query the table which has the results of search performed on the end nodes. The impact on performance is huge when the data is on remote server and each access requires transmitting all the intermediate queries and their results through the network. The above stated performance problem can be tied to the famous performance antipattern **Circuitous Treasure Hunt** (Smith and Williams. 2000)

In large customer environments we deal with huge result sets, one object invokes an operation on another object, that object in turn invokes an operation on another object, and so on, until the desired result is obtained. Then, each operation returns, one by one, to the object that made the original call. The performance of the systems will deteriorate due to such chaining of the method invocations among different objects. This chaining of the method invocations at different objects requires an extra processing to identify the final operation to be called and invoked, especially in distributed object systems where objects involved may reside in other processes and on other processors. The impact on performance degradation will be even greater, when every method invocation causes the intermediate objects to be created and destroyed. Allocation and De-allocation of memory on intermediate objects are performed frequently and consumes system resources.

5.2.2. Overusing database server for running code

In an ideal scenario it is more efficient to perform processing actions close to the data, rather than transmitting the data to a client application for processing.

In our workflow as depicted in Figure 1 we noticed that performing parsing of events and several other operations on the database end resulted in database server spending a lot of time in processing rather fetching data and serving client requests. As the database is a shared resource for both the event service and the search service it can become a bottleneck during high use. If in a cloud environment where Database Transaction units are charged the runtime costs would be huge as the datastore would be metered.

Moreover, moving the processing into computing resource which are scalable horizontally would always be better.

By doing so we should take into consideration of not moving the processing, if doing so can cause the database to transfer far more data over the network.

Rule check:

1. Add a check to monitor database activity, make sure to add rules that run a mixture of suspected scenarios with a variable user load. Telemetry data can be used to support this test.
2. Check the source code for DB activity that reveals significant processing but very little data traffic.

5.2.3. An excessive number of requests is required to perform a task

Small amount of information is sent in each message. The amount of processing overhead is the same regardless of the size of the message. With smaller messages, this processing is required many more times than necessary

Rule check:

Consider a software entity that exchanges a huge number of messages with remote entities.

1. Check for inefficient use of bandwidth, by checking if the software entity under inspection is sending high number of messages without optimizing the network capacity. The process node on which this software entity is deployed needs to be checked for utilization of the network lower than the given performance threshold.

5.2.4. Stuffing of the Session

User session during the web site visit can be tracked using the Session object. It generally starts with putting very little information in the session, but over a period the session object keeps on growing. At times unnecessary/redundant information is stuffed into the session object. The objects placed in the session will last till the session object is destroyed.

This impacts the number of users that can be served by the application at that instance.

Rule check:

1. Get details of what goes into the session object and filter out unnecessary information
2. Track objects that can be removed from the session when the usage is over
3. Check for objects that can be defaulted to request scope.

The above mentioned antipatterns are frequent causes of application performance issues. The teams usually start with the right intentions but over a period, things will start slipping. Some of the common reasons

5.2.5. Role of Concurrency Models on Performance

Performance throughput can be improved to a great extent by appropriately designing various concurrency models such as thread pool, thread-per-connection, or thread-per-request. The design should be efficient enough for threads to be able to process new incoming client requests even while other threads are blocked waiting to receive a response from a backend server. Due to the cost of thread creation, context switching, synchronization, and data movement, however, it may not be scalable to have many threads in the server.

Each of the above-mentioned concurrency models have the following limitations:

Thread pool—In a thread pool model, the number of threads in the pool limits the throughput. For example, if all threads are blocked waiting for replies from backend servers no new requests can be handled, which can degrade the throughput of busy middle-tier servers.

Thread-per-request— In this scenario a thread will be created for every incoming request from a client. Server can create a number of threads as per request. This concurrency model may not scale when a high volume of requests spawns an excessive number of threads.

Thread-per-connection— is the concept of reusing the same HTTP Connection from multiple requests. This model may result in server running out of threads if many clients connect to the server at once. If the server is slow in processing a client request, a single client may create many connections and threads on the server, further slowing it down. Moreover, if a server is busy processing a client's request, that client can open a new connection to send a new request. Also, the server has no way of knowing when a given (persistent) connection can be closed. If the browser doesn't close it, it could "linger", tying down the Thread Per Connection thread until the server times out the connection

Let us further consider the problem with thread per connection

- **CPU** – Thread switching is considered very expensive. The OS may switch between threads at any time and needs to save the entire thread state so that it can restore it when it switches back. For 10,000 threads, the overhead of switching takes up more than 40% of the CPU resources.
- **Memory** – Each thread would need a stack for all its function parameters, return values and local variables, which is large enough to prevent a stack overflow. If we consider a standard stack size of 1MB, for example, we will be dealing with 10GB of memory for 10K connections.
- **I/O** – We see that most of the server activity is I/O, like sending a request to another microservice or calling a database server. Therefore, at any given time, most of the threads will be idle, waiting for some I/O to return.

How the use of event loops helps dealing with above issues

In today's market, we have access to many technologies which have implemented a paradigm known as event loops. These servers use a single-thread which runs through a loop of CPU-bound code, using callbacks to manage I/O completion. In these cases, I/O is implemented using the operating system's asynchronous APIs. This method deals with all the drawbacks previously discussed:

5.3 Extraction of Architectural Performance Models from Execution Traces

Real-world execution traces collected can record performance problems that are likely perceived at deployment sites and usually triggered by complex runtime environments and real-world usage scenarios. By analyzing large-scale and diverse execution traces collected from deployment-site computers, performance analysts and developers can gain useful knowledge for system design and optimization

However, finding performance problems from real-world traces is challenging. The problems can be rooted subtly and deeply into system layers or other components far from the place where delays are initially observed. Performance analysts should spend great efforts to confirm the existence of subtle problems, and to figure out how they were caused and spread. Given many real-world execution traces where bad performance may be amortized over various underlying problems, such performance-analysis activities become harder or even infeasible.

To tackle challenges of identifying deeply rooted problems, we propose a new trace-based approach consisting of two steps: impact analysis and causality analysis. The impact analysis measures performance impacts on a component basis, and the causality analysis discovers patterns of runtime behaviors that are likely to cause the measured impacts. The discovered patterns can help performance analysts quickly identify root causes of perceived performance problems.

5.4. Extraction of architectural performance models from execution traces

The goal of performing architectural validation as mentioned in section 5 is to recognize potential trouble spots in the application runtime behavior that can lead to performance and scalability problems. To achieve this, we would need a solid set of architectural rules to be defined by the software architects.

6. Implementing Architecture Validation into Build Process

The goal of performing architectural validation as mentioned in section 5 is to recognize potential trouble spots in the application runtime behavior that can lead to performance and scalability problems. To achieve this, we would need a solid set of architectural rules to be defined by the software architects.

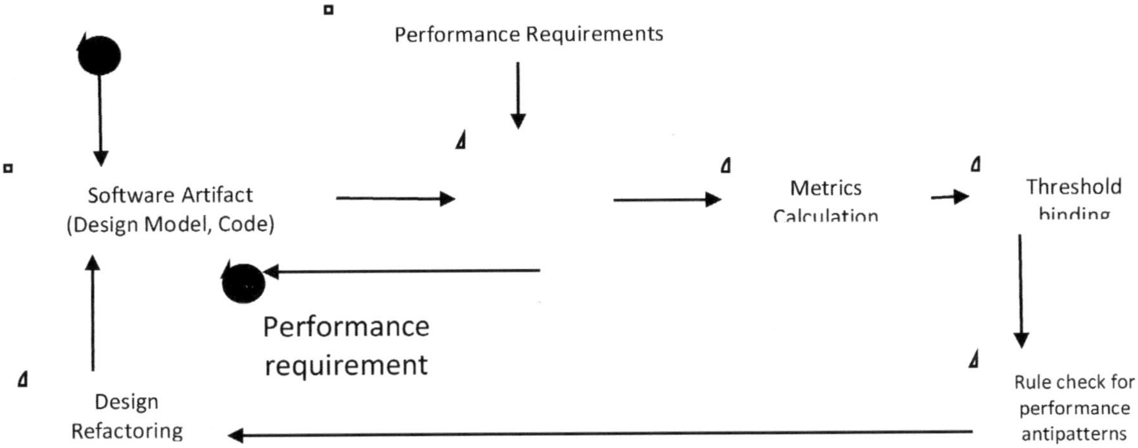

Figure 4: Performance architecture validation cycle

Our Proposed approach starts with the design model or existing version of the application, that does not fulfill certain performance requirements like the response time for a given service. To make sure the performance goals are met for the application it is required to conduct performance analysis. For an application that is in design phase, we can incorporate performance considerations using performance modelling techniques and for the application in development phase we can make use of performance monitoring methodologies to aid in improving the performance of the application. Based on the requirements gathered and previous programming experience we can add architecture rule checks to find the performance bottlenecks at an early stage and provide valuable feedback to avoid performance issues at later stages of the development cycle.

As part of the agile development methodology, it is required to test using stable system on regular and continuous intervals. Therefore, we would need to trigger automated architecture rule check framework within the build process. The results as with functional tests can be formatted as Junit or HTML reports. In case of execution errors we could use logs or tracing data. In addition to the results obtained from functional tests, performance-test results are analyzed and recorded for each build, and it is this integration of continuous testing with the agile ideal of continuous improvement that makes this method so useful. Developers can collect feedback on specific components in a sort of continuous feedback loop, which enables them to react early to any detected performance or scalability problems.

Choosing the apt tracing and diagnostic tools to measure performance and to determine architectural metrics can be substantially hard. The biggest problem with the current profiling tools, from the most basic to the most sophisticated is that they do not perform any meaningful analysis on the data collected. The most sophisticated tools merely perform statistical analysis on performance metrics and give average resources consumed by the different components/classes. When profiling large enterprise applications, the amount of information recorded can be truly overwhelming. It can be difficult and time consuming for developers that have to analyze the data produced by these tools in search of particular problems. Furthermore, even when developers manage to identify issues often they are unsure as to how to go about the issue.

Another problem with the current tools is that they tend to focus on identifying low level performance bugs that exist in the system. The tools, however, do not focus on analyzing the system from a design perspective. Thus, design flaws can easily go unnoticed. While identifying and fixing low level bugs in the system will very often improve the system performance, it is common that this is not enough to meet performance requirements.

To be able to deduce the run-time design from an application we need to identify the relationships that exist between the different components that make up the system. These relationships can be captured by recording run-time paths. There are commercial application monitoring tools, such as DynaTrace. Which uses its own PurePath technology which captures timing and context for all transactions across all application tiers. It has support for both Java and .NET environments. These paths maintain the order of calls between components they also capture communication patterns between the components. Such communication patterns can be analyzed to identify inefficient communication between components. We can also deduce performance metrics (such as CPU and memory usage) on the component methods. Below is a sample architecture validation rule snippet available through Dynatrace

```
▼<archival>
  ▼<rules rulesDashboard="RulesDashboard">
     <rule name="OnePurePath" description="Verifies that there is at least one PurePath" dataset="//purepaths
     <rule name="3APIs" description="Verifies that there are 3 APIs" dataset="//apis/api" verifyType="null" e
     <rule name="10MethodCalls" description="Verifies that the sum of all method call counts is not greater t
     source="count"/>
     <rule name="CallsHandleInternal" description="Verifies that there is a method call to handleInternal()"
     source="method"/>
   </rules>
  ▼<transactions transactionDashboard="TransactionDashboard">
     <transaction transactionDashboard="TransactionDashboard" pattern="*" rules="OnePurePath,3APIs"/>
     <transaction pattern="test.*" rules="CallsHandleInternal"/>
     <transaction pattern=".*NA=.*" rules="10MethodCalls"/>
     <transaction name="ByTraceName?testHomeHandler" rules="*"/>
   </transactions>
 </archival>
```

Figure 5: Architecture validation rule checks using Dynatrace

Tracing and Monitoring tools like Dynatrace have also enabled REST API which allows us to programmatically query for all the required information using Java.

In our management platform workflow, we encountered a major performance mishap, due to one of the third-party plugin which had few design flaws. Due to which the entire management platform was failing to function. To avoid such mishaps, we worked on coming up with a performance rule check framework with relevant architecture validation rules in place. The rule check framework would analyze a plugin deployed on the management platform and would monitor its interaction with the database and several other core services of the management platform. As this rule check helped maintain the overall performance of the platform, we would recommend this mechanism of including this architecture validation process as part of the performance engineering process.

Below is a graph with few response values extrapolated for the search result component that we have seen in figure 2. As seen in the below graph we see the difference in the response time of the search component has improved in the consecutive builds after incorporating few design changes based on the rule checks.

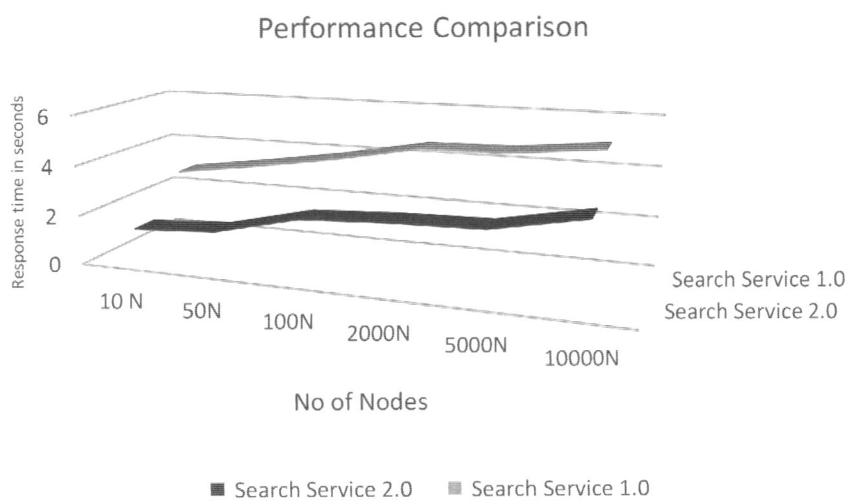

Figure 6: Performance comparison of search implementation between 2 different builds

7. Conclusion

In the grand scheme of things, you would need to take one of the three options to increase any given application's performance and scalability:

- Invest time in improving the performance of the application right from the initial stages of the development lifecycle

- Migrating the application or individual tiers to nodes with greater capacity- which is also known as Vertical Scaling.
- Instead of adding more resources, which is in the case of vertical scaling, a web application or its tiers are decoupled so that demand is spread out among multiple nodes- which is also known as horizontal scaling.

Which of the above three approaches should be considered depends on a series of factors, including the specifics of you web application, expertise of the team, initial design considerations of the application and what is more attainable given the resources you have in hand.

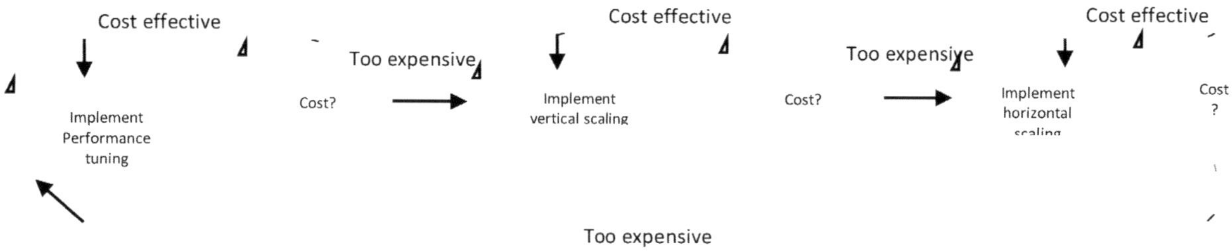

Figure 7: Decision tree for performance implementation

As depicting in the above figure, what factor is too expensive totally depends on the current state of the application. If the decision is made to implement performance tuning, it is very much required to a have well experienced team which can incorporate several checks right from the design phase, if that is not feasible it can be easier to skip to the next step of vertically scaling an application or vertically scaling its different tiers. By the same notion, if the service providers or data centers are unable to provision vertical scaling then it would be easier to skip to the step of implementing horizontal scaling on the application tiers or horizontally scaling tiers in themselves. If neither of the scaling options are possible and if there is an experienced team, sticking to performance tuning using the approaches mentioned in this paper maybe a better alternative.

8. References

Balsamo, S., Di Marco, A., Inverardi, P., Simeoni, M. 2004: Model-based performance prediction in software development: a survey. IEEE Trans. Softw. Eng.

Bernardi, S., Donatelli, S., Merseguer, J. 2002: From uml sequence diagrams and statecharts to analysable petrinet models. In: WOSP, pp. 35–45

Cortellessa, V., Di Marco, A., Inverardi, P. 2011: Model-Based Software Performance Analysis. Springer, Berlin

Woodside, C.M., Petriu, D.C., Petriu, D.B., Shen, H., Israr, T., Merseguer, J. 2005: Performance by unified model analysis (PUMA). In: WOSP, pp. 1–12

C. U. Smith, L. G. Williams.2000 “Software performance antipatterns”. WOSP.

Simchi-Levi, D.; Trick, M. A. (2013). "Introduction to "Little's Law as Viewed on Its 50th Anniversary"".
Operations Research. https://iso25000.com/index.php/en/iso-25000-standards/iso-25010/59-performance-efficiency n.d.

2000, Smith and Williams. “Software performance antipatterns”. WOSP.

ISO 25000 Standards. 2018. https://iso25000.com/index.php/en/iso-25000-standards/iso-25010/59-performance-efficiency

ISO 25000 Standards. 2018. https://iso25000.com/index.php/en/iso-25000-standards/iso-25010/59-performance-efficiency

Growing Engagement – How to Shape and Grow Your Team or Organization

Author
Levi Siebens

Abstract
Over the past several years there has been a shift for some organizations as they look to align their management philosophies with their shift to agile development practices. This has lead to different philosophies (Management 3.0, Managing For Happiness, etc) which focus on the employee and their engagement instead of viewing them as a machine to output some specific task. Overall, this shift has been a positive one which leads to better structured organizations that have higher performance and happier employees.

In this talk Levi will discuss why focusing on people over processes is a philosophy that works in any organization, regardless of the development methodology. In addition, he will go into the specifics of his experiences as both a Director of Quality and Engineering and as a Manager (Dev and Test) to give insight on what works well and what does not.

Biography
Levi has been through several different organizational alignments and changes over the past few years, including several mergers, acquisitions, organizational expansions and sustaining. His background in Psychology helps to dive deep into why specific management practices work best in a given organization. Levi is currently a Director of Engineering at XMedius.

1. Introduction
Creating an environment that individuals want to work in is a challenging thing to do for any organization. Measures show that in most workplaces, roughly 30% of an organization is considered to be an engaged worker. This means 30% of employees are passionate and feel like what they do matters to the company (Three Levels of Employee Engagement, Dailypay.). Often, this lack of engagement is created by top down control based management structures that many individuals do not want to be part of. This paper will examine the traditional forms of management and how they tend to fail in creating an engaged workplace. Then it will examine the philosophies and practices related to Management 3.0 which improve engagement in any organization.

2. Traditional Management

In most business environments there tends to be one of two management structures used which are based on a hierarchical / top down structure of command and control. Author Jurgen Appelo calls these two style Management 1.0 and Management 2.0 (Appelo, 2016, 6) recognizing that these two philosophies have built upon each other over the past decades. To illustrate their fundamental philosophy, let us look at some questions asked under these philosophies by high ranking individuals in an organization.

"How can we motivate our workers?"

If we tell our workers what to do, they will be motivated.

"How can we change the organization's culture?"

We must dictate what the culture should be. We need to tell individuals what to do.

"How can we change the mindset of managers? How can we get them to trust their teams?"

Simply tell the managers what to say and have a consistent message. Teams will come around as they are told to do the same thing repeatedly.

"How can we get teams to take responsibility?" (Appelo, 2016, 4)[1]

Tell them they need to be responsible.

"Notice that *all* these questions...are asking, 'How can we change ***other*** people?'" (Appelo, 2016, 4) Both the questions and the method of coming to answers focuses explicitly on how can individuals behaviors be modified through giving commands to others, similar to how factory workers have been managed in the past. To examine this further and see where this creates issues with engagement, let us look at the specifics of Management 1.0 and 2.0.

2.1. Management 1.0.

While not as common in the tech environment today, Management 1.0 can be seen where developers talk about being "code monkeys" (produce as many lines of code as possible) or testers who believe their job is to execute a specific number of test cases a day. As Jurgen puts it, "[the] common practice is that [organizations] are managed like machines, with their workers treated as gears and levers....[T]he organization consists of parts and that improvement of the whole requires monitoring, repairing, and replacing those parts." (Appelo, 2016, 6) Essentially, people aren't treated like people. They are something produce a specific amount of output and replaced when they serve their purpose.

When trying to answer the questions above, the focus is on modifying the individual pieces or replacing them. Want to change the organization's culture? Fire anyone who doesn't fit and

---

[1] Questions from book, answers are mine.

create bar a to ensure anyone coming in will fit. Want trust? Tell people they need to trust more. The change will always be in the modification of the individual much like modifying a cog in a machine.

This kind of management frustrates employees, is ineffective and reduces the employees desire to care about their job. It provides leaders with the illusion that they have control over individuals through short term gains in productivity, reinforcing that what they are doing is right. However, the only way to see continued "improvement" out of the organization is to increase the intensity on how behaviors are modified. It may look like increased demands on output or using fear to motivate employees which further frustrates and disengages employees. As the environment becomes more frustrating the employees engagement continues to drop in a negative spiral.

Overall, Management 1.0 does not give the freedom necessary to create an engaged workplace but can provide the illusion of productivity that makes leaders believe that what they are doing is having an impact.

2.2. Management 2.0.

Management 2.0 improves on the existing 1.0 model by recognizing people are not simply machines. "[Management 2.0] correctly understands that improvement of the whole organization is not achieved by merely improving the parts...[however], they prefer to stick to the hierarchy and have a tendency to forget that human beings don't respond well to top-down control and mandated 'improvements'". (Appelo, 2016, 7) Think of it this way, Management 2.0 correctly identifies that you need to treat people as, people. However it sticks with the Management 1.0 style of leadership where decisions are driven from the top down.

Looking at the questions above, a Management 2.0 philosophy would answer the question, "How do we change the culture?" by thinking through individuals and groups of people. But, once a change has been determined that change would come as a top down mandate of what the culture should be. To someone in the Management 2.0 style of leadership, every problem has a solution. That solution will take into account some context of the environment, but the actual decisions will come from those who are at the top.

While not treating individuals like a machine is a large improvement on Management 1.0 philosophies, it still runs afoul of the same top down management problem. Leaders (managers, directors, VPs, CTOs) define what and how everything should be done and employees feel they are simply there to do whatever their boss says. This creates the same sort of dissatisfaction and lack of engagement as individuals want to be part of decisions and participate in the creation of the environment they work within. In the end the solutions provided from the top down do not adequately address change in the proper way creating a greater sense of disengagement.

2.3. Traditional Management Summary

At the end of the day these methodologies (Management 1.0 and Management 2.0) take a "one size fits all" approach (Management 3.0 in 50 Minutes) of top down decision making. This does not create an engaged workplace as individuals want more than to be told how to do their work, how to define their culture and how to take responsibility. Many leaders default to these top down styles of management as it is easily understandable and seems like a simple answer for how to manage others. "See problem, determine issue with problem, fix problem" is a common way we work within in engineering. However, as HL Mencken says, "For every complex problem there is answer that is clear, simple and wrong." (Appelo, 2010, Loc 676) In this case, the wrong way of creating an engaged workplace is to believe that a simplistic top down management structuring will do this. To truly create an engaging workplace, which individuals truly want to work within, is a complex problem in which leaders need to understand the context of their environment and the people (Management 3.0 in 50 Minutes). Leaders must stop thinking about how to only tell individuals to change their behaviors and start thinking differently.

So how can we think differently? We can start by thinking of an organization as a complex web of interconnected individuals, as a system.

3. Systems and System Thinking

To understand what it means to think in terms of systems, we must first understand what a system is. Let us look at a few questions to highlight what is considered to be part of a system:

- *Are the people part of the system?* ***Yes.***
- *Are the processes within the organization part of the system?* ***Yes.***
- *Is the physical space (or distributed space) the people exist in part of the system?* ***Yes.***
- *Is what the group / team / organization accomplishes part of the system?* ***Yes.***

Anything which impacts the group of individuals that makes up an organization defines the system (people, processes, physical space, etc). With this in mind, let us compare visually our more traditional view of management structuring versus a more complex model.

3.1. Traditional Management Visualization

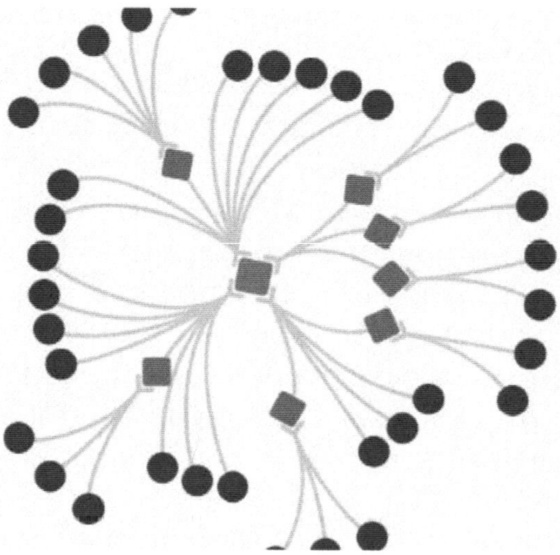

(Design System Intermediaries, Medium)

The diagram above demonstrates a more traditional view of management and organizational structuring. There is a leader at the center (CEO, VP, etc) who has leaders which report to them (Director, Manager) who have individuals who do the work reporting to them (QA, Dev, Devops, etc). The squares would be considered the leaders and the circles are considered the frontline employees. This is how most people think of their organization and the interactions within them. However, as the questions above highlighted, this hierarchical structure is only one piece of what goes into defining a system as a system is the totality of interactions, individuals and the environment they exist in. To better visualize a complex system, let us look at how a system model of a social network is visualized.

3.2. System Model of Social Network

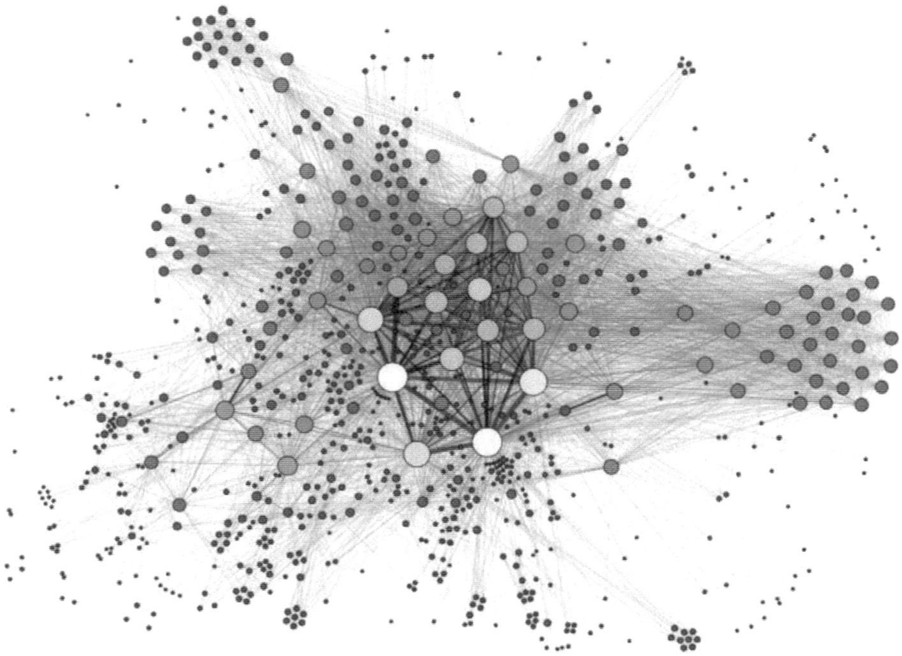

(Social Network Visualization, Wikimedia)

As can be seen here, the relationships between individuals are much more complex than a simple hierarchical diagram. This type of system level visualization which highlights all the interactions between individuals provides a better representation of what a system of people is like and how they interact. It is not simply a VP who interacts with a manager, or a manager who interacts with an Individual Contributor[2]. There is a complex web of interactions which go into creating an engaged workplace. Change any one of the nodes in the diagram and that will have a cascading impact which is hard to predict across the system due to its complex nature.

The complexity that occurs within a system is why top down styles of management are ineffective at creating an engaged workplace, as they reduce the interconnected group of people to a simple hierarchical structure. While that traditional view is much simpler, it excludes many aspects that are critical to creating engagement. It also has decisions flow from leaders which are not directly connected to areas of change. Visually in the social network system graph above, it'd be as if one of the center white dots attempts to improve engagement for one of the furthest / darkest dots. There would be an impact and a change, but the distance from the context and the complexity of the system will blunt the effectiveness of the change desired.

---

[2] Front line employee, or someone who delivers work.

System thinking requires thinking about the different aspects of a system and its interactions with an understanding and respect for its complexity. Management 3.0 takes system level thinking and provides some general principles and practices that guides us in creating an engaged environment and workplace.

4. Management 3.0

The goal of Management 3.0 is to use specific paradigms and practices to better treat an organization as a system of complex interactions. The core of Management 3.0 is system thinking, which Jurgen Appelo defines as "a problem-solving mindset that views 'problems' as part of an overall system. Instead of isolating individual parts, thereby potentially contributing to unintended consequences, it focuses on cyclical relationships and nonlinear cause and effect within an organization....Its main contribution is for people to concentrate on problematic systems instead of problematic people....[It] can give managers a more complete picture of their organization from various interesting but subjective angles." (Appelo, 2010, Loc 1599) In addition, it better reflects the complexity and interactions of different disciplines within the workplace (QA, Devops, Dev, Product) which are often considered to be silos.

In summary system thinking focuses on looking at an organization holistically to better understand the methodology and impact of making changes. It also focuses on the group and their interactions, not on individuals, as a recognition that a person's behavior is driven by their individual personality and the system they are part of[3]. Management 3.0 reflects these principles by identifying six aspects of any system that, when managed correctly, increases engagement without the top down structuring of Management 1.0 and 2.0. To demonstrate these principles, we must meet Martie, the management monster. The following sections walk through each of Martie's aspects detailing what the principle is and examples of how these principles can be applied to any organization.

[3] This concept is nearly identical to Lewin's equation which states a persons behavior is a function of their personality and enviornment (B = f(P,E)) - https://u.osu.edu/studentemployment/2015/01/28/bfpe/

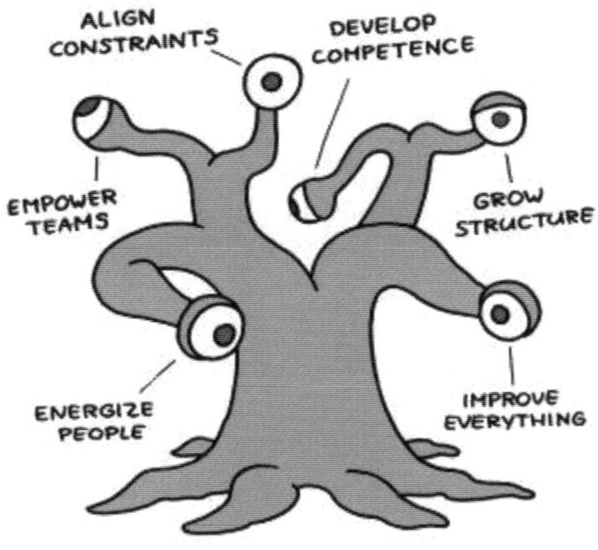

(Martie)

4.1. Energize People

Martie's first aspect is to energize the individuals that are part of the system. The question we are trying to answer here is "What motivates people within the system you're working in?" Remember, it is not just "How do I get Suzy to do her job better?" The right question to ask is, "What changes would impact the entire system to increase motivation and engagement for Suzy and other employees?" This is a very complex question with many different answers, however there are some guiding principles which can help.

To start with, you must understand some of the common needs and desires that occur for most everyone in a business environment. Jurgen Appelo provides a great summary of those items as what he calls 10 Intrinsic Desires. They are as follows:

- Acceptance: Need for approval
- Curiosity: Need to Think
- Power: Need for influence of will
- Honor: Being loyal to a group
- Idealism: The need for purpose
- Independence: Being an individual
- Order: Or stable environment
- Social Contact / Relatedness: Need for friends
- Status: Need for social Standing
- Competence: The need to feel capable (Management 3.0 in 50 Minutes, 19:58)

To increase engagement it must be understood which of these desires are being fulfilled and which are not. If all of these desires are being met within the system that you are part of, then the entire system thrives and engagement is high. If there is an issue with an area (one person has control over others, violating the desire of power) then that kind of behavior will cause issues throughout. If Suzy demands loyalty in every interaction, then people may simply agree all the time and never raise issues, "because Suzy said so." Or, everyone may start avoiding Suzy as she is not someone who can be trusted. Scenarios like this have much more complex causes and outcomes, but this example highlights the violation of one of the principles.

When there seems to be an issue within the system, leaders should step back and ask, "What desire may not be filled in the current system for an individual or individuals?" This helps to better understand the complexity of desires and their overall impact across the group of people. Interestingly enough, helping to energize people can be done in some easy ways when targeting specific desires. For example:

- Desire For Status / Acceptance / Honor: If only specific individuals in the organization are praised for their work, there may be a desire for Status (recognition) and Competence. So change the system! Distribute giving accolades by allowing people to give each other positive feedback. (Appelo, 2016, 23)
- Desire For Curiosity / Competence: Create structures that give time for learning (hackathons, discovery days, etc). Get individuals to share ideas on what they want to do and then let them work on it, *even if* it appears to not have significant business value.
- Desire For Order: Have a chaotic environment, but you don't understand why it is happening? Use a happiness index where employees can report each day how happy / sad / frustrated they are (Try The Happiness Index, Luis Goncalves).
- Desire For Power / Independence: Employees frustrated about a lack of power and influence, sit with them and use a technique like Dynamic Facilitation (Dynamic Facilitation, Co-Intelligence Institute) to let them feel truly heard regardless of what actions come out of the conversation.

Creating an environment of open conversation where solutions for problems come from those closest to the issues has been an area of focus for my current organization. Using the principles of dynamic facilitation (open communication, collaborative discussion, no single authority) myself and others have worked through a variety of issues that could have been driven as top down decisions. These ranged from how to structure agile, test methodologies and the release retrospectives. This kind of open discussion turned situations which were top down driven into conversations that empowered the individuals to make changes that were better than anyone in leadership could have driven. Leaders were still present, but their goal was to help the conversation be as open as possible, not to move to a specific solution or outcome. This built a positive cycle empowering individuals and creating independence.

There are more suggestions for how to address the different desires, but the key is that they are addressed in a way that improves the overall system. In turn, this increase the engagement of individuals.

4.2. Empower Teams

The second aspect of Martie, is ensuring that teams are empowered to make decisions. As Jurgen put's it, "Delegation of control is the only way to manage complex systems. There is no other option. If we didn't have delegation, the president of the United States would have to be the person with the highest mental processing ability in the entire country! Obviously, the United States have performed quite well without usually having such a person in the Oval Office." (Appelo, 2016, 11)

The key principle in empowering teams is that managers do not have to be the smartest or most knowledgeable in the system. In fact, it is often better to delegate authority down to individuals who actually do the work as this ensures the person who has the most knowledge of the situation is the one making the decision. Do we delegate all authority away for every decision? Of course not. But the goal is to delegate authority as much as possible to empower people to solve their own problems, creating better solutions than could have been done by a manager.

So how to do this? While it seems simple to say "Go forth and do the thing!" It is more helpful to create clear communication around what is being delegated and to ensure there is a shared understanding of the boundaries. This leads us to delegation poker.

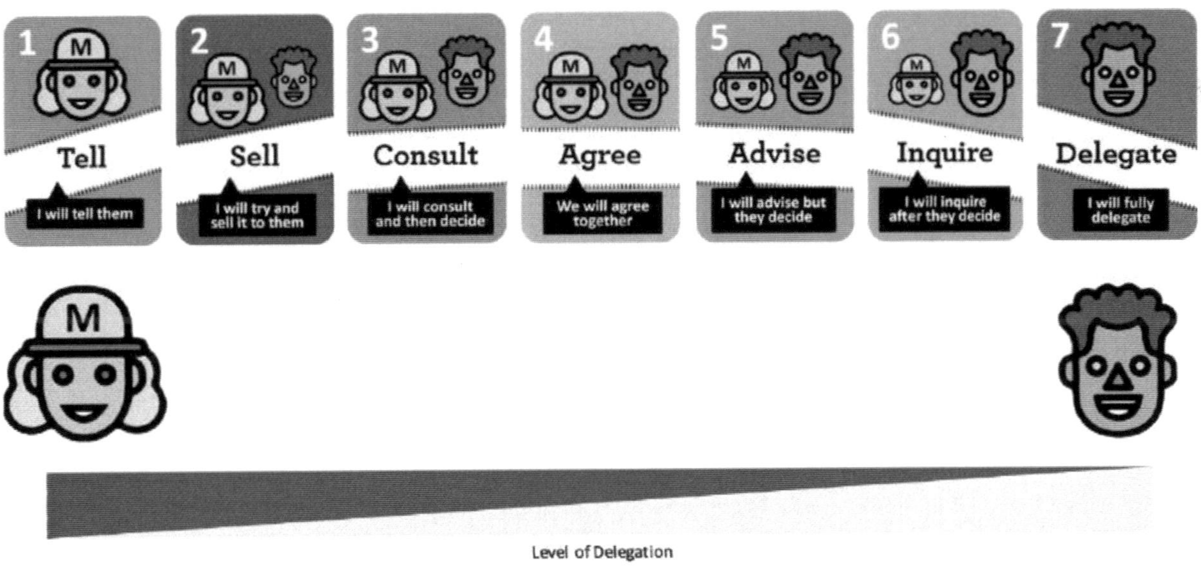

(Delegation Poker, Vivid Breeze)

Delegation poker is a way of having a group discussion around the responsibilities for a given set of tasks. It breaks down the scale of delegation from Tell (Manager Decides) to full Delegation (Employee(s) decide) and recognizes that there are several levels between those extremes. For example, there are times where the manager will Advise (Employee makes the decision, but the manager gives input). The Advise level may be used in adopting a new framework or tool within the organization. Looking at a different level of delegation, the manager may Sell an employee on the decision (telling them of a decision, but providing the reasons why). An example for the Sell level may be a change in the annual review process. Managers in this scenario are going to lay out the guidelines around reviews and demonstrate value to the employees to sell them on the change. At any delegation level, the key is understanding where the responsibility lies.

In practice using delegation poker has created a higher level of engagement in the organizations I've been a part of. Much like planning poker in agile, it creates a dialog to share what their expectations around the responsibilities for various work that needs to be done. This includes allowing the employee to challenge me as a manager if I am not giving enough freedom. I've used delegation poker with groups of testers who were trying to determine how a blocking issue could be driven to conclusion. I was attempting to delegate and empower as much as possible, but the individuals felt they could not address the issues on their own. With a little bit of conversation, we clarified that there was a difference in our delegation levels and reach a consensus that an advise position would help us move forward the best. In the end, I would give input but they would retain the accountability over the decisions being made. It empowered the team to move forward, provided the help they needed and allowed them feel more connected to the work then if I had solved the problem for them.

4.3. Align Constraints

Martie's third aspect is aligning constraints. Simply put, aligning constraints is answering the question of, "What is our purpose? Why do we exist?" Often the simple answer many people give is to make money and be profitable. This can be motivating for a team or organization for a time, but does not motivate long term. So to really align constraints and have a shared purpose across an organization there must be a shared set of values which both individuals and the organization are passionate about. Another way to think of it is, "We want everyone who is involved in a business to find it valuable." (Meaning and Purpose. Management 3.0) That value which individuals place on what they do and why they exist, is their purpose.

So often a purpose turns into a mission statement created after hours of meetings in a conference room with a few high ranking individuals in the organization (and we wonder why people aren't motivated by it?). These "mission statements" fall short because they don't engage the core desires for the group and do not give a true sense of the purpose for the business to exist. Thus they become just another statement placed on a piece of paper and hung on an office wall or cubicle to be ignored.

So how to do this differently? It starts with creating a shared sense of value. This means the corporate values should not be laid out by the CTO, messaged through directors, driven by managers and followed by employees. Instead, value should be created collaboratively (See Managing For Happiness On Value Stories) (Appelo, 2016, 78). Leaders should be part of the process as they are part of the system, but they should not be the owners, drivers and dictators of the overall value. All of the individuals working together to define these values leads to a shared sense of purpose and vision for the organization.

However, defining an overall purpose is only part of the process as once purpose has been defined it must be communicated. This is a second place where many organizations make a critical mistake. Often organizations focus is on creating a written statement that a person can read, memorize and post on a wall. The question is, is that the way most individuals remember information? The answer is no. As Jurgen Appelo puts it, "Use stories, metaphors, pictures or video" for goal setting instead of a mission statement." (Management 3.0 in 50 Minutes, 35:00) The use of a story or images gives a much stronger connection to the message being communicated and creates something everyone can remember.

The last mistake that organizations make as they attempt to align constraints is forgetting the most simple step. Ensure everyone understands and is communicated the overall purpose. Jurgen Appelo's test is this, "You should be able to ask any person in the organization at any time, what is it we are trying to do." (Management 3.0 in 50 Minutes, 36:16) This goes not only for what the teams and organization are delivering, but what their purpose is as well. So often the message gets communicated to a few individuals or broadcast in a large meeting after 45 minutes of presentations and quickly forgotten. Thus the message must be communicated clearly and often to ensure it has been communicated well.

4.4. Develop Competence

Martie's fourth aspect is about developing competence both in individuals and the system. While delegating authority and allowing individuals within the system to shape it helps engagement, it does not mean that every individual will develop the skills necessary to perform well in their role or within the system. One of the key places managers can help is to create structures and opportunities which allow employees to grow both in knowledge and skills. Just a few examples are:

1. Self Development (Learning On Own)
2. Coaching / Mentoring (Grow Directed With Others)
3. Training / Certification (Grow Through Courses / Externally)
4. Culture / Socialization (Creating A Culture Of Knowledge Sharing)
5. Tools / Infrastructure (Tools The Help Growth)
6. Supervision / Control (Monitoring Growth)

7. Management (Driving Accountability of Growth and Guiding Growth) (Management 3.0 in 50 Minutes, 40:45)

These different types of learning can be applied and customized as necessary to a system which will improve engagement and understanding. As an example, take the concept of a career model. Career models can be one of the most stifling things to an individual's growth if it dictates too narrowly how an individual should grow. However, in my experience, creating career models that reflect both how growth occurs (learning basics, developing / learning depth, mastery (Shuhari, Wikipedia)) and guides employees towards the depth and breadth of their field, can positively transform the entire system. Seeing all of engineering having a clear understanding of how to progress in their job while having clarity on their specific roles (Dev, SDET, QA, etc) allowed individuals to understand how they fit within the system while having the flexibility to grow in a variety of directions. The career model kept employees from feeling like cogs in a machine (Management 1.0) while providing enough structure for them to feel secure, which was transformational in my organization.

4.5. Growing Structure

Martie's fifth aspect is similar to developing competence. Instead of growing individuals competence, the focus is on growing the structure and environment around those individuals. The goal is not to create another meeting that people should attend to fill their day and feel "connected" to their team members. Instead, it is about creating structure that improves the overall communication across the organization (Grow Structure, Slideshare). There are numerous ways of improving structure, however there are a few specific practices which have been shown to positively impact an organization's structure and engagement.

First, there is the concept of a community of practice. These are typically "a group of professionals who share a common interest..., a common concern, or a passion about a topic." (Appelo, 2016, 113) They are a self organizing group and it is their passion for the area that pulls them together. Some groups even reference these as "communities of passion". (Appelo, 2016, 113) The goal is always to share information and learn from others that span different teams, business units and even disciplines (Appelo, 2016, 113). This can improve the overall system by improving the communication and rapport across the different areas of an organization. The passion for the topic creates open communication and often forms new relationships that cross organizational boundaries. These benefits all comes from something as simple as getting a group of people together around a shared purpose.

The best example I've seen of a community of practice was started by a peer of mine. The organization had a distributed set of SDETs who reported into development managers with no management connection to the quality organization. My peer took the initiative to gather those who were either knowledgeable in automation, passionate about automation or both to start informal conversations on how the organization could be improved. There was no specific goal that had to be accomplished and no direct oversight from management. This allowed the group to grow and focus on the issues most relevant to those delivering automation. The group was able to effectively grow and drive standards and frameworks across the organization because it was comprised of individuals who understood what needed to be done and was empowered to impact the organization as they saw fit.

A second practice which grows structure is the simple concept of a huddle. This is an informal meetup for peers (note, not managers) to get together and make decisions. (Appelo, 2016, 114) The discussions may spawn more formal meetings or the group may simply come to a conclusion without needing any additional follow up. But, the key is creating an environment where individuals are encouraged to communicate to one another without requiring a manager to be there and make a final decision. These informal peer meetings increase the cross team communication and better enable decisions to be made.

These are just two examples of how to improve the overall communication, and there are many other ways (guilds, shared meals, etc) (Appelo, 2016, 121). All of these are focused on creating a better structure where individuals communicate freely with one another.

4.6. Improve Everything

Martie's last aspect is improving everything. Those familiar with agile will be familiar with the concept of improving everything (continuous improvement) as a process for growth. In Management 3.0 this concept is the same idea as in agile, but applied to a complex system. Improving everything is a great way to constantly grow, however it only works well with a few guidelines. First, if change is constant then the system ends up in chaos and never falls into a regular pattern. This creates stress within the system and often on individuals by violating their desire for stability. Second, if the desired change is not understood and measured, then very often there will either be the wrong kind of change or a lack of understanding if there was effective change. A simple model for examining how to improve things is as follow:

1. Anticipate (Looking Forward, Imagining, Understanding)
2. Adapt (Look Backwards and Respond to change)
3. Experiment (Explore and get feedback) (Management 3.0 In 50 Minutes, 13:30)

These three principles encapsulate many of the frameworks for making change and continual improvement (Plan/Do/Check/Act (Continuous Improvement Models Learning Resources), Fail Fast (Continuous Improvement Models), etc). The key is to start with understanding where you are going (Anticipate) and where you have been (Adapt). Once that is understood, the experimentation is almost ready to begin. The key for experimenting is to explore some questions before starting the action. For example, questions that should be asked are:

- What is the improvement desired?
- What change will be made?

- How will the outcome be measured and understood?
- How can quick feedback be gained?

Once those questions can be answered you have the guidelines and data to run the experiment. This should be done transparently and with respect to the system (no random psychological experiments on employees just to see how they react). It all starts with understanding where you are at (past / present), where you want to be (future) and how to measure the change has been effective and it leads to growing the organization in a positive way.

5. Conclusion

"Adapt what is useful, reject what is useless, and add what is specifically your own." - Bruce Lee (Goodreads)

Thinking in terms of systems is a way of recognizing the complexities of an organization and working within it instead of trying to control it. It reminds us that while a system is made up of individuals, it is the interaction between those individuals and their environment which truly defines an organization. Yet, no theory or practice is ever perfect in quantifying the intricacies of any individual system. Nor will Martie's six aspects apply to every system equally. That is why we must always focus on Martie's sixth aspect (Improve Everything) and mind the words of Bruce Lee. Use what works for your system! Build on it, improve it and make it better than ever before! For those pieces that don't apply, discard them without a thought. By continuing to seek holistic improvement and building upon what works for *your* system, you will find a path forward that grows both individuals and your organization each and every day.

References

Appelo, Jurgen. 2016. Managing For Happiness. Wiley.

Appelo, Jurgen. 2010. Management 3.0. Addison-Wesley Professional.

Continuous Improvement Models Learning Resources. ASQ. http://asq.org/learn-about-quality/continuous-improvement/overview/overview.html (accessed Aug 19, 2018).

Continuous Improvement Models. Investor In People. https://www.investorsinpeople.com/continuous-improvement-models-four-great-options-for-you/ (accessed Aug 19, 2018).

Design System Intermediaries. Medium. https://medium.com/eightshapes-llc/design-systems-intermediaries-955ef18c9409 (accessed Aug 19, 2018)

Delegation Poker. Vivid Breeze. https://vividbreeze.com/delegation-poker/ (accessed Aug 19, 2018)

Dynamic Facilitation. Co-Intelligence Institute. https://www.co-intelligence.org/P-dynamicfacilitation.html (accessed Aug 19, 2018)

Grow Structure. Slideshare. https://www.slideshare.net/jurgenappelo/what-is-agile-management/46-View_5_Grow_StructureMany_teams (accessed Aug 19, 2018)

Management 3.0 In 50 Minutes. Youtube. https://www.youtube.com/watch?v=2LPkbGpWMNs (accessed Aug 19, 2018).

Martie. https://1qjpt15fhlq3xjfpm2utibj1-wpengine.netdna-ssl.com/wp-content/uploads/2015/03/Martie-scrum-300x271.jpg (accessed Aug 19, 2018)

Meaning and Purpose. Management 3.0. https://management30.com/modules/meaning-and-purpose/ (acccessed Aug 19, 2018)

Quotes by Bruce Lee. Goodreads. https://www.goodreads.com/quotes/30620-adapt-what-is-useful-reject-what-is-useless-and-add (accessed Aug 19, 2018).

Shuhari. Wikipedia. https://en.wikipedia.org/wiki/Shuhari (accessed Aug 19, 2018).

Social Network Visualization. Wikimedia. https://commons.wikimedia.org/wiki/File:Social_Network_Analysis_Visualization.png (accessed Aug 19, 2018).

Three Levels of Employee Engagement. Dailypay. https://business.dailypay.com/blog/the-three-levels-of-employee-engagement-and-how-they-impact-your-bottom-line (accessed Aug 19, 2018)

Try The Happiness Index. Luis Goncalves. https://luis-goncalves.com/happiness-index-agile-retrospective/ (accessed Aug 19, 2018)

How to Automate Testing for Next-Generation Interfaces (BOTs, Alexa, Mobile)

Author

Andrew Morgan (andrew.morgan@infostretch.com)
Sanil Pillai (sanil.pillai@infostretch.com)
Anu Raturi (anu.raturi@infostretch.com)

Abstract

Today's IT systems communicate with customers through multiple points of engagement and various interfaces, ranging from web, mobile and voice, to bots and apps like Alexa or Siri. These systems need to provide seamless hand-offs between different points of interactions, while at the same time providing relevant and contextual information at speed. To accomplish this, your project team must be able to successfully pair device hardware capabilities and intelligent software technologies such as location intelligence, biometric sensing, Bluetooth, etc. Testing these systems and interfaces is becoming an increasingly complex task — traditional testing and automation processes simply don't apply to next-generation interfaces.

This white paper will shed light on the landscape of these new, hyper-connected systems and their testing nuances, help you understand next-generation testing challenges that you need to address, and share the best strategies on how to effectively test them.

Biography

Andrew Morgan is the Director of Product Marketing at Infostretch. He is an experienced leader in strategic analysis, opportunity assessment, and roadmap execution. With his guidance and expertise, he has helped companies expand their digital initiatives to unprecedented levels.

Sanil Pillai is the Head of Innovation at Infostretch. He is an experienced engineering leader for digital and enterprise applications. He has built and managed offshore and onsite engineering teams, managed mobile projects for Fortune 500 clients, and has deep technical and functional expertise. At Infostretch, Sanil has established agile development and Continuous Integration methodologies, tracking metrics and monitoring processes to ensure continuous improvement in the development organization.

Anu Raturi is the Director of Infostretch Labs. He is an experienced engineering leader for digital and new tech applications. He has built and managed offshore and onsite engineering teams for Large Scale Companies as well as startups. At Infostretch, Anu has established innovative technologies in Automation and AI practices to ensure continuous improvement in the development organization adapting technical innovation.

1. Introduction

In today's hyperconnected world, connectivity is not limited to the mobile device alone. A plethora of smart devices and variety of sensors have expanded the connected ecosystem. Applications are increasingly leveraging data collected from peripherals like camera, BLE (Bluetooth Low Energy), etc. to add new capabilities. Testing such new age applications is challenging as current testing frameworks are not capable of testing the end-to-end functionality of such applications. Today, the enterprises are no longer confined to mobile and web presence alone to connect with customers. Consumers have shifted to smart devices and wearables and expect the companies to serve them on all the channels. Hence, it has become mandatory for enterprises to have an omnichannel presence so that they can reach out to maximum number of consumers. Rising consumer expectations and new business models like Phygital – 'Seamless integration of online and physical channels' have led enterprises to develop applications across a range of new interfaces such as wearable devices, chatbots, voice bots, virtual reality, smart TV applications, etc.

Today, applications have become the face of the organization to interact with their customers. So while developing these applications, it is equally important to ensure that these applications work perfectly. Any service failure due to undetected defects during the development and testing phase is a huge reputation risk and can harm the brand image of the organization. In this white paper, we look at the various challenges encountered by enterprises to ensure that the new age applications are able to function correctly. This white paper discusses approaches to overcome the testing challenges posed by the addition of inputs from peripherals like camera, Touch ID, Apple Pay, GPS, BLE, etc.

This white paper also defines the approach to test chatbots and voice bots which have gained tremendous adoption in the recent years. Chatbots are now becoming common and are now available on all major platforms such as Skype, Facebook, Slack, etc. Similarly, adoption of voice assistants like Amazon Echo and Google Home has also increased multifold. This has compelled the enterprises to reach out to their customers through these interfaces. This white paper discusses the challenges faced while testing these bots as well as defines the major factors to be considered while testing them.

2. Mobile Automation

Agile practices and DevOps have put Test Automation into a very different ball game from an automation coverage perspective. Higher coverage will definitely help faster release of better, quality products.

Mobile technology has made giant leaps with hardware capabilities including faster CPUs, larger memory and built-in sensors. With customers going digital, technology change has created new business models as well as new use cases around leveraging new hardware capabilities. Almost all mobile applications have at least one feature using device hardware capabilities. Popular frameworks like Appium have limitations in automating test scenarios involving mobile hardware, sensors etc.

A couple of scenarios involving device hardware like camera, Bluetooth, touch sensor is mentioned below:

- Check deposit features using mobile banking application enables the user to deposit check by capturing check image using camera. Data like the amount, payee, etc. is captured using OCR (Optical Character Recognition). Testing of this feature includes scenarios like scanning a check with a different amount, different handwriting or maybe a blank check. Automated end-to-end scenarios coupled with different test data can validate the functioning of the application across multiple devices and operating systems combinations. There is also a need to test using actual devices and cloud devices. While testing such applications on cloud-based devices, performing actions like putting different checks in front of device camera for scanning is necessary.
- Fitness applications connect with various BLE peripherals like heart rate monitor, temperature sensor, activity tracker, etc. Apart from Bluetooth connectivity related scenarios, it is important to verify the application's behavior for different test data values e.g. application behavior such as a case of abnormal heart rate. It is difficult to simulate scenarios involving different combinations of BLE peripheral events coupled with varying data for cloud-based devices.

  Some applications might be using device's biometric authentication system (i.e. Apple's Touch ID). Testing of such applications may include scenarios like how the app behaves in cases of successful and unsuccessful biometric authentication on devices without having biometric hardware.

2.1. Infostretch Mobile Automation Framework

Infostretch has developed a Mobile Automation Framework to help customers automate test scenarios involving device hardware. This solution works for real devices as well as cloud devices. Infostretch Mobile Automation Framework doesn't need application source code. Infostretch Mobile Automation Framework works on an application binary. Also, the framework can accept commands from any automation script and hence can be used in conjunction with any user interface (UI) based test framework, enabling customers to achieve highest level of test automation.

Solution Overview

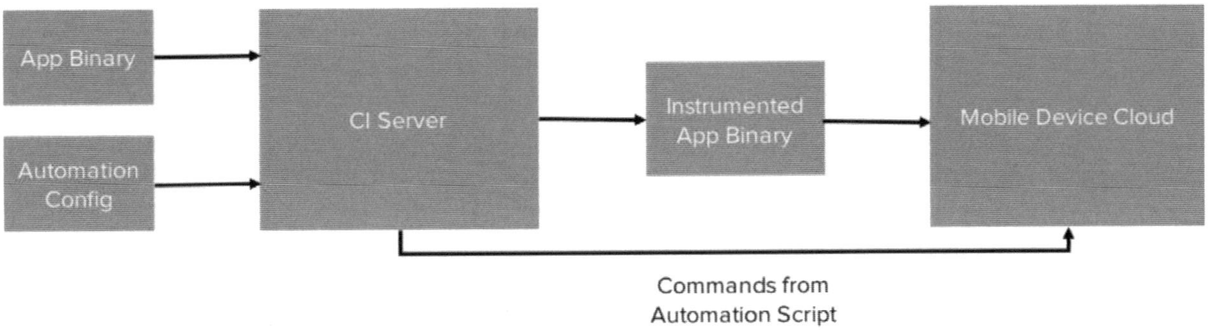

Diagram: Overview of the process flow for integrating and optimizing Mobile Automation

While writing the automation project, the peripherals that are required to be tested using the Mobile Automation Library are specified in the Project Configuration file. Based on the peripherals specified, the continuous integration (CI) server will prepare a customized mobile test automation library. This custom library is then integrated with the application under test. This application is then installed on actual devices or cloud-based devices for test case execution. Once the test suite is triggered, automation script will send command to Mobile Automation Library to simulate different hardware / sensor conditions based on the test case requirement.

Peripherals currently being supported in the Mobile Automation Library are:

- Camera
- Touch ID (Fingerprint-based authentication)
- Apple Pay (Biometric authentication for payments)
- GPS (Location Coordinates)
- BLE (Bluetooth Low Energy)
- System Date & Time

2.2. Mobile Automation Architecture

Mobile Automation Library's capability of simulating various hardware conditions is the heart of the framework. This library gets injected in the application binary (source code not required) at runtime, just before the test suite is triggered by CI. The injected library monitors the system calls and messages between the OS & application. The library gets commands from an automation script via REST API or Socket Communication and then changes or spoofs the data or conditions based on the test case execution.

A high-level diagram below explains the working of the solution:

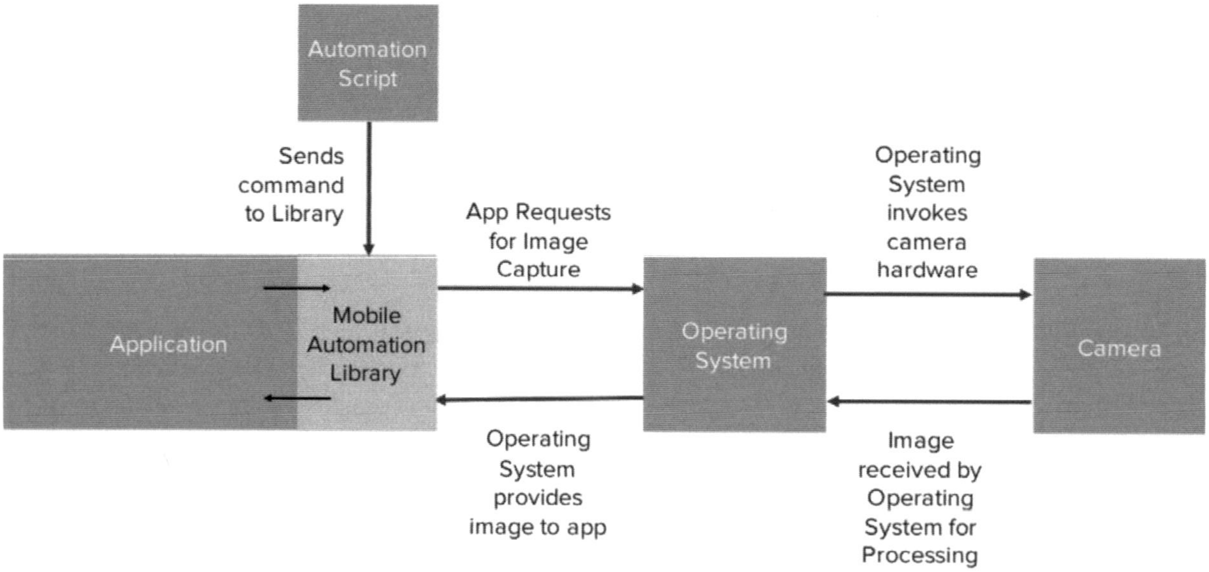

Diagram: Application-Hardware Communication Flow

The diagram above depicts how an application requests an image from the camera peripheral and how the request gets fulfilled subsequently. The application requests the operating system to capture an image. The operating system uses camera hardware to capture a picture, process it and then returns it back to the application. Mobile Automation Library constantly monitors the communication between the application and operating system regarding camera capture operation. While running the test automation script, whenever the operating system will capture an image and send it to application under test, the Mobile Automation Library will replace that image with a simulated image. The application will always get our simulated image which will be appropriate for the automation scenario. By using this approach, we can provide images of different checks covering various test data as required by test scenario.

3. Automated Bot Testing

3.1. Overview

The term "bot" refers to both chatbots as well as voice-based bots. It represents the automated technology that understands user's queries and then responds accordingly or performs an action. If I am interacting with a financial assistant bot and ask, "What is my net worth today?", the bot will be able to understand what my intent was and then provide the corresponding figure as the response.

Before we move to testing of bots, we will discuss the common concepts and terminologies required for understanding. In the industry, bots can be classified into three types:

- Chatbots
- Voice Bots
- Hybrid Bots

Chatbots: They interact with users through text-based messages. Popular channels of chatbots are Facebook Messenger, Skype, Slack, SMS, etc.

Voice Bots: They interact with user using voice-based responses. Popular channels of voice bots are Amazon Echo (Alexa), Siri, Google Home, etc.

Hybrid Bots: They react to users' questions using both text or voice. Very limited number of bots are available in the market that have capabilities of replying using text as well as voice. In near future, industries will see a wider adoption of such bots that allow users to communicate using both types of interactions – text and voice.

Bots cannot only answer questions posed by the users but can also initiate proactive communication (text/voice enabled) based on certain predefined triggers. For example:

- A weather bot would provide you the weather forecast for the day every morning at 6:00 am.
- A finance bot would alert you whenever your stock has reached to your defined level.

3.2. Need for Automated Testing of Bots:

Manual testing is time consuming and costly: Testing the bot manually is a cumbersome and time-consuming task due to the different flows created in the decision table defined for bot's responses. For example, take a simple bot which takes five steps to finish a transaction. In that decision flow, each step has four different options, and further flow is limited, there would be 256 unique flows which would need to be tested. We already know the limitations of the manual testing as it creates boredom and is often error prone.

Lack of Automation Framework: Bot development platforms don't provide automated testing capabilities. Current automation frameworks - e.g. Selenium provides limited options for testing of the bot.

3.3. Automated Testing of Bots:

Let's define "What" to test for the bot. We will confine our scope to the chatbot and voice bot only, as the hybrid bot is the mix of these two bots.

Types of testing for bots:

- Core Testing
- Peripheral Testing

Core Testing: While testing any kind of bot - irrespective of its type (chat/voice/hybrid), a few core parameters should be tested to ensure that the bot is able to converse effectively with the users.

Understanding User Intent: Success of any bot relies on right understanding on what the user is trying to say. User converses with the bot using natural language, so, by processing the user's utterances, the bot must be able to understand the user's intent. So, when the user asks – "who won the Super Bowl game last year?", the bot should be able to identify that the user's intent is to "know the winning team".

Formulating Appropriate Response: Another important aspect of the core testing is ensuring bot's response is understandable by the users. We need to test the bot's response when a specific intent has been triggered. So, taking the example above, against the intent of "knowing winning team", the bot's response must be to return the correct winning team information using natural language. If the user has asked for last year's winning team, the bot should respond with the name of the 2017 Super Bowl Championship winning team. So, we need to verify that the bot's response is in line with the user's intent.

Peripheral Testing: This testing is specific to the type of bot under test. There would be different parameters to be tested for chatbot vs. voice bot. A list of parameters is shown below in the table. Peripheral testing is equally important as core testing, as it is a significant contributor in ensuring quality around overall user experience while interacting with bots.

3.4. Factors to Be Tested for Bots:

Factors to be tested for chatbots:

1. Different Response – Same Query:
   Smart bots would react differently to the same query. When a user mentions "thanks" it would reply as – "Welcome" or "My Pleasure" or "No problem"
2. The bot's understanding of Intents:
   Different users ask the same query in different ways. For example, User 1 asks – "Growth of my portfolio" whereas User 2 asks "Percentage change in my portfolio"

3. Typo Errors Understanding:
   How far a bot can understand the typo error from a user without polluting with other intent.
4. Response time from the bot:
   How much time your bot is taking to respond back to your user's queries. Timeout defined for the bot response must also be aligned to that during automation
5. Multiple Queries in single sentence:
   How does your bot handle multiple queries in single statement? User asks – Show me the suspicious transactions value and total loss in 2017
6. Mixed Languages Query:
   Can your bot understand the multiple languages that has been asked? User may write - Combien avez-vous facturé pour mon POS system?

Factors to be tested for voice bot:

1. Different accents, gender:
   How does a bot behave for different accents & gender combinations - American female, British male?
2. Same meaning different utterance:
   Yes, yeah, true, exactly, certainly, etc. can be used interchangeably. The bot must understand them.
3. Different pronunciations:
   People often pronounce "assessory" instead of accessory – does your bot understand the essence of user's intention?
4. Punctuations:
   How bot interprets the punctuations: Woman, without her man, is helpless – vs – Woman! Without her, man is helpless?
5. Background Noise:
   Check for the effect of noise on the bot's capability to understand user's intent.
6. User speaking at distance:
   Effect of user speaking from distance, or in case of listening device being stationary (e.g. Echo) and user is moving and speaking – how does that impact bot's behavior?

3.5. Approaches for Automation of Bot Testing:

Mimicking the user's action:

Under this approach, user's actions are mimicked and the bot under test would interact with an automation script that is playing the role of a user. Infostretch's Automation Testing of Bot Framework has a capability to test chat and voice bot using this approach.

While testing the chatbot, our framework extracts the test data from MS Excel and does the response validation based on the response from the bot under test.

While testing the voice bot, our framework extracts the test data from MS Excel, converts the text to speech, and checks the response from the bot under test. For Peripheral testing, we apply conditioning such as varying distance, generating noise to simulate real-time conditions in our framework or allow user to do conditioning in the test data itself.

Headless Testing:

Under this approach, it is required to spoof the response from channel and interact directly with the bot server to understand the response to validate it. Infostretch's Automation Testing of Bot Framework has a capability to spoof the response for chat and voice bots. For test data, we rely on the MS Excel or CSV or allow specific format.

In both approaches – Mimicking or headless, using the framework we can do intent validation and response validation.

For test data, we have utilized MS Excel for flow and test data both. An advanced approach to that is to bifurcate both. Utilizing the mind map diagram for the flow and business rules/logic of the bot, while for the test data, utilizing MS Excel or TDM would serve the purpose. Our framework follows a specific format derived from mind map and creates the test scenarios based on the test data. So, any change in the business logic gets reflected in the Mind map diagrams (which is popularly used for development of a bot) and for the testing of the data, it relies on MS Excel or any test data server.

Summary

As the adoption of newer technologies like chatbots and voice bots increases, the number of applications built upon these technologies will continue to multiply. Enterprises are increasingly trying to reach out to their customers on these new platforms. Along with bots, the application architecture is also undergoing a huge shift as sensor data collected from peripherals like camera, BLE, GPS is being leveraged to improve the functionality of the mobile applications.

This white paper lays down a fundamental approach to test the evolving mobile application by automating the end-to-end testing cycle of the application using Mobile Automation Library. It allows cloud-based testing of mobile applications by mocking the functionality of the sensors to speed up the testing of applications.

Bot Testing Framework discussed in this white paper lays down a structured approach to identify the key parameters to be tested to ensure that the bots are functioning as per design. It discusses the specific factors to be considered while testing chatbots and voice bots. The white paper also defines different approaches that can be employed for testing of bots. Using the methods discussed here, it is possible to accelerate the testing cycle of bots; thereby shortening the overall time to market for bots.

References

QMetry Bot Tester: https://www.qmetry.com/qmetry-bot-tester/
QMetry Bot Check: https://www.qmetry.com/qmt-bot-check/

Enhancing Product Security Design Through Product Performance Testing, a New Dimension in Testing

Authors

Vittalkumar Mirajkar (vittalkumar_mirajkar@mcafee.com)
Sneha Mirajkar (SMirajka@cisco.com)
Narayan Naik (Narayan_Naik@mcafee.com)

Abstract

Performance testing is an indispensable part of testing life cycle. In endpoint software's, it is one of the key requirements to be met. Traditional performance testing scope has been around measuring response time, latency and resource availability for high frequency features, e.g. system start-up time, system shutdown time, in web services its request and response (turnaround) times.

Performance optimization has always been concentrated around the high frequency code paths. The logging associated with these paths are also optimized to great degree to increase performance. When an error condition occurs, i.e. a deviation from a known positive path, the optimized code flow diverts to forensic code flow and as much information of the current system state is captured.

Test designers rarely consider the most vulnerable area of performance testing – that of less optimized internal error condition reporting and logging code. These vulnerabilities can be identified and tested using targeted resource utilization tests which force application code to switch from a high frequency code path to a forensic code path. These tests are specifically designed to identify performance flaws that make the system vulnerable to a low-rate denial-of-service(DoS) attack. Low-rate DoS attacks are particularly concerning because they require less attack resources to be deployed against an application to achieve the desired effect.

In this paper, we discuss how we design specific resource utilization tests, which help us expose lesser optimized code areas which could lead to potential DoS attack entry points. We have effectively used this technique to explore how better designed test scenarios for resource utilization, can aid in uncovering performance bottle necks, security vulnerability and DoS attack entry points. The end results of this testing help not only fixing performance issues but also making design changes, making the overall product robust to attacks. This method of testing is applicable to any software. Test case efficiency of these tests are designed not only to help uncover performance issues but also to identify potential vulnerabilities.

Biography

Vittalkumar Mirajkar is a Software Architect at McAfee, with 12+ years of testing experience ranging from device driver testing, application testing and server testing. He specializes in testing security products. His area of interest is performance testing, soak testing, data analysis and exploratory testing

Sneha Mirajkar is a Software Engineer at Cisco, with 10+ years of experience in software testing and extensive hands-on in test automation using PYTHON, Selenium, PERL, QTP, VBscript, web services testing and functional testing. She has expertise in cloud testing (SAAS) and IAAS, AWS applications.

Narayan Naik is a Software Engineer at McAfee, with 11+ years of experience in exploratory testing and performance testing. He holds an expertise in providing consultation to enterprise customers for features and compatibility of various security products and security solutions deployed. His areas of interest are inter-compatibility test areas, performance testing and encryption product lines.

1. Introduction

Performance design considerations for a software product is as important as the product design itself. What do we test to ensure the product meets all the unforeseen performance challenges it may face in the field? During the product design phase, the emphasis is centered on meeting larger performance guidelines and less emphasis is given to functional deviation paths. These overlooked performance considerations come back to haunt us by making the system performance sluggish and in some cases, leading up to a DoS attacks resulting in complete failure of the product or system being over whelmed by it (Changwang Zhang 2012).

2. Performance Testing – What We Know

2.1. For Desktops and On-Premise Servers

Desktop applications and on-premise server applications are covered by the same general performance criteria guidelines, just at a different scale.

For Windows systems, Microsoft has "The Windows Assessment and Deployment Kit (Windows ADK)" (Microsoft 2018). It's a collection of tools which helps you to customize Windows images for large-scale deployment. It also aids to test the quality and performance of the system under test.

ADK assessments are tasks that simulate user activity and examine the state of the system. Assessments produce metrics for various aspects of the system and provide recommendations for making improvements. ADK has a standard set of assessments.

- ✓ Boot performance (full boot and fast startup)
- ✓ Hibernate and standby performance
- ✓ Internet Explorer startup performance and security software impact
- ✓ File handling and memory footprint
- ✓ Windows Store Apps

Software vendors add their software to the system's initial state and run ADK assessment test to see how the system is holding, this however does not exercise the software under test(SUT) but records the effects of its presence in system during ADK assessments. Parts of the SUT does get executed, however they are not the target of specific test execution. The larger goal is to record the effects of SUT's presence in the system when nothing unexpected is happening. Drawback of this test includes the following:

- Writing custom ADK assessments requires the tester to have a working knowledge of ADK.
- Default assessments rarely expose functionality issues of SUT. There is no targeted functional test executed, no corner case looked at. These tests are good for baseline testing but lack some key components for more robust performance testing.

Example:

- These tests do not cover functional test areas or any error conditions the software would be subjected to or targeted towards.
- The SUT is tested with no-load condition, not even an optimal load condition is considered.

2.2. Performance Testing of Cloud Based Applications

Cloud computing is changing the way applications are deployed, monitored and used by the end users. Cloud offers a virtually infinite pool of resources for computing, storage and networking resources where applications can be scaled as desired. So how do you measure the performance of these applications in the cloud?

Performance is a key factor in testing a web application as it directly impacts the end user experience. Performance testing in cloud is different from that of traditional on-premise hosted applications. Traditionally, the main aim of performance testing is to measure the various parameters such as system throughput, latency with changing number of parallel users accessing your application with different load profiles and various other performance metrics.

Some of the cloud metrics which are important are storage, processing, bandwidth and number of users accessing it at any given point. Scalability, availability, fault tolerance and reliability are the other factors which define a robust cloud infrastructure.

Below are the types of performance tests commonly performed on cloud applications:

- ✓ Stress, load and performance test
- ✓ Browser performance test
- ✓ Latency test and targeting infrastructure test
- ✓ Failover and capacity test
- ✓ Soak test

These tests help to characterize the quality aspects of the application like reliability, security and latency. Some of the areas overlooked in cloud performance are: DB latency, latency between two services, I/O delay, load on individual services, resource availability of each services.

Example:

- When a get request received by DB server in cloud that triggers the maximum number of permitted reads, there arises a situation of DB read request capacity being throttled. This leads to performance dip owing DB latency. This situation is not considered when the performance suite is designed as only turnaround time matters most.

3. Code Execution Frequency

When a software application is designed, it is expected to follow specific standards and attain certain performance expected characteristics. This ensures that all user flows are designed with same amount of scrutiny and critical flows are further combed through for fine tuning. Even though there are open source and commercial tools available for static and dynamic analysis of code (Softwaretestinghelp 2018) (Anderson 2008), they help achieve 100% code test coverage, review coverage and to a great degree, help uncover issues but shed little light on the frequency of the flow execution under real conditions.

We conducted a survey questionnaire to help us understand experienced software developer's perspective on code frequency when they write code. The survey (Survey by authors 2018) helps us confirm our understanding of the SUT from a black box testing perspective. The developer's responses helped us segment the SUT into areas where we can begin to target our testing. The segments are defined as shown in the table on the next page.

Code Section	% of code lines in overall code base	% of frequency of execution w.r.t entire code base	Examples
High Frequency actions	~20%-30% of code base	~70-80+ % of process time	• Core functionality blocks • DB executing a lookup request • Antivirus monitoring Disk I/O • Firewall inspecting every packet traversing IN/OUT of the machine
Mid Frequency actions	~20%-25% of code base	~10-15+ % of process time	• Lesser called functions • Configuration loads • Garbage collector / teardown code / sequencing / schedulers
Low Frequency actions	~45%-50% of code base	~5+% of process time	• Initialization Routines • Error condition handling • Service start, shutdown, restarts • Content loading or DB initialization
Rare code paths	~5% -10% of code base	~1%-2+% of process time	• Service crash and recovery. • Unexpected exit handling

A simplistic every day example to understand the frequency analogy is that of a ***motorcycle***:

- **High Frequency Use -** wheels which spin all the time, the engine, fuel injection system etc. Parts which need to run all the time.
- **Mid Frequency Use -** gear shift, breaks being applied, handle correction for direction.
- **Low Frequency Use –** use of the rearview mirror, ignition ON/OFF, turn indicators being used.
- **Rare Frequency Use -** crash guards.

4. Logging

Incorporating logging in code flow is an important, integral part of any commercial software. Logging information helps developers not only to debug issues better, but also helps quality analyst and service/support engineers to do first level of investigation in case of escalations. Logging also helps immensely in code maintenance. It is rare that a commercially released application will not have any form of logging.

The following represent a broad categorization of logging typically incorporated into all sections of code (Yuan, Park and Zhou 2012).

- Fatal
- Error
- Warning
- Information
- Debug

Each logging category has different verbosity levels (Yuan, Park and Zhou 2012) associated with them. The detail of less critical events (i.e. debug) will include events from higher category levels, i.e. debug captures everything which is captured by fatal, error, warning and information. Depending on the software module (e.g. Kernel Mode, User Mode or Web application); different default logging levels are enabled. In most open source software, on an average a line of log code exists for every 30 lines of code.

In a production system, logs are sometimes the only source of problem identification and troubleshooting of an event. Studies have shown that the use of log messages for troubleshooting on average, speed up root cause analysis by 2.2 times (D. Yuan 2011). This motivates developers to add more logging information as it gives a flow of thread-start, code flow and the unfolding of events as they happen. Logging is also crucial to system administrators as they are first responders and assist end users when a system malfunctions.

What to log? How much to log? How little to log? (D. Yuan 2011), there has been no formal study around this and it depends on experience of the developer.

4.1. Developer Bias in Code Modules and Logging

Logging is an integral part of software programming practice as it helps to save important runtime information by adding statements in source code as shown below:

Log (level, "logging message %s", variable);

A logging statement typically consists of a logging function and its parameters, including text messages, variables, and a verbosity level.

When we examine a typical code path for any functionality, you may observe something like the simplified snippet below:

```
if (testExpression1)
{
  // statements to be executed if testExpression1 is true
}
else if(testExpression2)
{
  // statements to be executed if testExpression1 is false and testExpression2 is true
}
else if (testExpression3)
{
  // statements to be executed if testExpression1 and testExpression2 is false and testExpression3 is true
}
.
.
else
{
  // statements to be executed if all test expressions are false
}
```

The positive or expected outcomes usually log minimal information to convey the event was a success and for rightful reason, this is expected for performance optimizations. It is when this expected condition fails, and an alternate option path is executed that additional information needs to be captured. To better understand the unfolding events, we tend to focus on capturing current system state information before we attempt the next step. The application moves from performance optimized code to a non-optimized forensic flow, i.e., logging. This switch is implicit, necessary and built into the design of the software.

However, the developer then has a choice of how much or little to log (D. Yuan 2011), invariably when software defects are uncovered in any state of the lifecycle, developers will often enhance logs to capture a better understanding of system state at the time of failure. This approach reduces the diagnosis time for future system anomalies. There are several logging libraries, such as syslog (C. Lonvick 2001) and log4j (The Apache Software Foundation 1999-2018) that provide better logging interface (e.g., multiple verbosity levels). However, in the end, it is the developers' decisions on when, what to collect and log.

4.2. Area of Interest

For the purposes of this paper, the high frequency code paths are of interest, specifically, the isolation of a single code flow or a sub flow, which under normal conditions would be executed most number of times. Our focus is to record its behavior and inherent design characteristics to build targeted test cases that force the code from the optimized state to deviate to the forensic (log) state.

Following are some of the guidelines we use to identify high frequency code execution flows and record the events that unfold when execution is in positive flow, as well as when a deviation flow is executed.

- Can the software be broken down in to individual modules, individual functions/code flows, sub flows?
- Are these sub-flows part of multiple flows? A sub-flow reused in multiple flows is an indicator for high frequency code. How easy is it to simulate a high frequency execution flow with minimal effort without complex dependencies?
- Is there an event type that needs to be recorded against a positive flow and a deviation flow? What is the data recorded? How different is it in both conditions?
- Are the events status recorded locally? Updated on a remote server? What is the frequency of server – client update?
- Is there queue maintained when one flow is triggered and another trigger for same code flow is waiting for execution? If there is an event wait queue, execution wait queue, any buffer that is used. Can this be tested?
- Do the logs collected roll over? Is roll over applicable for all event types?
- Are there UI action alerts involved? Are these actionable alerts or informational alerts? What is the queue like when multiple actionable alerts are queued?

The outcome of subjecting a software module to the above list helps us pick those basic functional tests which can target the high frequency code flows and their potential deviation paths. The goal is to pick the most basic feature and design tests to use its intended behavior under unexpected conditions.

Example:

- When a restricted action is performed on an enterprise managed machine, the event is blocked and event type is logged in a central management DB capturing system information, user details and the restricted operation performed. This information is stored in a remote DB. Can we perform restricted action on the managed machine to flood the database? Can we tweak the test, as to send more information to the server?

Email scanners on mail exchange servers scan incoming emails for malicious file attachments. This is a basic feature. If the attachment is a compressed file, the scanner would decompress it and then scan it. This is a sub-flow. Now, if the file attached is a super compressed file, the exchange server will need to decompress it and this action can consume the entire CPU and disk space; this is a DoS attack. For the right reasons, when decompression exceeds a certain size or CPU utilization, it gets flagged as DoS. What about small, clean but nested compressed files or a Zip bomb (Peter 2004-2009)?

4.3. Introduction to Soak Testing

Once a high frequency code flow and its normal (positive) and deviation paths are identified, the next step is to subject the path for targeted soak tests. A widely accepted definition of soak testing is "soak testing involves testing a system with a typical production load, over a continuous availability period, to validate system behavior under production use."

In simplified terms, our goal is to do high volume testing of high frequency code flow for normal and deviation events. This type of testing helps to simulate months of activity on the system in short duration of time.

Below figures explain a hypothetical case of soak testing.

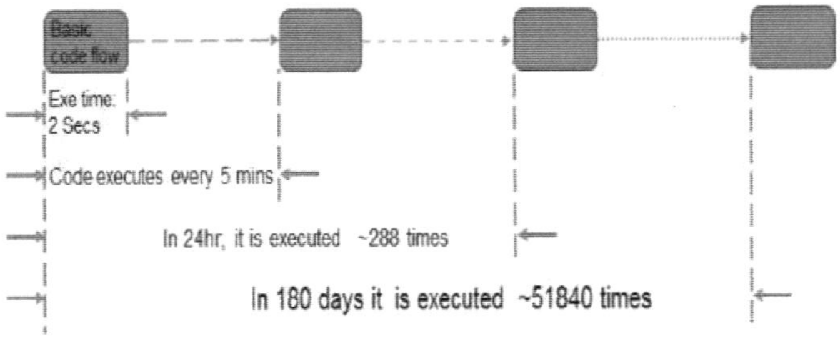

Figure 1 represents a basic code flow execution under a positive condition, which we would expect to be triggered approximately every 5 minutes in the production system. The code itself takes approximately 2 seconds to execute under normal operating conditions. In a 24-hour period we would expect this event to be triggered approximately 288 times in the production system.

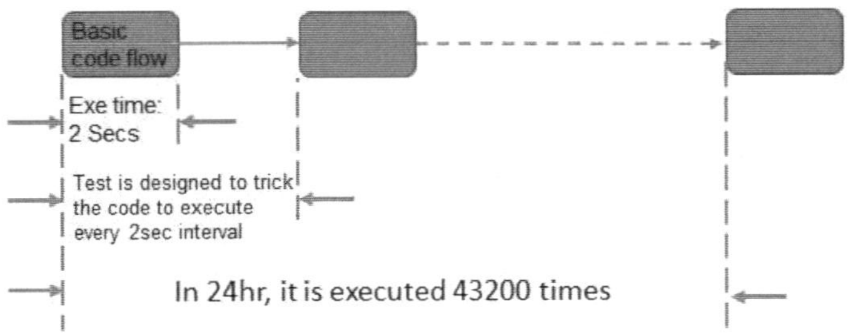

Figure 2 represents soak tests which focus on time compressing the event trigger from 5 minutes to every 2 seconds. In a 24-hour period we would expect this event to be triggered 43,200 times in our test system, simulating 150 days of production environment.

With this trend, in 36hrs we would have 64,800 executions. This could be soak test under ideal conditions.

Figure 3 represents further time compression of the event by continuously triggering of the same block of code. This represents positive flow (non-deviant) soak test

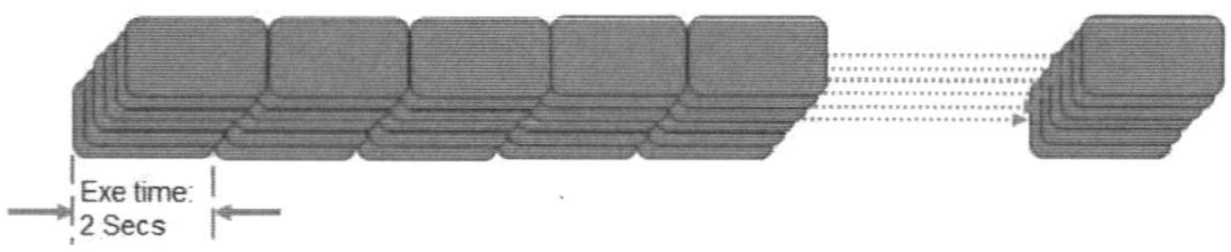

Figure 4 represents the parallelization of the continuous testing of the same positive flow of code. This test also begins to represent a positive flow, DoS simulation.

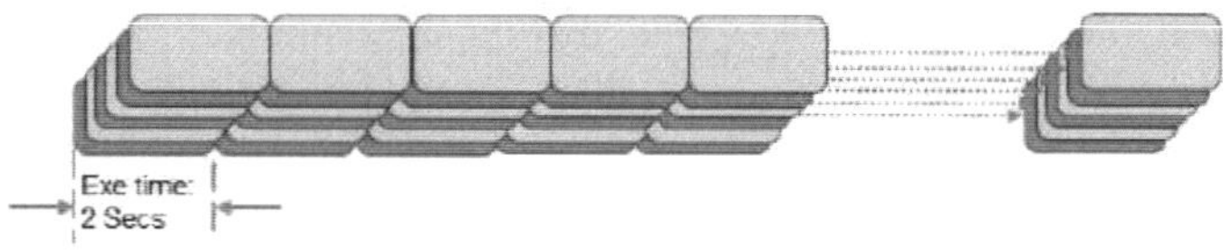

Figure 5 introduces the deviation flow test being executed in the soak test. This scenario begins the transformation from the positive flow, DoS simulation to the deviation flow, DoS simulation.

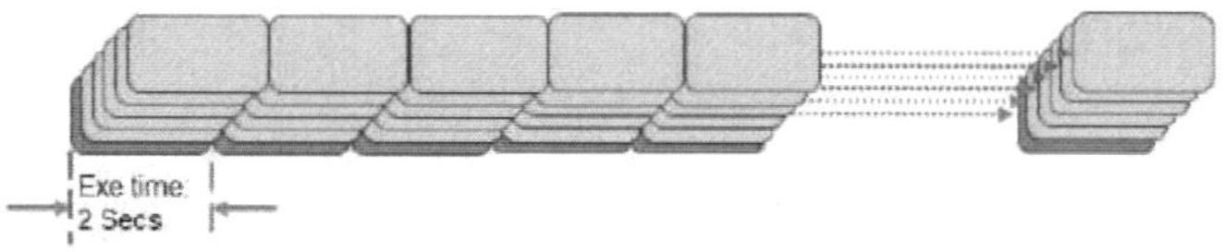

Figure 6 illustrates one positive flow, among a series of deviation flows. This is a full deviation flow, DoS simulation.

These soak variants (Figure 4, Figure 5 and Figure 6) not only help expose soak issues that Figure 2 and Figure 3 could expose but in addition also expose if there are any other hidden performance issues. This is our area of interest for this paper. In real world, code flow requests are both synchronous and asynchronous in nature. The above described approach though simplistic, still holds good for both conditions.

4.4. Guidelines for Running Soak Tests

Below are guidelines on how long to run the tests, and how to identify if this soak scenario, if extended could result in a DoS attack.

- For Windows environment, perfmon (Rusen 2016) is used to record resource utilization counters. Private Bytes and handle count is a good set to begin with. Note: Private Bytes refer to the amount of memory (RAM) that the process executable has asked for. Handle count is the number of logical associations with a shared resource like a file, window, memory location, etc.
- Duration: 25% of the time is for pre-cooling (this is a test ramp up time when SUT is subject to no load. It is expected to be in running condition and waiting for specific path trigger),100% run time, 25% of time should be post-cooling (this is the state where all the

load is taken off and SUT is expected to cool down, in best case resource come to a base level as exhibited by pre-cooling time behavior). Example: 4hrs test duration, 1hr will be pre-cooling and 1hr will be post cooling. Total 6hrs.

The figures below depict hypothetical cases of both a clean soak run and a run which shows signs of resource leak.

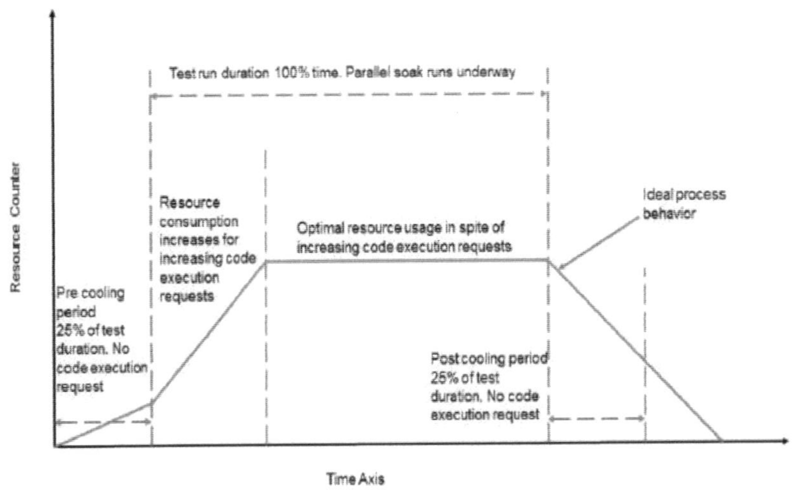

Figure 7:
This illustrates an ideal process resource utilization graph.

1st spike in memory or handle consumption: When actual test starts the memory and handle counts begin to ramp until optimal resource usage is achieved. This results in a flattening of the curve. In an ideal case, the memory and handle graph for a process will flatten after increasing for about 30-40 mins of peak tests. For some processes, it may take 1-2 hrs as well.

Decreasing trend: Once the test is over, resources consumed are freed, displaying ideal behavior

Figure 8:
This illustrates a process resource utilization graph which shows resource leaks as well as potential DoS scenario Resource utilization keeps increasing with increasing code executions requests.

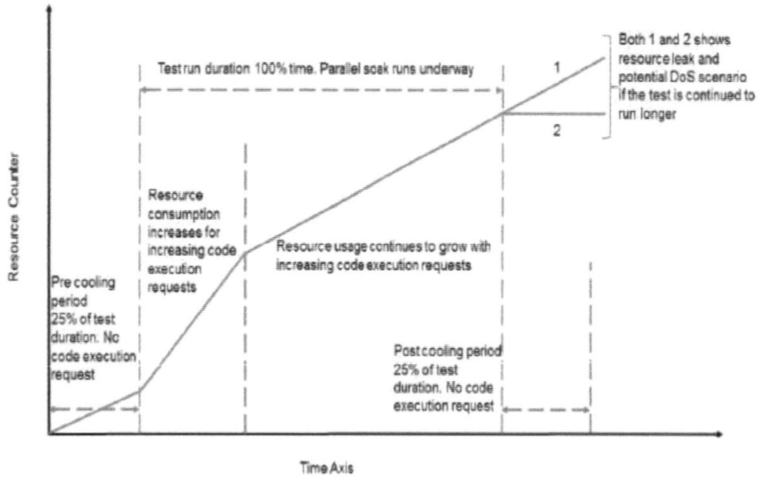

The cases mentioned (line 1 and 2) post code execution requests stop, in both cases, if the code execution requests would have continued, it would have been a potential DoS due to over utilization of resources.

Resource leak and DoS indicators:

- For Private Bytes: If we see an increasing trend in consumption of Private Byte at the rate of 500KB/hr. for more than 4hrs, it's a concern. (This rise is monitored after initial jump in resources.)
- For handle count: 25 handles/hr. for consecutive 4hrs is a concern.
- If graph shows slow growth rate, but consistent increase, a re-run of the test with increased time duration is recommended. Probably it is a small resource leak not resulting in DoS.
- If graph shows huge jump e.g. 250 handles/hr. and keeps growing, it's a clear concern. It is both a resource leak as well as if the tests are run long enough could result in DoS.

Reference to previous runs:

- Every test run is unique, and every operating system (OS) resource consumption is unique.
- Same test, same process on different OS's consume resources differently. On same OS, process resource consumption comparison in different test runs is valid. e.g. OS A vs OS B memory consumption cannot be compared for same test. However, different test runs of same test on OS A vs OS A, resource consumption can be compared.

4.5. Case Study of How to Build a Soak Scenario

On a popular OS type, we created two types of files: type A and type B. Both files are text files with varying content. Each file type creation triggers specific code flow execution. Below are couple of simulation run graphs when we tweak file name for long and short names and we measure a system process private bytes.

System configuration: 8GB Ram, 8 Core, 100GB HDD

We used a sample python script to create different file types i.e type A and type B files for this simulation.

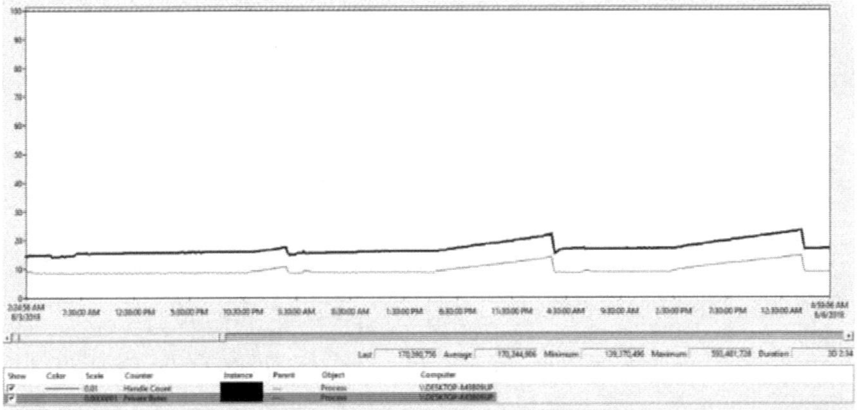

Test Duration: 3 Days, 2 Hours, Private Bytes: Max value ~565MB

Figure 9:
Type A files are created with maximum allowed file name character. Default maximum length of file name is 256 characters.

Analysis:
The system and application are stable with no memory leaks.

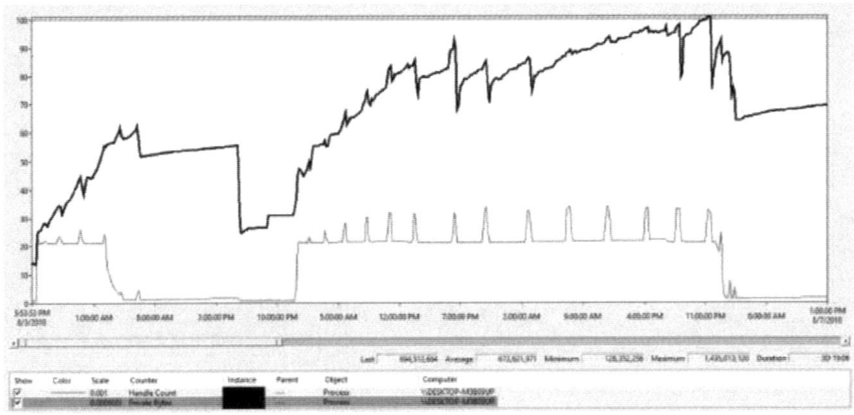

Test Duration: 3 Days, 19 Hours, Private Bytes: Max value ~1.3GB

Figure 10:
Type B files are created with short file names (8-15 characters)

Analysis:
With each type B file creation, memory consumption keeps increasing and continues to grow. We do not see optimal resource utilization level reached. Private bytes show signs of memory leak.

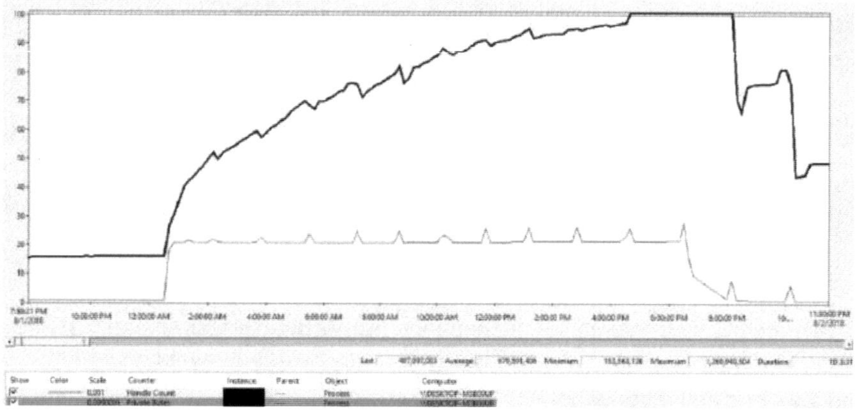

Test Duration: 1 Day, 3 Hours, Private Bytes: Max value ~1.2GB

Figure 11:
Type B files are created with maximum allowed file name character

Analysis:
By stacking multiple type B file creation events along with max length of file name we have started converting Figure 10 scenario to deviation flow. Private bytes show signs of high memory leak.

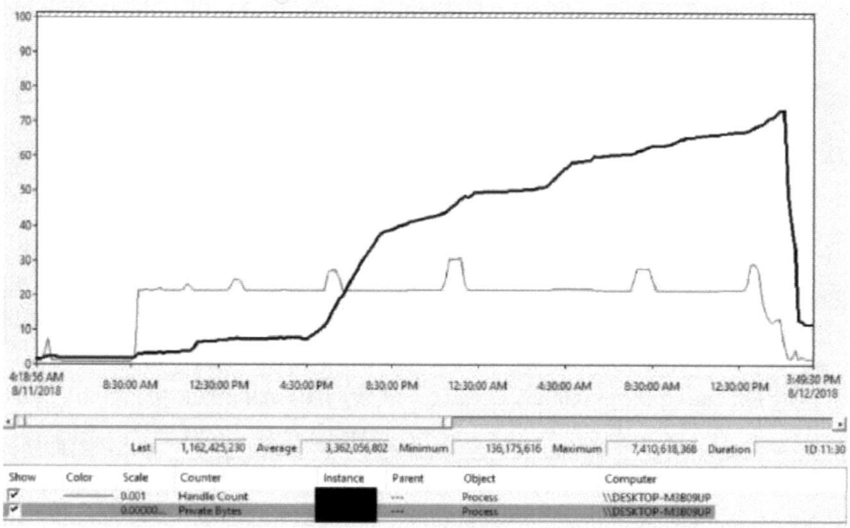

Test Duration: 1 Day, 11 Hours, Private Bytes: Max value ~7GB

Figure 12:
Parallel soak of type B file creation with maximum allowed file name character

Analysis:
Figure 11 test is converted to a parallel soak scenario (Refer Figure 6 and Figure 8) and we see signs of high memory leak and after this point a critical service failed. DoS scenario was hit. When we restarted the system, the service fails to restart, as it is unable to load file creation log entries, SUT has broken down.

5. Parallel Soak Testing and How It Is Linked to Security Testing

Functional testing dominates the testing landscape with little to no scope for non-functional test areas. For Security and Performance testing, standard test templates are followed which do not cover much beyond what is traditional. Due to aggressive project time lines, security testing and performance testing has not had its fair share of attention

- **For Security Testing:**
  Standard templates or models are used, and security testing is planned. Standard tests are, threat modelling, penetration testing and to lesser percentage privilege escalation. DoS attack does not have dedicated test slot. It is, in most cases a post release test.

- **For Performance Testing:**
  Performance testing is heading towards being a check box item in overall testing life cycle. Major emphasis is given to standard test templates defined or assume positive conditions in test environment. These tests are a good start for projects doing performance testing for the first time.

The gap in performance testing gives scope, where a DoS attack could be possible by exploiting the basic built in feature of the module. When soak testing is planned, it is planned only for positive linear flow and never considers a parallel soak conditions. This switch in our approach to run parallel soak test, help us expose potential DoS scenarios and as well as soak issues. The strength of the test is to use basic functional test case, and re-wire the conditions to expose issues which otherwise are waiting to be exploited in field.

There are multiple reasons why this area of testing is overlooked or has never been exposed. Among them are:

- The level of expertise required range from advanced to expert level functional testing knowledge.
- Understanding of how to leverage functional test cases to expose alternative code path weakness.
- Having a good understanding of logging involved at each failure stage is the key to parallel soak testing. This helps to better select the most vulnerable, high frequency code flows for test.
- Time. Product release cycles are under immense pressure, but making time for this type of testing, even periodically, is the key.

6. Key Takeaway of Parallel Soak Testing Approach

Parallel soak tests exhibit high test case effectiveness. Every test case is effective until it fails, once a fix is in place, chances of this modular test case failing are greatly reduced. There have been multiple attempts to define test case effectiveness mathematically (Chernak 2001), as-well-as to define test case efficiency (Naidu, Vasudeva 2012). Both definitions can be used to justify parallel soak test effectiveness.

We would use *"Test case efficiency"* with respect to detecting defects as a closer measure to evaluate soak testing contribution to test life cycle. Our definition is "the number of defects found per test case designed".

Test case efficiency = (Total actual defects found / Number of times a test case is run) * 100

- Number of times a test case is run = Number of times a specific test case is run against the application. Minimum value being 1.
- Total actual defects found = Total Actual defects found using this test case (which is intended defects + other defects found)
- Intended defects = Intended defects to be found by each test case, which at minimum per test case, will always be 1. This value cannot be zero, simply because you write a test case to find a defect, at the very minimum 1 defect, else the test case should not exist.

Our Observations:

- A value of 0 indicates the test case never found a defect, or all defects detected by it have been fixed, hence making the code immune to this test.
- A higher number would indicate multiple defects found by a single test case. This makes the test case one of the most effective and efficient test cases to be executed on every run.
- For a well-designed soak test case, the test case efficiency will always be a greater then 1, as it not only helps to expose performance issues but also, it exposes design flaws and security issues. For a functional test case, this value ideally will always be '1'
- For every test release cycle, when we evaluate test case efficiency after at least one run, a '0' would indicate time for designing a new test case.

Given a higher "test case efficiency" factor, return of investment to uncover defects is higher in soak tests when compared to standard functional tests.

Conclusion

Targeted parallel soak tests help expose resource utilization issues and low-rate DoS vulnerabilities in applications. Traditional performance and security testing do not cover this particular application security vulnerability/performance weakness. These tests can be achieved by simple rewiring of existing functional tests and adjusting the current performance testing approach. By doing these simple adjustments to the existing testing regiments, the parallel soak testing of deviation flow has a high rate of test case efficiency and yield positive return on investment (ROI) for the organization.

References

Anderson, Paul. 2008. "The Use and Limitations of Static-Analysis." CrossTalk-Journal of Defense Software Engineering 21. https://pdfs.semanticscholar.org/e716/7b08d27f1b92c42e573d0e59bf2d2810844d.pdf.

C. Lonvick. 2001. "The BSD syslog Protocol." tools.ietf.org. August. Accessed July 24, 2018. https://tools.ietf.org/html/rfc3164

Changwang Zhang, Zhiping Cai, Weifeng Chen, Xiapu Luo, Jianping Yin. 2012. "Flow level detection and filtering of low-rate DDoS." Computer Networks, Volume 56, Issue 15 (Elsevier BV) 3417-3431. doi: https://doi.org/10.1016/j.comnet.2012.07.003

Chernak, Y. 2001. "Validating and improving test-case effectiveness." IEEE Software, vol. 18, no. 1 81-86. http://ieeexplore.ieee.org/stamp/stamp.jsp?tp=&arnumber=903172&isnumber=19528

D. Yuan, J. Zheng, S. Park, Y. Zhou, and S. Savage. 2011. "Improving software diagnosability via log enhancement." In Proceedings of the sixteenth international conference on Architectural support for programming languages and operating systems (ASPLOS) 3-14. http://opera.ucsd.edu/paper/asplos11-logenhancer.pdf.

Microsoft. 2018. "Get started with Windows 10." Download and install the Windows ADK. April 30. Accessed July 24, 2018. https://docs.microsoft.com/en-us/windows-hardware/get-started/adk-install.

Naidu, Vasudeva. 2012. Test Case Effectiveness - What does it say? February 14. Accessed July 20, 2018. http://www.infosysblogs.com/testing-services/2012/02/test_case_effectiveness_-_what.html.

Peter, Bieringer. 2004-2009. Possible Denial-of-Service caused by decompression bombs. Accessed July 15, 2018. http://www.aerasec.de/security/advisories/decompression-bomb-vulnerability.html.

Rusen, Ciprian Adrian . 2016. How to start the Performance Monitor in Windows. December 2. Accessed July 15, 2018. https://www.digitalcitizen.life/basics-about-working-performance-monitor.

Softwaretestinghelp. 2018. Top 40 Static Code Analysis Tools. August 8. Accessed August 10, 2018. https://www.softwaretestinghelp.com/tools/top-40-static-code-analysis-tools/.

Survey, Vittalkumar Mirajkar, Sneha Mirajkar, and Narayan Naik. 2018. "Study to understand Code Execution frequency." SurveyMonkey. July 25. Accessed August 24, 2018. https://www.surveymonkey.com/r/RKKKD52.

The Apache Software Foundation. 1999-2018. Apache Logging Services - Log4j. Accessed July 24, 2018. https://logging.apache.org/log4j/2.x/.

Yuan, Ding, Soyeon Park, and Yuanyuan Zhou. 2012. "Characterizing logging practices in open-source software." ICSE 2012 102-212. http://opera.ucsd.edu/paper/log_icse12.pdf

This page intentionally left blank.

Quality & Risk Management Challenges When Acquiring Enterprise Software Systems

Authors

Ying Ki Kwong, PhD, PMP, Office of the State Chief Information Officer, State of Oregon (ying.k.kwong@oregon.gov)
Philip Lew, PhD, PMP, CEO, XBOSoft (philip.lew@xbosoft.com)

Abstract

Much has been written about quality and risk management from the perspectives of organizations that design, develop, and implement software systems. However, many enterprises no longer build software systems internally but, instead, acquire them from contractors. For an organization that acquires software systems, project management needs to be done from a different perspective, and quality and risk management needs a different focus and emphasis than the organization responsible for building the systems. This paper marks the tenth anniversary of a PNSQC 2008 presentation entitled "Management of Outsourced Projects." Many of the topics discussed then continue to be relevant today. The major difference between then and now, however, is the popularity of agile development methodologies. Agile, with some of its primary tenets including focus on short iterations, needs to be adapted in order to work successfully in an environment where organizations acquire software built by a third party. In this paper, the authors categorize problems and issues that arise when fitting Agile into these environments and discuss areas where Agile needs to be adapted in order to be successful. We conclude with the observation that system development life cycle (SDLC) methodologies like Agile is one facet of delivering enterprise system projects successfully in large organizations.

Biography

Ying Ki Kwong is the Statewide Quality Assurance Program Manager in the Office of the State CIO in Oregon state government. Prior to this role, he was IT Investment Oversight Coordinator in the same office and was Project Office Manager of the Medicaid Management Information System Project in the Oregon Department of Human Services. In the private sector, Dr. Kwong was CEO of a Hong Kong-based internet B2B portal for trading commodities futures and metals. He was a program manager in the Video & Networking Division of Tektronix, responsible for worldwide applications & channels marketing for a line of video servers in broadcast television applications. In these roles, he has managed software based systems/applications, products, and business process improvements. He received the doctorate from the School of Applied & Engineering Physics at Cornell University and was adjunct faculty in the School of Business Administration at Portland State University. He holds the PMP certification since 2003.

Philip Lew, CEO of XBOSoft, oversees strategy, operations and business development since founding the Company in 2006. In a span of 25 years he has worked as a developer, product manager, and held roles at the executive level both in USA and Europe. He also serves as an Adjunct Professor at Alaska Pacific University. He has spoken at conferences such as STPCon, PNSQC and Better Software East-West, StarEast-West while his papers have been published in ACM, IEEE, Project Management Technology, Network World, Telecommunications Magazine, Call Center Magazine, TeleProfessional, and DataPro Research Reports. Philip Lew is a certified PMP and holds a BS and a Masters Degree in Operations Research and Engineering from Cornell University and a Ph.D. in Computer Science and Engineering from Beihang University. He loves bicycling and has traveled the world visiting more than 60 countries to quell his passion for exploration and learning.

1. Introduction

In many organizations, enterprise software systems are acquired and not built internally. In these projects, the software development is outsourced to contractors and may span all aspects of the system development life cycle (SDLC). Even when a prime contractor is experienced and has a good track record of delivering projects successfully, a project that involves the acquisition of an enterprise system is a complex undertaking and so high risk for an organization acquiring the enterprise system ("acquiring organization").

Many times, there may be conflict between contracting model and SDLC. This is especially true with Agile, where requirements are supposed to be discovered and clarified as a project progresses, yet the acquiring organization wants a product delivered by a specific date that meets stated requirements and business needs.

From the perspective of the authors, a root cause of this problem is that Agile development methodologies, without adaptation, may not be compatible with procuring software systems from contractors. Remember that Agile, first proposed in 2001 via the Agile Manifesto [Beck 2015], is an alternative to development methods that emphasizes nailing down detailed requirements up-front with detail documentation throughout a project's life cycle. Challenges of adopting agile methods in the public sector can be found in the literature [Nuottila 2016], including papers that focus on systems acquisition and contracting [SEI 2016 and USGAO 2014].

Understanding these issues is critical to solving the problem of poor or failed system delivery projects. As such, this paper categorizes and describes challenges in quality & risk management from the perspective of an acquiring organization:

- Requirements & SDLC Congruency
- Organizational readiness;
- Contractual considerations;
- Business aware testing;
- Organizational dynamics

The authors believe a better understanding of these challenges would be the first step toward solving this problem. We will leverage lessons learned from the authors' experience in the public and the private sectors; with emphasis on improving quality, reducing risk, and minimizing technical debt in Agile or Agile influenced projects. Whether dealing with internal staff or with contractor staff, our main theme will be "trust but verify". As such, the reader can leverage lessons learned in each section depending on their specific context.

2. Context for Major IT Projects in Large Enterprises

A description of the context of major IT projects in large enterprises may be useful. Of particular importance would be the general solution approaches available and the challenges in large complex enterprises.

General Solution Approaches. Major IT projects are major capital investments for the acquiring organization. For each project, management makes its decision to invest, typically on the basis of a business case. Such a business case is usually supported by high-level business requirements and an analysis of available solution approaches in terms of their relative costs, benefits, and risks for the organization. Available solution approaches emphasize system integration and generally fall under three categories:

- Commercial-off-the-shelf (COTS) system with customization. This is usually based on a major software product or a suite of software products. Examples include enterprise resource planning (ERP) system or electronic document management system (EDMS) that have been implemented for similar enterprises in the same or similar vertical industries.
- Transfer system with customization. This is usually based on a system or a suite of systems that have been implemented for a specific enterprise.
- Custom developed system. This is often viewed as higher cost and higher risk, but may be the only viable approach if no COTS or transfer system based solution is available.

As an example, at any one time in Oregon state government, there are usually about 20 major IT projects in execution, with prime contractors on board and working. As of May 2018, only one of these projects selected a fully custom developed approach. The Top 5 projects by budget are in the following state agencies:

1. Department of Human Services - $335 million, transfer system with customization
2. Department of Justice - $130 million, transfer system with customization
3. Department of Transportation - $90 million, COTS system with customization
4. Oregon Health Authority - $28 million, COTS systems with customization
5. Department of Administrative Services - $20 million, COTS system with customization

The scope of customization may include integration or interfaces with existing or legacy systems, as well as conversion of data in systems being replaced. In addition, configuration, scripting, and custom coding are usually necessary. Even for a COTS or transfer system based solution, there may be significant coding efforts to deliver functionality not in the base system. As such, a "gap analysis" between the functionalities of the base system and the system to be delivered is of great importance during procurement and during development.

Challenges in Large Enterprises. Major IT projects are usually change initiatives that aim to significantly improve or transform an enterprise. For the acquiring organization, challenges include:

- Insufficient participation of subject matter experts - Cross-functional processes, business rules, and applicable regulatory requirements are often too numerous and complex for a few individuals to fully represent them. Yet, it is often impractical for the most qualified individuals to participate when needed, because these individuals may be indispensible in their normal duties.
- lack of familiarity with "to be" business processes or new operational paradigms - Personnel within the acquiring organization are experts of the organization's "as is" business processes, but these are the business processes being changed. For IT systems based on COTS or transfer systems, prime contractor staff are often the experts of "to be" business processes implicit in the base system.
- unobvious tradeoffs between cost / risk of customization vs. benefits that can be realized – Well meaning customization to support organization specific needs may have significant risks associated with cost, schedule, and other risks. On the other hand, exclusive use of functionalities "out of the box" may entail workarounds that are operationally time consuming or costly when in production use.

In the public sector, additional challenges that may be less common in the private sector include:

- competitive procurement processes - The prime contractor and the solution approach must be selected based on a fair, competitive request-for-proposal (RFP) process, because of public procurement statutes and rules. Such an RFP must be supported by requirements and a statement of work (SOW) that defines tasks, deliverables, and their acceptance criteria. Because these artifacts become exhibits of an executed contract, unclear requirements or SOW may face vendor questions or protests during the RFP process. More importantly, they may lead to contract disputes, cost escalation, or law suits later.
- lead time for contract review / approval - The RFP and the resulting contract and subsequent amendments must be approved by all participating funding partners, e.g. federal agencies in the case of state government. This review / approval process introduces significant lead time (usually many weeks) for contract amendments; typically contain changes to scope (requirements), schedule, and cost.
- Independent quality assurance and certification – The acquiring organization may need to pass independent reviews or be certified by one or more government agencies. Among Oregon state agencies, independent quality assurance by a third-party is mandated by

state statute and, if applicable, federal agencies funding the work. There are also specific requirements when a system must connect to certain government systems, e.g. federal Social Security Administration, federal Internal Revenue Service, state division of motor vehicles, and federal or state law enforcement authorities. Systems for managing payments in federally supported programs, e.g. Medicaid and social services, must be approved and certified by the appropriate federal agency or agencies before production use.

Certain human factors and organizational dynamics are also of great importance, because they may negatively impact project performance in significant ways. For the prime contractor, it is driven more by profitability than the best possible solution for the acquiring organization. So, prime contractor staff would tend to do the minimum required by the contract or steer toward new tasks or contract amendments with additional costs to the acquiring organization. For the acquiring organization, it is not a given that the assigned staff want the change desired by management. They may not share the same vision of change as management or may interpret that vision differently. They may have a desire to minimize change of "as is" business processes and so resist alignment with functionalities of a base system "out of the box" (which would mean larger scope of customization). Also, they may not necessarily feel fully motivated or empowered in assigned work teams.

3. Requirements & SDLC Congruency

From a software engineering standpoint, requirements are central to high quality system delivery. However, before the acquiring organization can have a prime contractor on board, one must be procured that is capable of delivering the system – often based on a COTS or transfer system, as discussed in Section 2.

Requirements for Procurement vs. Requirements for Development. For the acquiring organization, it is very important to differentiate between the following:

1. High-level requirements necessary to procure the prime contractor including competitive RFPs;
2. Detailed requirements necessary to support design, development, and implementation.

For (1), an acquiring organization must develop high-level requirements that describe strategic intents, business objectives, general features-functions needed, conceptual relationships with other data systems and data sources, and high level workflows and user scenarios. Frequently, this work may involve consultants or contractors. If contractors are involved, these should not be the prime contractor to be procured, as it represents a conflict of interest.

For (2), detailed requirements are usually done by the prime contractor, with participation of the acquiring organization's management and staff. This work may involve development of user scenarios or use cases, analysis of features-functions needed to meet business needs, modeling and validation of business processes as needed, and documentation to support the work of cross-functional teams and third-party reviews as needed. This type of work is accompanied by solution architecture based on software products chosen to support the general solution approach selected, as described in Section 2.

Requirements That Fail to Represent All Business Needs. A "technically good" system does not necessarily guarantee that the larger mission or objectives of the enterprise can be achieved. But even SDLCs such as Agile that incorporate the users into the development process do not necessarily guarantee that the delivered systems support the overall objectives of the enterprise. This is true especially for very large projects in large enterprises in which not all users or the relevant subject matter experts can be represented when needed. Indeed, a central challenge to the acquiring organization is in assuring requirements are sound, faithfully reflect business needs, and can be expected to give rise to features-functions that have reasonable return on investment (ROI), both in financial or non-financial terms.

Iterative Requirements. With good engineering and project management practices, subsequent work (Design, Build, Deploy, and Operate / Optimize a system) can be done on the basis of good traceability to Requirements with the participation of the end user or product owner. In the schematic SDLC representation of Figure 1, Waterfall SDLC [Jones 2012] may well have arrows from Build back to Design or from Design back to Requirements, but the general directionality is Design after Requirements and Build after Design. Agile and other iterative SDLCs (e.g. the Unified Process) would leverage the learning achieved from earlier software releases to enable refinements of Requirements and Designs in subsequent phases, iterations, or sprints.

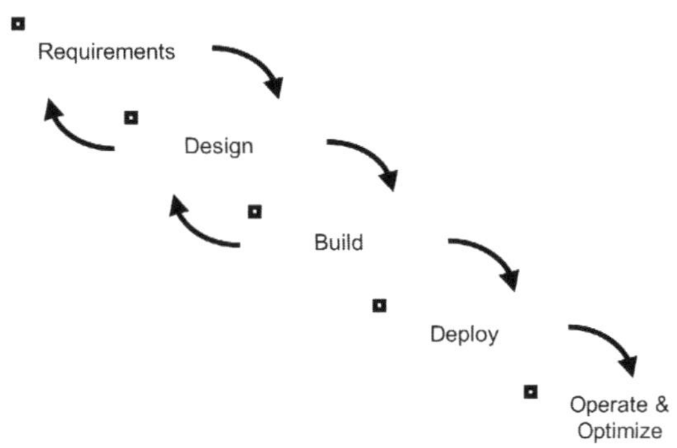

Figure 1: Generic System Development Life Cycle (SDLC) for a single phrase, iteration, or sprint in a project. A project with multiple phases, iterations, or sprints has multiple instances of this.

Where there are multiple major software releases and numerous minor software releases to be delivered over many iterations or sprints, it is important for the acquiring organization to be proactive with reviews of user scenarios, use cases, detailed requirements, and testing. It is necessary to adopt a "trust but verify" mindset when working with the prime contractor throughout the project's life cycle.

With contractors that develop software using an Agile methodology, yet with a waterfall type contracting vehicle, it is critical to allow extra time for the iterations in the requirements phase where the contractor involves the acquiring organization's project management team and the end user organization. As shown in Figure 1, this can be accomplished through iterative Requirements, Design and Build. These iterations can be time boxed with reviewable artifacts in order to support a controlled process that is part of enforceable contracts.

4. Organizational Readiness

In many acquiring organizations, the capture, analysis, and documentation of detailed requirements are increasingly in scope for the prime contractor. However, even when high quality resources to support all facets of a project can be expected from the prospective prime contractor, it does *not* follow that the acquiring organization can bring a prime contractor on board at any time without substantial preparation. The extent of this preparation varies depending on policies for IT investment due diligence, competitive procurement, budget cycles, and other considerations in the acquiring organization; as well as the level of management discretion allowed and accountability expected. More often than it should, the authors have seen that insufficient work is done by management and staff of an acquiring organization in preparation of the on-boarding of the prime contractor. The important lesson learned is: regardless of the quality of the prime contractor, few projects can expect to be successful without certain preparation to assure organizational readiness. This preparation includes:

- *Project Charter & Governance*. All major IT investment should put in place a project charter that identifies purpose of a project, executive sponsors, steering committee members, a project manager, and a project management team.
- *Business Case*. A major IT project is a major capital investment and should have a carefully prepared business case that identifies business drivers and justifications for undertaking the project. The business case should contain an analysis of solution alternatives that identifies their relative benefits (both financial and non-financial), costs, and risks. It should conclude with the solution alternative selected, key success factors, and risks.
- *Detailed Planning Artifacts*. Relevant artifacts include: requirements and statement of work to support procurement, a high-level project plan, communications plan, and other supporting plans.
- *Procurement Process*. Proposals are solicited using formal RFP or other processes. Proposals received are evaluated, possibly using predefined evaluation / scoring criteria. This is followed by contract negotiation with the apparent winner of the competitive process, legal reviews, and contract execution.

Note that when working with a contractor who is using an Agile development process, communications plan and other supporting plans need particular attention. Agile requires frequent communication -- sometimes on a daily basis. As part of the planning documents, processes need to be put in place for the contractor and the acquiring organization (including end users who will ultimately be using the system) to have frequent interaction and collaboration.

5. Contractual Considerations

From the perspective of the acquiring enterprise, project success is at least partly tied to the effectiveness of the contract. In this respect, it is important for the acquiring enterprise to consider the following:

- Procurement models;
- Terms & conditions including penalty or liquidated damage clauses;
- Degree of contract modifications anticipated during the project's lifecycle.

Procurement Models. Procurement models primarily refer to whether the contract will be deliverables based or time-and-materials based. If the requirements are well understood, stable, and can be well documented, a deliverables based contract is most appropriate; but this is not usually the case. Therefore, many enterprises (especially in the private sector) may feel that time-and-materials contracts are more easily set up and administered. This model is more supportive for Agile methods, because there is no need to have detailed requirements completely specified in the beginning of the project, allowing for discovery along the way. However, the acquiring enterprise must be willing to accept the risk associated with contractor non-performance and potentially flawed time and cost estimates.

On the other hand, a deliverables based contract does not give complete protection against cost overrun. This is because requirements may not be sufficiently detailed, and enhancements of requirements as the project progresses frequently entail additional costs. Also, the prime contractor would have included a price premium or slack in its cost proposal to deal with uncertainty or error in estimation.

This situation contrasts with a time-and-materials contract in which there is no specific upfront assurance of the cost and time required to deliver a specific set of features-functions. In short, there are positive and negative for either approach. What we have found that works is a combination of the two approaches where a time boxed iterative approach is used, but with specific deliverables after multiple iterations. The iterative approach in the beginning of the project allows for requirements discovery while both sides develop a better understanding of everything from the requirements to the technical difficulties involved. This is followed by specific milestone based deliverables that enable work in progress to be reviewed iteratively.

Terms & Conditions. Terms and conditions in the contract that awards performance (such as early completion) could be a useful incentive for the contractor; as are clauses that delay, retain, or otherwise reduce payment due to non-performance (such as late completion). Especially important would be payment terms (e.g. Net 30 upon invoice), provision for progress payment for deliverables work in progress, retainage (e.g. 15% holdback on all accepted deliverables invoiced until after User Acceptance Test (UAT) and formal acceptance of the system). This makes the UAT a critical part of any contract. More on UAT will be discussed in the next section.

Contract Statement of Work (SOW). Considerations for developing a SOW include the following:

- Deliverables need to have well defined acceptance criteria. In other words, the contract should specify what is included and not included in each deliverable.
- There is a need for contract language that balances specificity with flexibility to enable dynamic response to certain project unknowns, e.g. approved scope expansion or schedule changes.
- For requirements that may not be stable (e.g. requirements that have not been thoroughly vetted or rapidly changing business conditions), it may be necessary for the acquiring organization to budget extra funds for on-demand work by the contractor, through change requests, task orders, or contract amendments.
- The SOW needs to be consistent with the SDLC anticipated. If the contractor and acquiring organization agree to time boxes or an iterative process, the SOW and contract should reflect this directly.

The last point requires further discussion. Unfortunately, many organizations use SOW templates that assume a sort of "big bang" Waterfall SDLC, with major deliverables assumed to be a single instance of the detailed requirements, architecture, design, or testable software release. Referring to Figure 1, the contract / SOW template may implicitly assume a single unidirectional pass through the Generic SDLC model. From the perspective of the acquiring organization, this approach may be the result of historical practices, or it may seem "simpler" to have fewer contractual deliverables. When the contractor is using Agile methods, this practice is extremely problematic in two ways:

- First, it may encourage the prime contractor and the staff of the acquiring organization to actually adopt a "big bang" Waterfall SDLC; with all the schedule, budget, and scope / quality risks associated with delayed identification of defects in requirements and designs.
- Second, it may create mismatch of expectations around key deliverables (e.g. detailed requirements, architecture, design, and testable software releases); as far as what specific work products can be reviewed by the acquiring organization by what time. This is especially problematic in federally or state government funded projects in which independent quality assurance or independent verification & validation (IV&V) by a third party may be mandatory.

The overall result is a mismatch of development methodology with deliverable and expectations. This is a recipe for trouble. In summary, you cannot expect to have fixed timelines and deliverables without detailed requirements, and you cannot expect requirements not to change or at least be elaborated. Make sure the contract structure and deliverables are in alignment with expectations in SDLC and development methodology.

6. Business Aware Testing

Owing to the real-world challenges described in Section 2, major IT projects in large enterprises, including those that use iterative or Agile SDLCs, may discover defects in functional requirements late in the project's life cycle -- perhaps as late as User Acceptance Testing (UAT). This situation is not necessarily the fault of the prime contractor and the specific choice of SDLC. These types of defects are costly to fix and represent major risks to quality, schedule, and cost. To reduce defects at the time of system launch, we introduce the term Business Aware Testing. Business Aware Testing emphasizes testing from the business point of view, not only from the end users, but also from the acquiring organization's business needs.

A useful model for visualizing testing is the "V-model" that relates different types of testing to different aspects of the system, as depicted in Figure 2.

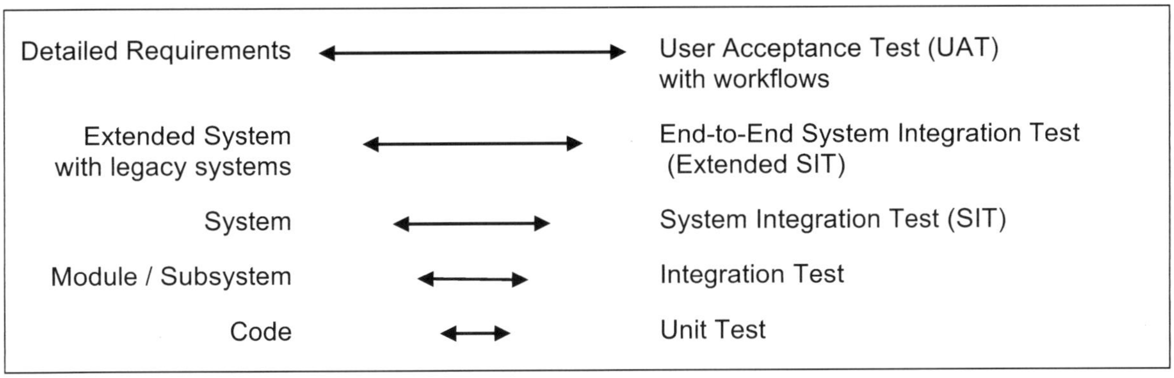

Figure 2: The V-Model for testing.

A good prime contractor would have planned for ample testing activities; especially in unit test, integration test, and system integration test. In the spirit of "trust but verify", it is important for the acquiring organization to organize a testing effort of its own, separate and independent from the prime contractor and their development and testing teams. When doing this, the following considerations are important.

Testing by Type. For the acquiring organization, there are three types of testing that are especially important conceptually:

- Functional Testing: features-functions, user scenarios, use cases, workflows, etc.
- Non-Functional Testing: performance, load, stress, etc.

- Regulatory Compliance Related Testing: connectivity to government systems, certification, attestation, etc.

In the context of functional testing, there are more specialized types of testing that tend to be a mixture of the three types of testing identified above:

- Security Testing
- Data Conversion Testing
- Accessibility Testing
- Extended System integration Testing (with interfaces / integration with legacy systems)
- User Acceptance Testing

Iterative / Agile SDLC with Waterfall Overlay. To assure accountability and in the spirit of "trust but verify," it is important for the acquiring organization to insist on testable code releases from the prime contractor that the acquiring organization can independently develop test scripts and run tests that can be traced to known detailed requirements. The authors believe a waterfall like overlay on the prime contractor's iterative or Agile SDLC, called "IterFall", would be advisable for accountability. See Figure 3 below.

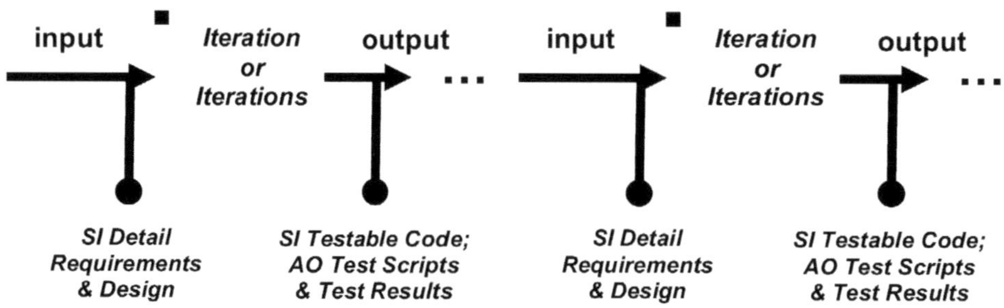

Figure 3: Iterative SDLC with Waterfall Overlay, called "IterFall" by the authors. In this figure, one or more iterations (sprints) would produce a software release that the acquiring organization or a third-party can test. Here, "SI" denotes system integrator (prime contractor) and "AO" denotes acquiring organization.

Entry & Exit Criteria. For the acquiring organization, User Acceptance Tests (UAT) and Pilot of a major system involve coordination between different parts of the organization. Having well defined entry and exit criteria are not only important for mutual understanding between the acquiring organization and the prime contractor, they are important for the acquiring organization to effectively communicate with internal stakeholders and to manage the participation of staff and contractors resources in UAT and related activities. Examples of typical entry and exit criteria from a major IT project of the state of Oregon are given in Figure 4.

Project Time Frame	Typical Entry Criteria	Typical Exit Criteria
System integration Test (SIT) or Extended SIT	• As determined by prime contractor.	• Prime contractor completed all SIT test cases • Level 1 Defect = 0 and Level 2 Defect = 0
User Acceptance Test (UAT)	• SIT Exit Criteria met • Acquiring Organization's test cases ready	• Level 1 Defect = 0 • Level 2 Defect = 0 or as agreed with prime contractor • Shape Metric requirement met (see below)
Pilot	• UAT Exit Criteria met and Federal approval to start Pilot received • Data conversion completed & checked • Server recovery exercise complete at hosting facility • Business / people ready, especially training • Rollback strategy complete	• Level 1 Defect = 0 • Level 2 Defect = 0 or as agreed with prime contractor • Shape Metric continues to trend downward (see below)

Figure 4: Sample entry and exit criteria for SIT/Extended SIT, UAT, and Pilot in a state of Oregon major IT project. "Level" in this table refers to severity level of a defect. (See text below.)

In Figure 4, "Level" refers to severity level, which classifies defects in terms of their impact on overall system operations. This table assumes four levels of severity: Level 1 = critical software defects / total application failure, Level 2 = major software defects, Level 3 = minor software defects, and Level 4 = cosmetic defects that do not affect operation [Jones 2012]. In a contract, severity levels may need more precise operational definitions, in order to avoid disputes. It turns out dispute around assignment of defect severity level is common during UAT, with the prime contractor pushing for lower severity level than that assigned by the acquiring organization's testers. This is understandable as earlier acceptance means earlier payment is possible from the prime contractor's perspective. Within the acquiring organization, there may be enormous pressure to accept the system so it can be launched and the project closed – sometime before system quality has stabilized, unfortunately.

Empirical Shape Metric for Defect Counts. In order to understand if system quality has stabilized, it is important to track the temporal trend of total defects discovered by testing against some specific set of test scripts or test cases. Figure 5 depicts schematic defect trend in time that would need to be observed before a system can be considered production worthy for applications that are considered mission critical and/or must conform to strict regulatory compliance.

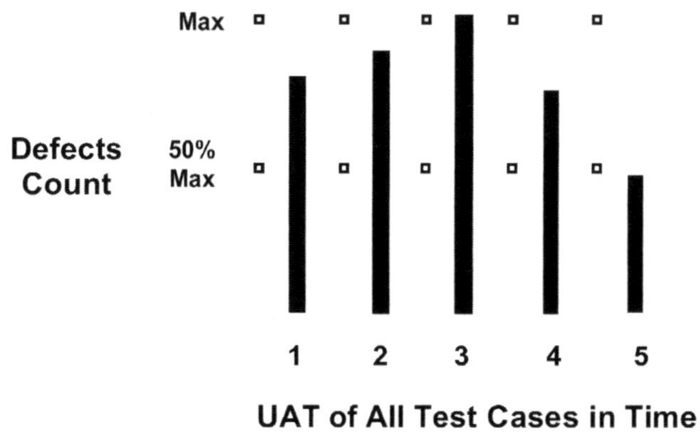

Figure 5: Sample Defects Shape Metric, which is a time series of Defects Count when a fixed number of test scripts are run multiple times.

It is possible to develop contract language to formalize understanding around defects shape metric between the acquiring organization and the prime contractor. Below is sample language from an executed contract between the state of Oregon and a major system integrator:

1. There will be at least five data points gathered during UAT. Agency will designate data points in its UAT Test Plan;
2. Defects discovered at the final data point must be less than or equal to 50% of the Time Series Maximum. "Time Series Maximum" is the data point representing the highest number of Defects discovered during the execution of the UAT test cases designated as data points;
3. There must be at least two data points following the Time Series Maximum; and
4. Data points must show that the total number of Defects is declining.

Lessons Learned From Testing. Some of these lessons learned may seem like common sense. However, there is a pattern of history repeating itself that the authors have observed. One reason is organizational dynamics and politics that sometime motivate premature system launch. Another reason may be general lack of awareness of certain types of risks among staff and management of the acquiring organization or the prime contractor.

- Systems should not be placed into production when there are critical defects that require complex workarounds or have no workaround.
- Empirical defects trends are important for go-live decisions.
- Interfaces to legacy systems and integration with other existing systems may be complex and high risk. Time and time again, interfaces with existing / legacy systems have delayed a project's ability to move to pilot or to go-live enterprise wide. Interfaces and integration with existing systems must be tested.

- Data conversion (with shadow data repositories that often lack good inventory and documentations) may be complex and high risk. Time and time again, data conversion has delayed a project's ability to move to pilot or to go-live statewide. Data that need to be converted must be identified early, and converted data must be checked.
- Security testing and reviews need to be done by trained specialists that apply appropriate test protocols, methods, and tools. Applicable standards may be industry specific or mandated by relevant government entities [End Note 1]. Also relevant are standards, policies, and procedures of the acquiring organization.
- Disaster recovery plan needs to be in place, tested, and validated.
- Regression testing needs to be done after bug fixes. Lack of test automation is a challenge against sufficient regression test or even "smoke test" after bug fixes or software upgrades; which include upgrades or patches of underlying COTS products / platforms, middleware, and operating systems.

7. Organizational Dynamics

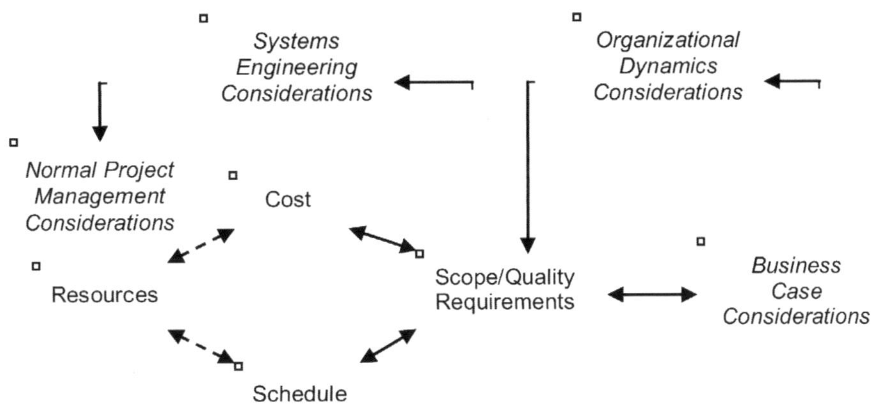

Figure 6: Project management considerations are not simply the management of the triple constraints of scope, cost, and schedule, based on system engineering considerations. Scope/quality requirements are affected by changes in business case considerations and are susceptible to the influence of organizational dynamics.

Referring to Figure 6, "normal project management" is predicated on the management of a baseline project plan, which is the science and art of balancing the triple constraints of scope, cost, and schedule. When the business case and "to be" system requirements are stable, the challenge of balancing the triple constraints is mainly influenced by system engineering considerations. However, a stable business case with corresponding stable requirements is not a valid assumption in many projects, especially those that aim to transform operational paradigms or other important aspects of the enterprise. In these situations, requirements are susceptible to the influence of organizational dynamics. This means human factors of individuals and groups -- operating in the context of the organizational culture of the enterprise -- play an important role in shaping and morphing the requirements. Some lessons learned regarding organizational dynamics are:

- Projects need to deal with enterprise-wide paradigm change early, especially with respect to business process change, staffing change, and other changes that are in conflict with prevailing organizational practices or culture.
- Projects need to adapt and adjust scope / quality requirements with evolving changes in the business and external environment that may affect the business case; not ignore or resist them on the ground of scope creep or change control.

There is a fundamental tension between change management from the perspective of project management (which emphasizes change control) and organizational change management (which emphasizes necessary and beneficial change to the enterprise). The acquiring organization must balance change to project scope, schedule and budget with change needed by an enterprise, but the latter frequently requires time and organizational learning to develop and to refine [Crawford 2014]. In Agile, as in other SDLCs, a major IT project in a large acquiring organization must [Sills 2017]:

- develop project roadmaps that integrate relevant business functions and IT;
- put in place project governance that integrates all work teams and relevant business functions;
- coordinate cross-team / cross-function dependencies methodically and carefully;
- assure end-to-end functionality of work products across all work teams and relevant business functions.

Given organizational culture, it is not a given that all enterprises can do these things well to properly support Agile or, for that matter, another SDLC chosen to deliver a major IT project. In other word, SDLC is just one facet of success in delivering a major IT project in a large complex enterprise.

8. Conclusion

In this paper, we have examined various aspects of assuring good quality & risk management for large organizations when acquiring enterprise systems, with emphasis on the use of Agile methods. In this context, an acquiring organization needs to pay particular attention to:

- how requirements are to be discovered and refined, given the general solution approach chosen;
- organizational readiness before the prime contractor should come on board;
- alignment between contract and SDLC, especially in relation to ongoing verification & validation of prime contractor work products;

- business aware testing, especially in relation to end-to-end functional testing and defects management during UAT;
- human factors and organizational dynamics that may cause real-world circumstances to deviate significantly from those assumed by life cycle reference models and processes, especially those that assume stable requirements and business case as given.

When working with a prime contractor, it would be important to adopt a "trust but verify" mindset during all aspects of a project. A project that aims to bring about major business process changes and operational paradigm shifts [End Note 2] is especially challenging and need to review business case and requirements frequently with those participating in project governance. Real-world complexity – including but not limited to availability of subject matter experts, contracting models, resources for end-to-end functional testing, and organizational dynamics / culture -- may render Agile (or other SDLCs for that matter) not a good fit for the acquiring organization.

Large IT projects in large enterprise are among the most complex human endeavors. A viable solution that meets business needs requires good cross-team / cross-functional coordination that takes into account human factors and organizational dynamics. There is no "silver bullet" for successful delivery of major systems. The choice of SDLC, including Agile if chosen, is one facet of good management and systems engineering / systems integration.

References

[Beck 2015] K. Beck, M. Beedle, A. van Bennekum, A. Cockburn, W. Cunningham, M. Fowler, J. Grenning, J. Highsmith, A. Hunt, R. Jeffries, J. Kern, B. Marick, R. C. Martin, S. Mellor, K. Schwaber, J. Sutherland and D. Thomas, *Manifesto for agile software development*, June 2015. Available: http://www.agilemanifesto.org.

[Crawford 2014] L. Crawford, A. Aitken, and A. Hassner-Nahmias, *Project Management and Organizational Change*, Newtown Square, PA: Project Management Institute, 2014, ISBN: 978-1-62825-043-5, page 1-3.

[Jones 2012] C. Jones and O. Bonsignour, *The Economics of Software Quality*, Boston: Addison-Wesley, 2012, ISBN: 978-0-13-258220-9. See page 246 for relevant paragraphs on Waterfall SDLC and page 281-282 for relevant paragraphs on defect severity levels.

[Nuottila 2016] J. Nuottila, K. Aaltonen, and J. Kujala, "Challenges of adopting agile methods in a public organization," International Journal of Information Systems and Project Management, Vol. 4, No. 3, 2016, page 65-85; and references cited therein. Available: http://www.sciencesphere.org/ijispm/archive/ijispm-040304.pdf.

[Sills 2017] D. Sills, K. Tunks, and J. O'Leary, "Agile in Government – Scaling Agile for Government," *Agile in Government: A playbook from the Deloitte Center for Government Insights*,

Deloitte Development LLC, 2017, page 8-13. Available: https://www2.deloitte.com/insights/us/en/industry/public-sector/agile-at-scale-in-government.html.

[SEI 2016] Software Engineering Institute, "RFP patterns and techniques for successful agile contracting," Report No. CMU/SEI-2016-SR-025, November 2016. Available: https://resources.sei.cmu.edu/asset_files/SpecialReport/2016_003_001_484063.pdf

[USGAO 2014] United State Government Accountability Office, "Healthcare.gov – ineffective planning and oversight practices underscore the need for improved contract management," Report No. GAO-14-694, July 2014. Available: https://www.gao.gov/assets/670/665179.pdf.

End Notes

[End Note 1] For examples, see: https://www.pcisecuritystandards.org/pci_security/standards_overview for an overview of payment cards industry security standards; http://owasp.org for Open Web Application Security Project (OWASP) which provides a Testing Guide; https://www.hhs.gov/hipaa/for-professionals/security/index.html for HIPAA Security Rule that applies to the U.S. healthcare industry; and https://fedramp.gov for security standards of cloud services used by U.S. federal government agencies.

[End Note 2] The term "paradigm shift" originated in philosophy of science. See T. Kuhn, *The Structure of Scientific Revolutions, Second Edition,* Chicago: The University of Chicago Press, 1970. Besides the physical sciences, this term has been widely used in different fields (e.g. technology, marketing, and social sciences) to mean a major change in thought pattern or approach of individuals or organizations.

Acknowledgment

The authors acknowledge helpful discussions with (in alphabetical order of last names): Edward Arabas, Nicholas Betsacon, Bob Cummings, Capers Jones, Patricia McQuaid, Alex Pettit, and Wallace Rogers.

This page intentionally left blank.

Automated Visual Regression Testing with BackstopJS

Authors
Angela Riggs (riggs.ang@gmail.com)

Abstract
During the software development life cycle, there are many types of testing that are done to ensure the quality of work. While back-end testing is fairly standardized, testing your front-end work is more difficult - verifying implementation across a variety of devices, or making sure new style changes don't introduce style regressions across the site.

But how do you test front-end regressions? Manual testing is an option for smaller sites, but much less efficient as websites become bigger and more complex. After failing to scale exploratory testing and trying other tools that weren't the right fit, we finally landed on BackstopJS, an open-source npm package that allowed us to create a system for automated visual regression testing.

In implementing this tool, we had to overcome some challenges as we began to meet our initial goal of verifying front-end quality. Once BackstopJS was in place, new challenges came up that needed to be solved as well:

- Refining a broad testing tool into a more specific approach
- Ramping up a testing tool into the software development workflow
- Lowering the barrier of use to encourage other teams and developers to adopt it

As these challenges were solved, the result was a robust process for automated visual regression testing that is easily customized and iterated, and offers the ability to catch and fix mistakes before they become our clients' problem.

Biography
As a QA Engineer, my role is at the intersection of Testing, DevOps, Architect, and Scrum Master. I approach my work with determination and a positive energy, holding myself and my team to a high standard. I have an enthusiasm for learning and advancing, and appreciate that my field calls on my curiosity and attention to detail. I understand the importance of acknowledging and balancing competing needs to ensure individual, team, and project success.

I believe in people over process, but also enjoy creating useful foundational processes that promote clear understandings around development workflow. I take pride in both my technical and interpersonal skills, and work hard to be a leader who offers empathy, support, and thoughtful problem-solving to my team and my company.

Outside of work, I enjoy meandering through nature, or through the aisles of Powell's. I also have an enthusiasm for karaoke, and long debates about what can truly be categorized as a sandwich.

1. Catching Visual Regressions

Automated visual regression testing started as a solution to a specific problem for our engineering team. One of our websites was experiencing content loss and style regressions on deploys to staging and production. Unfortunately, we became aware of these challenges because the client would find them and tell us. We needed a better way to catch these regressions so we could rollback, fix the issue, and redeploy in a timely manner.

Our initial solution was to deploy during low-traffic periods, and to follow up the deploys immediately with exploratory testing. This was inefficient and mostly ineffective, as the website had so many pages and sub-pages that it just wasn't reasonable to test this way and expect to catch regressions.

We needed a way to easily check large portions of the website for regressions, and we needed something pretty quick. Some of the initial options required too much configuration before tests could be run, or necessitated writing out all of the tests for each page of the website manually. The time and effort to do that meant that it wasn't much of an improvement from the exploratory testing.

After researching a few options, BackstopJS stood out as the best solution for our problem. It was quick to set up, configure, and start running. It also offered a visual report that compared before and after screenshots side-by-side, which made it easy to see where any differences were.

Most of the setup involved creating a list of URLs for BackstopJS to iterate through for its screenshots. Because the regressions were inconsistent, 60-70 URLs were included in the configuration file. For each URL, a screenshot of the header, footer, and main content section were captured. Before a deploy, the reference command would be run, which captured the present-state screenshots for staging and production environments. The developer would deploy to staging, and the post-deploy BackstopJS command would be run to capture screenshots of the updated site and compare for style regressions. Once it was verified that the deploy went well - or the regressions had been fixed - the developer would deploy to production, and BackstopJS would be run on production to check for regressions.

With this tool in place, style regressions could be caught and fixed before they became a problem for our client. But there were a few more challenges ahead that needed to be solved in order to get the best use out of automated visual regression testing.

2. Narrowing the Scope

The initial problem had been solved, but the current setup required a lot of overhead to run the tests. Because so many URLs were being tested, there were around 400 screenshots per run. This broad sweep approach worked for catching regressions, but there were a few drawbacks. The screenshots included a lot of false negatives, which was tedious to parse through and verify whether a regression had occurred. The tests also took quite a long time to run, and would actually time out and fail about halfway through unless npm's "no timeout" argument was included in the command.

From start to finish - running the references, deploying, running the tests, and reviewing - the process took about 45 minutes to an hour. This hardly made it more worthwhile than manually testing for regressions. A more effective workflow was needed to reduce the time and effort involved, and to take advantage of this automated testing tool.

Looking through the website, there were a handful of templates repeated across the site. This was helpful - the number of URLs in the configuration could be reduced, and still have all of the templates represented in the testing. The height value in the viewport was adjusted to 3000px, and each URL was given a single CSS selector to trigger the screenshot. The height change meant that the captured screenshot was tall enough to cover the whole page, instead of getting coverage via multiple CSS selectors.

These configuration changes drastically reduced the overall running time, removed the risk of timing out, and reduced the number of screenshots per run from 500 to under 100. This iteration made automated visual regression testing much more useful for wider use, and it was set up on all of our projects. Instead of just being a reaction to bad deploys on a single project, it was implemented as a smoke test for all deploys to staging and production.

3. Lowering the Barrier for Use

With the overall configuration improved, there was one challenge left to tackle. Although running the tests had become more efficient, maintaining and updating the configuration was still problematic. Each environment required its own configuration file, which meant four separate files to update and keep in sync. The extra effort here made it hard to iterate the tests as greenfield sites were built, which prevented widespread adoption of BackstopJS during feature development.

To solve this, the configuration setup was changed to use a single JavaScript file instead of the default JSON format. This format change allowed for arguments to be defined and passed in to the BackstopJS commands. It also allowed for an environment argument to be passed in for the URL to test, instead of having to reference separate configuration files. Alongside this change, there was a file with an array of URL paths to iterate over, which was also included as an argument in the BackstopJS commands.

These changes made the workflow much more convenient to use, but had an unexpected side effect that still presented a blocker for developers. Because the setup was very customized, it required a number of arguments to be passed in for executing the tests. This resulted in lengthy and cumbersome commands. To improve this experience, a Makefile was created for running BackstopJS. This took the commands from something like `backstop reference --configPath=backstop.js --pathFile=paths --env=prod` to `make prod-reference`. This was much more intuitive, and much easier to remember.

With these final improvements to the configuration and setup, the barrier of use was lowered for developers, which meant they were willing to add it to their local development workflow. Now, style regressions had the potential to be caught long before any deploys to production!

4. Successfully Transitioning to Automated Testing

With BackstopJS in place, we were able to reliably and efficiently test for style regressions. However, we learned that introducing the tool wasn't a magic solution. Although it was the right tool for the job, there was still work to be done to make it an effective part of the general workflow.

The first introduction of BackstopJS did offer automated testing as an alternative to inefficient manual testing, but the way it was used didn't really end up saving time or effort. By minimizing how much BackstopJS actually needed to test, we were able to reap the benefits of having automated testing in place of the former manual testing. And because we took the time up front to adapt the configuration and keep it simple to run, automated visual regression testing was adopted for use throughout the development workflow, from feature work to deploys.

The challenges we solved and the lessons we learned while adopting BackstopJS can be applied to many processes of researching and adopting any new testing tool. Replacing manual testing with automated testing is not a one-size-fits-all solution. Not all tools are the right solution for your problem, and even the right solution may not work right out of the box. Transitioning to automated testing requires iteration and feedback, and buy-in from the people who will be using or benefiting from it. Find the right tool, figure out how to make it work for your needs, and make it easy to people to use.

Why is Communication So Difficult?

Authors

Peter Hartauer, QualityMinds GmbH
(peter.hartauer@qualityminds.de) @certifiedtester

Abstract

Communication is essential for a successful project. Acceptable results can only be reached when all participants are communicating effectively. However, it is often difficult to establish this level of communication.

This talk encourages all project participants to think about their own methods of communication. It uses a real-world example to point out one specific problem: the "Chinese Whispers" cumulative error, which is characterized by people talking only to the person next in their hierarchy. It results in distorted information and creates an outcome quite different from the input. The talk will present the issue in a humorous way and give some solid advice.

Biography

Peter Hartauer is a quality engineer and a tester by heart - because good products are fun.

In the beginning of his career, Peter worked in a large multinational company in Erlangen, Germany. As a consultant for customers in the public sector and in internal projects he became riveted on testing, working his way up from manual tester to test manager in a multicultural project. In 2011, he started working as a trainer for the ISTQB, REQB, IQBBA and IBUQ certification classes.

Peter is an active member of the testing community: He follows the newest trends in testing, attends conferences, organizes the Nuremberg's Testers Meetup and contributes to the Ministry of Testing Community. His Twitter handle is @certifiedtester.

Summary:
2005 - 2008: Apprenticeship at Siemens IT Solutions and Services GmbH
2008 - 2011: (Junior) IC Consultant at Siemens AG
2011 - 2016: Trainer and Software Process Engineer at Knowledge Department GmbH
2016 - now: Team Lead Testing Essentials at QualityMinds GmbH

1. Introduction

Communication is the most important thing in a project. More than testing. More than coding. More than planning. More than managing. It's all about communication. We communicate all day, discussing problems and try to solve them. Spoken and written words carry the information we want to share with other people.

To this end we need to ensure that we communicate effectively. That's the difficult part, because usually communication is more than words. It contains emotions, facial expression, gestures and much more. It is also driven by the context, the relation to the person you are speaking to.

After all, communication is important. It can improve the project, the outcome of the project, and the quality of the product. If you can convey all the things you want to say with your words then your expectations and intent can be understood more easily by others. So why does it so often fail?

2. So, What's the Problem?

In my years as a software tester, as a Scrum Master, and as a consultant and a trainer for many companies in Europe, I realized that a lot of the communication is not respected enough by people. Information often flows in one direction only without any feedback and not really wanting a response. In hierarchical organisations especially there is a missing culture of communication. The results are sometimes catastrophic: wrong outcomes, buggy products and much more.

2.1. NLP as a start

A lot of the defects in communication are systematic. That means we are doing them over and over again, because we are "programmed" to act like that. But, systematic also means that there is a pattern. And where there is a pattern, there is a possibility to break that pattern. There are a lot of books, blogs, and other resources dealing with communication defects and how to solve them. One of the most popular is Neurolinguistic Programming (NLP). It was developed in the 1970's for the treatment of psychological illnesses. It was intended to help the therapist to understand the patient more clearly. NLP deals with three main defects in communication I often encounter even today.

Generalization is one of the defects you may encounter. Last week I heard the following sentence in a company's jour fixe: "If we don't deliver on time, the product will fail." It's a special case of generalization because the product will not be successful even if you deliver on time. The failure or success of the product depends on a complex combination of different factors like costs, time, environment, quality and more.

Another defect is deletion where necessary information is omitted. In a management conference the speaker said: "You have to believe me and carry out the orders I give you." The funny part was, the speaker used the deletion by intent. He wanted to show how problematic it is to obey orders without knowing everything. He purposefully didn't give any information on what would happen if somebody didn't follow his instructions. The deletion is the missing consequence and the free interpretation. Everybody was looking for a safe space, so everybody obeyed the speaker. They painted their faces with green paint. Five minutes later it was time for lunch, but people with green faces were not allowed in the dining room. It turned out that the paint was very difficult to remove, so the dining room remained almost empty while the queue for the toilets grew. The speaker said to me: "Look at the sheep. And they think they are leaders."

The third defect is distortion. It is generated by the speaker, often unintentionally. "I always have to do all the stuff." But who is saying that? "I have to work at least to 8pm because everybody will say, that I'm lazy if I don't." Really? Perhaps you have good time management. Perhaps you carry out the work much faster than others because you're more intelligent?

2.2. Biases to Intensify them

There are more than 130 biases you can find while surfing the web. The swimmers body illusion, the availability bias or the sunk cost fallacy. All of them influence the way we behave, the way we communicate. One of the biases is the authority bias. I will explain this bias, because it will be important in understanding the Chinese Whispers defect I want to explain later.

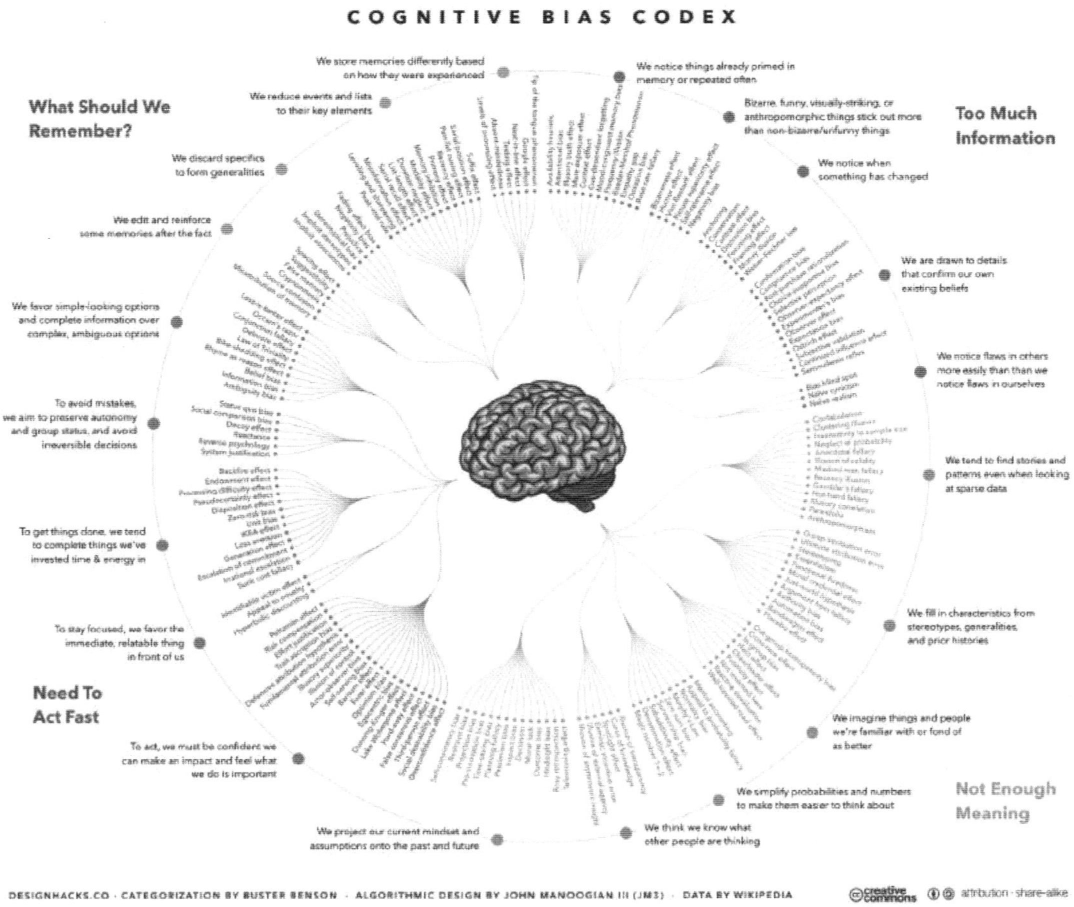

The authority bias is one which predisposes us to respect authorities much more than we trust ourselves and so we stop thinking. It is related to the example of deletion. The speaker used his authority and everybody stopped thinking. To explain it a little bit more concretely, just think about your latest tests. If a "simple" tester says: "The product is crap. I found so many defects that it will be catastrophic if we release right now!" Would you trust them? If a test manager with a high reputation in the company says: "The product is crap. I found so many defects that it will be catastrophic if we release right now!" Would you trust them more? And why? Is the manager smarter than the tester who executed the test and really saw the problems in the product?

3. How the Improve Quality with Communication

Let's assume that the quality of your communication directly affects the quality of the product. Wouldn't you set up a communication test? What if this wasn't just an assumption, but product quality really does improve with good communication? We take classes in better coding, better architecture, professional project management, better testing, better everything. Instead, what we really need is better communication classes. Many people think we are good speakers because we use our speech every day, almost always in spoken or written formats. Consider what would happen if you were no longer able to use words to transfer information. What would you do?

To increase the complexity further, imagine trying to give this information to a person without a direct line of communication. A person that you don't know. How would you do this? Sign language? Prototypes? How would you effectively communicate?

In a lot of projects and companies I have encountered the tapper and listener syndrome. It is another bias that leads to the Chinese Whispers defect. You start omitting this information because you assume that others already have the same knowledge as you. Why is it called tapper and listener? There was an experiment that divided people into two groups. The first group were tappers, and the other were listeners. The tappers were given a list of songs like "Happy birthday" or "The Star Spangled Banner". Then they have to tap the rhythm of the song and the listeners have to guess the song. In advance the tappers and listeners were asked about the probability the listener would guess the song correctly. The tappers said that the others would be right 50% of the time. So, one of two songs is guessed right. The listeners were more sceptical and thought that they would be right 25% of the time. While conducting the experiment, the quota of correctly guessed songs was about 2%! The most disappointed group was the tappers. Why? They couldn't believe that the listener misinterpreted "The Star Spangled Banner" as "Happy Birthday". Why did this happen? The tapper has the information, the listener doesn't. The tapper has the melody in mind while tapping, the listener only hears some sort of freaky Morse code.

4. Chinese Whispers

Perhaps you know this game from kindergarten, from your youth, or perhaps from your kids. Five or more children sit in a row and the child at one end of the row thinks about a word. Then this word is quietly whispered into the ear of the child sitting next to the first. Then the second child gives the information received to the next child. And so on until the last child receives the information. This child has to loudly speak out the "word". And in most cases, it is definitely not the word provided by the first child.

If an easy word is chosen, like "Needle" or "Bus", it is more likely that the correct information is transported. That's because it is an easy to speak and mostly unambiguous word.

You can increase the difficulty if you choose a word that rhymes with, or sounds similar to, another. If you choose "Book" you can get "Hook". Or if you choose "Mouse" you can get "House". In that case the information transforms to something else. And there is definitely a difference between my giving a "book" or a "hook".

To create real chaos the child could choose a complex word. For example: "Surreptitiously". I'm pretty sure that this word wouldn't make it through Chinese Whispers correctly. Most often the result would be something Germans call "Wortsalat" or "Buchstabensalat". It literally means "word salad" or "letter salad". Everything is scrambled. If this happens it is great fun for the kids!

Why don't the children ask their neighbours to repeat the whispered words if they don't think they've understood the word correctly? Why not ask if the word is understood correctly? Well, that's the only rule in the game: No asking, no repetition.

5. The Story of Chinese Whispers

So, what does this game have to do with reality? Why is this game relevant to quality and testing? Let me take you to a project of mine from some years ago…

The project was at a big IT-consulting company that was, in turn, part of an even bigger company which produced lots of different goods, from electronics to machinery. The project's objective was to create an IT-asset management system for the company itself as well as a number of external customers. The system should be capable of managing orders from employees if they needed something for their work. The most important categories were IT equipment, telephone infrastructure, moving of offices, file sharing and access rights, servers, room bookings and office furniture. There were other things as well but as you can see, the system should be capable of everything.

The system was a complex client-server application with a lot of different rules, databases and connected systems orchestrated by JBoss. The team had to connect to the current LDAP and Active Directory. To make it even worse, there was an IT management system capable of performing some of those tasks in one division of the company that didn't want to give up their system. So, it had to be integrated.

The development time was about 5 years in total. The number of parallel users was estimated to be more than 5.000. The budget, of close to 2 million Euros, was far too low.

Over the years the team produced a working system in several releases, but it was not finished. In spite of that the CEO deciding in a management jour fixe that the first customer should be given access to the system within two weeks. Everybody was so enthusiastic at the beginning that the manager decided a risk management strategy would not be necessary.

The company was very hierarchical and you had to follow the defined way of "communication". You were only allowed to talk to your subordinates and to your one and only supervisor. Therefore there was a perfect chain of children sitting next to each other. Oh, sorry: People.

After testing the system, our tester (let's call him Bob) raised a warning that the system was in a non-deliverable state. He did this via email because the team was distributed all over Germany. This is the email Alice, the test manager, received:

> Hi Alice,
> I'd like to inform you about the latest test results:
> I have executed 250 test cases and only 53 were successful without errors.
> All major risks are still not mitigated. In my opinion there is no chance for a successful roll out. We haven't been given enough time to fix the errors and the product will not work at all. Please inform everybody.
> Bob

Let us analyze that email. What does Bob do well, and not so well? At first, he takes the initiative to speak out about a problem. He mentions that there are problems and even included figures. So, there is no defect in the words he used. Bob does state a personal assumption but makes it clear to Alice that this is what it is - an assumption. The only big problem is the request for action, where Bob says "everybody" without specifying who this included, is a deletion.

After further emails were exchanged between the developer (Charlie) and Bob, Alice writes an email to Daniel, the Development Lead:

> Hi Daniel,
> Bob and Charlie informed me that meeting the deadline is impossible. The testing department won't give this release a go ahead until all major bugs are fixed and all critical (priority 1) test cases are successfully executed.
> Alice

This email is interesting, because it is the beginning of the Chinese Whispers. So, let's take a closer look at it. She states the impossibility of meeting the deadline, without including what would go wrong. This is a deletion of what problems might arise. This information is in the next sentence, but the consequences of releasing the product anyway are still not included. By generalizing in this way, Alice reduces the criticality.

Hi Eric,
Alice informed me that an on-time release of our product is going to be difficult. They have too many bugs and have problems executing all the important test cases. We should monitor the situation by keeping an eye on development and testing.
Daniel

Daniel informs the project manager Eric and the next defect strikes. Daniel seems to have massive respect for Eric. Authority bias combined with a fear of asking softens the "impossible" to a "difficult". This is the point where everything is going wild and crazy. In this project everybody acted this way. You can see an increasingly soft tune in the emails. The following email is from the project manager (Eric) to the business unit manager (Franck) and his email to the CEO (Gerry):

Hi Franck,
it seems there are some difficulties in testing and development. Something about some bugs that occurred and too little time to test everything. I think we should go on with our plan but keep our metrics in mind, so we can react.
Eric

Hi Gerry,
you wanted some information on the new release. Eric told me that some bugs occurred, and they need to test further to execute the test cases. I think we are on a good way. Will you tell Hannah, so she can inform our customer?
Franck

What happened? I will call this a cumulative error. Everybody acted the same way and softened the message. The impossible situation morphed into being on a good way! And accordingly, Gerry goes on to send this email:

Hi Hannah,
good news from our development and testing department! We are on a good way and keep the work up with our actual release.
Can you inform Irene?
Gerry

At the end, the customer representative (Irene) receives the complete opposite of the initial warning.

5.1. The Big Bang

As you can see, this conversation went really strange and had an interesting outcome. At least we can learn from their mistakes. For the company it went terribly wrong. After deploying the system to the customer an undocumented and untested function dropped the customer's database and caused a stop in production and a loss of 1.6 million Euro. The CEO was not amused with the outcome and wrote the following email:

> Hi Alice, hi Daniel,
> can somebody explain to me what happened after releasing our new version?
> I THOUGHT WE HAD A GOOD DEVELOPMENT AND TESTING DEPARTMENT???
> Why did this happen? What should I tell our customer? His systems were going down and we have had a massive data loss. We cannot afford such bad work! Why was I not informed about these massive problems?
> Crisis meeting in 15 minutes in my office! Gerry

6. Lessons Learned

Who is guilty? I don't want to blame a single person. Instead I want to focus on the important details. As it is a cumulative error there are a lot of factors contributing to this situation. But there are some indicators that can give you a clue that there is something strange happening.

6.1. Subject Line of Emails

An interesting part was the subject line. It was growing. From:

"Test results"

To:
"FW: FW: FW: FW: FW: FW: FW: RE: Test results"

In addition, all of the previous emails were attached! The first indicator and lesson learned is that you should read all the emails throughout. Especially if the email was forwarded multiple times. I advise you to stop the chain if there is the second "FW:" in the subject line. Furthermore, read the whole email. Don't expect that the latest comment has all the information.

6.2. Don't Trust the Rabbit

If there is only a vague expression of detail in an email, then ask the people directly. This concerns all words like "some", "good", "maybe", "eventually", "only", "always", "sometimes" and so on. Ask for the real meaning and if there are exceptions. Fighting generalization is like cutting the heads off a hydra.

6.3. Talk About the Risk

If you see a risk, you are the one to talk about it! Even more so if you are a tester or test manager. It is your job to inform others about potential risks. If the risk is too big, and you expect severe damage, then ignore communication rules. Talk directly to the people who are affected and whose decisions are based on your information.

6.4. Don't Play the Game

There are a lot of companies playing that Chinese Whispers game. Don't be part of it. If you are forced to play it, explain the risks. You lose information every time it is transferred via another person. That's normal, that's human. That's a common linguistic defect. But it is systematic. And you now know the root cause and can do something against it.

7. Conclusion

This event as described may appear to be exaggerated. I wish I could say "Yes, it is fiction!". Sadly, it is not. All of this did happen and it was a pity to see the cumulative effects. It was a big lesson for me and has changed the way that I act as a tester or test manager. Quality improvement is not only testing, reporting, finding bugs and debugging, reviews and all the other tools we have. Quality is based on communication. The same problem can occur whilst creating requirements and communicating them to developers. It can occur during estimations. It's everywhere!

I want you to think about your method of communication. The way you distribute information. I would encourage you to improve your communication skills, to watch for biases and linguistic defects. Then you will have taken a further step "On The Road To Quality".

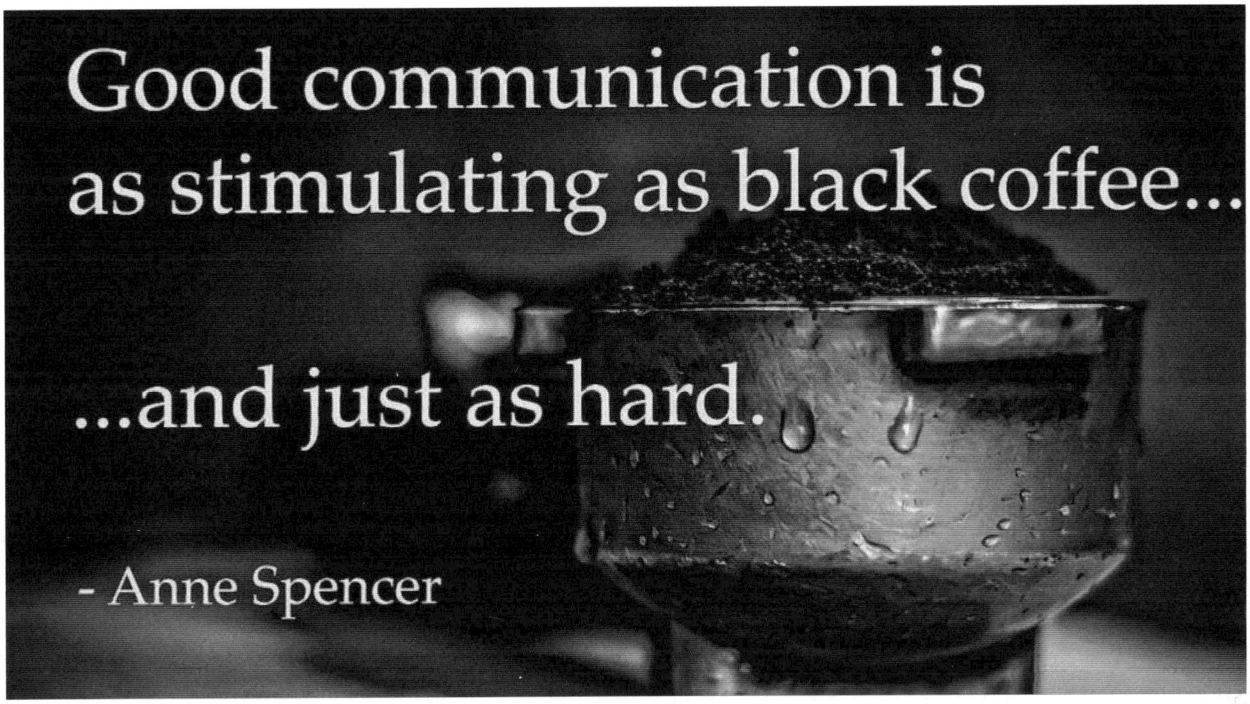
Good communication is
as stimulating as black coffee...
...and just as hard.
- Anne Spencer

Structure, Design, Extensible and User Experience – Foundations for an Automation Framework

Authors

Arvind Srinivasa Babu (Arvind_Babu@mcafee.com)
Abhishek Sharma (Abhishek2_Sharma@mcafee.com)
Hemant Prasad (Hemant_Prasad@mcafee.com)

Abstract

Our team works on a native application that is deployed on tens of millions of machines worldwide. Frequent release commitments, new features and the agile process, stresses our need to increasingly speed up our validation process and our use of automation.

Over the course of the past decade, we developed couple of frameworks focused on features, services, or just simply automating our test suites. This worked well in the short-term but was unable to scale with our validation processes, which grew with every feature and release.

In this paper, we will highlight some of our pitfalls and how we overcame them by structuring our automation suite, segregating design, test suites, and considering the user experience in adding new test cases and extending the framework itself.

Biography

Arvind Srinivasa Babu is a Software Development Engineer and Software Security Architect at McAfee, with over 9 years of experience designing and implementing software. He leads the development of different features across server and non-server technologies while also building in security controls for the product. His areas of interest span network programming, user interface design and applications, cloud solutions, system programming, product security and mobile development.

Abhishek Sharma is a Senior Principal SDET at McAfee, Bangalore. He has over 9 years of experience in embedded as well as application software verification. Prior to McAfee, Abhishek led the Software Common Components verification team in Software Center of Excellence in Aerospace domain at Honeywell. Abhishek holds a Master in Computer System Engineering specialization in Intelligent Systems from Halmstad University.

Hemant Prasad is a Software Development Engineer at McAfee, Bangalore. He has 10 years of experience in analysis, design, and development of enterprise level products at McAfee. Hemant holds Master of Computer Applications from NIT, Karnataka, Surathkal. His area of interests is networking, system programming, and debugging and crash dump analysis.

1. Introduction

Automation[1] is the task of repeatedly performing a set of actions without any manual intervention. Automated testing is the principle in which the validation of software modules is performed automatically as new code changes are introduced in the software. As the software lifecycle keeps evolving, the critical ask for every software project is to deliver software faster and with highest quality. As per our observation over several years, automation has taken center stage in the domain of Software Quality as it drives faster delivery with highest quality confidence. While new greenfield projects have the advantage of developing automation as the new code is put in place, there are organizations that have had the struggle of moving legacy code from manual testing to testing with automation.

Our product is a native application that supports various platforms including Windows, Linux, MacOS, HP-UX, Solaris, AIX and all their flavors and versions with varying hardware architectures. Our software has been deployed over tens of millions of computer nodes with various network topologies and infrastructure. While it has been of paramount importance for our team to keep providing customers new features and product versions with the highest quality, we must also keep delivering updates with an ever increasing pace. Over the past decade we have had various challenges in automating the testing of our product and have employed various "Automation Frameworks" and have also developed our own.

In this paper, we will focus on our experiences in the past, what we have learned from it and what we have done to utilize our learnings. The paper is organized into various sections starting from where we were and leading up to where we are with our automation testing efforts. Section 2 will focus on our history, the challenges we faced in a non-automated world, how we incrementally set up smaller automation fronts, re-architected the product and along with it developed our initial home-grown automation framework. Section 3 will focus on how what constitutes an automation framework based on the learnings we obtained from our past experience. Section 4 will detail what we identified as foundations for any framework that needs to be developed for a product. Section 5 will discuss in detail on how to apply this Structure, Design, Extensibility and User-experience (SDEU) philosophy to a product.

2. The Challenges of Automating "LEGACY" Code

Our product has been deployed worldwide in tens of millions of end nodes and it has been successfully adopted for more than 15 years. Our product also supports over 200 flavors of operating systems including Windows, Linux, MacOS, HP-UX, AIX, Solaris, etc. These metrics speak to the efficiency of our quality process, which has continuously provided a better customer experience. Our team has constantly changed in size in the past 15 years and averages between 10-15 engineers at any given time. This is the team that has designed, developed and validated the product across various process lifecycles, platforms and release timelines.

Before we embraced automation, all validations were done through manual testing. A small change in one of the core modules would easily render a manual validation effort of five to six months. We did have a few unit tests that barely provided us 3% functional coverage due to an architecture that needed to support multiple hardware platforms and operating systems.

Our initial attempt at automation was to increase our code coverage through unit testing for legacy code. While this certainly helped in increasing our functional code coverage by 10%, but it was still not enough. However, the core modules were actively tested through unit testing while functional verification tests and build verification tests were still being performed manually. This helped reduce a couple months' efforts as core modules were not often worked upon and when we did work on them, the unit tests helped flag any anomalies with newly introduced code.

The above process worked well for a two to three year period, but a four month validation effort to verify a few lines of code changes was still affecting our delivery rate. We also started transitioning our lifecycle process from waterfall to a semi agile process since the validation duration was bottlenecked with manual testing. This was leading to story sizing issues as well as spikes in every sprint. We decided to tweak our process to fit our validation efforts. This was the time we decided to step in and build an automation framework, a home-grown project that could automate and validate test cases within the python framework. This was keyword-driven automation suite to allow individuals to write new tests easily. It worked for a couple of years but as team members changed and new features came in, the framework couldn't scale up to meet the demand for new keywords and it eventually failed to enable team members to automate new features (Figure 1).

After being in the field for nearly a decade, we wanted sleek and manageable product code that could support various platforms and operating systems, so we decided to re-architect our product to position ourselves with embedded devices as well as the other platforms we already support. This also allowed us to move our architecture to service-oriented architecture and a new automation framework to specifically verify services. We mirrored our development of the new automation to our new service-oriented design of the product and added service verification tests to gain more coverage of our new services. While this new framework proved useful during the development of our product, as we approached our release milestones, we started to build security controls into the product. The automation framework failed miserably since it was not able to perform the validations it could during development and the entire effort done to build the service verification framework had to be dropped altogether.

The third iteration of the automation framework focused more on automation infrastructure resources and on enabling testing in a rigid environment where the automation code, test suites, test cases and infrastructure details resided as part of code. Although this rigid automation style restricts who can modify the automation framework, this mode of automation served its purpose for a few years where the validation efforts were reduced to a month with the automation focusing on positive test paths for feature validations that usually run to the better half of a day.

While our third iteration is no way perfect, it served us well for some time where team could avoid manual verification of basic functionalities and focus on verifying the new features being delivered. We identified the challenges and limitations in the automation framework over the period. The next sections will cover the identified challenges and how we overcame those while making our journey towards end objective of continuous integration and release cycle.

2.1. Challenges

We identified a lot of problems and challenges when attempting to automate our validation plans. A few of the challenges we faced are as follows:

2.1.1. Tools

There are a wide variety of tools to solve problems, which we face in validating products and solutions. The bigger challenge has been in deciding the best tools andfit it into our product's life-cycle process. As our product has been in the market for more than two decades, we realized that the most important factor is the amount of work required to adopt newer tools and frameworks.. This adds cost and complicates long term support of the product. Moreover, identifying commercial off-the-shelf(COTS[5]) softwares that continues to evolve and provide enhancement over the years, is a challenge.

2.1.2. Automation Development

As product grows, so does the automation suite/framework associated with it. Without proper maintenance or process it can quickly overgrow the product and become a complete mess. Building automation frameworks without a long-term vision for support and maintenance, the life of the automation framework is only as long as the developer who wrote the automation framework. It becomes non-reusable to more modern features and cannot support legacy features.

2.1.3. Design

A lack of automation design leads to quick fixes and short-term solutions but causes long term problems in maintaining the automation code. The automation suite/framework cannot scale or extend to support product engineering teams to validate future versions.

2.1.4. Code Structure

The most common approach we have observed is the quick fix approach to solve a problem or automate a component of the product. This leads to the framework code and the automation code for the business logic of the product component to be clubbed together, making the code non-reusable and rigid in its extensibility.

2.1.5. Software Builds

The idea of automation is to get results faster. A Continuous Integration (CI) process would result in giving faster results per check-in and can just run with unit tests, but the automation needs formally generated builds, which generally run into several hours depending on the language in which the product was implemented and size of the project. The delays in getting builds causes a lot of delay in finding out issues with newly checked in code, thereby causing overall delay in getting automation results.

2.1.6. Backwards Compatibility

As product support runs long term, maintenance activities cause older versions to be supported with hotfixes or patches. The automation framework without versioning results in breaking older version validations due to addition of new code to support new/modified features. For example, a product is having a mainline development in version 4.0.0 and there are maintenance activities in its 3.0.0 and 2.0.0 versions. Automation codebase without versioning has been tuned to work with 4.0.0. If a hotfix or patch has to be delivered to 2.0.0 versions (as 2.0.1 or 2.0.x), he automation framework would miserably fail as the codebase contains automation code for 3.x and 4.x features.

3. What Consitutes an Automation Framework?

As we started to realize the challenges we faced in our past, we ultimately decided to ask the question "What constitutes an automation framework?" There is certainly a plethora of tools and each one of them solves a unique problem. But there is no tool that serves all purposes. We attempted several homegrown solutions to develop an all-in-one automation framework but as highlighted in the previous section, each attempt had brought about its own challenges. The other question that kept coming up was "For what purpose does the automation really bring value?" Should the automation framework focus only on faster delivery of validation results or should it also allow developers to be more vigilant about their code changes breaking something. We had unit tests running in our CI part of the pipelines, we also had a mix of tests automated for end-to-end workflows and the rest was covered as part of our manual validation efforts. So how do we keep things simple and automate our validations across white-box, grey-box and black-box testing as efficiently as possible?

We started to derive the foundations from what we have learned from our past encounters and we used that to build the foundations for the new framework. The automation framework will exist in any product that wants to automate their validation process. We define an Automation Framework as a codebase that controls, monitors one or more tools and independently facilitates execution and verification of test cases.

4. Foundations for an Automation Framework

We believe that any Automation Framework that is being developed should be founded on these four critical principles. An Automation Framework should encapsulate:

- Structure
- Design
- Extensibility
- User Experience

4.1. Design of an Automation Framework (D)

Any product being developed requires a simple but robust design to allow more features to be built into it. The same principle applies when designing an automation framework. It is essential for framework developers to model the framework in such a way that the product can exist for decades. Designing a framework to solve a short-term problem will give a life-expectancy for that short-term only. Most of our previous iterations in designing the framework aimed at solving short-term problems and that framework lasted only a few years.

A strong design for an automation framework should:

- Be modularized.
- Be able to handle automation of standalone test cases as well as test scenarios requiring complex configurations and setups.
- Abstract the underlying tools employed to validate a test case.
- make it easier for test automation engineers to add new test cases.
- Allow rapid integration of new as well as old technologies or frameworks from other scripting languages.
- Be extensible to accommodate multiple component architectures.
- Be able to integrate with continuous integration tools such as Jenkins[4] or Teamcity[3].

A strong design is what allows developers of products to keep building new features easily into a product. The same principle is often overlooked when writing for automation. A robust design provides inputs when structuring your framework, as well as provides extensibility and simple user-experience to write product test case automation.

4.2. Structure of an Automation Framework (S)

When a product is developed for more than a decade it shouldn't be surprising when you end up with millions of lines of code. This would lead to your automation code as well to grow into a complex framework. The structure of your Automation Framework is defined as the boundary within which your automation code can be segregated. We believe this is one of the most important aspects to consider when writing the framework as well as when writing the test cases.

Here are some few pointers when defining the boundaries for your framework.

- Never combine product test cases with framework code.
- Apply versioning to your framework so that users know exactly which version of framework has what capabilities.
- Define packages (if applicable) to organize your framework code. Monolithic framework requires high maintenance.
- Maintain separate repository for your product test case automation code, if possible in the same branch as where the product development happens.
- Identify product features and their interdependencies and model your product test cases to mirror the dependency matrix of the features.

Maintaining a structure discipline in your framework and test code allows your framework to scale and be maintainable as your product's features grow.

4.3. Extensibility of an Automation (E)

Any framework that is being developed should have provision to extend its capabilities at any given point of time. A framework that is designed to be rigid will ultimately solve the short-term problem but will fail on the long-term. A few items to consider for extending your framework:

- Allow addition of new features to framework.
- Allow addition of new product test cases.
- Allow complex reporting mechanism on success and failures.
- Allow addition of new programming languages.
- Allow addition of new tools or substitute old ones.
- Minimize or avoid rewrite of product test cases.

4.4. User Experience (U)

Each of the below user profiles will have different expectation when using the automation framework.

- Automation Framework Developer.
- Test Case Automation Developer.
- Product Developer.

4.4.1. Automation Framework Developer (AFD)

This user is primarily responsible to add or maintain the framework and provide integration and reporting mechanism for other types of users. A good experience for an AFD can be characterized by

- Ease of maintainability of framework codebase.
- Ease of addition or removal of feature support.
- Ease of addition or removal of external tools.
- Abstraction of product test cases from framework codebase.
- Versioned framework releases to track and maintain framework capabilities.

4.4.2. Test Case Automation Developer (TCAD)

The predominant user of an Automation Framework would be the product's test case automation developer. This can be any quality assurance engineer including the automation framework developer themselves. A good experience for a TCAD would be

- Ease of integrating test cases into automation framework.
- Platform agnostic way to acquire infrastructure resources to perform validation.
- Ability to write automation code that is coherent with the manual test case execution workflow.
- Framework that allows multiple technologies or architectures when automating different features.

4.4.3. Product Developer (PD)

The product developer is primarily the initiator of new product features and their inputs might be essential in adding new framework features to support automation of test cases. A good automation framework experience for a product developer would be

- Faster results of unit tests.
- Faster results of product feature validation.
- Faster results of end-to-end testing.

5. Applying SDEU Philosophy to Non-Server Technologies

While the Structure, Design, Extensibility and User-Experience (SDEU) philosophy can be applied to any product or automation, we will be focusing on applying this to automation of non-server technologies.

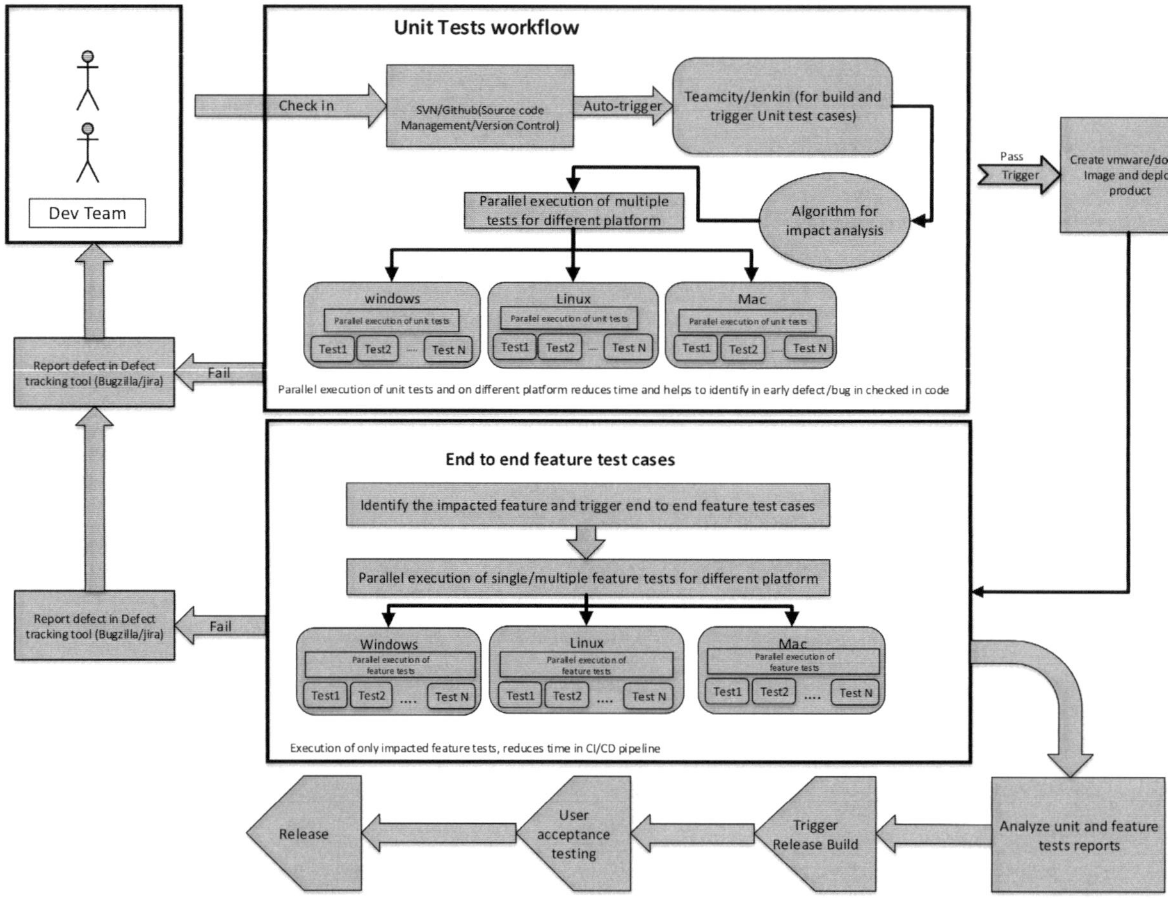

Figure 1: Overview of apply SDEU on an Automation Framework End-to-End.

5.1. Identify the Structure of the Framework

- Gather the infrastructure requirements to perform validation of your product.
- Design the framework for reusability. Make components for your framework that can be re-used everywhere. Group utilities and build your framework on top of that.
- Identify your Continuous Integration (CI) pipeline and how to fit your automation to make Continuous Delivery (CD) of your product.
- Define an integration mechanism to allow automation engineers to seamlessly automate their product.

5.2. Differentiate Test Cases from the Framework Itself

- Never combine the automation framework with product test cases. The framework needs to be agnostic of the product to maximize reusability.
- A product test case will entirely focus on the product, whereas the framework would abstract the complexity of management of underlying tools.

- If possible, maintain versioning of the framework to facilitate addition of features and updating of tools as and when necessary.

5.3. Optimizing Build Process

While the build time of a product is entirely dependent on the technology or language used to develop the product, it does take considerable time and delays to validate code changes leading to duplication of a CI process and a build process.

Generally, when a build is triggered, debug and release configurations of the product are built sequentially. While there are no relations between the two configurations and can in fact be built in parallel, a small optimization is to modify the build script to build the configurations in parallel. (A MS-Build script can allow parallel jobs to build Visual Studio solutions or adding -j in a make file can produce a significant difference, depending on the size of your product and dependencies between its various components.)

5.4. Segregating White Box, Grey Box and Black Box Testable Code Base

Not every line of code written in the product needs to be validated through black box manual testing. Blocks of code that can run without any resource dependencies like server setups etc. can be unit tested.

- Identify areas of code like utilities or helper modules that can be unit tested independently of the product's core business logic.
- The business logic may contain some blocks of code that can be unit tested, but based on our experience a lot of code changes that happen in this layer of a product's architecture are better grey box tested Most of the automation code will be written for this layer.
- The end-to-end system verifications tests, or integration tests of our product from deployment to uninstallation falls under black box testing. This part of testing also needs to be supported from a framework perspective.

Having a clear demarcation between our product's utilities, platform support matrix and business logic helps build a reliable framework.

5.5. Keep Unit Tests Simple

The purpose of unit test[2] is to test whether individual units of source code or modules with associated data or procedures are fit for use. The definition of "unit of source code" varies from individual to individual and on the implemented programming language. In C or C++ development of our product, we have had debates on defining units of code, for e.g. a non-static function in a .c or .cpp file or exposed functions through DLL. In Java, it is the public methods of a class.

Based on our experience, it's impossible to keep adding, updating and deleting unit tests for every piece of code written during development when features are added, modified or removed. To keep things simple, any non-business logic of your product needs to be unit tested and the tests need to be updated accordingly, based on the code change that goes in. Usually utilities, helpers, configuration of files and folders fall under the unit-testable category.

In C/C++, macros allow unit testers to make hidden static functions exposable based on some preprocessor definition at build time to expose the function to be unit tested. This allows unit tests to cover almost 100% of the code. Executing these unit tests falls under automation framework purview and the framework needs to expose methods to integrate new tests.

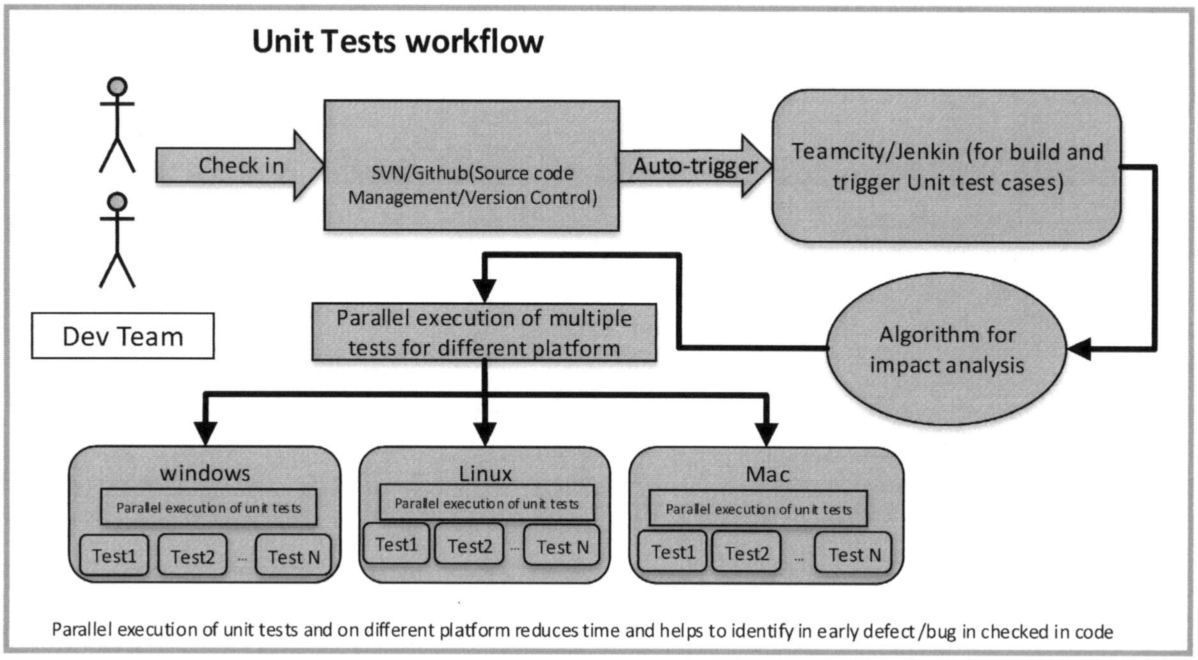

Figure 2: Unit Testing in the Continuous Integration Pipeline.

5.6. Identify Tools for Grey Box and Black Box Testing

A single tool or script written in one of the popular scripting languages like Perl or Python might never solve automation efforts for all features. The design of our automation framework should be accommodating in including different tools and provide a seamless switch between different tools and help in configuring them.

A product is made up of hundreds of features. Some of them may be independent and others interdependent on other features. As an automation framework developer, it is essential to identify the best tool to collectively test a particular feature or group of features and build the tool into the framework. This essentially granulizes the framework itself and helps to maintain regression tests for features.

For system level tests and end-to-end tests, infrastructure orchestration, tools to deploy the product and run integration tests if our product is part of a larger solution, should be taken into consideration when designing our framework code.

5.7. Defining Pipelines for Components and Features of the Product

A pipeline in an automation framework is something we define as the process of setting up all necessary infrastructure and resources to validate a sub-component or feature of the product. Splitting up the product into features and related group of features helps in maintaining a strong automation pipeline to validate code changes and perform regression testing when required. The granularity of the feature allows selective validation of just the feature(s) being impacted by code change.

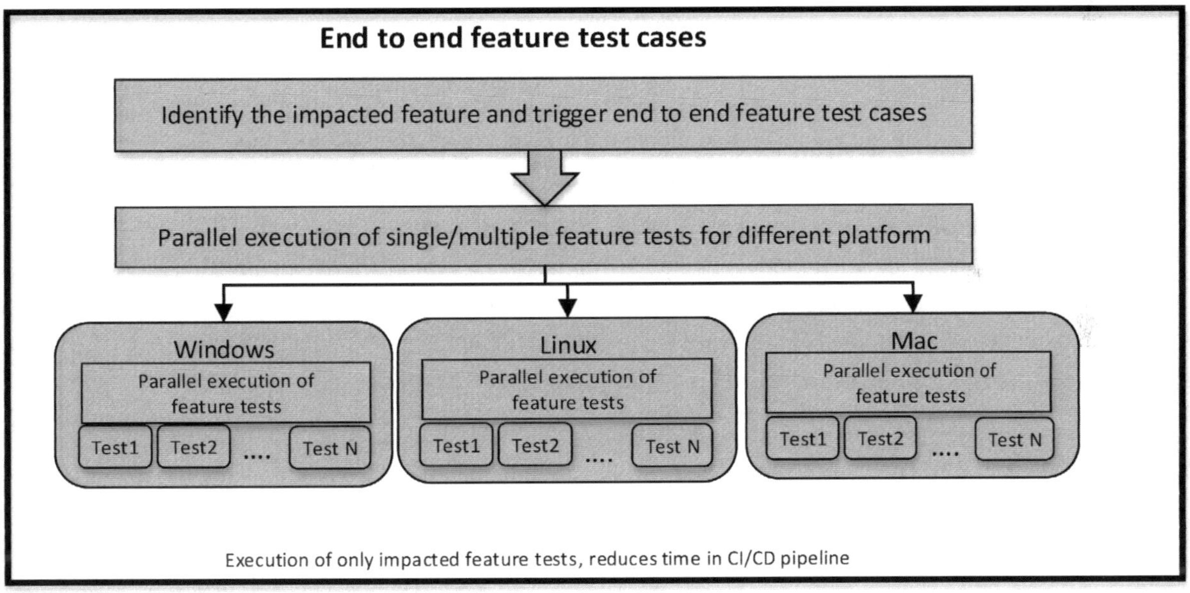

Figure 3: Feature Verification Tests in a Continuous Delivery pipeline.

5.8. Defining End-to-End Automation Pipeline

While a feature pipeline helps in validation of existing and new features in the long run, integration tests and system tests deal with a whole other infrastructure and resource complexity, which should be run independently and at regular intervals (maybe per day once or twice a week depending on the build time of the product). The inputs for building an end-to-end automation framework would rely on parameters and configuration information collected and tests modeled from at least one round of manual testing.

5.9. Framework Implementation to Connect the Dots

With all the different components of the framework in place and the tools necessary to run our automation suites and tests, the framework implementation should focus on two main areas.

5.9.1. Abstracting the Underlying Tools

For a TCAD engineer who engineers the test cases into the framework, the seamless experience would be where the engineer need not worry about what tools to use and what not to use. The framework's integration kit would hide away the complex details and that is one of the focus areas when implementing the framework. For e.g., to execute unit tests, the framework would hide away the CI server like Teamcity[3] or Jenkins[4]. The TCAD engineer or Product Developer simply integrates the unit tests to run with the Framework's integration kit and the framework would take care of executing it in a Teamcity CI agent or Jenkins agent.

5.9.2. Make Extending the Test Code Developer Friendly

For a TCAD engineer, writing framework code as part of product test cases should be avoided and the roles and responsibility of a TCAD engineer should be solely to automate the test cases for the business logic of the product. Any and all code that is required to ensure the test case can be easily automatable is brought under the framework implementation and the functionality required is exposed via the integration kit under a suitable package or component. This allows both the Automation Framework Engineer as well as a TCAD engineer to keep a productive pace in developing more test cases and build on top of the framework.

5.10. Automate Away!

With a clear segregation of different areas of the products validation areas, separate repositories for framework and product automation code, pipelines being set up for regression of features, system and integration tests gives a holistic perspective to automation engineers keeping a maintainable source code that is easy to scale and extend.

Conclusion

We briefly went over the challenges faced when developing an automation framework from scratch and our inferences from the challenges. We formulated a philosophy that can be built into any product line or technology based on the structure of an automation framework, its design, and focus on it extensibility, all culminating in a seamless user experience to automate test cases. After applying this to our product, we have had significant improvement both from a unit testing perspective and automation codebase. We were able to improve our unit test coverage to 27% conditional focusing on the areas demarcated as utilities and helpers. We were able to set up pipelines to validate our install and uninstallation steps and other core business logic of our application and run system level automation validations. While there is still a lot of work ahead of us in converting our manual regression tests to automation code, we have made it simpler for anyone in the team to pick up and automate the product's test cases.

References

1. Test Automation : https://en.wikipedia.org/wiki/Test_automation
2. Unit Testing: https://en.wikipedia.org/wiki/Unit_testing
3. Teamcity: https://www.jetbrains.com/teamcity/
4. Jenkins: https://jenkins.io
5. COTS: https://en.wikipedia.org/wiki/Commercial_off-the-shelf

Security Tsunami! SDL Fundamentals and Where to Start

Authors

SAFEcode.org
Tania Skinner (Tania.Skinner@intel.com)
John Martin (John.P.Martin3@Boeing.com)

Abstract

In the world of secure development, there are 10,000 + things you can do... What are the fundamentals and where should you start? A healthy, secure development program is an ever-evolving suite of skills, tools and process coupled with an intricate understanding of an organization's capabilities, culture, and appetite for risk. SAFECode, an industry consortium of companies seeking, analyzing and sharing best practices in secure development, will present a set of broad secure development practices that have been effective in improving software security in real-world implementations across diverse product lines and various development methodologies. Learn about SAFECode member's key SDL practices and actionable guidance for how to prioritize and apply these fundamentals to your organization.

This paper is an abbreviated version of the SAFECode publication "Fundamental Practices for Secure Software Development" that is the result of best practice sharing amongst SAFECode members including Intel, Microsoft, Boeing, Siemens, Adobe, Dell EMC, Security Compass, Symantec, Veracode, Manicode and CA Technologies. The full paper has many contributors from across SAFECode member companies.

Biography

SAFECode.org: The Software Assurance Forum for Excellence in Code (SAFECode) is a non-profit organization exclusively dedicated to increasing trust in information and communications technology products and services through the advancement of effective software assurance methods. SAFECode is a global, industry-led effort to identify and promote best practices for developing and delivering more secure and reliable software, hardware and services.

Tania Skinner graduated from the University of Illinois at Urbana-Champaign in 1992 with a BS in Computer Science. She joined Intel as a Software Engineer developing software for transistor level reliability testing and analysis. Through the years Tania has filled many roles on software projects from developer to database administrator to project manager. She eventually landed in the Corporate Quality group where she was responsible for leading a variety of cross-corporation SW development measurement and process improvement initiatives. Today, Tania is a Product Security Strategist & Researcher, responsible for leading and continuously improving Intel's Security Development Lifecycle (SDL) for all product development (including all HW, SW, FW development).

Tania is also Intel's representative on SAFECode's Technical Leadership Council. Outside of Intel, Tania is Galactic Central Command to the very busy Skinner family. Tania specializes in secure development, software engineering, benchmarking, continuous improvement and the art of herding cats.

John Martin, CISSP, CISM, is Boeing's Security Program Manager with responsibilities ranging from DevSecOps to Commercial Software Security. His career spans the years between Blue-Box MF generators, through the era of automated hacks, and into our modern age of industrialized paranoia. Unlike more statesman-like peers, he suffers the disadvantage of being alive. He is, unfortunately, a frequent speaker on the topic of commercial software security. In his spare time, he designs specialized NSA-proof tin-foil hats designed to keep the implant signals in. John was named by SANS as one of the 10 Difference Makers in security for 2016. John represents Boeing on SAFECode's Technical Leadership Council.

1. Introduction

In developing the most recent version of the SAFECode Fundamental Practices for Secure Software Development paper[1], it became obvious to the team of contributors that the paper may seem intimidating to those who are new to the world of secure development. Those experienced in applying and evolving secure development practices will appreciate the depth of the full publication, but those who are just dipping their toes into the SDL ocean may find the details overwhelming and struggle with 'where do I start?' This shortened paper, presented in layman development terms, will attempt to

- demystify the secure development practices for the beginning secure development professional
- provide actionable guidance on where to start in applying secure software development practices
- provide guidance on planning the rollout of an SDL in your organization.

Secure development practices, or SDL (Security Development Lifecycle) as commonly referred to in the industry, fundamentally boil down to a few essential steps:

1. **Know what you need to protect, and protect it**
2. **Use secure code and components**
3. **Validate that protections are successful**
4. **Manage issues**
5. **Continuously improve**

Every SDL needs to address each of the steps listed above – with varying levels of breadth and depth. An SDL needs to cover all of the steps identified above, but doesn't initially need to address all of the specific techniques identified within each of these topic areas. Don't expect to start with a highly mature set of secure development practices, as there is a lot to do, but rather start with some solid foundational pieces and plan on constantly evolving and maturing your practices.

2. Know What You Need to Protect and Protect It

2.1. Know What You Need to Protect

A key consideration in applying secure development practices is understanding what, if anything, needs to be protected. Consider software that manages personal medical records. Clearly there is some very important information to protect and the software must be designed and implemented appropriately. Conversely, a simple text-editor could probably leverage the security of the underlying operating system. The first step in understanding what secure development practices to apply, is understanding what you need to protect. This is best achieved through a common secure development practice called Threat Modeling. Threat modeling enables the development team to identify data that needs to be protected, the ways in which an attacker could access the data, and the security features that are necessary to protect the data. These security features perform functions such as user identification and authentication, authorization of user access to information and resources, and auditing of users' activities as required by the specific application.

Threat modeling is started early in the development lifecycle before the core architecture or design is finalized and requires the participation of the system's architects and a security expert. During threat modeling, specific architectural or design changes will be identified to protect the data. There are many different models and methods for doing threat modeling.

Further Reading:

- More information about the benefits of threat modeling, some of the methodologies in use, simple examples and some of the pitfalls encountered in day-to-day practical threat modeling, as well as more complete references, may be found in the SAFECode paper "Tactical Threat Modeling." [2]
- Adam Shostack provides some very basic and layman friendly helpful information introducing threat modeling at https://misti.com/infosec-insider/threat-modeling-what-why-and-how.[4]

2.2. Protect It

Once you understand what information you have to protect and you have identified some methods for protecting it, you must apply secure design principles to the product's design. It is critical that the product architecture/design for any product is evaluated from the security perspective. Architecture/design flaws often cannot be fixed with a few lines of code, but rather require a re-architecture, a typically expensive proposition. Experienced practitioners have learned the hard way how best to design a product to prevent these kinds of bug. These practitioners have developed volumes of secure design principles and practices to guide your application's design. These include things like fail safely, the principle of least privilege, an encryption strategy, and defense in-depth, to name a few. Learn from others past mistakes and avoid them by applying secure design principles and practices. Make sure that all of your organization's architects and designers are well versed in the secure design principles and practices. Architecture/Design reviews should include a checklist of secure design principles and practices that designs are reviewed against. Some obvious items to include on your checklist are:

- Never trust input from an unknown component
- Always use secure protocols
- Never roll your own secure algorithm or crypto

Further Reading:

- More information on secure design principles and practices is provided in the full SAFECode Fundamental Practices for Secure Software Development[1], see section: Design.
- The principles of secure system design were first articulated in a 1974 paper by Jerome Saltzer and Michael Schroeder (The Protection of Information in Computer Systems)[5]
- ISO/IEC 27034-1 provides a method for identifying and incorporating Application Security Controls into a software project.[9]

3. Use Secure Code and Components

Whether software is built as a monolithic block of code or as a highly modularized framework of components and micro-services, the following secure-coding principles are critical to achieving a well-written, secure software product.

3.1. Secure Coding

When developers write software they can make mistakes. Left undetected, these mistakes can lead to vulnerabilities that can compromise that software or the data it processes. A goal of developing secure software is to minimize the number of these unintentional code-level security vulnerabilities. This can be achieved by defining coding standards, selecting the most appropriate (and safe) languages, frameworks and libraries, ensuring their proper use (especially use of their security features), and performing both automated and manual code vulnerability analysis.

3.1.1. Establish Coding Standards and Conventions

Every software development language has strengths and weaknesses that need to be understood by the development team. For example, C++ requires significant memory management and input validation but there are also many commercial and Open Source code vulnerability analysis tools that can help with reviewing the code. Conversely, Golang avoids most memory issues but has few automated code analysis and test tools. Once a language choice is made, appropriate coding standards and conventions that support both writing secure code and the re-use of built-in security features and capabilities should be created, maintained and communicated to the development team.

Where possible, use built-in security features in the frameworks and tools selected and ensure that these are on by default. This will help all developers address known classes of issues, systemically rather than individually.

3.1.2. Use Safe Functions Only

Many programming languages have functions and APIs whose security implications were not appreciated when initially introduced but are now widely regarded as dangerous. Although C and C++ are known to have many unsafe functions, many other languages have at least some functions that are challenging to use safely. For example, dynamic languages such as JavaScript and PHP have several functions that generate new code at runtime (eval, seTtimeout, etc.) and are a frequent source of code execution vulnerabilities.

Developers should be provided guidance on what functions to avoid and their safe equivalents within the coding standards. Additionally, there are resources such as Microsoft's freely available banned header file that, when included in a project, will cause usage of unsafe functions to generate compiler errors. It is quite feasible to produce code bases free of unsafe function usage.

3.1.3. Use Current Complier and Toolchain Versions and Secure Complier Options

Using the latest versions of compilers, linkers, interpreters and runtime environments is an important security practice. Development tools and compilers are constantly evolving and incorporating automated checks for newly discovered vulnerabilities. For example, many C and C++ compilers automatically offer compile-time and run-time defenses against memory corruption bugs. Such defenses can make it harder for exploit code to execute predictably and correctly.

Enable secure compiler options and do not disable secure defaults for the sake of performance or backwards compatibility. These protections are defenses against common classes of vulnerabilities and represent a minimum standard.

3.1.4. Use Code Analysis Tools to Find Security Issues Early

Tooling should be deployed to assist in identifying and reviewing the usage of dangerous functions. Many static analysis tools plug directly into the integrated development environment and helps developers find security bugs early and effectively without leaving their native development environment. Many of these tools will identify common issues such as unbounded functions, potential buffer overflows, etc.

3.1.5. Handle Data Safety

Input validation is one of the single most important coding practices. You have probably heard about SQL injections, a common attack that can be achieved when code accepting user input doesn't validate that the input satisfies pre-defined size and type constraints. All user-originated input should be treated as untrusted and handled consistently throughout the entire system. Additionally, input from micro-services and 3rd-party components should also be treated as untrusted. For example, in web applications the same input data may be handled differently by the various components of the technology stack; the web server, the application platform, other software components and the operating system. An attacker could potentially inject malicious data at any input. If this data is not handled correctly it can be transformed into executing code or unintentionally provide access to resources.

There are many different techniques for safely handling input, including encoding and data binding, and many different problem areas. This secure coding area is addressed in great detail in the SAFECode Fundamental Practices for Secure Software Development paper.

3.1.6. Handle Errors

All applications run into errors at some point. While errors from typical use will be identified during functional testing, it is almost impossible to anticipate all the ways an attacker may interact with the application. Given this, a key feature of any application is to handle and react to unanticipated errors in a controlled and graceful way, and either recover or present an error message.

While anticipated errors may be handled and validated with specific exception handlers or error checks, it is necessary to use generic error handlers or exception handlers to cover unanticipated errors. If these generic handlers are hit, the application should cease performing the current action, as it should now be assumed to be in an unknown state. The integrity of further execution against that action can no longer be trusted.

Error handling should be integrated into the logging approach, and ideally different levels of detailed information should be provided to users as error messages and to administrators in log files.

When notifying the user of an error, the technical details of the problem should not be revealed. Details such as a stack trace or exception message provide little utility to most users, and thus degrade their user experience, but they provide insight to the attacker about the inner workings of the application. Error messages to users should be generic, and ideally from a usability perspective should direct users to perform an action helpful to them, such as "We're sorry, an error occurred, please try resubmitting the form." or "Please contact our support desk and inform them you encountered error 123456." This gives an attacker very little information about what has gone wrong and directs legitimate users on what to do next.

3.2. Use Secure Components

Today's modern applications contain a vast amount of third-party components. The majority of these third-party components are open source components.

Open source components are here to stay, and you must have a plan for 1) identifying components used, 2) assessing the security risk of these components, 3) monitoring components used, and 4) mitigating vulnerable components in your products. The management of security risk in third-party components is a complicated topic with many different approaches from highly governed internal repositories of acceptable components to security risk evaluations of components to automated scanning tools and scheduled security releases. SAFECode has an entire publication dedicated to this topic. Whatever the approach you take, you need to understand the risks and have a plan for selection, identification, monitoring and maintenance.

Further reading:

- SAFECode publication: Managing the risks inherent in the use of third-party components[2]

4. Validate That Protections are Successful

An essential component of an SDL program, and typically the first set of activities adopted by an organization, is some form of security testing. For organizations that do not have many security development practices, security testing is a useful tool to identify existing weaknesses in the product or service and serve as a compass to guide initial security investments and efforts, or to help inform a decision on whether or not to use third-party components. For organizations with mature security practices, security testing is a useful tool both to validate the effectiveness of those practices, and to catch flaws that were still introduced.

There are several forms of security testing and validation, and most mature security programs employ multiple forms. Broadly, testing can be broken down into automated and manual approaches, and then further categorized within each approach. There are tradeoffs with each form of testing, which is why most mature security programs employ multiple approaches.

As in other areas of development, automated security analysis allows for repeatable tests done rapidly and at scale. There are several commercial or free/open source tools that can be run either on developers' workstations as they work, as part of a build process on a build server or run against the developed product to spot certain types of vulnerabilities. Automated tools are adopted because of the speed and scale at which they run, and despite having false-positives, they allow organizations to focus their manual testing on their riskiest components, where they are needed most.

There are many categories of automated security testing tools. Some common automated testing tool categories: Static Analysis Security Testing (SAST), Dynamic Analysis Security Testing (DAST), fuzzing, software composition analysis, network vulnerability scanning and tooling that validates configurations and platform mitigations. Each category will be briefly introduced with an assessment of ease to implement for organizations newly venturing into this space. Note that no single tool will find all security flaws and mature organizations use a suite of tools.

The full publication SAFECode Fundamental Practices for Secure Software Development includes much greater detail and depth on security validation tools and methods. Below is a summary of some of the techniques and tools that may be utilized for security validation.

Technique	Type	Difficulty to Implement	Security Expertise Required	Cost
Static Code Analysis	Automated	Easy	Low	$$
Dynamic Analysis Scanning	Automated + configuration	Easy	Low	$
Fuzz Parsers	Automated + configuration	Difficult	High	$$$
Perform Automated Functional Testing of Security Features/Mitigations	Automated	Varies	Low	$
Manual Verification of Security Features/Mitigations	Manual	Varies	Moderate	$$
Verify Secure Configurations and Use of Platform Mitigations	Automated	Easy	Some	$
Penetration Testing	Manual	Difficult	High	$$$

Table 1: Summary of Security Validation Techniques

4.1. Use Static Analysis Security Testing Tools

PROS: good coverage efficiently, finds problematic patterns, can be tuned

CONS: may not cover all languages, can be noisy (false positives)

Static analysis is a method of inspecting either source code or the compiled intermediate language or binary component for flaws. It looks for known problematic patterns based simply on the application logic, rather than on the behavior of the application while it runs. SAST logic can be as simple as a regular expression finding a banned API via text search, or as complex as a graph of control or data flow logic that seems to allow for tainted data to attack the application. SAST is most frequently integrated into build automation to spot vulnerabilities each time the software is built or packaged; however, some offerings integrate into the developer environment to spot certain flaws as the developer is actively coding. SAST tends to give very good coverage efficiently, and with solutions ranging from free or open source security linters to comprehensive commercial offerings, there are several options available for an organization regardless of its budget.

4.2. Perform Dynamic Analysis Security Testing

PROS: ease of use, few false positives, good coverage

CONS: un-credentialed scans may produce false negatives

Dynamic analysis security testing runs against an executing version of a program or service, typically deploying a suite of prebuilt attacks in a limited but automated form of what a human attacker might try. These tests run against the fully compiled or packaged software as it runs, and therefore dynamic analysis is able to test scenarios that are only apparent when all of the components are integrated. Most modern websites integrate interactions with components that reside in separate source repositories – web service calls, JavaScript libraries, etc. – and static analysis of the individual repositories would not always be able to scrutinize those interactions. Additionally, as DAST scrutinizes the behavior of software as it runs, rather than the semantics of the language(s) the software is written in, DAST can validate software written in a language that may not yet have good SAST support.

4.3. Fuzz Parsers

PROS: deep test capabilities of known APIs and I/O

CONS: laborious to setup and determine root causes

Fuzzing, a specialized form of DAST (or in some limited instances, SAST) is the act of generating or mutating data and passing it to an application's data parsers (file parser, network protocol parser, inter-process communication parser, etc.) to see how they react. Fuzzing is a very advanced security validation technique.

4.4. Verify Secure Configurations and Use of Platform Mitigations

PROS: ease of use, few false positives, good coverage

CONS: un-credentialed scans may produce false negatives

Most security automation seeks to detect the presence of security vulnerabilities, but as outlined in the secure coding practices section, it is also important that software make full use of available platform mitigations, and that it configure those mitigations correctly. These tools are very strong in finding security issues like patch levels, secure configuration settings, secure and HTTP Only cookie flags, and that a server's SSL/TLS configuration is free of insecure protocol versions and cipher suites. Regular validation that software and services are correctly using available platform mitigations is usually far simpler to deploy and run than other forms of security automation, and the findings have very low false positive rates.

4.5. Perform Automated Functional Testing of Security Features/Mitigations

PROS: utilizes existing functional validation capabilities

CONS: Should not be perceived as comprehensive security validation

Organizations that use unit tests and other automated testing to verify the correct implementations of general features and functionality should extend those testing mechanisms to verify security features and mitigations designed into the software. For example, if the design calls for security-relevant events to be logged, unit tests should invoke those events and verify corresponding and correct log entries for them. Testing that security features work as designed is no different from verifying that any other feature works as designed and should be included in the same testing strategy used for other functionality.

4.6. Perform Manual Verification of Security Features/Mitigations

PROS: Flexibility, leverage prior findings, good training tool

CONS: more laborious, not comprehensive security validation

Manual testing is generally more laborious and resource intensive than automated testing, and unlike automated testing it requires the same investment every time that it is performed in order to produce similar coverage. In contrast to automated testing, because human testers can learn, adapt and make leaps of inference, manual testing can evolve based on previous findings and subtle indicators of an issue.

Just as security features should be included in existing unit tests and other automated functionality verifications, they should be included in any manual functional testing or code review efforts that are performed. Organizations employing manual quality assurance should include verification of security features and mitigations within the test plan, as these can be manually verified in the same way that any non-security feature is verified. Organizations that rely more heavily on automated functional testing should still perform peer review and occasional manual spot-checks of security features to ensure that the automated tests were implemented correctly because mistakes in some security features are less likely to be caught and reported by users than mistakes that result in erroneous outputs. For example, a user is likely to report if a text box is not working but is not likely to identify and report that security logging is not working.

4.7. Perform Penetration Testing

PROS: can discover complicated vulnerabilities, mimics attackers methodologies and tools

CONS: the most laborious and time-consuming form of security testing, not comprehensive coverage

**Many consulting companies exist that specialize in penetration testing services. For security-critical applications, contracting out penetration testing may be the best option.*

Penetration testing assesses software in a manner similar to the way in which hackers look for vulnerabilities. Penetration testing can find the widest variety of vulnerabilities and can analyze a software package or service in the broader context of the environment it runs in, actions it performs, components it interacts with, and ways that humans and other software interact with it. This makes it well suited to finding business logic vulnerabilities. Skilled penetration testers can find vulnerabilities not only with direct observation, but also based on small clues and inferences. Using their experience testing both their current projects, and from all previous engagements, they also learn and adapt and are thus inherently more capable than the current state of automated testing.

However, penetration testing is the most laborious and time-consuming form of security testing, requires specialized expertise, scales poorly and is challenging to quantify and measure. Large development organizations may staff their own penetration test team but many organizations engage other companies to perform penetration testing. Whether using staff or consultant testers, it is appropriate to prioritize penetration testing of especially security-critical functions or components. Also, given the expense and limited availability of highly skilled penetration testers, performing penetration testing tends to be most suitable after other, less expensive forms of security testing are completed. The time a penetration tester would spend documenting findings that other testing methodologies can uncover is time that the penetration tester is not using to find issues that only penetration testing is likely to uncover.

Further Reading:

- More information on secure design principles and practices is provided in the full SAFECode Fundamental Practices for Secure Software Development[1], see section: Testing and Validation.

5. Manage Issues

5.1. Issues Discovered During Development

Practices such as threat modeling, third-party component identification, SAST, DAST, penetration testing, etc. all result in artifacts that contain findings related to the product's security (or lack thereof). The findings from these artifacts must be tracked and action taken to remediate, mitigate or accept the respective risk. While we all desire to ship defect free products, there will inevitably come a time when you will be faced with a decision on whether or not to ship a product with a vulnerability. Before you find yourself in this unpleasant situation, you should have a predefined policy and model for assessing risk and making an informed, risk based decision. This model should include things such as (this is not an exhaustive list):

- Severity of the vulnerability
- Likelihood of exploit
- Potential for brand damage
- Remediation options

It is essential that you adopt a consistent formal process for assessing the risk with a decision maker with the appropriate level of authority to accept the risk and a system to track such decisions and any closing actions needed.

Further Reading:

- More information on managing security issues is provided in the full SAFECode Fundamental Practices for Secure Software Development[1], see section: Manage Security Findings.

5.2. Issues Discovered in Released Software

Despite the best efforts of software development teams, vulnerabilities may still exist in released software that may be exploited to compromise the software or the data it processes. Therefore, it is necessary to have a vulnerability response and disclosure process to help drive the resolution of externally discovered vulnerabilities and to keep all stakeholders informed of progress. This is particularly important when a vulnerability is being publicly disclosed and/or actively exploited. The goal of the process is to provide customers with timely information, guidance and, where possible, mitigations or updates to address threats resulting from such vulnerabilities.

Many companies establish a dedicated team, called PSIRT (Product Security Incident Response Team) whose primary function is to respond to and manage security vulnerabilities in released product. There are many industry papers regarding vulnerability response and disclosure process and/or PSIRT that provide a wealth of information and guidance.

Further Reading:

- More information on managing security issues is provided in the full SAFECode Fundamental Practices for Secure Software Development, see section: Vulnerability Response and Disclosure.
- FIRST PSIRT Services Framework: https://www.first.org/education/FIRST_PSIRT_Service_Framework_v1.0[7]
- ISO/IEC 29147 [10] – Vulnerability disclosure (available as a free download). Provides a guideline on receiving information about potential vulnerabilities from external individuals or organizations and distributing vulnerability resolution information to affected customers
- ISO/IEC 30111 [11] – Vulnerability handling processes (requires a fee to download). Gives guidance on how to internally process and resolve reports of potential vulnerabilities within an organization

6. Continuously Improve

Secure development practices are constantly evolving as technology, tools and attack techniques evolve. It is essential that you establish feedback loops that evaluate the outputs of your secure development practices and identify improvement needed to your policies, processes and or tools. The Cost of Quality [8] model principles apply to security just as they do to quality--security vulnerabilities found early in development cost a lot less to fix than those found later in development. We want to prevent security vulnerabilities from being introduced, but when they are present, we want to identify and fix them as early as possible. Performing root cause analysis on issues found will help us identify the gaps in process/policy and prevent them from re-occurring. An example:

- A buffer overflow vulnerability is identified in a released product with a root cause of improper usage of an unbounded function. POSSIBLE improvements: make sure static code analysis software scans for these by default and identifies them, update policies requiring teams to run static code analysis software and address findings, update coding standards to ban usage of unsafe, unbounded functions.

This type of analysis and secure development practice evolution is critical to identifying gaps and closing those gaps. In addition, as the secure development practices you have adopted become standard practice and are woven into development, you will want to assess other practices, policies or tools that can strengthen the security posture of your products and/or improve efficiency. If done well, your secure development practices should be constantly evolving, just as the attackers and attack techniques are.

7. Planning the Implementation and Deployment of Secure Development Practices

An organization's collection of secure development practices is commonly referred to as a Secure Development Lifecycle or SDL. While the set of secure development practices described previously in this paper are essential components of an SDL, they are not the only elements of a mature SDL. A healthy SDL includes all the aspects of a healthy business process, including program management, stakeholder management, deployment planning, metrics and indicators, and a plan for continuous improvement. Whether defining a new set of secure development practices or evolving existing secure development practices, there is a variety of factors to consider that may aid or impede the definition, adoption and success of the secure development program overall. Below are some items to consider in planning the implementation and adoption of an SDL:

- Culture of the organization
- Expertise and skill level of the organization
- Product development model and lifecycle
- Scope of the initial deployment
- Stakeholder management and communication
- Efficiency measurement
- SDL process health
- Value proposition for the secure development practices

7.1. Culture of the Organization

The culture of the organization must be considered when planning the deployment of any new process or set of application security controls. Some organizations respond well to corporate mandates from the CEO or upper management, while others respond better to a groundswell from the engineering team. Think about the culture of the organization that must adopt these practices. Look to the past for examples of process or requirements changes that were successful and those that were not. If mandates work well, identify the key managers who need to support and communicate a software security initiative. If a groundswell is more effective, think about highly influential engineering teams or leaders to engage in a pilot and be the first adopters.

7.2. Expertise and Skill Level of the Organization

If an organization is to be successful in implementing an SDL, some level of training is necessary. The entire organization should be made aware of the importance of security, and more detailed technical training must be provided to development teams that clearly articulates the specific expectations of individuals and teams. If individuals do not understand why these practices are important and the impact of not performing these practices, they are less likely to support them.

Additional training will likely be needed, depending on the expertise in the organization. For each of the secure development practices, consider the expertise/skill level needed and the coverage of that expertise in the organization.

7.3. Product Development Model and Lifecycle

Along with a specification of the secure development practices, it is essential to consider when the practices are required. When or how often a practice is applied is highly dependent on the development model in use and the automation available. Although security practices executed in sequential and logical order can result in greater security gains (e.g., threat model before code is committed) and cost effectiveness than ad hoc implementation, in agile or continuous development environments, other triggers such as time (e.g., conduct DAST monthly) or response to operating environment changes (e.g., deployment of a new service or dataset) should be considered.

Not everyone is nor needs to be a security engineer, and the SDL framework should provide engineers with clear actionable guidance, supported by efficient processes, carefully selected tools and intelligent automation, tightly aligned with the engineering experience. To facilitate change at scale, security process and tools must be integrated into the engineers' world and not exist as a separate security world, which is often seen as a compliance function. This not only helps to reduce friction with engineers, it also enables them to move faster by integrating security tools into the world in which they live and operate.

Table 2: SDL Framework for All Development Models

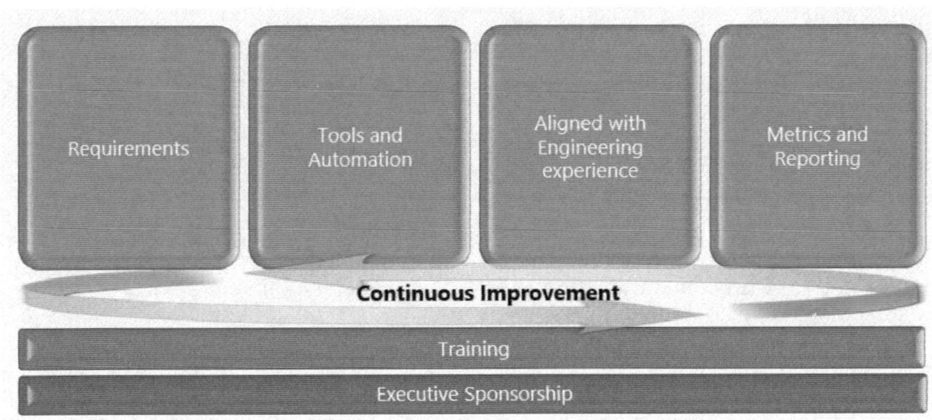

7.4. Scope of Initial Deployment

Often, the teams implementing the secure development program are resource constrained and may need to consider different ways to prioritize the rollout across the organization. There are many ways to manage the rollout of the SDL. Having a good understanding of how the project planning process works and the culture of the organization will help the secure development program manager make wise choices for the implementation and adoption of secure development practices. Below are some options to consider:

- Will the initial rollout include all secure development practices or a subset?
- Consider the product release roadmap and select an adoption period for each team that allows them time to plan for the adoption of the new process. It may be unwise to try to introduce a new process and set of practices to a team nearing completion of a specific release.
- The initial rollout might also choose to target teams with products of higher security risk posture and defer lower risk products for a later start.
- Consider allowing time for transition to full adherence to all SDL requirements.

7.5. Stakeholder Management and Communications

Deploying a new process or set of practices often requires the commitment and support of many stakeholders. Identify the stakeholders, champions and change agents who will be needed to assist with the communications, influencing and roll-out of the program. Visit these stakeholders with a roadshow that clearly explains the value and commitment to secure development practices and what specifically they are being asked to do.

7.6. Compliance Measurement

In implementing a new set of security requirements, the organization must consider what is mandatory and what (if anything) is optional. Most organizations have a governance or risk/controls function that will require indicators of compliance with required practices. In defining the overall SDL program, consider the following:

- Are teams required to complete all of the secure development practices? What is truly mandatory? Is there a target for compliance?
- What evidence of practice execution is required?
- How will compliance be measured? What types of reports are needed?
- What happens if the compliance target is not achieved? What is the risk management process that should be followed? What level of management can sign off on a decision to ship with open exceptions to security requirements? What action plans will be required to mitigate such risks and how will their implementation be tracked?

7.7. SDL Process Health

A good set of secure development practices is constantly evolving, just as the threats and technologies involved are constantly evolving. The SDL process must identify key feedback mechanisms for identifying gaps and improvements needed. The vulnerability management process is a good source of feedback about the effectiveness of the secure development practices. If a vulnerability is discovered post-release, root-cause analysis should be performed. The root cause may be:

- A gap in the secure development practices that needs to be filled
- A gap in training/skills
- The need for a new tool or an update to an existing tool

In addition, development teams will have opinions regarding what is working and what is not. The opinions of development teams should be sought, as they may help identify inefficiencies or gaps that should be addressed. Industry reports regarding trends and shifts in secure development practices should be monitored and considered. A mature SDL has a plan and metrics for monitoring the state of secure development practices across the industry and the health of the organization's secure development practices.

7.8. Value Proposition

There will be times when the funding for secure development practices support will be questioned by engineering teams and/or management. A mature secure development program will have good metrics or indicators to articulate the value of the secure development practices to drive the right decisions and behaviors. Software security is a very difficult area to measure and portray. Some common metrics can include industry cost-of-quality models, where the cost of fixing a vulnerability discovered post-release with customer exposure/damage is compared to that of finding/fixing a vulnerability early in the development lifecycle via a secure development practice. Other metrics include severity and exploitability of externally discovered vulnerabilities (CVSS score trends) and even the cost of product exploits on the "grey market." There is no perfect answer here, but it is a critical aspect of a secure development program to ensure that the value proposition is characterized, understood and can be articulated in a way that the business understands.

Further Reading:

- More information on managing security issues is provided in the full SAFECode Fundamental Practices for Secure Software Development [1], see section: Planning the Implementation and Deployment of Secure Development Practices

8. Moving Industry Forward

One of the more striking aspects of SAFECode's work in creating this paper was an opportunity to review the evolution of software security practices and resources in the seven years since the second edition was published. Though much of the advancement is a result of innovation happening internally within individual software companies, SAFECode believes that an increase in industry collaboration has amplified these efforts and contributed positively to advancing the state of the art across the industry.

References

SAFECode. "Fundamental Practices for Secure Software Development, Third Edition". SAFECode.org. https://safecode.org/wpcontent/uploads/2018/03/SAFECode_Fundamental_Practices_for_Secure_Software_Development_March_2018.pdf (accessed August 19, 2018)

SAFECode. "Tactical Threat Modeling". SAFECode.org. https://www.safecode.org/wp-content/uploads/2017/05/SAFECode_TM_Whitepaper.pdf (accessed August 19, 2018)

SAFECode. "Managing Security Risks Inherent in the Use of Third-party Components". SAFECode.org. https://www.safecode.org/wp-content/uploads/2017/05/SAFECode_TPC_Whitepaper.pdf (accessed August 19, 2018)

Shostack, Adam. "Threat Modeling: What, Why, and How?". https://misti.com/infosec-insider/threat-modeling-what-why-and-how (accessed August 10, 2018)

Saltzer, Jerome and Schroeder, Michael. "The Protection of Information in Computer Systems". MIT.edu. http://web.mit.edu/Saltzer/www/publications/protection/ (accessed October 2017)

ISO/IEC 27034-1 provides a method for identifying and incorporating Application Security Controls into a software project.

FIRST. "FIRST PSIRT Services Framework." FIRST.org. https://www.first.org/education/FIRST_PSIRT_Service_Framework_v1.0 (accessed July 26, 2018)

ASQ. "Cost of Quality." ASQ.org. http://asq.org/learn-about-quality/cost-of-quality/overview/overview.html (accessed August 10, 2018)

International Organization for Standardization. "ISO/IEC 27034-1". ISO.org. https://www.iso.org/contents/data/standard/04/43/44378.html.

International Organization for Standardization. "ISO/IEC 29147". ISO.org. https://www.iso.org/contents/data/standard/04/51/45170.html.

International Organization for Standardization. "ISO/IEC 30111". ISO.org. https://www.iso.org/contents/data/standard/05/32/53231.html

This page intentionally left blank.

How to Get There from Here: REI's Journey Toward the Right Data and Environments for Their Enterprise Testing Ecosystem

Authors

Bob Stuart (bstuart@rei.com)
James Wilson (jamwils@rei.com)

Abstract

Like any retailer, REI is in an industry that changes frequently and increasingly leverages technology to differentiate itself and improve efficiency. The pressure to keep up with this is, like many companies, felt deeply within the QA department. REI QA found itself having a great staff and desire to help the company improve its delivery capability, and in 2015 REI showed its support for QA by hiring its first director of QA. Priority #1 was an improved QA practice, but it was clear that some combination of technology, environments and data needed to be dealt with. But how to get there from here?

In this case study you will read of REI QA's multi-year journey toward the lofty goals that so many aspire to: intentionally managing test data and test environments. You will learn of the reasons for change, projects that have been put into action, the reasoning and business justifications, lessons learned, organizational adjustments, achievements to date and what is next in the roadmap.

Biography

Bob Stuart is a QA System Engineering Lead and subject matter expert at REI with 10+ years of experience in IT test environment planning, scheduling, architecture and management. His career has covered the spectrum from hands-on desktop support, to server and network engineering, seven years in the SAP application space and, prior to QA, being a charter member of the ITSM team to launch Release and Change management for the REI enterprise. Bob has a mathematics degree from Seattle Pacific University, and multiple network engineering and IT process certifications.

James Wilson is a Sr. Project Manager at REI on the IT Enterprise QA team. He has enjoyed a career in IT and technology companies in a variety of roles, such as management consulting, project management, business systems analysis, and technical communications. Along the way he led SDLC adoptions, PMO lifecycle rollouts, agile and waterfall projects, and many vendor product evaluations. He successfully implemented adoption of new technologies and processes by applying some key principles: 'begin with an end in mind', 'light many small fires' to bring about big changes, don't be afraid to make mistakes, and never stop learning. He holds an MBA as well as a Masters in Management Information Systems, both from the George Washington University.

1. Introduction

REI QA was, for years, a department within IT that was largely an 'order taker' group and struggled to influence software delivery and project management. In 2015 QA hired its first director and was given a seat at the table for improving software delivery and project execution. Starting with that first year there were two parallel tracks of work that moved forward.

1.1. Assess and Improve QA Core Practice

This effort consisted of a strategic hire of a QA lead with the experience and skills to consolidate, document and roll out a standardized set of practices and deliverables. This was executed well and gave a boost to the team in the form of standardized practices, process and document templates.

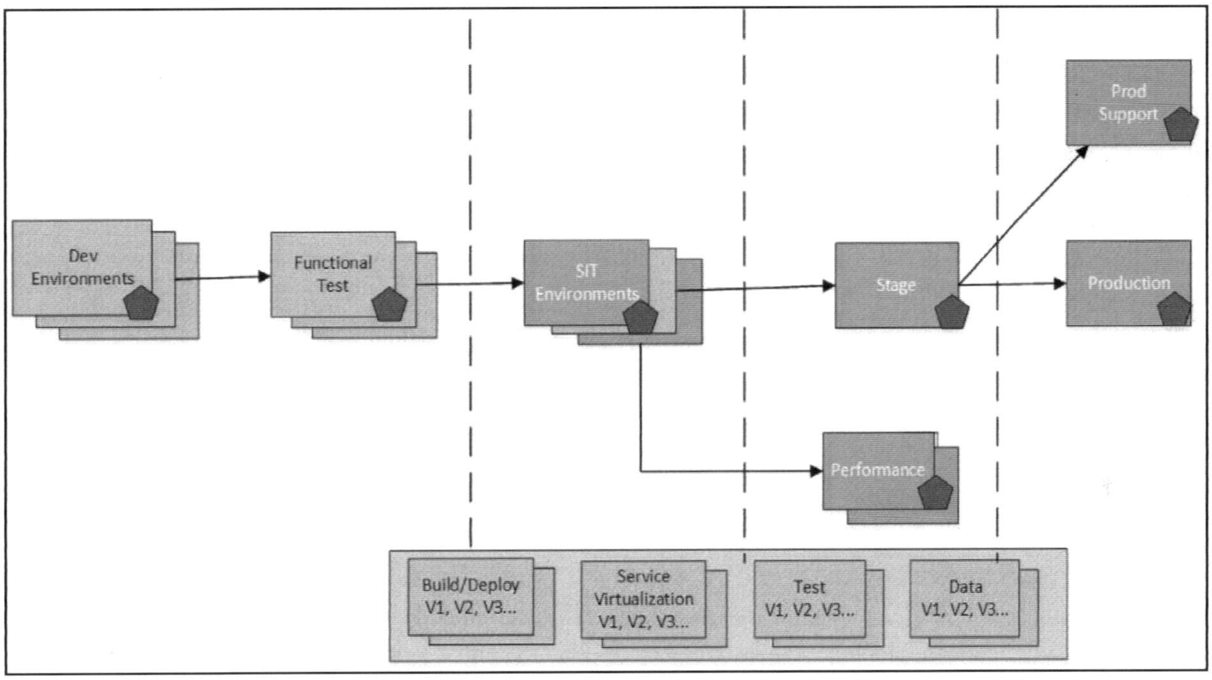

Figure 1

1.2. Test Environment Planning

The concern of this track was the quickly accelerating work starting up to 'move to the cloud'. This began with a QA leadership alignment effort in which an approach to future test environments was designed, based largely on the static, on-prem environments of the past (see Figure 1)

From the environment alignment effort (1.2) a project was sponsored to draw up the requirements---from a QA perspective--for a well-designed *hybrid test environment* (on-prem and cloud infrastructure). The end goal was to have a blueprint for test environments that could be executed when ready to migrate to the cloud. This effort was led by a niche consultant and documented each team's capability and concerns with going to the cloud. The output of this project was shelved leading into 2017.

Lesson learned #1: Looking back, 2016 was full of cloud hype and our team was being [possibly overly-] proactive and taking on responsibility for planning things over which they ultimately had no control. The company was not ready to migrate to the cloud, so it was a matter of missed timing.

2. A Good Start – Define the Problem

Just as the hybrid test environments blueprint was completed, events led to the team being without a director for the last half of 2016. It was in this period that the team began to plan for the 2017 budgets and, in the absence of a hybrid environments project, the focus shifted to more textbook TDM (Test Data Management): refresh, synthetic data, fencing/reservation, etc. A number of meetings were held with vendors and there was cautious optimism that QA might be able to sponsor a TDM project.

In the vendor meetings it became clear that a business benefit was needed in order to move forward, so an effort was launched to assess the impact of test data issues on the QA team. The goal of the assessment was to develop a business case upon which a TDM project might be chartered. The assessment used a two-pronged approach, focusing on two areas:

2.1. Waste Analysis

This was a survey of the team to discover how much time was spent across all portfolios to prepare and deal with test data. The average was approximately 12% of the QA team time, which was much less than the informally tossed around 25% industry average. This rings true, given the omission of the non-QA time (software developer, DBA, etc) spent on data manipulation. The dollar impact to QA per year was estimated to be ~$1.2M of the team's time spent on non-value-add test data management.

2.2. Pain Points Survey

This was an anecdotal survey of the QA Team regarding any and all known data issues. The line items were organized into similar categories and rated on overall impact to the team. The consolidated pain points details are shown in *Table 1*.

Top Issues that cause problems	Issue Count
Changed data	13
Data not sync'd	15
Data setup problems	7
Environment Availability	1
Environment Configuration	1
Environment Issues-Need more detail	4
Inability to identify data with correct attributes	1
Missing data	4
No QA support	1
Stale Data	1

Table 1

3. Assessing Solutions

After attempting to define the problem and not delve into solutions, it was time to discuss what technical people love—solutions to problems. The solutions under consideration were a blend of classic "TDM" and more technical solutions. The following definitions were used by the team for this exercise

3.1. Solution Coverage

In this stage of the process the team collectively assessed how well they felt each of the possible solutions might solve the various pain points. Each solution was discussed, and the relative merits or applicability to the problems was debated. The end result was a pivot-table driven mathematics exercise of lining up the problems and the solutions, with the resulting score representing how well the collection of solutions could solve each problem. It was felt that this score would indicate which solutions to pursue and in what order.

Term	Definition
Dynamic data	ad hoc or on-demand, at time of test, non-static data, disposable (could be programmatic); self-service
Term	**Definition**
Gold copy	planned, based on Prod usually, highly analyzed to ensure validaty E2E, contract testing
Subsetting	planned, not full copy of db, culled/scrubbed for dupes or edge cases, can be sliced by time or process
Refresh	planned or ad hoc, copy from other instance (prod usually), can be full copy or tables, etc
Data fencing	planned, data reservation, protection of data so others can't use or change it
Service Virtualization	Full service logic, record & respond, generates dev artifacts/versioning, data can be managed in background
Mocks	Minimal logic, returns 'canned' response, may have limited exception handling or error checking
Stubs	No logic, returns 'canned' response, no exception handling or error checking
Db Virtualization	Minimal pointers that access full copy of data, all data with no subsetting
Masking	Can be deterministic or not; change fields to hide real member/customer data; must be done across core TDM systems concurrently
PII Data	Those personally identifiable information (PII) data elements determined by REI business owners and Enterprise Architecture that put customers and the company at risk

Table 2

Table 3 shows the final "Solution coverage across all problems" in the bottom row, which we viewed as the best indicator of what QA should focus on as solutions

		Solutions											
Top Issues that cause problems	**Issue Count**	**Dynamic data**	**Synthetic data**	**Gold copy**	**Subsetting**	**Refresh**	**Data fencing**	**Service Virt.**	**Mocks**	**Stubs**	**Db Virtualization**	**Masking**	**Solution coverage by pain point**
PII data	**36**	0	5	4	5	0	3	4	5	5	4	5	**40**
Data not sync'd	**15**	4	4	3	0	4	3	5	5	5	4	NA	**37**
Changed data	**13**	5	3	0	3	4	4	5	5	5	4	NA	**38**
Data setup problems	**7**	4	5	4	3	2	2	5	5	5	4	NA	**39**
Missing data	**4**	0	5	5	0	2	0	5	5	5	5	NA	**32**
Environment Issues	**4**	NA	NA	NA	NA	NA	NA	NA	NA	NA	NA	NA	**0**
Inability to identify data with correct attributes	**1**	3	3	4	2	0	0	3	3	3	3	NA	**24**
Stale Data	**1**	0	4	4	0	4	0	3	3	3	5	NA	**26**
Environment Availability	**1**	NA	NA	NA	NA	NA	NA	5	3	3	NA	NA	**11**
Environment Config	**1**	NA	NA	NA	NA	NA	NA	3	3	3	NA	NA	**9**
No QA support/coverage	**1**	NA	NA	NA	NA	NA	NA	NA	NA	NA	NA	NA	**0**
Solution coverage across all problems		**16**	**29**	**24**	**13**	**16**	**12**	**38**	**37**	**37**	**29**	**5**	

Table 3

4. Decision Factors

The team concluded the assessments as 2016 ended, just in time for a new director to take the helm of Enterprise QA. After reviewing the available information and options the decision was made in early 2017 to pursue PII data masking and database virtualization (DV). This decision was influenced by several factors:

4.1. Logical Order of Projects

Service virtualization (SV) had the highest scores and was seen as a big boost to overall software development and testing, yet ultimately needs a robust data plan behind it. There was not enough budget to pursue one of the enterprise TDM tools, so the team considered point #4.2

4.2. Pragmatism

The DV toolset was already purchased and stood up in a proof-of-concept fashion--and the QA team was welcomed to take this ball and run with it. Thankfully, the database team was a great partner in supporting QA's interest in establishing a robust foundation for getting data and environments in the hands of testers.

4.3. Risk Management

The DV platform purchase included a robust data masking toolset, which got the attention of Enterprise Architecture. This was one of the key use cases/issues called out in the QA assessment (and in Architect interviews), so pursuing DV while simultaneously dealing with data security was seen as a huge win.

4.4. Strategic Alignment

The new director came in with a vastly different perspective on test data and test environments and how they can help drive software development and testing--it was certainly different from the original team alignment of the previous year. This change in perspective resulted in significantly reducing the focus on infrastructure and cloud test environments, and focusing on providing core testing capabilities and capacity for the enterprise.

5. The North Star

5.1. Shifting of the Tides

The new director arrived having previously seen the impact that targeted solutions can have on the QA practice and software development overall. Soon after arriving she worked with the QA engineering team to develop a target state for test environments--referred to as our "North Star", or "Polaris". This was a set of graphics and a slide deck showing multiple approaches to test environments for the cloud use case. This became necessary in order to help clarify the software testing/delivery approach being communicated throughout IT.

Figure 2 was created to illustrate how QA partners with other teams that already own or specialize in delivering infrastructure and providing systems needed for software delivery across the REI landscape. This illustration was very cloud oriented, reflecting the focus at that time, but easily maps to on-premise infrastructure.

The vision is that QA will sit alongside other teams in a shared VPC (virtual private cloud) and provision the many databases and services needed to conduct effective testing. This view of the future presumes a high degree of collaboration and alignment between QA and these other teams.

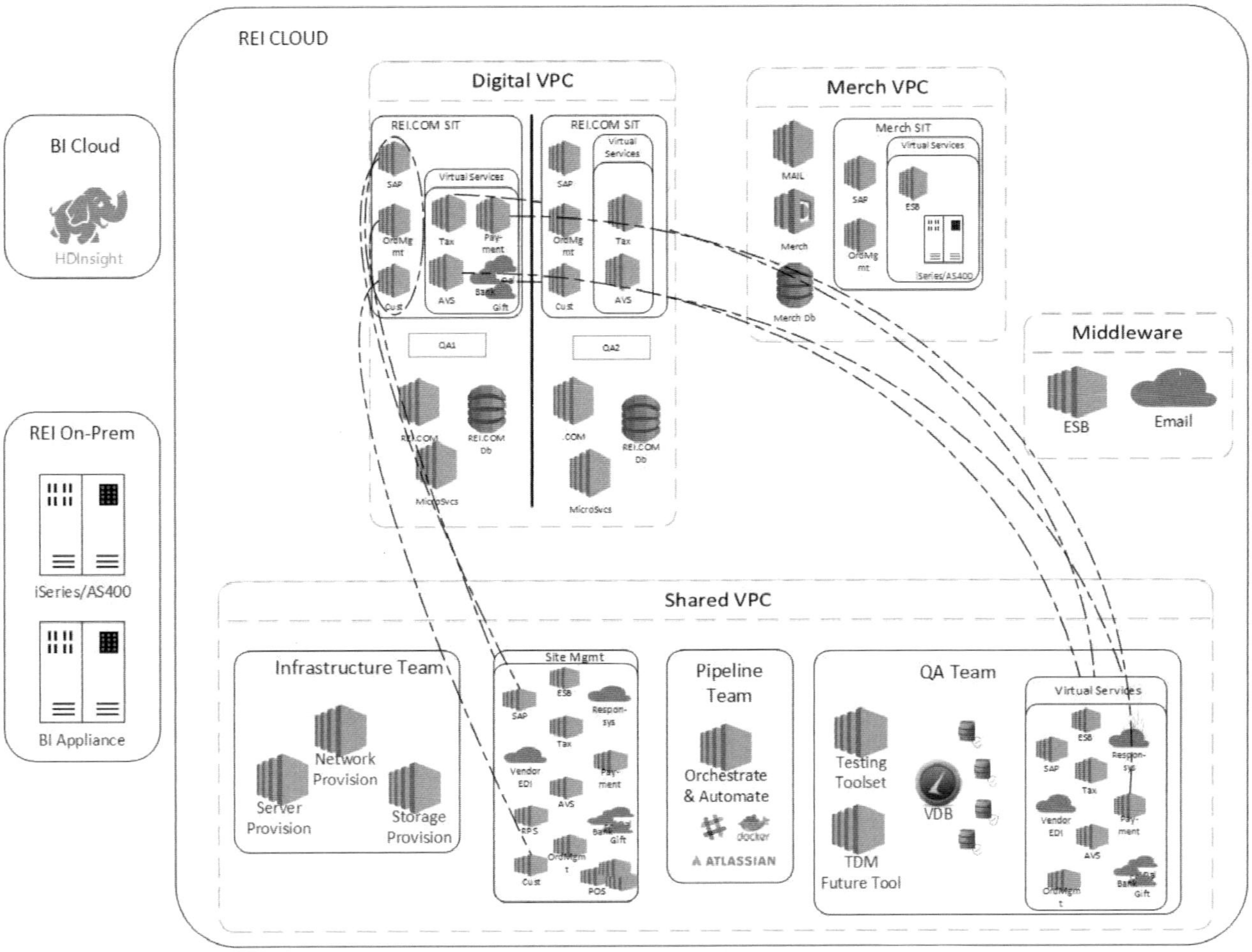

REI CLOUD
Digital VPC
REI.COM SIT
Virtual Services
QA1
QA2
Merch VPC
Merch SIT
Middleware
ESB
Email
BI Cloud
HDInsight
REI On-Prem
iSeries/AS400
BI Appliance
Shared VPC
Infrastructure Team
Network Provision
Server Provision
Storage Provision
Site Mgmt
Pipeline Team
Orchestrate & Automate
ATLASSIAN
QA Team
Testing Toolset
VDB
TDM Future Tool
Virtual Services

Figure 2

5.2. The Roadmap

In addition to the North Star artifacts, a 3-year roadmap of projects was developed to help keep the focus on reaching tangible milestones in the maturity of the program.

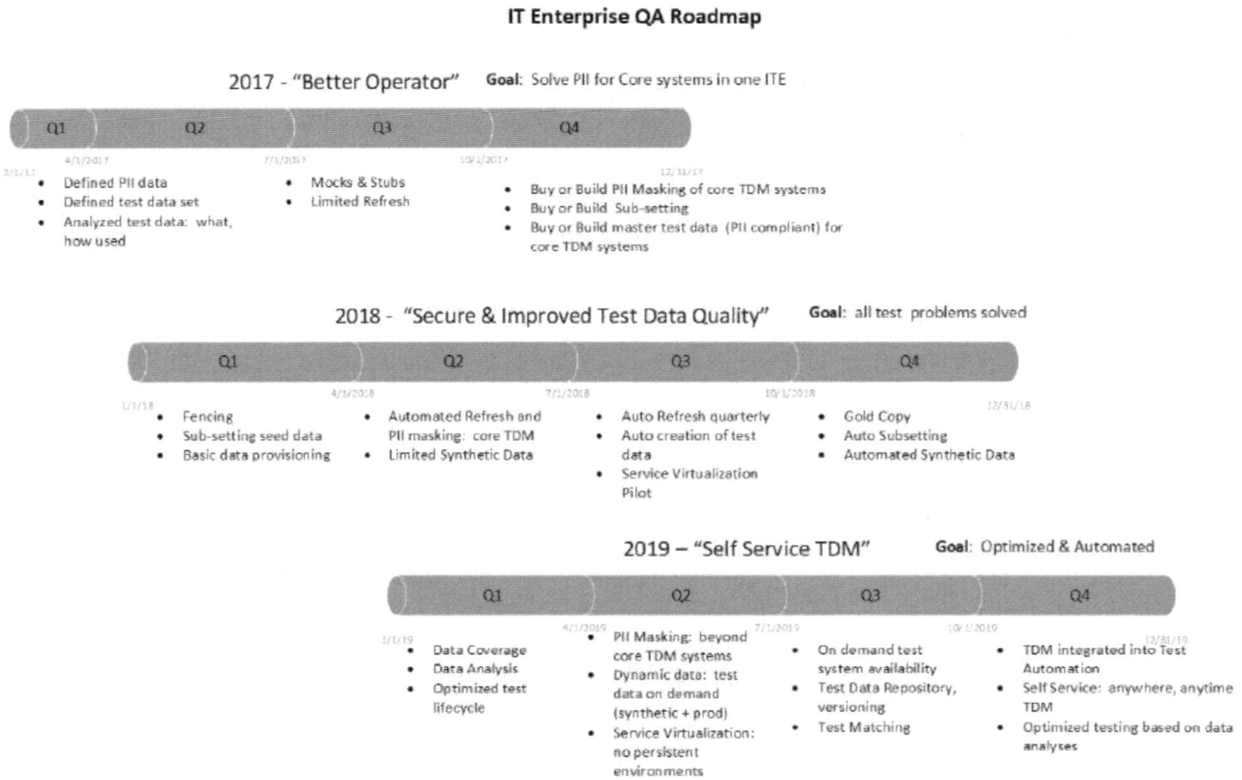

Figure 3

5.3. New Tenets Brought Forward

5.3.1. No Persistent Environments

In a cloud model there is likely no (or a very rare) use case for having persistent, static test environments. Given the expense of creating most environments, it behooves the organization to know why and when to create a persistent environment, especially if it is on-prem. We understand the usual exceptions are PERF testing environments and, depending on comfort level, prod support environments that mimic the production footprint.

5.3.2. QA Does Not Plan, Design or Provision Infrastructure

QA needs to see themselves as a consumer of infrastructure and yet act as a key partner to help ensure teams get what they need for testing. Regarding the provisioning of whole applications for test, it remains to be seen what role QA will have. They key is that QA will work to provision infrastructure or apps only where there is an ongoing gap.

Lesson learned #2: Be ready to redefine what a "test environment" is. Proliferation of servers and databases does not equate to improving your testing capability. Making more copies of systems and environments is usually expensive and unsustainable. Focus on the needed features and functionality.

5.3.3. QA Does Not Plan, Design or Provision Platforms, Tools and Data Which Enable All Forms of Testing

This is the "other side of the coin" from point 5.3.2. The focus must be on A) what you can control, B) what enables your core competency, and C) what prepares QA to be a strategic partner for software delivery in the future.

5.3.4. The Project Roadmap Focus

It become the collective QA understanding that the cumulative effect of smaller projects will be significant (something about *sum of the parts*). This shift in thinking was evidenced in the shift away from pursuing the "big bang" (and big dollar) type of projects, and instead focusing on targeted, affordable solutions to use as building blocks.

Since early 2017 these artifacts and the evolution in thought have resonated with QA partners across IT, specifically Enterprise Architecture, Site Reliability Engineering, and the software engineer community.

Lesson learned #3: Roadmaps are living documents, don't get too attached to them. The combination of the new tenets and re-calibration of the technologies that QA should own resulted in an overhaul of the roadmap after the first year. Present example: we deferred the textbook TDM focus (refresh, subset, synthetic data provisioning) and reprioritized database virtualization and service virtualization projects, because they were achievable with the small team and budget, and were already on the roadmap.

6. Navigating the Projects – Year #1

6.1. Getting Going

So the 2017 goal was set: mask the PII data in five systems of record and virtualize the databases for four of those systems (Yes, the math might seem funny, but the DV tool did not support virtualizing an AS400 database, but it can mask it!). The systems chosen to be masked/virtualized were not chosen at random, we focused on the core systems of record that impact the vast majority testing: ecommerce, customer, order management, ERP and warehouse management. There was not a detailed use case review made that drove the decision, it was more of a common sense consensus that drove the decision.

These projects definitely "take a village". The team chosen for this project included a project manager, a SME/lead, a functional QA analyst, and a QA SDET--plus a substantial amount of support from a senior DBE.

6.2. Value Add

So the The PII data masking depended on the DV platform, so we focus on that first. DV brings with it a lot of goodness that is not present in physical databases, and this is what was socialized as the benefits:

- Access to updated production data
- A regular database refresh cycle can be configured and automated, frequently
- Teams can consume refreshes as needed or choose to retain their changes
- Teams have the ability to bookmark and roll back to previous versions of the database
- Teams can share versions of their database with others
- Vastly smaller storage requirement for each virtual database

6.3. The Big Challenge - Masking

Like any new technology there is a lot to be learned along the way, but the database team had already set the foundation of the DV platform in 2016. Setting up the platform was relatively easy compared to the data masking. To accomplish the database masking, the team followed a pattern for each app:

1. Do the work to get the virtual database ingested
2. Conduct an initial interview with the app teams that knew their own data, and step through a review of the data that appeared to be in the database
3. Develop detailed data rules
4. Execute masking (a <u>very</u> iterative process)
5. Review with the app team to confirm that data masking was successful

6.4. Minor Lessons and Decisions Made Regarding Our Masking Project

- While the focus is so often on software developers, when it comes to handling data you will need a ROCK SOLID database engineer (DBE) to help with the database work. There is no substitute for a capable DBE
- The decision was made to retain the vendor's team to accomplish the data masking project. We 'got lucky' and made this decision before we learned the lesson:
  - *Your typical database engineer has heard of the various methods and tools needed for data masking in one or more platforms, but you will likely need an experienced data masking specialist to make it an effective use of your time across all the various platforms and structures.*
- You will get a big boost from having an analyst (QA functional analyst works great!) that knows the data to help review and accomplish data masking.
- No matter how good you are, databases live on servers and take up space so you will need to be prepared for the cost of infrastructure.
- Project success was defined as successful masking, but standing up an application server and conducting testing was decided to be out of scope for the first project
  - *The validation was performed using database query tools and manual inspection, but the decision was made to defer connecting apps to the databases to a later phase*
  - *This required many iterations of manual inspection, and the number of iterations were increased due to the number of times the VDB's had to be started from scratch.*

Lesson learned #4: You can't use *'slices'* of people's time effectively. Resource availability for our core team was a major constraint, but it did work for each application owner. The SME, Analyst and SDET on the core team were fully allocated to projects, so their time and contributions were constrained. You should plan for a dedicated team to begin masking across the enterprise.

7. Projects Year #1

Rounding the turn into 2018, the team is focusing on several projects: 1) operationalize the DV platform, 2) DV adoption, and 3) SV (Service Virtualization) Pilot.

7.1. Operationalize DV

In a phrase, this is the year that VDB's get real. With PII data masking already largely being accomplished in 2017, the focus for the 2018 Operationalize project is to automate from the point of intake of the production database all the way to the template VDB, from which other VDB's may be provisioned. For this work the vendor was again retained to focus on the tool config required for automation, and scripting required for user security. Again in 2017, our assigned DBE has been critical to project success

7.2. Adoption of DV

The focus of this branch of the project is usage by the application teams. The approach we used is to socialize and evangelize, and we also set a goal of migrating one of the shared end-to-end test environments to VDBs by end of year. We believe the teams will eventually see the need, but we have tried to set some interim goals and ask for their help to achieve them.

Lesson Learned #5: The benefits of VDB's will sell themselves to some degree, the biggest challenge is getting your champion who will do whatever is necessary to support you supporting them. Our champion from each system saw the value it gives them and was willing to do the work necessary to move their team along the journey with us

7.2.1. DV Successes

Thus far there have been several champions that have stepped forward and gotten their teams using VDBs:

- Marketing/Customer Systems team needing to overhaul annual reward/dividend process - they very happily embraced a masked, stand-alone database for a major code re-factoring effort
- SAP team has "seen the light" and is seeking to replace all non-prod databases with VDB's.

Lesson Learned #6: Watch for unplanned wins. There is an unintended benefit from the SAP team replacing all their non-production databases: eventually reclaiming ~50TB ($250,000) of enterprise class storage. The team knew there would be savings, and sometimes you just get lucky on your first try. The flip side of this is be wary of easy wins as there is often some off-setting work required to achieve the win

7.3. Service Virtualization Pilot

This was REI's first foray with an enterprise SV tool. This project is seen as an "enabler" project, which has several major benefits we hope to leverage:

- Enable teams to test without needing the other systems for integrations
- Test reliability, predictability and environment control
- Testing new development before a missing integration dependency is ready for testing
- Elimination of data dependencies
- Strategic value - gets us one step closer to being able to test in the cloud

The approach for this project has been similar to the database virtualization project in terms of it being a collaboration of a key consultant with our core QA team. The difference with SV is that the team is much larger. The first service that was virtualized required four REI resources plus the consultant, researching app config details, going back and forth to a lab of physical hardware, trying various methods to handle security and certificates, etc. It was quite a flurry of activity, but it was a great way to start.

Lesson learned #7: - SV will require a broad team with similarly broad skills, knowledge in the various services you want to virtualize, and access to technical configuration information—get as much done ahead of time as you can. Lesson 7b: plan focused working sessions and just make whatever progress you can when you get the right people in a room together.

8. Sharing the Love

8.1. Upping Our Social Game

Our team dedicated time in the first half of 2018 to begin spreading the word through REI regarding the benefits of virtualization and QA's readiness to partner with them. The director developed more formal team and personal goals around planned events:

- Quarterly engineering internal meet-ups (good reason to have beer)
- Quarterly "Innovation days": a couple of days of dedicated to team members just trying something and producing something with demonstrated value. "Winners" are eligible to receive some funding to take the concept farther

8.2. Taking Ownership

Regarding having vendors lead the way on evangelizing our projects and roadmap, you've heard it said many times, and REI is no exception: "culture eats strategy for breakfast, lunch and dinner"[4]. We were engaging the DV vendor to evangelize the products within the company, but we realized that we needed to take the reins and share this with the company ourselves.

Lesson Learned #8: Our approach of *show, not tell* is proving to be effective at building our most valuable asset: interest and buy-in. You can leverage your vendor partners for a lot but consider making yourselves the face of the projects to your company.

9. Next Steps

9.1. Finishing 2018

As we round the bend into the latter half of 2018, our team is focused on wrapping up the stated project phases, and several other efforts:

- Select one end-to-end test environment and make plan to convert to virtual databases
- Continue the effort to develop a library of virtual services
- Launch an REI EPIC program to recognize and capture savings
- Develop a business case for a formal support program with dedicated resources

9.2. The Next Trip Around the Sun

In the coming year our group is planning to achieve several expansions to the existing projects. These plans include:

- Design and setup of final SV infrastructure
- Project to finalize full infrastructure for DV platform
- Capacity management and forecasting for DV storage
- Alignment and partnering with the Digital and Site Reliability groups to include virtualization technologies in automated provisioning of systems, apps and pipeline testing
- Self service

[1] https://www.google.com/url?q=https://www.torbenrick.eu/blog/culture/organisational-culture-eats-strategy-for-breakfast-lunch-and-dinner/&sa=D&ust=1532056980167000&usg=AFQjCNEAr5yaEHtgTGjqsJNvikhRJ_s1sA

10. Summary Conclusions

REI's journey is not necessarily unique, but the effect of these streams of work within the company is very encouraging and potentially transformative. In just these few short years QA has gone from being the tail wagged by the dog, to more of a partner and needle-mover within the software engineering ecosystem of the company.

There are a few thoughts to conclude with:

1. Keep in mind this is indeed a journey. What transformed our organization is having a leader who is focused on forward path, and who is willing to accept levels of uncertainty and variability that many 'leaders' won't.

2. Temper the uncertainty by having an overall vision and end state target, and then apply small steps and adjustments, learning as you go.

3. Carve out smaller units of work, be willing to learn from small mistakes, fail fast and fail forward. Make incremental progress and celebrate small wins.

4. You won't have control over a lot of variables, such as key resource availability, conflicts with project and operational priorities (e.g., I can't make your workshop this week because ...fill in the blank). Prepare to just roll with the punches but focus on actually delivering the smaller targets.

5. Expect resistance to some of your ideas and initiatives. As a mitigation, keep the North Star (end state) in focus: don't lose sight of where you're trying to go. Evaluate your progress frequently and be willing to adjust your path—but ensure you are always driving to the North Star

6. Most of all, be positive and confident that you'll get there. And you will.

Effective CI Using Automated Quality Checker

Authors

Ruchir Garg, Red Hat (rgarg@redhat.com)

Abstract

Continuous Integration is the need of the day for dynamic software, where time to market is the key. To achieve this, it's necessary that all incoming code Merge Requests (also known as Pull Requests) meet the quality criteria and doesn't break the master build. These checks cannot be only manual, and hence all repetitive steps need to be automated. This paper talks about automated checks that ensure that the incoming code meets the recommended coding guidelines, contains enough unit tests, references the feature it adds or the issue it fixes, maintains backward compatibility, contains documentation (if needed), etc. The comprehensive list of possibilities is dependent on the criteria defined by the team. Failure to meet such criteria results in rejected merge request. Once these checks pass, the reviewer has to only review the code and the artifacts of the automation manually. This cuts down on the review time drastically and prevents wastage. It also helps to keep the quality quotient high and the software always ready for continuous deployment.

Biography

Ruchir Garg is a Principal Engineer at Red Hat, where he is working on creating a new developer experience for enterprise developers. He has previously worked as a security consultant and as an automation architect, developing brand new test automation frameworks. Ruchir has spent more than 15 years of industry experience developing, testing and supporting software products in various domains like embedded, mobile, wireless and desktop applications. Ruchir holds a degree in Electrical Engineering from Nagpur University, India.

1. Introduction

Dynamic software with frequent release cycles are dependent on Continuous Integration (CI) and Continuous Deployment (CD). In the cut-throat world of fierce competition, a delay in the release cycle due to an ineffective CI or a CD can negatively impact the businesses. In this paper, we'll focus on CI and discuss various ways of making it effective by leveraging automation and reducing the manual steps to the minimum. We'll also discuss how data generated by a CI system could be used as quality metrics.

2. Opportunity

Making CI effective, though most are already doing it, is a challenge. An effective CI system, to a large extent, depends upon automated quality checks. These checks should not only ensure complete regression (reactive), but should also ensure that the new code is not adding to the technical debt (proactive). Most automated quality checks focus excessively on the former, but ignoring the latter would eventually lead to a situation where regression will forever play catch-up with new code.

The proactive approach, too adds value but only when its automated, or else it may slow things down. For the scope of this presentation, let's refer to this automated CI plugin as the ***checker***.

3. Opportunity

Dynamic software with frequent release cycles are dependent on Continuous Integration (CI) and Continuous Deployment (CD). In the cut-throat world of fierce competition, a delay in the release cycle due to an ineffective CI or a CD can negatively impact the businesses. In this paper, we'll focus on CI and discuss various ways of making it effective by leveraging automation and reducing the manual steps to the minimum. We'll also discuss how data generated by a CI system could be used as quality metrics.

3.1. Avoid technical debt

All new code must come with its own set of new tests, else it adds up to technical backlog and increases testing gaps. The *checker* must automate this check and take necessary action in case the minimum conditions are not met. let's consider the following few cases:

When: No tests written for the code being submitted.

What: The code merge request is Blocked and is also marked as such.

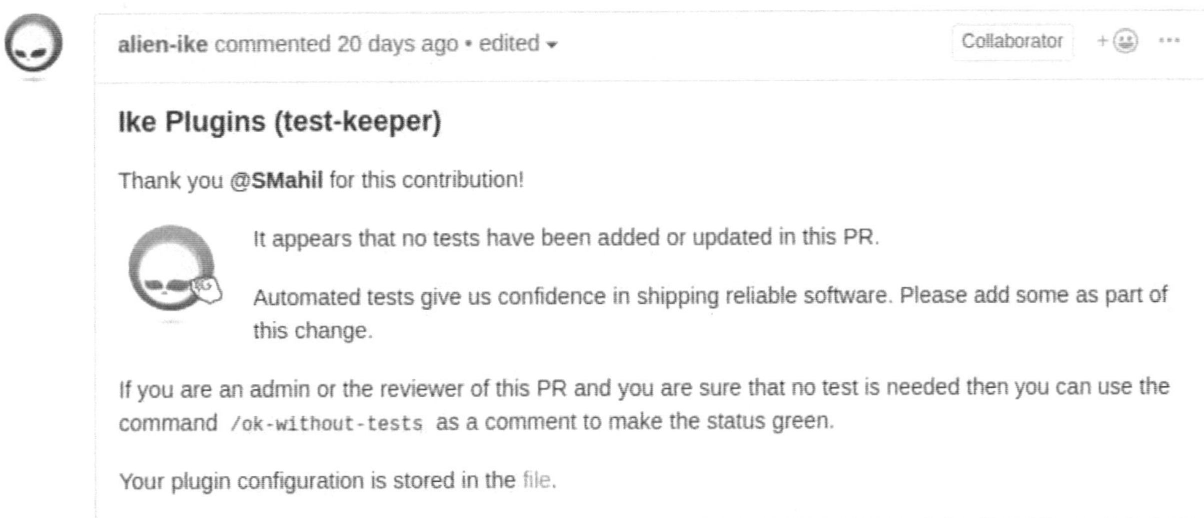

Figure 1: Checker blocking a merge request due to missing tests

How: This could be achieved by scanning the files submitted as part of the merge request and identifying the files added that represent tests. For example, assuming a project source directory has all tests nested under the "tests" directory, so additions to files under that directory could be assumed as new tests.

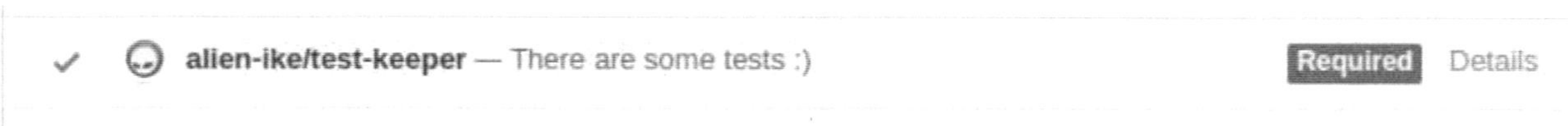

Figure 2: Checker marking the request when the author adds some tests

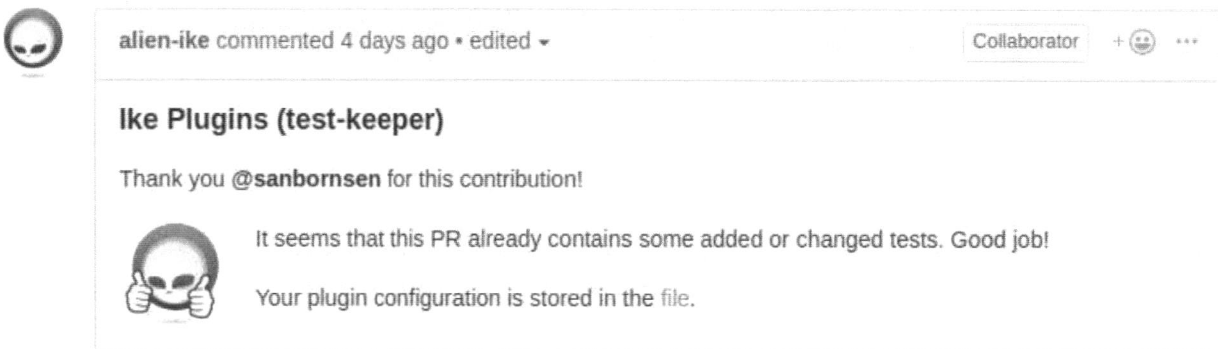

Figure 3: Checker lauding the author when the code is submitted along with the tests

Why: This process enforces a habit of writing tests along with production code. It ensures that people don't spend precious time reviewing incomplete and possibly dysfunctional code. It also makes regression easy to manage and hence increases code maintainability.

3.2. Don't Break the Working Code

While it's important to ensure tests are written for new code, it's equally important to ensure that the old code continues to work as before. No amount of fancy new code can justify a breaking change at the customer's end. The CI system must automate this regression based on existing tests:

When: The new code submitted breaks an existing test.

What: The code merge request is Blocked and is also marked as such.

How: Configure the CI system to automatically run the existing tests (unit, integration, functional) against the build that is generated using the new code. Let the build fail on a test failure.

Why: This process ensures that the new code doesn't destabilizes the existing code and the current user experience is maintained. This check provides a safety net to engineering and instills confidence to roll out code more frequently without worrying about the outcome.

3.3. Maintain Code Coverage

Now that it's ensured that all new code is submitted with additional tests, we also need to ensure that the new tests added are sufficient too:

When: A fairly large amount of new code is submitted with a single new test.

What: The code merge request is Blocked and is also marked as such.

How: Configure the *checker* to automatically calculate the code coverage metrics. This could be done using tools like Codecov[5] or Gcov[6]. A simple goal could be that adding new code should not bring down the code coverage percentage any lower than before. The checker can compare the coverage numbers and then take appropriate action.

Why: This ensures that the new code not only adds new tests, but also adds sufficient amount of tests. With this system in place, it would be difficult to game the system by adding minimum tests and getting away with it.

3.4. Ignore Non-Production Code

Not all merge requests carry code that runs in production environment. Examples of such requests could be automated tests, non-production configuration changes, documentation, etc. Such requests could safely be ignored by the checker:

When: A new merge request is made that only contains test scripts.

What: The code merge request is Ignored by the *checker.*

Figure 4: Checker skipping a merge request containing only non-production code

5 https://codecov.io/
6 https://gcc.gnu.org/onlinedocs/gcc/Gcov.html

How: Configure the *checker* to specify directories that contain only non-production code. Commits to such directories would be assumed to contain non-production code and hence, would be ignored.

Why: This ensures that non-production code is spared the unnecessary scanning as the process to treat such code could be totally different than production code.

Note: It is quite possible that, even with all the check customization, there could be merge requests that carry production code, but doesn't require additional tests (e.g. config file changes). In such cases using a keyword, reviewers and administrators can bypass the otherwise mandatory quality checks.

3.5. Manage the Process

Reviewer's accountability: A merge requests submitted requires a review from a peer, before it gets merged with the master branch. While we've been talking about the authors responsibilities, the reviewer, too has its own responsibilities. The reviewer needs to provide feedback within a stipulated time. A feedback provided towards the end of the sprint is undesirable as it would be then too late to make the changes and the author might be hurried into delivering the fixed code.

Work-in-progress = Ignore: Any merge requests that are marked for work-in-progress are to be skipped from the quality checks or peer review, as they are still not ready. The checker can take care of this by looking up strings like *WIP/work-in-progress* either in the title/description/labels.

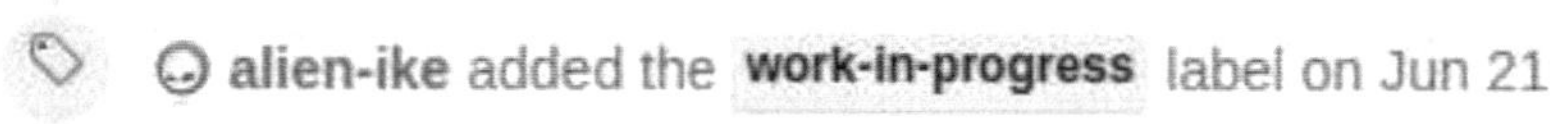

Figure 5: Checker adding a "work-in-progress" label to the merge request

Figure 6: Checker blocking the merge request unless the "work-in-progress" label is removed

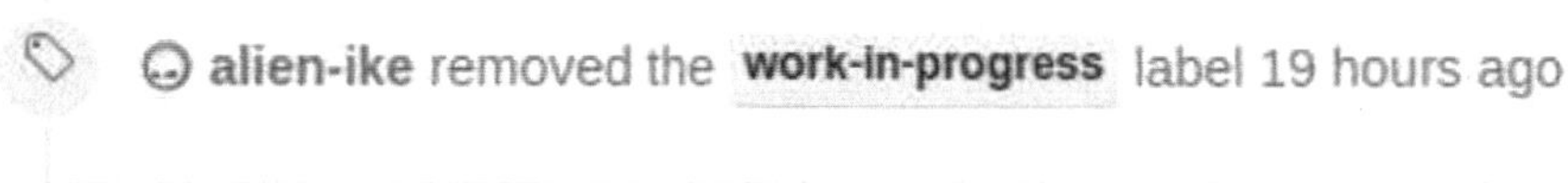

Figure 7: Checker removing the "work-in-progress" label from the merge request

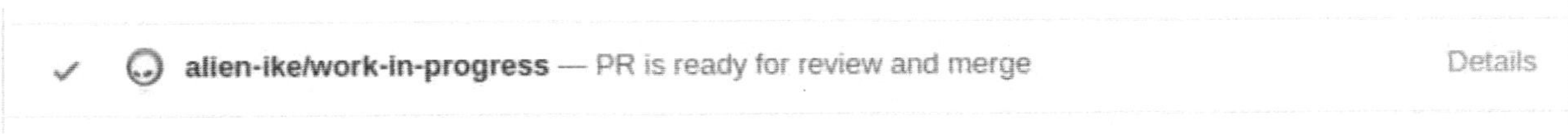

Figure 8: Checker unblocking the merge request

Reason of the merge request: When a merge request is submitted for review, it must either be to implement a story or to fix a defect. Random requests with no references are not encouraged as the reviewer would also need some context before reviewing the work. The *checker* ensures that this process is followed by ensuring that a reference hyperlink to the user story or the defect that is addressed is provided in the merge request.

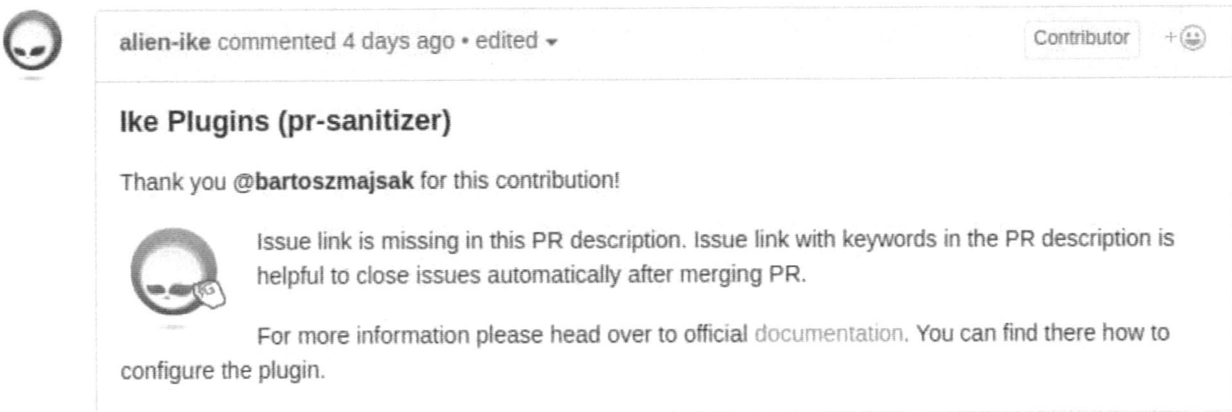

Figure 9: Checker marking the merge request as a link to the issue it fixes is missing

Optionally, the presence of minimum description text could also be enforced by counting the characters entered by the author in the description field.

3.6. Deep Insights

Having an automated quality *checker* has its advantages, beyond great quality software; quality metrics!

Each quality check failure could be captured as a metric and collection of such data can indicate deeper insights into the real issues that teams might be facing. Consider the following:

a) A large number of merge requests that are blocked due to missing or insufficient tests indicate a skill gap. It's possible that the team need additional training to start writing tests.

b) Sizable regression failures indicate careless coding practices and may require a stringent peer-review system to fix. This metric also indicates the number of potential breaking defects that were prevented from reaching the production system.

c) A peer feedback to the merge request could be captured using special flags representing defects. For example, feedback reported like this:
"/defect-high Missing null check"

   This could be tracked as a defect against the code. Similarly, the author can mark a defect resolved like this:

   "/defect-high-fixed Missing null check"

   As a precondition to merge the code, all defect counts against the request must be zero:

   i. All defects reported and fixed as reviews could be termed as early defects, which are the preferred type of defects.

   ii. Early defects are the ones that failed to reach production. Similarly, an escaped defect is that defects that slipped your checks and processes to reach production.

   iii. Using an automated CI process, keeping a count of such defects is possible.

d) Since the code and tests are tracked as part of single merge request, it's possible to create an automated map between the code churned and the tests that cover it. Let's call it code-test matrix. This could be used in future for effective and smart regressions.

e) If the code and the defect tracking is consolidated in a single system, then tracking back a defect to its original source of introduction could also be tracked. Since the code commit history is maintained at all times, a late defect while being fixed, could be traced back to its original source of injection. Not to play a blame game, but to learn about the reason the defect escaped in first place.

4. Results

An automated quality *checker* that not only performs regression, but also ensures process compliance results in a self-sustaining model of development that always keeps pace with the pace of development. The resultant product is of high quality with reduced probability of finding defects in production. The metrics that it can offer also acts as a feedback to allow continuous improvement of the continuous integration system.

5. Final Words

The changes suggested in this paper require a system that may have to be developed grounds-up as it may not be available off the shelf. Folks using GitHub, you can look at the open source *Ike Prow Plugin*[7] developed by Red Hat. This may give you a head start, but remember the plugin is still in its early days and all functionality discussed in this paper may not be available. Here is the recommended workflow in the form of a flowchart:

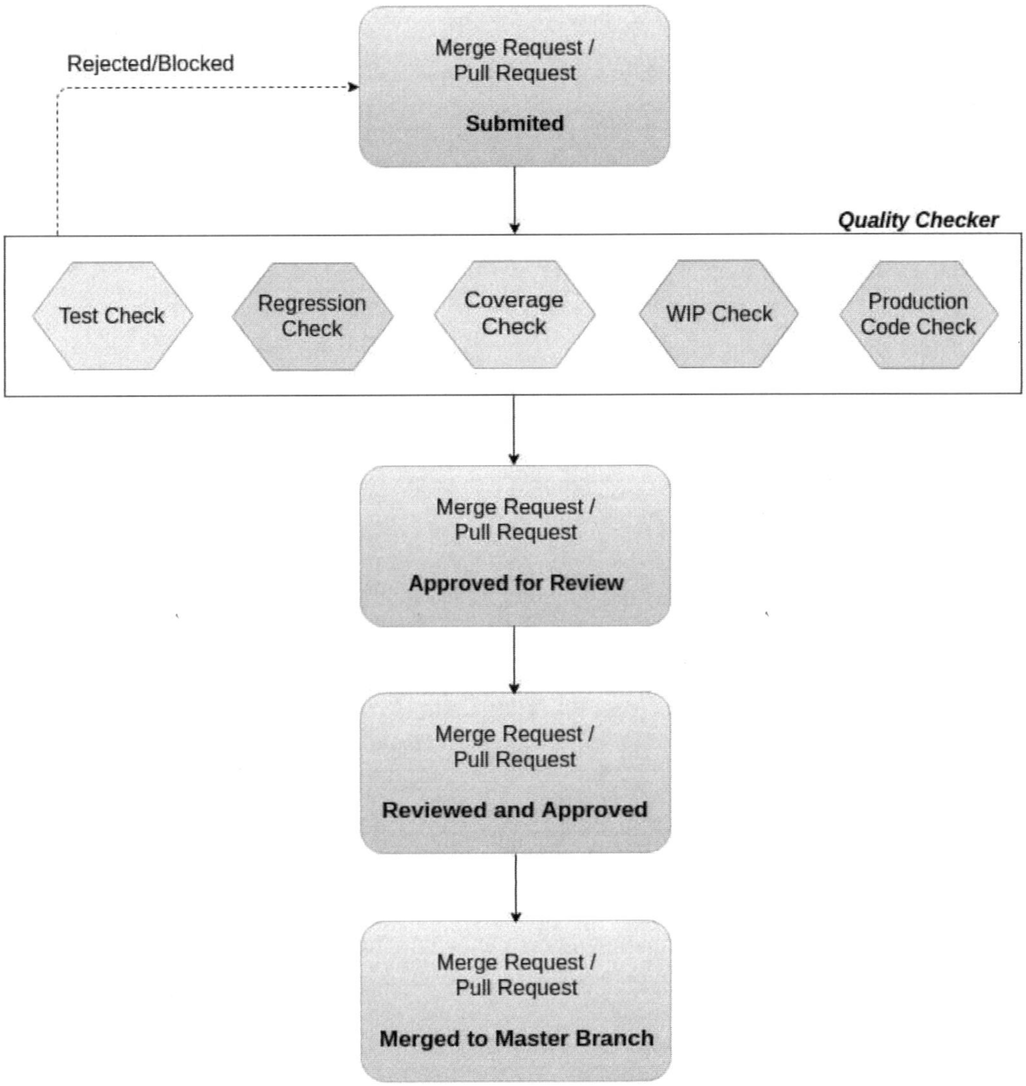

Figure 10: Recommend workflow

7 Arquillian – Ike-prow-plugin: http://arquillian.org/ike-prow-plugins/

Such a system will extensively depend upon the API availability of the source repository system in use, and processes used in different organizations vary, so a one-size-fits-all approach will not work. Developing such a system will require investment and hence management commitment is needed to charter on this journey.

References

Arquillian – Ike-prow-plugin (The *checker*): https://github.com/arquillian/ike-prow-plugins

This page intentionally left blank.

$, $$, $$$ Which QA Tools Are Worth It at Their Respective Price Points

Authors

Victor La (via@paraport.com)

Abstract

Making the right tooling decisions can impact how effective you are when managing, testing and maintaining an application. Regardless of whether a tool is - open source, free or paid - all tools have their pros and cons. The roles and duties of Quality Assurance are vast and ever changing. However, there will always be a need to: manage test cases, verify information and automate workflow. But there is no need to reinvent the wheel! There are a number of tools/vendors/ consultants out there that will probably satisfy the needs of your team. The true dilemma becomes: "What is right for my team?", "Am I really getting what I need out of this?", "How much does this cost?" Culminating to a simple question: "Worth it?" The process is simple! Compare different tools at different price points to see which tool is the most worth it to us at its given price point.

Biography

Victor La is a Quality assurance Engineer who has spent the last 9 years working in the financial services industry & the last 3 years as a Quality assurance engineer and advocate at a Seattle FinTech organization. Victor strives to create operational efficiencies in his work testing: Big data, UI performance, UI/UX, Web APIs & Desktop and Web applications. He is passionate about improving process with free or cheaper alternatives & coaching the next generations of test engineers. When he is not tinkering around with various products, he enjoys cooking, traveling & enjoying life. Feel free to contact victor at vla@paraport.com.

1. Our Dilemma

Concepts like continuous integration and continuous deployment become reality and achievable when there are sets of tests that can be run: On Commit, Ad Hoc, Scheduled, etc. However, in order to get to that point everyone needs to be part of the conversation. From the developers, dev-ops, sys-ops, Software Development Engineers in Testing (SDET) to manual testers. The right tooling decisions can impact how effective a team is when managing, testing and maintaining an application. Regardless of if a tool is open source, free, or paid, all tools have their strengths and weaknesses. It's hard to know what tool is right or wrong for your organization, without having to spend precious time testing and evaluating each tool. However, is that entirely necessary? In the age of google, the internet and YouTube. There are easy ways to find whether a tool fits your needs without having to spend hours, days and weeks testing and evaluating. Chances are, as long as you are diligent and have your personalized set of criteria, a few hours of research and a few YouTube / plural sight videos later, you will emerge from your den with an idea of which tool is right for you. Your personalized criteria will help you quickly sort through the numerous number of tools, venders, consultants out there. The original dilemma of: "What is right for my team?", "Am I really getting what I need out of this?", "How much does this cost?" quickly boils down and becomes a data point in our criteria. Only tools that are able to meet the baseline should be evaluated, otherwise any time put into the effort would be for nothing. This process will turn the selection of a testing tool from a feel into an engineered science, and ultimately help us decide, is it worth it!

2. Our Focus on WEB APIs

There are many layers that make up a full stack application. From the UX/UI used by users to the database(s) used to store information provided by the user and stored by the application. Web application programing interfaces or Web APIs act as an interface that allows anyone the ability to access features, logic or data through the use of HTTP protocol. It can be appropriate to think of APIs as pieces of software modules that enable systems to communicate, start process and initial tasks with other systems or programs. According to Forbes contributor Louis Columbus, "2017 is quickly becoming the year of the API economy. Businesses are now realizing that APIs can be used to create new business models and new opportunities for income streams." Through the use of API keys, business and entrepreneurs with an idea or program allow access to registered users and track their usage of the API as a means to bill the user while protecting the system as a whole from fraud and abuse. The more users and the more your API is used, the more in revenue your API is able to earn. ProgrammableWeb.com, one of the world's leading sources of news and information about internet-based APIs is currently reporting more than 19,910s publically accessible APIs. This does not even include APIs that are used in a private business to business (b2b) capacity. Since 2005, there has been an exponential growth in the number of APIs that are open to be used. The graph shown in exhibit 3 illustrates the level of growth seem in APIs since 2005.

3. Why WEB APIs

The level of growth Web APIs has seen over the last decade presents quality assurance engineers (QAE) and software developers with an interesting problem - How do we going to keep all of the chief information officers (CIO) & chief technology officers(CTO) of the world happy by constantly and consistently releasing quality APIs and how are we supposed to test and maintain all of these APIs as we release them to the public to be used by the masses? There are many ways to go about testing your own APIs, such as: Unit Tests, PowerShell & manually. Luckily for us, there is no need to reinvent the wheel on how to test web APIs. Vendors and companies out there that have invested a significant amount of time and resources and are more than happy to sell you a product for you to be able to verify, test and maintain your Web APIs. So then, the question really becomes - Is it necessary to pay a company or is it to the advantage of your organization and your team to spend a little time and energy to create a self-hosted mechanism to test? Culminating to the ultimate question – Is it worth it?

4. The Sea of Solutions

There is a proverbial sea of solutions out on the marketplace that advertise their tools and solution can help you achieve continuous delivery and rapid deployments of your projects. With Web APIs being a mature and well understood framework and understood problem, many problems and uncertainties that usually come with a new technology have already been solved and addressed. A quick search on Google for the phrase "Testing Web APIs" yields over 482,000,000 results, with the top results coming from many popular providers and vendors that are used by many of the large fortune 500 companies of the world. A screenshot of these results can be seen in exhibit 4. Through a bit more surfing, poking and prodding of the wares, you can easily discover that for the most part, many of these vendors and products offer a free version and a subscription based version. The goal for our process it to be completely tool & process agnostic. Ideally, our criteria can be used to access thousands of tools and processes and provide a score that will help you decide whether or not a tool deserves a second glance.

5. Our Criteria

Before we set out to examine and uncover the dark secrets of these applications and vendors, it is imperative that we arm ourselves with the means to properly evaluate and rate the products in order to stay objective. In order to achieve a holistic picture of a given application we will look at five different categories and see how the product lives up to our standards by assigning it a score between one and five. (One being the WORST and 5 being the best) Our five categories are as followed:

1. Features
2. Price
3. Ease of use
4. Community Support
5. Repeatability

5.1. Feature Rich

The features we look for in an application fall into two sub-categories, needs & wants. It is important to understand this distinction. An example of a need might be that the application must be compatible with Windows & IOS, where a want might be having a Chrome plugin. As many of the applications usually have some sort of tiered payment system. We will evaluate each tool's features at its highest price point and attempt to break down the major features, both the "needs" of the application as well as the nice "wants" that the application may or may not have. Through experience and from colleges, I've compiled a list of needs & wants that we will look for when examining a tools features:

Needs:

Web or Console UI	**API**	**CD / CI**	**Asynchronous**
Monitoring	**Documentation**	**Windows/ Mac/ Linux**	**Repeatability**

Wants:

Easy to set up	**Multiple Language support**	**Multiple Format support**	**Plugins**
Playback	**Open Source**	**Free/ Cheap**	**Cloud**

While the list is not 100% exhaustive, it does give us a good picture of features we need and want to look for when evaluating a tool. Before beginning your search for a tool, it is highly recommend that you compile a list of your individual needs & wants. The exercise should only take you 5 mins but will give an anchor point when doing a quick evaluation of a tool. Our scoring system will follow the below rubric:

1. Lacking in both needed features and wanted features.
2. Has a number of needed features with very little wanted features.
3. Has all needed features but only a few wanted features which may lead to the tool being cumbersome to use
4. A feature rich application of both needs and the majority of your wants
5. A feature rich application of all needs, wants & even bonuses

5.2 Price Matters

While features are certainly important, so is how much we are paying for those features. Many of the vendors and the applications promise the holy grail of web API testing. From creating, administering to even automating your web API testing. However, behind the glitz and the glamor is a platform that requires a great deal of time and money to set up. While it is easy to see and evaluate the price seen on the "pricing" page of a tools website. It is much harder to calculate the amount of costs that you may incur from using a tool. Cost to set up a self-hosted server, training costs and support, at the end of the day, will affect the bottom-line of any business or organization. Our hope is to uncover all costs associated with using a tool and thus score it from 1-5 using the below criteria:

1. Costs are astronomical: Cost of tool exceeds $5,000 a year, Servers need building / maintenance / support staff & consultants needed

2. Costs are high, total costs per year will exceed $5,000
3. Costs are moderate, but totals cost per year will not exceed $5000
4. Costs are low and total cost per year will not exceed $1000
5. There are no costs, 100% free to use

5.3. It's Bought, Now How Do I Use This...

Let's attempt to look a week into the future after we've purchased the tool and signed the licensing agreement. Our goal is to look at the: "What needs to happen to get this thing working." Implementation can be difficult and time consuming and working with a new technology can be rough, especially if the tools do not follow best practices or have detailed documentation. It would be naive for us to believe that a tool will just work out of the box. There are a number of factors that should be considered at this stage. Those factors are as followed:

Factors

Physical	Human
Does the Hardware exists to support my tool?	**Do I have anyone to build out infrastructure if I need it?**
Does my tool require specialized components?	**Do i have someone who would be able to support this tool?**
Does our current tooling already support a Web API Testing Framework?	**Is there anyone else I will need to involve during the set up?**

Many of the factors above all have a common theme, which is, who am I or what am I missing in this conversation. It is important to remember, that Rome was not built in one day, nor by one man. It takes a village, and in this case, an organization to: set up, use and perfect a tool. Take 5 mins to ask yourself the above questions. Your answers should then be evaluated against the below scale:

1. I have not talked to enough people in the organization, there are 6 or more people I need to consult before I should proceed any further | infrastructure is not set up nor is there an appetite to invest in additional hardware.
2. Infrastructure will need over 50 hours of work & people will need to be hired
3. Infrastructure exists however will need some investment for scaling purposes | People in the org have had some experience with the tool
4. Infrastructure is in place with only minimal changes needed & People are on board with setting up the new technology
5. Infrastructure in place & people are already skilled at using the tool

**Example of people who you may want to speak with:

1. Developers
2. Infrastructure
3. Dev-Ops
4. Sys-Ops
5. Security

5.4. Community Support

Sometimes it's just easier to run a google search in order to quickly answer a question. While documentation can be great. Sometimes it's even better to have a mature community and well documented patterns on popular knowledge repositories (E.g. stack overflow). Other community support sources we will be looking for are: Libraries, best practices guides, mods, templates, etc.

The following items will be counted as community support tools:

Official Documentation	Stack Overflow	Community FAQ	Blogs
Guides	templates	libraries	Open Source

In this 5 min exercise. Think of a common and simple question you may have when using or setting up a tool. Some example questions would be:

1. "When trying to POST app returns 500 -insert tool name"
2. "-insert tool name- continuous integration"
3. "Best way to use -insert tool name-"

Your questions should be similar in nature and should try to address any shortcomings that you've identified thus far down this process. Once your questions have been documented, perform a search on the tools community site, google , stack overflow and evaluate whether or not your question was answered and if there is any supplementary tools or processes that can take you one step further. As for the score, we will evaluate the community support based on the below criteria:

1. Searches yield little or no information
2. Searches does not provide much help or references outdated material
3. Search yields the answers that you seek after a little digging
4. Searches yield a plethora of answers & provides follow up instructions on how to proceed
5. Searches yield a plethora of answers, best practices, and even provides ways to solve it

5.5. Automatable?

In the age of Continuous integration (CI) and Continuous delivery (CD), just being able to run functional tests is not enough. Ideally, a Web API testing platform should allow a team to make quick iterations and most importantly, give the team the ability to add features and refactor without fear of breaking changes. While automation may not be important to you now, or in the near future. It is important to understand the technology is moving faster and faster. The ability for a dev to change code at a moment's notice and have those changed into production minutes later is increasingly valuable. Our criteria on how repeatable a tool is as follows:

1. The tool does not support automation and is for manual testing only
2. The tool can be used for automation, however, tests can only be performed on an ad hoc basis
3. The tool supports automation through the use of its own internal UI
4. The tool supports continuous integration with your desired CI framework
5. The tool supports CI/ CD development on numerous frameworks

6. Tips and Hints

There are a number of very popular tools out there on the market place but sometimes it's easier to see if there are any tools that your organization already owns but just not utilized. For example if you use Smartbear as a service provider, it would be good for you to know that Smartbear partners with SoapUI and provides this service as part of their package of testing utilities. Other major vendors who provide testing applications as part of their contracts would be: Parasoft, Apache & Progress. So it is worth some time exploring some of your existing relationships to see if there is something that you are already paying for but not utilizing.

Scoring:

Scoring should be relatively straightforward. Every tool you evaluate will be out of 25. I would recommend any tool that scores lower than a B (80%) to be tossed aside as it would not be worth your time exploring the tool any longer. Where anything that scores 80% or greater should be evaluated at your own discretion. The scoring will look a little something like this

Tool: Postman

Quality	Score
Feature Rich	X/5
Price	X/5
Ease of use	X/5
Community Support	X/5
Automation	X/5

Total: X/25

Tools:
Below are some popular tools that I've done research on in the past.

Postman	Visual Studio	Fiddler	Soap UI	REST-Assured
apigee	jMeter	Tricentis	Katalon	Karate DSL

7. Closing Remarks

The scoring and the evaluation methods detailed above do not have to stop at Web APIs. For the most part, the questions are agnostic enough for you to be able to slightly modify them and apply them to an array of tools. In addition, the questions should be general enough for anyone to be able to use them. From a QA manager to an individual contributor. I myself am not in a managing role, however, I have had a great deal of fun finding ways to make the lives of those around me a little easier. I encourage all to do a little homework and to think about what is important when it comes to your tooling and how you'd like to test now, tomorrow and in the future.

Happy testing!

References

Columbus, Louis. "2017 Is Quickly Becoming The Year Of The API Economy." Forbes. January 29, 2017. Accessed June 18, 2018. https://www.forbes.com/sites/louiscolumbus/2017/01/29/2017-is-quickly-becoming-the-year-of-the-API-economy/#573b4f796a41.

Pw_honcho. "About ProgrammableWeb." ProgrammableWeb. May 22, 2014. Accessed August 20, 2018. https://www.programmableweb.com/about

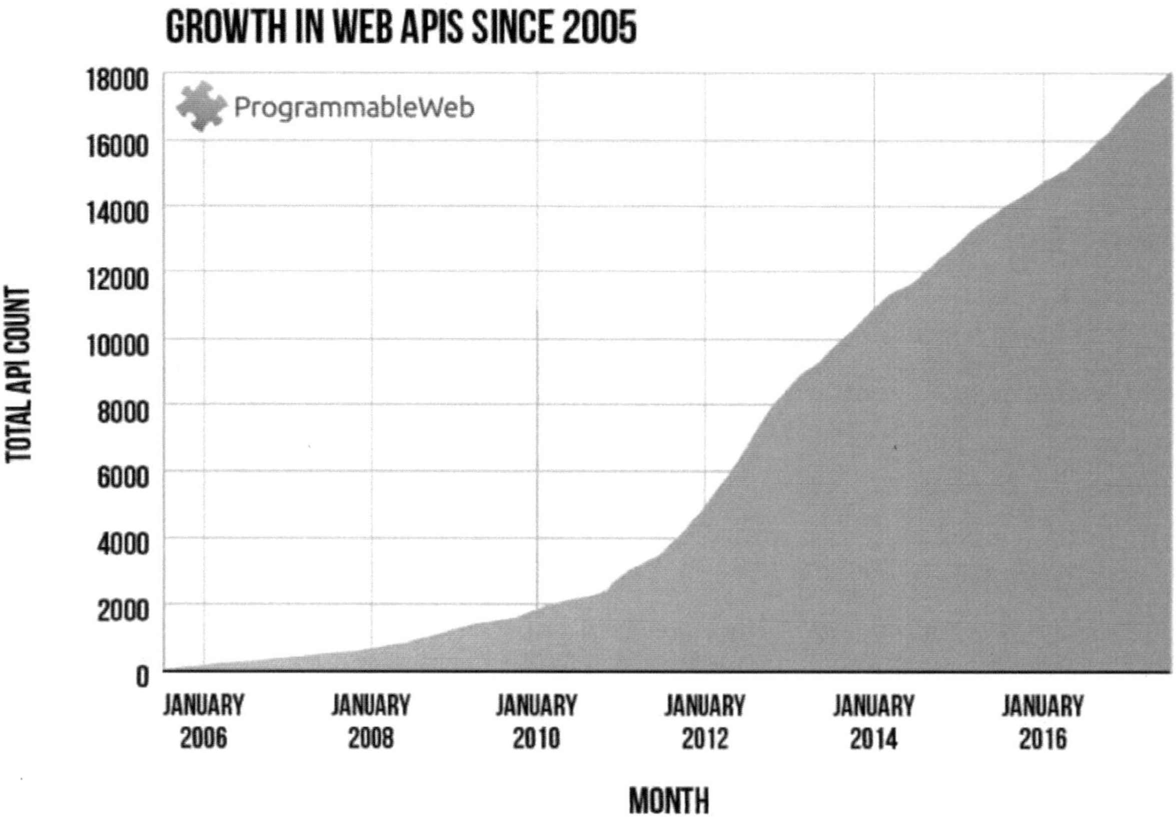

Exhibit 3

This page intentionally left blank.

Collaborating with Students to Produce High-Quality Production Software

Authors

Sam Murthy (murthys@wcsu.edu)
Andrew Figueroa (figueroa039@connect.wcsu.edu)
Steven Rollo (rollo003@connect.wcsu.edu)

Abstract

Agile and DevOps processes are generally considered beneficial to collaboratively producing high-quality software. Thus, employers currently seek people with skills in these two areas, even for entry-level positions which new Computer Science (CS) graduates often fill. However, undergraduate CS programs generally only provide opportunities for students to practice core CS concepts in simple classroom exercises and projects, instead of providing immersive experiences. Industry internships do expose students to real-life development and maintenance (often with emphasis on maintenance), but interns rarely experience the entire product life cycle; many do not even get to see the "big picture".

In this paper, we share the experience of a hands-on co-curricular lab where students learn many practical aspects of collaboratively building high-quality production software alongside faculty members. The important bit is that the process of learning and practicing is itself agile-like, in the sense that students are incrementally taught concepts and given opportunities to realize hands-on why a certain process step is necessary and what some of the alternatives might be.

The lab was founded by a faculty member and has thus far engaged 12 CS undergraduate students including sophomores, juniors, and seniors. The faculty member generally moderates discussions and introduces new concepts, but no distinction is made among any team member based on their standing (faculty or student). The lab is not part of any coursework, and all participation is voluntary. The lab has thus far developed two products, but this paper focuses on just one product—called *ClassDB*—and provides the perspectives of the faculty member and two student collaborators.

The following is a summary of the lab's progress in ClassDB: Development began in Summer 2017 with pre-production versions released throughout summer, and the first production version released by the term's end. 20 students used the software during Fall 2017, and 20 more used it in spring after a major update in winter. The software is rolled out to about 50 students this fall and is being prepared for use by about 4,000 students across the university system. All source code, tests, issues, and documentation are available in a public GitHub repository at http://bit.ly/ClassDBRepo

Biography

Dr. Sean Murthy is a member of the CS faculty at Western Connecticut State University (WCSU) as well as the founder and director of the Data Science & Systems Lab (DASSL, read dazzle). He has extensive experience in software engineering and has developed several commercial software products including a few for Fortune 100 companies.

Andrew Figueroa is a CS undergraduate student at WCSU presently in his senior year.

Steven Rollo graduated from WCSU in Spring 2018 with a BS degree in CS and is now employed at Fiber Mountain. Prior to graduation, Rollo completed two internships in software engineering and systems integration at Seagate Technology. Murthy, Figueroa, and Rollo are all members of DASSL where they co-develop ClassDB, Gradebook, and other products.

1. Introduction

In the past few years, the software-engineering industry has seen rapid and extensive changes in tools, approaches, and more importantly mindset. The changes are due to an explosion in the number of tools that boost accessibility, productivity, and software quality. They are also due to improved access to reliable information on technology, tools, and processes, as well as due to wider adoption of agile and DevOps processes in both engineering and management.
Due to these changes, employers are naturally seeking people with skills in newer tools and approaches and expect employees to have or develop an "Agile and DevOps mindset", even in entry-level positions which new Computer Science (CS) graduates typically fill. However, universities have yet to change their programs to meet employers' needs, largely because they focus on teaching core CS concepts such as programming, algorithms and architecture. In fact, a typical undergraduate program requires students to complete just one course in software engineering. Some programs offer courses on software quality, but only as an elective. CS 320 at Whitworth University is one such elective course (Whitworth University 2018).

A common limitation of most undergraduate CS courses is that they can only afford to have students practice simple exercises and projects, instead of providing an immersive experience. Students who obtain industry internships do get exposure to real-life development and maintenance (often with emphasis on maintenance), but they rarely experience the entire product life cycle. In fact, many interns report they did not get to see the "big picture".

We believe the typical undergraduate CS program is structurally unable (at least presently in the US) to prepare new graduates to fully contribute to products and processes in this "agile era". We fear that the new graduates' inability to fully and readily participate results in delayed hiring, and the delay can create a vicious cycle where the graduates fall behind more as time passes.

Our solution to this problem is a *hands-on co-curricular lab* to introduce undergraduates to practical aspects of building software, including an introduction to a lightweight "Agile and

DevOps process". The emphasis is on faculty and students collaborating to build, deploy, document, and maintain high-quality production software. (See Section 2.2 for a definition of terms.)

The solution was conceived by, and is led by, a CS faculty member (the first author of this paper) as part of the Data Science & Systems Lab (DASSL, read *dazzle*) (DASSL 2017b) Western Connecticut State University (WCSU). The lab runs throughout the year, with special sessions in summer and winter.

Since its founding in Spring 2017, DASSL has engaged 12 undergraduates, including the second and third authors of this paper. It has developed two products, including *ClassDB* (DASSL 2018a) which is now in production for about 50 students, with plans to soon open it to about 4,000 students across four universities and 12 community colleges in the Connecticut State Colleges and Universities system. Also, including this paper, DASSL has thus far produced four peer-reviewed publications (Murthy 2018b, 2018a, Figueroa, and Rollo 2018), two of which have student co-authors.

More importantly, each participating student has an online portfolio that readily demonstrates their accomplishments to prospective employers. Indeed, DASSL alumni report that their lab participation has given them a competitive edge and that employers have appreciated their familiarity with modern software-engineering processes and toolchains. (Section 6 provides some examples.)

In this paper, we share our experience with faculty-student collaboration to build and maintain high-quality production software at DASSL. We mainly use ClassDB to provide examples and share our perspectives as significant contributors to DASSL.

The rest of this paper is organized as follows: Section 2 introduces ClassDB and DASSL as well as some terms. Section 3 outlines the educational and engineering processes used at DASSL. Section 4 highlights the "team culture". Section 5 describes DASSL's effort specifically in two areas to maintain high quality. Section

2. Background

This section provides some background about the ClassDB application and DASSL, and also introduces some terms. The information about ClassDB is limited to the needs of this paper, but details are available elsewhere (DASSL 2018a; Murthy, Figueroa, and Rollo 2018). Also, later sections of this paper add details.

2.1. ClassDB

Instructors can use ClassDB in teaching courses where students interact with databases. It can be used in both introductory courses where students learn to write queries, and in upper-level courses where students perform analytics and other advanced data-management activities. In addition, ClassDB itself provides many case studies for data management and software engineering courses, as evidenced in WCSU courses CS205 and CS305 (WSCU 2013).

Instructors use ClassDB to provide database sandboxes to students and student teams. Each student has full control of their own sandbox. Likewise, each student team has its own sandbox and all team members have full access to their team's sandbox. No student is able to read another student's sandbox, but an instructor can read any sandbox. Instructors can also consult the detailed activity logs ClassDB maintains to review student progress and analyze the logs to provide customized feedback to students.

Task	**API call**
Add 'edwall' as a student	SELECT ClassDB.createStudent('edwall', 'Ed Wall');
Create team 'dragon'	SELECT ClassDB.createTeam('dragon');
Add 'edwall' to team 'dragon'	SELECT ClassDB.addToTeam('edwall', 'dragon');
List currently registered students	SELECT UserName FROM ClassDB.Student;
List activity summary for 'edwall'	SELECT * FROM ClassDB.getUserActivitySummary('edwall');
List my DDL activity (any user)	SELECT * FROM public.MyDDLActivity;

Table 1: Example calls to ClassDB API

ClassDB runs entirely within a server instance of a database management system (DBMS). Unobtrusive by design, its existence is ordinarily not apparent to any DBMS user, including instructors, but especially to students. It includes no user-interface elements (UI) and is usable through its application programming interface (API) from any pre-existing DBMS client application. The ClassDB API includes about 100 functions and views, a majority of which are accessible to instructors and a few are accessible to students. Table 1 shows some example calls to the ClassDB API.

ClassDB is implemented in PostgreSQL ("Postgres") using SQL with procedural extensions (PostgreSQL Development Group 2017). The current version of ClassDB—Version 2.2—is comprised of 2,788 lines of code (LOC) indicating that ClassDB is not a small application, given it is implemented in a declarative language: 2,788 LOC in SQL translates to between 11,152 LOC and 27,880 LOC in the C programming language according to Caper Jones's Programming Language Tables (Wallshein 2010; Jones 2007).

The core of ClassDB is built using the following DBMS concepts: schemas (each sandbox is a schema), role-based access control, triggers, and server logs. The use of role-based access control (Ferraiolo and Kuhn 1992) is particularly important to simplify the system implementation but still provide the safeguards necessary to maintain both data privacy (no student can see another student's data) and data integrity (not even the instructor can alter student data). Contrary to what the small LOC count might suggest, the use and careful choreographing of these concepts makes ClassDB a relatively complex system.

2.2. DASSL

DASSL is a research group with broad focus on data science and data-intensive systems, including the creation and maintenance of software applications in these areas. Much of the work at DASSL is in collaboration with CS undergraduates. (WCSU does not have a graduate CS program.)

Membership is open to all WCSU faculty and students. Students wishing to join are generally expected to have completed CS205 (an introductory data-management course), and most students who have completed CS205 will likely also have completed CS140 and CS170 (WCSU 2013) which introduce Java and C++ respectively. In this scheme, students are able to join DASSL after their 3rd semester, but due to a variety of reasons, students are more likely to join after their 4th semester. Some students have even joined DASSL in their senior year.

The first author of this paper is the *lab director* and is involved in all lab activity. The other two authors are charter student members of DASSL and have been involved in most DASSL activities to date.

Participation in DASSL is *not* part of any coursework, and all participation is voluntary. Students do not pay any fee or receive academic credit, and the faculty member does not receive any pay. When funds exist, some students receive a small stipend if their role includes helping the lab director run DASSL.

DASSL builds non-trivial applications that address real needs of real end users, with emphasis on end-to-end engineering including analysis, design, development, testing, documentation, deployment, and maintenance. Most DASSL products are free and open source, and are generally distributed under a Creative Commons Attribution-NonCommercial-ShareAlike license (Creative Commons 2013). As a rule, all work products are stored in GitHub repositories (DASSL 2017a), with many repositories being public.

2.3. Quality Orientation

We now introduce key notions of quality that drive software development at DASSL. Specifically, we introduce the terms in this paper's title: "collaborating with students to produce high-quality production software".

By "collaborating with students", we mean both faculty members and students working as a team using tools and processes comparable to those used in professional software development. Specifically, both faculty and student members are expected to participate in all software-development activities and subject their work to the same quality-assurance processes.

By "production software", we mean:

- Software meant for use by people other than its developers, and actively used by others beyond the semester or year in which the software is initially released.
- The development process has clear activities of design, implementation, testing, documentation, release, deployment, and maintenance.
- Software is developed and maintained with a process and fervor comparable to what a company in the business of producing such software might use and possess. This criterion is particularly important because one of DASSL's goals is to introduce undergraduates to practical aspects of building software.

By "quality software", we mean software that is useful, usable, and maintainable. We omit discussing the usefulness aspect of ClassDB, because that is not this paper's focus. By usability, we mean ease of deployment, operation, and maintenance. By "maintainable", we mean low effort to find and fix issues as well as to make enhancements.

By "high-quality software", we mean software that has few issues that prevent it from being useful, usable, and maintainable. At this point, we have not defined quantitative limits for the number, nature, and severity of issues that define "high quality", but we are in the process of developing a simple model.

3. Processes

In this section, we outline the educational and engineering processes at DASSL.

3.1. Educational

Summer and winter sessions: In addition to regularly scheduled meetings throughout the academic year, DASSL holds special sessions during summer and winter breaks. Students state their intent to join these sessions 1-2 months prior and discuss previous experience, interests, and availability with the lab director.

DASSL has thus far held three special sessions:

- Summer DASSL 2017 lasted six weeks and engaged eight students. It entailed 6-hour in-person meetings four times a week for six weeks, for a total of 144 hours (the equivalent of three university courses).
- Winter DASSL 2018 ran for two weeks and focused on developing ClassDB 2.0. It involved two returning students and two new students.
- Summer DASSL 2018 was 10 weeks long with three returning students and two new students. The main focus was to create ClassDB 2.1 and 2.2 as well as work on conference publications and presentations.

Meetings: DASSL holds occasional meetings to keep track of progress, share ideas, and provide an open environment to discuss project concerns. A majority of the meetings are online, which is particularly helpful during summer and winter. During the academic year (fall and spring terms), DASSL meets in-person once a month. These meetings discuss topics relevant to DASSL and also discuss issues in DASSL products.

DASSL Day: DASSL students publicly present their work once a semester. In addition to helping students develop skills in technical and scholarly communication, this event serves as a recruitment tool for new students, and a means of informing university administrators of the lab's progress and contributions.

Agile-like learning: Students are introduced to key concepts and tools in an agile-like manner that emphasizes iterative learning through practical scenarios rather than initial mastery of the theory. Because there are few concrete requirements to join DASSL, none involving prior knowledge of specific tools, an agile learning process is essential to reduce onboarding time and allow students to start contributing early.

3.2. Engineering

Milestone-driven development: Prior to starting development on a project or a product's release, an informal list of desired topics or features is created as a wiki page (DASSL 2018e). The list is discussed, refined, and expanded (with links to additional wiki pages if necessary). Once consensus develops, the list becomes a "to do" list for a new "milestone" and is assigned a completion date and the resulting product version number. These milestones function much like "sprints" in a traditional agile process. The wiki page for ClassDB Milestone 2 (DASSL 2018c) illustrates our approach.

Issue-driven development: Issues are logged and managed in GitHub Issues (DASSL 2018b). Each issue is classified by *nature* (wrong, missing, extra) and *priority* (low, medium, high). Where appropriate, issues are grouped into "epics". (ZenHub 2018b, 2018a). Section 5.2 details our issue-management process.

Developers self-assign issues to work on and generally choose the next pending issue with the highest priority. However, students new to DASSL tend to work on "easy to address" issues such as those needing changes to a single region in a single file. Regardless of issue classification, all changes committed to the repository are tagged with issues so that both issues and changes can be traced to each other.

Version control: We require every artifact—both code and non-code—to be under version control. To further ensure that work-in-progress does not interfere with a previous release, we use the GitFlow strategy (Driessen 2010) and maintain two long-lived branches named "master" and "dev". The master branch contains only code that is released, whereas all work-in-progress is maintained in the dev branch or in a sub-branch of the dev branch. Once a milestone's tasks are complete, the dev branch is merged into master, and that commit is tagged as a "release".

Pull Requests: Pull requests (PRs) are GitHub's mechanism to let a contributor inform other contributors that they wish to merge changes in their own branch into another branch. We require PRs to merge changes to the master or the dev branch on the server (DASSL 2018d). All PRs require approval from at least two other contributors, but it is common for all team members to review every commit. Every PR is expected to leave the dev branch stable with exceptions clearly noted in PR comments and discussion.

Code reviews: We review all code and non-code artifacts, including test scripts, prior to merging into the dev branch. Examples of issues identified in reviews include repeated and overly-verbose code, typographical errors, formatting inconsistencies, and unclear internal documentation. This attention to detail often results in many revisions and review cycles, but we have found these cycles to be very productive and illuminating for both the submitter and the reviewers. Also, frequent commits, each with meaningful and incremental changes in an "agile" fashion, make reviews easier and more productive.

Testing: We require any code that implements new functionality to include corresponding unit tests, and code that modifies existing functionality to also update existing unit tests. We also require that all code revisions pass both existing and new unit tests after the dev branch is locally merged into the branch of interest. Both the code submitter and all reviewers perform these tests in their own local repositories as part of code review. Presently, unit tests are run manually, and we are investigating test automation.
In addition to unit tests, we also have a separate test suite which performs a full system test on the privilege levels that each kind of ClassDB user has.

Agile-like development: The combination of short development cycles, milestone-driven development, and issue-driven development has the effect of causing incremental changes to the product. Table 2 shows a summary of activity for each version of ClassDB. The data for versions 2.0 and 2.1 shows the number of PRs match almost one to one with the number of issues addressed (defects fixed plus enhancements made). The table also reflects the conscious change we made from Version 1.0 to 2.0 to reduce the number of issues addressed in each PR.

	V1.0	V2.0	V2.1	V2.2
Commits	355	204	234	60
Branches	51	30	21	14
Pull requests	52	29	23	14
Defects addressed	62	31	11	5
Enhancements	NA	2	12	7

	V1.0	V2.0	V2.1	V2.2
Tables	3	4	3	3
Attributes	34	34	15	15
Functions	25	59	84	85
Views	0	14	16	16
Triggers	2	6	7	9

Table 1: Activity across ClassDB version object by type

Table 3: Number of ClassDB

Table 3 illustrates an effect of our agile-like approach on the functionality added with each release of ClassDB, using the number of database objects as a proxy. The significant increase in the number of functions and views from Version 1.0 to 2.0 is mostly due to the large number of API shortcuts added to slice user activity logs, all of which are based on just three functions and one view. The significant drop in the number of table attributes from Version 2.0 to 2.1 is due to a persistent table being replaced with a temporary table as part of improving product quality.

Figure 1 shows how LOC is distributed across production and test scripts, clustered by product version. The significant increase in LOC from Version 1.0 to 2.0 corresponds to the growth in the number of functions and views. Section 5, specifically the discussion related to Table 4, further analyzes the data in Figure 1.

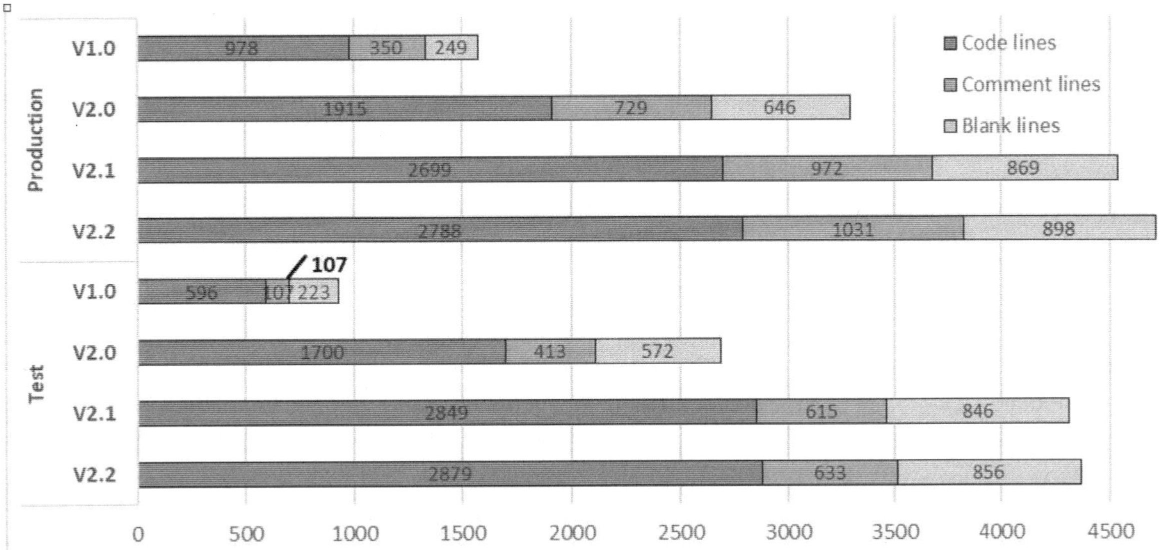

Figure 1: Distribution of LOC in ClassDB by file purpose (production and test), clustered by version

4. Team Culture

We now share the ethos consciously practiced and improved at DASSL. These are the principles that guide DASSL and enable its progress.

Mindset is a skill; the team is a product: As outlined in Section 2.2, students join DASSL any time between their sophomore year and senior year, leading to a large variation in skill levels among them. Thus, DASSL aims to help students develop a *mindset* they can use to produce high-quality work regardless of their skill level. This is done by encouraging a strong team culture where everyone has equal standing and anyone can take leadership of any task. Also, all members are free to (and are encouraged to) participate in the planning, development, and review process of any part of a DASSL product.

Acknowledge others' contributions and provide feedback: Team members are encouraged to interact with other members in a collaborative manner, providing honest suggestions, concerns, and complements as appropriate. This discourse is aided by GitHub Issue and PR systems which allow members to give feedback on others' work. ClassDB PR #214 (DASSL 2018d) is an example of this approach in practice.

Document everything: Everything is documented: code via comments, function usage and API in docs, data and software design, development methods, design rationale, and so on. This effort is aided by the ClassDB Wiki (DASSL 2018e) which allows any contributor to easily create and update docs.

The "documenting everything" approach greatly improves productivity. Because there are large time gaps between development cycles, the extensive documentation allows contributors to quickly refresh their memory, both in terms of how ClassDB works (external docs) and what the code does (internal docs).

Think first, code later: DASSL strongly encourages discussing and planning changes prior to coding. We have several examples of practicing this philosophy, including large-scale changes that have been discussed for days or weeks before implementation.

An example is the addition of disconnection activity logging to ClassDB in response to Issue #206 (DASSL 2018b). At its core, this enhancement required a single line of code that changed a Postgres configuration parameter, but several other changes were needed to fully implement disconnection logging. After an extensive analysis of the issue, we concluded that the best approach was to add several new columns to a particular table. In the process, we identified several additional issues such as NULL constraints on one of the new columns which required special attention to porting data in existing ClassDB installations. By identifying such issues prior to implementation, we were able to come up with a robust design that helped us easily add new features and also upgrade existing ClassDB installations.

Focus on building systems, not on writing programs: Although students develop core CS and programming skills at DASSL, end-to-end engineering is the DASSL objective. An example of this approach is our effort to maintain a property called **idempotence** in all ClassDB scripts which allows a script to be safely run any number of times. Running an idempotent script for the first time makes all necessary additions and modifications but re-running does not make additional modifications or cause errors.

In addition to greatly reducing testing effort, script idempotence is beneficial to users because it permits easy installations and updates without having to remove any existing installation, and it is generally more forgiving than non-idempotent code. Further, maintaining idempotence improves code quality because it increases our awareness of what each line of code does.

Code like the world is watching (because it is): We expect to display not only our final product, but the discussions and processes we use to get there as well. Posting code in a public repository and using various GitHub features to discuss and comment our decisions compels us to be conscious of our actions and decisions. For example, we closed ClassDB Issue #233 due to its changes being outside the scope of the current milestone, but we left the discussion public so all could see the reason behind our decision.

Always be learning, adopting, and adapting: Every member of DASSL is encouraged to continuously learn new tools, methods, and then to use their learning to address new issues as well as to improve existing solutions. This approach has helped us adopt new tools and methods throughout the development of ClassDB. For example, during the development of ClassDB 2.0, we quickly evaluated GitFlow and switched to it from a standard Git workflow. Similarly, when the university provided us Microsoft Teams (Microsoft 2018), we quickly evaluated it and incorporated it into our process starting with ClassDB 2.1.

Reciprocal, equitable, and voluntary participation: These three participation traits play a large part in successful teamwork at DASSL. All three traits are evident in practically every ClassDB issue and PR, the discussion on ClassDB Issue #206 being particularly demonstrative:

- Reciprocal: Team members respond to initiatives from others and return favors when helped by others.
- Equitable: On the whole, every team member adds equal value. Members adding too little may be viewed as not contributing their fair share; those adding too much could be perceived as dominating.
- Voluntary: Every team member willingly participates in team activities and does not feel they are being forced.

Reciprocal and equitable participation occasionally adds a bit more work to all team members, but in our experience, it also tends to produce better solutions faster, keep every team member more aware of the product details, and generally strengthens the sense of team and teamwork.

5. Focus on Quality

In this section, we discuss two specific aspects of our effort to produce high-quality software.

5.1. Maintainability

At a high level, DASSL emphasizes the following code characteristics and enforces them during reviews:

- Function and block structure: Organize code into functions and blocks; avoid lengthy functions.
- Code format: Choose identifier names to reflect their purpose; consistently indent code.
- Code chunks: Write code in chunks; perform one related task in each code chunk; keep chunks small.
- Comments: Comment each code chunk; say something that is not obvious in the code.
- External documentation: In the documentation, describe every API entry point available to end users.

We now present a brief quantitative analysis of LOC data to illustrate the impact of enforcing the code characteristics outlined. We use data generated from the FOSS counting tool *cloc* (Danial 2018) in this analysis.

Table 4 presents a summary of the number of files and LOC in production scripts broken down by version and line type. The Count section of Table 4 shows the raw number of files and lines, with values in parentheses showing percentage growth over the previous version. For example, the number of code lines grew 96% Version 1.0 to 2.1, but it grew only 40% from Version 2.0 to 2.1.

The Distribution section shows the proportion of each line type: Generalizing across versions, 59% of all lines are code lines (not comment or blank); 21% of lines are comments; and 20% of lines are blank. The Ratio section provides an alternative view of this distribution showing that across all versions, the source files contain one comment line and one blank line for approximately every three code lines.

Table 4 quantitatively supports our approach to writing code in small chunks and commenting chunks. The consistency of the ratios across four versions also shows the consistency of our coding and review practices. It is important we note that we did not set out to consciously arrive at the specific ratios seen in Table 4. In fact, this data was gathered for the first time only after ClassDB 2.1 was released.

The Density section of Table 4 shows the average number of lines of each type per production script, with the minimum and maximum number of lines shown in parentheses. Although the average values indicate small files, which in turn point to higher maintainability, the value ranges indicate the existence of "heavy hitters". Indeed, an analysis of Version 2.1 shows that just four scripts contribute 66% of all code lines and provides us a list of candidate files to refactor. However, refactoring files can be non-trivial because that also requires refactoring unit tests, and potentially documentation as well in some cases. It will also likely change the dependencies between scripts and thus require a revision to the product installation process.

	VERSION 1.0	VERSION 2.0	VERSION 2.1	VERSION 2.2
Count (growth % from previous version)				
Files	12	23 (90%)	24 (4%)	26 (8%)
Code lines	978	1915 (96%)	2699 (40%)	2788 (3%)
Comment lines	350	729 (108%)	972 (33%)	1031 (6%)
Blank lines	249	646 (159%)	869 (34%)	898 (3%)
Total lines	1577	3290 (108%)	4540 (38%)	4717 (4%)
Distribution: % of total lines				
Code lines	62%	58%	59%	59%
Comment lines	22%	22%	21%	21%
Blank lines	16%	20%	20%	20%
Ratio of non-code lines to code lines				
Comment to code	1 per 2.8	1 per 2.6	1 per 2.7	1 per 2.7
Blank to code	1 per 3.9	1 per 3.0	1 per 3.1	1 per 3.1
Density: average LOC per file (also min-max LOC)				
Code lines	82 (4-284)	83 (2-347)	112 (2-610)	107 (2-610)
Comment lines	29 (7-64)	32 (8-134)	41 (8-163)	40 (8-152)
Blank lines	21 (3-69)	28 (4-109)	36 (4-184)	35 (3-184)
Total lines	131 (14-417)	143 (16-590)	189 (14-957)	181 (13-936)

Table 4: A summary of LOC data for ClassDB production code (corresponds to the first cluster in Figure 1)

5.2. Issue Management

We now present how we organize issue reports to help us analyze product quality and prioritize work.

We expect team members to log every potential issue they observe and require each issue report to include the following parts (the first three parts are required):

- Title: For defects, the title concisely describes the problem; for enhancements, it states the requirement.
- Description: The description clearly states the problem and where possible include links to the issue location. We also encourage submitters to include proposed solutions in issue descriptions.

- Nature: Each defect is classified as Wrong, Missing, or Extra (or a combination). Enhancements and non-issues are explicitly tagged as such. We use issue nature to summarize how many defects are addressed and how many enhancements are made in a release. (See Table 2.)
- Related issues and PRs: Citations that tie the issue to other issues or PRs so the issue can be addressed comprehensively.

As part of issue management, the lab director assigns the following additional information to each issue. We do not prevent any member from changing any of the assigned metadata, but prefer (and encourage) all members debate any assignment in issue threads before changing the metadata:

- Priority: The urgency (high, medium, low) with which the issue needs to be addressed.
- Milestone: The product milestone in which the issue is to be addressed.
- Pipeline: A coarse-grained issue bucket, a feature available in ZenHub.

We presently do not assign severity and effort estimate to issues, but we are incrementally introducing these and other concepts to the team.

As summarized in Table 2, we have thus far addressed 118 issues in ClassDB, including 104 defects and 14 enhancements. However, we emphasize that the count of 104 defects does not indicate poor quality, because only 42 of those defects are logged after the first release, and none of those defects have been "show stoppers". In fact, to date, we have seen only one issue (Issue #200) in the deployed system that prevented the use of a part of a system. We consider this a "low severity" issue because it did not impact the overall system functionality or usability, and its occurrence required a power outage, disk crash, or other rare event. Yet, we addressed this issue as high priority because it prevented the use of a particular function an instructor is likely to perform frequently.

6. Perspectives

We now present individual perspectives of the three authors about their experience at DASSL. The writing in the rest of this section is intentionally in first-person singular.

6.1. Andrew Figueroa (Student)

DASSL presents its members with unique opportunities to analyze, build, and maintain data-intensive systems in ways that are not possible in a classroom environment, or even an industry internship. Much of what leads to this has been described earlier in this paper. However, one aspect not yet mentioned is that by participating in DASSL, students such as myself are given real responsibility of a major project.

Classroom experiences are an inherently "sheltered" environment: instructors generally have a solution in mind and can provide detailed feedback when students are headed in the wrong direction. Tasks have a specific set of requirements that must be met. Additionally, there is only one element at risk if an attempt goes wrong: a student's grade. Although grades are an important aspect, the effects of a single failed attempt are often remedied by the ability to make multiple attempts and by the weight of other assignments.

However, experiences at DASSL differ in that there is no immediately clear potential loss: all work performed is voluntary, ungraded, and not as time-sensitive as in a classroom. However, this is replaced with the responsibility of collaboratively undertaking research or developing a system that will undergo an actual publication or release. A mistake could result in the whole group having to later lose precious time fixing it. Even worse, some mistakes could result in major research efforts being for nothing, or security vulnerabilities in production software. Additionally, at least for our software projects, the entire process is publicly viewable. At times this fact is stressful, but this is also a significant part of what makes the whole experience as educational and enjoyable as it is.

Responsibility, among the other aspects of DASSL's culture, encourages me to always gradually improve as opposed to simply meeting the requirements (which for the types of projects implemented in DASSL, are usually either non-concrete or are set by us in the first place). The effects of this encouragement can be seen through the consistent quality improvement of code, documentation, and discussions in ClassDB contributions in which I have been involved.
One of my early contributions to ClassDB was Commit 494ed85 as part of PR #9. Although I had a basic understanding of using Git and GitHub, this commit shows several practices I now avoid, such as a non-specific subject line and including multiple unrelated changes in a single commit. Also, this PR itself has several issues such as having over 50 commits with major changes to a script and changes to unmentioned files. Contrast this PR with the later PR #92 in which all included commits were related to each another, had descriptive subject lines, and each commit made just one significant change. PR #92 also includes a detailed description of the changes made, their effects, and potential situations where the changes may behave unexpectedly.

Beyond developing software products, DASSL has encouraged me to participate in writing several papers that summarize the work done at DASSL, including this paper. I would otherwise have not even considered writing any academic papers during my undergraduate years. Beyond helping to further develop my understanding of the topics at hand, these papers have presented me with several opportunities that I would otherwise not have even imagined having, not the least of which being attending and presenting at an ACM conference in London, UK (Murthy, Figueroa, and Rollo 2018). Prior experience presenting new topics to other DASSL members and presenting DASSL work to other students and faculty at WCSU helped prepare me for this international conference and led to it being a success.

6.2. Steven Rollo (Student)

I strongly feel DASSL helped me develop a competitive software-engineering skillset by providing opportunities to participate in challenging real-world projects. Learning the modern software-engineering practices described in this paper is attractive to any employer because modern workflows are based around these tools and techniques. While it is possible to grasp basic tool usage in the classroom, developing mastery requires practice in real-world scenarios. DASSL provides a unique opportunity for students to extensively learn and practice a full range of software-engineering techniques with strong emphasis on teamwork and team communication, which I found to be particularly valuable. Prior to my participation in DASSL, I put little effort into developing an effective teamwork skillset. Between never being assigned group work in class and only working on relatively small personal projects, it felt unnecessary to develop these skills. The Summer 2017 session of DASSL placed a large emphasis on effectively documenting work, communicating issues, and developing a working relationship with other team members. Learning these skills allowed me to function effectively in the team projects I participated in at DASSL.

My experience at DASSL also shows that learning these skills requires practice and is evident in the progression of my work at DASSL. For example, large improvements in clarity can be seen between Issue #18 and Issue #243 I logged respectively during Milestones 1 (2017) and 3 (2018) of ClassDB. The title of Issue #18 ("The object name should be recorded in the student table on sql_drop events") is relatively unhelpful. Also, the problem stated in the issue description is only tangentially related to the title. Overall, though this issue does contain helpful information, it failed to communicate the actual problem effectively. In comparison, Issue #243 is much more effective. This issue's title explicitly states what exactly is wrong with the product. The issue description then provides a diagnosis of the problem, an example of what causes the problem, and three possible solutions. I was able to gain the ability to communicate in such a mature way only due to the practice from my experience at DASSL.

I feel these improvements in communication skills greatly helped me when I looked for a job after graduating from WCSU. My ability to communicate effectively has made me more confident about my ability to work on a team, instead of just being a lone programmer. When interviewing for a job, I was able to easily convince others that I have experience working in an agile environment. Additionally, I was able to quickly grasp the workflow of the department I was interviewed at, which allowed me to make a more informed choice about my suitability to work there.

6.3. Sean Murthy (Faculty Member)

I believe the student perspectives in Sections 6.1 and 6.2, and similar feedback from other students, testify to DASSL's effectiveness in preparing students for software-engineering careers by helping them learn and practice modern tools and processes of software engineering. I am pleased to lead this effort.
I feel my experience in commercial software development as well as my experience teaching a variety of CS topics have been helpful in leading DASSL. The following factors have also played a significant role:

- Spend much of summer and winter breaks with students: I spend about 80% of the break with students.
- Work long hours, about 8 hours a day: For example, I spent about 115 hours on just development and management of ClassDB 2.0 (over 5 hours a day). In addition to product development and management, I customize plans for each student because every student learns differently and is motivated by different things. I also meet each new student member one-on-one about one hour each week.
- Lead by example: Participate in every aspect of product development and management; submit own work for review; share critical review of own work to set a model for students and to make students feel comfortable enough to submit their work for review.
- Earn and maintain student trust: Always have student interest in mind and practice it visibly in both words and deed. No action or activity should hurt students' main purpose of being at a university. No activity can be solely to the benefit of a faculty member unless separate and appropriate employment terms are negotiated with students.
- Continuously learn new tools and techniques.

I feel the DASSL process is repeatable but is not necessarily scalable or easily sustainable because It takes considerable amount of time to provide high-quality mentoring while also producing high-quality work. Also, DASSL tasks are in addition to publication, teaching preparation, administrative tasks, family time, and other commitments that need equal or greater attention.

The following factors are also potential hindrances to scalability and sustainability:

- Small student pool: Many students are interested in the benefits of DASSL, but few are able to spend the necessary effort, largely because they need to work or they do not live on or near campus.
- Different engagement mode for new members: Online meetings can help enlarge the student pool, but intense daily in-person meetings are necessary for new students. Additional online engagement with seasoned students requires additional time and energy on the part of faculty members.
- Large portfolio: The lab needs to start a new product or module about every two years in order to expose students to different stages of product life cycle, which results in a large product portfolio over time.
- Short engagement and availability: Engagement is only over summer and winter breaks, and students spend at most four term breaks in DASSL, which results in frequent changes to the team composition.

The following actions can address the aforementioned challenges to scalability and sustainability:

- Increase faculty participation: Small faculty size makes additional faculty participation hard. However, different faculty members can (and do) organize DASSL-like effort. For example, Dr. William Joel involves students in his Graphics & Interactive Technologies Research Group at WCSU (Joel 2010).
- Maintain "anchor students": Anchor students are those with commitment to quality and have the industry to learn a variety of topics. It is especially helpful if anchor students join the effort soon after their third semester so they are around to gain extensive practice which they can use to lead sub-projects and semi-independently assist new student members.
- Offer paid positions: Paid positions recognize students who contribute significantly to the cause. They also permit students to continue in the lab instead of pursuing "non-tech jobs" elsewhere for sustenance.
- Raise funds: Stipends can increase both faculty and student participation, but stipends obviously require funding. Funding can realistically be from prospective employers who stand to gain from these efforts.
- Add an "engineering bent" to the academic program: Most CS courses rightfully focus on programming, algorithms, architecture, and other core concepts. Yet, there is scope for introducing the concepts of requirements, design, milestones, and other engineering aids early in the academic program. I use this approach for term projects in the CS205 and CS305 courses I teach (WCSU 2013).
- Offer an early "DevOps" course: A course targeting 4th-semester students to introduce topics such as version control, testing, issue management, and continuous integration can be quite helpful. Such an early course provides students additional opportunities to practice "DevOps" in labs and in later courses in the academic program. I am scheduled to teach such a DevOps course in Spring 2019.

In short, the continued success of DASSL and similar efforts requires support from university administrators and the industry. The combined effort can improve the quality of CS education and of software in the large.

7. Summary

Employers expect employees to possess an "Agile and DevOps mindset" and produce "high quality" software using sophisticated tool chains. Increasingly, they do not exclude even new CS graduates from this expectation. However, undergraduate CS programs are structurally unable to produce new graduates who meet this requirement. Hands-on co-curricular labs can fill this gap by introducing students to key aspects of building high-quality software and help meet employer expectations. Alternatively, employers will likely prefer new graduates who possess these skills over those who do not.

Being such a hands-on lab, since Spring 2017, DASSL has infused 12 undergraduates with many of the modern skills and the mindset employers seek. It does so by engaging students in every stage of the product life cycle using much of the same processes and tools professionals use. In the process, students collaborate with faculty members to build and maintain non-trivial products that meet a relatively high standard of quality. As illustrated in Sections 2-5, ClassDB is one such high-quality product DASSL has produced.

Efforts such as DASSL are reproducible and repeatable, but are not easily scaled or sustained. Their continued success depends on a sustained "critical mass" of compatible students, and on faculty members with significant experience building high-quality production software. Also, both faculty and students need to spend (or lose) considerable amount of time, energy, and money outside regular academic commitment. Small changes in CS programs and support from administrators and industry beneficiaries can address these and other impediments.

8. Acknowledgments

We thank the faculty and administrators of Western Connecticut State University, particularly the CS department, for encouraging DASSL. We thank Kevin Kelly, a student member of DASSL, for assistance with compiling some of the data included in this paper. We are also thankful for the generous educational licensing policies of GitHub and ZenHub. Finally, we thank the reviewers of this paper for their feedback on drafts.

References

Creative Commons. 2013. "CC BY-NC-SA 4.0." Creative Commons - Attribution-NonCommercial-ShareAlike 4.0 International. 2013. https://creativecommons.org/licenses/by-nc-sa/4.0/legalcode.

Danial, Al. 2018. Cloc. https://github.com/AlDanial/cloc.

DASSL. 2017a. "DASSL GitHub Repositories." GitHub Organization. 2017. https://github.com/DASSL.

DASSL. 2017b. "Data Science & Systems Lab Home Page." 2017. http://dassl.github.io.

DASSL. 2018a. "ClassDB Documentation." 2018. https://dassl.github.io/ClassDB/.

DASSL. 2018b. "ClassDB Issues." 2018. https://github.com/DASSL/ClassDB/issues.

DASSL. 2018c. "ClassDB Milestone M2." 2018. https://github.com/DASSL/ClassDB/wiki/Milestone-M2.

DASSL. 2018d. "ClassDB Pull Requests." 2018. https://github.com/DASSL/ClassDB/pulls.

DASSL. 2018e. "ClassDB Wiki." 2018. https://github.com/DASSL/ClassDB/wiki.

Driessen, Vincent. 2010. "A Successful Git Branching Model." January 5, 2010. https://nvie.com/posts/a-successful-git-branching-model/.

Ferraiolo, David F., and D. Richard Kuhn. 1992. "Role-Based Access Controls." National Computer Security Conference 15: 554–63.

Joel, William. 2010. "Graphics & Interactive Techniques Research Group." January 5, 2010. http://www.wcsu.edu/cs/sample-page/computer-science-research/computer-science-grg/.

Jones, Capers. 2007. Estimating Software Costs: Bringing Realism to Estimating. 2nd Edition. McGraw-Hill Education.

Microsoft. 2018. Microsoft Teams. Microsoft Corporation. https://products.office.com/en-US/microsoft-teams/group-chat-software.

Murthy, Sean. 2018a. "Employing FOSS Tools to Improve Learning and Increase Opportunities." Presented at the Northeast Regional OER Summit 2018, University of Massachusetts, Amherst, MA. https://drive.google.com/drive/folders/1I8gd_dQEIzgfaawltCXgXL6vXazgvlb3.

Murthy, Sean. 2018b. "Shared Governance by Design: Employing FOSS Tools to Improve Learning, Reduce Cost, and Increase Opportunities." Presented at the 4th Annual Conference on Shared Governance and Student Success, Southern Connecticut State University, New Haven, CT, April 13.

Murthy, Sean, Andrew Figueroa, and Steven Rollo. 2018. "Toward a Large-Scale Open Learning System for Data Management." Presented at the Fifth Annual ACM Conference on Learning @ Scale. London, UK. https://doi.org/10.1145/3231644.3231673.

PostgreSQL Development Group. 2017. "PostgreSQL 9.6.9 Documentation." 2017. https://www.postgresql.org/docs/9.6/static/index.html.

Wallshein, Corinne C. 2010. "Estimating Software Effort Hours for Major Defense Acquisition Programs." Dissertation, George Mason University. http://ebot.gmu.edu/bitstream/handle/1920/6025/Wallshein_Dissertation_Spring_2010.pdf.

WCSU. 2013. "Computer Science Course Catalog." 2013. http://www.wcsu.edu/catalogs/undergraduate/sas/courses/computer-science/.

Whitworth University. 2018. "Mathematics & Computer Science Course Catalog." 2018. http://catalog.whitworth.edu/undergraduate/mathcomputerscience/#courseinventory.

ZenHub. 2018a. "An Intro to ZenHub Epics." 2018. https://help.zenhub.com/support/solutions/articles/43000010341-an-intro-to-zenhub-epics.

ZenHub. 2018b. "ZenHub." 2018. https://www.zenhub.com/

How to Fix "Test Automation" for Faster and More Valuable Quality Knowledge

Authors

Matt Griscom, MetaAutomation LLC (matt@metaautomation.net)

Abstract

I From years in the trenches of "test automation," I found it broken. Applying "automation" to "test" creates mismatches leading to inefficiency, poor communication, and quality risk. I discovered and recorded the MetaAutomation pattern language to fix it and make quality feedback much faster, more reliable, richer, and more valuable across the larger team and distributed teams. The base pattern is simple and familiar: it enables self-documenting checks with complete details driving and measuring the System Under Test (SUT), creating very trustworthy structured artifacts that give deep knowledge of SUT behavior for rich communication and analysis. Any team member can drill down through the hierarchy from business-facing steps to technology-facing steps of the check result. Every completed or failed step shows milliseconds-to-completion, and the artifact shows blocked steps too. The hierarchy supports data-driven timeouts for any step. Manual testing becomes more fun and effective with complete clarity on automation actions and results. MetaAutomation shows how to maximize scale. It solves the flaky check problem, cuts defect escapes, and on check failures it sends directed notifications to team member(s) that need to know so issues needing attention from a team member are resolved at correct priority. This paper discusses how to prioritize and optimize automated checks and how to fill out the quality automation problem space to empower the QA team as the glue that binds the larger team together. Working samples on metaautomation.net show single-process, multi-process, and multi-tier checks.

Biography

Matt Griscom has 30 years' experience creating software including innovative test automation, harnesses, and frameworks. Two degrees in physics primed him to seek the big picture in any setting. This comprehensive vision and a love of solving problems that are important yet challenging led him to create the MetaAutomation pattern language to address the quality automation problem space of the software business. Matt blogs on MetaAutomation, consults, and recently published his third book on MetaAutomation. He also hikes, kayaks, runs, helps run an awesome Toastmaster group, and lives with his wife and two kids in Seattle. Matt loves helping people be more effective in doing software quality and is available by email at matt@metaautomation.net.

1. Introduction

Consider these four questions:

1. Does the SUT do what we need it to do, and do it fast enough?
2. Can automation verify requirements of behavior and perf on the SUT, and do it fast and thoroughly enough to ensure that quality always moves forward?
3. Can the whole team access highly detailed and trustworthy information on that, in role-appropriate ways?
4. Can we notify the developers and QA people who need to know, while avoiding non-actionable emails and improving response times to un-block the team as needed?

This paper, and the corresponding talk, is about enabling "Yes!" to the questions. The journey requires questioning some common understandings and practices.

1.1. A Better Way

Imagine the state of "test automation" applied currently to measure and report quality on the SUT.

By contrast, imagine an ideal solution for the business with automation: measuring, recording, and reporting detailed information to fulfill those four questions. This ideal solution reconsiders everything that we know or think we know about the profession and practice.

It helps to start with the "big picture" and define the space for the problem at hand. I call this problem space "quality automation," with automation to serve quality between the technology-facing interface of driving and measuring the SUT, and the business-facing interface of serving information to the people of the business. Quality automation serves the interests of software quality: driving it forward, while managing quality risk, with automation where that applies to answer the four questions.

1.2. Break With the Past

Zooming in from the big picture to the component details shows that some practices are broken.

First, there was Glenford Myers' mistake with his 1979 book "The Art of Software Testing." Myers was explicit:

> *Testing is the process of executing a program with the intent of finding errors.*
> *(Myers, 1979, p. 5)*

He elaborates on the topic at length, including this on the next page:

> … since a test case that does not find an error is largely a waste of time and money… (Myers, 1979, p. 6)

I summarize the mistake as "Testing is only about finding bugs." The book was published so long ago, and the impact of software on people's lives was so drastically different then as compared to now, that the mistake was a very minor one at that time and approximately correct – yet flawed. The importance of the flaw was magnified in the following 40 years, while the influence of such an important book from so long ago was magnified as well.

2. The Problem with "Test Automation"

Applying SUT automation to test birthed the obvious phrase to describe that union: "test automation." Unfortunately, the implication of the phrase — that automation produces the same value as manual testing, just faster — lives on today. Automation applied to functional quality for "test" does not work like industrial automation does for building furniture, or flight deck automation does to help pilots fly a plane; it is very different.

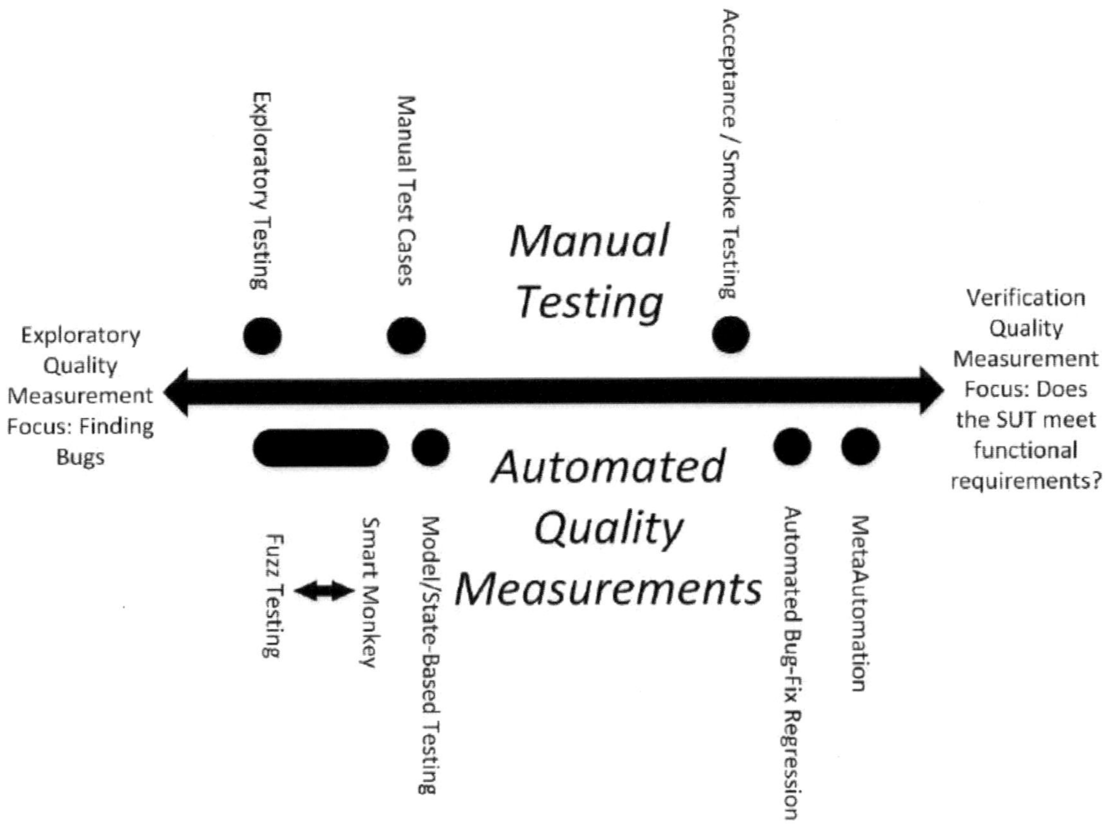

Figure 1: Two important focuses for automation and manual testing, and how some practices align towards one or the other

By linguistic relativity (a.k.a. the Sapir-Whorf hypothesis) "test automation" locks us into a very expensive misunderstanding about what automation can do for quality. This misunderstanding limits the productivity of the QA role and minimizes their importance to the larger software team.

The need for manual test will never go away because humans are unmatched in perceptive intelligence towards deciding whether some bit of SUT behavior is actionable or not (and, the rise of AI will not replace people for at least a decade). But, automation can be very valuable, and much more so if it is not constrained by misunderstandings.

Therefore, I use the phrase "quality automation" to describe the problem space (as discussed above) *and* the service of automation towards bringing value in that problem space. Quality automation is much broader in capabilities than "test automation" ever was or ever could be and does not have the baggage. One could replace the mistaken phrase "test automation" with "SUT automation" but since automation around reporting and communication depends so closely on what "SUT automation" does, I prefer to just replace "test automation" with "quality automation."

As a side note, there are other positive movements in software quality that are complementary to quality automation: Analytics and A/B testing remain powerful and important trends. Shift-left testing is a clever idea to getting quality results faster and closer to developers — if system testing is not neglected.

My personal favorite is bottom-up testing: system testing done first at the least dependent layers of the SUT, e.g., a database layer with no mocks, and then working up to the more dependent layers, e.g., a GUI. This is powerful for quality automation, because higher-impact and higher-risk issues are found much faster this way. Complete system testing can be addressed at a lower priority because issues found in the most dependent layers are low-risk to change or fix.

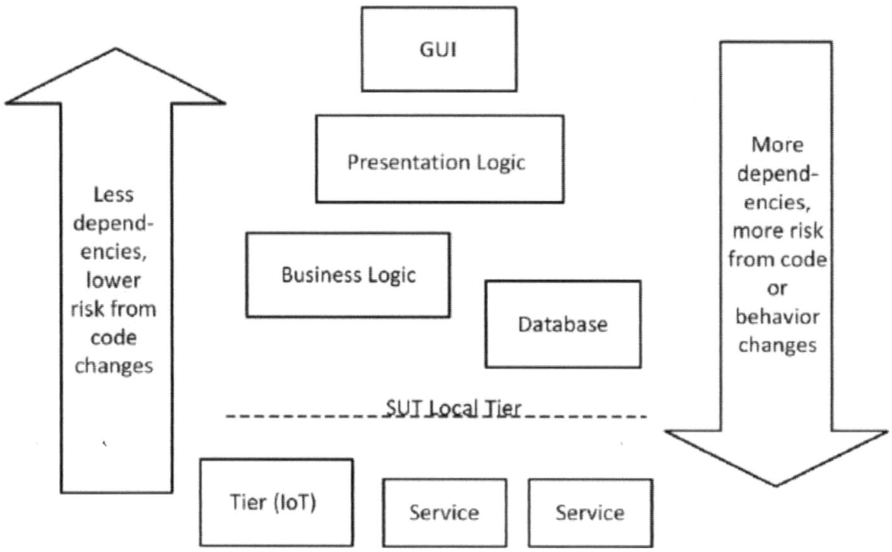

Figure 2: Dependency vs. Quality Risk

The focus of this paper is on repeatable checks, because those are of core importance to getting trustworthy quality results fast. The Hierarchical Steps application towards SUT automation, which creates a structured record of all data on driving and measuring the SUT, is also generally applicable towards model-based testing or other "big" tests with automation.

3. MetaAutomation

Simply put, patterns are solutions to a problem in a context. A prescriptive pattern language is a set of patterns with intra-pattern dependencies to address a complete problem space.

MetaAutomation is a pattern language that describes an ideal platform-independent, language-independent solution to the quality automation problem space. All patterns in MetaAutomation are based on existing practices, but it combines them in ways both old and new to achieve the ideal. It is not an unchanging pattern language; it will become a living pattern language with extensions and refinements as needed with input from the community it serves.

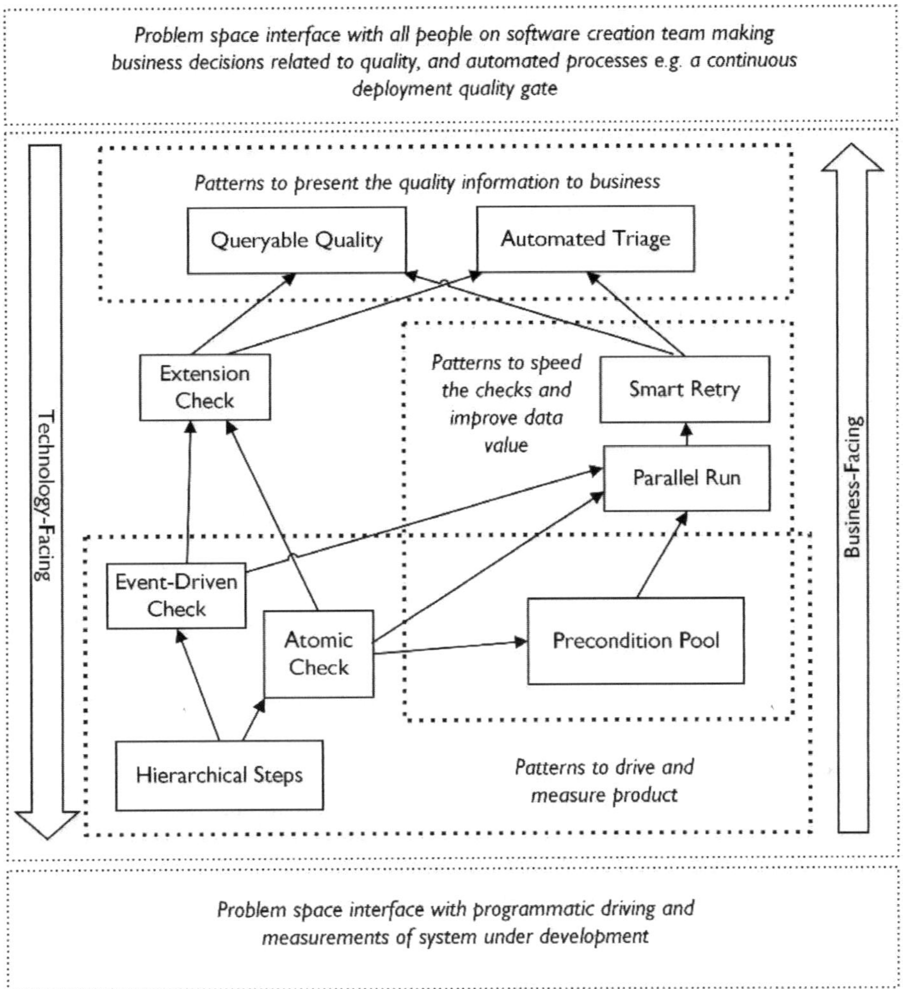

Figure 3: The MetaAutomation pattern map filling the quality automation problem space

Everybody uses the Hierarchical Steps pattern, whether they work in software or not; it is a natural way of describing, communicating, or executing any repeatable procedure. Applying this pattern to quality automation is the most fundamental — and radical! — change that MetaAutomation recommends. Implementing it is not trivial, so working open-source samples are available on GitHub, linked from the MetaAutomation.net web site.

Milliseconds-to-completion for every step in the hierarchy is automatically recorded. In case of check failure, the failed steps going from leaf step up to root are noted, and blocked steps show the quality risk of unmeasured SUT behavior. Each step can have a data-driven timeout for that step, too, configured directly in the artifact of a check run to serve as a guide for the next run of that check.

A check is a kind of test that is suited for automation; there are no extra steps or measurements, nor any assumption of powers of observation that a person might bring to a manual test but that SUT automation cannot do.

Atomic Check is familiar already to people who are skilled at SUT automation for quality. Simply put, it is about measuring a functional requirement in a way that is as simple as possible. Atomic checks have priority from functional requirements (from prioritized business requirements) first and implementation order second.

Event-Driven Check is like Atomic Check, but where the SUT is triggered by events that cannot necessarily be controlled in the same way as, e.g., API or service calls.

Precondition Pool is about managing check preconditions outside the check, to simplify and speed the check. This pattern is a generalization of the pattern of managing such check preconditions as environments in which checks are run, to also managing user accounts, documents, databases, or anything else the check needs but which is ancillary to the focus of the atomic check and can be managed asynchronously and out-of-process.

Parallel Run is widely used; it is just running checks in parallel across multiple processes and/or machines.

Smart Retry is like the Retry pattern where a check is retried on failure, but smart because the data (from applying the Hierarchical Steps pattern) is readily available to the automation to determine root cause of a failure, whether it as just been reproduced, and whether a retry is in order, e.g., in case of a timeout on a GUI thread or external dependency. When the Smart Retry implementation is correctly configured, it solves the flaky-check problem.

Extension Check is a check based on the detailed artifacts (results) from an earlier check, for example, to verify that certain performance criteria are met.

Automated Triage directs notifications based on root cause of an actionable failure. For example, it might notify a developer if it is determined – based on the artifact of a check, or a reproduced failure – that a developer "owns" the feature involved with that root cause.

Queryable Quality is an implementation of an intranet site to show all the data that quality automation provides on the SUT, including behavior, verifications, the performance measurements with every step, etc. This is like an information radiator for QA, but much richer in data and highly interactive. This is where team members might review a run of a set of checks or view the steps of a check or checks and drill down from the business-facing steps near the root to the technology-facing leaf steps that drive and measure the SUT.

4. Conclusion

Coming back to those four questions:

1. Does the SUT do what we need it to do, and do it fast enough?

For software that matters to people, it is both unethical and poor business practice for the team to ship anything that does not meet these criteria (other than explicitly alpha or beta software). Quality in software is becoming more important every year. The mistakes and inefficiencies of "test automation" are holding software quality back; software teams need a smarter approach to ground their quality efforts.

It is time to leave behind any illusion that manual test and automated verifications are effective at the same things.

2. Can automation verify requirements of behavior and perf on the SUT, and do it fast and thoroughly enough to ensure that quality always moves forward?

By using the wrong tool for the job — log statements — conventional "test automation" drops valuable information of SUT behavior on the floor, so it cannot answer the question in a detailed or even trustworthy way. Even BDD automation drops any information behind the keywords. Starting with the Hierarchical Steps and Atomic Check patterns, MetaAutomation shows how to record and present this information with no need to even look at the code, cut false positives, cut defect escapes and non-actionable SPAM notifications, and do it with specific guidelines and techniques to do it as fast as possible.

3. Can the whole team access highly detailed and trustworthy information on that, in role-appropriate ways?

The structure and detail of Hierarchical Steps extends from the business-facing steps at and near the root of the hierarchy, to the technology-facing steps at the leaf nodes. On an intranet site, team members can drill down into details of SUT behavior and verifications as needed to get an unprecedented view into behavior and performance.

For manual testers, it means that they do much less repetitive testing because they know exactly what the quality automation system did with the SUT, and they know exactly where exploration is needed. Manual testing becomes more fun and more effective.

For the whole team, defect escapes are reduced because the details of what is measured is highly trustworthy and accessible; what is not measured is discoverable by comparing SUT behavior with the quality portal that implements the Queryable Quality pattern.

4. Can we notify the developers and QA people who need to know, while avoiding non-actionable emails and improving response times to un-block the team as needed?

MetaAutomation shows how to record and communicate the detailed, structured, and highly trustworthy information, and the solutions that are needed to make these things happen. It shows the QA role how to assume the central role that they deserve: the backbone of communication and collaboration around SUT behavior, and the role that enables the larger team to ship higher-quality software faster.

References

Myers, Glenford. 1979. *The Art of Software Testing*. John Wiley & Sons, Inc.

This page intentionally left blank.

On the Road to Reliability for Android Robots in a Physical World

Authors

Krishna Saxena, Jesuit High School in Portland, Oregon
Torin Perkins, Central Catholic High School in Portland, Oregon
Catherine Lee, Sunset High School in Portland, Oregon
James Menezes, Westview High School in Portland, Oregon
Bo Li, Logic Technology Development, Technology and Manufacturing Group, Intel Corp.

bytesofkitkats@gmail.com
bo.a.li@intel.com

Abstract

Robotics software reliability is very crucial to control robot hardware while interacting with the physical world to accomplish a set of missions. The software needs to tackle senor errors, incorrect functionalities, software exceptions and uncertainties from the external environment. This paper depicts the challenges of attaining software reliability in Android robotics through the experiences of FIRST Tech Challenge (FTC) robotics team, the Bytes of Kitkats.

The software fault tree analysis (FTA) and software failure modes and effects analysis (SFMEA) are accomplished to prepare the statistical testing to evaluate and improve the software reliability. Software reliability is employed to predict the software reliability growth model (SRGM) through the stochastic process. The objectives are to build the software reliability model with finite or fixed number of inherent defects and accelerate the software reliability improvement process to ensure the robot behaves consistently in the field. Through the case study of building and testing Android robots with different motors, sensors and 3D-printed attachments, authors categorized sensor reading uncertainties (e.g., the position of robot and surrounding objects, etc.) and multiple uncontrollable environmental factors from the physical world in software reliability modeling.

Biography

Authors are high school students from the Bytes of Kitkats robotics team which was formed in 2013. In 2016, the team received Oregon championship award in FIRST LEGO League (FLL), a LEGO robotics competition for elementary and middle schools. In 2016, the team moved to FTC. The team has been recognized many times for being an exemplary team in the robot software development and innovate designs in Oregon, US FTC West Regionals and FTC world Championship events. In addition to striving for hardware and software excellence, the Bytes of Kitkats are also focusing on outreach activities in educating young students in Portland communities, other US states and countries oversea about robotics through camps, specific topic workshops, community open houses, and mentoring younger robotics teams.

Bo Li works in software developments and managements for Logic Technology Development in Technology and Manufacturing Group (TMG) at Intel. He joined Intel in 1999 after receiving Ph.D. from Georgia Institute of Technology. Since then, he has been focusing on software development, reliability, and testing. Outside of work, he mentors robotics teams in the community for high school and middle school students to foster more passions and knowledge in Science, Technology, Engineering and Mathematics (STEM).

1. Introduction

It has long been recognized that experiential and hands-on education provides superior motivation for learning new material by providing real-world meaning to the otherwise abstract knowledge. Robotics has been shown to be a superb tool for hands-on learning, not only of robotics itself, but of general topics in Science, Technology, Engineering, and Mathematics (STEM). Learning with robotics gives students an opportunity to engage with real life problems that require STEM knowledge. Mataric et al [1] describe the approach to enabling hands-on experiential robotics for all ages through the introduction of a robot programming workbook and robot test-bed aiming at providing readily accessible materials to K-12 for direct immersion in hands-on robotics. Additionally, the success of learning science through robotics is also explored by Chow et al [2] based on their experiences.

FIRST is among the broad spectrum of avenues for pursuing robotics at the pre-university level to promote STEM around the world. FIRST stands for "For Inspiration and Recognition of Science and Technology" and FIRST is an international youth organization to develop ways to inspire students in engineering and technology fields [3]. The FIRST Tech Challenge (FTC) is designed for students in grades 7–12 to compete using a sports model. Teams are responsible for designing, building, and programming their robots to compete in an alliance format against other teams. The robot kit is programmed using Java. Teams, including coaches, mentors and volunteers, are required to develop strategy and build robots based on sound engineering principles. The ultimate goal of FTC is to reach more young people with a lower-cost, more accessible opportunity to discover the excitement and rewards of STEM.

1.1. Background for FIRST Tech Challenge Robot Programming

The FTC competition field is 12′ x 12′. Each match is played with 4 randomly selected teams, 2 per alliance. 4 18″ x 18″ robots must be able to navigate around each other without breaking when hit by another robot.

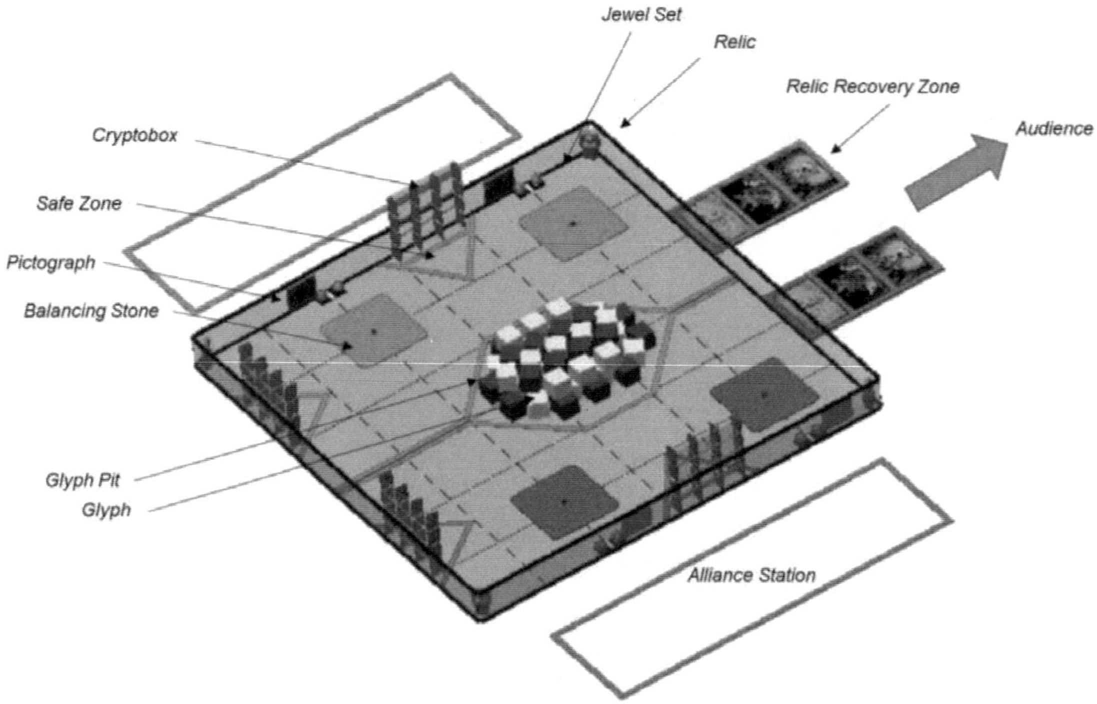

Figure 1: FTC field seup for the 2017-18 FTC season [4]

Figure 1 shows the field setup for the 2017-18 FTC season. The FTC robot game is composed of two phases: (1) the autonomous phase and (2) the user control tele operation phase. There are 2 red and 2 blue balancing stones being mounted on the field. Teams must balance their robot on their balancing stones prior to the start of the match. Teams also preload one glyph per robot. Field personnel then randomize the location of the jewels. They also randomly select one of three pictograph designs and install them on the field walls. During the autonomous period there are many ways for teams to score using only pre-programmed instructions in the phone mounted on the robot. If only one jewel is left on the platform at the end of the autonomous period, the alliance corresponding to that color will earn 30 points. Each glyph scored in a cryptobox earns the alliance 15 points. The pictographs have a coded message indicating which of the cryptobox column is a key. If a robot can decode this message and place a glyph in the cryptobox key, their alliance earns a 30 point bonus. Each robot parked in a safe zone earns their alliance 10 points.

In FTC, the robot motions are controlled by Android phones. The Android phone sends commands to different types of motors in order to make the robot move. To aid with decision making, the phone also can receive input from internal and external sensors. The Android device on the robot is programmed from a computer, using Android Studio and the FTC software development kit (SDK), which adds functionality to control motors from the Android phone. Both autonomous and user control tele operation programs are loaded onto the robot, and then are run from the Android phone. During the autonomous phase, the robot moves based solely on its autonomous program. During the user control tele operation phase, the Android device on the robot is connected to another Android device through Wi-Fi connections. This second Android device is connected to two joysticks and transfers joystick input to the Android phone on the robot. From there, the drivers of the robot can use their joysticks to drive the robot. Teams use the Android software platform on the mobile phones located both on the robot and with the driver to run their programs that control the robot. During the tele operation period in this FTC season, the robot needs to collect glyphs and stack them up into the cryptobox to score points. A diagram illustrating the interaction among different components of this system is shown below (See Figure 2):

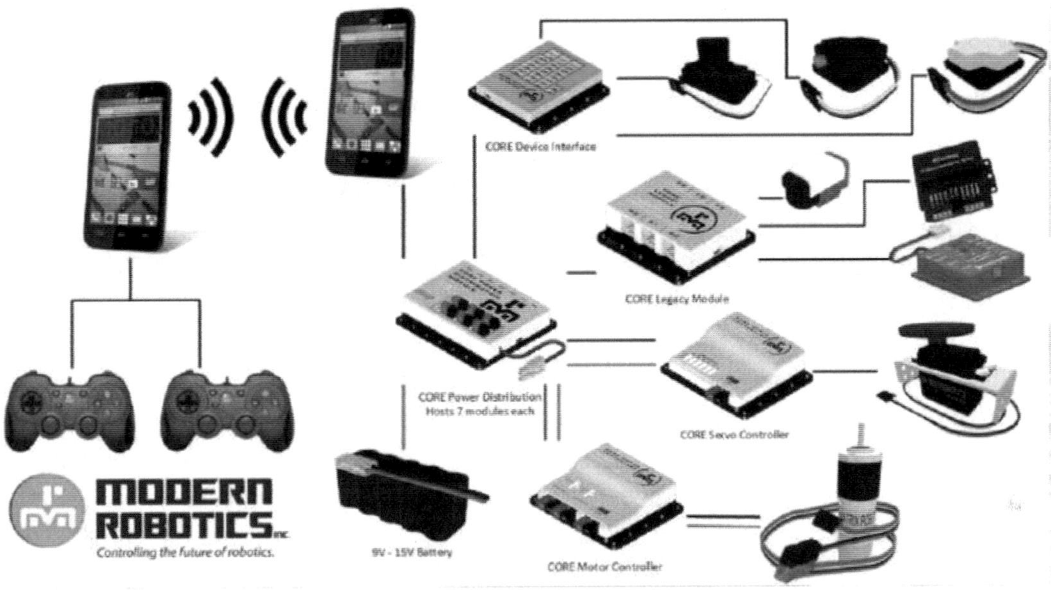

Figure 2: The control system of an FTC robot and its subsystems consisting of joysticks (used by drivers). Android smartphones with pre-loaded software programs, core components (e.g. external sensors, motors, power, etc.) to detect and control FTC robot [5]

1.2. Introduction to FTC Software Reliability

Software reliability is often defined as the probability of failure free operation of a computer program in a specified environment for a specified period of time [6]. FTC software reliability is very crucial due to the high expectations of consistent performance during FTC competitions for the new and updated versions of autonomous and tele operation control software. Software reliability is also a very time critical requirement, and the software failure can significantly impact FTC competition results.

Through the case study of building and testing a robot with motors and sensors in FTC, we characterized the robot sensor reliabilities and variable environmental factors in the physical world (e.g., the robot setup and locations, glyph pile setup, and balance stone conditions, etc.). Software reliability for FTC robots is difficult due to the difficulty in isolating the precise point of failure and evaluating the fault conditions for defect removal. In addition, robot design consistently evolves in terms of its hardware and physical capabilities during the competition season. Moreover, field conditions vary, so the robot has to be able to adapt to a variety of conditions with reliable software functionalities.

This paper presents two main challenges in accomplishing software reliability for FTC robotic competitions. The first challenge is ensuring that the software defects are removed effectively and the software can be adapted to the new capability and environment changes rapidly to reach the software reliability target. The second challenge is ensuring that the robot can utilize the software algorithms to minimize effects of sensor variability and analyze the physical world inputs to make right decisions in varieties of different situations. Since there are so many factor changes between each run of the robot, the software algorithms have to be tested thoroughly to ensure the robot can consistently make the right decisions and have very reliable performances.

2. On the Road to Software Reliability in Android Robots

In this paper, we used the fault tree as a logic diagram to display the interrelationships between a potential critical event (top event) in a system and causes for this event. The goal is to find critical events concerning fault introduction and take appropriate actions to reduce the probabilities of these events and the subsequent probability of the top event. A Fault Tree forms a logical representation of the manner in which combinations of basic events, often made up of failures at the component level, could lead to a hypothesized failure of a system. We then think about these potential problems and how to detect, prevent, or mitigate the problems before they create a catastrophe which is to drive software failure mode and effects analysis (SFMEA). Reifer was widely credited for introducing the SFMEA to software engineering for requirements analysis in 1979 [7]. During SFMEA, possible design failure modes and sources of potential nonconformities must be determined in multiple software artifacts. A complete FMEA for a software-based system should, however, include both hardware FMEA and software FMEA, and the effects should be assessed on the final system functions.

Software FMEA in practice is often performed at different levels (i.e., system, subsystems, and components) which corresponds to architectural partitions or levels of abstraction. As design and implementation proceed, more details of the system are revealed, which enables more meaningful low-level analysis. Neufelder identified 8 viewpoints: functional, interface, detailed, maintenance, usability, serviceability, vulnerability, and software process [8]. The functional viewpoint is mostly useful for software FMEA, the interface viewpoint is for software/software and software/hardware interface FMEA, and the detailed viewpoint is applicable to design and implementation FMEA. The outcome of an FMEA is documented in a worksheet. Failure modes need to evaluate (a) severity which is subjective rating and measures how bad or serious the effect of the failure mode is, (b) occurrence which is the likelihood that the failure cause occurs in the course of the intended life, and (c) detection which is a subjective rating that quantifies the likelihood that a detection method will detect the failure of a potential failure mode before the impact of the effect is materialized. The combination of the severity, occurrence, and detection ratings is used to prioritize potential failure modes and root causes. The software FMEA team then agrees on a threshold of these factors and need to address all items above the threshold.

After the fault tree and software FMEA analysis, Software Reliability Growth Models (SRGMs) are considered to predict the defect density. Over the past decades, many researchers have discussed SRGM assumptions, applicability, and predictability. The basic assumption in software reliability modeling is that software failures are the result of a stochastic process, having an unknown probability distribution. Software reliability models specify some reasonable form for this distribution, and are fitted to data from a software project. Once a model demonstrates a good fit to the available data, it can be used to determine the current reliability of the software, and predict the reliability of the software at future times.

This paper employed the shortcut model prediction approach based on input answers to key questions. The Shortcut Defect Density Prediction Model [9] assumes that the defect density is a function of the number of risks versus strengths regarding this release of the software. The shortcut model includes factors that affect failure process. Using real-life data sets on software failures, this proposed approach is evaluated and compared to the real existing data from FTC competition matches. As a result, the applicability of the model is validated on these software failure data.

The software size is estimated in terms of 1000 source lines of code (Kilo-SLOC or KSLOC) first, then the associated defect density was selected based on the shortcut model. Here is the sequence of actions to get the predicted defect density. Table 4 shows Strength and Risk Survey for the shortcut model:

a. Count the number of yes answers in the Strengths. Assign 1 point for each yes answer. Assign 0.5
   point for each "somewhat" answer.
b. Count the number of yes answers in the Risks. Assign 1 point for each yes answer. Assign 0.5 point for each "somewhat" answer.
c. Subtracting the result of risk points from the result of Strength points.
d. If the result ≥ 4.0, predicted defect density = 0.110,
   If the result ≤ 0.5, predicted defect density = 0.647,
   Otherwise predicted defect density = 0.239 in terms of defects per normalized effective KSLOC.

The resulting defect density prediction is then multiplied by the normalized effective KSLOC (EKSLOC) to determine the defect density. EKSLOC is a weighted average of new, modified, reused, and auto-generated code. Here is the formula to normalize KSLOC for software reliability model effectiveness:

EKSLOC = New KSLOC + (A × major modified KSLOC) + (B × moderate modified KSLOC) + (C ×

Minor modified KSLOC) + (D × reused KSLOC without modification) + (E × auto-generated KSLOC)
where

- Reused code: Previously deployed on a previous or similar system without modification.
- New code: Code that has not been used in operation.
- Modified code: Reused code that is being modified.
- Auto generated code: Code that is generated by an automated tool.

The new code is 100% effective. Code that is reused without modification is fractionally effective as there may still be a few latent defects in that code. Code that is reused with modifications will have an effectiveness that is between these two extremes. Reused code that is subject to major modifications, for example, may be almost as effective as new code. Reused code with minor cosmetic changes, for example, may be slightly more effective than reused code with no modifications. Auto-generated code typically has an effectiveness that is similar to reused and not modified code since it is generated by a tool.

Multiplier	**Ranges**	**Function of**
A—major modification	≥ 40%	Magnitude of requirements change.
B—moderate modification	20% to 40%	Magnitude of design change and cohesiveness of design.
C—minor modification	5% to 20%	Cohesiveness of code (ability to change it without breaking an unrelated function).
D—reused	0% to 30%	Cohesiveness of design. How long the reused code has been in operation.
E—auto generated	0% to 10%	The ability to program the automated tool to provide code as per the design and requirements.

Table 1: Typical Effectiveness Multipliers

Normalized EKSLOC is then normalized for languages (Table 2) so that it can be multiplied by the predicted defect density that are in terms of defects/normalized EKSLOC to generate the predicted number of defects.

Language type	**Normalization conversion**
High order language such as C, Fortran, etc.	3.0
Object oriented language such as Java, C++, C#	6.0
Hybrid	4.5

Table 2: Typical Ratios for Different Languages and Assemblers

3. Case Study: FTC Android Robot Software Reliability Analysis and Improvements

By using several case studies including the development of robots in the context of FTC competitions, the robot software reliability fault trees, software FMEA and shortcut model were utilized to improve the robot software reliability in the competition field. The thorough fault event analysis and software functional FMEA analysis are crucial to effectively characterize the software reliability behavior to cover three main perspectives including the software World, the Physical World, and how they interact with each other.

3.1. FTC Robot Autonomous Glyphs Collections and Delivery to Cryptobox

We executed the case study for FTC Robot autonomous glyphs collection and delivery to cryptobox to illustrate the software reliability improvement processes.

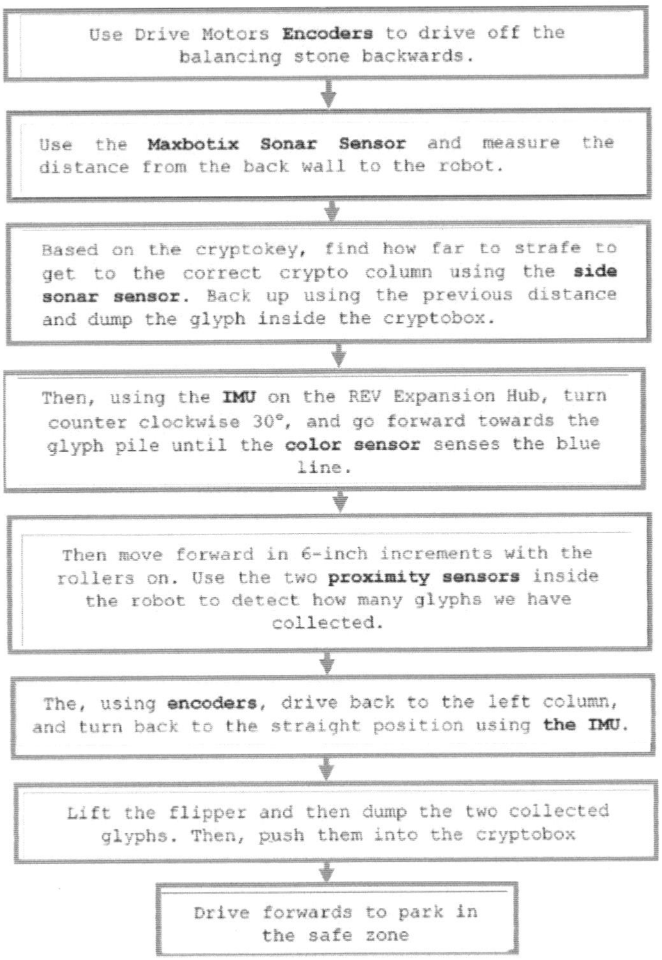

Figure 3: Robot Software Flowchat in Autonomous Period

Figure 3 shows the robot software flowchart for the software controlling FTC robot movements. The robot left the balance stone with one glyph within the robot. The target is to collect as many as possible (e.g., 2 or 3) of glyphs and deliver them to the cryptobox while the robot can't hold more than 2 glyphs at the same time. Figure 4 shows how the sequence of robot movements through the autonomous time period.

	Using **phone camera**, Vuforia SDK, OpenCV, identify the jewel, and flick it; Identify the crypto key.
	Use **encoders** on the drive motors to drive off the balancing stone.
	Use a Maxbotics **sonar sensor** to detect the robot's distance from the wall, and based on this distance, we strafed to the correct crypto column and dump the glyph.
	Using the Inertial measurement unit (**IMU**) on the expansion hub, we will turn about 45 degrees, making sure that we face the glyph pit.
	Use a **color sensor** to go forward until either the red or blue line. Then move forward while moving the rollers at the same time.
	Use two **proximity sensors** inside the robot to detect how many glyphs are collected from the glyph pile.
	Use **encoders** to go back to the cryptobox, the same way it came.
	Use an **IMU** to make the robot straight. Then lift the flipper lift and deposit the collected glyphs. Then move back into the cryptobox and score them.

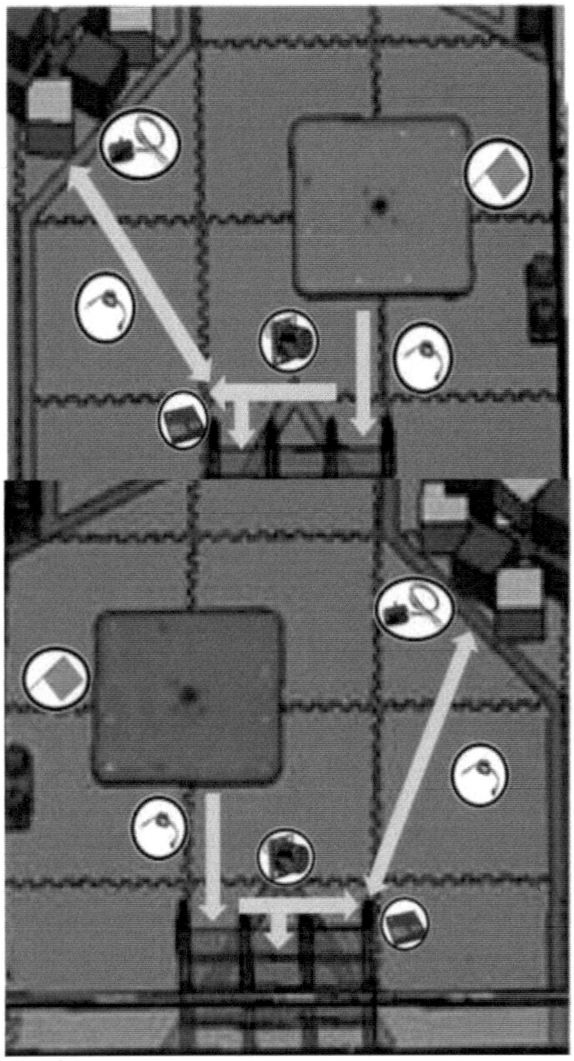

Figure 4: The Autonomous Glyphs Collections and Delivery to Cryptobox

The following graph (see Figure 5) shows how many glyphs the robot can deliver to the cryptobox throughout the 2017-2018 competition season for our robot. The team did a major software change before Houston World FTC championship competition in April'2018 in order to enable the robot ability to score more points during the autonomous time period. The shortcut software reliability model was employed to complete the defect predictions, and the team decided to complete the major software redesign with the understanding of the risk of small number of defects. Figure 5 illustrates that the software reliability is stable when the robot design and software algorithm intends to deliver only one glyphs to the cryptobox. The only incident happened during SC # 3 (Oregon State Championship Match #3) when the robot was positioned on the balancing stone incorrectly and later on was added to Fault Tree Analysis (Figure 6). Prior to Houston World Championship, the software was rewritten for ~ 50% of the code, the robot is capable of delivering 2 or 3 glyphs to the cryptobox. The testing spiral was rerun to cover scenarios based on fault tree analysis and software FMEA results for 4x2x3=24 test cases (Table 3). The differences among balancing stone, robot initial positions and cryptobox destination columns reflected the uncertainties in the physical world.

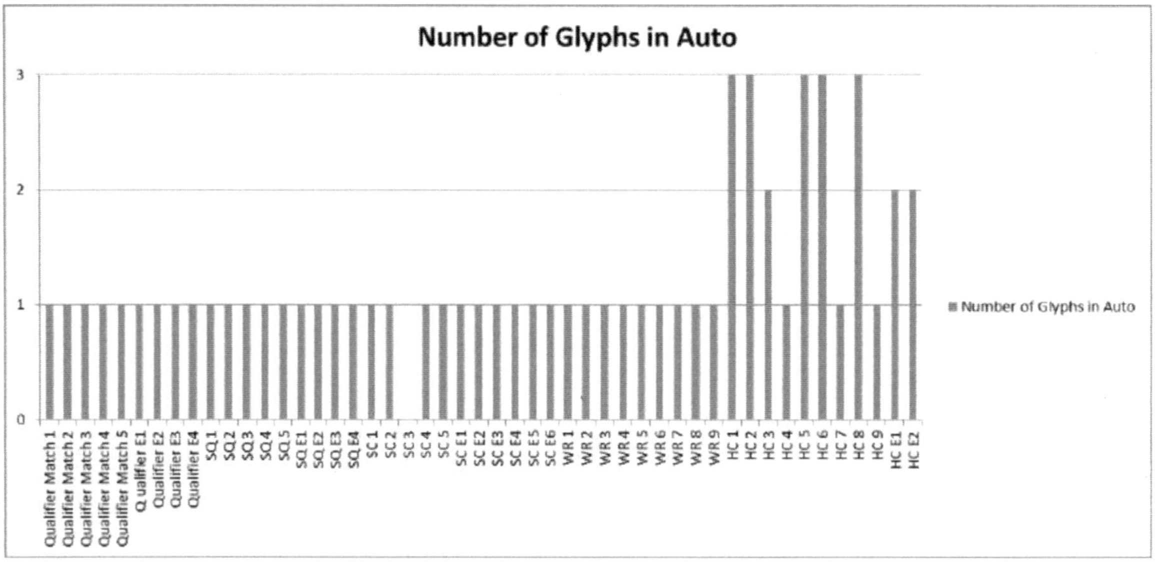

Figure 5: The number of glyphs that the robot can deliver in autonomous

(Qualifier Match: 1st level Oregon Qualifier Match
Qualifier: 2nd level Oregon Qualifier Match
SQ: Super Qualifier, 3rd level Oregon Qualifier Match
SC: State Championship, 4th level Oregon Qualifier Match
WR: US West Regional Match
HC: Houston World Championship Competition)
HC E1/2: Houston World Championship Semi-Final)

Balancing Stone Selection (4 Balance Stones)	Cryptobox Destination (either near alliance station or far away. See Figure 1)	Jewel Flick
a. Red stone 1 (Left, Face Alliance Station)	a. Column 1 @ far Crytobox b. Column 2 @ far Crytobox c. Column 3 @ far Crytobox	a. Jewel on Left b. Jewel on Right
b. Red stone 1 (Right, Face Alliance Station)	d. Column 1 @ near Crytobox e. Column 2 @ near Crytobox f. Column 3 @ near Crytobox	
c. Blue stone 1 (Left, Face Alliance Station)	g. Column 1 @ far Crytobox h. Column 2 @ far Crytobox i. Column 3 @ far Crytobox	
d. Blue stone 2 (Right, Face Alliance Station)	j. Column 1 @ near Crytobox k. Column 2 @ near Crytobox l. Column 3 @ near Crytobox	

Table 3: Test Scenario Summary for Glyphs Collection and Delivery in Autonomous

After these rigorous testing for different functionalities, the software reliability experienced one critical defect of the sensor failure with the wrong reading (HC #9) which caused the robot not able to collect more glyphs and then later on recover from this autonomous period fall out using the joystick remotely triggered software functions to recover the robot. Please note that HC #4 and #7 matches only delivered 1 glyphs because the glyphs pile is randomly setup and the robot intake mechanism can't collect 1 or 2 more glyphs through the pre-defined robot traveling path within 30 second autonomous. For HC #4 and #7, it is considered to be working successfully. Hence, the Mean Time between Failure (MTBF) is 720 seconds when considering both failures for SC#3 and HC #9. The # of defect matches the shortcut model prediction. The fault tree analysis (FTA) is shown in Figure 3. The software that we use to create the fault tree is from http://www.fault-tree-analysis-software.com/fault-tree-analysis [10]

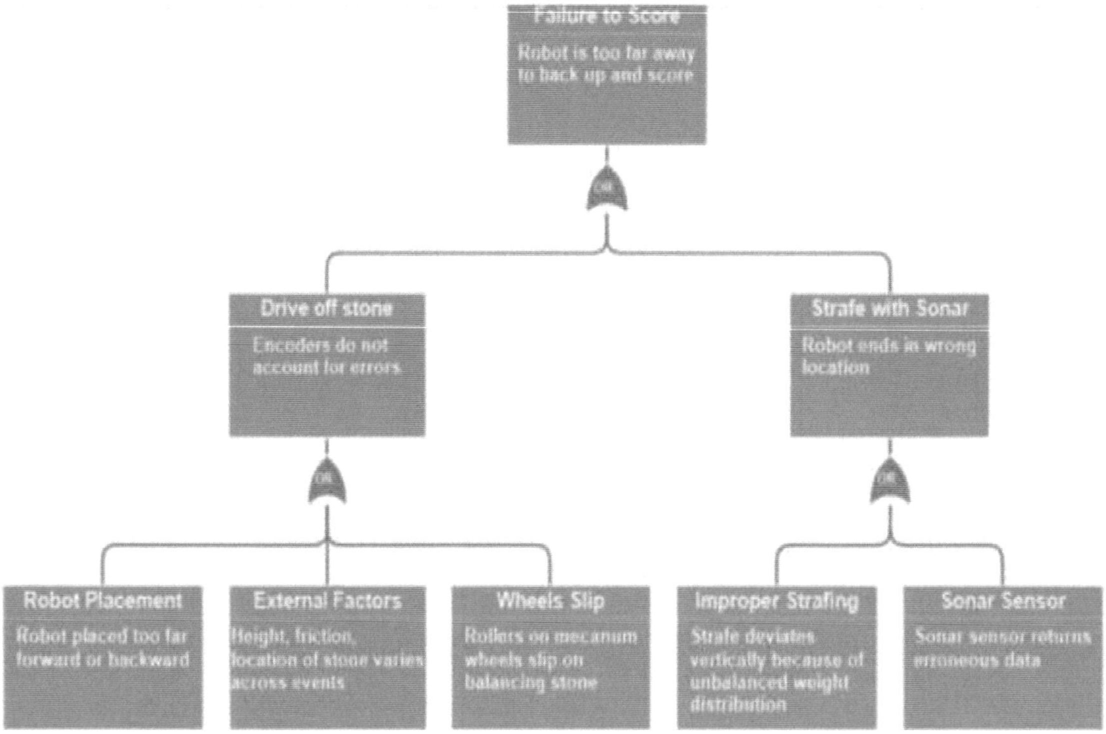

Figure 6: The Fault Tree to Collect and Deliver Glyphs to Crystobox in Autonomous

After we did fault tree analysis, we complete the Software FMEA for different viewpoints. Here is a sample software FMEA events for fault sequence and fault data category from the functional view point.

Fault Category	Definitions	Key Fault Events Being Addressed
Functionality: Fault sequence/ order	A particular event is initiated in the incorrect order or not at all.	Fault Event: The robot lifting level in the software was set to zero at the incorrect lifting position due to the autonomous program stopped by the glyph Solution: Developed the software reset program and trigger the one button manual reset at the beginning of the tele operation (TeleOpe) session to recover in 1 sec.
Functionality: Fault data	Data is corrupted, incorrect, etc.	Fault Event: The robot back sonar sensor reading incorrect data caused the wrong traveling distance. Solution: added the error protection in the software program to cap within the threshold for the traveling distance to avoid hitting the balance stone.

Table 4: Sample of Software FMEA Functionality Categorization and Action Implementation

The shortcut model was employed in the software reliability growth model and calculating the predicted defects. Here are answers to Table 5 shortcut model questions through the survey within Bytes of Kitkats team. The score delta between the software reliability "Strength" (9.5 points) and "Risks" (3.25 points) categories is 6.25 points > 4. Hence, the software defect density is expected to be 0.11 in terms of defects per normalized EKSLOC based on IEEE Recommended Practice on Software Reliability guidance. This information guided the team to do the following in order to reduce the risk so that the defect density can be reduced to lower value (0.11): a) The code reuse is considered in the robot hardware and software redesign for the world championship event. b) The team also ensures the software code is up to date and avoid using legacy code >10 years.

Strength		9.5 points
1	We protect older code that shouldn't be modified.	Yes (1)
2	The total schedule time in years is less than one.	Yes (1)
3	The number of software people years for this release is less than seven.	Yes (1)
4	Domain knowledge required to develop this software application can be acquired via public domain in short period of time.	Yes (1)
5	This software application has imminent legal risks.	No (0)
6	Operators have been or will be trained on the software.	Yes (1)
7	The software team members who are working on the same software system are geographically collocated.	Yes (1)
8	Turnover rate of software engineers on this project is < 20% during course of project.	Yes (1)
9	This will be a maintenance release (no major feature addition).	No (0)
10	The software has been recently reconstructed (i.e., to update legacy design or code).	No (0)
11	We have a small organization (<8 people) or there are team sizes that do not exceed 8 people per team.	Yes (1)
12	We have a culture in which all software engineers' value testing their own code (as opposed to waiting for someone else to test it).	Somewhat (0.5)
13	We manage subcontractors—Outsource code that is not in our expertise, keep code that is our expertise in house.	No (0)
14	There have been at least four fielded releases prior to this one.	No (0)
15	The difference between the most and least educated end user is not more than one degree type (i.e., bachelors/masters, high school/associates).	Yes(1)
Risks		**3.25 point**
1	This is brand new release (version 1), or development language, or OS, or technology (add one for each risk).	Yes (1)
2	Target hardware/system is accessible within 0.75 points for minutes, 0.5 points for hours, 0.25 points for days, and 0 points for weeks or months.	0.75
3	Short term contractors (< 1 year) are used for developing line of business code	No (0)
4	Code is not reused when it should be	Somewhat (0.5)
5	We wait until all code is completed before starting the next level of testing	No (0)
6	Target hardware is brand new or evolving (will not be finished until software is finished)	Yes (1)
7	Age of oldest part of code >10 years	No (0)

Table 5: The shortcut model software reliability answers to survey questions

	New KSLOC	**Major modified KSLOC**	**Moderate modified KSLOC**	**Minor modified KSLOC**	**Reused KSLOC**	**Auto generated code in KSLOC**	**Total EKSLOC**
Weight	100%	40%	30%	15%	5%	1%	
Software prior to April, 2018	5	0	0	0	0	0	5
Software post April, 2018 (HC)	2.5	0	0	0	2.5	0	2.5 + 0.125 = 2.625

Table 6: EKSLOC Normalizations for FTC Robot Software

Once the effective KSLOC is predicted, the last step is to normalize the EKSLOC based on the language used to develop the code (See Table 6). Some languages such as object oriented languages are denser than other languages. For FTC robot software, the Object oriented language Java was used. Hence, the normalization conversion factor is 6.0.The total EKSLOC is then shown as follows with the language type and normalization for FTC robot software reliability defect density predictions. The defect density prediction guided us in defining our robot redesign strategy and also the timing to redesign the software for the increased robot capabilities before the world championship competition to gain more scoring capabilities. The software reliability model helped us to evaluate the defect density with 1.73 defects (See Table 7). This guided the team to evaluate the risk of critical defects with the comparison against the original robot design and hardening process (3.3 defects in Table 7), and then make the informed risk-taking decision to redesign the robot hardware/software for the world championship event in Houston, TX. The team used the fault tree and FMEA to improve the robot software reliability in less than a month so that the robot can perform well in the field for the world championship competitions. Furthermore, this process helped the team to grow knowledge and skills to improve the software reliability and can be employed in other fields in the future.

Total EKSLOC	KLSOC	Normalization for this language	Normalized EKLSOC	Predicted defect density	Predicted defects = predicted defect density × normalized EKSLOC
Software prior to April, 2018	5	6	5	0.11	5 X 6 X 0.11 = 3.3
Software post April, 2018 (HC)	5	6	2.625	0.11	2.625 X 6 X 0.11 = 1.73

Table 7: Final computation for FTC Software Reliability EKSLOC Normalizations

3.2. Autonomous Image Detection Through Android Phone Camera Image and Reliable Software Algorithms

The accurate detections of VuMark and the two jewel locations are the keys to do the flicker action as part of the autonomous period. While a lot of FTC teams came up with designs to leverage different color sensors and complex software program, we utilized Android phone camera image and reliable software algorithms to find VuMark and the two jewel locations at a much faster speed of 0.25 second. As a result, this team eliminated unreliable sensor mount and reading errors, and also greatly simplified the software complexity to accomplish tasks reliably.

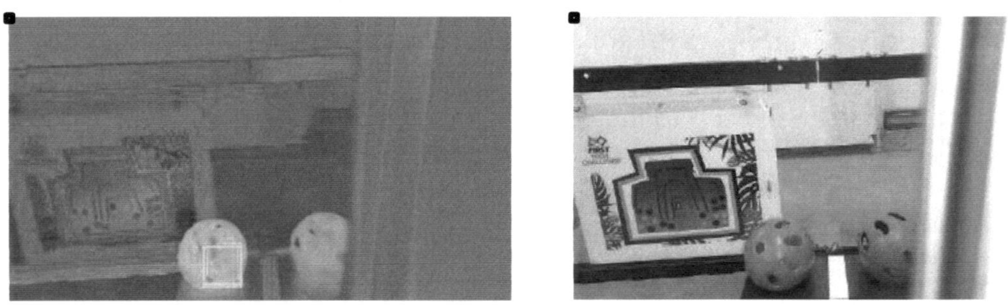

Figure 7: Self-correction Image Detection through Android Phone Camera Image (Left: ROI (Region of Interest) with BGR format; Right: Image of VuMark and the two jewels)

When we designed the solution to this complex problem, we found that the robot controller phones have cameras that can be accessed for computer vision purposes. As part of the design, we installed the phone mount on the robot frame. When we ran the autonomous code to initialize Vuforia software, the phone camera can view both the VuMark and the two jewels very reliably. Vuforia Software Development Kit (SDK) was then utilized to identify the VuMark to determine the correct crypto key. We then take the image in RGB format using Vuforia. Before inputting this image into OpenCV, we converted the image from RGB to BGR, as OpenCV only processes in BGR format. Afterward, we converted the world coordinates to 2D image coordinates using Vuforia SDK. Once we know the coordinates of the center of the image, we identified the location of the Region of Interest (ROI) – the location of the left jewel in the image (See Figure 7). The rectangle containing the ROI is from (505,540) to (600, 640), as the center of the image was around (360,400) and the ROI covers almost 75% of the jewel. The ROI image is converted from BGR to Hue, Saturation, and Value (HSV) format. We then use OpenCV's histogram analysis API to give the histogram of the color of pixels in the ROI. We count the number of red pixels in the histogram, if there are more than half red pixels, we declare that the left jewel is red, otherwise it is blue. This case study is to show how to use the phone's camera to attain software reliability with very minimum hardware dependencies.

After we designed the phone camera based solution, we also completed fault tree analysis and took actions to address key fault areas to improve the software reliability and enable the consistent FTC robot performance in the field. In this case study, the ambient light fault event was addressed using the innovative software and hardware integrated solution. After creating a sample OpMode that plotted a histogram of BGR values using OpenCV, we saw that the histogram changed significantly when lighting conditions were changed which can be used to address ambient light fault event from Figure 8. After color representations, we chose to use HSV for color detection because the hue will be the same independent of the lighting conditions. The Opmode in FTC SDK is able to convert colors from the typical Red, Green, Blue (RGB) to Hue, Saturation, Value (HSV) format. To confirm the reliability of HSV, we conducted 3 tests to make sure that the correct jewel gets flicked consistently. During the testing, the image was taken by the phone camera and the OpenCV was used for color conversion and saving of the image:

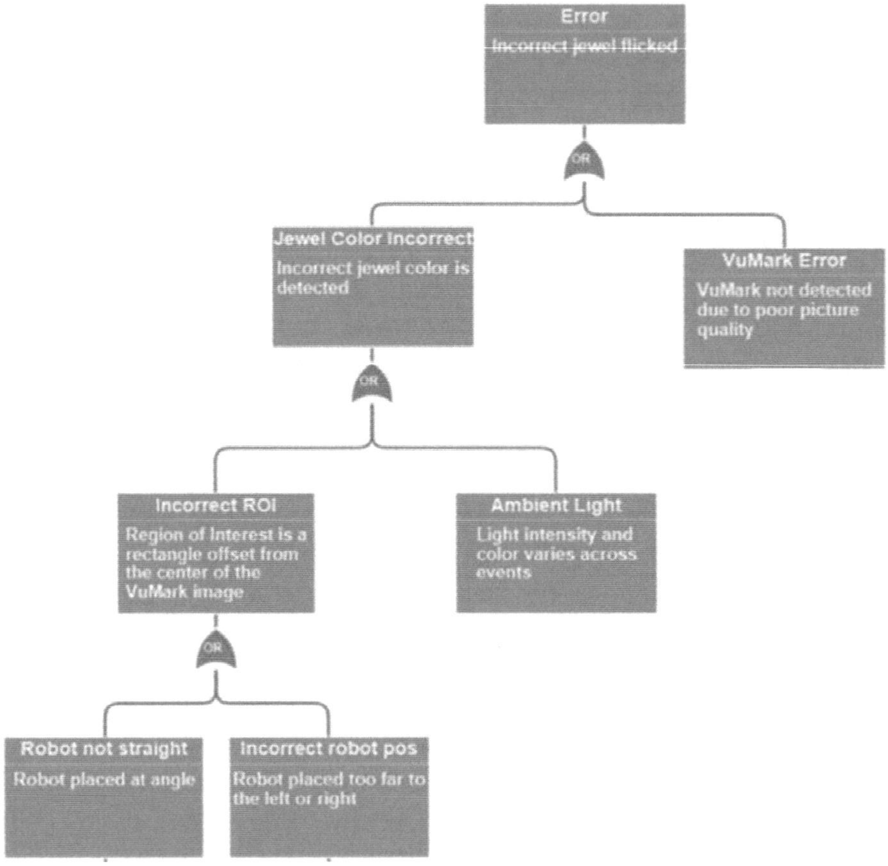

Figure 8: Jewel Flicker Fault Tree Analysis

In order to quantify the results of the previous test, we ran another set of tests. In the new tests, we changed the brightness of the ambient light and apply a color filter over the lights. The figure below provides an example of the method where a green film covers the only light source besides the phone's flash (Experiment setup see Figure 9).

Light Condition	**Image taken by Robot (camera flash is ON)**	**HSV image (shown as RGB)**	**Correct Jewel Flicked?**
Dark		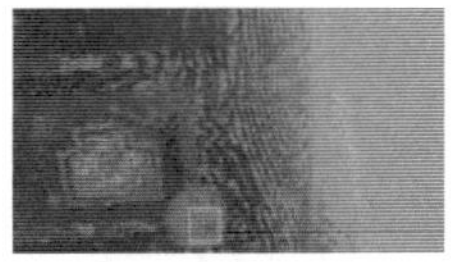	Yes
Normal		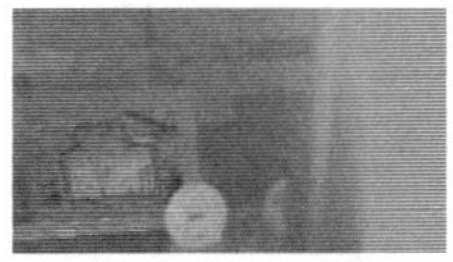	Yes
Very Bright		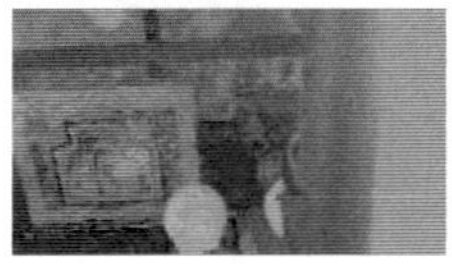	Yes

Table 8: Different light condition testing for jewel flicker missions

Figure 9: New testing setup to test effects for the brightness of the ambient light and color filters

This table shows that regardless of the intensity or color of light, the algorithm accurately predicts the color of the jewel. Using HSV enables the robot to predict the color of the jewel with 100% accuracy.

Trial	Luminosity (lx)	Description	Correct Jewel
1	180	Only flash	Yes
2	501	Standard conditions	Yes
3	2400	Light focused on VuMark	Yes
4	1100	Flash and focused green light	Yes
5	320	Flash and focused red light	Yes
6	95	Flash and focused blue light	Yes
7	1400	Standard and focused green light	Yes
8	450	Standard and focused red light	Yes
9	190	Standard and focused blue light	Yes
10	72-160	Pulsing light	Yes

Table 9: HSV Prediction Accuracy for Software Reliability

4. Summary

This paper presented our approaches to improving software reliability in Android robots that integrates robot software and physical worlds together. Case studies were used to analyze fault trees, Software FMEA and the shortcut model for software reliability defect predictions in Android robots for the robot performance improvements in FTC robot competitions. The detail fault trees were analyzed to consider multiple factors including sensor reading and the environment uncertainties within Android robot and the field. With the evolvement of robot performances and capabilities, the software reliability theoretical model of the expected defect removal and software reliability growth model were generated based off the shortcut model for FTC robot software reliability characterizations. It was found that by comparing the software reliability model data and the robot performance in the field, the software reliability model is a very powerful tool to guide the team to close software reliability gaps in critical areas for consistent robot performances and also decide the robot redesign strategy and timing. Furthermore, the paper also presented the method to improve the software reliability through Android phone internal image process to minimize dependencies on the external physical sensor readings and the mechanism to mount the sensor. HSV based color processing methods were employed in order to ensure that prediction algorithms could accurately make decisions based on the input image data without being affected by the light conditions. All of these methods can be utilized in industries to improve software reliabilities when handling the physical world uncertainties and complicities.

Acknowledgments

Authors wish to thank reviewers, Keith Stobie and Kingsum Chow, for their invaluable assistance and discussions on software reliability. In addition, authors also wish to thank Oregon Robotics Tournament & Outreach Program (ORTOP) whose assistances are very crucial for the success of FTC events in Oregon.

References

[1] Mataric, Maja J., Koenig, Nathan and Feil-Seifer, David. 2007. Materials for Enabling Hands-On Robotics and STEM Education, In AAAI Spring Symposium on Robots and Robot Venues: Resources for AI Education, Stanford, CA.

[2] Chow, Kingsum, Chow, Ida, Niu, Vicki, Takla, Ethan and Brillhart, Danny. 2010. Software Quality Assurance in the Physical World. Proceedings of the Pacific Northwest Software Quality Conference. Portland, Oregon. USA.

[3] http://www.usfirst.org/ (accessed August 1, 2018).

[4] https://firstinspiresst01.blob.core.windows.net/ftc/game-manual-dw-part-2.pdf
(accessed June 1, 2018).

[5] http://roboaztechs.org/technical-resources/ftc/ftc-robot-wiring-guide/
(accessed August 1, 2018).

[6] Musa, J.D. and Okumoto, K. 1984 A logarithmic Poisson execution time model for software reliability measurement. Proceedings of the *7th* International Conference on software Engineering.
230-237, Orlando.

[7] Reifer, Donald J. 1979. Software Failure Modes and Effects Analysis, IEEE Transactions on Reliability. R-28 (3) 247-249.

[8] http://www.softrel.com/softwarereliability.pdf
(accessed August 1, 2018).

[9] IEEE Standard Association, 2016, IEEE Recommended Practice on Software Reliability.

[10] http://www.fault-tree-analysis-software.com/fault-tree-analysis
(accessed August 1, 2018).

Diverse Teams Are Essential for Quality Software

Author

Rebecca Long (Rebecca@futureada.org)

Abstract

It has been shown that having diverse teams lead to increased problem-solving abilities. Solving complex problems is pivotal to software engineering and producing high quality software. It is natural to conclude that creating diverse software teams is a key element on the road to software quality. Rather than only thinking of quality in terms of testing by quality assurance engineers, Team composition is critical to quality software output. This paper will challenge you to consider the broader aspects of the other factors that play into creating quality software discuss ways you can create a diverse software team. It will also highlight examples of what Future Ada, a Spokane based non-profit, is doing to help build a strong diverse workforce.

Biography

Rebecca Long is a software engineer with 15 years experience focusing on quality assurance and DevOps. She is currently working at RiskLens, a cyber-risk quantification software company in Spokane as their Lead DevOps Engineer, Washington. She holds undergraduate and master's degrees in computer science with her thesis on social engineering and phishing within a financial institution. As a leader in the Spokane tech community for most of the last decade, she finally launched her dream of a non-profit called Future Ada in 2018 which supports and advocates for women and non-binaries in STEAM (science, technology, engineering, art, and mathematics). She lives with two cats, who are the true masters of the household.

1. Introduction

As software professionals, we are driven by the desire to problem solve and create innovative solutions for the world. We care about what we produce and want it to be of the highest quality we can manage. It's common practice to include various types of testing in our software development lifecycle (SDLC). This could include unit tests, integration tests, end-to-end tests, UI tests, etc. We know testing helps to find bugs and other missed items during development or planning and results in higher quality output when found earlier than later.

Quality is more than just a low bug count though. It involves creating the right product, the right way, at the right time, for the right audience. Quality needs to be injected throughout the SDLC not just when it's time for testing. As early as the initial planning and brainstorming phase, quality needs to be on the forefront of everyone's mind. Is the problem being solved the right problem to tackle? Are we thinking of the problem from every angle? Who is our audience and what pros/cons would they have in using our product? This problem-solving phase is critical to the success of a project.

The makeup of the team at the problem-solving table is a critical element to the process and resulting quality product produced. Each team member has their own technical background to bring to the table, but they also have their own personal experience, upbringing, perspectives, and cultural background to share as well. Each of these different aspects contribute to the problem-solving process that takes place during software development. When the team members are all from similar backgrounds and experience, their perspectives will also be similar and thus only provide a limited view on the world. When the team members are of a diverse set of people, their perspectives will be wide and varied which ultimately helps the problem-solving process and can improve the quality of the software being developed.

2. The Lack of Diversity in Tech

The tech industry struggles with a lack of diversity. There aren't enough underrepresented people coming into the industry and there are too many who leave early. While the tech industry is still booming, the solutions being developed and the distance we could go could still be improved through a more diverse workforce at the wheel.

2.1. Historical Diversity

We executed the case study for FTC Robot autonomous glyphs collection and delivery to cryptobox.

Figure 1: Augusta Ada Byron Lovelace (Sydell 2014)

The computing industry owes a lot to women for their multitudes of major contributions. Famous mathematician Augusta Ada Byron Lovelace (commonly known as just Ada Lovelace) is credited with inventing the first computer programming language (Gürer 2002). The ENIAC programming team had six women on it. Admiral Grace Hopper coined the term "computer bug" and invented the first computer compiler (Sanders 2009). Women math majors were common in the 1930's and those same women jumped at the chance to contribute more during World War II by working on computers (Sydell 2014).

Despite women's major accomplishments in this field they rarely were credited or acknowledged. Programming was still seen "as menial labor, like factory work, and it was feminized, a kind of "women's work" that wasn't considered intellectual" (Mims 2017). It wasn't until the 1960's that the industry was professionalized and recognized as an intellectual career. This shift began attracting men and pushing women out of the field. Women earning computer science degrees peaked in 1984 at a mere 37% and has only been declining ever since (Mims 2017).

2.2. Modern Demographics

Since the peak in the mid-1980's, the industry has become filled with an increasing number of white men. Despite recent efforts to counter this trend, we are still seeing the number of underrepresented groups diminish.

2.2.1. Gender

Multiple studies have shown that the number of women in the tech industry has been steadily dropping since the 1980's with the more current numbers showing we are down to only 15-20% (Gardner 2014, Henn 2014). In 2008, Harvard Business Review published "The Athena Factor" which found that women's careers often stall at the mid-point and that "after 10 years of work experience ... 41% of women in tech leave the industry, compared with 17% of men" (Gardner 2014). Most of the women who leave are not leaving the workforce but instead switching industries which could imply that part of the diversity problem lies with the industry culture.

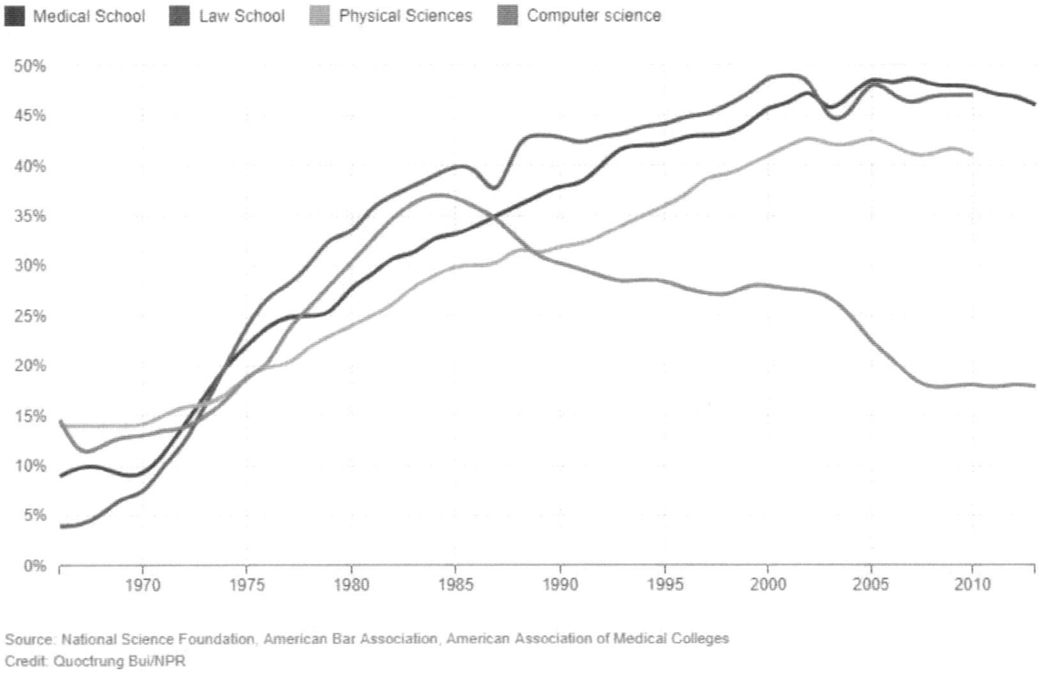

Figure 2: Number of women in computer science over time (Henn 2014).

2.2.2. Race

Representation of minorities in tech is even worse than the gender gap. According to the U.S. Equal Employment Opportunity Commission (EEOC), "high-tech sector in 2014 employed a larger share of whites (68.5% tech vs. 63.5% private sector), Asian Americans (14% tech vs. 5.8% private sector) and men (64% tech vs. 52% private sector). It also employed a smaller share of African Americans (7.4% tech vs. 14.4% private sector), Hispanics (8% tech vs. 13.9% private sector), and women (36% tech vs. 48% private sector)" (Rayome 2018). Additionally, 83% of tech executives are white (Rayome 2018).

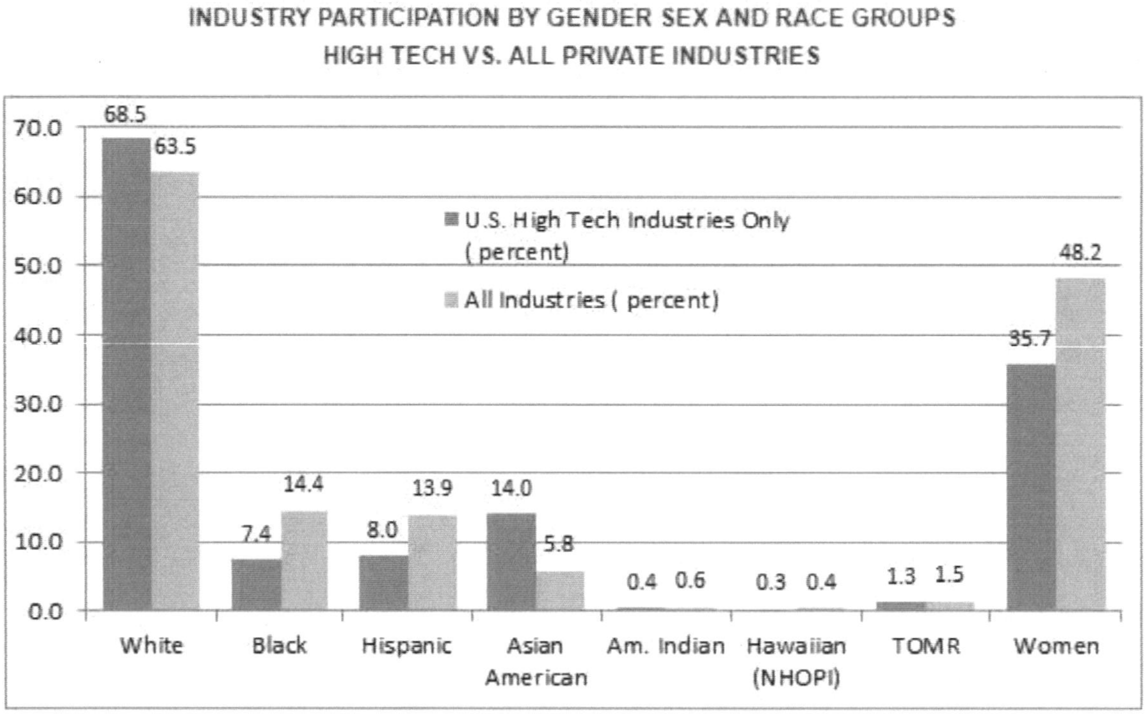

Figure 3: Equal Employment Opportunity Commission stats on race and gender in high tech (EEOC 2014)

2.2.3. Impact on Software Development

A great example of what a lack of diversity can do on an engineering team is to look at the airbag industry. The team who developed airbags was all-male and thus designed airbags to work for the average height and weight of a man. Unfortunately, the "tragic consequence was that women and children were killed when those early airbags were deployed" (Catlin 2014). Without women at the table during the design and testing phase, it wasn't until after many accidents happened that finally in 2011 a female-crash-test-dummy was required to be used (Shaver 2012).

Another excellent and less tragic example is when Google initially launched the YouTube app for Apple. They noticed that:

> *"... approximately 10 percent of the uploaded videos were upside down: "Were people shooting videos incorrectly? No. Our early design was the problem. It was designed for right-handed users, but phones are usually rotated 180 degrees when held in left hands. Without realizing it, we'd created an app that worked best for our almost exclusively right-handed developer team."" (Brown 2016).*

We need to ensure everyone is at the table for solving the world's problems. When we have a homogeneous team doing the work, the perspectives available are limited which ultimately leave holes in the solutions developed as seen with the airbags. Missing something as big as "the impact of airbags on women" can result in costly errors. The quality of the product is lowered and worse yet the perception of your product and company is reduced as well.

3. Benefits of Diversity

There are many direct and indirect benefits to have diversity on your teams and in your leadership. Diversity leads to broader perspectives for problem solving which ultimately leads to greater innovation and better bottom lines.

3.1. Greater Innovation

Research shows that "socially diverse groups (those with a diversity of race, ethnicity, gender and sexual orientation) are more innovative than homogeneous groups" (Seiter 2017). A Harvard Business Review research study has highlighted how diversity does play a critical role in innovation. In the study diversity was broken into two categories: inherent and acquired. Inherent diversity representing the traits you are born with such as gender, ethnicity, and sexual orientation. Acquired diversity being what you gain from experience such as working in another country. They considered companies who had leaders exhibiting at least three of each type of diversity as having two-dimensional diversity (2-D). In these environments, the ideas and values of diverse employees are heard and promoted up the chain. The study found that "Employees of firms with 2-D diversity are 45% likelier to report a growth in market share over the previous year and 70% likelier to report that the firm captured a new market" (Hewlett 2013).

Another study, this time by the Boston Consulting Group (BCG), showed that teams with diverse leadership have a direct positive impact on innovation resulting in higher revenue from new products and services (Lorenzo 2017). This same study also showed that "innovation performance only increased significantly when the workforce included a nontrivial percentage of women (more than 20%) in management positions" and that "having a high percentage of female employees doesn't do anything for innovation … if only a small number of women are managers" (Lorenzo 2017).

3.2. Better Financial Bottom Line

As the Kapor Center for Social Impact's 2017 study calls out:

> *"Diversity in tech matters—for innovation, for product development, for profits, for meeting future workforce demands, and for closing economic and wealth gaps. But unfairness, in the form of everyday behavior (stereotyping, harassment, bullying, etc.) is a real and destructive part of the tech work environment, particularly affecting underrepresented groups and driving talent out the*

door. With a concentrated focus on building inclusive workplace cultures, tech can save billions of dollars in financial and reputational costs, keep great talent, and finally make progress on its diversity numbers" (Kapor Center for Social Impact 2017).

As called out in the book *Inclusion*, a 2015 McKinsey report states:

"In the United States, there is a linear relationship between racial and ethnic diversity and better financial performance: for every 10 percent increase in racial and ethnic diversity on the senior-executive team, earnings before interest and taxes (EBIT) rise 0.8 percent" (Brown 2016).

4. Increasing Diversity on Software Teams

Here are industry and research backed methods to help increase diversity on your team. There are many levels needed to effectively approach this problem. Only doing one or two things will be a good starting point but try to be mindful of each of the areas listed.

4.1. Educate Staff

Diversity can be a tricky subject for many. It is important to educate your leadership and team members on the importance of it. Developing an annual or semiannual mandatory training on diversity, inclusion, and equal employment opportunities can help with this understanding and reduce the "chances of unfavorable situations" (Forbes Coaches Council 2018).

4.2. Create an Inclusive Culture

It is important to create a culture of inclusion on your teams. This will naturally draw in diverse members as everyone will feel safe and included regardless of age, race, gender, or background. Even if you don't have a diverse team today building this culture will allow different folks to feel welcome as soon as they walk through the door (Forbes Coaches Council 2018).

4.2.1. Inclusive Language

A powerful way to start building an inclusive culture is to start with the language you and your team use. While you may not purposefully mean to be excluding anyone, much of the common language used in day to day conversations are microaggressions and can be harmful to an inclusive culture. Microaggressions are "the tiny, casual, almost imperceptible insults and degradation often felt by any marginalized group" (Seiter 2017).

Inclusive language is defined as:

"Language that avoids the use of certain expressions or words that might be considered to exclude particular groups of people, esp gender-specific words, such as "man", "mankind", and masculine pronouns, the use of which might be considered to exclude women" (Dictionary.com 2012).

Incorporating inclusive language in conversations can include the following (Seiter 2017):

- Don't use "guys" to refer to men and women
- Use gender-neutral terms
- Avoid statements that perpetuate stereotypes
- Respect the language people call themselves
- Be thoughtful about the imagery you use
- Avoid negative or demeaning language around different groups of people

Swapping out commonly used words for more inclusive ones can help a lot at creating an environment where everyone feels welcome.

Exclusive Term	*Inclusive Term*
Mom & Dad	Parents, Caregivers
Boys & Girls	Children
Guys	Folks, People, Y'all
Men & Women, Ladies & Gentlemen	People of all genders
Brothers & Sisters	Siblings
Crazy, insane, nuts, psycho	Person with psychiatric disability; mental illness
Impaired, invalid, crippled, afflicted	Person with a disability
The handicapped, the disabled	People with disabilities
Retarded, slow, idiot, moron	Person with intellectual, cognitive, developmental disability

Table 1: Exclusive vs Inclusive Terms (Seiter 2017)(Unitarian Universalist Association 2018)

4.2.2. Unconscious Bias

We all have unconscious bias (also known as implicit bias) which are social stereotypes about certain groups that get formed outside our conscious awareness. These biases often are the root of much of today's discrimination which is ultimately an unconscious act stemming from our misconceptions around the belief "that the norms and experiences of our own social group— whether defined by race, class, gender, sexual orientation, disability, religion, or some other qualifier— are, or should be, the same for every other social group" (Brown 2016). While we can't help having unconscious bias, we must acknowledge this reality and then work to be mindful of it and prevent it from getting in the way of interacting with and respecting others.

4.2.3. Empathetic Leadership

It's important for everyone on a team, but especially leadership, to have emotional intelligence and empathy. This is a form of social awareness that allows being "able to assess situations from multiple perspectives" (Harlan 2017). To relate to one-another as human beings, versus the older workplace model of checking your emotions at the office door. Life and your humanity does not stop just because you are at a desk. For employees to feel safe in bringing their full selves to work they need empathy and understanding from others. This is especially important for when major life events spill over into our work life – kids must be picked up from daycare early because they have a fever, the emotional impact from a divorce, disorganization that comes from moving, distraction that comes from pregnancy or adoption, or the toll from the death of a loved one. All these things can impact all employees, even the rock stars. Creating a safe environment where they can share what's going on in their life to empathetic and understanding peers and leaders helps everyone, not just the underrepresented groups. Having this social awareness and empathy can help you pause before judging and improperly dealing with situations that may arise (Harlan 2017). It is becoming clearer that "higher emotional quotients have greater sensitivity and empathy, are rated as more effective, receive higher performance ratings, develop high-performing effective teams, and create a healthier … culture" (Pinkus 2016).

4.3. Recruitment and Hiring

Outside of offering equal pay to women and minorities, there are some other tactics to keep in mind when looking for diverse job candidates.

4.3.1. Job Postings

When seeking out women and other underrepresented groups to join your team, it's best to be mindful of recruitment strategies. Does your job ad highlight things like cold beer, ping pong, and endless video games? While it's great to have a fun, laid back culture, these things often attract younger, predominantly male applicants and turn away folks with kids or those interested in starting a family (Geek Feminism Wiki). The phrasing of titles also can be problematic as the industry favors descriptions like "rockstar" and "ninja" which women are less likely to identify with. Additionally, listing the skills needed for the job under "required" can turn away women who believe they must meet 100% of those qualifications. Listing skills in more general terms instead of specific technologies and under a "preferred" heading will help pull in more diverse candidates (Geek Feminism Wiki). It can be helpful to have a diversity statement on your website and job posting so potential applicants can see your commitment to this issue.

4.3.2. Seek Underrepresented Candidates

Search for women and minorities to apply for your open postings. Send the job listing to community organizations advocating for diversity in tech and encourage employees, especially those of underrepresented groups, to share with their networks.

Be sure if you attend a conference or career fair for recruitment, the image you are presenting is inclusive for everyone. Do not have "booth babes" but instead bring along technical women who can also help speak to the culture of the company. Be mindful of phrasings and the jokes told in front of potential candidates.

4.3.3. Hiring Panels

Hiring panels should be made up of diverse employees to help sort the candidates. Blind resume reviews can be helpful to focus on skillsets rather than gender or age by removing names and dates before sorting. It has been shown that gender bias still exists in STEM when determining the best qualified candidate. A 2012 study showed that with two identical resumes, one with the name "John" and one with the name of "Jennifer," employers in STEM viewed "John" as more qualified and even offered "John" a higher initial salary with mentoring opportunities (Moss-Racusin 2012).

4.3.4. Interviews

Standardize interview questions ahead of time before bringing in any candidate. Ensure the entire hiring panel agrees on what the questions are and why they are being asked. Be sure to discuss and secure what hiring criteria to use prior to any interviews and then commit not to change the criteria part way through the process.

4.4. Retainment

4.4.1. Equality

Women and minority employees need be held to the same standards as other employees. This includes equal pay for salaries, raises, and bonuses. Have equal job expectations for employees. Be sure underrepresented groups have equal promotional opportunities and take note if there is a lack of diverse team members moving up the corporate ladder. If women and other underrepresented groups see only white men being rewarded for their hard work, those employees will start looking for opportunities elsewhere where they will be appreciated for their contributions.

4.4.2. Growth Opportunities

Provide mentoring opportunities to employees of underrepresented groups. Internal corporate mentor programs are great, but if your employer doesn't offer one consider informal mentoring options. Consider being a coach, mentor or sponsor for a woman or other minority member of your team. Each of these roles are different and each are important for success: "a coach talks to you, a mentor talks with you, and a sponsor talks about you" (Catalyst 2014).

Sponsor training events for women and minorities to send them to conferences or other seminars to help their career. Make sure all employees are receiving some form of sensitivity, anti-harassment, and unconscious bias training.

4.4.3. Work/Life Balance

Providing a culture that promotes a healthy work/life balance is key to drawing and retaining diverse employees. Corporate cultures that encourage 50, 60, 70+ hour work weeks are not friendly to families or those wanting to start a family and quickly lead to burnout. A company that has balanced parental leave policies that protect a parent's job following the birth or adoption of a child shows a commitment to employees and an understanding that employees also have lives outside work. Offering flexible schedules and remote options can also provide more opportunities for parents to work on your teams. This opens a large candidate pool of talent to pull from as well.

Ultimately, all employees benefit from a commitment to work/life balance. A study called *How Men Flex* found that "men respondents believed that work flexibility helped them be more productive, happier, less stressed, more motivated at work, more effective at home, and more committed to their employers" (Brown 2016). Promoting a healthy work/life balance helps not just underrepresented members of your team but all employees. Happier and healthier employees benefit the company via lower turnover rates, fewer sick days, and greater loyalty.

4.5. Executive Efforts

For those in executive leadership positions, you are in a unique position to make larger impacts on the organization's culture and stance regarding diversity and inclusion. The first recommendation is to hire a dedicated, experienced human resources person. Second is to consider hiring a Diversity and Inclusion (D&I) expert. Both roles will help guide you on setting up a safe environment that fosters inclusion.

Having clear, strong anti-harassment and anti-discrimination policies in place is key. It is critical that these policies are posted for all staff to have easy access and to ensure the policies are well understood by everyone. It is recommended to have a zero-tolerance policy for misconduct to show these issues are taken seriously. The organization must understand that a "lack of action [with sexual misconduct] implies tolerance, harming their investments in the long term and damaging that company's chances of success" (Lodico 2017).

When problems do eventually happen, it's important to have a safe reporting path for individuals to utilize. If the reporting process isn't safe, where the employee feels there will be negative repercussions for filing the report, you will only hear of problems after they are too big to remediate.

4.6. Community Involvement

As an individual, a team, or an organization who is committed to diversity and inclusion, make efforts to reach out to the community and help promote these values. Help to recruit women and minorities into the industry. Help teach tech skills to the youth to help create a diverse next generation of tech professionals. Show up at diversity events, sponsor scholarships, and offer internships to underrepresented groups. These steps can help show your community that you take the issue of diversity in tech seriously and want to make a big picture difference.

5. Community Organizations Here to Help

Thankfully there are many organizations around to help you make your team diverse and inclusive. These groups are good to connect with. Attend their meetings, volunteer, sponsor events. Learn from their examples. Supporting the work they do will ultimately help our whole industry bring in and retain underrepresented groups. Establishing good rapport with organizations like these, especially ones local to your company, will provide an avenue to learn from and to recruit from.

5.1. Future Ada

Figure 3: Equal Employment

Future Ada (named after Ada Lovelace) is a Spokane based non-profit established in early 2018 (Future Ada 2018). Our mission is to secure space for women and non-binaries in STEAM (science, technology, engineering, art, and mathematics). We purposefully decided to go with STEAM, inserting "art" into the traditional STEM fields. We believe:

> *"the STEAM movement isn't about spending 20 percent less time on science, technology, engineering, and math to make room for art. It's about sparking students' imagination and helping students innovate through hands-on STEM projects. And perhaps most importantly, it's about applying creative thinking and design skills to these STEM projects so that students can imagine a variety of ways to use STEM skills into adulthood" (Feldman 2015).*

We are making strides to help increase diversity and inclusion in all the STEAM fields, not just technology. Our initial focus has been on the tech industry, however, as most of our founding members are from tech. Projects we are involved with currently include bringing in other national resources to Spokane such as Django Girls, Girls Who Code, and Write/Speak/Code. We also created a scholarship for women interested in attending one of our local university computer science programs and are building a mentorship program with the same university to help prepare women and non-binary students for industry. Support from industry and our communities are critical to our success in helping advocate and encourage underrepresented groups to go into and stay in STEAM.

5.2. Other Community Opportunities

There are many other wonderful organizations and conferences who are working toward helping and supporting diversity in technology.

Women in Tech Organizations:

- Women Who Code: https://www.womenwhocode.com
- Girls Who Code: https://girlswhocode.com
- The Anita Borg Institute: https://anitab.org
- Black Girls Code: http://www.blackgirlscode.com/
- Django Girls: https://djangogirls.org/

Diversity and Inclusion Organizations:

- Project Include: http://projectinclude.org
- Compassionate Coding: https://compassionatecoding.com
- <div>ersity: https://hirediversity.us/
- Better Allies: https://maleallies.com

Conferences:

- Grace Hopper Celebration of Women in Computing: https://ghc.anitab.org
- Women in Cybersecurity (WiCyS): https://www.wicys.net/
- The Diana Initiative: https://www.dianainitiative.org/
- Write/Speak/Code: https://www.writespeakcode.com/

6. Conclusion

As software quality assurance professionals, we understand the creativity and innovation that goes into software engineering and software testing. We build software to solve problems, to help people, to help our communities. Software is built for people and built by people. As such, it is critically important that we have those creating the software also be representative of the world around us, the world that will be using the software. Diversity is a key element in developing high quality software as diverse team members are the best way to have broad perspectives and be maximally innovative.

There are many steps individuals, teams, and organizations can take to reach a team full of diverse employees creating high quality software. Simple steps such as using inclusive language and being mindful of unconscious bias make huge differences. Bigger steps such as fostering an inclusive environment with strong work policies, safe reporting methods, and empathetic leaders take more work but are worth the effort. All these efforts lead to a stronger, more innovative team which will ultimately produce better software and better bottom-lines.

Luckily, there are some universities that are having success increasing the number of women in their computer science programs. Harvey Mudd increased their computer science ratio to be 48% women and Carnegie Mellon increased theirs to 42% as of the year 2000 (Catlin 2014). This is good news for potential new hires to help diversify your teams.

6.1. Future Research

This paper has connected dots between research into how diversity and inclusion impact teams in general and the assumed impact that would have on software specific teams. Next steps would include doing specific research to prove the conclusions drawn here, that a diverse team produces higher quality software.

6.2. Call to Action

Every day more research comes out to show benefits to having a diverse team and an inclusive workplace. I encourage everyone to help create an inclusive environment at your office and on your team. Help create a space where diverse individuals want to be. We can all play a part in helping to create a safe space for diversity and we all will reap the rewards of creating a better workplace and producing higher quality software.

References

Brown, Jennifer. *Inclusion: Diversity, The New Workplace & The Will To Change.* Hartford, CT: Purpose Driven Publishing, 2016.

Catalyst Inc. "Coaches, Mentors, and Sponsors: Understanding the Difference." Knowledge Center. Last modified December 11, 2014. https://www.catalyst.org/knowledge/coaches-mentors-and-sponsors-understanding-differences (accessed August 2018)

Catlin, Karen. "Women in Tech: The Missing Force." Writeup of her talk at TEDx College of William and Mary on April 6, 2014. Last modified May 1, 2014. https://medium.com/women-in-tech/women-in-tech-the-missing-force-e4709f348610

Dictionary.com. "Inclusive Language." Last modified 2012. http://www.dictionary.com/browse/inclusive-language
U.S. Equal Employment Opportunity Commission (EEOC). "Diversity in High Tech." Last modified 2014. https://www.eeoc.gov/eeoc/statistics/reports/hightech/

Feldman, Anna. "STEAM Rising." Future Tense. Last modified June 16, 2015. http://www.slate.com/articles/technology/future_tense/2015/06/steam_vs_stem_why_we_need_to_put_the_arts_into_stem_education.html

Forbes Coaches Council. "13 Effective Ways to Educate Employees on Diversity." Leadership. Last modified June 28, 2018. https://www.forbes.com/sites/forbescoachescouncil/2018/06/28/13-effective-ways-your-organization-can-educate-employees-on-diversity/#4624a51756ab

Future Ada. Last modified 2018. https://www.futureada.org/

Gardner, Sue. "Why women are leaving the tech industry in droves." Opinion. Last modified December 5, 2014. http://www.latimes.com/opinion/op-ed/la-oe-gardner-women-in-tech-20141207-story.html

Geek Feminism Wiki. "HOWTO recruit and retain women in tech workplaces." For Employers. http://geekfeminism.wikia.com/wiki/HOWTO_recruit_and_retain_women_in_tech_workplaces (accessed August 2018)

Gürer, Denise. "Women in Computing History." *SIGCSE Bulletin* 34, no. 2 (June 2002): 116-120. https://dl.acm.org/citation.cfm?id=543843

Harlan, Danielle. *The New Alpha*. McGraw-Hill Education LLC, 2017.

Henn,Steve. "When Women Stopped Coding." Planet Money. Last modified October 21, 2014. https://www.npr.org/sections/money/2014/10/21/357629765/when-women-stopped-coding

Hewlett, Sylvia, Melinda Marshall, Laura Sherbin. "How Diversity Can Drive Innovation." Harvard Business Review, December 2013. https://hbr.org/2013/12/how-diversity-can-drive-innovation (accessed August 2018)

Kapor Center for Social Impact. "Tech Leavers Study." Last modified April 27, 2017. http://www.kaporcenter.org/wp-content/uploads/2017/04/KAPOR_Tech-Leavers-17-0427.pdf

Lodico, Phil. "Sexism in Tech Is Dying: Are You Still Part of the Problem?" Sexism. Last modified August 8, 2017.
https://www.entrepreneur.com/article/298166
Lorenzo, Rocio, Nicole Voigt, Karin Schetelig, Annika Zawadzki, Isabell Welpe, and Prisca Brosi. "The Mix That Matters: Innovation Through Diversity." Last modified April 26, 2017. https://www.bcg.com/en-us/publications/2017/people-organization-leadership-talent-innovation-through-diversity-mix-that-matters.aspx

Mims, Christopher. "The First Women in Tech Didn't Leave – Men Pushed Them Out." Tech. Las modified December 10, 2017. https://www.wsj.com/articles/the-first-women-in-tech-didnt-leavemen-pushed-them-out-1512907200

Moss-Racusin, Corinne A., John F. Dovidio, Victoria L. Brescoll, Mark J. Graham, and Jo Handelsman. "Science faculty's subtle gender biases favor male students." *PNAS* 109, no 41 (October 9, 2012): 16474-16479.
http://www.pnas.org/content/pnas/109/41/16474.full.pdf

Pinkus, Ari. "A Call for More Inclusive, Empathetic Leadership." Learn. Last modified November 8, 2016.
https://www.nais.org/learn/independent-ideas/november-2016/a-call-for-more-inclusive,-empathetic-leadership/ (accessed August 2018)

Rayome, Alison DeNisco. "5 eye-opening statistics about minorities in tech." Last modified February 7, 2018.
https://www.techrepublic.com/article/5-eye-opening-statistics-about-minorities-in-tech/

Sanders, Lucy. "The History of Women in Computing." Blog. Last modified February 14, 2009. https://www.ncwit.org/blog/history-women-computing

Seiter, Courtney. "An Incomplete Guide to Inclusive Language for Startups and Tech." Last modified October 26, 2017.
https://open.buffer.com/inclusive-language-tech/

Seiter, Courtney. "The 3 Research-Backed Benefits of Diversity That Guide Our Team Growth." Diversity. Last modified July 14, 2017.
https://open.buffer.com/diversity-benefits/

Shade, Leslie Regan. "Anita Borg: American Computer Scientist." Biographies. Last modified 2018.
https://www.britannica.com/biography/Anita-Borg

Shaver, Katherine. "Female dummy makes her mark on the male-dominated crash tests." Transportation. Last modified March 25, 2012.
https://www.washingtonpost.com/local/trafficandcommuting/female-dummy-makes-her-mark-on-male-dominated-crash-tests/2012/03/07/gIQANBLjaS_story.html

Sydell, Laura. "The Forgotten Female Programmers Who Created Modern Tech." All Things Considered. Last modified October 6, 2014.
https://www.npr.org/sections/alltechconsidered/2014/10/06/345799830/the-forgotten-female-programmers-who-created-modern-tech

Unitarian Universalist Association. "Inclusive Language Guide." Ways to Welcome. Last modified 2018.
https://www.uua.org/lgbtq/welcoming/ways/200008.shtml

This page intentionally left blank.

High Maturity, But Yet You're Late?

Authors

Emanuel R. Baker, Ph.D. Software Eng'g Consultants, Inc., Los Angeles, CA 90077
erbaker@swengcon.com

Elizabeth Clark, Ph.D., Software Metrics Inc., Haymarket, VA 20169
betsy@software-metrics.com

Adrian Pitman, Capability Acquisition and Sustainment Group (CASG), Australian Department of Defence
adrian.pitman@defence.gov.au

Angela Tuffley, RedBay Consulting Pty Ltd., Redland Bay, QLD, Australia
a.tuffley@redbay.com.au

Abstract

Many organizations have adopted process improvement models (e.g., *Capability Maturity Model Integration* (CMMI)) and have seen marked improvements in quality and performance. Yet, a number of these organizations, including some who have achieved Capability Maturity Level 5, still fail to achieve their product or service delivery milestones. High maturity organizations create process performance models (PPMs) which theoretically are more accurate in predicting realistic delivery dates, but don't always succeed. PPMs rely on knowing the variability of constituent subprocesses and typically include in a Monte Carlo simulation model those that have a major impact on a given process performance goal. PPMs tend to focus more on components that can be characterized by subprocesses having variability. Risk factors don't vary over time and are typically not included. Yet, risk realization often becomes the primary cause of program slippage. The failure to include risk in PPMs is a major contributing factor to a project's lateness.

To combat this shortcoming, the Australian DoD Capability Acquisition Sustainment Group (CASG) has created a review methodology called Schedule Compliance Risk Assessment Methodology (SCRAM). It addresses 11 major categories of risk and enables an assessment review team to evaluate how both customer and development organization have addressed these categories to mitigate their impact on critical milestones. SCRAM establishes the probability of meeting critical milestone dates, and is a proven methodology that has been used very successfully on a large number of projects in a variety of technology and environmental domains (Air, Land, Sea). This paper describes what SCRAM is, how it can be used, and notable successes to date.

Biography

Emanuel R. Baker, Ph.D., a principal in two consulting firms (Software Engineering Consultants, Inc., and Process Strategies, Inc.) is certified by the CMMI Institute as a high maturity lead appraiser and as an instructor in the CMMI. He has over 45 years of experience in software engineering. Previously, he was Product Assurance Manager at Logicon and was the author of the original draft of DoD-STD-2168 on software quality assurance.

Elizabeth (Betsy) Clark is President of Software Metrics Inc., a Virginia-based consulting company she founded in 1983. Dr. Clark was a primary contributor to Practical Software Measurement (PSM) and to the SEI's core measures. She is also a principal contributor to Australian Defence's SCRAM development. She collaborated with Drs. Barry Boehm and Chris Abts to develop the COCOTS cost estimation model. She is a long-time consultant to the Institute for Defense Analyses and, more recently, to the Software Engineering Institute. Dr. Clark earned her bachelor's degree from Stanford University and Ph.D. in Cognitive Psychology from the University of California, Berkeley.

Adrian Pitman is a Director in the Capability Acquisition and Sustainment Group (CASG) in the Australian DoD. He has 52 years of Defence experience – 20 years as a member of the Royal Australian Air Force and 32 years in defence capability acquisition. Adrian initiated and is a co-developer of SCRAM. He has participated as an acquisition project team member in Engineering, Quality Assurance and Project Management roles on multiple projects. He is a SCRAM Principal, a ISO 9001 Lead Auditor and a former Defence Materiel Organisation CMMI Lead Assessor.

*Angela Tuffley is the Director and Principal Consultant of RedBay Consulting. She has over 35 years of industry experience, both in Australia and overseas, providing expert professional services in training, assessment and advice for the acquisition, engineering and support of software intensive systems. She is a co-developer of SCRAM and provides consultation on SCRAM, the adoption of the CMMI and ISO/IEC 15504 Information Technology Process Assessment (*Software Process Improvement and Capability Determination *(SPICE)).*

1. Introduction

Many organizations have adopted process improvement models (CMMI, for example) and have seen marked improvements in quality and performance. High maturity organizations, rated at maturity level (ML) 4 or 5, have successfully implemented PPMs that predict the ability to achieve quality and performance goals. Some models have been constructed to predict the ability to achieve critical milestones, such as delivery date. In spite of that, a number of these organizations still miss the mark when it comes to delivery of the product or service on the original promised date. During development, delivery often gets renegotiated with the result that the contractor delivers on the final renegotiated date and claims victory. Yet delivery didn't really occur when the customer originally wanted it.

High maturity organizations create PPMs which theoretically are more accurate in predicting realistic delivery dates. The problem is the basic structure of a PPM. They rely on knowing the process variability of constituent subprocesses and including in the model those that have a major impact on a given process performance goal. This data and the current performance of a constituent subprocess are typically inputs to a PPM to assess the probability of achieving that goal on the project of interest. Consequently, PPMs tend to focus more on issues of quality since aspects of quality can often be characterized by variable subprocesses. Risk factors are not easy to include since they don't vary over time and are typically characterized as point values of impact and probability of occurrence. Yet, risk realized, technical debt, and poor management decisions often become the primary causes of program slip. The inability to include these factors in PPMs is a major factor in a project's failure to meet the predicted delivery date.

To combat these shortcomings, CASG of the Australian Department of Defence created an assessment methodology called SCRAM (Schedule Compliance Risk Assessment Methodology). SCRAM addresses 11 major categories of programmatic problems. It enables a review team to evaluate how the development organization of interest addressed these factors to mitigate their impact on meeting critical milestones. For any critical milestone, SCRAM quantifies the potential risk (slippage) and determines the numerical probability of meeting that date. It is a proven methodology that has been used very successfully on a large number of projects in a variety of capability domains. This paper describes what SCRAM is, how it can be used to address these issues, and notable successes to date.

2. Statement of the Problem and Its Solution

The media abounds with stories about well-known programs that were late, over budget, and in some cases had quality problems as well. Some notable recent examples include the California High Speed Rail (HSR) project between San Francisco and Los Angeles, the Joint Strike Fighter (F-35), the rollout of the Affordable Care Act web-based user interface, and the Los Angeles Department of Water and Power billing program. Some of these have involved organizations that have been rated at ML 5. Nonetheless, these organizations were not able to create a schedule that guaranteed delivery of the product on the date that the customer originally required. Phase 1 of the HSR project is already several years late, for example.

As an organization matures, its ability to control development processes improves, thus improving product and service quality as well as creating more accurate schedules. An organization at ML 3 has significantly-improved capability to accomplish this over an organization at ML 2. The hallmark of a high maturity organization is its use of quantitative methods to quantitatively control project processes; use of this data to make predictions concerning the achievement of quality and process performance goals; and implement corrective action on the offending process. They create control charts to quantitatively control critical subprocesses and use the current data on the performance of these controlled subprocesses in PPMs to make predictions about, for example, residual defects in the delivered product and to predict if they will meet their schedule constraints. Yet, as noted above, even high maturity organizations miss the mark.

The problem is that most PPMs do not address risk directly. Anecdotally, several lead appraisers have indicated that none of them had ever seen a PPM that included risk or other issues that create schedule risk, for example, technical debt. As noted previously, risk is typically characterized by citing a fixed probability of occurrence and numerical estimate of impact (for example, on a scale from 0 to 1). Since most PPMs are built on parameters having variability over time or frequency of occurrence, risk does incorporate well into such models because it has fixed values. Yet, there are PPMs to predict the ability to meet schedule, but because risk is rarely considered, they often fail to make accurate predictions.

SCRAM, because of its explicit consideration of risk and factors related to risk, does a significantly better job of calculating the probability of meeting critical milestones. Moreover, the process of conducting a SCRAM reveals what was not considered in creating the schedule, an example of which is technical debt. Technical debt is the price a development team pays for omitting or reducing a part of a process, often for the sake of short-term expediency. When an organization, in the interest of shortening development time, reduces the number of peer reviews for example, there is a risk that some defects will go undetected. The price and interest that is paid is the amount of rework unaccounted for in the schedule that is often revealed later in development when it is more costly to correct.

Technical debt is only one aspect considered in a SCRAM Review (see Figure 2). The interview process in a SCRAM typically reveals other things, as well, that were either not considered, or were poorly considered, when the schedule was created. By accounting for these omissions or poorly estimated effects, SCRAM is able to come up with a more accurate estimate, and identify where the root cause of schedule slippage occurred.

SCRAM can be effectively applied during the proposal phase to determine the probability that the customer-desired delivery can be met, and if not, what strategies can be applied to better align capability with the desired date. It can be used during development to assess the probability that critical milestones will be met. It can also be used as a diagnostic tool when it becomes apparent that a critical milestone will not be met. Acquiring organizations can use SCRAM to assess the probability that their contractor will meet the desired delivery date.

3. Overview of SCRAM

A SCRAM Review is an independent, non -advocate and non-attributable engineering focused approach used to evaluate a program's schedule performance and identify risks to contractual schedule compliance. SCRAM was developed to benefit defense and industry decision makers and program managers by providing a method that assists experienced engineers and program controllers to consistently identify root causes of schedule slippage and recommend corrective actions.

SCRAM[8] uses two established scientific analysis techniques: Schedule Monte Carlo simulation to model estimation uncertainty and risk impacts and a dynamic software model to assist in forecasting schedule milestone completion based on objective data characterizing performance to date. SCRAM utilizes best practices from systems and software engineering together with schedule development and program execution. In addition, SCRAM facilitates improved organizational processes and practices based on feedback and systemic issues obtained from SCRAM Reviews.

There are three SCRAM delivery or application modes. These modes are:

- *Pre-emptive SCRAM* - conducted early in the Program life-cycle to avoid systemic issues and risks (e.g. ideally prior to contract award and/or an Earned Value Management - Integrated Baseline Review (EVM-IBR));
- *Assurance SCRAM* – conducted at any point in the program lifecycle to ascertain schedule performance is on track; and
- *Diagnostic SCRAM* - when a Program is experiencing significant schedule slippage i.e. a program is of interest or concern (similar to a US Nunn-McCurdy breach situation, i.e., one that requires notification to Congress if the cost per unit goes more than 25% beyond what was originally estimated, and calls for the termination of programs with total cost growth greater than 50%.).

In addition an organization acquiring a product or a service from a prime contractor can utilize SCRAM to independently evaluate if the contractor is likely to deliver when promised.

---

[8] SCRAM uses SLIM-Control, a commercially available tool from Quantitative Software Management in McLean, Virginia.

The SCRAM Review process, shown in **Error! Reference source not found.**, is typically conducted over a two-week period on site followed by a written detailed report two weeks later. The SCRAM process is in accordance with the guidelines described in International Organization for Standardization/International Electrotechnical Commission (ISO/IEC) 15504 – Information technology process assessment.

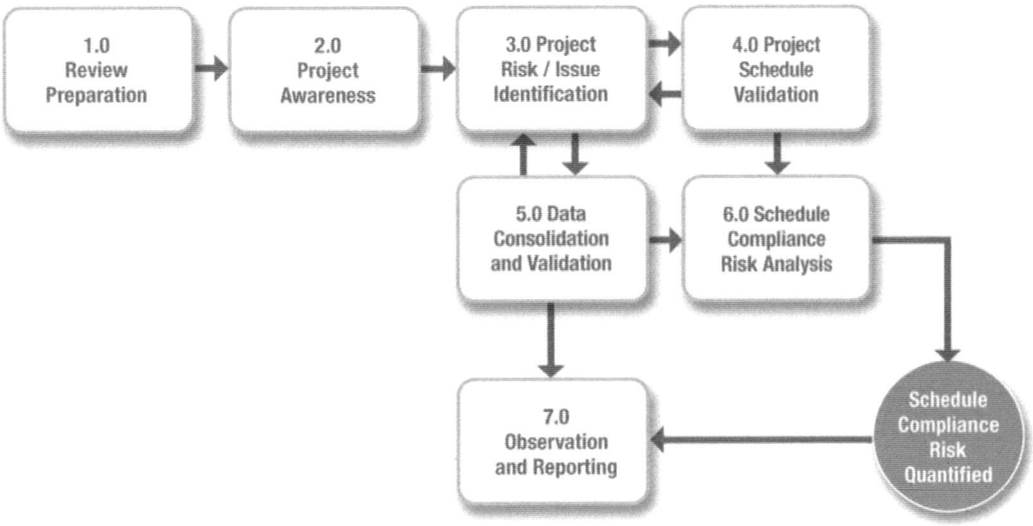

Figure 1: High Level SCRAM Review Process.
Copyright 2018, Commonwealth of Australia

A SCRAM Review is conducted with seven Key Principles. These are:

- **Minimal Disruption**: information is collected one person at a time through interviews that typically last an hour. Artifact reviews (plans, detailed schedules) are conducted offline.
- **Independent**: SCRAM Team members are organizationally independent of the program under review. Some SCRAM Reviews have been joint contractor/customer team to facilitate joint commitment to resolving the review outcomes.
- **Non-advocate**: all significant issues and concerns are considered and reported regardless of the origin of the issue (customer or contractor).
- **Non-attribution**: the information source is not attributed to any individual instead focusing on identifying and mitigating the issues/risk.
- **Corroboration of Evidence**: significant findings and observations are based on at least two independent sources of corroboration.

- **Rapid turn-around**: only one to two weeks are spent on-site with an executive out-briefing presented at end of second week and a written report two weeks later.
- **Sharing Results, Openness and Transparency**: particularly for the parametric modelling component of a SCRAM Review, the organization under review may witness the data analysis process and challenge the results, and a preliminary out brief of findings is delivered prior to departure from the review site. This principle builds cooperation, trust and confidence in the schedule forecast.

SCRAM Reviews, data gathering, analysis and reporting in SCRAM Reviews are structured around the Root Cause Analysis of Schedule Slippage (RCASS) model shown in

Figure *2: Root Cause Analysis of Schedule Slippage (RCASS).*
Copyright 2018, Commonweath of Australia

. RCASS organizes program information into categories related to planning and executing a program.

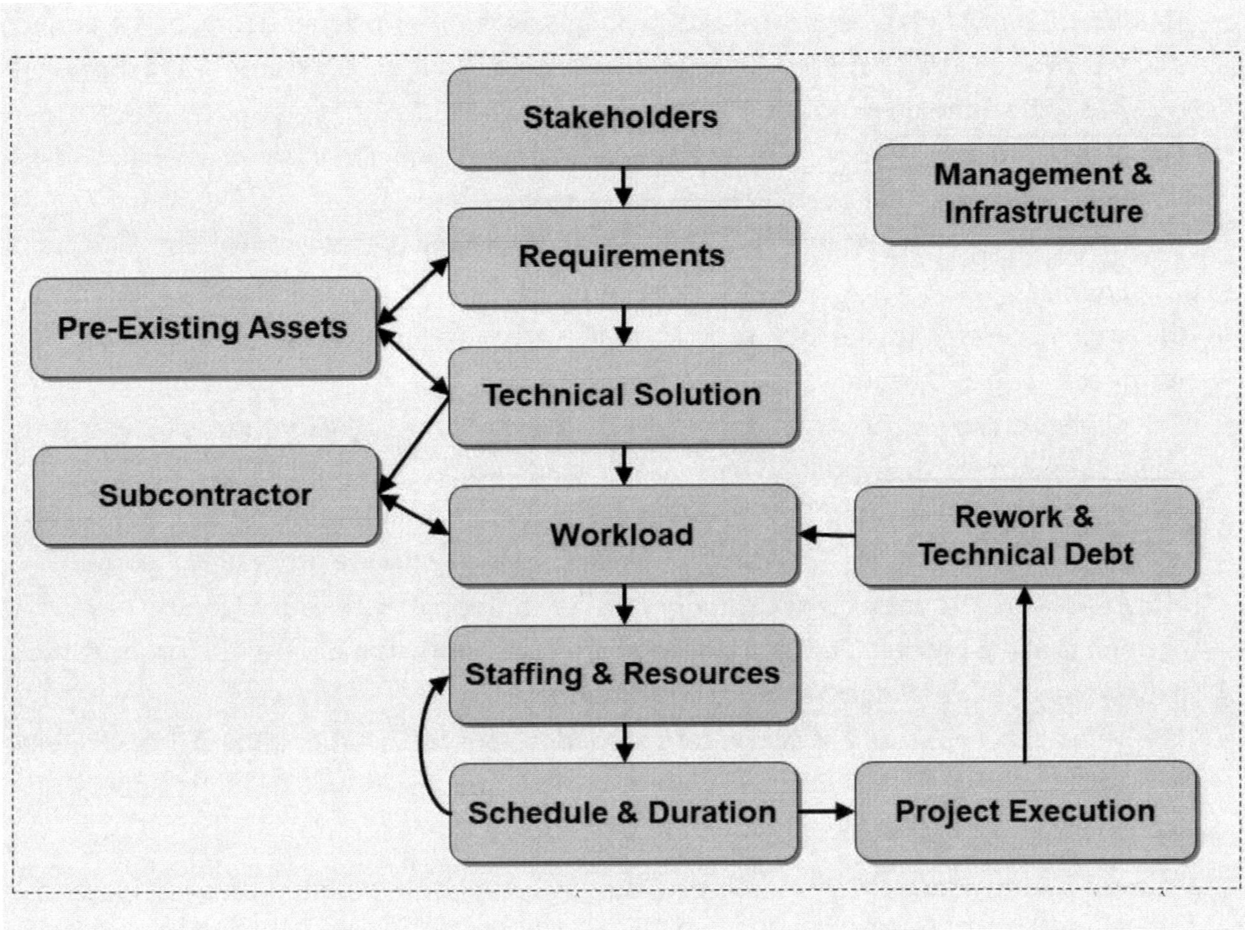

Figure 2: Root Cause Analysis of Schedule Slippage (RCASS).
Copyright 2018, Commonweath of Australia

- The *Stakeholders* category reflects program turbulence and entropy because of difficulties in synchronizing the program's stakeholders: i.e., users, customers, system engineers, developers, maintainers, and others, relative to meeting commitments.
- The *Requirements* category reflects understanding and stability of the functional requirements, performance requirements, constraints, standards, for example, used to define and bound what is to be developed.
- The *Technical Solution* category reflects the design considerations and approaches needed to ensure that the chosen solution is architected, logically and physically designed to align with the business enterprise architecture, satisfy functional and non-functional requirements (quality attributes) and optimized to meet system development and sustainment life-cycle objectives.

- The *Pre-Existing Assets* category reflects products developed independently of the project that will be used in the final product, i.e. an asset that can reduce the amount of new work that has to be done on a project.
- The *Subcontractor* category reflects subcontractor products or services that will be delivered as a part of the overall deliverable system.
- The *Workload* category reflects the quantity of work that has to be done.
- The *Staffing and Resources* category reflects the availability, capability and experience of the staff necessary to do the work as well as the availability, and capacity of other resources, such as test and integration labs.
- The *Schedule and Duration* category reflects the tasks, sequencing and calendar time needed to execute the workload by available staff and other resources.
- The *Project Execution* category focuses on schedule, management and monitoring and controlling the execution of the program in accordance with the program schedule.
- The *Rework and Technical Debt* category reflects additional work caused by the discovery of defects in the product and/or associated artefacts, work that is deferred for short-term expediency (technical debt) and their resolution.
- The *Management and Infrastructure* category addresses factors that impact the efficiency and effectiveness of getting work done, e.g. work processes, use of management and technical software tools, or management practices.

A SCRAM review is conducted by a team of typically five people certified to participate in a SCRAM. It includes a certified team leader, two team members technically qualified to participate in a SCRAM for the type of project involved, a source material expert (SME), and a scheduling expert. Certification is granted by CASG after participation in a training program, demonstration that the candidate understands the SCRAM methodology, and passing an exam.

4. SCRAM Successes

SCRAM has been used for over ten years and has proven its value in a variety of application domains including aerospace, maritime, communications, space, training, logistics, and mission planning. The RCASS model is general and is applicable to software-intensive programs and to programs with no software involvement (e.g., ship maintenance). SCRAM reviews span both acquirer and contractor organizations. Much of SCRAM's success is due to the non-advocate, collaborative and transparent approach that serves to build trust and reduce defensiveness from programs and projects being reviewed. The following comments from the government Joint Program Office for the largest defense program ever undertaken, the F-35 Joint Strike Fighter, provides testimony to SCRAM usefulness:

"The SCRAM reviews were very collaborative...When we went forward with the results to our senior leadership, it was a jointly endorsed assessment. You gave us plenty of time to concur with your assessment or not. In short, we felt SCRAM was great."

- William Urschel, F-35 Software Director, Joint Program Office (2012-2015)

Nowhere is the transparency and collaborative nature of SCRAM as important as when using program data to forecast critical milestone dates. In our experience, the first question typically asked by any program when asked to provide data for forecasting is "how can this hurt us?" This is a natural and understandable concern because data is often gathered and used to make forecasts without a full understanding of the context surrounding the data. People often take data and "run with it." In contrast, part of the SCRAM forecasting methodology is to spend great care ensuring that data is understood, is summarized correctly, that any apparent anomalies are explained or corrected and only then, is data entered into the dynamic forecasting model. In addition, contractors are given the opportunity to observe the modeling and are presented with the results prior to anyone else seeing them (including the government program office). This goes a long way to dispelling concerns. Equally important, it greatly increases the likelihood of having valid, correct data.

Over the years, the SCRAM milestone forecasts have proven to be quite accurate. SCRAM Reviews included forecasts for the F-35 onboard software (approximately nine million lines of source code) and the off-board support software encompassing logistics, training, and mission planning. A testimony as to the accuracy of those forecasts was provided by Lt. Gen. Christopher Bogdan, the former Program Executive Officer for the F-35 Program:

"SCRAM gave us new techniques for measuring the progress of software development and for predicting how long the software development was going to take. In 2014, I briefed the SCRAM results to the Defense Acquisition Board. Of all the organizations that were making estimates, the SCRAM estimates, in hindsight, were the most accurate."

-- Lt. Gen. Christopher Bogdan, Program Executive Officer, F-35 Program (2012-2017)

Perhaps no other evidence is more telling of the value of SCRAM than the fact that several complex, multi-phase programs have requested multiple SCRAM Reviews over a period of years at their cost and on their own initiative. In the words of one program staff member:

> ***"We know when our program is going off the rails but we often don't know why. The SCRAM Team can bring independent eyes to quickly identify why things are starting to go off track. That's been very helpful for us"***
>
> ***Mr. Robert Jackson, Chief Engineer, ANZAC System Program Office, Australian DoD***

5. Conclusion and Summary

The private and public sectors of commerce have been plagued by projects that are delivered late, over budget, and sometimes lacking the required quality. Industry has adopted models and standards to improve quality and the ability to deliver on time and within budget (such as the CMMI and ISO 9000), but still many projects fall behind schedule even when developed by organizations rated high on the CMMI or ISO 9000. SCRAM has been demonstrated to be a very effective method to determine the ability to meet critical milestones, and can be used to great effect by development contractors and by acquiring organizations to monitor their contractor's ability to meet critical dates. It is a very effective adjunct to the CMMI, ISO 9000, and other process improvement models and standards.

We believe there is no reason to abandon the use of PPMs. SCRAM experience indicates that it is a highly valuable addition to the program management toolkit. Currently under development by the SCRAM development team is a detailed taxonomy of technical implementation risks called TIRA (**T**echnical **I**mplementation **R**isk **A**ssessment). For example, decisions that are made concerning the development approach to be taken (e.g. custom vs commercial off-the-shelf (COTS) based development) can result in a specific set of risk areas. The risks identified in TIRA will facilitate development teams in better identifying the risks that may impact their projects and its schedule and to take steps to mitigate those risks.

References

Nunn-McCurdy Breach, *Defense Acquisition Guidebook, Chapter 10*

Pitman, Adrian; Tuffley, Angela and Clark, Betsy. SCRAM: A method for assessing the risk of schedule compliance [online]. In: 22nd Australasian Software Engineering Conference: ASWEC 2013. Barton, A.C.T.: Engineers Australia, 2013: 45-58.

Chrissis, Mary Beth, Konrad, Mike, and Shrum, Sandy. *CMMI for Development*, Addison Wesley, Third Edition, 2011.

Chaos Engineering and Testing for Availability and Resiliency in Cloud

Authors

Krithika Hedge (krithika_hedge@mcafee.com)
Amith Shetty (amith_shetty@mcafee.com)

Abstract

As enterprises embrace the cloud for large-scale distributed application deployments, it has become crucial to making sure that systems are always available and resilient to failures. We are quick to adopt practices that increase the flexibility of development and velocity of deployment. But as systems scale, we expect part of the infrastructure to fail ungracefully in random and unexpected ways. We must design cloud architecture where part of the system can fail and recover without affecting the availability of the entire system.

We make our architecture fault-tolerant and resilient by adopting multi-availability zone deployments, multi-region deployments, and other techniques. However, it is equally important to test these failure scenarios to be confident about surviving in these disruptions and recovering quickly. Functional specifications fail to describe distributed systems because we cannot characterize all possible inputs, thus the need to validate system availability in production with chaos engineering.

This paper explains how our teams can take small first steps in learning and building Chaos Engineering and Testing tools for cloud deployment in Amazon Web Services. If adopted and experimented in a controlled manner, we will be able to learn system behavior in a chaotic state and design preventive actions to recover from disaster situations and reduce the downtime.

Biography

Amith Shetty is a Technical Lead, at McAfee, based in Bangalore, India. He has over 10 years of experience in building applications in Microsoft .NET technology stack. He is experienced working on highly scalable, fault tolerant cloud applications with Amazon Web Services.

Krithika Hegde is a Senior Software Development Engineer at McAfee, with over 8 years of experience in product development and Integration Activities She has participated in various product life cycles and been a key contributor to various releases within McAfee. She is passionate about leveraging technology to build innovative and effective software security solutions.

Atul Ahire is an SDET at McAfee, with more than 6 years of experience in Software Development, Test Automation, Build Release and Deployment. His areas of interest include Cloud solution design, deployment, and DevOps.

1. Introduction

Over the years we have seen drastic changes in the way systems are built and the scale at which they operate. With the scale comes the complexity and there are so many ways these large-scale distributed systems can fail. Modern systems built on cloud technologies and microservices architecture have a lot of dependencies on the internet, infrastructure, and services which you do not have control over. It has become difficult to ensure that these complex systems are tested to be always on, resilient and fault tolerant. Confidence in distributed system behavior can be determined by experimenting with worst-case failure scenarios in production or close to production.

When we develop new or existing software, we toughen our implementation through various forms of tests. We often refer to this as a test pyramid that illustrates what kinds of tests we should write and to what extent. This pyramid at a minimum consists of Unit Tests, Integration Tests, and System Tests.

When creating unit tests, we write test cases to check the expected behavior. The component we are testing is free of all its dependencies and we keep their behavior under control with the help of mocks. These types of tests cannot guarantee that the system as a whole is free of errors.

Integration tests test the interaction of individual components. These are ideally run automatically after the successfully tested unit tests and test-interdependent components. We achieve a very stable state of our application with these tests, but only under real conditions of production environments, we see how all the individual components of the overall architecture behave. This uncertainty is increased with the adoption of modern microservice architectures, where set of possible system states grows exponentially over time.

Chaos Engineering is the discipline of experimenting on a distributed system to build confidence in the system's capability to withstand turbulent conditions in production. Chaos Testing is a deliberate introduction of disaster scenarios into our infrastructure in a controlled manner, to test the system's ability to respond to it. This is an effective method to practice, prepare, and prevent/minimize downtime and outages before they occur. Traditional testing methods mentioned above are necessary for every system. Most of these testing methods determine the validity of a known scenario under a given condition, whereas Chaos testing is one of the ways to generate new knowledge by experimenting complicated scenarios which these tests are not expected to cover.

2. Principles of Chaos Engineering

The term Chaos Engineering was coined by Engineers at Netflix. The idea of Chaos engineering is instead of waiting for systems to fail in production, perform experiments and proactively inject failures to be ready when disaster strikes. Chaos Engineering is all about running experiments and these experiments are designed based on the following principles (Principles of Chaos Engineering 2018).

Figure 1: Principles of Chaos Engineering

1. Define system's normal behavior: The Steady state can be defined as some measurable output like overall throughput, error rates, the latency of a system that indicates normal behavior.
2. Hypothesize about the steady state: Make assumptions about the behavior of an experimental group, as compared to a stable control group.
3. Vary real-world events: Expose experimental group to experiments by introducing real-world events like terminating servers, network failures, latency, etc.
4. Observer Results: Test the hypothesis by comparing the steady state of the control group and experimental group. The smaller the difference, the more confidence we have in the system.

3. Real-World Example of Chaos Experiment

Let us look at some examples that can be considered for experiments. Injecting failures such that individual pieces of the infrastructure become unavailable is a good way to learn about decoupling in systems.

1. Let us assume that our application performs compute-intensive operations like mathematical calculations. Resources like CPU and memory are limited on standalone machines. When number of computations increases, the application will be forced to handle lack of resource. We can test the precautions taken by the development team to handle the resource exhaustion verify that steady state remains unaltered throughout the experiment.
2. Let us say we are building a music streaming service with microservice architecture. This application has a recommendation service which recommends music to users based on history. When these services are built as loosely coupled independent services, deployed separately, it is a common scenario for services to go down for shorter or longer duration of time, or not reachable over the network. As a common practice, we can fall back to graceful behavior, subtlety return recommendations from a cache or a list of static content to the user in this scenario. We can use chaos experiments to simulate this failure of network or instance and find out if the system behaves as expected.

With such cost-effective experiments, we will be able to disprove our hypothesis and find weaknesses in system behavior.

4. Chaos Engineering in Practice

Chaos experiments should be designed by considering a collection of services as a single system to understand the behavior of the system rather than testing individual components in the system. Following is the overview of the process involved in designing chaos experiments (Casey, et al. 2017).

4.1. Prerequisites

1. As stated in principles, chaos engineering is all about discovering the unknowns, if you know that your system cannot withstand failures, fix those problems first.
2. Have monitors in place which can provide visibility into the steady state of the system and help in making conclusions about experiments. There are two classes of metrics which can determine your steady state.
    a. Business metrics: Business metrics are the numbers that indicate activities in the system, that have a direct impact on the revenue. For example, in e-Commerce systems, how many checkouts are successful over time? Metrics can also be answers to questions like, is each customer happy with response time of the application and not quitting before checkout? Typically, these metrics are harder to implement than system metrics. These metrics should be a matter of continuous monitoring in contrast to the calculations at end of the month.
    b. System metrics: System metrics measure and monitor the overall health of the system. For example, CPU usage, memory, disk usage, response time, error rate of the APIs etc. These can help to troubleshoot performance issues and sometimes functional bugs.

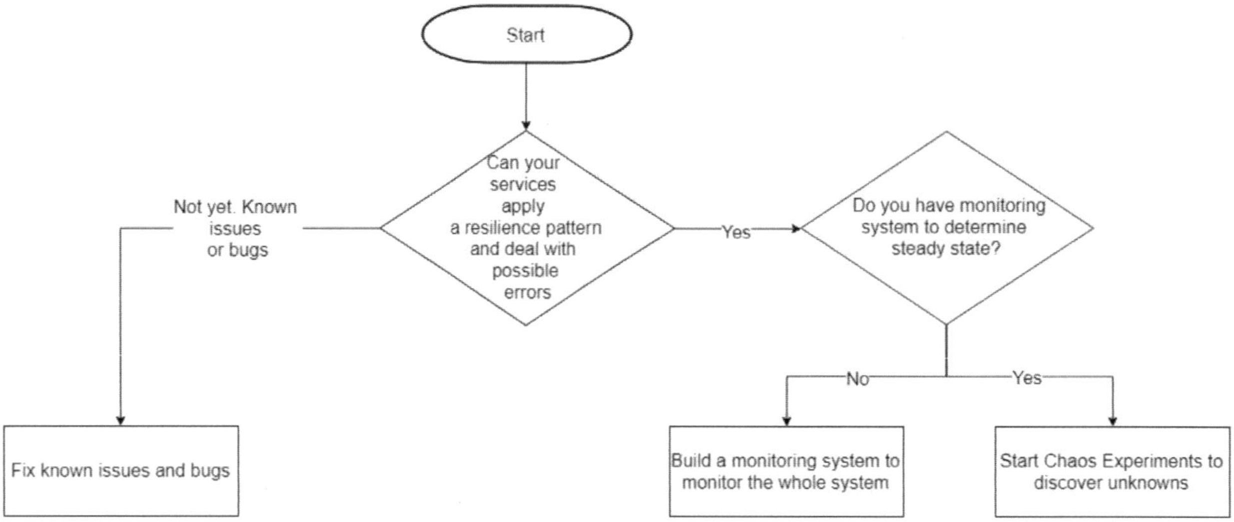

Figure 2: Prerequisites

4.2. Designing Experiments

Let us look at the process involved in designing chaos experiments in general.

4.2.1. Pick a Hypothesis

System behaviors are generally categorized as acceptable behaviors and unexpected behaviors. The normal state of the system should be considered as the steady state. The goal of this step is to develop a model that characterizes the steady state of the system based on business metrics. If a system is new, steady state is determined by regular testing of the application and collecting metrics over time which can portray the healthiest state of the system.

Once we have the steady state behavior and metrics, we can derive Hypothesis for the experiment. Hypothesis chosen here will be believed as the output of the experiment. If we have a strong hypothesis about the steady state, designing experiments becomes easy as we precisely know what experiments to create instead of creating uncontrolled Chaos. Since Chaos Engineering is to ensure the reliability or the graceful degradation of systems, the hypothesis for the tests should be in line with the statement "the events we will inject into the system will not result in a change from the steady state."

4.2.2. Choose the Scope of the Experiment

While planning the experiments we need to carefully consider how far we need to go to learn something useful about the system. We define the area which can get affected by the experiment as its blast radius and it should be as minimal as possible. The scope of the experiment should be determined to minimize the impact on real customers if running on production and in general. Although running tests closer to production will yield better results as the real events often happen to occur in production, not containing the blast radius can cause customer pain. Start experiments in test environments initially, and start with the smallest possible tests, until you gain confidence and then simulate bigger events.

4.2.3. Identify the System/Business Metrics

A central metric system could be capturing metrics for multiple services. Out of these metrics, identify the correct metrics which you can use to evaluate the results of the experiments chosen.

We should be very particular about evaluating the result of a test by relating it to a metric. For example, if our hypothesis states that an instance under our load balancer in auto scaling group is terminated, it should have no impact on the system. "No impact" is measured by checking the metrics. Number of failed requests for orders should be zero, the response time of the service falls in the expected range etc. Metrics will also help to identify when to abort the experiments if there is a larger impact.

4.2.4. Notify Teams

It is important to discuss and notify the teams which handle the service about the experiments going to be carried out so that they are prepared to respond. This is required at initial stages of adapting Chaos Engineering. Once all teams are used to these types of experiments, teams gain confidence and they will start incorporating correct measures to withstand these tests in the development phase and they would start perceiving these exercises as normal events. If experiments are run in production, we should inform support and community staff which may start receiving questions from customers.

4.2.5. Run the Experiment

At this step, we start executing our experiments and start watching metrics for abnormal behavior. We should have abort and rollback plan in place in case the experiment causes too much system damage or impact real customers. Alert mechanisms should be in place to act upon if there is too much variation in the critical metrics and handle customer impact. Our experiments should simulate real-world events. Experimenting and fixing events such as CPU exhaustion, Memory overload, network latency and failure, functional bugs, significant fluctuations in the input, retry storms, race conditions, dependency failures, and failures in communication between services can increase confidence in the reliability of the system.

4.2.6. Analyze the results

Analyze the metrics once the experiment is complete. Verify if the hypothesis was correct or there was a change to the system's steady state behavior. Identity, whether there was any adverse effect on customers or the system, was resilient to the failures injected. Share result of the experiment with the service teams so that they can fix them. The harder it is to deviate from the system behavior with the experiments, the higher the trust in the reliability of the system. Look at recurring patterns in design or issues that need to be addressed and encourage teams to test for resilience early in the product lifecycle.

4.2.7. Increase the Scope

As our experiments with smaller inputs and scope start succeeding, we can start increasing the scope. For example, smaller tests can target one host at a time under a load balancer. Start scaling it to take down two or more in further experiments. to test for resilience earlier in their lifecycle.

4.2.8. Automate

Initial experiments can be started with the manual process as it is safer to run manual tests than ruining a buggy script with unknown outcomes. As we gain confidence it the system we should start automating the tests so that we can save time and execute tests frequently.

4.3. Sample Inputs for Experiments

Experiments vary depending on the architecture of the systems being built. However, in a distributed system and microservices architecture deployed on cloud following are the most common experiments that can be automated with open source and commercial tools.

- Turning off instances randomly in availability zone (or data center)
- Simulating the failure of an entire region or availability zone.
- Resource exhaustion: Exhausting CPU and Memory on instances.
- Partially deleting stream of records/messages over a variety of instances to recreate an issue that occurred in production.
- Injecting latency between services for a select percentage of traffic over a predetermined period.
- Function-based chaos (runtime injection): randomly causing functions to throw exceptions.
- Code insertion: Adding instructions to the target program and allowing fault injection to occur prior to certain instructions.

The opportunities for chaos experiments are boundless and may vary based on the architecture of your distributed system and your organization's core business value.

5. How We Got Started

In this section, we will focus on a few applications which our teams are responsible for and the chaos experiments carried out to find weaknesses.

5.1. Identity Service

Application: Identity service is one of the key services which is part of our Management Platform. This acts as central service to provide Authentication and authorization to all other services so that each application need not build its own authentication service. This service generates OAuth based identity and access tokens. This service becomes critical service as the other services depend on the token generated by this. Thus, it was crucial for us to make sure this service is always available and resilient to failures.

Architecture: To make this service highly available, we chose to deploy this on AWS and make use of managed services to reduce the operating cost.

1. Stateless application servers containing microservice were deployed on EC2 instances in 3 availability zones (AZ-#).
2. Application servers are placed under Elastic Load Balancer.
3. Auto-scaling enabled with Minimum one system in each availability zone and auto-scaling rules set to scale based on a number of parameters.
4. Cold stand-by set up in a secondary region to failover in case of region failure.
5. 6 node Cassandra cluster across 3 availability zones with Quorum consistency.

Deployments: Following is a typical deployment model for high availability in AWS

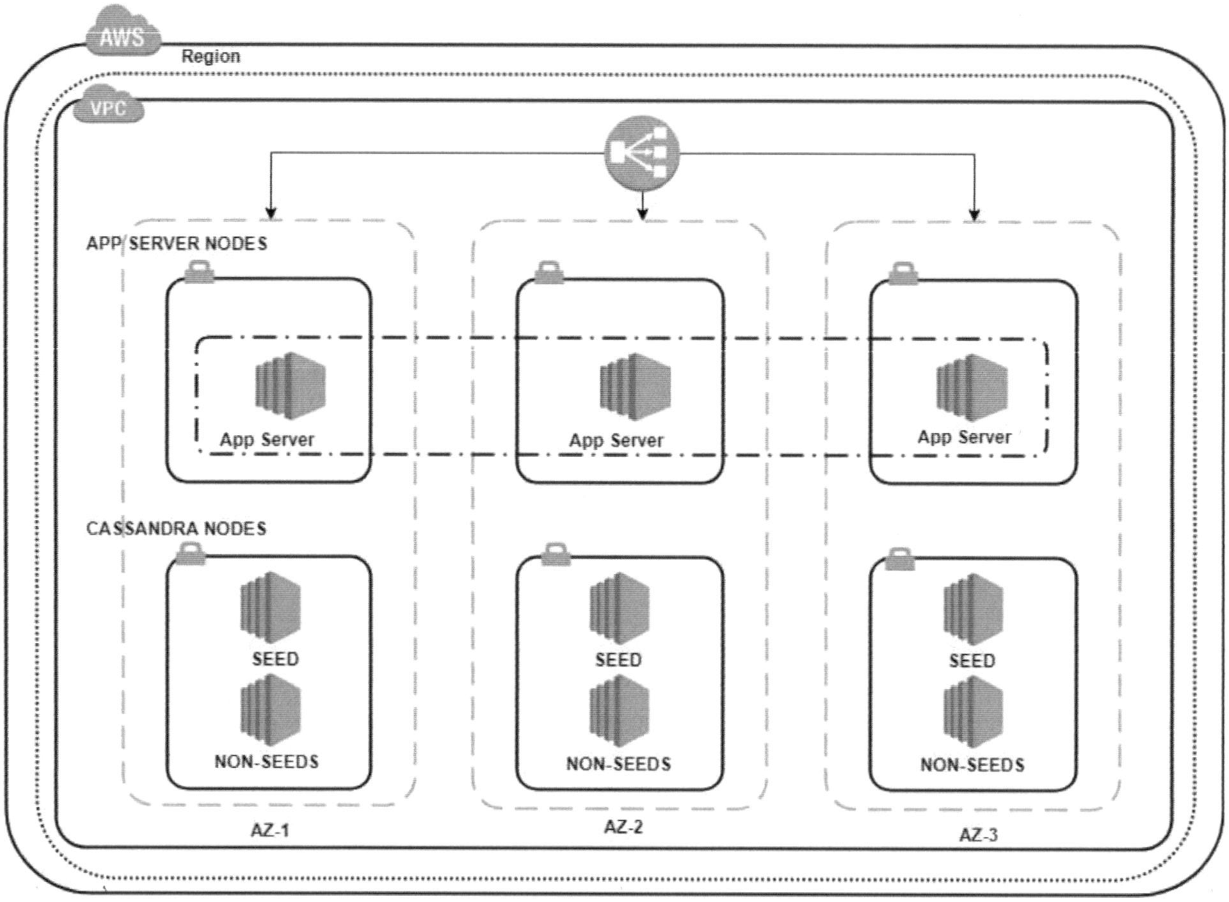

Figure 3: AWS Deployment Diagram

5.1.1. Experiment – Host Failures

Target: Identity Service

Experiment Type: EC2 instance failure

Steady State: All requests to token endpoint (API serving tokens) return tokens with no failures

Hypothesis: If a single instance of EC2 hosting the identity service application fails, rest of the services should be able to handle the request. There will be no impact on the tokens generated. A new EC2 instance should come up with the application deployed on it and join the load balancer. While the new instance is coming, we might see an increase in response time for the requests.

Blast radius: Contained to a Single instance

Metrics: Kibana dashboard showing number of failed requests to token endpoints

Simulation: During the initial days of the experiment we started this in manual mode. The manual test was as simple as terminating one of the EC2 instances from AWS console. Our API test automation suite (Gatling tests) was continuously sending requests to token endpoint throughout the duration of the experiment.

Results and Findings: When the EC2 instance was shut down, auto-scaling group configuration and scaling policies determined the change and started the process of launching a new instance. Requests coming in during this duration were handled by other two instances and we did not see any failed requests, which proved our hypothesis correct. As you can notice in the below screenshot from Kibana dashboard, all requests results returned 200 and none of the requests returned response error codes such as 500.

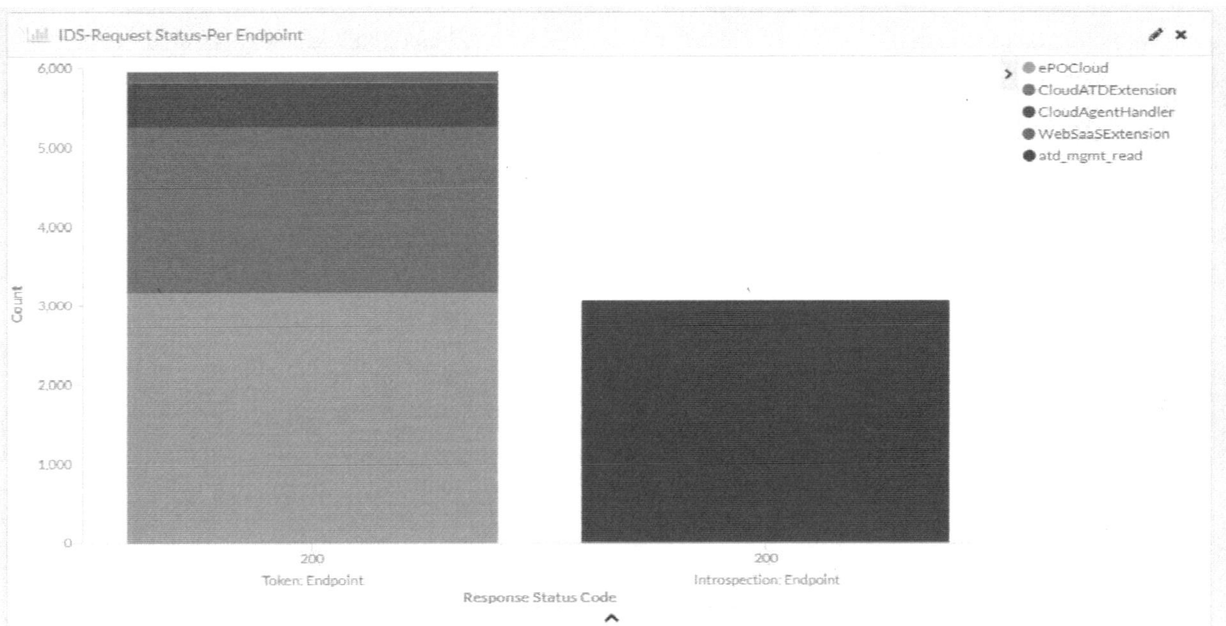

Figure 4: Steady state of requests from Kibana

It can be observed from the below reports that more than 2000 requests show response times greater than 800 ms. This increase in response time was observed at the time when one instance was terminated.

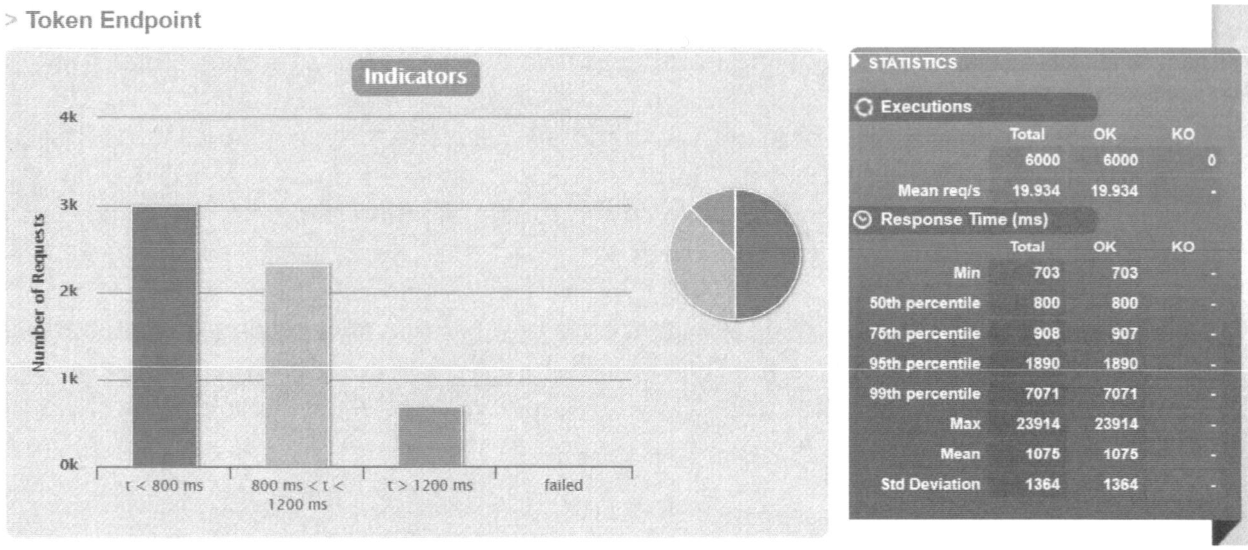

Figure 5: Status of requests

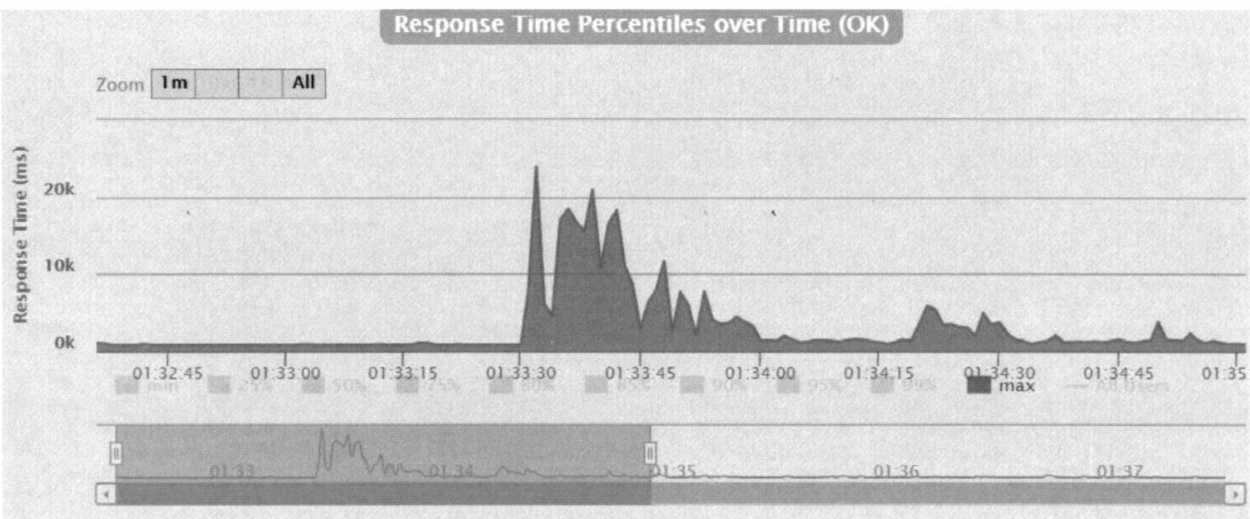

Figure 6: Increase in response time with a single machine

Once we gained confidence in such manual tests, we moved on to use Chaos Monkey for terminating random instances in the setup. Once the experiments are stable we started scaling up the scenario by increasing the number of instances that fail and repeat the experiment.

5.1.2. Experiment 2

Target: Cassandra DB Nodes

Experiment Type: Un-reachable DB nodes and DB node restarts

Steady State: All requests to token endpoint (API serving tokens) return tokens with no failures

Hypothesis: Our Cassandra data store runs with a setup of 3 nodes. Key-space is initialized with replication-factor of 3. Read and write operations are processed on a QUORUM consistency level, i.e saving a new record will succeed only if at least two of the 3 nodes receive the new record. A select query will return record only if at least two of the three nodes return the record. If there is a problem with one of the nodes and it is not reachable by other DB nodes or the application server, service should continue to work as the consistency level is set to QUORUM.

Blast radius: Single Cassandra DB node

Metrics: Kibana dashboard showing number of failed requests to token endpoints

Simulation: We started this experiment in manual mode by blocking access to Cassandra Port – 7000 through AWS security groups. This made the node unable to communicate with other nodes in the ring. API test tool was continuously sending token requests.

Results and Findings: With QUORUM consistency set, the application can perform queries on DB without error when one node is not available. No failures were observed on the dashboard which proved our hypothesis.

Automation: We started using a tool like Blockade and Muxy to simulate these failures. Blockade is a utility for testing network failures and partitions in distributed applications. Blockade uses Docker containers to run application processes and manages the network from the host system to create various failure scenarios.

5.3. Order Management System

Order management system is a collection of multiple microservices facilitating customer orders for Endpoint solutions. This solution consists of a collection of REST APIs, built as microservices communicating with each other over HTTP. Order Data Service and Product Catalog services are two among other microservices in this system. Order Data service makes a call to Product catalog service to fetch information about Product SKU being placed.

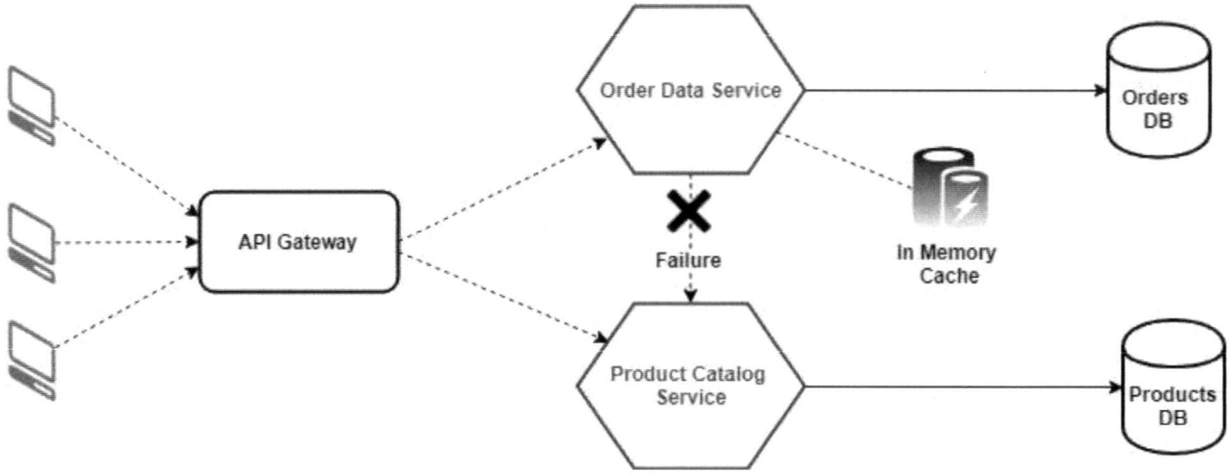

Figure 7: Services interaction

5.2.1. Experiment – Network Failure, Retry Storms

Target: Product Catalog Service

Experiment Type: Network Failure, Retry Storms

Steady State: All orders received by order data service are successfully accepted for processing.

Hypothesis: If product catalog service goes down because of a node failure, or order data service is not able to connect to product catalog service, a retry mechanism will try again for 3 times. If 3 retries fail, order data service should call In-memory cache to get details of the product which is being placed.

Blast radius: Contained to product catalog service

Metrics: Dashboard showing number of orders failed to process

Simulation: To begin with, we took manual steps. We blocked access to port 8443 on the instance where product catalog service was hosted. Test tools started sending requests to order data service. In later stages, we used Blockade and Latency Monkey for this experiment.

Results: When the number of requests were low, order data service was able to handle the retries and return the cache for product catalog response after 3 retries. However, as the number the requests started increasing we started seeing an interesting failure scenario. Our CPU utilization on the order data service started spiking up and requests started to fail.

Findings: So, what went wrong with the retry mechanism? This unavailability or failure to connect is not due to any problem in the service, but due to some reasons like network failure or server overload. Such issues are ephemeral. If we call the service again, chances are that our call will succeed. Such failures are called transient failures. Simple retry mechanisms work when transient failures are of short duration. However, if the duration is longer, our application will end up retrying, waiting and retrying till the maximum retry count is hit and thus wasting resources. So, we should have some mechanism to identify long-lasting transient faults and let this retry mechanism not come into play when we have identified the fault as a long-lasting transient fault.

Fixing: Circuit Breaker pattern is a better approach to handle the long-lasting transient faults. In this pattern, we wrap the service calls in a circuit breaker. When the number of retry failures reaches above a certain threshold value, we change the status of the circuit to OPEN, which means the service is not available at the time. Once the circuit reaches the OPEN state, further calls to the service will immediately return failure to the caller instead of executing retry logic. This circuit breaker will have some timeout period after which it will move to HALF-OPEN state. In this state, it will allow a service call which will determine if the service has become available or not. If the service is not available, it goes back to OPEN state. If the service becomes available after this timeout, the circuit breaker moves to the CLOSED state. The callers will be able to call the service and the usual retry mechanism will come into play again.

This helped in reducing all the retry execution in case the fault is long lasting and thus saving resource and providing more immediate feedback to the order data service.

6. Benefits of Chaos Engineering

6.1. Customer

- Benefits of chaos engineering at the top level can be measured by overall system availability. Companies pioneered in Chaos Engineering like Netflix, Amazon defines their availability for most of the services in terms of 4 to 6 9s or even more. Four nines availability mean that a system is available 99.99% of the time (or less than 1 hour a year). Translating these numbers into actual outage time can indicate why availability matters the most. Frequent chaos experiments make systems more resilient to failures and increase these numbers which makes happy customers.

6.2. Business

- Can help prevent extremely large losses in revenue and maintenance costs. Outages can cost companies millions of dollars in revenue depending on the usage of the system and the duration of the outage (Chaos Engineering : Breaking Your Systems for Fun and Profit 2017).
- Increases confidence in carrying out disaster recovery methods. Most teams do not have enough confidence in full-scale disaster recovery as they perform these tasks

only in extreme disaster cases. If the whole system has adopted principles of chaos engineering, disaster recovery practices can be performed more often to gain confidence.

6.3. Technical

- The insights from chaos experiments can mean a reduction in incidents.
- Helps teams to see how systems behave on failure and prove that their hypothesis is valid
- Chaos Engineering also tests the human involvement in the system like the response of engineers to the incidents. It can verify when an outage occurs if the right alert was raised and the appropriate engineer was notified to take appropriate action.
- Increases engagement of engineers to make applications highly reliable as they put more effort to make application reliable to sustain the chaos tests from the early stages of the development.

7. Tools & Techniques

Following are various open source and commercial products available for performing chaos experiments:

1. The Netflix Simian Army (The Netflix Simian Army 2011): Simian army consists of several services in the cloud for generating various kinds of failure.
    a. Chaos Monkey: Randomly terminates virtual machine instances and containers that run inside of your environment. The service operates at a controlled time (does not run on weekends and holidays) and interval (only operates during business hours).
    b. Chaos Kong: Simulates AWS region failure by injecting failures for all resources in a region. Best suited for disaster recovery testing to determine Recovery Time Objective (RTO) & Recovery Point Object
2. Chaos toolkit: This tool kit aims to be the simplest and easiest way to explore building your own Chaos experiments. Built as a vendor and technology independent way of specifying chaos experiments by providing Open API. https://docs.chaostoolkit.org/
3. Kube-Monkey: This is an implementation of Chaos Monkey for Kubernetes cluster. It randomly deletes Kubernetes pods to experiment with the resiliency of cluster. kube-monkey runs at a pre-configured hour on weekdays and builds a schedule of deployments that will face a random Pod failure sometime during the same day.
4. Pumba : Chaos testing and network emulation tool for Docker containers and clusters.
5. Gremlin; Gremlin offers a failure-as-a-service tool to make chaos engineering easier to deploy. It includes a variety of safeguards built in to break infrastructure responsibly
6. Chaos lambda: Chaos Lambda increases the rate at which EC2 instance failures occur during business hours, helping teams to build services that handle them gracefully. Every time the lambda triggers it examines all the Auto Scaling Groups in the region and potentially terminates one instance in each. The probability of termination can be

changed at the ASG level with a tag, and at a global level with the Default Probability stack parameter.

7. Chaos monkey for spring boot: This project provides a Chaos Monkey for Spring Boot application and will try to attack your running Spring Boot App.
8. Blockade: Blockade is a utility for testing network failures and partitions in distributed applications. Blockade uses Docker containers to run application processes and manages the network from the host system to create various failure scenarios. A common use is to run a distributed application such as a database or cluster and create network partitions, then observe the behavior of the nodes. For example, in a leader election system, you could partition the leader away from the other nodes and ensure that the leader steps down and that another node emerges as leader.
9. WireMock : API mocking (Service Virtualization) as a service which enables modeling real-world faults and delays.
10. ChaoSlingr : ChaoSlingr is a Security Chaos Engineering Tool focused primarily on the experimentation on AWS Infrastructure to bring system security weaknesses to the forefront.
11. Muxy: Muxy is a proxy that mucks with your system and application context, operating at Layers 4, 5 and 7, allowing you to simulate common failure scenarios from the perspective of an application under test; such as an API or a web application. https://github.com/mefellows/muxy

8. Best Practices

Many organizations are reluctant to break the systems on purpose considering the risks involved as the experiments are run in production. We can follow some of the best practices that have evolved from the experience of people in the chaos community to mitigate the risks.

- **Minimize the blast radius:** Begin with small experiments to learn about unknowns. Only when you gain confidence, scale out the experiments. Start with a single instance, container or microservice to reduce the potential side effects.

- **Build v/s Buy:** Perform a study of on the tools available. Compare features available and time and effort required to build your own tools. Do not pick tools which perform random experiments as it would become difficult to measure the outcome. Use tools which perform thoughtful, planned, controlled, safe and secure experiments.

- **Start in the staging environment:** To be safe and get confidence in tests, start with staging or development environment. Once the tests in these environments are completely successful, move up to production.

- **Prioritizing Experiments:** Chaos experiments while running in production can have an impact on core business functionality. Several factors need to be considered while prioritizing the experiments.

- Categories your services as Tier1 (critical) and Tier 2(Non-Critical). This can be determined by factors such as the percentage of traffic a service receives, ability function with or without a fallback path etc. Start experiments with Tier 2 services to verify if the unavailability of these services is handled gracefully and core business functionalities are not affected. If an attack on Tier 2 service brings the system down, then this service need to be badged as a critical service.
- If your system is resilient to instance failure, start those tests firsts and then move on to experiments like latency injection and network failures which may require special tooling.
- Among the categories chosen above, prioritize the experiments which can be executed safely without causing business impact.

- **Be ready to abort and revert:** Make sure you have done enough work to stop any experiment immediately and revert the system back to a normal state. If experiment by any chance causes a severe outage, track it carefully and do an analysis to avoid it happening again.

- **Calculate cost and Return on Investments**: Business impact of the outages can vary based on the nature of the business. Impact on revenue in case of outages can be calculated by number of incidents, outages, and their severity. Compare this with the cost of chaos experiments and other alternate ways of reducing outages to arrive at a conclusion.

- **Don't do the experiments if the problem is known to exist:** Brainstorm with the team to understand systems known weaknesses. If you know that an experiment can result in failures or cause outage to the customer, do not perform it. Fix the known issues and then experiment. Perform your experiments in the following order.

    1. Known Knowns - Things you are aware of and understand
    2. Known Unknowns - Things you are aware of but don't fully understand
    3. Unknown Knowns - Things you understand but are not aware of
    4. Unknown Unknowns - Things you are neither aware of nor fully understand

9. Limitations

1. Unplanned, careless chaos can cause damage to applications and impact the customer experience.
2. Executing large-scale experiments in the cloud can become expensive
3. Failures in abort conditions and strategy can lead to downtime.

10. Conclusion

In today's interconnected, internet-based world, no system is safe from system failure. Most of the Organization's experience with the cloud and the distributed system has not been without glitches and some of them are major. Infrastructure can be volatile and can fail in ways dissimilar to the ones we had learned to expect using a data center. Apart from Infrastructure failures, APIs and services in large micros services ecosystem can fail for several reasons and it is important to make this system resilient and highly available. The key takeaway is that we need to plan and design around failures. Resiliency must be baked into our designs and plans.

One of the best ways for the failures to not impact customers, employees, partners, and your reputation, is to proactively find it and address it before they occur. Chaos engineering is one of the optimal and cost-effective ways to do this. Organizations that build distributed internet applications should consider chaos engineering as part of their Resiliency strategy.

The opportunities for chaos experiments are boundless and may vary based on the architecture of your distributed system and your organization's core business value. Cost of deploying chaos experiments can be significantly lesser than hiring several system admins to fix problems when they occur. Running chaos experiments on a regular basis is one of many things you can do to begin measuring the resiliency of your APIs. Making sure you have good visibility (monitoring) and increasing your fallback coverage will all help strengthen your own systems.

References

Casey, Rosenthal, Hochstein Lorin, Blohowiak Aaron, Jones Nora, and Basiri Ali. 2017. Chaos Engineering. Building Confidence in System Behavior through Experiments. O'REILLY.

2017. "Chaos Engineering : Breaking Your Systems for Fun and Profit." Gremlin. 12. https://www.gremlin.com/media/20171210%20%E2%80%93%20Chaos%20Engineering%20White%20Paper.pdf.

2018. Chaos Engineering: the history, principles, and practice. 06. https://www.gremlin.com/community/tutorials/chaos-engineering-the-history-principles-and-practice/.

2017. Netflix Technology Blog - Chaos Automation Platform. https://medium.com/netflix-techblog.

2018. Principles of Chaos Engineering. 05. http://principlesofchaos.org/.

Ratis, Pavlos. 2017. awesome-chaos-engineering. https://github.com/dastergon/awesome-chaos-engineering.

2011. The Netflix Simian Army. 07. https://medium.com/netflix-techblog/the-netflix-simian-army-16e57fbab116.

This page intentionally left blank.

From a Controlled Chaos to a Well-Oiled Machine: Agile & Develops Complement Each Other

Author

Rajasree Talla, Program Manager, New Relic Inc.

Abstract

Current thinking in the software industry demands that companies be ready to release a product whenever our customer is ready - not when the company is ready. It's also important to build and deliver software that's designed from the customer's viewpoint. It's no longer about, "Here's a cool feature that makes us look like awesome coders." It's about releasing increments that allow us to deliver features or capabilities that customers find valuable. Incorporating DevOps practices is desirable to deliver products faster, so you can get feedback faster, get to revenue faster, and compete effectively. Hearing from customers and going through transition of practicing DevOps, informed it's not easy and there is no prescribed way. This journey uncovered how closely being agile and practicing DevOps need to work together in order to achieve the true value.

This paper explains a company's journey to become a well-oiled machine -- how internal processes, tooling improvements, incorporating feedback loops supported with agile mindset helped us achieve this transformation providing incredible value to us as an organization and also to end-users. Key focus areas include the approach taken with these tracks:

- Adopting continuous integration, delivery & deployment
- Iterative development and agile mindset
- Incorporating feedback loops: build, measure and learn
- Building the muscle of continuous improvement

Biography

Rajasree Talla has about fifteen years of experience in software industry and has been part of agile transformations and practicing DevOps in various companies. With a passion in customers experience, she is keen in ensuring end user workflow remain the focal point of organizational transformations. Strong advocate of lean methodologies, being agile and continuous improvement. Trained as SAFe Agilist, Scrum master, Project management professional (PMP). She has masters in Engineering and technology management from Portland State University. She is co-author & editor of Planning and Roadmapping Technological Innovations: Cases and Tools . Enjoys speaking about DevOps & agile transformations and is a speaker at DevOpsdays.

Linkedin: https://www.linkedin.com/in/rajasree-talla/ Twitter: @rajasree_talla

1. Practicing DevOps

1.1. Why DevOps?

Customers expect companies to deliver software faster with a predictable cadence. Organizations expect to get feedback faster, revenue faster and also compete effectively. It is important to try to reduce the gap between development and feedback. This expectation doesn't differ much with various industry sectors like science, health, technology, consumer applications. One common question is 'How to enable organizations to be high performing?' Most of the companies try to align teams to optimize performance.

"In high-performing organizations, everyone within the team shares a common goal—quality, availability, and security aren't the responsibility of individual departments, but are a part of everyone's job, every day." (Kim, Debios, et al. 2016)

Focusing on a common goal and keeping customer experience intact is important. Removing the handoffs and barriers within the organization plays a key role. Not just the product development team, operations team is also part of this equation. That is where DevOps practices play a prominent role.

DevOps is the practice of operations and development engineers participating together in the entire service lifecycle, from design through the development process to production support. (Mueller 2018)

DevOps 'Infinity loop'

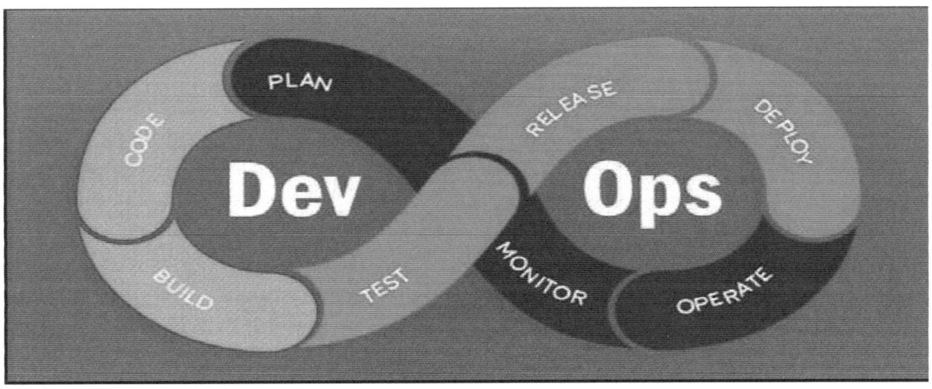

(Kulshrestha 2017)

Looking at what are the pieces in software lifecycle workflow in a simplified way in the image above. Communications and collaboration are keys to practice DevOps. Having feedback loops back to development from operations will have this effect of this infinity loop. Planning for a project developing code, testing & release cannot be is isolated from operations - deploying the code, monitoring. Feedback from monitoring the experience should flow back to planning. Tools

& internal process changes are required to optimize this flow. Many tools are available in market to optimize & automate this workflow. The benefit of having this working will lead us to not only high performing teams working on a common goal, but also help us with a consistent user experience seeking feedback along the way.

1.2. State of DevOps Report

Every year companies analyze what's new in DevOps practices to help them practice DevOps. We chose to review Puppet State of DevOps report 2017 by Puppet to understand challenges of practicing Devops. This is generated in collaboration with DORA (DevOps research and assessment). This analysis is from survey of responses from various IT industries. It's important to understand the current trend while adopting DevOps practices at an organization. This will help you serve as a resource for best practices and customize to your company needs. Below were key findings with the 2017 DevOps report. (Forsgren, et al. 2017)

- Transformational leaders share five common characteristics that significantly shape an organization's culture and practices, leading to high performance
- High-performing teams continue to achieve both faster throughput and better stability.
- Automation is a huge boon to organizations.
- DevOps applies to all organizations
- Loosely coupled architectures and teams are the strongest predictor of continuous delivery.
- Lean product management drives higher organizational performance

1.2.1. Why DevOps at Puppet?

Puppet is one of the leading configuration management tools used to practice DevOps.While Puppet's portfolio was evolving, the need to respond to customer's feedback also increased. Puppet team was making a significant effort to cut down on release cycles and react to learnings and feedback from field as quickly as possible. Being part of many DevOps transformations, Puppet understands the benefit of shifting the organization to adopt DevOps practices. In this case, 'learning & feedback', 'design for customer needs', ' focus on continuous improvement' , 'reduce time to market' served as key interests for this shift (Kersten 2017). With the support of our leadership Puppet was able to succeed through this transformation (Gazitt 2017)

2. Challenge in Hand

2.1. Context – Product

It is important to know the baseline before jumping into how we shift to adopt new practices. At Puppet we were looking at adopting DevOps practices in entire product and engineering organization. Major effort was in shifting the flag ship product "Puppet Enterprise". For context on the problem, this product is a commercial on premise offering of Puppet. Major releases of Puppet Enterprise product are scheduled to be generally available every six months. Let's discuss about some pain points before the transformation.

2.2. Unpredictable Releases

Releases were always planned with a fixed scope in hand. Scope here is the features we need release with attempt to detail and plan. There was some predictability with respect to the date of the release. New product iterations were released every six months. As a program manager of Puppet Enterprise, I always experienced a tension in the room about feature completion by this release time. Adjusting the release timeline according to the feature completion was the only solution. This approach led to release date and scope time adjustments at the very end of the release cycle. Not a great start to ideal go to market or customers experience.

2.3. Minimal Feedback at Development

Puppet already had a few mechanisms to capture feedback at early stages of a feature during discovery, definition, and early design. Technical advisory boards, market research are used during the discovery, definition of the customer problem & Puppet's opportunity. Usability research called test pilots is used during later part of definition, early design where users can provide feedback on prototypes. Not all features were generating prototypes. Once the feature is in development until its completion there was no feedback incorporated. This created a scenario where we had to sometimes to do a new patch release immediately to incorporate feedback and it was not the ideal customer experience.

2.4. Long Hardening Cycle – 6 to 8 Weeks

Hardening cycle was about eight weeks. Hardening here includes integration, performance, exploratory testing. It also includes time taken to get the release bits ready and stages. Risk was always high as we integrate all components work in the first couple of weeks of those eight weeks. There was at least two weeks spent on integrating all the component's code to the main release branch (Johnson 2017) (Talla 2017). Doesn't make it effective because most of the difficult tasks were pushed to end of the release cycle.

2.5. Water – Scrum – Fall: Handoffs

Puppet teams delivering this product were organized as scrum teams. They were practicing usual scrum rituals (standups, sprint planning, backlog grooming) and using tools to accommodate the same. Only developers were working from one backlog. Teams were focused on development, testing, documentation tasks separately. Centralized design, quality assurance and documentation team supported the development team (Gazitt 2017). Deliverable at end of a two week sprint was not a value add for user. It was an engineering task that will not make users realize value add directly unless the entire project is complete.

2.6. Continuous Integration System Always Red

Lot of great work went in to making sure existing continuous integration system automated and kept was up to date. These tests were acceptance level tests covering different components. Only throwback was that, it was failing most of the times with breaking code (Johnson 2017). Sometimes with transients that are intermittent failures which cannot be reproduced easily. Bringing it to complete green was an impossible task even at end of release cycle. We had to disable few tests and ignore transients to ensure release happens on time. Basically this system failed to serve the purpose. It helped with finding the problems just not at the right time.

2.7. Code in Production Only After Launch

Puppet's IT operations team uses Puppet to configure, deploy and maintain systems. Not every company has internal customers. They could be a great source of feedback. Pushing through most of the testing to end of the release cycle did not help. IT operations team were not able to install the builds before launch. It was a missed opportunity, but also reflects the quality of builds until right before launch (Talla 2017) (Gazitt 2017).

3. Bright New World!

There were lot of challenges in hand to shift this system at Puppet. Instead of focusing on efficiency, team started to look at what's being effective means at Puppet (Talla 2017). It took about eighteen months to see the complete benefit of adopting the DevOps practices. Puppet Enterprise now delivers a release every sprint (2 weeks) to customers as beta builds. Explained next are the key shifts noticed.

3.1. Continuous Integration Green

Getting the continuous integration system to all tests passing were the first tasks. We already had a system and making it work is all we had to do. This required pushing integration testing to further down in the workflow. Code is integrated as soon as it written. Thus reduced the cycle time between developer check in and integration into the main branch (Johnson 2017).

3.2. Continuous Delivery & Deployment

Releases are cut every weeks at the same time and day. These releases are installed by site reliability engineering team in to operations staging & production on day# 0. Code was actually in production every two weeks (Talla 2017). Beta program got the builds in to customer hands every two weeks

3.3. Minimum Hardening for GA – Less Than a Week

There is no separate time in the release cycle for integration. We integrate the code the mainline, the final destination as we go. Hardening is used for release preparation, allowing our go-to-market team to get things ready to launch day (Talla 2017).

3.4. Small Batches of Work

This required shift to iterative development. Deliverable at end of sprint are small stories with user value. Slicing of the feature in to such small batched of work became crucial to see value out of this framework. Started embracing agile mind set all along (Gazitt 2017).

3.5. Feedback in Entire Release Cycle

Customers or end users using this product via Puppet enterprise beta program every two weeks. Did not have to wait until the end of the release cycle. We are able incorporate feedback cycles into design, development & early delivery (Talla 2017).

While this transition wasn't easy, there was definitely no secret sauce or standard recipe to adopt DevOps practices. Every organization has unique needs and its own way to make this work.

4. Approach

We were challenged by our leadership to actually adopt the practices recommended by Puppet preaches and promotes to customers on DevOps. With a small group of cross functional team including myself as a program manager were trying to determine how and where should we start this transition.

4.1. Interviews & Findings

It was important to understand the problems from the people that were facing them. We had to understand the pain points. So we started interviewing various disciplines across the organization trying to understand where to focus, their perception of DevOps and also trying to find the low hanging fruits.

4.2. Tracks & Approach

Many good points were brought up and the cross functional group started sifting through the conversations, grouping the pain points. We separated these into three almost parallel tracks for execution

- Adopting continuous integration, delivery & deployment
- Iterative development and agile mindset

- Incorporating feedback loops: build, measure and learn
- Building the muscle of continuous improvement

4.2. Adopting Continuous Integration, Delivery, Deployment

To make other tracks work, it was important to get the tooling and automation in place for continuous integration, delivery & deployment work. Here is a view of how these three will impact the release cycle

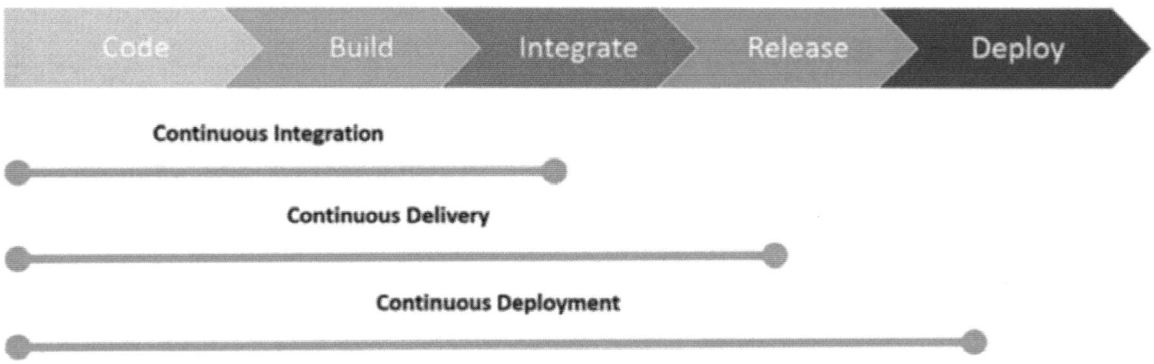

(Tiwari 2018)

4.2.1. Continuous Integration (CI)

CI system was already in working. We had to make shifts to advance the CI system and internal processes. All developers were asked to promote code early and often. Depending on the component most of the promotions were automated. This reduced the feedback time for developer check-ins. automated testing became a requirement at component level that mimics the integrated environment before merging to mainline. Getting CI green (passing all integration level tests) became everyone's responsibility instead of a single team owning the pipeline (Johnson 2017). This became the measure for quality of code.

4.2.2. Continuous Delivery (CD)

Implementing continuous delivery was major piece to get this adoption work. We had to look at the entire release process and make it as lean as possible. We reduced number of milestones and also heavy water fall stylish milestones. We tag a release every alternate Wednesday at end of sprint cycle. Rule of thumb was, if CI is red due to a code change, revert the change and there is always next release cycle to fix it. Don't hold up the release for that. Also implemented release branching as part of continuous improvement. Releases became predictable with this shift. The quality of builds being delivered as part of continuous delivery are at quality of a general availability build (Talla 2017)

4.2.3. Continuous Deployment

Started using IT operations team as our customer #0. As soon as the release is out this build is deployed in staging environment. Depending on the deployment and basic smoke testing build is pushed production on the day of the release. Every sprint a new build tagged as release is also available on the Beta website for the customer. Customers who signed the beta agreement were able to deploy the build on day#0 of the release. Production deployment was still a manual step. Continuous deployment forced the builds to have the quality of generally available release. Hardening cycle was completed reduced from six weeks to a week.

4.3. Iterative Development: Being Agile

This track was the most difficult as it needed a mindset shift on many areas of day to day work Inheriting the agile principles improved the quality of work. Teams were organized into autonomous self-sustaining teams (Broza, The Agile Mind-Set: Making Agile Processes Work 2015).

User design, testing & documentation teams started working from one backlog towards same goal. Centralized team structure for testing, design, documentation was dismantled. All the work items were present in scrum board.

Starting from how we define work to how execute and release software had to change. Product managers and UX designers started breaking the work into stories with user value. With continuous delivery & deployment it was possible to iterate (producing small batches of user value and adjust deliverables with feedback) on the feature before the big splash generally available release. Every team has unique challenges while decomposing a feature into increments of value. Keeping the feature value proposition intact while slicing the user stories was important.

Without disrupting existing work, selected couple of teams to test this shift. Focused on concepts that are biggest bang for the buck. We were already doing sprints and scrum rituals. Key changes at team level include

- Definition of done & acceptance criteria per story
- Getting use interface work into sprints
- Sprint demos & review stories with product owner, field engineers, usability team were significant
- Some teams had a definition of ready before starting development on a story
- Documentation and release notes developed incrementally as we develop user stories.

These changes shifted team's mindset. Testing is not just one person's responsibility. Team tested each other's story at component level manual testing. These new tests generated via test planning were automated for future use. It suddenly became a shared game instead of throwing over the wall. These best practices were shared among the teams. (Broza, The Agile Mind-Set: Making Agile Processes Work 2015).

We are able to get flexibility with the scope focusing on objective of learning and feedback After a complete release cycle of six months it was clear that leadership and parts of organization that enable go to market are shifting towards agile mindset and iterative approach (Broza, The Human Side of Agile - How to Help Your Team Deliver 2012).

4.4. Feedback Loops: Build, Measure & Learn

The most important benefit of iterative development is incorporating feedback into product development. This is incorporating feedback loops in a smallest batch of work we can produce. Below is how feedback loops were incorporated in to feature lifecycle

- Discovery of the feature technical advisory board and market research
- Definition & early design : Test pilots conducted by user interface designers
- Development : Customer #0 , beta, early access to partners
- After delivery measuring success, feature adoption and capturing feedback for future iterations.

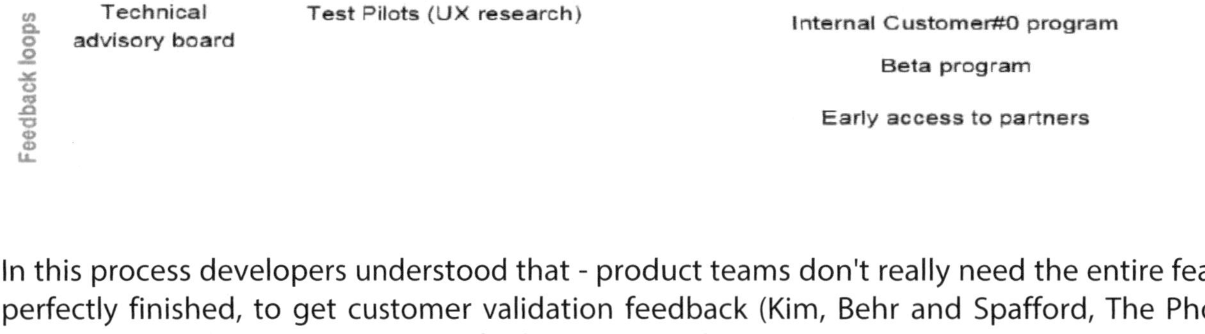

In this process developers understood that - product teams don't really need the entire feature, perfectly finished, to get customer validation feedback (Kim, Behr and Spafford, The Phoenix Project 2013). Sharing increments of value generated curiosity in our customers, and prompted them to provide helpful feedback, which made it easier for teams to develop software that was most useful to customers.

4.5. Continuous Improvement

At end of every sprint teams started doing retrospectives at team level & release level (Broza, The Agile Mind-Set: Making Agile Processes Work 2015). It is not possible to get everything working with guided set of principles for the first time. Internal process changes and molding the adoption to success was only possible with the ideas that came up from the retrospectives. Also fail fast mechanism helped us get to the releases every sprint quickly. This transformation of practicing DevOps was done incrementally and it is still evolving as a well-oiled machine. Building the muscle of continuous improvement is key for any organizations success.

5. Learnings & Conclusion

Many interesting facts were inferred from this transformation of a controlled chaos to a well-oiled machine. As an organization our prominent key learnings include

- Understand how to be effective before being efficient (Broza, The Human Side of Agile - How to Help Your Team Deliver 2012). This is important while developing any internal process or trying to get to high performing teams
- Business deadlines are unavoidable. Go to market activities are important for a successful product launch and get revenue. Agility may not work in all cases.
- User story definition to delivery in a single sprint is challenging. Depending on the feature this challenge varies. This is an art that can gained with experience.
- Tooling & process is not enough for a transformation to be successful - being Agile is actually a shift in mindset.
- Getting a cross-functional team together doesn't mean agile. Completing a story is shared effort is important to get the value of it.
- Shift to customer lens by incorporating feedback loops helps the organization including developers gain confidence in the code.

In a nutshell, streamlining internal processes support the transformation. Being agile is a mindset shift & practicing DevOps is a cultural shift. It is proven being agile & practicing DevOps complement each other.

References

Broza, Gil. 2015. *The Agile Mind-Set: Making Agile Processes Work.* 3P Vantage Media.
—. 2012. *The Human Side of Agile - How to Help Your Team Deliver.* 3P Vantage Media.

Forsgren, Dr. Nicole, Gene Kim, Jez Humble, Alanna Brown, and Nigel Kersten. 2017. *2017 State of DevOps Report.* Accessed July 23, 2018. https://puppet.com/resources/whitepaper/state-of-devops-report.

Gazitt, Omri. 2017. *Practicing DevOps at Puppet.* 11 December. Accessed July 23, 2018. https://puppet.com/blog/practicing-devops-puppet.

Johnson, AJ. 2017. *How our approach to code integration led to shared responsibility & CD.* 24 October. Accessed July 23, 2018. https://puppet.com/blog/how-our-approach-code-integration-led-shared-responsibility-cd.

Kersten, Nigel. 2017. *What is DevOps.* 30 January. Accessed July 23, 2018. https://puppet.com/blog/what-is-devops.

Kim, Gene, Kevin Behr, and George Spafford. 2013. *The Phoenix Project.* IT Revolution Press.

Kim, Gene, Patrick Debios, John Willis, and Jez Humble. 2016. *The Devops Handbook : How to create World class agility, reliability, security in technology organizations.* IT Revolution Press .

Kulshrestha, Saurabh. 2017. "How do I learn Devops." Edureka. *How do I learn Devops.* Accessed 2018. https://www.quora.com/How-do-I-learn-DevOps.

Mueller, Ernest. 2018. *DevOps Foundations: Lean and Agile.* 23 July. https://theagileadmin.com/tag/devops/.

Talla, Rajasree. 2017. *Continuous delivery at Puppet: from controlled chaos to a well-oiled machine.* 14 September. Accessed July 23, 2018. https://puppet.com/blog/continuous-delivery-puppet-controlled-chaos-to-well-oiled-machine.

Tiwari, Ajay. 2018. "Continuous Integration Vs Continuous Delivery Vs Continuous Deployment." Saviant Integration solutions. *Continuous Integration Vs Continuous Delivery Vs Continuous Deployment.* India. Accessed 2018. http://www.saviantconsulting.com/blog/difference-between-continuous-integration-continuous-delivery-and-continuous-deployment.aspx

This page intentionally left blank.

Is the Testing Role Relevant?

Authors
Sriratna Josyula (ratnaj@zillowgroup.com)
Jonathan Li On Wing (jli@zillowgroup.com)

Abstract
Testing is one of the fields of Software Engineering that has been very rapidly evolving over time. The latest evolution is the departure of the traditional testing roles. Various companies like Microsoft that had previously a ratio of 1:2 Software Development Engineers in Test (SDETs aka Testers) to Software Development Engineers (SDEs aka Developers), have converted their SDETs to generic Software Engineers.

Until about 5 years ago, product testing involved some combination of manual and automated testing that ran into hundreds, if not thousands of test cases. Turnaround time for test, would be anywhere from few days to few weeks. Once shipped, if a product had a major bug, it would be part of a service pack or the next version, testing for which would again consume the same amount of time as before.

Fast forward to the current day - software is largely shipped as services, instead of as products - which makes it very easy for bugs to be fixed if found. This is one of the biggest reasons that has caused companies to take a very different approach towards testing.

As a result, we see shorter test passes, faster ship cycles and fewer resources dedicated to testing. But, that does not mean that software can be shipped without being properly tested. This paper is an effort to shed light on what lies in the future for testing as a discipline and how to stay relevant in this field.

Biography
Sriratna Josyula is a Senior Software Test Lead at Zillow, in Seattle WA. She earned her Master's in Computer Science from University of Southern California. She has over 9 years of experience, working in various roles in test, starting from Validation Engineer to SDET to QA Manager, on products spread across the networking stack, from router firmware to advertising technologies.

Sriratna is passionate about all things related to quality. Her interests lie in improving software quality practices, project management and product management.

Jonathan Li On Wing is a Senior Engineering Manager at Zillow, in Seattle, WA. He earned his B.Sc. Cum Laude in Software Engineering from McGill University specializing in Artificial Intelligence and

Requirements Analysis. He has 12 years of industry experience in various roles working at small and large companies such as Microsoft, Oracle, Expedia, Groupon, and SMART Technologies.

Jonathan's interests lie in Human-Computer Interaction, Automated Testing and Software Life Cycle Processes. He believes in bringing testing upstream and has been improving software testing processes in several companies. Jonathan sees himself as a customer advocate and enjoys challenging everything.

1. Introduction & Motivation

Traditionally, the role of a person in test, whether it be a Software Tester, Software Test Engineer, Software Engineer in Test, or Software Development Engineer in Test was to sufficiently test a product and to "sign-off" that a piece of software was ready to be released. The term "Signing-off" came from other realms of engineering where an engineer had reviewed the specifications, verified that the project was compliant with any rules and regulations, verified that the project met the specifications, and to state that it was safe for usage.

This often led to a "throw over the wall" type of mentality, where Software developers would sometimes deliver sub-par quality software, just because they were not being held responsible for its quality. This was not only just a bad practice, but it also caused projects to often miss release deadlines because of time spent going back and forth between testing and development.

In the past decade, there has been a push to curb this mentality and make quality a team-oriented goal. There was a shift on accountability, where engineering teams were held accountable and not individual roles. However, if the engineering teams owned quality, why were there test roles? At that time, the thinking was that testers would still be the primary source of testing work -- both manual and automated -- but there would be an expectation that developers would help and that the throw over the wall mentality would disappear.

1.1. Evolving Role of the Tester

As the ownership of quality shifted towards the entire engineering team, the distinction between developers and testers got fuzzier. Companies started obscuring between the roles of developers and testers, and titles were merged. Teams went from having ratios closer to one tester per every two developers, to one tester per team.

Now, with the push towards Service Oriented Architecture and increased usage of telemetry the need for a specialist in manual and automated testing seems to be fading away. So, what does that mean to the testing role? Is it still relevant? Is it to disappear? What is the future? In this paper, we will discuss our thoughts of these questions.

First, we will look at what has led us to this point and study what some companies have done. We will then discuss what our belief of the next evolution of testing is, and how best to stay relevant. We conclude with a summary of our thoughts.

2. Evolving Approach Towards Testing

Historically, especially when we consider waterfall style methodologies, verification was performed by "testers". This was often the last step before the software was released. Typically, there would be a test plan written by testers and then that plan would be followed. These tests traditionally were manually executed, but later progressed to use more automation.

Nowadays, testing isn't a specific step in most lifecycles. It is a part of the development process, and it isn't as vigorous, detailed or specific. Testing tasks are shared across the team, and focus towards risky areas, likely scenarios, and happy paths.

2.1. Implications of Shared Testing Tasks

Making testing a "shared" responsibility had effects on both the testing role itself and product development. For the role, some companies have started merging testing and development roles into one. In some cases, testers would need to interview for development roles or be laid off. This will further be expanded in Section 3.

The implications on product development is that *shallower testing* is performed; hard to think of unhappy paths, the bread and butter of a testers' job, are often ignored. James Bach and Michael Boulton contrasts *deep testing* versus *shallow testing* in their Rapid Software Testing courses as: Testing is deep to the degree that it has a probability of finding rare, subtle, or hidden problems that matter.

Deep testing requires substantial skill, effort, preparation, time, or tooling, and reliably and comprehensively fulfills its mission.

By contrast, shallow testing does not require much skill, effort, preparation, time, or tooling, and cannot reliably and comprehensively fulfill its mission. (Bach & Bolton, *Rapid Software Testing*, 2017)

2.2 Why is There a Shift?

The main reasons why we see a shift in how companies approach testing is mainly because of (but not limited) to the following:

- Developing Software as a Service (SaaS) - building web services and applications instead of desktop applications.

- Shared Responsibility - quality is no longer just owned by the tester.
- Speed - moving fast and getting a product out faster to market is often prioritized over quality.
- Analytics and Telemetry - increased ability to monitor and find bugs in production.
- Partial Roll Outs - slowly dial users to use new functionality.
- Continuous Integration & Deployment - it is easier to ship or roll back changes.
- Microservice Architecture - moving away from monolithic applications.

2.2.1. Software as a Service (SaaS)

Developing desktop software applications typically involved long ship cycles and longer time to update (even more so in the period of installation via physical media). Additionally, one could not always guarantee that a user would install the update. Therefore, there was emphasis on the quality of every shipped version. With the shift to developing and deploying software as a service, software is very easily deployed, updated or rolled back. This meant that certain compromises could be made on quality, as long as some basic quality criteria were met.

2.2.2. Shared Responsibility

Many technology teams have moved to Lean and Agile methodologies, and this methodology challenges the need for separate development and test groups. They encourage having one team with a shared common goal. Everyone on the team is treated equally responsible and encouraged to take on any task.

2.2.3. Speed

Software is being built at a much faster pace than before, and companies want to get as many features out as possible, and as fast as possible. This does not necessarily mean that quality is not important. However, risk can be assessed, and a question can be raised as to how much testing is good enough. At a certain point, it will cost more to find a bug than to release the software as is.

2.2.4. Analytics and Telemetry

Tools and applications to help monitoring production code have been on the rise and becoming more sophisticated. Many tools now exist to help investigate production issues and to catch issues early on. With some such monitoring software even using advanced machine learning techniques, production issues can be identified even before they occur. Moreover, such analyses cannot only be done in production, but also in test environments. These tools help in making software more reliable and stable even before it is released to production.

2.2.5. Partial Roll Out

A/B testing has been widely used to test features to test experiments and see which version performs well and which one doesn't. This same framework can be used to limit user exposure to new features, thereby providing the advantage of releasing a new feature early, while also minimizing risk by not releasing it to 100% of a company's user base. By having good metrics, monitors, and alerts as mentioned above, companies could release a feature to 1% of users and see if there are any errors, bugs, or issues.

Gradually, they can dial up to 100% of users.

Additionally, this methodology has allowed companies to be able to cause brownouts where features can be quickly turned off while the engineering team fixes the bugs.

2.2.6. Continuous Integration & Deployment (CI/CD)

With modern build processes, each commit an engineer does, can automatically build, launch a test environment, apply a battery of tests, and ship it to a set of environments (including production).

Additionally, triggers could be set to automatically rollback to previous versions should bugs be found.

2.2.7. Microservice Architecture

Moving to microservices architecture has helped in a few ways. First, by breaking products into small logical services makes testing features and functionality easier. That is, it is easier to test in isolation, and a microservice architecture's goal is to isolate functionality into its own service.

Second, it is easier to ship a small web service to see how it performs and roll back if necessary. Third, based on our personal experiences, there seem to be less logical bugs in this type of architecture.

3. Case Studies

We chose to include these companies in our Case Studies because they are our current/ former employers. *These comments and studies are based on our experiences working at these companies and from the references cited. These comments are not official responses from companies.*

The purpose of these case studies is to highlight the transformation that is happening to the traditional software testing role.

We will consider three companies that we have had experiences with, Zillow, Expedia, and Microsoft. Although we talk about three companies, we believe that these changes are happening at various other companies as well, based on articles we read and speaking with engineers.

3.1. Zillow

Zillow has seen its test discipline re-structure from being a heavily SDET owned operation towards a developer **owned**, but test owner **driven** testing.

Most teams at Zillow now have a test owner (Test Lead or an SDET and/ or a Test Engineer) who is responsible for the overall test quality of the team's products.

Each test owner usually works with a team of about 8 developers. Test owner leads the testing effort, but responsibilities can vary between teams. Engineering teams decide what would be the best way to distribute test efforts among the team and proceed with the same for testing their features. For some teams, test owners take charge of test planning, execution, while developers write the test automation, for some others, test owners do the actual manual/automated testing, and for some other teams, test owners drive planning, test code reviews and releases. In most cases, developers own writing and maintaining test automation.

3.1.1. Zillow's Transformation of the Testing Role

Originally, Zillow had a Testing org (as well as Development and Product Management orgs). Testers did manual testing and wrote test automation. Zillow mostly hired SDETs and had an offshore manual testing team to do sitewide test passes.

As the company started growing, it re-structured orgs and as a result, broke into individual product teams, with each team having a Group Manager. Developers, Testers and Product Managers reported to the Group Manager. Most of these testers were SDETs and they wrote test automation, test plans, did some manual testing, and directed the offshore manual testers. SDETs spent most of their time doing manual testing and directing the manual testers. Management realized that Development teams were not taking ownership of quality or automated tests and were just pushing it over to the testers.

So, Zillow moved automated test responsibility to the developers, and switched to hiring test leads. Test leads would direct testing for the team, but Development teams would own the automated tests. Test Leads would also direct manual testing for offshore team. Even in this model, the role of the Test Lead varies by needs of their Development team. The role of test leads really is to make sure that their team is thinking about quality and doing the right thing for continuous improvement.

3.2. Expedia

At Expedia, testing role varied from one organization to another. In general, though, SDETs were the main drivers of quality. They owned test planning and the test automation platform. They built test frameworks and test automation themselves. They executed tests and logged most of the bugs. To be able to meet testing demands, developer to tester ratio was around 3 to 1.

Expedia has been going through a change in its approach to testing. There are groups that have already transitioned completely from having dedicated testers. In those teams, SDETs would need to change roles to be a developer, with a small focus on testing or find other teams that needed SDETs.

In teams that still have SDETs, it would be rare to have more than one per team. SDETs would focus on test architecture, worked alongside developers to write test automation, run tests, and mentored SDEs on how to write good tests.

3.3. Microsoft

At the time that we were at Microsoft (over 5 years ago), SDE:SDET ratio on the teams that we were on, was about 2:1. SDETs owned all the work related to test planning, test automation and maintenance.
However, from approximately about 3 years ago, Microsoft has moved to a "Combined Engineering" model, where SDETs no longer exist or exist only in very specialized teams.

The concept of Combined Engineering is that an engineer is responsible for his/ her feature end-to-end – from "from unit testing, to integration testing, to performance testing, to deployment, to monitoring live site" (Shah, 2017).

4. Future of Software

In the future, this is what we envision the role of someone in Software Testing would be:

- To not just test in the traditional way, but to be an evangelist for quality.
- Coach and mentor your team on how to think about quality in the tasks they do.
- Focus on quality of customer experiences and not just on code quality.
- Risk assessment.
- Ask questions about the testability of a system.
- Push for quality upstream, right from planning for a new product or feature.
- Quality gates for when code is checked in.
- Unit test coverage
- Think of Test Driven Development
- Automate the "right" things!
- Excessive UI automation is never good.
- Learning new technologies and seeing how it can help them in their role and beyond.
- Analyze production issues to find issues or commonalities, and determine if it is a bug.

4.1. Evangelize the Importance of Quality

In the never-ending quest to move fast to release software, quality often is forgotten. Since quality/ testing efforts are taken up towards later phases of a project (usually following product planning and development) it is common that there is not enough time between getting a final build ready to test and the product release date. This puts testers in a difficult situation - Should they be asking for more time to test? Should they fit in as much testing as possible within the time left? What if they find blocking issues that need fixing, and the product goes back into development, giving them even less time to test and sign- off?

This is where evangelizing for quality becomes important.

Help your team understand that quality is everyone's responsibility and not just the tester's. Coaching and mentoring your engineering team on quality, and how the team can improve, will become an important part of someone in a dedicated role for quality.

After all - a well-scoped and properly developed product is always better and faster to test, than otherwise!

4.2. Have a Growth Mindset!

Technologies for development and deployment of software are continuously evolving to become better and faster. To continue being relevant and thrive alongside this change, professionals in the field of quality need to have an awareness and an overall understanding of these technologies. Testing practices need to adapt based on technologies used to develop and deploy software. It is more important now than ever, to stay aware of upcoming technologies, and find out if there are any tools or services you can use to help with testing.

4.3. Drive a Quality Mindset!

Technologies for development and deployment of software are continuously evolving to become better and faster. To continue being relevant and thrive alongside this change, professionals in the field of quality need to have an awareness and an overall understanding of these technologies. Testing practices need to adapt based on technologies used to develop and deploy software. It is more important now than ever, to stay aware of upcoming technologies, and find out if there are any tools or services you can use to help with testing.

Understanding the product and being involved in product and design discussions right from the beginning is key to successfully planning for test and delivering on the same. Someone in test should:

1. Work with product/ project manager to get product specs written and reviewed by the entire team. Ensure that the scope of the project is correctly defined and prevent "scope creep".

2. Work with your engineering team to
    a. Assess risk
        i. What is the *most* critical feature in the product?
        ii. What would take the most time to test?
        iii. Which component is prone to having more bugs?
    b. Is the product testable? If not, understand what the reasons are, and plan for getting needed resources ahead of time to make testing possible before release.
    c. Define quality gates and acceptance criteria before the product moves over into test -
        i. Is Unit testing being done? This is the least expensive of all types of testing (remember the Testing Pyramid?) and extremely important.
        ii. Are test plans defined, and on time? Do they cover the needed product behavior as defined in the Product spec?
        iii. Ensure that test automation is a planned activity as part of release of the project.
    d. Be involved in the design and architecture
        i. Does the design make sense?
        ii. Are we using the right technologies?

4.4. Be a Customer Advocate

In many cases, a finished/ built product is delivered to a tester to test it out, but a professional in the field of quality (or testing), should have the right understanding about why a product is being built and, how to test it effectively.

- Why is our company/ team building this product?
    - What is the purpose of this specific product or feature?
- What customer problem does it solve?
    - What alternative approaches exist to solve this problem?
- Who are the types/ groups of users that will use this product?
    - How should I cater testing to ensure proper usability of this product?
- Do you believe that the finished product serves the customer as expected? Not just in terms coding requirements, but also in terms of user experience?
- How is the end user experience using this product (or feature)? How easy is it to use?

With all the emphasis given to and time spent improving software development processes and coding practices, it can be easy to overlook if a finished product or feature will serve the customer as expected. But remember – asking right questions at the right time during product development is key to a project's success. If a product isn't solving a user's need as expected, a thoroughly developed and well-tested product is of little use!

4.5. Remember That Internet of Things (IoT) is Here

Looking at the current trend and the pace at which IoT is expanding, it is only fair to assume that it's here to stay. Testing software services end-to-end may include testing using devices of multiple operating systems, user interfaces, screen sizes, versions. Testing various aspects of a service, like accessibility, performance, scalability, usability, security, compliance, software upgrades can get much more complicated than before and will need careful planning and execution on behalf of testers.

4.6. Don't Forget Security Testing

As a direct result of having a diverse set of devices embedded in a service's workflow, there will be multiple places where data is exchanged between devices. Each of these interactions will involve devices that may use different security protocols to communicate, making it more challenging to test. Information security will be a big area for testers to focus on, not only to ensure that devices are communicating securely, but also to ensure client and customer data privacy.

4.7. Get Comfortable with Software That Can Write Software

Not too distant in the future, test automation may not be written by testers or developers, but by software. What does this mean for testers? Should this be perceived as a threat to a tester's role or be considered as help? We think this can be a new opportunity for testers - this can be a tool that will help testing to move fast, without compromising on quality. Testers need to put in checks and balances in place for such software, to ensure that such software is testing the right things in the right way.

5. Conclusion

All evidence points towards a big shift in the testing role. More companies are re-thinking their approach to testing due to the reasons mentioned above (in Section 2) and joining the movement to get away from a traditional software-testing role. Does that mean that a career in testing is obsolete? No. Quality is important and relevant. So is delivering a high-quality customer experience for any product or service.

This means that a testing role will still exist in most companies. However, it may not look like what it does right now. Focus of this role will shift towards "quality" rather than just "testing". We believe that testers will go from typical individual contributor – in-the-weeds – roles to more leadership and consulting type roles. This may look like specialized virtual teams that focus on software quality for an entire company or specialized roles in quality, for a set of teams. There may still be certain companies that need manual software testers with specific skills, but demand for such roles will continue to wane.

The expectation of writing automation or running manual tests will be shared, but where testers will excel is by being "quality stewards" - influencing and growing the team and organization to develop a quality mindset.

We believe that this transformation not only sets up a career in software testing for longer-term success but also is beneficial to product and company success.

References

Allanabana, Fazal, et al. 2016. "Product Integration Testing at the Speed of Netflix." Netflix Technology Blog. https://medium.com/netflix-techblog/product-integration-testing-at-the-speed-of-netflix- 72e4117734a7 (accessed August 23, 2018)

Bolton, Michael. 2017. "Deeper (1): Verify and Challenge." http://www.developsense.com/blog/2017/03/deeper-testing-1-verify-and-challenge/ (accessed August 24, 2018)

Crowdsourced Testing. 2018. "Crowdsources Testing." Crowdsourced Testing. https://crowdsourcedtesting.com/ (accessed August 25, 2018)

ISO\IEC\IEEE. 2013. "The Role of Testing in Verification and Validation." *ISO\IEC\IEEE 29119-1:2013 Part 1: Concepts and definitions:* Section 5.1.1.

Page, Alan. 2016. "What's so special about specialists?" Testastic – The ramblings of a software quality philosophist. https://testastic.wordpress.com/2016/09/05/whats-so-special-about-specialists/ (accessed August 23, 2018)

Reddy, Jogannagary, et al. 2016.
Schaffer, André. 2018. "Testing of Microservices." Spotify. https://labs.spotify.com/2018/01/11/testing-of- microservices/ (accessed July 19, 2018)

Shah, Munil. 2017. "Evolving Test Practices at Microsoft." Microsoft. https://docs.microsoft.com/en- us/azure/devops/learn/devops-at-microsoft/evolving-test-practices-microsoft. (accessed August 23, 2018)
Splunk. 2018. "Predictive Analytics dashboard." Splunk Docs. https://docs.splunk.com/Documentation/ES/5.1.0/User/PredictiveAnalyticsdashboard (accessed July 18, 2018)

Thonangi, Uday. 2014. "Why did Microsoft lay off 'Programmatic testers'?" https://www.linkedin.com/pulse/20140806183208-12100070-why-did-microsoft-lay-off-programmatic- testers/ (accessed August 23, 2018)

Ulrich, Adam. 2006. "What's the difference between SDE and SDET at microsoft?" AdamU WebLog. https://blogs.msdn.microsoft.com/adamu/2006/01/27/whats-the-difference-between-sde-and-sdet-at- microsoft/ (accessed August 25, 2018)

Wikipedia. 2018. Crowdsourced testing. https://en.wikipedia.org/wiki/Crowdsourced_testing (accessed August 25, 2018

Additional by Abstraction: A Conversation About Adding Value to an Automated Test Suite Through Dynamic Coding and Abstract Concepts

Author

Jerren Emery (jerren.r.every@huntington.com)

Abstract

Many current automated test suites are brittle and not adept to handle change. This often occurs when people get pressed for time and begin to focus on short-term goals. This focus on the short-term can mean that your team will not be successful long-term as technology or your application goes through drastic changes.

The goal of a test development team should be to make a test suite that can stand the test of time. Common code development techniques such as Orthogonality, DRY(Don't Repeat Yourself), Metaprogramming, Refactoring, TDD (Test Driven Development), Dynamic Failures and Data Setup/Cleanup can help us create a more robust test suite that delivers value to the user.

Biography

Jerren Every is currently working as an Automation Developer Analyst-Senior on the Automation Architecture team at Huntington National Bank. His focus is on mastering the art of automation within design and deployment in a dynamic/fast paced agile environment. Jerren has received Professional Scrum Master, Professional Scrum Product Owner and Professional Scrum Developer certifications as well as the Certified Software Tester and Certified Software Quality Analyst certifications. With a strong knowledge of scrum ideology, QA ideology and automation ideology, Jerren is driven to help others embrace and understand these concepts. Jerren graduated from the Ohio State University with a degree in Psychology and enjoys bridging the gap in conversations between business minded individuals and technical minded individuals.

1. Introduction

This paper is an overview of the ways in which an automated test suite can be developed to be dynamic and robust by utilizing: Orthogonality, DRY(Don't Repeat Yourself), Metaprogramming, Refactoring, TDD (Test Driven Development), Dynamic Failures and Data Setup/Cleanup.

These ideologies are largely part of the standard body of knowledge for development for a variety of technologies. The source for definitions in this paper is the Pragmatic Programmer[9] which is consistently rated as one of the best software development books on the market. The challenge is that it is difficult to find examples on how to apply these ideologies within a testing framework.
With that being said, my goal in writing this paper is to start a conversation about how we can utilize these coding practices in a testing framework in order to develop more robust and dynamic tests that require minimal effort to maintain. The test frameworks in which I have utilized these ideologies include: database testing frameworks, mainframe testing frameworks, web testing frameworks and REST testing frameworks.

The structure of this paper will list first the ideology being discussed followed by a definition, then a section of examples of how to implement this ideology within a testing framework, and last any constraints that the ideology may have.

2. Making Code Orthogonal/Decoupling

2.1. Definition

Orthogonality is a term stolen from Geometry, two lines are orthogonal if they meet at right angles. In a programming sense parts of code are orthogonal if changes in one do not impact changes in the other (Hunt, 34).

Orthogonal code is beneficial as your team will not have to change existing code as new code is developed. (Hunt, 34).

Orthogonal code will reduce risk in the following ways (Hunt, 34).

A. Bad code is isolated.
B. Changes are isolated.
C. Easier to unit test.
D. Layer of abstraction between services and code.

2.2. Implementation

---

[9] Hunt, Thomas. 1999. *The Pragmatic Programmer: from journeyman to master*

The main way decoupling is beneficial in an automated test suite is through providing an abstraction layer between your internal code and any external functionality. Some examples of external functionality are:

A. Excel
B. Watir (Web Application Testing In Ruby)
C. Databases
D. Rest Client
E. Mainframes

Most often in test suites we see step definitions directly interacting with the services mentioned above. This non-orthogonal design will make it difficult to change and test your code.

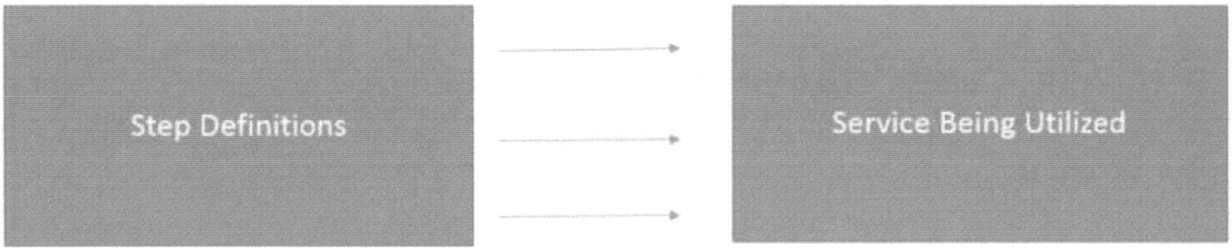

Orthogonal Code – Step Definitions reference a helper method which interacts with the service being utilized. Changes to the service only impact the helper.

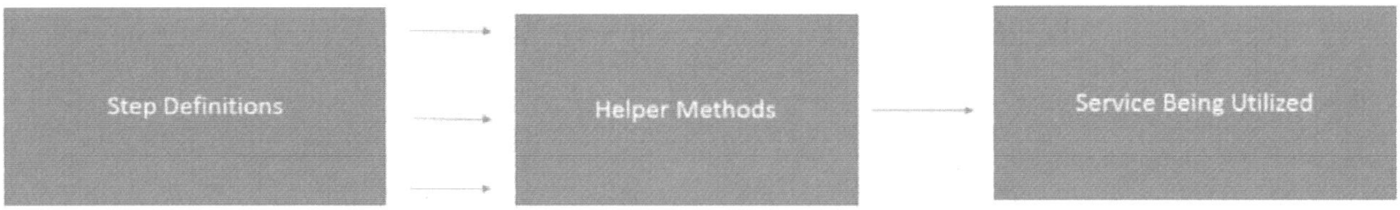

Another big benefit of utilizing these helper methods is that you now have a bit of functionality that is easy to unit test.

Unit testing is the act of testing a single section of functionality without outside interference. Within Ruby, RSPEC is typically utilized to unit test code.

2.3. Constraints

There is a balance that needs struck between complexity and orthogonality.

3. DRY (Don't Repeat Yourself)

3.1. Definition

In programming we want to be as lazy as possible, this means that we should take steps so that we do not repeat the same code. If the same logic is utilized twice this logic should be extracted into a method and stored so that it can be reused later on down the road.

3.2. Implementation

The concept of DRY seems simple enough, most of the difficulty comes when you start making alterations that impact what others have developed. I would recommend first fostering a culture where no individual owns portions of code but the whole team shares that responsibility. I would also recommend discussing the changes you are making with the team and showing the value that the changes are providing.

3.3. Constraints

Making changes to code often times has unintended consequences. Ensuring that unit testing is performed on your code is a good way to ensure that your changes don't impact the external functionality of the code.

4. Metaprogramming

4.1. Definition

The process of taking details out of the code. Developer should utilize metadata from the end user to set the arguments for the methods, the methods should be dynamic enough to allow for maximum reuse.

4.2. Implementation

Within a Ruby/Cucumber test automation suite most of the details get into our code externally from the Gherkin level passing in arguments to the step definition. But what some teams miss is that while we are passing data from the Gherkin level to the step definitions, the data passed should only be enough to make the end user capable of understanding what the test is validating.

For example, it makes sense that the expected business logic that needs validated is housed at the Gherkin level like:

Given the user inputs 2 + 2

When the user selects calculate

Then the application returns four

The more meaningful form and less evident way of metaprogramming is utilizing data keys where business logic is not concerned. In the example below the business can define what it means by valid credentials, and our code can go retrieve that test data and utilize it. This is beneficial as it prevents hard coding of values where it is not necessary and you can utilize the same data object in multiple flows.

Good Example:

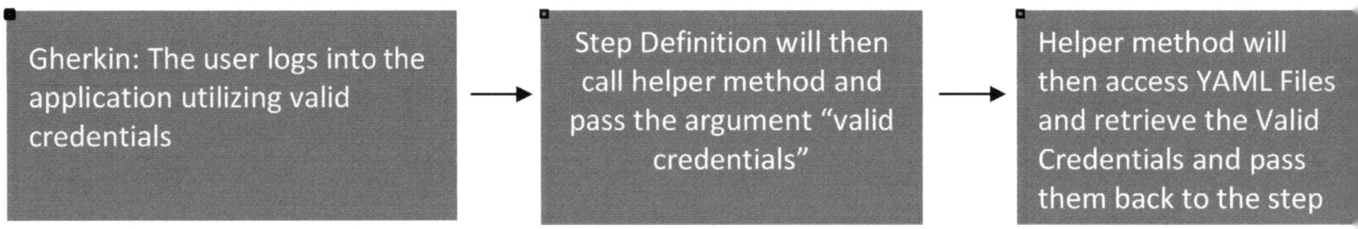

We can contrast the above with the unnecessary hard coding seen below. In addition to being brittle this has little value to the end user. When they read this test they don't know what the JackSmith user is or what status his account is in.

Bad Example:

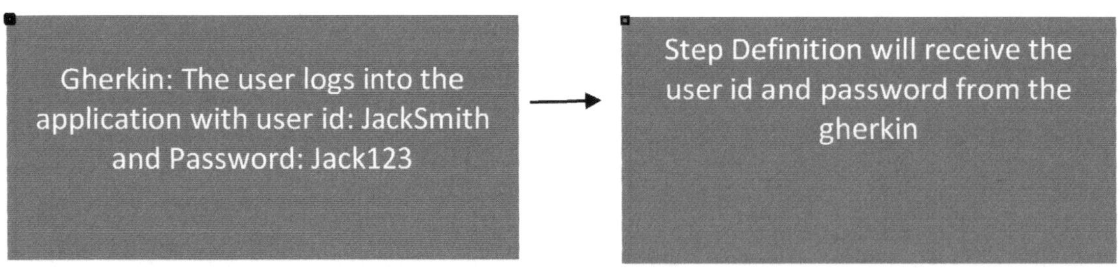

4.3. Constraints

We should be careful only to take the details out of the code when it makes sense.

I would also caution that when utilizing metadata/metaprogramming we should write our test in a way that only valid data should pass the test. Otherwise we risk having false positives in our testing suite.

5. Refactoring

5.1. Definition

Refactoring is the process of improving the structure of code without changing how the actual code functions.

5.2. Implementation

In the previous three sections we have discussed orthogonality, metaprogramming and DRY ideologies. All of these ideologies are examples that overlap with the ideals of refactoring. Ruby is a text manipulation language. Most often in test automation we are either manipulating input text, or validating data returned to ensure it meets our expectation. How we structure the code that supports this input preparation and output validation is where refactoring becomes important and the three previous ideas lay a good groundwork to begin refactoring.

5.3. Constraints

Refactoring is meant to be an organic process that happens as it provides value. Software is meant to be soft and change is supposed to be constant. One should not "own" code and one should not be defensive when code is critiqued.

Having a refactoring session is very beneficial in bringing about change to a test suite. These meetings should be discussions about finding improvements, not as a time to point blame.

6. Test Driven Development

6.1. Definition

TDD- Test Driven Development is the process of developing code through testing. The benefit being that the software you develop is much more likely to be robust and less error prone. Additionally you have developed unit tests that can be utilized for the life of the functionality you have implemented.

Test Driven Development Steps:

A. A programmer writes a test for a bit of functionality that is not yet developed. The test is ran and it fails.
B. The programmer then writes the code that he thinks will satisfy the unit test
C. The test is ran and it passes or fails
D. If the test passes the programmer can then refactor the code or move on to additional functionality.
E. If the test fails the programmer can make modifications as needed.

6.2. Implementation

Within Ruby, RSPEC is the most common framework for implementing unit tests that you can utilize for TDD. The Unit test developed provide continual benefit as you can test the validity of your code long after the code has been developed.

6.3. Constraints

Most often the constraint with utilizing TDD come about through managerial concerns about implementing the new process.

7. Dynamic Failures/Timely Failures

7.1. Definition

Test your code to fail as early as possible (RSPEC). Once a failure occurs have code to ensure that steps are completed to roll back any changes made to your environment.
Ensure that failures occur in a manner that will direct the developer to the root cause of the issue.

7.2. Implementation

A programmer can implement simple checks on the input data that is provided to a method to ensure that the input data received is valid. This layer of checking when a method begins running provides an ideal separation of work for items.

Example:

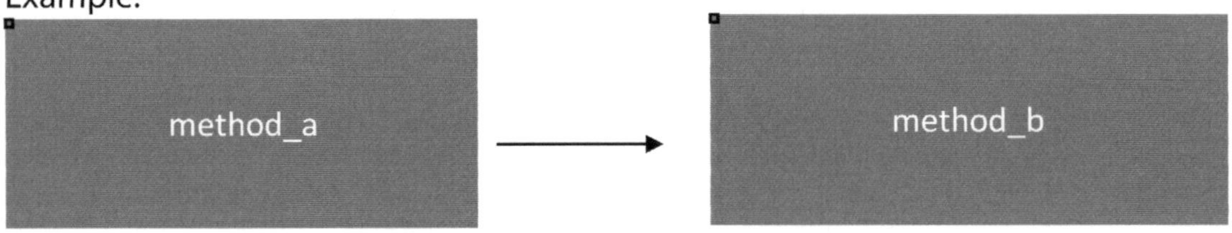

In the above example if method_b always accepts what method_a returns, method_b can be blamed for method_a's failure.

If instead method_b looked at what method_a returned to make sure it was valid any failure within method_b is sure to be caused by the logic within that functionality.

Rescue clauses within Ruby provide an easy way to catch a failure and continue on an alternate flow that allows for the failure to be addressed through additional steps or cleanup if need be.

7.3. Constraints

Rescue clauses should be used carefully. A true failure within the application that could be representative of a defect should not be caught by the rescue clause and should be passed to the tester as an issue.

Methods should not be so constrained by what they can receive as input that they lose a lot of flexibility.

8. Data Setup/Cleanup

8.1. Definition

Data necessary for a test should (as often as possible) be created and destroyed within the context of a test. The benefits being that each test is receiving clean data, and the test leaves less of a footprint once complete.

8.2. Implementation

In Ruby, hooks provide the ability to execute certain functionality before and after a test. For example; I worked on an account origination application and we had a tag invoked after hook that would remove account linking for a current user so that the test data would be able to utilize multiple times within the test suite. Without this after hook this test data would've been ruined after each test run.

8.3. Constraints

This process of test data setup and tear down is the gold-standard but can become inefficient, this should only be used where it makes sense by improving the quality and efficiency of a given test.

9. Conclusion

In conclusion we have discussed:

- Orthogonality and decoupling as a way to provide a layer of abstraction between the step definitions that run your tests and the services that support those step definitions.
- DRY as a way to minimize duplication and the ideology that the team owns the code not the individual
- Metaprogramming as a way to remove details from our code that would otherwise make our code base brittle.
- Refactoring as a process combining a bunch of individual ideas to modify the structure in which our code operates.
- TDD as a way to minimize risk when creating and updating test automation software.
- Dynamic/Timely Failures as way to make sure that the developer can quickly identify problem code rather than going down a stack trace goose hunt.
- Date Setup/Cleanup as a way to maintain robust tests that require minimal preparation prior to execution.

All of these ideals combined provide the groundwork for a robust testing framework that can be fun to work within and easy to modify when necessary. One point to consider is that any programming standard has a point where the usage of that ideal can make a test suite optimal and a point where it can make a test suite inefficient. The conversation each team has to have is how they can use these ideals effectively in the environment in which they operate.

References

Hunt, Thomas. 1999. *The Pragmatic Programmer: from journeyman to master.*

A Case Study in Improving Cross Functional Collaboration

Authors

Dain Peter Charbonneau, Parametric Portfolio (dcharbonneau@paraport.com)

Abstract

Testing should not be an island and we should not be throwing code back and forth over a wall, however this is what happens when there is poor or no cross functional collaboration. Cross functional collaboration is essential for successful agile environments.

Everyone has opportunities to encourage and implement behaviors that improve Cross functional collaboration. This also allows additional benefits such as getting out ahead of defects by driving quality upstream, encouraging earlier QA engagement, greater understanding of the product and user behaviors, and an improved ability to identify non-functional defects.

This paper examines practices that can be used for improving cross functional collaboration, adding to this are the authors experience with this practice, pitfalls encountered, and successes.

Biography

Dain Charbonneau has 11 years of quality assurance experience working in ecommerce and the financial service industry. Throughout his career, Dain has been a mentor and coach, worked on enriching sites through A/B and multivariate testing, led QA teams on feature development for large and small projects, and is currently working on an Agile team with a DevOps focus. Contact Dain at dcharbonneau@paraport.com.

1. Introduction

Cross functional collaboration involves people with different roles and expertise contributing to a common project or goal. These people may be grouped into a specific team for the duration of a task, project, or longer term for a company strategy or initiative. Additionally this involves people not dedicated to a specific team whose intentions are divided on many differ tasks and projects.

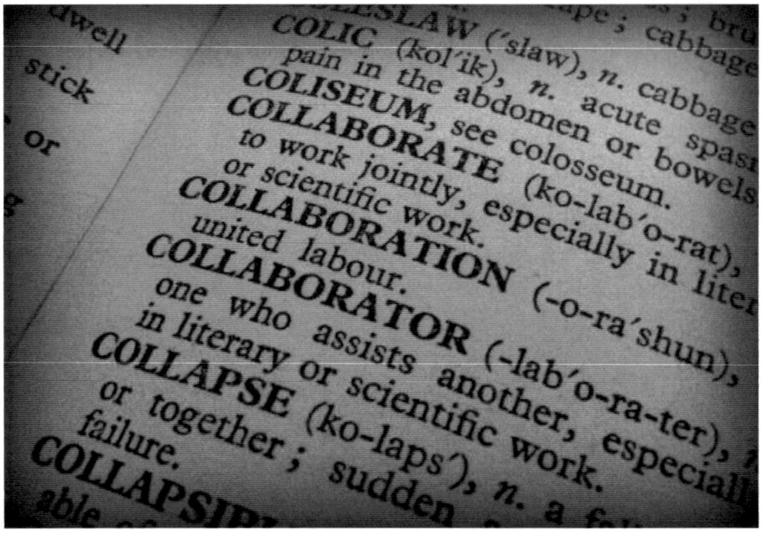

Image 1 (Pixabay, n.d.)

There are a number of benefits to a work culture that encourages and supports cross functional collaboration. A few of these benefits are:

- Improved project visibility across departments. This helps avoid gaps with what's delivered vs expectations.
- Identify misalignment of project goals earlier in the projects life cycle. This can reduce late scrambles adding missed features or pushing out features to future projects.
- Helps to improve the entire teams understanding of the feature and can aid in identifying bugs earlier.
- Gives people a stake in the project outside of their specific area.

An individual cannot always dictate exactly how a team functions, let alone additional teams one may have to work with due to common tasks and goals. But that does not mean an individual has no power to encourage cross functional collaboration. There are many opportunities for professions to incorporate practices that can develop, improve, and strengthen cross functional collaboration throughout the software development lifecycle.

2. Why Poor Cross Functional Collaboration is a Problem

A key component of Agile development is cross functional collaboration. A team can claim to be Agile, but with poor cross functional collaboration they are effectively tossing handoffs over walls to each other. Poor cross functional collaboration is a leading contributor to project delays and failures.

What is the problem?

- Poor cross functional collaboration negatively affects performance. (Schenk, 2016)
- A lack of collaboration is cited as a leading cause of workplace failures from a survey of 1400 corporate executives, employees, and educators. "86 percent cite lack of collaboration or ineffective communication for work place failures." (Stein, 2012)
- Cross functional collaboration is challenging when:
  - People are only partially dedicated to the project.
  - Team members are in different locations around the globe.
  - Poor tools and/or processes in place to support Cross functional collaboration.
- Moves teams closer to separate entities where code is tossed over the wall for each step of the process.
- Individuals don't feel they can implement change. Instead complain hoping and waiting for leadership to fix everything.

The blueprint for building an agile team with a strong culture of cross functional collaboration can be found in many books and all over the web. Examples are Martlew's book Changing the Mind of the Organization: Building Agile Teams, (Martlew, 2015) Adkins book Coaching Agile Teams: A Companion for ScrumMasters, Agile Coaches, and Project Managers in Transition, (Adkins, 2010) and web sites like Atlassian's Agile Coach. (Atlassian, 2018) Just because a team is functioning exactly to an agile blueprint does not mean that there are no opportunities for improvement. Teams are made up of unique individuals, no two teams will ever be the same and no blueprint will work perfectly for every team. A blueprint for agile can be an excellent guideline for implementation, but to excel a team should be adaptable, willing to try different things, and always looking for ways to improve.

3. Techniques to Improve Cross Functional Collaboration

Communication is key to successful cross functional collaboration. There are a number of practices that can help to encourage and improve communication across departments such as development, quality assurance, business stakeholders, project managers, and customers. Not all practices require a mandate from high up or a major overhaul of a work culture. Many practices can be introduced and encouraged on an individual level.

3.1. Developer Handoff Demo

A powerful tool that can be used to ensure a feature is really ready for testing and ensures the testing professional understand the feature is for the developer to demo their code. This involves having the developer explain their code to the testers and display how it works. This can easily be initiated and driven by the developer or testing professional and does not have to be limited to these two professions.

Image 1 (PXhere, 2018)

3.1.1. Why Use the Developer Handoff Demo?

The first benefit lies in the description, the developer has to show it working. There are many stories of experiences where a handoff should have never happened, the code was just not ready. This can waste countless hours troubleshooting, debugging, and filing bug after bug without the ability to fully test the feature. Developers may then waste additional time getting refreshed on the code to work on it again. Requesting a demo of the code at hand off can save time for everyone involved in this stage. Think of the time and effort saved if during the demo, it's identified that a piece of the feature is not working. For quality assurance, no time is wasted testing a feature that is not ready. As for the developer, the code is fresh, resulting in quicker turnaround time due to the reduced ramp up needed when reviewing to make corrections.

Another benefit a dev demo has is how they allow the testing professional to review the code with its creator. This is an opportunity to clear up any uncertainties the tester may have. This is an opportunity to ask questions while the code is fresh in the developers mind. The tester should walk away from the demo with a good understanding of the item being handed off, how it works, and how to test the feature.

Finally, this is beneficial to the tester as they gain insight into how the developer uses the feature. Understanding how the developer uses a feature can help to identify areas overlooked with development and target test cases that are not covered with unit and integration tests. This can aid in setting priorities in testing to identify bugs quicker.

3.1.2. Only When It's Needed

A developer handoff demo should not be requested for everything as they take time and add meetings to the schedule of those involved. Questions should be asked prior to requesting one to ensure the dev handoff demo is being used effectively: Is the code extremely complex? Is there confusion with some portion of it? Does the tester understand the feature? A no to any of these questions is a good indication that a code handoff demo can be useful. Be smart in knowing when a demo can be of benefit and use this tool effectively.

3.1.3. How It's Used in the Office

In my current workplace this is encouraged by leadership whenever a tester needs to improve their understanding of the feature being handed off. If there is confusion with the feature, we request a demo from the developer. A request is not always made to initiate a demo, developers will also choose to demo their feature if they feel it's needed with the feature being handed off. Most of the time I find it sufficient to do the demos while pairing at a desk, only requesting a conference room as needed for larger groups.

3.2. Test Case Reviews

Another technique that encourages collaboration between testers, developers, and feature experts are test case reviews. This is where the tester walks through the test cases with the parties responsible for the code and any feature experts.

3.1.3. Why Have Test Case Reviews

Developers should know their code better than anyone else, they wrote it. There are likely product owners or business associates that know the features expected behaviors better than anyone. Fellow testers will have insights based on their experiences and different understandings. A test case review provides opportunity for attendees to bring insights with testing and additional risks that tester was unaware of or was overlooking.

3.2.2. Key for Effective Test Case Review

Attendee engagement is key for this to be successfully. Be smart with who is being invited to attend the review. Include those that are willing to speak up and help generate ideas no matter how obscure an idea may be. If all attendees think the test plan looks good, challenge them to come up with ideas even if there are low priority edge cases that may never get tested. Try to keep these review groups small with involved players as this helps to avoid ideas being drowned out by stronger personalities.

3.2.3. Benefits of Test Case Reviews

Test case reviews provide attendees with insights on how and to what extent QA is testing. Because they are being asked for feedback on the test methods and coverage, attendees can get a sense of having a stake in the testing. This is important for the developer and tester relationship because they are most effective as a team working to make the code better vs the destructive environment of us vs them.

3.2.4. Test case reviews in practice

For my current team, we strive to have test case reviews for most projects. My team has been fantastic in these reviews with calling out additional tests or questing existing ones. These reviews can be difficult for the testers with test cases being challenged and called out. We need to understand this is an opportunity to learn and improve rather than being defensive. The result is improved testing coverage, improved understanding of the feature and project, and allows everyone to learn and grow from each experience.

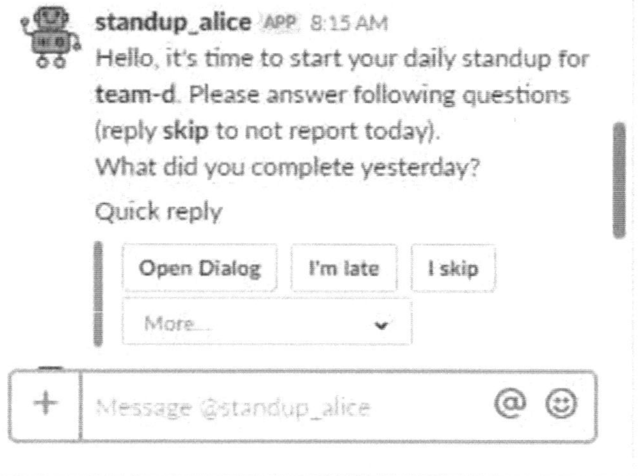

Image 2 Standup_Alice bot in slack to support asynchronous stand-ups.

3.3. Daily Stand-Ups Can Be Effective Even if They Do Not Fit the Mold

A very common agile practice are daily stand-ups. Daily stand-ups are short regular meetings that are part of agile methodologies. The intent is to have everyone standing so people do not get comfortable and to keep the meeting short, preferably under 15 minutes. The meeting consists of everyone answering three questions: What did you do yesterday? What do you plan to do today? And do you have any roadblocks or impediments?

When executed well, these can be a great resource for collaboration on your team. They provide insight and understanding towards the big picture and allow for visibility on blocking issues. When not utilized or executed poorly, an individual's focus can become tunneled to their current work which can result in missing the overall picture. The stand-up is an opportunity to gain awareness of what the team is doing as a whole, bring to light issues, and set up collaboration among the attendees.

Typically, when implemented, stand-ups follow agile best practices guidelines. However, for stand-ups to have long lasting effectiveness, teams should constantly evaluate what's working, be willing to try new things, and make adjustments for areas that are identified as broken.

3.3.1. Keeping Stand-Ups Small

What happens when a team or project grows too large, to the point where stand-ups are excessively long losing their effectiveness? Too many involved they will become disengage and feel that their time would be better spent elsewhere. One option is to consider shrinking the stand-up back down by splitting up into to smaller groups. Each group would then have a designated spokesperson that would meet with the designated people from the other groups to relay any information pertinent to all. This process is known as a Scrum of Scrums. This does not mean bringing more people together is always wrong, just be sure the situation calls for a larger stand-up and try to avoid making a habit of it. It's suggested for when groups get very large to no longer call the meeting a stand-up, but to rebrand it to help set expectations that differ from a stand-up for the meeting.

3.3.2. Asynchronous stand-ups.

Another option to managing large stand-ups and involving global remote attendees are asynchronous stand-ups. These are stand-ups that are typically managed through a chat bot. The bot will ask the three standard stand-up questions, or more if defaults are changed, and at a designated time will share all answers through the chat. An example of a bot for asynchronous stand-ups is the Standup Alice bot in Slack. Image 3 shows the slack bots initial greeting to start the gathering of information.

During large team stand-ups, people will lose focus and may miss key points. But with asynchronous stand-ups there is a record saved so it can always be referenced. This is also beneficial to those who are unable to attend the stand-up but have an interest in it. Conflicting meetings are not a problem as the stand-up content can be reviewed as availability allows. This is also convenient for remote team members, attendees around the globe do not need to join stand-ups at weird hours due to different time zones.

There are risks to be aware of with asynchronous stand-ups. Blocking issues may not be addressed right away, since asynchronous stand-ups do not always happen at the same time for everyone. Since brainstorming is not done face to fact, they may be a reduction in ideas generated. There is also the loss on interpersonal team building that occurs from coming together in person.

3.3.3. Hybrid Stand-Up

To combine the benefits of a traditional stand with the advantages of an asynchronous stand-up, consider a hybrid stand-up. This starts with an asynchronous stand-up, after which everyone still comes together in person or video conference for remote attendees. This provides an opportunity to address questions or concerns from the asynchronous stand-up. This also keeps the face to face interaction short as the three questions have already been answered and reviewed by everyone. Only clarification questions and issues are discussed. For those who are unable to attend and interested, there is still the record for review.

3.3.4. Personal Experience with Stand-Ups

Having experienced recurring oversized stand-ups where attendees would become disengaged and discussions were not relevant to most in attendance, I have a strong preference for scrum of scrums and asynchronous meetings. With my last experience of an extremely large stand-up, we had good intentions with different teams forming a joint stand-up for a specific project. However, the net result was the majority of people's time being wasted. Once it was acknowledged that this was not an effective use of our time, we broke back up into smaller stand-ups with pertinent information being shared by the leads. Currently my team is executing the hybrid stand-up. When we do this right, it has helped to keep everyone informed and engage with our colleagues in Argentina. This also keeps the face to face time short and effective. When done wrong, the traditional strand up takes place after the asynchronous and the effectiveness is lost. We continue to work on and improve our implementation of this.

Image 3 (PXhere, n.d.)

3.4. Engage Stakeholders and Users

There can be disconnects between stakeholder expectations and what is being delivered. Perhaps there was a misunderstanding, perhaps something was missed or left off the acceptance criteria, or perhaps it was unreasonable with the time and resources allocated. But the result is the same, when delivery arrives, the stakeholders are disappointed. One way to help avoided this is by engaging stakeholder and internal users throughout the development process with demos.

3.4.1. Demo to Stakeholders and Users

Providing visibility through the development of a project to users and stakeholders can provide a number of benefits. Demos help to ensure everyone is on the same page with deliverables. There are no surprises at the end. If there are concerns with anything, these concerns come out much sooner in the product life cycle. This feedback loop helps to establish and manage expectations, identify disconnects, and if changes are needed due to disconnects, development does not waste time ramping back up as they are currently engaged

What if there is nothing to demo but still want to build engagement with the project?

- Share metrics.
- Talk about the benefits the feature will provide.

Attendees are taking time away from their work to come see the demo. It's important to keep demos on time, focused, and to the point. The goal is not to bore everyone, you want to engage attendees, build excitement for the project, and invite involvement and engagement.

3.4.2. Situational Settings for the Demo

My office uses different techniques for this demo depending on situations. There have been quick demos at the end of stand-ups with stakeholders attending. We pair at a desk for short demos to an individual stakeholder. Last, conference rooms are used for short demos as part of a meeting or more formal demos that are the purpose of the meeting.

3.5. Pairing with User Acceptance Testing (UAT) & Test in Production with Partner Users

When handing off for User Acceptance testing there is the old throw it over the wall methodology. Evolving past this old methodology, there are better ways to hand off for UAT.

3.5.1. Demo the UAT Handoff

Similar to how the developer demos a feature to the tester, the tester can demo the feature to those conducting UAT. First demonstrating what the user needs to do to access the feature. For example, if the feature is in a test environment, the first part of the demo will be how to access the environment. The next part of the demo is showing the feature. This helps prevent confusion with how to access the update and establishes exactly what was included with the feature.

3.5.2. Pairing During UAT and with Partner Users

The second option that can be used is pairing during UAT. This is where the testers sits down and watch the users use the feature. Done right and improved understanding can be gained on how the product is used by the user. If a bug is encountered, the tester will have a clear understanding of it rather than getting a vague email and trying to reproduce it. Last, this provides opportunity for quick feedback and discussion if there are concerns. Below are suggested tips for effective pairing.

- Don't influence the experience by showing or explaining expectations.
- Have the stakeholder use the product without giving steps. Provide them with a task and see how the task is completed. Many times, a behavior outside of expectations will be observed. If the user can not figure out how to complete the task on their own. Then there may be a UX design flaw.
- Ask about scenarios that are not used. Are there better ways or does the user not know about capabilities.
- Conducting multiple sessions with different users, especially if there are multiple groups that use the feature. Do different groups use the different ways?
- Smaller "focus groups" with 2 to 3 people max. Larger groups will drown people out, especially with direct reports in the room. People seem to be less vocal on opinions when their boss is present.
- Have multiple sets of keyboards and mice set up. This encourages getting others involved rather than only one person driving with the mouse and keyboard.
- Consider inviting a developer or two to attend. Developers can also learn for observing how the feature is used in the real world.
- Prepare what if questions. E.g. If a feature breaks what do you do? If someone asks you to do something, how do you do it? If you could improve something about this flow, what would it be?

Pairing can be an effective exercise and should not be limited to the UAT process. Depending on the workplace and industry this exercise can be an effective tool for testing in production with partner users.

3.5.3. Pairing During UAT and with Partner User's Personal Experience

Depending on who the user is, many companies need to set up focus groups to observe their users with new features. It's much easier with my company, all that is needed is to set up a meeting. This is due to the end users being the portfolio managers and traders in the building. It has been an effective tool in improving developments understanding on how products and features are being used and in creating effective solutions.

3.6. Building Work Relationships

3.6.1. Advantages of Building Working Relationships

Positive working relationships allow employees to be more comfortable in interactions with colleagues. This can be extremely important when collaborating with people across different teams and departments. Getting to know coworkers such as subject matter experts and developing working relationships only pays dividends in the future. Take advantage of opportunities during and outside of work to get to know colleagues and develop working relationships. Establishing a positive working relationship will encourage behaviors like collaboration and team centric thinking.

The challenges are amplified when attempting to improve cross functional collaboration with colleagues in different offices or regions. If possible put in the extra effort for face to face interactions when the opportunity to meet in person exists. Set up team activities outside of work to build working relationships among different offices and regions.

3.6.2. Personal Experience Example

When a new colleague visited from Argentina, the team made it a point to do outside work activities. While not everyone attended all the team lunches, happy hour, and dinner that was set up, everyone did make it a point to make it to multiple engagements. This was done to help establish interpersonal relationships with the team's new colleague and to create building blocks for communication and collaboration in the future.

4. Conclusion

Cross functional collaboration is an important component for productive work environments, successful projects, and effective teams. Without effective collaboration, there is a shift from agile to a silo style development and the us vs them mentality. This can lead to longer delays, roadblocks, incomplete projects, and increased hostility in the workplace. A culture of cross functional collaboration can combat these issues and lead to improvements in projects and their development life cycle. Building working relationships across functions with face to face interactions, providing information and feedback between cross functional roles, and having bigger picture engagement all contribute to a culture of collaboration. There are many opportunities to build engagement between departments and employees in different functions through the development life cycle. Taking advantage of opportunities and molding them to best fit your people and company will contribute in creating a more enjoyable and collaborative work environment.

References

White, Stephen. 2016. "Why Your Team Should Try Asynchronous Daily Stand-ups" Medium, entry posted November 4, https://medium.com/@stevoscript/why-your-team-should-try-asynchronous-daily-stand-ups-87f1b809e5c8 (accessed July 16, 2018).

Appelo, Jurgen. "Daily Meetings with Remote Teams (Stand-ups Don't Work, But Daily Cafes Do)" Agility Scales Blog, entry posted July 4, 2017, https://blog.agilityscales.com/daily-meetings-with-remote-teams-stand-ups-dont-work-but-daily-cafes-do-35c6d3902f3b (accessed July 16, 2018).

Stein, Nick. "Is Poor Collaboration Killing Your Company? [Infographic]" SalesForce Blog, entry posted Sep 12, 2012, https://blog.agilityscales.com/daily-meetings-with-remote-teams-stand-ups-dont-work-but-daily-cafes-do-35c6d3902f3b (accessed August 18, 2018).

Schenk, Tamara. "How Cross-Functional Collaboration Impacts Performance" CSO Insights, entry posted Oct 20, 2016, https://www.csoinsights.com/blog/cross-functional-collaboration-impacts-performance/ (accessed August 18, 2018).

Atlassian. "The Agile Coach: Atlassian's no-nonsense guide to agile development."Atlassian Agile Coach, https://www.atlassian.com/agile (accessed August 18, 2018).

Adkins, Lyssa. 2010. Coaching Agile Teams: A Companion for ScrumMasters, Agile Coaches, and Project Managers in Transition. Addison-Wesley Professional.

Martlew, Christopher. 2015. Changing the Mind of the Organization: Building Agile Teams. Troubador Publishing Ltd

Pixabay (n.d.). Dictionary Book Collaborator Words. [image] Available at: https://cdn.pixabay.com/photo/2015/12/23/22/16/collaboration-1106196_960_720.jpg [Accessed 25 Aug. 2018].

PXhere (n.d.). Collaborative meeting conversation. [image] Available at: https://get.pxhere.com/photo/meeting-conversation-convention-academic-conference-205854.jpg [Accessed 25 Aug. 2018].

Pxhere (2018). Coworkers in a business discussion. [image] Available at: https://pxhere.com/en/photo/1434347 [Accessed 25 Aug. 2018].

Better Testing Through Process Automation

Authors

Rick Tracy, Hapalion Consulting & QualityMinds
(hapalion@gmail.com)

Abstract

Automating testing is currently still one of the top priorities among CIOs, and it remains a popular topic in the industry. Yet though it's not a new concept applying seems to still be in its infant, chaotic stages, and this is causing distress for both managers and practitioners of testing. This paper will explore some of the underpinnings of this dilemma and propose a new way forward, namely thought automating the processes surrounding testing instead.

We will take a short look into one large financial company's attempts to automate their testing for their data warehouse, and explore what went wrong and what was learned from it. Exploring the theory behind the automation is an important step on that journey, and so both the mentality and the application of that theory will also be presented as it was used by our team. Lastly we will look at where this led us to and why we believe this is a better way forward for testers and development teams as a whole.

This topic is still highly theoretical, with few companies in our experience moving towards this new paradigm. New tools are being created to facilitate it however and the more practical examples we see and testing minds involved we have the more refined we can make this. We look forward to spirited discussions and quality minded observations at PNSQC and beyond.

Biography

Rick is a freelance Tester and Scrummaster working in the finance and medical sectors and with Quality Minds and Hapalion Consultancy.

These positions have given him a variety of experience with different international audiences for test processes and reporting and plenty of experience doing it with more and less effective results. Rick's work passions lie in technique, optimization and communication, and occasionally the optimization of communication. He enjoys designing training programs and teaching and has focused most of his lectures on how to communicate ideas between different stakeholders and perspectives.

While he has a reputation for always having a story to tell, Rick prefers an interactive lecture or debate to a chalkboard presentation.

1. Introduction

Let's get this out of the way first: automation is not automatic. Regardless of whether you are changing a verification check into a test step, a manual activation into a triggered one, or a communication form into a report, creating automation takes work. Every moment spent automating is one less spent testing, so seeing it as an investment is advised and prioritizing accordingly is a must.

That said, we are in an age of ever-increasingly complex systems, products, and organizations, and we simply do not have the time to look over every aspect manually. We also have better and easier to use tools than ever before to aid us in exploring and testing items. So ignoring automation is something we cannot do.

This paper is a summation of what I've learned throughout my time going from 100% manual testing to figuring out what automation style works best with my work. It will cover the basis for automation, the arguments for and against, the balance needed to achieve it and the lessons learned as we created it. However, this paper seeks to go one step further and advocate for a different form of automation, one that focuses more on the strengths of both man and machine and how to utilize each in the best possible manner.

2. The Story So Far

To begin, I'm going to take you back to the days of 2012, where my foray into automation began. I was working for an international bank in the back office, where we processed around a million or more transactions per day through a global financial system pulling in records every minute from all around the globe (or the four corners of the world, for flat earth enthusiasts). This, as you may imagine, requires quite a large system of inputs, checks, databases, checks, reporting flows, checks, and tests. And that's just running it day to day.

We primarily focused on baseline cases in our team, but we were surrounded by six other project teams working on the exact same system and structure, meaning anything they altered would impact us and vice-versa. As you can imagine, this create quite the Wild West scenario, not only for architects and requirement engineers but also developers and testers. Every three months we were requested to put out a release of new inbound streams, new reports, and new functionality within the datawarehouse and to keep it all at the highest form of quality we could manage. Given that we were seven teams all depositing code in various states of readiness into one package, that highest form was not nearly as high as we wanted it.

After a while enough of us were upset about the quality degradation. Gathering a team of testers, developers, and business analysts we created our very first Agile Development team and set to work on what would later be called the Integration Quality team. Step one was to figure out how to bring a huge system with voluminous data into a reasonable scope for analysis. One brainstorm session later and Milestones was born.

Milestones was a Table Data Comparison tool built entirely from scratch using APEX oracle inputs and triggered commands. It was also our first foray into automation, as we found we could easily turn collecting data into comparing data. The result was a tool which could read each table in our system and compare the impact of any introduced changes. While we had to load our tables manually, and define each table with the columns we wanted to compare, this did free up time and effort in making these queries manually and running them on volatile and ever-changing test environments.

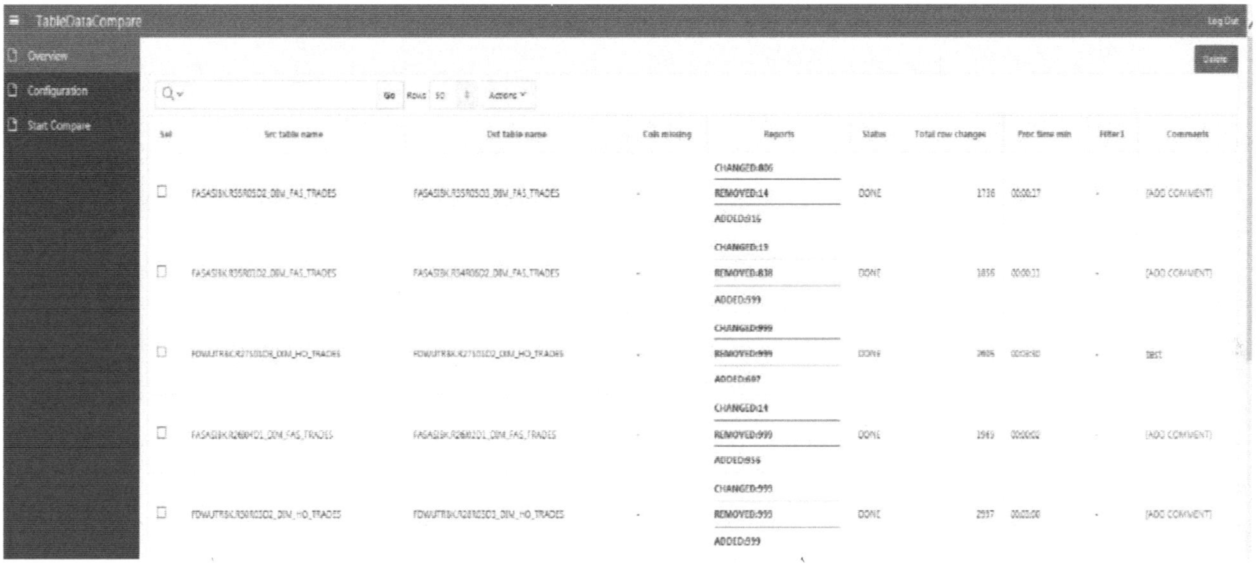

Image 1: Milestones Table Comparison Tool

This tool sped up our analysis considerably and since it was used by a single team across teams we had a potential solution for many of our top issues in quality. However, once testers from each team began using it, flaws were discovered which almost tanked the whole project. Table configurations were still different per team depending on the changes they introduced, environments didn't match, and worst of all, the comparison done from Milestones only showed that there was a difference, not what caused it or whether it was expected or not. Trying to add useful manual checks to the program caused a significant slowdown, so many ended up using both, costing more time.

```
(select 'Old',PROPERTY_NAME,PROPERTY_VALUE,DESCRIPTION from DATABASE_PROPERTIES_OLD
minus
select 'Old',PROPERTY_NAME,PROPERTY_VALUE,DESCRIPTION from DATABASE_PROPERTIES)
union all
(select 'New',PROPERTY_NAME,PROPERTY_VALUE,DESCRIPTION from DATABASE_PROPERTIES
minus
select 'New',PROPERTY_NAME,PROPERTY_VALUE,DESCRIPTION from DATABASE_PROPERTIES_OLD)
order by property_name;
```

Script Output × | Query Result ×

SQL | All Rows Fetched: 8 in 0,009 seconds

	'OLD'	PROPERTY_NAME	PROPERTY_VALUE	DESCRIPTION
1	Old	DICT.BASE	3	dictionary base tables version #
2	New	DICT.BASE	2	dictionary base tables version #
3	Old	DST_PRIMARY_TT_VERSION	22	Version of primary timezone data file
4	New	DST_PRIMARY_TT_VERSION	23	Version of primary timezone data file
5	New	EXPORT_VIEWS_VERSION	8	Export views revision #
6	Old	EXPORT_VIEWS_VERSION	9	Export views revision #
7	New	NLS_CURRENCY	$	Local currency
8	Old	NLS_CURRENCY	Eur	Local currency

Image 2: Example of a manual script

Trying to turn a comparison program into a tester for integration tests was not working on this scale. Many testers started looking for additions to the program or designing their own. What could have turned into a failure instead set off a chain of innovation, and soon testers were coming with unique solutions to familiar problems.

One of those was a reset protocol for all environments, which would use a single repository of table settings from the Integration Quality (IQ) team to align any test environment in minutes. This script could be run manually or kicked off from Milestones once integrated. It didn't slow down the comparison process and solved one of our most insidious issues of alignment. This was immediately added and implemented into our process, and testers used it gleefully and often.

```
delete from TABLE_1;
delete from TABLE_2;
delete from TABLE_3;
delete from TABLE_4;
delete from TABLE_5;
delete from TABLE_6;
delete from TABLE_7;
delete from TABLE_8;
delete from TABLE_9;
delete from TABLE_10;

Insert into TABLE_1 (select * from BKP_TABLE_1);
Insert into TABLE_2 (select * from BKP_TABLE_2);
Insert into TABLE_3 (select * from BKP_TABLE_3);
Insert into TABLE_4 (select * from BKP_TABLE_4);
Insert into TABLE_5 (select * from BKP_TABLE_5);
Insert into TABLE_6 (select * from BKP_TABLE_6);
Insert into TABLE_7 (select * from BKP_TABLE_7);
Insert into TABLE_8 (select * from BKP_TABLE_8);
Insert into TABLE_9 (select * from BKP_TABLE_9);
Insert into TABLE_10 (select * from BKP_TABLE_10);
```

Image 3: Example reset script

Next step was to get the comparisons to give more direct and specific results, rather than a bland comparison. In order to do this testers looked into how they tested their specific cases, and we went for a batch/report generator validation automation style. This means taking batch commands and adding them to the validations, so that we could put both into Milestones and run specific cases. This combined both the comparison function and the reset function and used validation rules we injected to decide if the next step would turn on or not. This was our first step towards what eventually would revolutionize how we did automation.

5. Automation in Theory

Take a look at the following two pictures and see if you can detect the differences:

Image 4: Comparisons

Most of you will see the airplane, the time and the number on the bus first. Some will also see the missing head of the light or the color of the shirt of the walking man on the right. These are not the only changes, but they are the ones we see without taking the picture pixel by pixel.

The theory behind automation in comparisons is that a computer can do that low-level comparison by taking each component (in this case, the pixels) and comparing them, noting differences. This is a solid conclusion; Milestones did as much with any table comparison we had it do. So why don't we automate every comparison?

Mainly it has to do with what you see first. Most people looking at this picture will not look for any and all changes. They see a sky, a clock, and a bus. We are drawn to the important aspects of the picture, the ones which will have the most impact. So we immediately see a plane has entered the sky, the time has changed and the bus number is altered. Major impacts on major features.

Automated comparison will find things that a tester doesn't on first glance, but it will not prioritize like we do. It will tell you everything, and you have to tell it what's important. So while it is useful in a 100% coverage of comparison, it is slow and cares about every alteration equally. In order to automate a comparison to make it like a professional did it, we have to program priority, impact, features, and all other things we as people do automatically on first glance. That's a lot of extra work.

This shows us that people have a good and easy grasp of the priorities and features while computers have a good grasp of the details. It also sets the stage for our overhaul of automation as a theory. But before we went there we had to explore what else automation could do for us.

Automation comes in many forms, but the ones most commonly presented are key command logs (copiers), external based automation (cloud or database call connections), and background functionality scripts (prompts followed by data processing). Searching for the right ones to use takes understanding what they are best at.

Copiers are good for tasks that are repetitive in static environments. They work really well if the command is universally executable and all data is present. That is also their weakness: there can be no shift in interface that disrupts it and if any part of the data or source doesn't exist it will fail. It took only one insistent screensaver to push us away from using this for our automation goals.

Connection automation calls up commands and triggers from an external source, often a static one or a default one, much like our reset script did. It isolates automation to counter the weaknesses of copy automation, and has major strengths in reliability of data, maintenance, and repeatability. It is not flawless however, as connections can be poor, no environment that needs alterations is ever truly static, and single point of failure issues.

Then there was prompt automation, which always looks great on the outside. For a user, all you have are a few prompts and results, much like the original Milestones. This makes them very user-friendly and functional. Unfortunately, like many systems that are outwardly calm, the inside is pure chaos, and getting something to run that smoothly means programming for each eventuality or accepting poor function, both of which cost more time.

So it looked like nothing in theory was going to cover everything we needed to automate our tests. Too many variables, too many places it could go wrong, and a system far too large to efficiently program every eventuality. Still, we Dutch are stubborn, so we decided to just dive in and see what the teams could come up with in practice.

6. Automation in Practice

In practice, we needed a process that wasn't GUI reliant, but was also flexible enough to present results in a useful manner. Through experimentation we'd found that automation worked best for us in blocks of functionality, for specific cases and for general integration. But with each team working on different changes, it had to be automation that had maximum customization options without being cumbersome to run and taking forever.

We started playing around with a few test suites focused on customized validations and total control of the test process. These programs worked on the user scale: not coding each action but grouping all functionality into small processes like moving a mouse, searching for items, running general logic and even customized functions. With this we could create GUI, background, and connection automation whenever and wherever we wanted in the process.

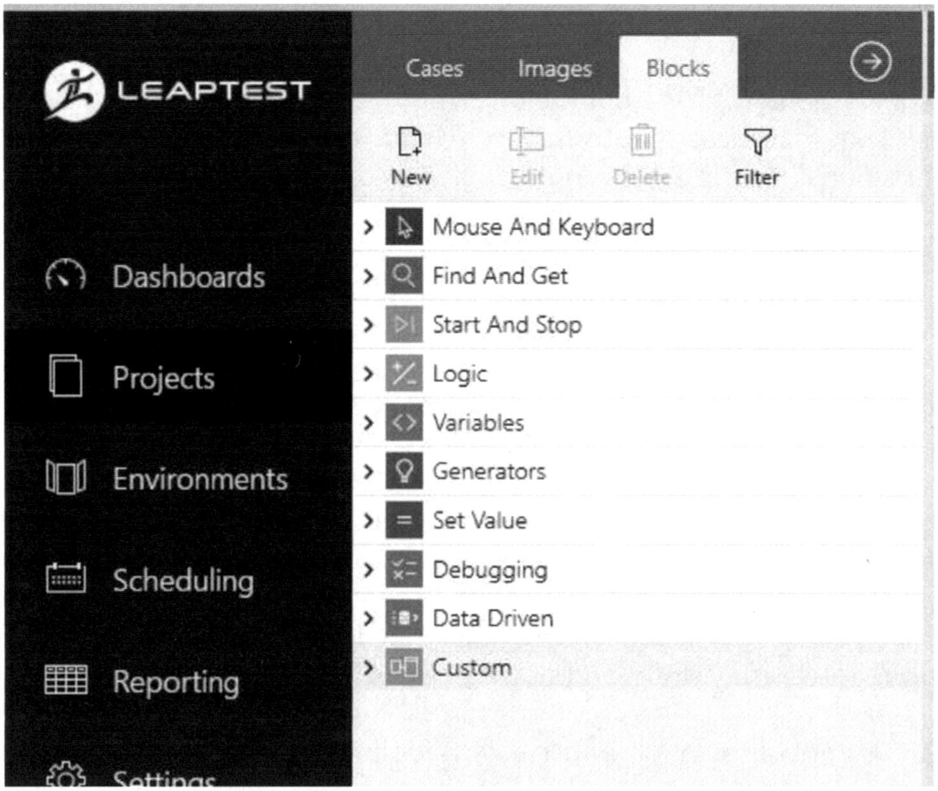

Image 5: Example of a customizable test suite (Leaptest)

This kind of experimentation allowed us to make any automation process our own. We started automating annoying manual procedures like logins, opening programs and starting batches. Small functions wrapped in little blocks allowed us to quickly automate things that just took time, not thought. We originally used it to get the process out of the way so we could automate the testing and verifications, but then the team reflected on what had just been accomplished. Had we just redesigned the purpose of the test suite to automate a process instead of a validation?

7. A New Kind of Automation

There is a prevailing image of automation as replacing test work. This is a flawed premise, not only in that humans and machines operate differently as shown above, but also misses automation's best feature: companionship. Automation should ***augment*** testing, and by looking at the parts that we didn't like to do anyway, we were able to focus much more of our attention on things we were better at. We created Process Automation.

The team started to focus in earnest on creating shared process steps using the customization functions from suites and from our own systems. We would debate on whether this was a step that:

- Was easily automated
- Didn't require much brain work
- Wouldn't reveal bugs
- Didn't contribute to finding out the quality of the system.

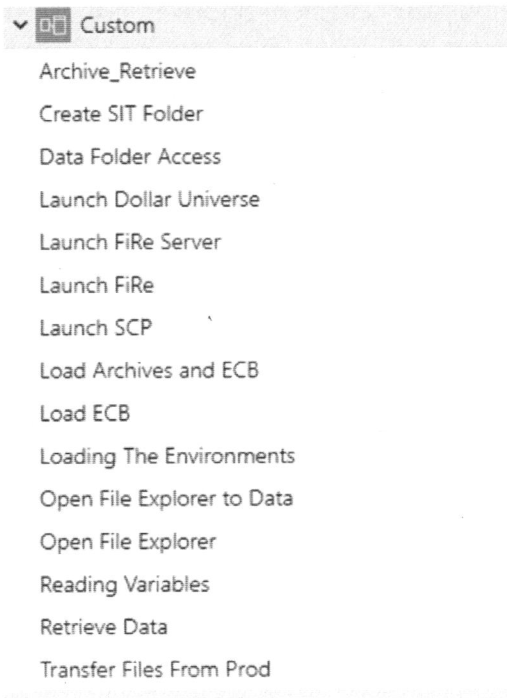

Image 6: Examples of Automated Processes

If it passed muster, we'd automate it, and before we knew it we had a process that would practically run itself. All a tester would have to do would be to throw the blocks together for the test they needed, and it would run it with an updated setup in an updated environment with the latest data. And once built the first time, the process could be saved for faster recall and repeatability later.

We found that this not only made automation much simpler and enjoyable, it also saved us significantly more time than automating the tests and checks. For an hour's work a tester saved themselves and everyone thereafter at least five minutes of work (or waiting) per test run. That investment paid off quickly in a large system with seven teams.

It wasn't without its pitfalls though, and that is what we are looking at going forward. For one, the process can and does fail, and when it does we don't know what happened or why the more abstract our process automation got. So we started implementing activity logs in any significantly complex automation, as much for maintenance as for debugging. We then sent this log to our DevOps team who used it for monitoring for failures in production, adding more value from our process.

We also learned that automating functionality of a process that large can grow out of hand very quickly. We had to implement functionality in larger blocks, while keeping a repository of the individual tasks kicked off by them for universal maintenance. We're still not sure what to do about the constant growth of functions without in essence recreating the entire system, but it does give us insights into improvements to our existing system by pointing out repetitive functions, combination potential, and sensitive points of possible failure.

Maintenance is often a sore point of automation, so we wanted make sure we learned quickly what the most efficient manners were. Storing values in the code was quickly dismissed in favor of simple excel sheets we could load in with values, and passwords were defined globally so a user wouldn't have to enter it each time it was required in different sections of the process. I'm sure a security tester is having a fit at that last one; if so, we're definitely open for suggestions on how to improve this point!

Automated SIT Template

Value	Variable
I:\1. Regression Data & Results\	SIT Folder
20170228 1703 March Release	Data Folder
I:\1. Regression Data & Results\Production Files	Data Transfer Site
5	Number of Entities
5201 RXF	Entity 1
utc_dnb	Entity 1 Schema
6016	Entity 2
dubrn_dnb	Entity 2 Schema
6006	Entity 3
par_dnb	Entity 3 Schema
6005	Entity 4
sch_dnb	Entity 4 Schema
5201 FDW	Entity 5
utc_dnb	Entity 5 Schema

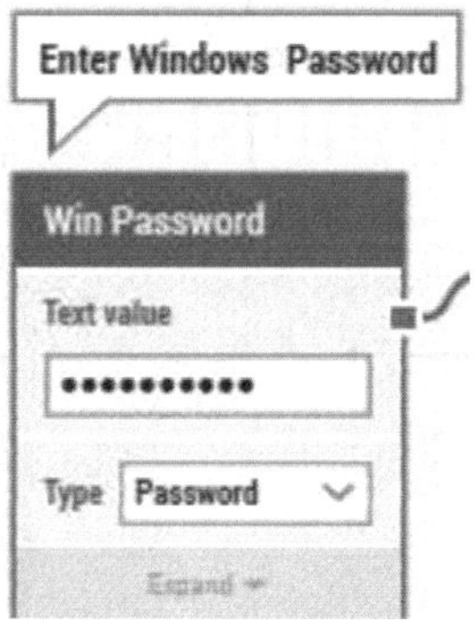

Image 7: Excel and password examples

Lastly, we quickly found that processes are very similar throughout our system. I postulate that that's true in many systems. We found several places where functionality was near enough to another that they could be filled and activated simpler with one function than with several repeated ones. It took us from looking locally to looking globally.

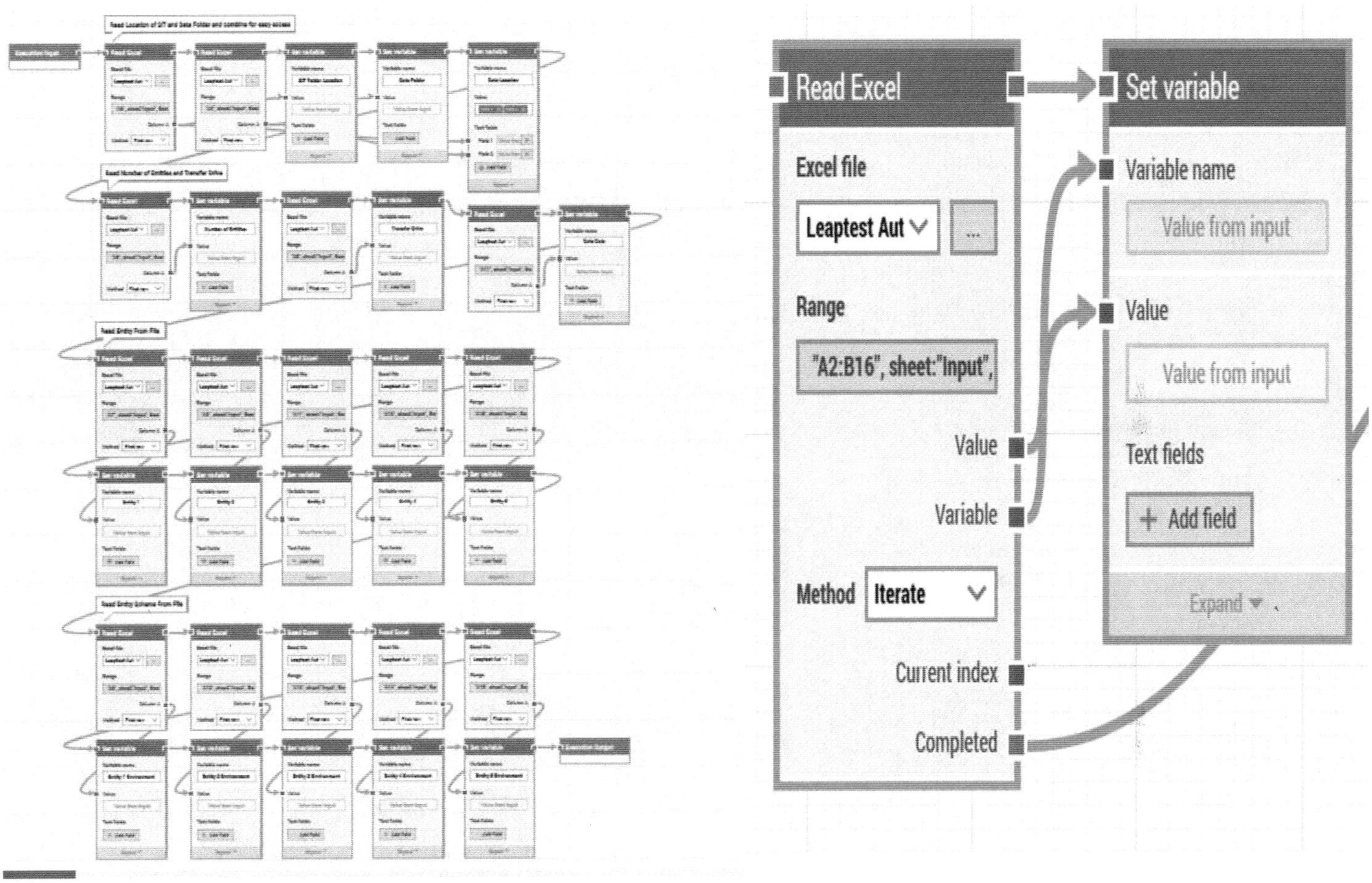

Image 8: Simplification of functionality

8. Conclusion

Automation is a tool. As such, it is up to the user how he or she uses it. We've found that automating tests is a large endeavor with many pitfalls and ignores the selection skills of professionals in favor of massive amounts of data. Because of this we want to push for more process automation, letting technology do what it does best to augment the test process.

In order to do that we want to assist you with the following tips:

- Focus on what you want to produce, and let the automation produce it.

- Look at how you do things now and decide what you want to improve on and what can stay the same (and automated!)
- Think about your approach; learn from others and from new technology before diving in. Learn especially about the strengths and weaknesses of your team and your tech.
- That said, don't be afraid to experiment to find things no one has before or new applications for old approaches.

Lastly, don't hoard automation. Automate the process for others as well as for yourself. This helps in recycling of tests, saves others time in designing how to monitor the process, and even gives your users a break by granting them an easy to use tool for User Acceptance Tests.

By doing this our hope is that more people can build the automation necessary to make their testing and overall system quality continuously better and set out faster On The Road To Quality!

The Path Beyond Cucumber 3.0

Author

Thomas Haver (tjhaver@gmail.com)

Abstract

Cucumber is a tool that supports Behavior Driven Development (BDD), a software development practice that promotes collaboration. Cucumber will execute specifications written in plain language and generate reports to reveal the behavior of software against expectations. In the Fall of 2017, the Cucumber core team formally released Cucumber version 3.0.0, introducing changes that will shift how developers use the tool. Among those changes are Cucumber Expressions, updated Tag Expressions, Retry & Flaky Status, Strict Mode, and a new Events API. This paper will present the new features of Cucumber and how to integrate them into an existing automation suite.

Biography

Thomas is presently serving as a Senior Application Architect for Huntington National Bank. He is responsible for the conversion from manual testing to Ruby/Cucumber automation for the entire enterprise. Originally accountable for the development and maintenance of automation frameworks for Digital Channels, he now leads the automation effort for 73 applications across Huntington that encompass testing, metrics & reporting, data, and environment. Thomas leads the training & technical support for both on-site employees as well as offshore contractors. He has developed test strategies and assisted in coordination between multiple lines to improve delivery effectiveness & resource flexibility.

1. Introduction

The goal of Behavior Driven Development (BDD) is to combine automated acceptance tests, functional requirements, and software documentation into a single format that's understandable by the entire team (North, 2006). The core feature of BDD is collaboration, through which a shared understanding of delivering features to the user is independent of role. In BDD, the "definition of done" is agreed to by the entire team. The development team focuses on making requirements pass in the form of tests. These tests are typically written in a business readable format to emphasize the purpose of creating a shared understanding.

Originally developed by Aslak Hellesoy in 2008 (Hellesoy, 2017), the tool called "Cucumber" can be leveraged to support BDD in creating automated tests, executable specifications, and living documentation. In describing the tool, Aslak wrote, "Cucumber was born out of the frustration with ambiguous requirements and misunderstanding between the people who order the software and those who deliver it" (Hellesoy, 2014). The business readable language for implementing Cucumber scenarios is called Gherkin. Chris Matts is credited with originally inventing the "Given-When-Then" keyword format for examples written as test scenarios (Wynne & Hellesoy, 2012). The Gherkin template implies "Given" some initial context, "When" an event occurs, "Then" ensure some outcome. Following BDD principles, the features written in Gherkin are intended to drive development, not follow it. The top-layer of Cucumber is the Gherkin, and will be the starting point for discussion of this paper.

The development team behind Cucumber implemented changes in five core areas for Cucumber 3.0: (1) Cucumber Expressions; (2) Tag Expressions; (3) Retry & Flaky Status; (4) Strict Mode; and, (5) new Events API (Wynne, 2017). Cucumber Expressions are intended to replace Regular Expressions for matching patterns of user behavior in Gherkin. The Tag Expressions replace prior tag standards to enhance readability. The Retry & Flaky status are intended to identify tests that flicker from pass to fail. The Strict Mode will provide more options with Gherkin that is unimplemented or unfinished. Lastly, the new Events API has been updated to model the execution of automation as a series of distinct events.

2. Cucumber Expressions

Cucumber Expressions are simple patterns for matching Step Definitions with Gherkin steps. The Cucumber development team wanted to replace Regular Expressions with something more user friendly and powerful (Wynne, 2017). Cucumber Expressions are an expression language for matching text and the syntax is altered for legibility. In comparison, Regular Expressions were previously used for more flexibility and control. The development team for Cucumber reasoned that automation developers don't need all the power of Regular Expressions, and that legibility is more important to Gherkin (Wynne, 2017).

Whereas Regular Expressions use capture groups to extract pieces of text, Cucumber Expressions use output parameters (Hellesoy, 2017). An output parameter is simply a name between curly braces. The sample scenario below shows a simple example of using a Cucumber Expression versus earlier versions of Cucumber.

@cucumber_expressions_example

Scenario: sample scenario for cucumber expressions using an integer
Given the user navigates to the **Example Search** page
And the user fills in "**money**" for **search field**
When the user selects the **3**rd **predictive question** result
And the user waits for **2** seconds
Then the user validates the url of the browser window contains **search**

It's not advisable to use explicit sleeps in test automation, but for the purpose of this example it fits. Prior to Cucumber 3.0, the underlying step definition would be implemented like this:

When(/^the user waits for (\d+) seconds$/) **do** |*time*|
 sleep *time*.to_i
end

The step would accept one or more digit characters as a parameter, and the sleep method call would wait a certain period of time. With the advent of Cucumber Expressions, the integer is a built-in parameter type. The step definition would now look like this:

When(**"the user waits for {int} second(s)"**) **do** |*time*|
 sleep *time*
end

The above expression passes an Integer from the Gherkin by explicitly calling for an "int" in the step definition. However, the expression would match 2 seconds but not 1.5 seconds. Integers are not the only new parameters added – Float is a valid, built-in parameter type:

When(**"the user waits for {float} second(s)"**) **do** |*time*|
 sleep *time*
end

Now the associated sample scenario will accept fractions of a second because the parameter type was changed to Float.

@cucumber_expressions_example
Scenario: sample scenario for cucumber expressions using an integer
 Given the user navigates to the **Example Search** page
 And the user fills in "**money**" for **search field**
 When the user selects the **3**rd **predictive question** result
 And the user waits for **1.5** seconds
 Then the user validates the url of the browser window contains **search**

Another change was made to the step definition example in addition to using a double quoted String in place of "Regexp" and a parameter type. Cucumber Expressions allow for optional text. The step definition, "**And the user waits for 1 seconds**" is grammatically incorrect. Surrounding the text with parentheses makes the text inside optional.

When(**"the user waits for {float} second(s)"**) **do** |*time*|
 sleep *time*
end

@cucumber_expressions_example
Scenario: sample scenario for cucumber expressions using an integer
 Given the user navigates to the **Example Search** page
 And the user fills in "**money**" for **search field**

When the user selects the **3**rd **predictive question** result
And the user waits for **1** second
Then the user validates the **url** of the browser window contains **search**

Before Cucumber 3.0, typically a non-capturing group with optional repetition parameter would be used.

When(/^the user waits for (\d+) second(?:s)?$/) **do** |*time*|
sleep *time*.to_i
end

Using an Integer parameter is more appropriate when decimals will never be needed. Cucumber Expressions also allow for alternative text. Sometimes the Gherkin needs two or more options from non-capturing groups to make the Step flow. Instead of using pure regexp to indicate multiple options within a non-capturing group, a forward slash works between two or more options:

Step for Cucumber < 3.0:
When(/^the user selects the (\d+)(?:st|nd|rd|th)? (.*) result$/) **do** |*index, page_element*|

Step for Cucumber 3.0 and beyond:
When(**"the user selects the {int}st/nd/rd/th {page_element} result"**) **do** |*index, page_element*|

The current built-in parameter types are:

{int}	# for example 71 or -19
{float}	# for example 3.6, .8 or -9.2
{word}	# for example bacon (but not bacon cheeseburger)
{string}	# for example "money" or 'money'.

The quotes are removed from the match.

Custom Parameter Types can be defined to represent types for any Cucumber suite. The benefits are: (1) automatic conversion to custom types; (2) document and evolve ubiquitous domain language (living documentation of variables); and, (3) enforce certain patterns (Wynne, 2017 and Hellesoy, 2017). Start by creating a Parameter Types Ruby file in the Support directory. Under Parameter Type (reference shown below), "name" is the name of the parameter type, "regexp" (Array format) list of regexps for capture groups, "type" is the return type of the transformed, "transformer" is the lambda that transforms a String to another type, "use_for_snippets" is a Boolean that can be used for snippet generation, and "prefer_for_regexp_match" is a Boolean that should set preference over similar types (Wynne, 2017 and Hellesoy, 2017).

```
ParameterType
  name: 'name',
  regexp: //,
  type: Type,
  transformer: lambda {|foo| foo.to_type_change},
  use_for_snippets: true or false,
  prefer_for_regexp_match: true or false
)
```

Custom parameter types are new to Cucumber 3.0. In prior versions, regexp for each step was the common practice. Now it's possible to develop a set of parameters relevant to the application under test, as a form of business logic documentation about application specific criteria. An example is shown below:

```
ParameterType(
  name: 'page_element',
  regexp: /.+/,
  type: String,
  transformer: lambda {|s| s.gsub(/\\"/, "'")},
  use_for_snippets: true,
  prefer_for_regexp_match: false
)
```

The example using "**page_element**" for snippets on web applications is not an ideal implementation. When Cucumber encounters a Gherkin step without a matching Step Definition, it will print a Step Definition snippet with a matching Cucumber Expression as a starting point. Thus, the regexp will match one or more characters, so "page_element" will be recommended for snippet generation everywhere. Therefore, it's important to utilize as specific matchers as possible. Examples would be account numbers of a specific length, dates in a particular format, or word characters that must be phrased in a redundant manner

Regular Expressions will not disappear from Cucumber. A regular expression used with a capture group for an integer, such as **(\d+)**, the captured String will be transformed to an Integer before being passed to the step definition. The Cucumber Expression library's support for Regular Expressions pass capture groups through parameter types' transformers, same as Cucumber Expressions. Cucumber will no longer suggest Regular Expressions in snippets. Cucumber Expressions will instead be recommended.

Step for Cucumber < 3.0:

```
When(/^the user waits for (\d+) second(?:s)?$/) do |time|
 sleep time.to_i
end
```

Step for Cucumber 3.0 and beyond:
When(/^the user waits for (\d+) second(?:s)?$/) **do** |*time*|
 sleep *time*
end

At the time of this writing, there are multiple unresolved issues with Cucumber Expressions as currently implemented. For one, RubyMine has a difficult time recognizing the Cucumber Expressions, giving the appearance of unimplemented steps when using that particular IDE. Another is when several parameter types share the same Regexp, only one of the parameter types can be preferential. If two parameter types are defined with the same regular expression that are both preferential, an error will be thrown during matching. Execution will have infinite hang-time with an invalid match with Parameter Type from the Gherkin. Typos will ultimately wreck execution. Both "use_for_snippets" and "prefer_for_regexp_match" parameters don't get passed through with the ruby interpreter using RubyMine. Lastly, Flags for regexp area are not recognized; instead, multiline, ignore case, and extended will throw a Cucumber Expression error that the Parameter Type cannot use that option.

3. Tag Expressions

The new Tag Expressions are Boolean expressions of tags with the logical operators "**and**", "**or**", and "**not**". The new Tag Expressions replace the old syntax with a new, plain language readable syntax to specify which scenarios to run. The intention was for Cucumber can store and reuse commonly used cucumber command line arguments for a project in a **cucumber.yml** file (Wynne, 2017). Now, defining a template requires a name and the command-line options to execute with a profile.

Tags are identified within Feature files or Hooks by an "**@**" symbol. Cucumber uses them as a query language; they help organize features and scenarios, as well as selectively run tests. The new Tag Expressions are used to: (1) run a subset of scenarios and (2) specify a hook that should be executed or excluded for a subset of scenarios (Wynne, 2017).

The command line arguments for execution are stored in the **cucumber.yml** file. Defining a template requires a name and various command-line options to execute with the profile. The execution of a profile requires the **--profile** or **-p** flag. The default profile is named **default** (the profile will execute if a profile is not specified). All common profiles exclude any **Features** or **Scenarios** with the **@wip** or **@manual** tags by using the tilde (**~**) in front of the tag.

default: --format pretty --tags ~@wip --tags ~@manual
run: --format pretty --tags @run --tags ~@wip --tags ~@manual
regression: --format pretty --tags @regression --tags ~@wip --tags ~@manual
jenkins: --format json -o cucumber.json --tags ~@wip --tags ~@manual
devops: --format json -o cucumber.json --tags ~@wip --tags ~@manual

Cucumber uses tags in multiple ways. With hooks, tags can be added to "**Before**", "**After**", "**Around**", or "**AfterStep**" (Wynne & Hellesoy, 2012). This will execute hooks for only those scenarios with the given tags. A Feature Tag is located above the feature header. Multiple tags can be applied to a feature (separated with a space or newline). A Scenario Tag is located above the scenario header. Multiple tags can be applied to a scenario (separated with a space or newline). Any tag that exists on a Feature will be inherited by each Scenario, Scenario Outline, and Example. The new Tag Expressions for Cucumber 3.0 and beyond will use Boolean expressions of tags with the logical operators "**and**", "**or**" and "**not**".

Tag Expressions for Cucumber < 3.0:
sample_or_tags_profile: --format pretty --tags @smoke_test,@pbi12345,@pnsqc
sample_and_tags_profile: --format pretty --tags @smoke_test --tags @pbi12345 --tags @pnsqc
sample_excluding_tags: --format pretty --tags ~@manual --tags @smoke_test

Tag Expressions for Cucumber 3.0 and beyond:
sample_or_tags_profile: --format pretty --tags '@smoke_test or @pbi12345 or @pnsqc'
sample_and_tags_profile: --format pretty --tags '@smoke_test and @pbi12345 and @pnsqc'
sample_excluding_tags: --format pretty --tags '@smoke_test and not @manual'

A parentheses can be used for clarity or to change operator precedence:
sample_parantheses_profile: --format pretty --tags '@regression and not (@wip or @manual)'
sample_parantheses_profile: --format pretty --tags '(@pnsqc or @smoke_test) and (not @manual)'
sample_parantheses_profile: --format pretty --tags '(@smoke_test) and (not @manual) and (not @wip)'

All new Cucumber profiles must use Strings around the tag expression and use logical operators. The optional parentheses are best used for clarity or precedence. Multiple usages of the **--tags** flag in a profile is still allowed. The new syntax also applies to the aforementioned tagged Hooks. There are no changes to how tags are written in Features or Scenarios. There is no change in behavior due to underlying code changes in the Rakefile, Cucumber Profile, or Hooks. There is, however, one warning to note: Cucumber will yield a warning in the console to update the profile usage of tag expressions, but the old way of identifying tags won't be deprecated until **cucumber –v 4.0.0** (Wynne, 2017).

4. Retry and Flaky Status

A Retry flag has been introduced to retry any scenario that fails a given number of times. Scenarios that pass on a subsequent execution are given a "flaky" status. The Cucumber development team wanted to address flickering scenarios, since they reasoned automation developers were implementing their own solution to retry failed scenarios (Wynne, 2017). Retry is now an optional command line argument, which will accept integer values. Any scenario that fails is assigned the "flaky" status upon success after a prior failure. Example execution result is shown below:

Flaky Scenarios:
cucumber **<u>features/gherkin/sample.feature:3</u>**

3 scenarios (1 flaky, 2 passed)
23 steps (1 failed, 2 skipped, 20 passed)
1m1.651s

The usage of "retry" is questionable because it already exists as a keyword in Ruby, which can lead to confusion and potential misuse. Also, Flaky status is not present in outputted HTML report or JSON report, but the execution result is present for **Rerun**.

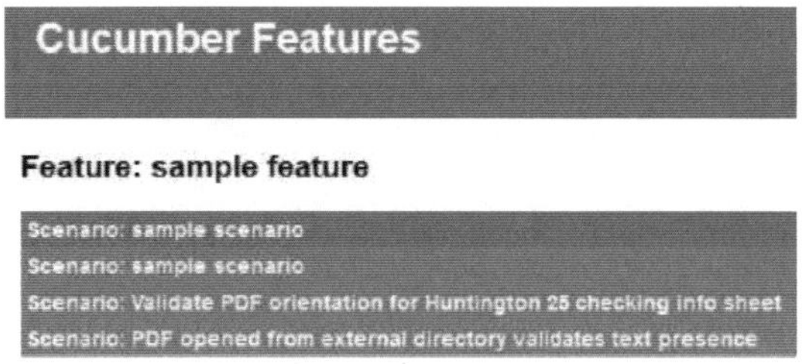

5. Strict Mode

The updated Strict Mode is more flexible about enforcing rules on the result of Scenarios compared to prior versions of Cucumber. The Cucumber development team changed the original strict mode, which failed if there were any undefined, pending, or failing results. One consequence of the old implementation was any execution in continuous integration (CI) tool such as Jenkins resulted in failures from the execution of many scenarios if just a single issue was present (non-zero exit code). The new Strict Mode implementation is intended to provide more flexibility for execution (Wynne & Hellesoy, 2017). Details of the command options are shown the table below:

Strict Mode Changes	
Command	**Effect**
-S, --[no-]strict	Fail if there are any strict affected results (that is undefined, pending or flaky results).
--[no-]strict-undefined	Fail if there are any undefined results.
--[no-]strict-pending	Fail if there are any pending results.
--[no-]strict-flaky	Fail if there are any flaky results.

A Scenario with an undefined step will have two different exit codes depending on **Strict** mode. If the profile has nothing defined, the exit code is 0. If the profile has --**no-strict-undefined**, the exit code is also 0. If the profile has --**strict-undefined**, the exit code is 1. The console yields a Cucumber exception for that step.

Profile with nothing defined:

```
 Then undefined step

2 scenarios (1 undefined, 1 passed)
5 steps (1 undefined, 7 passed)
0m13.087s

You can implement step definitions for undefined steps with these snippets:

   Then("undefined step") do
     pending # Write code here the phrase here into concrete actions
   end

Process finished with exit code 0
```

Profile with strict undefined set:

```
  Then undefined step
    Undefined step: "undefined step" (Cucumber::Undefined)
    features/gherkin/sample.feature:66:in 'Then undefined step'

Undefined Scenarios:
cucumber features/gherkin/sample.feature:63

2 scenarios (1 undefined, 1 passed)
5 steps (1 undefined, 7 passed)
0m17.919s

You can implement step definitions for undefined steps with these snippets:

Then("undefined step") do
  pending # Write code here the phrase here into concrete actions
end

Process finished with exit code 1
```

A Scenario with a pending step will have two different exit codes depending on **Strict** mode. If the profile has nothing defined, the exit code is 0. If the profile has --**no-strict-pending**, the exit code is also 0. If the profile has --**strict-pending**, the exit code is 1. The console yields a Cucumber exception for that step.

Profile with nothing defined:
Then pending step
TODO (Cucumber::Pending)
./features/step_definitions/custom_steps.rb:19:in '/^pending step$/'
features/gherkin/sample.feature:66:in 'Then pending step'

2 scenarios (1 pending, 1 passed)
5 steps (1 pending, 7 passed)
0m19.316s

Process finished with exit code 0

Profile with strict pending set:
Then pending step
TODO (Cucumber::Pending)
./features/step_definitions/custom_steps.rb:19:in '/^pending step$/'
features/gherkin/sample.feature:66:in 'Then pending step'

Pending Scenarios:
cucumber **features/gherkin/sample.feature:63**

2 scenarios (1 pending, 1 passed)
5 steps (1 pending, 7 passed)
0m18.079s

Process finished with exit code 1

A Scenario with a flaky step will have two different exit codes depending on **Strict** mode. If the profile has nothing defined, the exit code is 0. If the profile has --**no-strict-flaky**, the exit code is also 0. If the profile has --**strict-flaky**, the exit code is 1.
Profile with nothing defined:

Flaky Scenarios:
cucumber **features/gherkin/sample.feature:63**

2 scenarios (1 flaky, 1 passed)
14 steps (2 failed, 12 passed)
0m36.332s
Process finished with exit code 0

Profile with strict flaky defined:
Then flaky step

Flaky Scenarios:
cucumber **features/gherkin/sample.feature:63**

2 scenarios (1 flaky, 1 passed)
11 steps (1 failed, 10 passed)
0m21.935s

Process finished with exit code 1

A Scenario with all failure types will have two different exit codes depending on **Strict** mode. If the profile has nothing defined, the exit code is 0. If the profile has --**no-strict-** the exit code is also 0 so long as pending or undefined occurs first. Even in **--no-strict** mode, a flaky scenario followed by a pending or undefined step will yield an exit code of 1. If the profile has --**strict**, the exit code is 1 regardless of order.

For any implementation beyond Cucumber 3.0.0, new profiles for strict mode conditions can be created in the **cucumber.yml** file. However, that would require many additional profiles without being able to modify the existing profiles. Instead, any existing profiles prior to version 3.0.0 should remain the same, with optional **strict** parameters. The **strict** flag can be passed in dynamically via environment variable. Without being set, the **strict** environment variable will default to the **--no-strict** flag (the default in Cucumber as before).

Strict Mode will not show you Flaky status either or provide additional context in the output HTML or JSON report. The existing color schemes provided in the formatter will have to be used for guidance. Even in **--no-strict** mode, a flaky scenario followed by a pending or undefined step will yield an exit code of 1; the result should be exit code 0.

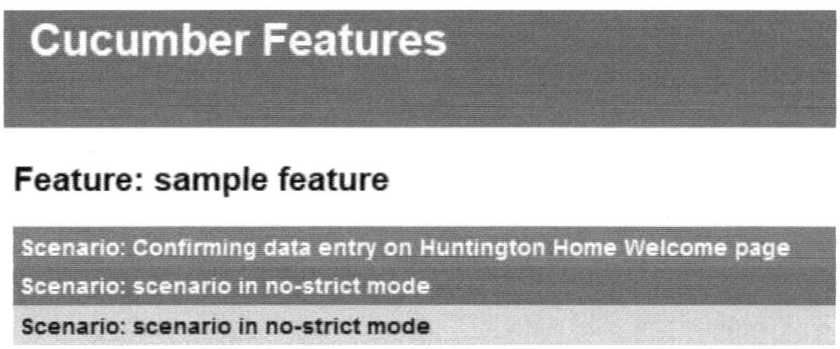

6. Events API

The Cucumber development team updated the test automation execution of compiling and running features into a series of accessible events. The intent was for events to be read-only, which are used by writing formatters and output tools (such as test result persistence stored in database tables). Many of formatters prior to version 3.0.0 have been rewritten to use the new API, though some still use the old formatter API. The events are described as follows (Wynne, 2017):

- **StepDefinitionRegistered:** "event when the **step_definitions** directory is read".
- **GherkinSourceRead:** "event when Cucumber reads a **Feature** file".
- **StepActivated**: "events are fired as each step is activated when the **Feature** file is compiled into test cases".
- **TestRunStarted:** "event describes what will run after the test cases are compiled".
- **TestCaseStarted:** "event fires for each test case before any steps run".
- **TestStepStarted:** "event (including hooks) fire for each Test Step".
- **TestStepFinished:** "event contains the result and duration of that step".
- **TestCaseFinished:** "event fires when all the steps have run, and includes the overall result of the test case".
- **TestRunFinished:** "event fires when all test cases are done".

There are still unresolved implementations for the new events API. The event, **TestRunFinished**, contains no data. Events API is a work in progress for many formatters. Lastly, the Cucumber Reports Jenkins plugin must be updated to parse Cucumber v. 3.0.0 results.

7. Additional Changes Beyond Cucumber 3.0

There are a few other changes to consider:

- Support for Ruby 1.9 and 2.0 has been dropped.
- Transforms have been removed in favor of Parameter Types (Cucumber Expressions).
- The Cucumber Core Team plans to open up contributions to more users in an effort to clean up the code base. The code base will be simplified.
- The old formatter API will be deprecated in Cucumber –v 4.0.0
- Existing Tag Expressions will be supported until Cucumber –v 4.0.0.

8. Appendix: Installation for Ruby with RubyMine IDE

Ruby-Cucumber can be installed via command line directly, bundle installation in the console, or within an IDE such as RubyMine. When the gem version is excluded from the command (e.g., –v 0.0.0), RubyGems will pull the most recent version by default. To install a specific version, include the –v tag in your install command with the specific version number. Alternatively, type "gem install cucumber –v 3.0.0".

```
Microsoft Windows [Version 6.1.7601]
Copyright (c) 2009 Microsoft Corporation.  All rights reserved.

C:\automation\hnb-web-template>gem install cucumber
Fetching: cucumber-3.0.2.gem (100%)
Successfully installed cucumber-3.0.2
Parsing documentation for cucumber-3.0.2
Installing ri documentation for cucumber-3.0.2
Done installing documentation for cucumber after 25 seconds
1 gem installed
```

For RubyMine, include 'cucumber' in the Gemfile so the bundle installation will install the other required project gems. If the version number is not included with the gem, bundler will install the most recent version. To update the project suite with PDF Reader, follow these steps in RubyMine: Tools -> Bundler -> Install -> click 'Install'.

```
source 'http://rubygems.org'

group :default do

  gem 'rake'
  gem 'cucumber', '=3.0.0'
  gem 'rspec'
  gem 'page-object'
  gem 'watir'
  gem 'selenium-webdriver'
  gem 'cuke_sniffer'
  gem 'rspec_junit_formatter'
  gem 'pdf-reader'
  gem 'certified'

end
```

For Console Bundle Installation (within the project directory), include 'cucumber' in the Gemfile so the bundle installation will install the other required project gems. If the version number is not included with the gem, bundler will install the most recent version.

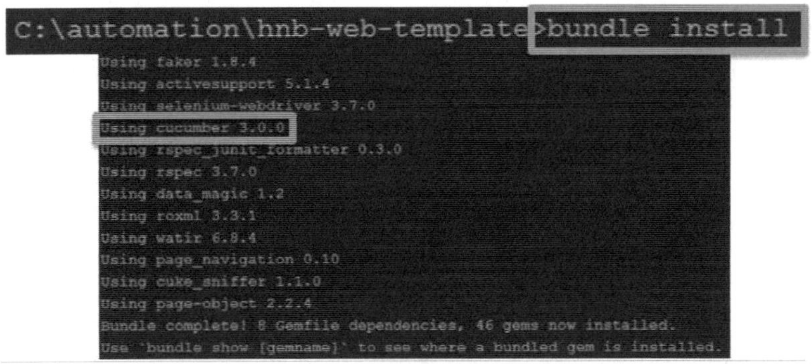

References

1. North, Dan. 2006 "Introducing BDD." Dan North & Associates. https://dannorth.net/introducing-bdd/ (accessed November 12, 2017).

2. Hellesoy, Aslak. 2017. "Why is the Cucumber Tool for BDD Named as Such?." Cucumber Limited. https://www.quora.com/Why-is-the-Cucumber-tool-for-BDD-named-as-such (accessed September 27, 2017).

3. Hellesoy, Aslak. 2014. "The World's Most Misunderstood Collaboration Tool." Cucumber Limited. https://cucumber.io/blog/2014/03/03/the-worlds-most-misunderstood-collaboration-tool (accessed September 27, 2017).

4. Wynne, Matt, and Aslak Hellesøy. The Cucumber Book: Behavior-driven Development for Testers and Developers. Dallas, TX: Pragmatic Bookshelf, 2012.

5. Wynne, Matt. 2017. "Announcing Cucumber-Ruby v3.0.0." Cucumber Limited. https://cucumber.io/blog/2017/09/27/announcing-cucumber-ruby-3-0-0 (accessed September 27, 2017).

6. Hellesoy, Aslak, 2017. "Parameter Types Examples." Cucumber Limited. https://github.com/cucumber/cucumber-ruby/blob/master/features/docs/writing_support_code/parameter_types.feature (accessed November 12, 2017).

7. Hellesoy, Aslak. 2017. "Announcing Cucumber Expressions." Cucumber Limited. https://cucumber.io/blog/2017/07/26/announcing-cucumber-expressions (accessed July 26, 2017).

8. Wynne, Matt. 2017. "Cucumber Expressions." Cucumber Limited. https://docs.cucumber.io/cucumber-expressions/ (accessed November 12, 2017).

9. Wynne, Matt. 2017. "Tag Expressions." Cucumber Limited. https://docs.cucumber.io/tag-expressions/ (accessed November 12, 2017).

10. Wynne, Matt. 2017. "Retry and Flaky Status." Cucumber Limited https://app.cucumber.pro/projects/cucumber-ruby/documents/branch/master/features/docs/cli/retry_failing_tests.feature (accessed November 12, 2017).

11. Wynne, Matt, Hellesoy, Aslak & various contributors. 2008-2018. Full Change Log: https://github.com/cucumber/cucumber-ruby/blob/master/CHANGELOG.md (accessed November 12, 2017).

12. Wynne, Matt. 2017. "Events API." Cucumber Limited. http://www.rubydoc.info/github/cucumber/cucumber-ruby/Cucumber/Events (accessed November 12, 2017).

13. Adzic, Gojko. Specification by Example: How Successful Teams Deliver the Right Software. Shelter Island, NY: Manning, 2011

QA in an Agile Development Team

Authors

Michelle Wu (mwu@paraport.com)

Abstract

Our company has been using the Agile Development process for almost 10 years. Our QA team plays an important role in making the development process successful. During these 10 years, we have been experimenting with various processes and approaches to make our development process more efficient; some work well for us, some do not work at all, and some need to be modified to fit our needs. In this paper, I would like to discuss what role our QA team plays in different stages of the software development lifecycle. What are the challenges we have encountered and how we have resolved them?

Biography

Michelle Wu is Parametric's Master Software Quality Assurance (QA) Engineer. She provides oversight and leadership of the company QA department. She has over 25 years of working experience in software testing. Prior to joining Parametric in 2006, Michelle had worked in software testing on firmware, drivers, printing software, access point management software. She earned B.S. and M.S. in Computer Science from California State University, Chico.

1. Introduction

Parametric is a financial company that do wealth management. We build proprietary software for our business to manage daily business workflows. Our development team supports over 36 applications running with 67 services on 14 databases. We started using Agile Development process over 10 years ago. Our QA team has been playing an important role in making the development process successful. During these 10 years, we have been experimenting with various processes and approaches to make our development process more efficient; some work well for us, some do not work at all, and some need to be modified to fit our needs. In this paper, I would like to discuss what role our QA team plays in different stages of the software development lifecycle. What are the challenges we have encountered and how we have resolved them?

2. Development Team Overview

First I would like to give an overview of our development team structure. Our development team consists of four subdivisions. The responsibilities of the development team are split into four and distributed amongst these subdivided teams; Project Teams, Performance Team, Maintenance Team, and Tools Team. There are 4 Project Teams and they are responsible for the development of new features and applications to support company operations and workflows. The Performance Team is responsible for the improvement and optimization of our application performance to ensure smooth operation of all the features. The Maintenance Team is responsible for resolving production escalations and supporting minor feature backlog items. Finally, the Tools Team is responsible for development and deployment tools.

These four subdivisions of the Development Team work in tandem to produce the most optimized and effective software applications and tools. With the exception of the tool team and one of the project teams, all of our development teams have one to two developers and only one QA. With the Agile development approach, we release new features and feature updates very frequently. Our development team has deployed over 250 feature updates to production in the year 2017. This makes the job of QA very challenging.

3. QA Lifecycle Overview

Before getting into the challenges, I will give a brief overview of the current QA workflow in our development team. Our QA workflow starts from the beginning of the product lifecycle. We begin with consulting the Business Analysis and Business Users to draw out acceptance criteria for the project. Based on the acceptance criteria, we develop test plans and test cases, followed by test cases execution, and user acceptance tests. Finally, we coordinate with the release team to release the project to production. QAs face different challenges in different phases of the QA lifecycle. In order to overcome and reduce the bad side effects of the challenges, we continuously adjust and modify our QA workflow to make the QA team more efficient. We will discuss each phase of the QA lifecycle in detail in the later section of this paper. For now, let us go over the challenges and explain how we adjusted the QA process and lifecycle to reduce the bad side effects of these challenges.

4. Challenges

4.1. Frequent Releases

As an Agile development shop, we release updates and new features frequently to production. Often times, we release updates for an application as frequent as a couple times each week. Because of that, the risk of breaking existing features becomes very high. In order to ensure that we do not break any existing features in a release, we have to run very extensive application regression tests. This places a massive overhead in the time and effort required to finish regression tests each time before the release. To address these challenges, we adjusted our project planning to get releases into smaller chunks. This will reduce the risk of breaking existing features and the impact of the release in production. Smaller releases means more frequent releases. However, this puts a large burden on the QA to regress the application features before every release. To resolve this, our QA team maintains a set of comprehensive regression test documents. We automate the regression tests as much as we can, specifically in the areas that would take a long time and effort to test manually. For example, data validation logic, mathematic calculation logic, etc. would be prime areas to automate. We also check developers' code commits to the source control to better understand what areas are being updated. This allows the QA to better plan regression tests to ensure that the updated areas are being tested sufficiently.

4.2. Developers are Always Ahead of QA in Completing Tasks

Another challenge that QAs normally face is that developers are always ahead of the QA in completing tasks. QAs always get pushed at the end of the development cycle to finish testing new and existing features.

When we first employed the Agile Development methodology, we used the fixed iteration method, which was 2 weeks cycle. This was because we wanted to find our team velocity. In addition, by using fixed iteration development cycle, developers will not acquire any non-planned tasks before the end of the iteration, and subsequently, developers will not be too far ahead of QAs. However, we found out later that fixed iteration would only work well if we could accurately estimate how much time we needed to finish the tasks for the iteration. We often either overestimated or underestimated the time and effort for the iteration. The team either ran of tasks to do or could not finish all the tasks we planned for the iteration.

We adjusted our process to plan our tasks based on project features. We do not use fixed iteration. Instead, we release when features are ready to be released. But by having a dynamic release cycle, the problem of developers finishing tasks ahead of QAs came back to us. In order to narrow this gap, we integrated more automated tests in our code to test features. These automated integration tests are run after the project has been built. We have also adjusted our project task breakdown process to make every feature task testable. By having testable tasks, QAs can work in parallel with the developers to test the task as soon as the developers have finished implementing it. In addition, developers help our QAs demonstrate features to the business users and run regression tests. Since we have developed a set of comprehensive regression documents that the developers can just follow, the ability to run regression tests has been made vastly easier.

4.3. We Are Not Building the Right Thing

Building a feature that does not meet user expectations is a mistake commonly made in product development. In order to ensure that we develop the right feature that meets business user needs, the QA is involved very early in the product development lifecycle. We meet with the developers, business analysts, and business users to review test cases. Test case review meetings provide the opportunity for business users to communicate their expectations and business workflow to developers and QAs.

Thought test case review, developers and QAs also communicate with each other how the features should work for the business users. And ensure that the test cases provide good feature coverage and the features are being tested correctly.

In addition to test case review sessions, we also demonstrate the features to business users as soon as the features are completed and tested. This allows development teams to get feedback from the business users and make necessary changes as early as possible. The further along the development cycle, the higher the cost is to make changes to the code. To further ensure the right features are built, QA conducts "Paired UAT" with the business users, which is a process in which the QA sits down with the business users to execute user's acceptance tests.

We also narrow the communication gap between us and the business users by co-locating with them. The development team, including QAs, sit right next to the business users. This allows QAs to demo new features to the business users and get feedback during the development process.

4.4. Agile Development Emphasizes Test Driven Development (TDD) No QAA is Needed

There is a myth that test automation is all that is required in software testing. While test automation is important in software testing, automation cannot completely replace manual testing. Manual testing is still needed for tests that are difficult and costly to automate. For example, end-to-end functional test.

End-to-end functional tests involve testing across applications and services. It is difficult to automate testing across applications as we need to pass data and commands between application projects.

5. QA Lifecycle at Parametric Portfolio Associates

5.1. Review Requested Feature

Our QAs work very closely with business analysts and business users (stake holders) to define acceptance criteria for feature requirements. We ensure that the acceptance criteria is clear and correct and that feature requirements are correctly translated to acceptance criteria.

5.2. Test Cases Development

Based on the acceptance criteria, the development team goes through a task breakdown process to break down the projects into testable tasks. While developers are implementing the features, the QA develops test cases and reviews them with the developers. We also often involve business users in our test case review meetings to ensure that we are testing the features correctly and ensure that QAs and developers have a good understanding of feature workflow.

5.3. Feature Testing and Regression

As developers finish a feature task, the QA will pick up the task and test the feature by running the test cases. The QA will also regress the feature with existing features of the application to ensure that the new feature does not break any existing features. This will offload the burden of running regression at the end of the project development cycle. Once the development team finishes implementing and testing a feature set, the QA will demo the features to the business users.

5.4. Demo

5.4.1. Why Do We Demo?

Demo is "Show and Tell". Regardless of how well the requirement and acceptance criteria are written, it is difficult for business users to picture how exactly a feature works. Demo is always the best way to communicate how a feature will function to the business user. By using the feature during demo, the business user can visualize how the feature functions and verify if the feature fits their workflow and if the user interface is intuitive. Demo also allows development teams to gauge user feedback from the business user earlier. This will minimize the cost of changes, as changes in the later stage of the development cycle cost significantly more. Finally, by demoing features as soon as they are ready to be used to the business users, the business users will be more involved with development cycle, leading to better communication and more effective product development.

5.5. User Acceptance Testing

User Acceptance Testing (UAT) plays an important role in ensuring that the development team built the correct product. The user acceptance testing phase takes place at the end of the development cycle after features have been demoed to the users. Developers will create a release candidate of the application and the QA will push the application to the test environment for business users to run tests on the application.

During feature demo to the users, the QA reviews acceptance criteria and test cases with the users as preparation for UAT. The QA also provides guidelines to the user in how to run tests and what they need to look for when running tests. UAT feedback, which can be bugs, feature updates, or new feature requests, are reported to the development team. These issues will be triaged and fixed accordingly.

After the bugs or features are updated, updates will be pushed to the test environment for another round of testing and verification.

This cycle will continue until the user has verified that all the features are working as expected. At this point, users will give their approval to release the updates to production.

5.6. Prepare for Release to Production

After getting business approval, the QA will run a final round of regression tests of the released application. After the regression tests have passed, the QA will submit release tickets to our application support ticket system. Then, the QA coordinates with the DevOps release team to prepare the release of the application to production.

5.7. Post Release Support

The QA's responsibilities do not end with the release of the application. After the application release, we run demos for the Maintenance team and Application team so that they understand how the new features work and are able to support production requests and escalation of the release features. QAs will also continue to support the features if a warm fix (bug introduced with workaround) or hot fix (work stopping issue) is needed after features are released. Finally, QAs also update our application regression test document with the new features so that these feature will be tested in the next release of the application.

Diagram 1 QA Lifecycle at Parametric

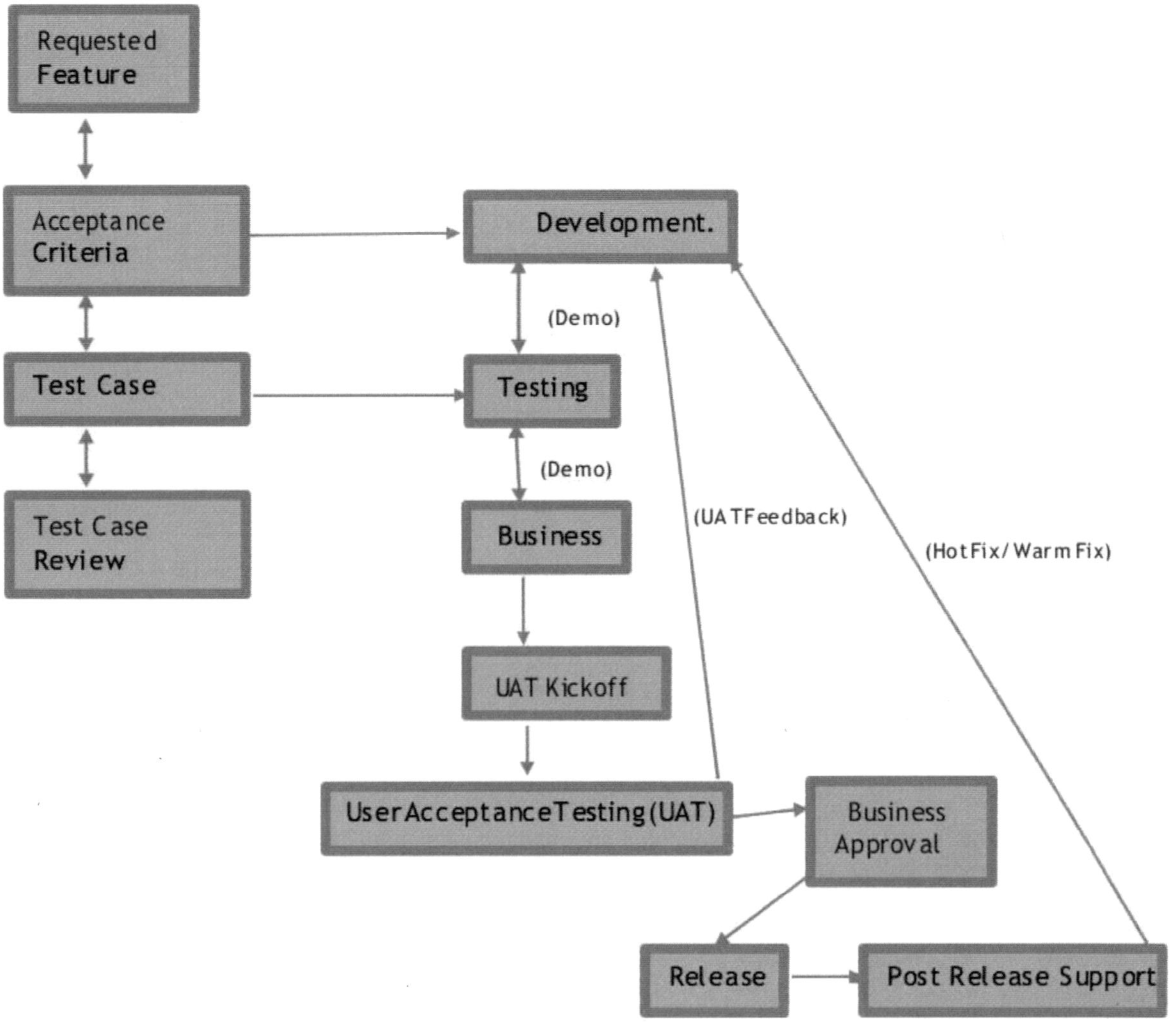

6. Conclusion

As mentioned in the beginning of the paper, we started using Agile Development process over 10 years ago. Ten years ago, QA lifecycle at Parametric was limited to test planning, application testing and regression testing. In these 10 years, QA lifecycle has expanded to start at the beginning of the product development cycle, which is feature analysis with business users and business analysts; and end at providing post-release support.

QA works very closely with the business users and business analysts to derive acceptance criteria for the project. We conduct test case review sessions with the business users and developers to ensure features are being built correctly to meet business users' expectations. In order to narrow the gap that developers finish all the tasks before QA, we adjusted our project task breakdown process to make every feature task testable. By having testable tasks, QAs can work in parallel with the developers to test the task as soon as the developers have finished implementing it. In addition, we integrated more automated tests in our code to test features. We also develop sets of application regression test documents to allow developers help with regression testing.

To further ensure that we build the product features right, we demo the application features to the business users as soon as they are finished. QA also plays a very important role in conducting and coordinating the user acceptance testing with the business users. We communicate feedback from the business users to the development team.QA responsibility does not end after we finished testing the application features. We co-ordinate the release to the production. QA also provides post-release support to the application support team and the maintenance team.

Our development and QA team have been working very hard to make the Agile Development process work well for us. We attended conferences and workshops every year to bring new technologies, new knowledges about Agile Development back to our team. We constantly slim line our development and testing processes to improve efficiency and accuracy. We will continue strive for improving our QA processes to make our development team more efficiency,

7. Appendix

The following are the major tools our development and QA team use for project management, managing project documentations, such as technical requirements, acceptance criteria, test cases and regression test documents, and application deployment tools.

7.1. Project Management

- Leankit/Jira
- Confluence (project stories, test cases)

7.2. Automation

- Unit Tests
- Integration Tests (Specflow)
- Postman (WebApi testing)

7.3. Logging

- Kibana
- Elk Stack/ Elastics Search

7.4. Deployment

- TeamCity (Build Agent)
- Octopus

Risk Based Testing: Communicating Why You Can't Test EVERYTHING

Authors
Jenny Bramble, WillowTree Apps. Inc.
jenny.bramble@gmail.com
http://twitter.com/jennydoesthing

Abstract
The idea of testing everything is a popular one, in fact, many stakeholders think that's exactly what their quality teams do. It usually isn't and can't be; but how can teams communicate this? Join Jenny Bramble as she helps to pave the way using the language of risk-based testing. By defining risk in two simple parts, the team and project have a tangible and usable metric. She shares how to apply this metric and use it to determine where the team should focus testing, making it more effective and efficient whilst communicating that effort through the creation of a risk matrix.

As a result, risk becomes the right language for the team to communicate clearly and concisely with everyone involved in the project by using agreed-upon words and definitions.

Biography
Jenny Bramble ended up--as many of us do--falling in a quality assurance career after trying a few other routes. She came up through support and DevOps, cutting her teeth on that interesting role that acts as the 'translator' between customer requests from support and the development team. Her love of support and the human side of problems lets her find a sweet spot between empathy for the user and empathy for my team. She's done testing, support, or human interfacing for most of her career. She has been interested in risk her entire career, finding it the foundation that all QA is built upon.

1. Introduction
One of the hardest parts of my career in quality assurance has been telling someone--anyone--that I'm worried about a feature that they really want to release. I'm an emotional person and favor talking in pictures and feelings over logic and rationale. This would often leave me in the sorts of situations where everyone involved walked away upset.

"Hey," I'd say to one of the developers on my team. "I feel bad about this feature that we're trying to push out for the next release."

"What do you mean?" he'd ask.

"It's just...I have a bad feeling." I might wave my arms about or shrug.

He'd look at me, look at his computer, and decide that it wasn't worth his time to try and force me to make sense.

This scene would repeat over and over in my days as a junior QA person and I never really understood why they didn't seem to understand me. I thought I was communicating well, and after a while, people would trust my 'gut instincts' about our projects. Yet, every time we'd get a new developer, new product owner, new project manager, new quality assurance person, or new intern, the cycle would start again.

What was going on? It turns out I was trying to communicate risk to my stakeholders (in this case, my developers) and because we were using different subsets of language, I was not able to effectively communicate.

2. What is Risk?

Risk--or our feelings about risk--while essential to every aspect of a project is not easy to communicate. We use words that mean something to us, but that may mean something entirely different to another person. Considering this is a metric that we use to define our scope of testing, this is a gap in our communication that can be very detrimental to our projects. If we can't talk about risk in a concrete, meaningful way, we are losing one of the best tools in our QA toolbox.

So, then, what is risk? Can we give it a value that we can use to compare different features and use cases?

Yes!

Simply put, risk is the impact of failure and the likelihood that failure will occur. The intersection of impact and likelihood gives us that value.

Once we can determine the impact of the failure that may occur and the likelihood of that failure, we can create a scale that we will use to assign a value to the likelihood and the impact which can be combined to give us a value that we can assign as risk.

Let's start with a definition of "failure" and its impact.

3. Failure, Impact of Failure, and Probability of Failure

Failure is anything that has an impact on the business. The most obvious examples are bugs that cause catastrophe--users can't login or can't perform basic functions. But, there are a lot of layers to the impact that failure can have. When we've determined what our failure cases are, we can move on to talking about the impact of these failures.

The easiest types of impacts to see are the technical failures. Examples here are features not working or behaving in unexpected ways from something as simple as 'users can't log in' to a more complex scenario such as 'the data returned are subtly off from the expected value.' We see these failures every day as we navigate the web or use mobile applications on our phones. They're the most obvious of failures to end users.

But, there are other types of failures. You can have a failure that impacts the business side of the house: maybe there's a feature released too early. Or a rule that's not been properly implemented. Or worse--legal language missing from a site that brings your company out of compliance.

Most importantly and most often overlooked, we can also have a failure that impacts the morale of our users; an emotional failure if you will. This happens when users have their workflow interrupted or something that causes them to need to do extra work. Even a flow that improves the time they need to spend on a task can be disruptive if it's not communicated clearly.

When we finally can sit down and talk about all the ways a use case, feature, or application can fail, we can start to have a real meaningful discussion on what the impacts are. This is the first time in the process that we start to level set and align everyone's expectations together. Once this is started, you will find your teams have a much easier time communicating.

The next area to focus on is probability. Simply put: how likely is it that this use case, feature, or application will fail in the ways we've described?

There is not always an obvious answer to this question. As with the impact, we end up making an educated guess. This means that our first step is to educate ourselves.

Begin by asking questions. Has this feature failed before? How did it fail? When? Have we handled that use case?

Has something similar failed before?

Are there any outside influences acting on our team that may make this feature more likely to fail?

Do we have any root cause analysis documents or defects that can tell us about past failures? Have we asked any of our team members who've worked in this area of the code before about it?

How likely is this use case to be encountered by end users? How many end users may see the failure?

All of these answers will give us information that we can use to determine the likelihood of the item failing in our present day. There's always the chance that we'll be wrong, but our job is to make these educated guesses by collecting as much information as is feasible and translating those answers to the team in a reasonable way.

If you are looking at your item and are concerned that you're not getting the full picture, there's a few other things you can do as well.

First, remember that there are other types of risks. Perhaps you want to indicate that user familiarity is a factor that will increase the risk or likelihood that you will see issues. Or you are concerned about the number of merges a particular feature has and you'd like to use that to weight the risk value. If you have any industry specific risks that come into play, you can use those as well. Anything that gives you enough information to make a decision but not so much that you create a lot of chaos or swirl is worth noting.

Second, look for more or less granularity. If you are looking too closely at the details then you may not be getting a good picture of the true risks. Similarly, if you're going too broad, you may miss individual pieces that need more attention. Maybe there's a particular use case that has a high impact of failure yet the overall feature tends to have a lower impact as there's several ways to access it. This would be valuable to call out separately.

Once these things have been hashed out, we can start using our rating system. By defining what we mean when we say risk, we've already started to create a stronger team. Using the same words with the same meanings, we're able to accurately communicate to our team members.

4. Building a Risk Matrix

Begin by deciding how you'll represent your concerns or feelings on the impact and likelihood. A scale of 1 to 10 is most often used, though you can use anything that makes sense to your team. Values of high, low, medium or t-shirt sizing can also work. If you have a team that is particularly emotion driven, a set of emojis can also be a fantastic visual way to represent the impact, likelihood, and resulting risk.

Create a matrix with one row for each of your use cases or features and a column for each item that will contribute to the overall risk value and a column for the over-all risk.

Item/Use Case	**Impact of Failure**	**Probability of Failure**	**Risk Value**

As you can see, it looks pretty simple. This is by design. The more complex a risk matrix is, the less likely it is that it will be filled out in a timely, useful manner.

Enter in all the use cases or features you want to look at. Remember that for each risk assessment session, you should focus on a subset of features, since doing all of them at once will muddy the waters and you may find yourself rushing to just get numbers down.

Item/Use Case	Impact of Failure	Probability of Failure	Risk Value
Upload a song to your account			
Set a song to "fans only"			
Add lyrics for a song			

With the team or with yourself, discuss the rating system. What does a catastrophic failure look like for these scenarios? What does an acceptable failure look like? What about a failure that is bad, but not earth shattering?

Once you have those things defined, you can enter in values for the Impact of Failure column.

Item/Use Case	Impact of Failure	Probability of Failure	Risk Value
Upload a song to your account	10		
Set a song to "fans only"	6		
Add lyrics for a song	2		

In this scenario, uploading a song is our golden path--our most important workflow. If a user is unable to upload a song at all, that constitutes an all-hands-on-deck emergency. But if they can't set a song to "fans only", that's not as big of an issue. It's still bad and we need to resolve it, but it isn't a severity one emergency.

If users are unable to add lyrics to a song, we are not as concerned. It'll be fixed, but perhaps in the next build not as a hotfix.

Next, we look at the probability of failure. This is where most of the discussion happens. When I run a risk assessment session, I will often time box these discussions to 3-5 minutes. You can discuss it longer, but if you restrict the time (or timebox it), people will often start to agree on a number.

Item/Use Case	Impact of Failure	Probability of Failure	Risk Value
Upload a song to your account	10	4	
Set a song to "fans only"	6	8	
Add lyrics for a song	2	3	

Here, we've determined that uploading a song probably will not break, but it's a workflow that we have in a lot of places and there's a chance of it failing as a result of other work.

Setting a song to "fans only" is brand new functionality and we've never had any gatekeeping in place like this. Therefore, it has a high chance of breaking or being implemented incorrectly.

Adding lyrics has a low probability of failure. It's a simple text page with no formatting and we haven't touched that code path in a long time.

Now that we have this, we can multiply the values together and get a value for risk.

Item/Use Case	Impact of Failure	Probability of Failure	Risk Value
Upload a song to your account	10	4	40
Set a song to "fans only"	6	8	48
Add lyrics for a song	2	3	6

We can clearly see and now clearly communicate to our team where we should be focusing our testing efforts. Setting a song to "fans only" is the obvious choice, with uploading songs a close second.

Now that we have these numbers in our hands, we can take them to other parts of our cross functional teams and say 'this is where our efforts will be focused and this is why.'

This lets us not only justify our decisions to our team but it can also let us argue for more resources such as more people working on a project or more time to complete the work we've been given. In short, risk drives these decisions and by clearly defining risk as impact of failure multiplied by probability of failure we can communicate risk via a risk matrix. This helps our team members make better, more informed decisions.

Summary

In summary, the language of risk-based testing, once it's defined by your team, is a powerful tool to use for communication. You can supplement the definitions with a risk matrix and find that you and your team communicate more clearly, precisely, and will lead to better testing of your application. In turn, this leads to high quality and higher confidence overall.

References

Heuristic Risk-Based Testing by James Bach
http://www.satisfice.com/articles/hrbt.pdf

Risk-Based Testing: Test Only What Matters by Rajnish Mehta
https://www.stickyminds.com/article/risk-based-testing-test-only-what-matters-0

Risk Based Testing, Strategies for Prioritizing Tests against Deadlines by Hans Schaefer
http://www.methodsandtools.com/archive/archive.php?id=31

Wave of risk perception
http://www.a-sisyphean-task.com/2018/06/the-wave-of-risk-perception.html

Hardening Your Development Process

Authors

Nicolas Guini (nicolas_guini@mcafee.com)
Andres More (andres_more2@mcafee.com)

Abstract

Every day, we can find new software security issues, exploits and new ways to misuse the software to do things never thought. Security criminals look every day at the software we produce and try to find a simple breach to exploit it and gain control to use it as they wish.

Many times, the security tests are not considered because it is difficult to see results, it is difficult to implement, or it costs time and money. But, when attackers find security flaws in our software, we regret the decisions made previously and we wish to have checked again with a security perspective.

For these reasons, it is important to add controls and security checks in our development process. The application of the Secure Development Process (SDL) added to a Security Maturity Model (SMM) helps our development teams find security infractions in the early stages before the software comes out into the open.

The purpose of this paper is to review an introduction to the life cycle of secure development and how it can be improved by verifying it with a measure of the security maturity model. We discuss how this process helps to find security problems in a new feature development. And a practical application of lessons learned to make this process faster and easier for development teams.

Biography

Nicolas Guini is a Software Security Architect at McAfee Argentina. Nicolas has a Computing Engineer Degree where worked with Security Tools for pentesting, a Specialization on Computer Security and two Ethical Hacking Certifications. Lecturer at OWASP and local universities.

Andres More is a Software Product Architect at McAfee Argentina. Andres has a CS degree where implemented mandatory security control at Linux's network stack, and a MSc in High Performance Computing where developed infrastructure to support performance optimization. Lecturer at OWASP and postgraduate courses in security at a local military institution.

1. Introduction

This section introduces software security and how it should be incorporated in a software development lifecycle, considering an agile implementation. Following sections go into detailing best practices around security on each different development activity.

1.1. Software Security

Software security is the idea of developing software so that it continues to function correctly under malicious attacks of vulnerabilities. Security is necessary to provide integrity, authentication and availability as non-functional requirements.

Software security best practices leverage good software engineering and involve thinking about security at early stages of the software development lifecycle, considering and identifying common threats, designing for security and subjecting all software artifacts to thorough objective risk analysis and testing.

Security and privacy perspectives should be included in all software and application development practices. Product security policies and processes must be applied, to proactively find and remove software security defects or vulnerabilities as early as possible.

1.2. Secure Software Development Lifecycle

Software Development Life Cycle

The Software Development Life Cycle (SDLC) is a process used by software engineers to design, develop and test high quality software [9]. It describes the stages and tasks involved in each step of a project to write and deploy software. A mature process should be documented so it can be properly communicated, incorporated, measured and ideally improved over its own lifecycle.

Secure Development Lifecycle

The Security Development Lifecycle (SDL) is a software development process that helps developers build more secure software and address security compliance requirements while reducing development cost [1], [4], [8].

The goals of SDL therefore are twofold:

- Reduce the number of security vulnerabilities and privacy issues.
- Reduce the severity of the vulnerabilities that remain unaddressed.

Agile SDLC

An agile SDLC favors collaboration thru frequent and incremental releases, made by self-organizing teams in direct interaction with end users, it was made popular after a manifesto were customer satisfaction is the top priority [11].
An agile implementation of a SDLC following the scaled agile framework [10] is depicted in Figure 1.

Investment themes are used to drive definition from a high-level plan of intent until concrete development stories, refining work items from a program backlog into a team backlog. Team ceremonies including daily syncs, sprint reviews and retrospective sessions drive the team pace on shippable increments until a finished product is completed.

Agile SDL
For a new product, the security process typically begins at project initiation. A seasoned security architect assesses a proposal for its security implications. The output of this engagement is any additional security features that will be added for software self-protection so that the software can be deployed in accordance with the different security postures.

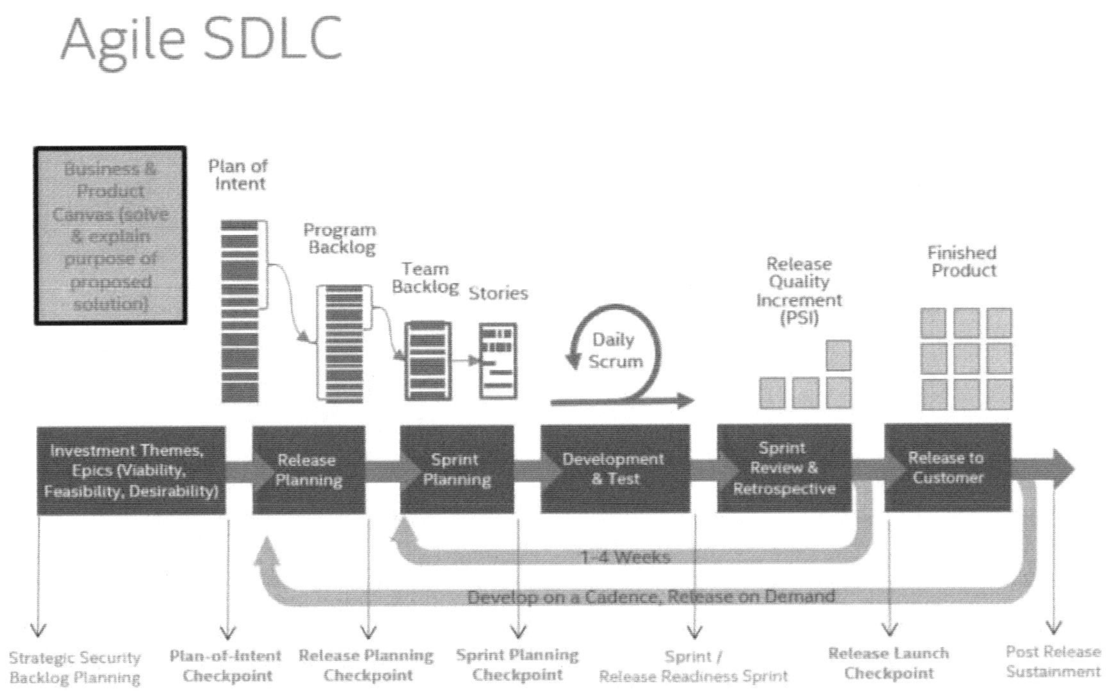

Figure 1: Agile SDLC

Any project that involves a change to the architecture of the product is required to go through a security architecture review. The proposed architectural changes are analyzed for security requirements, as well as analyzed within the whole of the architecture of the product for each change's security implications. A threat model is created or updated. The output of this analysis will typically be the security requirements that must be folded into the design that will be implemented. An architecture review may be a discreet event or may be accomplished iteratively as the architecture progresses (Agile).

The Agile SDL requires that designs that contain security features or effects are reviewed to make sure that security requirements will be built correctly. The Security Architect signs off when the design meets expectations. All functional items, including security design elements, are included in the thorough functional test plan. Like architectural reviews, a design review may be a discreet event or may be accomplished iteratively when design work occurs (Agile).
In tandem with architecture and design reviews, privacy reviews are conducted. A Privacy Impact Assessment (PIA) is performed to determine if any additional privacy activities are required to protect personal data. Privacy reviews cover the whole lifecycle of personal data and often extend beyond the product collecting the data and include backend systems and infrastructure.

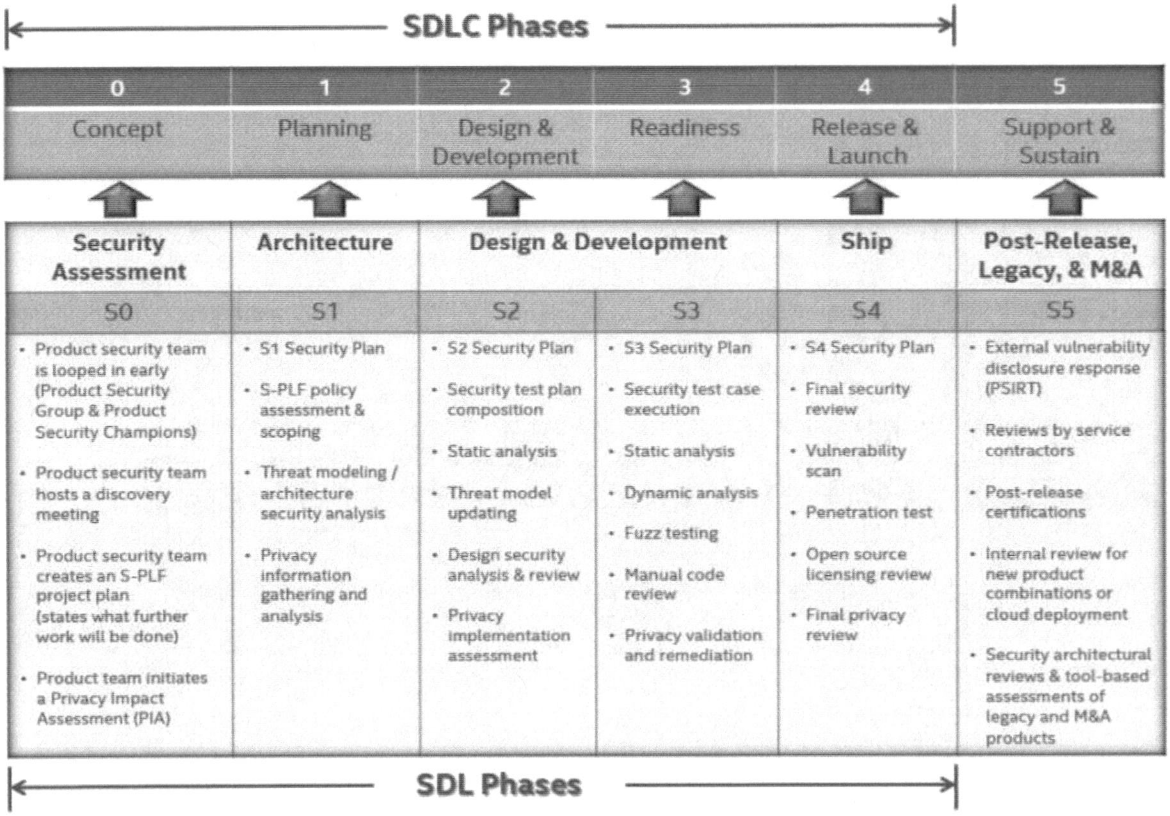

Figure 2: Waterfall SDL and Agile SDLC security tasks

The above chart shows how can a traditional Waterfall SDLC can be adapted to Agile methodology and security tasks can be applied on each phase. Integrated into Secure Development, security and privacy tasks are executed as seamless and holistic process designed to produce software which has an appropriate security and privacy attributes built into it.

The set of security tasks can be applied either as a Waterfall development or in Agile development, performing them across the iterations. For Continuous Integration, SDL activities are determined by certain triggers which are set by milestones, events, and time intervals.

Security Maturity Model

A Security Maturity Model applied to SDL is a multi-layered measurement approach that can be applied to any product to understand security practices. Is not different from other maturity models [12] but having security-related practices as the focus.

The McAfee Product Security Maturity Model [2] is how McAfee evaluates developing team's work and procedure related to implemented tasks, activities and findings before, during and after the development process. The McAfee's PSMM covers around 16 topics which are evaluated in all aspects related to secure development, since new initial requirements are defined, architecture and design of new changes are reviewed, the whole process is monitored, and final checks are executed.

Post-release activities should be discussed independently when considering security, as vulnerabilities on the field might impact not only the product but the customer relying on it. McAfee establishes a company-wide Product Security Incident Response team (PSIRT), who oversees all answers of product security concerns to customers including vulnerability handling.

Security Bulletins (SB) are security documents that ISVs publish when they fix some vulnerability on their products. An SB contains a brief description of each fixed vulnerability including affected products. Fixes and their release date are specified sometimes including workaround mitigations until patches are applied. McAfee follows this practice as well [3].

2. Tools and Automation

This section describes what and how security can be considered on each different task to be completed during process development stages. Lessons learned are included so other team can leverage.

2.1. Concept

2.1.1. Security Training

Training is a tool that avoid bugs up-front as they are not even created. Training should be considered a never-ending activity delivered to the team incrementally. Each training increments should cover topics around:

1. *Security Domain*: the team should be familiar with the security domain, including corporate practices around managing products on the same vertical.
2. *Used Technology*: the team should know language or framework specific hurdles around potential vulnerabilities when not implemented properly.
3. *Security Tools and Processes*: eventually the whole agile team should understand how to run security scans, how to test security communications, etc. Every task with changes to be required again should be documented for the rest of the team, and documentation on tasks should evolve when the tasks reoccurs.

2.2. Requirements

2.2.1. Definition of Done (DoD)

The definition of done explicitly defines to the team members what needs to be completed before closing an assigned epic or story. From a security point of view:

1. Critical code should be reviewed by a senior or security SME (Subject Matter Expert)
2. All code changes should be statically analyzed, and found defects addressed
3. New and modified interfaces should be dynamically tested using scanners and fuzzers.
4. New or modified dependencies (such as 3rd party libraries) should be reviewed.

Following the agile concept, we have established a flexible approach for DoD as well. There are different levels: Good, Better, Best. For instance, an epic might be in a good state if functionally is completed but not all peer review findings are addresses yet. With regards to security, an epic might not be in best state until security testing has confirmed proper cryptography is being used in a new communication channel.

This incremental DoD follows the idea of tracking technical debts but does it without splitting the tasks and helping the team to avoid postponing resolving it. The incremental DoD also allows integrating components on a complex product to delivery incremental value altogether.

2.2.2. End of Life Components

Most products today rely on multiple third-party components. Each component should be reviewed in search for vulnerabilities and signals of being out-of-maintenance. The company keeps track of whitelisted and blacklisted projects so the analyzed does not need to be repeated across teams.

Factors while analyzing the health of a dependency are:

1. User base (downloads, discussion posts quantity)
2. Frequency of releases
3. Known and patched vulnerabilities

For Java and Python based components we leverage and contribute into OWASP dependency checker [13], and recently added Safety [14] for Python as an early adopter in the community. A roadmap of component updates should be keep updated and each product release should incorporate upgrades to avoid vulnerabilities.

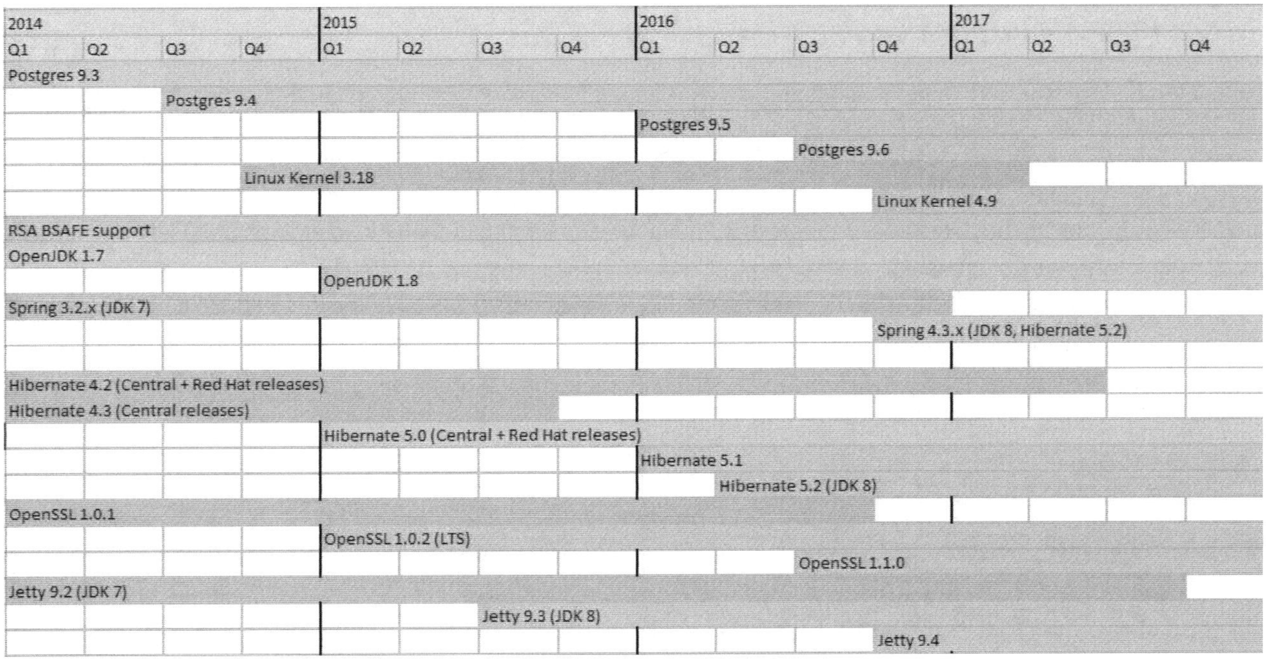

This is an example of how EOL libraries and their versions can be tracked.

2.2.3. SDL Kanban

The security architect creates a storyboard or Kanban with all mandatory, required, and optional SDL activities. Those activities can be ordered by sprints, how they can be implemented, and ordered by importance and/or effort.

Once this is prioritized together by the team, it should be captured in the product backlog itself. During this phase a standard questionnaire is used to dimension the SDL work for the release, for instance:

1. Is the target release vehicle a major update or just contains minor maintenance changes?
2. It the product architecture changed?
3. Is there any change on dependencies?
4. Is any new PII information being handled at the product?

Explicitly listing what security-related work not will be included in the release has been found useful to direct effort and communicatee with stakeholders.

A discovery meeting involving stakeholders and reviewing target features is also held towards early discussion of security concerns and identification of next steps on each case.

2.2.4. Privacy Impact Assessment (PIA)

Feature review from privacy point of view. Detailed documentation of information being collected, persisted and ship to cloud-based services if that is the case. Also details about how long the information will be stored and documentation on how to delete them if required.
For instance, product telemetry is the usual feature being considered here, a spreadsheet with each particular data attribute is kept updated with field name, purpose, examples, etc. Product documentation should clearly discuss what, when and why telemetry is sent. Product logging should include full telemetry payload as part of special log level to allow confirmation of telemetry content by customers. Opt-in and not opt-out.

2.3. Design

2.3.1. Security Plan

A security plan documents targeted tasks (also non-targeted ones) after prioritizing and ranking requirements. All tasks in scope are then added to the backlog thru user stories. The security plan should include user stories towards maintaining or increasing the product security maturity level.

2.3.2. Architecture and Design Security Analysis

A security architecture review fully documents the product's architecture. This architecture review is then used to produce the Security Design Review and Threat Model. These help to identify possible attack vectors early in the product development lifecycle before design. The security architecture review is intended to be a starting point to build security into the product.

2.3.3. Threat Modeling

A threat model uses the security architecture to identify all possible attack vectors. The attack vectors that exposer areas of potential security exploitation weaknesses (a.k.a. vulnerabilities) are then addressed by defining countermeasures to prevent, or mitigate the effects of, threats to the system early in the design phase. Threat models are used to prioritize the threat/attack vector based on risk and business requirements.

To identify those weaknesses, many methodologies can be applied, among them STRIDE is widely used for this purpose. STRIDE means **S**poofing, **T**ampering, **R**epudiation, **I**nformation Disclosure, **D**enial of Service and **E**levation of Privilege. Can be used to identify new threats answering typical questions around each component (or new integration).

It's recommended to divide the working project into multiple layers, from a very high-level scheme were the component under analysis is just a minimum part of the whole ecosystem, and then create new layers with more details (zooming in). Making an analysis of each layer and applying a detection methodology to each one, is the easiest approach to identify all possible vulnerabilities.

To reach this purpose Microsoft offers a specific tool, which is Microsoft SDL Threat Modeling Tool.

2.3.4. Privacy Information Gathering and Analysis

Privacy protects the confidentiality, integrity and availability of personal and corporate data. In this stage known what kind of data will be collected, how long and where, it's necessary to be compliant with standards regulations and company policies.

2.4. Implementation

2.4.1. Secure Coding Standards

Ensure secure coding standards and best practices are used throughout the development of the product.

One way to achieve that is trainings the development team and adding plug-ins with custom information to the development IDE.

One tool that can be used is Checksyle. Checkstyle is a tool that can be installed as a plug-in on the development IDE and checks Java source code for adherence to a Code Standard or set of validation rules.

Findbugs is another tool that can be implemented on the development environment. Findbugs is an open source tool that executes a static analyzer over Java code.

PMD also can be used for this purpose, it's open source code analyzer which finds common programming flaws. Supports multiple languages like Java, C, C++, Python and Ruby.

2.4.2. Static Analysis

Static analysis is a method of examining software for vulnerabilities at compile and/or build-time, reporting potential defects in source code. The analysis searches the code for known weaknesses such as buffer overflows, null pointer exceptions, among others.

A lot of tools exist on static analysis field, multi-language or specialized can be found on Internet. Coverity by Synopsis is one of them and can be integrated to a CI/CD plan, in a way that a developer make code changes and generates a new entry into the code repository. A dedicated Coverity servers is listening for new changes and if it found a new one, it triggers a static scan. Once the analysis finishes and new findings are discovered, it can trigger an email to the entire development team and assigned owners to fix them.

Other tools used for this purpose also are Checkmarx, Klockwork, Veracode. IDEs like Eclipse or IntelliJ also have integrated code inspection on compile time. A developer can install those IDEs, plus static code analyzer plug-ins such as Findbugs, to detect vulnerabilities, before submitting their code.

2.4.3. Threat Modeling (Updates)

On this phase we recommend looking again the Threat Model in order to find new changes, missing vectors due to design changes.

We found that a threat model update on this phase also can be useful to make because architecture changes can be in place due to unexpected conditions or requirement changes.

2.4.4. New Tools Evaluation

In a mature development team, multiple tools can be integrated during the development pipeline. All tools already implemented in the CI/CD process helps at the beginning to get new findings and then to keep the quality code standards.

Every day new tools are created and shared into the market. Testing or implementing those tools helps not only to get new findings

During the implementation phase, new tools can be used and tested.

Running different tools vs always running the same one.

2.5. Verification

2.5.1. Dynamic Analysis

Dynamic analysis tools find vulnerabilities in the binary executables and other runtimes, like Web applications at run-time, by executing the code over multiple test cases, reporting actual defects.

Most dynamic solutions test only exposed HTTP and HTML interfaces of Web-enabled applications, they're also called Web Application Scanning.

A difference to static code analyzers, dynamic tools need a running application. Most of tools implemented in this field are Web Application Scanners and for this purpose tools like Netsparker, ZAP Proxy, w3af, Burp Suite and homemade scanners can be used.

In case of Zed Attack Proxy Project (a.k.a. ZAP Proxy), it's an Open Source tool created by OWASP community helps to find security vulnerabilities in a web application automatically. This tool provides you an automatic web spider which helps you to collect the information and then make the analysis but, one of the most useful features that this tool provides, it is his proxy. Using the proxy, you can navigate thru your web page and collect only data for those modified web pages (or where the spider can't reach), and then analyze them. The tool also provides a Jenkins plug-in which can be installed.

2.5.2. Interactive Analysis

Interactive analysis is a different form to test your application security that stems from a combination between dynamic and static analysis technologies. This approach analyzes leverages information from inside the running application, including runtime requests, data flow, control flow, libraries, and connections, to find vulnerabilities.

2.5.3. Fuzz Testing

Fuzz testing or "fuzzing" is a subset of dynamic analysis. It finds vulnerabilities and system crashes in the running binary executables by probing all inputs, network protocols, and file formats with intentionally invalid data. It permutates the packet boundaries with illegal formats to see if the running program will trigger an error condition or fault. These error conditions can lead to exploitable vulnerabilities.

We found that not all tools support automatic generation of payloads after a JSON Schema, only after JSON examples of the payloads.

2.5.4. Manual Code Review

Security-focused manual code reviews involve humans to search for and find vulnerabilities and weaknesses in the source code.

Code review it's a fundamental step when a developer wants to add his own code to the main repository. Github has his own Code Review tool and it's widely used cross all development teams. CodeCollaborator helps to accomplish the objective and has the capability to integrate with other versioning software like SVN.

2.5.5. Vulnerability Scan

A vulnerability scanner is a tool used to find known vulnerabilities and exposures in a binary executable and the environment to which it is deployed and runs.

This stage where most of the tools can be found. The most used ones are based on environment scanner like OpenVAS by OWASP, Nessus and Nexpose.

2.5.6. Penetration Test

Pen testing requires sophisticated use of tools by human analysts to find and then prove vulnerabilities in executables and the environment in which they run.

On this stage mostly, custom scripts should be implemented and integrated with common tools and frameworks like Nmap, Metasploit.

We have made pre-build templates so team members can easily spin up new instances of the required tooling to perform security testing.

2.6. Release

2.7.1. Conduct Final Security Review

After the development a testing conduct a final security review helps to summarize and improve all security controls made during the development phase.

2.6.2. Retrospective

A retrospective review, from a security related perspective is useful. During this meeting, new tools can be discussed, how to track security tasks, know what was useless during the process, what can be improved or modified, what can be a good thing to start doing.

2.7. Response

2.7.1. External Vulnerability Disclosure Response (PSIRT)

It's very common that new vulnerabilities appear once the product is running in production. You can either document the vulnerabilities and their impact, and/or implement changes fixing the vulnerability,

A Security Bulletin is a document where the vulnerabilities are described and analyzed by the security experts. In this document information related to the vulnerabilities such as vulnerability ID, widely known as CVE, their impact on the software using an attack vector known as CVSS, and if it's a workaround or software fix update.

2.7.2. Post-Release Certifications

We have undergone multiple independently product certifications, as they are required by many verticals in the financial and aerospace industries.

FIPS requires evidence of using proper cryptography providers and their configuration, we recommend putting automation in-place to gather evidence without investment effort each time a dependency is upgraded. Performance gaps need to be considered and they are usually caused by lack of entropy pools being properly configured at platform level.

Common Criteria requires thorough architecture and design documentation. Finding an individual with experience in the paperwork is key.

FedRamp compliance is not a big difference when previous two certifications are completed, we have identified the requirement of having an antivirus and file integrity components in place at platform level as the main gap.

3. Conclusions

This section covers a quick summary of interesting talking points in previous sections.

The impact on having automation in place for defect identification and testing APIs and communication channel cryptography cannot be highlighted enough. Removing security issues in the code is cheap when they are identified earlier in the development process. Quick re-test of cryptography over communication channels allow the usual fine-tuning on default (and allowed for negotiation) algorithms and key sizes when undergoing compliance certifications such as Common Criteria and FIPS. The same happens with vulnerability scanners against dependencies, they should be hooked into build systems for best results.

The identification and tracking of EOL components helps planning of current and future releases, allowing to establish what not will be updated and how it would be mitigated if required up-front.

Having an agile mindset towards the application of DoD and the team training has allowed teams to harden components and add expertise incrementally and globally.

References

The authors would like to thank the Argentina Software Development Center for the provided support to make this research paper to happen. Also, the authors would like to recognize the product security expert community around McAfee who provided valued feedback on early and late drafts.

[1] Howard, Michael; Lipner, Steve (June 2006). The Security Development Lifecycle: SDL: A Process for Developing Demonstrably More Secure Software. Microsoft Press. ISBN 0735622140.

[2] James Ransome, Harold Toomey (October 2017). McAfee Product Security Practices. Available at https://www.mcafee.com/enterprise/en-us/assets/legal/product-software-security-practices.pdf.

[3] McAfee Product Security Incident Response Team (June 2018). McAfee Product Security Bulletins. Available at https://www.mcafee.com/enterprise/en-us/threat-center/product-security-bulletins.html.

[4] Microsoft (May 2012). Security Development Lifecycle, SDL Process Guidance Version 5.2. Available at http://www.microsoft.com/sdl.

[5] S. Lipner, "The trustworthy computing security development lifecycle," 20th Annual Computer Security Applications Conference, 2004, pp. 2-13.

[6] M. Howard, "Building more secure software with improved development processes," in IEEE Security & Privacy, vol. 2, no. 6, pp. 63-65, Nov.-Dec. 2004.

[7] Joshua Cajetan Rebelo, Patrick McEnany (October 2015), "Moving up the Product Security Maturity Model". Available at http://uploads.pnsqc.org/2015/papers/t-051_Rebelo_paper.pdf.

[8] NIST Special Publication (SP) 800-64, Revision 2, Security Considerations in the System Development Life Cycle

[9] IEEE Std 1074-2006 (Revision of IEEE Std 1074-1997) - IEEE Standard for Developing a Software Project Life Cycle Process

[10] Leffingwell, Dean (2007). Scaling Software Agility: Best Practices for Large Enterprises. Addison-Wesley. ISBN 978-0321458193.

[11] Jim Highsmith (2001). "History: The Agile Manifesto". www.agilemanifesto.org.

[12] "CMMI for Development, Version 1.3". CMMI-DEV (Version 1.3, November 2010). Carnegie Mellon University Software Engineering Institute. 2010. Retrieved 16 February 2011.

[13] OWASP Dependency Check.
https://www.owasp.org/index.php/OWASP_Dependency_Check.

[14] Safety. https://pyup.io/safety/

Automated Detection of Individual Anomalies and General Behaviour Changes in Timeseries Metrics

Authors

Tifany Yung, Groupon Inc (tiyung@groupon.com)
Renato Martins, Groupon Inc (rmartins@groupon.com)

Abstract

Metrics provide insight into system health, performance, and stability and must be monitored throughout the software release process to catch issues before they reach production. Therefore, a fast, effective method of identifying deviant metrics is necessary to more quickly identify and stop regressions. However, manual analysis of hundreds of metrics is time-consuming, subjective, and error-prone. Some automation can be achieved by alerts that trigger when metrics cross a hardcoded threshold, but smaller changes with a noticeable but less severe impact would not be picked up.

In this paper, we introduce a technique we developed to automate building a model of expected behavior for each metric based on its previous data and using it to compute variable thresholds for the current metric data. We then describe our experience using it in our own deployment process.

We found that all metrics flagged as deviant were confirmed by human analysts to be so, including subtle cases where the deviation was not immediately obvious. Our technique also streamlined our deployment process by reducing the number of metrics our analysts had to review by 92-98%, and manual review of the remaining 2-8% was only needed to use the flagged metrics to diagnose the problem.

Biography

Tifany Yung is a biomedical engineer and computer scientist with a minor in Applied Math and Statistics. She has a Master's in Computer Science from the University of Illinois at Urbana-Champaign, where she did research on software quality and test automation. She has now been working at Groupon for 2.5 years developing monitoring tools to improve early detection of regressions and new issues.

Renato Martins is a EE who has never developed hardware for a living. Renato also has a Master's Degree in Computer Science and an MBA. Renato started his career developing firmware for phones and accessories at Motorola. After that Renato spent 11 years at Microsoft on many quality-oriented roles where Renato worked on projects involving automotive systems, embedded OSs, Windows Phone, and then made a transition from the world of small computers to custom online tools used by Microsoft Support. Renato fulfilled his entrepreneurial aspirations by becoming the co-founder and CTO of Stringr.com where he built the platform from scratch. Renato now leads an engineering team at Groupon.com.

1. Introduction

Metrics provide insight into system health, performance, and stability and must be monitored throughout the software release process as new software is deployed first to the testing, staging, and then production environments. They are needed to catch issues before they reach the latter and affect end users, as well as to detect issues that do slip into production. However, manual analysis of hundreds of these metrics, usually by visual inspection of their graphs, is time-consuming, subjective, and error-prone.

Some automation may be achieved by setting alerts that automatically trigger when a particular metric crosses some critical threshold, but it may take time for the metric to reach them, or the metric may just never reach a level that triggers it, thereby allowing moderately severe issues to slip through. Therefore, it is still necessary to inspect metrics for anomalous behavior that occurs below the critical level.

One way this can be done, whether through manual inspection or an automated detection algorithm, is by comparing metric data from after a deployment, which we call test data against metric data from before the deployment, which is selected to exhibit the expected behavior of the metric and which we call model data. Another method, used by Elasticsearch's X-Pack extension [1], is to look for individual anomalous points within a dataset.

Many algorithms have been proposed to do one or the other. Some can find individual anomalous points, such as one algorithm that compares a data point to those around it and flags the point if it differs from its neighboring points by more than some threshold [2]. Others instead detect general changes in behavior between the model and test data, including algorithms that encode time series data as strings and generate detector strings that do not match the string for the model data [3], or use the edit distance between model and test data strings [5].

However, while solutions that detect individual anomalous points can help identify exactly when a metric deviated, they do not indicate whether the deviation was temporary noise or a change in the metric's behavior. On the other hand, algorithms that detect overall changes based on how different the encoded datasets are do not identify individual anomalies that could help diagnose whether a deviation is ongoing or was resolved.

In this paper, we describe an algorithm for automated detection of both individual anomalies and overall changes in metric behavior, which allows us to determine not only whether a metric's behavior has changed after a deployment, but also which data points in the time series contributed to the change. A model of expected behavior is built and used to predict the test data values, and anomalous points are identified based on how far off the predictions are from the actual observed values. Then, the number of anomalous points and how recent they are used to determine whether the test data exhibits different behavior from the model data. Human involvement is necessary only when alerts have been generated for the flagged metrics, and only to review them and make a call on the deployment based on them.

2. Methodology

The detection algorithm we describe below is entirely automated except for the one-time, initial configuration setup and runs as a cron job that sends notification emails listing the flagged metrics when alerts are triggered.

For the purposes of this paper, we will focus on the detection algorithm and minimize implementation details, such as configuration file formatting and the underlying statistical packages used, to what is necessary to understand the algorithm.

2.1 Initial Setup

The initial setup step involves the creation of configuration files that describe the metrics to be monitored and is the only manual step in the otherwise automated detection algorithm.

Configuration files contain a list of metrics and their metadata. Each job has its own configuration file, and we define a *job* as a set of related metrics to be monitored, e.g. metrics for the staging environment.

Metadata for each metric will be explained in the algorithm below as they turn up but include the source to retrieve the metric data from, time ranges to use for the model and test data, season size to use when modeling a metric that exhibits seasonal behavior, etc. These are fed as parameters into the algorithm and used to customize modeling and detection for each metric.

2.2 Modeling the Expected Behavior

For each metric to be monitored, the following steps are performed when building a model of the metric's expected behavior to compare against its behavior in the test data:

- Get the model data based on the data source and model data time range metadata given in the configuration file. The data source is queried for the metric values within the time range and returned as a *time series*, where the metric values are matched with their corresponding timestamps.

  For our own use case, we selected the metric's data from midnight to noon of the second most recent day of data available. This was done since our deployments almost never occur during that time range, so the metric should be most stable and best demonstrate the ideal behavior for that metric.

- Similarly, query for the test data that needs to be checked for anomalies and behavioral changes, also using the data source, as well as the test data time range.

  For our own use case, we select the most recent hour of data available for a metric as its test data. This time range was selected to give our deployed application just enough time to warm up and receive enough traffic to stabilize the metric, and to allow us to evaluate the deployment without losing several hours or an entire day while accumulating data.

- Remove outliers from the model data so that they do not affect the model. Here, we use the interquartile range (IQR) method to find outliers rather than the mean and standard deviation method, since the latter depends on the data being normal. However, since this is often not the case with time series data, as can be seen by visual inspection of the graphs of ours and other time series, we use the more generic IQR method.

  Using this method, we define any data point below *p25 - n*IQR* or above *p75 + n*IQR* as an outlier, where *p25* and *p75* are the 25th and 75th percentiles of the model data, respectively. For normally-distributed data, the commonly used value in statistics for n is 1.5, but since time series data often does not appear normal, we make n a parameter in the configuration file so that it can be customized depending on how sensitive we want the alert to be. Larger values of n generally result in less sensitive alerts that tolerate more deviation before flagging the metric.

- Build the time series model for model data.

  We use the autoregressive integrated moving average (ARIMA) class of models to model the data. Since ARIMA models are well-known and common models in time series analysis and statistics in general, we will not explain them in detail in this paper.

  The algorithm may select either an ARIMA model or a seasonal variant of it as the model to fit the model data to. Which one the algorithm chooses to use is determined as follows:

  - If a metric is marked as seasonal in the configuration file, the seasonal variant is selected. To use this model, the seasonal difference of the data is computed, and the resulting time series is used to build an ARIMA model.
  - Otherwise, the algorithm checks that the conditions for using ARIMA, such as stationarity of the data, are satisfied. If not, the data is processed so that the resulting time series satisfies the condition; else, the original time series is used. The model is then built using the resulting time series.

Note that, though the model orders are usually chosen by inspecting a graph of the data, we use an information criterion to estimate them so that we could automate the process of building the model. Maximum likelihood estimation is then used to estimate the best-fitting model coefficients. Since both are done via the Python statsmodels package, we do not go into more detail here on how model for the model data is developed.

- Compute the prediction errors between the actual observed model data points and the values predicted by the model. These are the *model prediction errors*, and we call the distribution of these errors the *model error distribution*.

  Models are expected to exhibit some prediction error, as the model may otherwise be overfitted and unsuitable for forecasting on new data. We use the model error distribution to determine approximately how much error is expected for a given model. This distribution will then be used to determine whether the errors for the model's prediction for the test data points are within the expected errors for the model, or if the test point value deviates significantly from the expected value and is likely an anomaly.

2.3 Finding Anomalous Data Points in the Test Data

Once the model for a given metric has been generated, we compare its predictions with the actual test data. If the behavior of the metric hasn't changed between the model and test data, the test data predictions should have approximately the same distribution of errors as the model data predictions. Any test point that is too far from the prediction would be flagged as an anomaly.

The following is done to determine whether the error between the actual value of a test point and its prediction is too large:

- Forecast the predicted values for the test data point values using the ARIMA (or seasonal ARIMA) model generated for the model data.
- Similar to what was done to get the model prediction errors, compute the prediction errors between the actual test data points and the predicted values from the model.
- Check whether each test point's prediction error is an outlier with respect to the model error distribution, using the same IQR method and parameter n to identify outliers as was used to remove outliers from the model data. Any test point whose prediction error is an outlier with respect to the model errors is flagged as an anomaly.

We do this because the model error distribution gives the approximate amount of error to expect from predicting with the model, since the model points are known to exhibit expected behavior. So if a test point's prediction error is too large, whether in the positive or negative direction, that point's actual value exhibits a greater deviation from the forecasted value than expected, and are thus anomalous.

2.4 Identifying Overall Changes in Metric Behavior

After identifying individual anomalies, we use the number of anomalies and their times of occurrence to determine whether a given metric is currently exhibiting different behavior from the model data.

Essentially, if most of the points in the test data are anomalous and the anomalies are relatively recent in the test data, then the metric behavior is flagged as anomalous. We consider how recent an anomaly is so that a metric isn't flagged for possibly unrelated behavioral changes if it was behaving differently earlier in the test data but has returned to expected behavior. Such anomalies may be caused by factors like unusually high spikes in traffic or load to the deployed application that are independent of the deployment itself.

- If the majority of the test data points are flagged as anomalies and the majority of those anomalies are in the more recent half of the test data, then that metric's behavior is flagged as changed.

  In our own default use case, we defined *majority* as at least half of the test data points, so a metric is flagged only if it has been consistently deviating. However, we also did not want the alert to trigger only when all of the test data points deviated since it is possible that there are still occasional test points that occur within expected levels. Requiring that multiple, but not all, test points deviate is done so that a temporary anomaly will not generate noisy alerts, but also so that the metric need only be deviating consistently and repeatedly, without errors having to be permanently elevated.

  For example, consider a latency metric that measures how long an application took to handle a request. A spike in the number of requests may cause the metric to deviate temporarily, even if it was unrelated to the deployment being tested and was resolved by itself. Or an actual performance issue in the deployment could cause the latency to increase most of the time but sometimes fall within the error range due to multiple requests that were not affected by the issue.

  In the case where a metric's trigger should be more or less sensitive, our algorithm does allow a value to be passed in in each metric's configuration. With this, a lower threshold for majority can be used to create more sensitive alerts that are triggered by fewer anomalies and vice versa.

- Send an email alert detailing which metrics were flagged for changes in behavior and which points in each of the metric's test data were anomalies (i.e., contributed to that metric's behavior being flagged as changed).

2.5 Making a Call on a Release

Once all metrics in a job have been analyzed, a single alert email is sent to the interested developers for all metrics flagged in that job.

Since the algorithm only automates the detection of anomalies and behavioral changes, human involvement is still required after it is run to make a call on whether to proceed with deploying a release to the next environment in the release process, or whether the build has an issue and needs to be blocked and reworked.

This involves reviewing the alert to determine what metrics were flagged and whether the anomalies and changes in those metrics were expected and/or acceptable since depending on the metric, some increases or decreases are considered improvements, or a new feature could cause a metric's behavior to change.

For example, if a computationally-heavy new feature was added, it may be expected that latency metrics would increase. Or if latency decreased, the release would be considered an improvement and allowed to proceed. However, if error rates also increased, the build may be blocked pending an investigation since that would suggest that the system is encountering problems that cause it to terminate early, thus decreasing latency.

In short, our algorithm analyzes the metrics and provides the results, but not the final call on a release, so the final decision on whether a release moves forward depends on the human analyst and whether they are able to use the information in the alerts to make a judgement.

2.6 Related Works

A similar approach to ours was proposed in an earlier work by Laptev et al. [4], where expected behavior is modeled by an ARIMA time series model and anomalous points are identified by the prediction error of a test point.

The primary difference is that Laptev et al. compared a given test point's prediction error with that of other test points and flagged a given point when its error was an outlier with respect to other test point errors. In contrast, we compare with the prediction errors of the model points and flag a given test point whose error is an outlier with respect to the model errors.

This is significant, as it allows our algorithm to flag an entire test data set whose overall behavior differs from the expected. It also allows us to detect when all test points are anomalous.

Additionally, if all test data points deviate from the model by approximately the same amount, even if the test point values are visibly behaving differently from the model, the test points would not be flagged due to all of them having approximately the same amount of prediction error. Therefore, none of the test points would appear to be an outlier when compared to each other.

Other differences also include our support for seasonal ARIMA models and our use of the IQR method of identifying outliers rather than the standard deviation method, so that the algorithm is viable even in the case where the prediction error distribution does not fit a normal distribution and thus cannot use the three-sigma rule.

3. Results

Using our own deployment process and its associated set of metrics, we ran this algorithm and also had our human analysts perform manual metrics analysis to compare the algorithm's ability to detect anomalies and overall changes against that of the analysts.

We found that the algorithm was at least as capable of identifying changes in metric behavior as manual monitoring by a human. In some cases, the algorithm was also able to pick up changes that were missed during a manual inspection of a metric's graph (e.g., a slow but persistent increase in a latency metric that suggested a growing problem but that was not steep enough to be flagged during a manual analysis). Some changes were too subtle for the human to notice, depending on the resolutions of the graphs they used for manual inspection.

We also greatly reduced the amount of time spent on inspecting metrics since we now need to manually review only the flagged metrics. The need to manually review metrics was not eliminated as it is still necessary to figure out, when diagnosing a problem with a deployment, what metrics were flagged and in which direction they deviated. There is no need, however, to analyze the data and make a decision on whether the metric is deviant.

This resulted in a reduction of about 92-98% in the number of metrics that our human analysts needed to review, where the type and magnitude of the issue in a deployment affected the number of deviant metrics that were flagged. For the purpose of the comparison, metrics that were not flagged were also reviewed to ensure that they did not exhibit deviant behavior that was missed by the algorithm. But when using this algorithm in practice, the non-flagged metrics, which made up 92-98% of the total number of metrics, need not be manually inspected.

Additionally, no further analysis of the metric's behavior needed to be done during the review; only a go/no-go decision on the deployment needed to be made based on which metrics were found to exhibit changed behavior.

Overall, use of this algorithm has allowed us to greatly reduce the time spent on metrics monitoring while increasing the rate of detection of both individual anomalies and overall changes in metric behavior. Use of the algorithm also made the metrics analysis results less subjective than "eyeballing" the metrics graphs since the data models and error distributions could be used to justify the decision on whether a metric's behavior changed.

3.1 Example Analysis

The figure below shows a graph of several of the metrics we monitor during the deployment process. The four metrics are the maximum (lightest grey), 99th percentile (lighter grey), 95th percentile (darker grey), and median (black) values at a given time of a metric being collected by our application.

The model data was taken from 6:00 to 9:00, and the test data was taken from 15:00 to 16:00.

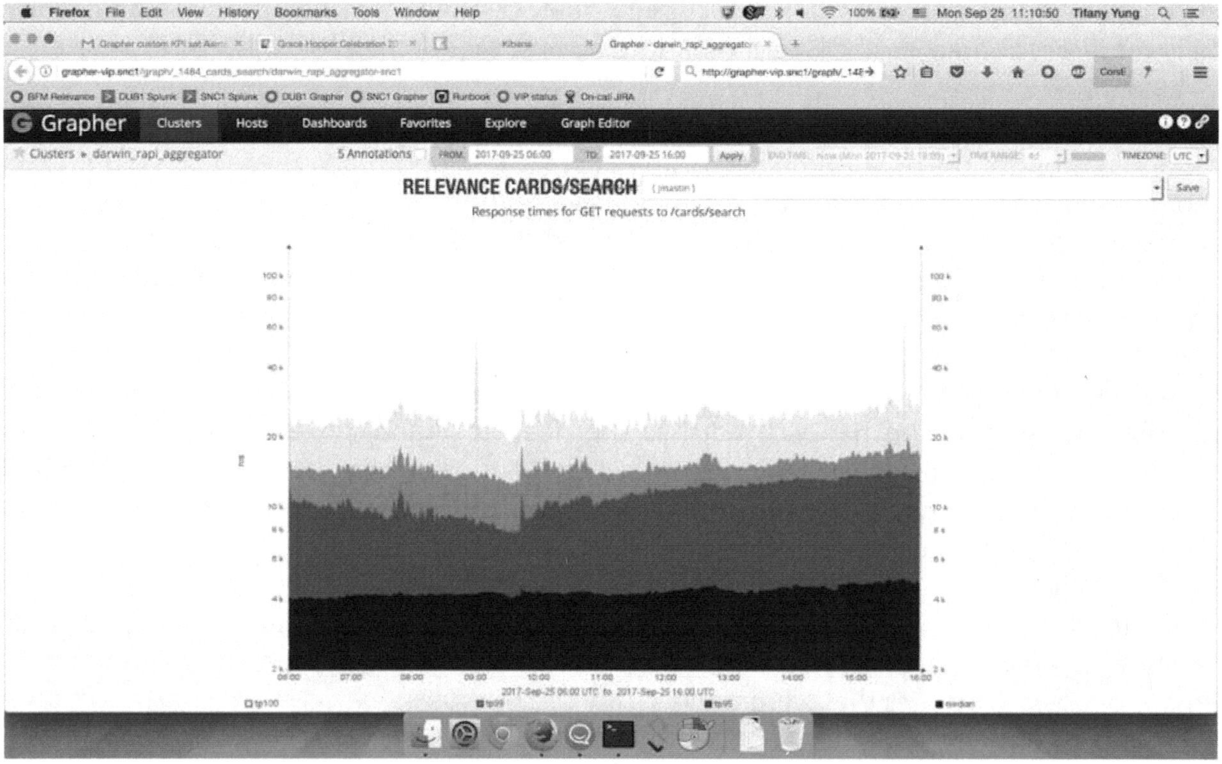

Based on a visual manual inspection, the 95th percentile appears to exhibit a visible increase from the model to the test data, while the 99th percentile and maximum metrics' behaviors may have changed, though it is hard to tell whether the increase is due to a few spikes from noise or if the increase is persistent. And without much closer inspection, for which there is not often time when analyzing hundreds of metrics for a deployment, it is not noticeable that the median metric also increased.

Meanwhile, our algorithm was able to correctly flag all four of the metrics for an overall increase in the test data when compared to the model data. Not only do the model parameters and other data provided by the algorithm reduce the subjectivity of the judgement, but the algorithm also runs in less time than it takes for a human analyst to retrieve and inspect the metric graphs; approximately one to two minutes compared to ten to fifteen seconds. It is also worth noting that since dozens of analyses can be run in parallel, the percentage reduction in time spent when using the algorithm is even greater for larger numbers of metrics.

4. Conclusion

In this paper, we have described a new algorithm to automate the detection of both individual anomalies and overall changes in metrics behavior. The algorithm offers an improvement on methods that detect only individual anomalous points by analyzing overall behavior within the data points being tested. It also improves upon previous methods that measured overall changes by using the individual anomalies to identify what times in the test data exhibited the most deviant behavior and contributed most to the change in metric behavior.

We found that the algorithm could identify changes in our deployment metrics at least as well as manual monitoring of metrics graphs by human analysts. In some cases, the algorithm was also able to identify more subtle changes in metric behavior that were missed during manual inspection, and reduced the time spent on analyzing metrics, in addition to reducing the subjectivity of the analysis.

4.1 Future Work

Future work would include expanding the types of models available beyond ARIMA and experimenting with other time series-specific models, and even non-time series models to better support the rare metrics that do not behave like typical time series.

We also plan to gather results and feedback from more teams, including those with fewer metrics but who still prefer to automate the monitoring process. While we have made most of the parameters involved customizable via the job configuration file, we would like to receive feedback on what other options other teams would like to have control over.

References

[1] X-pack: Extend elasticsearch, kibana & logstash — elastic. https://www.elastic.co/products/x-pack Accessed: 2018-03-02.

[2] Sabyasachi Basu and Martin Meckesheimer. Automatic outlier detection for time series: an application to sensor data. Knowledge and Information Systems, 11(2):137–154, 2007.

[3] Dipankar Dasgupta and Stephanie Forrest. Novelty detection in time series data using ideas from immunology. In Proceedings of the international conference on intelligent systems, pages 82–87, 1996.

[4] Nikolay Laptev, Saeed Amizadeh, and Ian Flint. Generic and scalable framework for automated timeseries anomaly detection. In Proceedings of the 21th ACM SIGKDD International Conference on Knowledge Discovery and Data Mining, pages 1939–1947. ACM, 2015.

[5] Li Wei, Nitin Kumar, Venkata Nishanth Lolla, Eamonn J Keogh, Stefano Lonardi, and Chotirat (Ann) Ratanamahatana. Assumption-free anomaly detection in time series. In SSDBM, volume 5, pages 237–242, 2005.

AI-Driven Test Generation: Machines Learning from Human Testers

Authors

Dionny Santiago (dsant005@fiu.edu)
Tariq M. King, Ultimate Software (tariq_king@ultimatesoftware.com)
Peter J. Clarke, Florida International University (clarkep@cis.fiu.edu)

Abstract

Although recent test automation practices help to increase the efficiency of testing and mitigate the cost of regression testing, there is still much manual work involved. Achieving and maintaining high software quality today involves manual analysis, test planning, documentation of testing strategy and test cases, and development of test scripts to support automated testing. To keep pace with software evolution, test artifacts must also be frequently updated to stay relevant. Current test automation is unable to generalize across applications and is unable to mimic human intelligence. As such, there is a significant gap between the current state of practice and a fully automated solution to software testing.

This paper investigates a practical approach that leverages artificial intelligence (AI) and machine learning (ML) technologies to generate system tests based on learning testing behavior directly from human testers. The approach combines a trainable classifier which perceives application state, a language for describing test flows, and a trainable test flow generation model to create test cases learned from human testers. Preliminary results gathered from applying a prototype of the approach are promising and bring us one step closer to bridging the gap between human and machine testing.

Biography

Dionny Santiago is a Principal Quality Architect at Ultimate Software, a leading cloud provider of human capital management solutions. Dionny provides expertise and leadership in software testing and contributes in various capacities including hands-on testing, technical problem-solving, training, and internal tools development. Test automation being one of his primary areas of interest, one of Dionny's goals is to advance the current state of the art; he is focused on research and development efforts to apply artificial intelligence and machine learning to software testing. Dionny is also currently pursuing his M. Sc. in Computer Science at Florida International University.

Tariq M. King is the Senior Director and Engineering Fellow for Quality and Performance at Ultimate Software. With more than fifteen years' experience in software testing research and practice, Tariq heads Ultimate Software's quality program by providing technical leadership, people leadership, strategic direction, staff training, research and development in software quality and testing practices. Tariq is a frequent presenter at conferences and workshops, has published more than thirty research articles in IEEE and ACM sponsored journals, and has developed and taught software testing courses in both industry and academia.

Peter J. Clarke is an associate professor in the School of Computing and Information Sciences at Florida International University. His research interests are in the areas of software testing, model-driven software development, and computer science education. He has published over 75 research papers in various journals and conferences, and has received research grants from the NSF and Ultimate Software Group Inc. He has served as the program co-chair for one IEEE conference, the co-chair for 11 faculty development workshops, and on the technical program committees for more than 50 conference and workshops. He is a member of: AAAS, ACM, AISTA, ASEE, AST and the IEEE Computer Society.

1. Introduction

Although test automation practices provide critical efficiency benefits to the software development process, there are many accompanying problems with the current state of the art. Test scripts do not generalize across applications, and may easily break in the presence of changes to the underlying application. Outside of model-based testing (discussed later), test scripts are hand-crafted by humans, and test execution and logging of results are the only fully automated parts of the testing process. Also, automated test script oracles are limited and can only detect defects based on the path and assertions that were coded explicitly in the test script. Consequently, current approaches do not provide for fully automated software testing and substantial manual effort is still required.

There exists a significant gap between machine testing and human-level performance. Human testers can perceive the state of an application, can act intelligently, and can observe resulting application state to uncover defects. To improve efficiency and reduce the cost of quality, there is a need for improving software testing and test automation, and for introducing more intelligent automated testing behavior that is capable of mimicking human behavior.

Advances in AI and ML have shown that machines are capable of matching or surpassing human performance across various problem domains (Bojarski et al. 2016, Moyer 2016, Xiong et al. 2017). As a result, we are witnessing the new uprising of self-driving cars. These systems are capable of perceiving the environment and surroundings of a vehicle, and are capable of mimicking intelligent human driving behavior. We are also seeing many intelligent systems that can communicate with humans and answer questions asked in spoken natural language, and even systems capable of beating top human players at classic board games such as Go.

As a testing community, we are lagging behind other software engineering fields when it comes to innovation. While there has been extensive research and work into semi-automated testing techniques, such as model-based test generation, these techniques do not: (1) mimic the thought and learning process of human testers; and (2) seamlessly generalize across applications and application domains. There is a need for building more intelligent software testing approaches akin to that of self-driving cars and other comparable intelligent systems.

This paper aims to stimulate research and innovation in software testing through the use of AI and ML. We present an example of our journey and experiences of applying existing AI research to testing. We also strive to provide critical takeaways for how quality professionals can get the necessary foundation to break into the AI world and start contributing to this ripe emerging field of intelligent automated software testing.

2. AI for Software Testing

Thanks to the continuing advances in AI and ML, the idea of being able to build intelligent systems that can test software, and that can improve their ability to test by learning from humans, may be closer than we think to being a reality. In this section, we provide an overview of ML, and we also establish a mapping between the software testing problem and ML.

2.1. Overview of Machine Learning

Machine learning is a sub-field of AI and is the science of getting computers to act without being explicitly programmed (Stanford 2018). Two major applications of ML are referred to as **unsupervised learning** and **supervised learning**. In unsupervised learning, unlabeled data is fed into a training algorithm with the goal of discovering patterns and relationships. Examples include clustering algorithms that attempt to organize data points into groups. Supervised learning, in contrast, involves **human-labeled training data**. A supervised learning workflow typically involves multiple iterations of constructing labeled training data, extracting features from the data, choosing an algorithm, training a model, evaluating the model using test or input data, and improving the model.

The diagram below portrays this workflow:

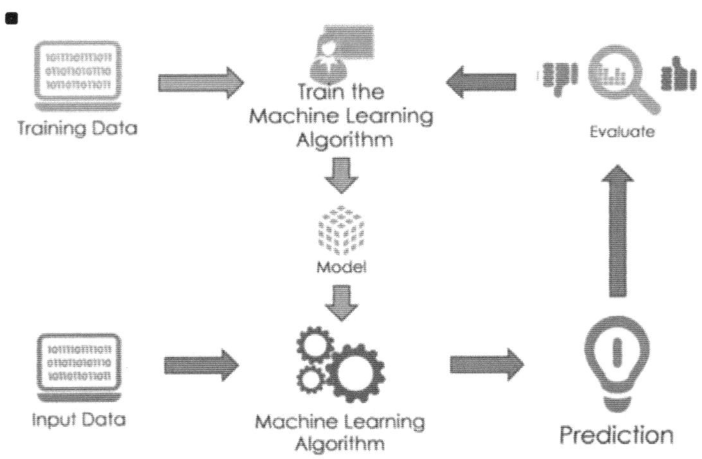

A common ML system is the artificial neural network (ANN). ANNs are computing systems vaguely inspired by biological neural networks, and are based on a collection of connected units called artificial neurons. There are many different types of ANNs, including convolutional neural networks (CNNs) and recurrent neural networks (RNNs). CNNs are commonly used for image recognition problems, and RNNs are commonly used for natural language processing (NLP) problems.

Another application of ML is **reinforcement learning**. This learning approach involves creating algorithms that are capable of learning by using reward systems. Useful actions are positively rewarded, whereas less useful actions may be penalized.

2.2. Relationship Between ML and Testing

There is a direct mapping from the software testing problem to a machine learning solution. The testing problem involves applying a test input to an application or function, then comparing the output to an expected result. This is precisely what machine learning does. A set of inputs (or **features**) is supplied to a training algorithm. In supervised learning, the correct answer is also supplied to the training algorithm with each set of inputs. The job of the machine learning system is to iteratively *(slightly)* reconfigure the "internal brain", each time getting better and better at providing the correct answers based on the provided input sets. Therefore, all of the existing and ongoing research and development that has gone into building these ML systems are providing a direct benefit towards further automating the software testing problem.

Self-driving cars and the technology that powers them can be mapped to the problem of software testing. Just as humans can teach learning algorithms how to drive a car, we can envision building a system capable of learning from a user's testing journey. Similarly, NLP and natural language generation research may map to test case generation. Lastly, game theory and reinforcement learning may map well to the problem of discovering a system and hunting for bugs. For example, reinforcement learning may be used to reward an intelligent system for uncovering a system crash or an exception.

Researchers and practitioners realize the potential for AI and ML to be leveraged to help bridge the gap between the testing capabilities of humans and those of machines (AIST 2018, AISTA 2018). Existing work on applications of ML to software testing has explored applying supervised ML to the testing problem (Arbon 2017). There is also an abundance of emerging research on new AI and ML techniques and algorithms. It is imperative that the testing community make a concerted effort to keep up with AI research and look for ways to innovate within the testing field.

3. Applying AI to Testing

In this section, we set out to provide a journey of how we have been able to leverage existing AI research and map it to specific software testing problems. We present two examples. For each example, we first focus on an AI research area; then we explore our experiences when trying to map the research to testing. Our goal is to let our experiences serve as a framework and as motivation for the reader to follow a similar approach.

3.1. Research: Object Recognition

There exist several problems and areas of research surrounding object recognition within images. Image classification involves visually inspecting an image and deciding whether the image belongs to a particular class. For example, given an image of a cat as input, an image classifier may return the label "cat" as an output.

In some cases, classifying an image with a single label is not sufficient. Suppose the input image contains both a cat and a dog. While assigning either label would be correct, we may instead want to produce two output labels for the single input image. Research efforts have been focused on ML algorithms that can produce multiple outputs. Lastly, in some cases, we are not just interested in generating classes for a given input image. Depending on the problem at hand, we may want to build a system capable of detecting the location of the object within an image.

The following image illustrates several object recognition research problems:

To get a feel for how the different training and prediction processes work, we encourage you to experience these algorithms for yourself. There are several image recognition tutorials and videos freely available online (see **Section 5**). We recommend starting with image classification tutorials that use the TensorFlow (Abadi et al. 2016) framework. TensorFlow is a popular and highly active open source ML framework developed and maintained by the Google Brain team.

3.2. Application: Perceiving Web Application State

The question we will explore in this section is: How can image classification and object detection be leveraged to aid in software testing?

To generate and execute test cases against a web application, the current state of the art involves constructing page objects that are coupled to the implementation details of a specific web application. Page objects often include references to document object model (DOM) and stylesheet information for a specific system under test (SUT). It is beneficial to shift towards an approach that leverages ML to raise the level of abstraction by which generated test cases interact with webpage components. Rather than interacting with elements using information that is SUT-specific, the goal is to be able to leverage ML to identify web components based on models that have been trained across various SUTs.

Having the ability to perceive web application state and recognize objects using ML-based approaches moves us one step closer to being able to write test cases devoid of any SUT-specific implementation details. Armed with enough example training data, we can leverage existing AI research and techniques for object recognition to raise the level of abstraction by which our automated test cases refer to objects. There are several benefits to this approach, including the ability for test scripts to self-heal if the SUT changes. For instance, while a change in the way the SUT renders a shopping cart button would likely break test scripts that leverage traditional DOM-based element selection strategies, a sufficiently trained ML model may be able to locate the new shopping cart button, allowing a test script that leverages ML-based element selection to continue execution. Also, by raising the level of abstraction, it becomes possible to reuse test cases across different SUTs.

With enough training data, an ML model could be trained to recognize various components of a web application state. An example of webpage decomposition and object recognition is below:

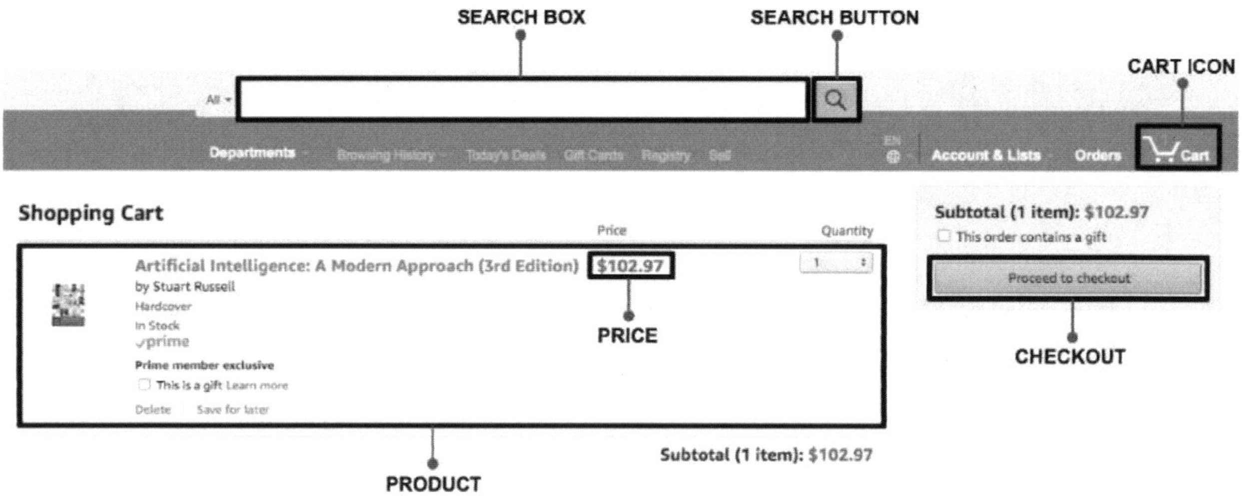

The diagram below shows another example of an actual ML-based classification system recognizing various components (Page title, widget labels, and error messages) on an arbitrary web page:

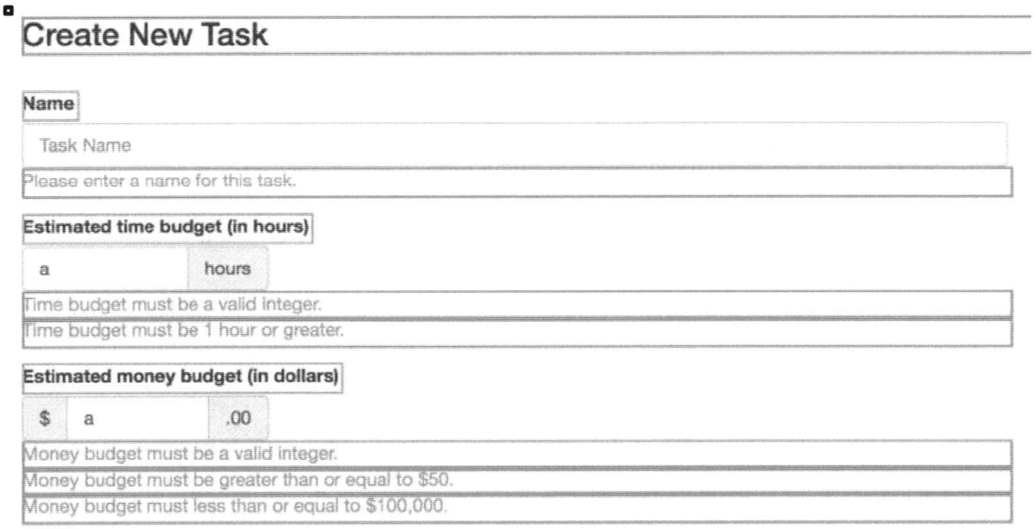

Picking up from the exercise we recommended in **Section 3.1**, we encourage readers to continue practicing by collecting many images of webpage components, labeling the images, and then building an ML system capable of classifying webpage components. Images can be collected and labelled using tools such as LabelImg (LabelImg 2018). Frameworks like TensorFlow and Keras (Chollet 2015) can then be used to train ML models using the generated training set. During our research, we have also found it worthwhile to collect information from the webpage DOM alongside with the component images. Since ML systems thrive on data, being able to extract more features from the raw collected data generally allows for more useful experimentation towards increasing the accuracy of the ML system's performance on the training data.

3.3. Research: Text Generation

Much research exists on generating sequential information using ML-based techniques. In the field of natural language processing (NLP), several approaches to text generation have been studied. A conventional approach is to treat text generation as a **sequence-to-sequence** problem. A sequence of text is fed into a trainable algorithm that in turn outputs a sequence of text. The training goal is that the concatenation of both sequences results in a plausible sentence. Since machines do not understand words, a common practice is to map words to integer values, resulting in what we may refer to as a **word encoding**. This means that both the input and output of the sequence-to-sequence problem are a sequence of integers. Word encodings are challenging to create and maintain as there are many possible words that may appear, especially when different languages are used.

An alternative approach is to create a **character encoding**, where each character (for example, each character from A-Z) is mapped to an integer. Although this simplifies the text-to-machine mapping process, it creates additional complexity from a training standpoint. There are many valid (and invalid) arrangements of character sequences that can first form words and eventually form sentences. In contrast, there are much fewer unique arrangements of complete words. ML-based text generation techniques that leverage character-based encoding typically require more training to reach stability and feasibility-of-use over word-based encoding approaches.

An example of an ML approach to sentence generation using word encodings is below:

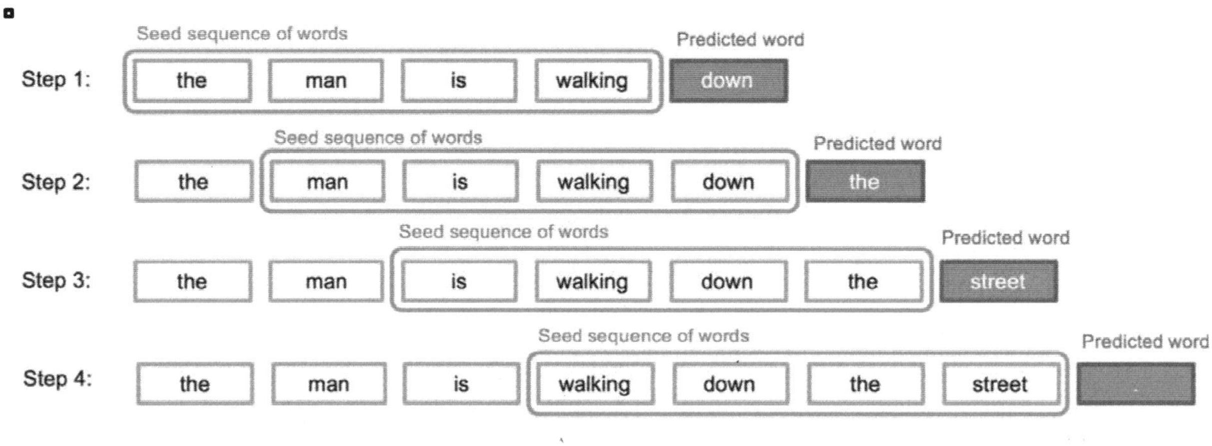

Research has shown that specialized ANNs are capable of being trained to handle sequence-to-sequence problems (such as text generation). Long Short-Term Memory (LSTM) recurrent neural networks (RNNs) are a particular type of neural network capable of generating sequential data with long-range structure (Graves 2013). For the interested reader, Jason Brownlee provides a great step-by-step tutorial that leverages tools such as Keras and TensorFlow to build LSTMs capable of generating plausible sentences for a problem domain based on training from classical texts (Brownlee 2017).

3.4. Application: Text Generation for Web App Testing

The question we will explore in this section is: How can text generation be leveraged to aid in software testing?

In **Sections 3.1** and **3.2**, we explored image recognition research and practical applications for software testing. Raising the level of abstraction by which we interact with objects in a web application sets the stage for the next step. Having the ability to recognize objects, the next task of interest is learning important test flows from human testers. A **test flow** is a sequence of actions performed onto a SUT, followed by a set of expected observations. The steps that a human tester follows while executing test flows may be modeled as follows:

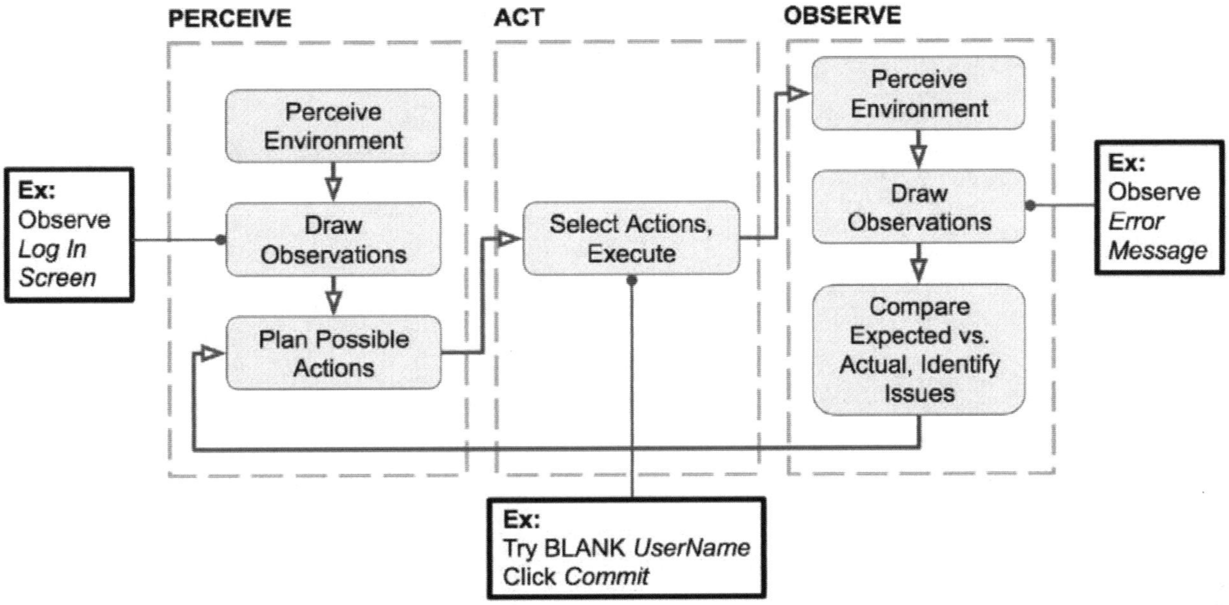

At a high level, we present the test flow execution process as a sequence of steps where each step belongs to one of three categories: **Perceive**, **Act**, **Observe**. Steps belonging to the **Perceive** category focus on establishing preconditions for a test flow, and involve drawing observations from the environment, and action planning before selecting an appropriate set of actions. Steps belonging to the **Act** category focus on selecting and executing appropriate actions based on the previously constructed plan. Finally, steps belonging to the **Observe** category focus on comparing expected vs. actual SUT behavior, and deciding on correctness. We support the continuity property of the testing process by allowing the results of the **Observe** steps to initiate a new **Perceive** stage, thus forming a cycle.

Presenting the test flow process using this framework is the first step towards the goal of being able to represent the process in a machine-understandable format. Next, we define a **language** that may be used to express concrete test flows that fit into our framework. The language must be expressive enough to allow covering essential test cases, yet constrained enough to reduce the data complexity of ML-based techniques to test flow generation.

The language must also promote the use of webpage component abstractions that utilize the system described in **Section 3.2** in place of SUT-specific information. This supports the generality of the approach.

The main building blocks of the language are **components**, **actions**, and **observations**. Components represent elements on a web page. Observations represent information about components that can be perceived from a given web page. Finally, actions are interactions that may be performed onto components. By interleaving observations and actions, the language allows for the specification of test flows. The language supports the use of abstract learned objects, instead of using specific input values and observed text values that may only be pertinent to a single SUT or only pertinent to a specific domain of software applications. The figure below shows how test flows (b) may be created for a simple form (a) by utilizing the language:

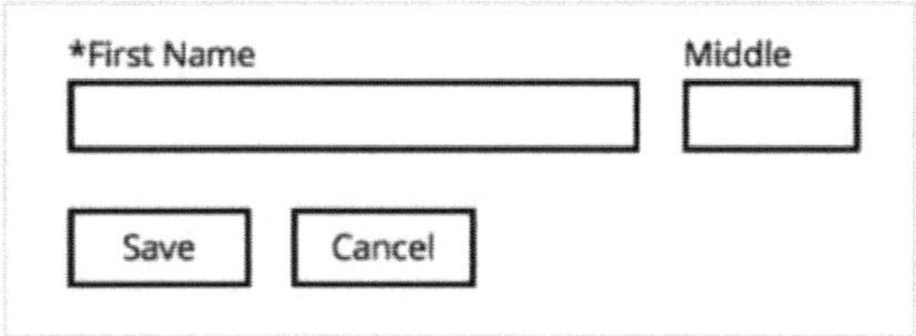

(a)

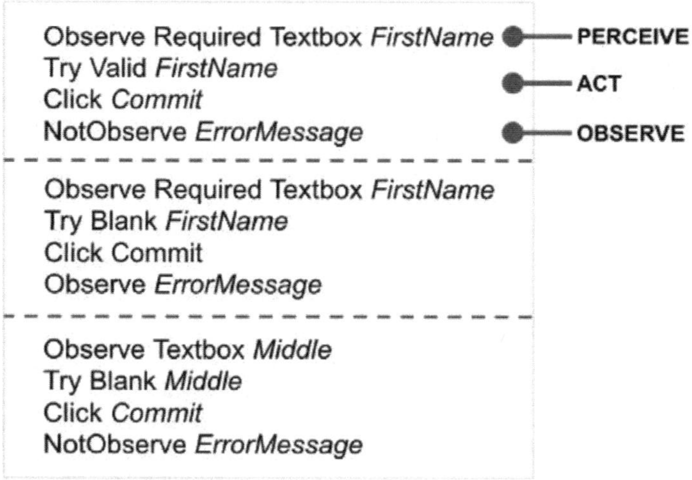

(b)

Going back to the shopping cart example from **Section 3.2**, the figure below shows how the language could be utilized for more complex scenarios:

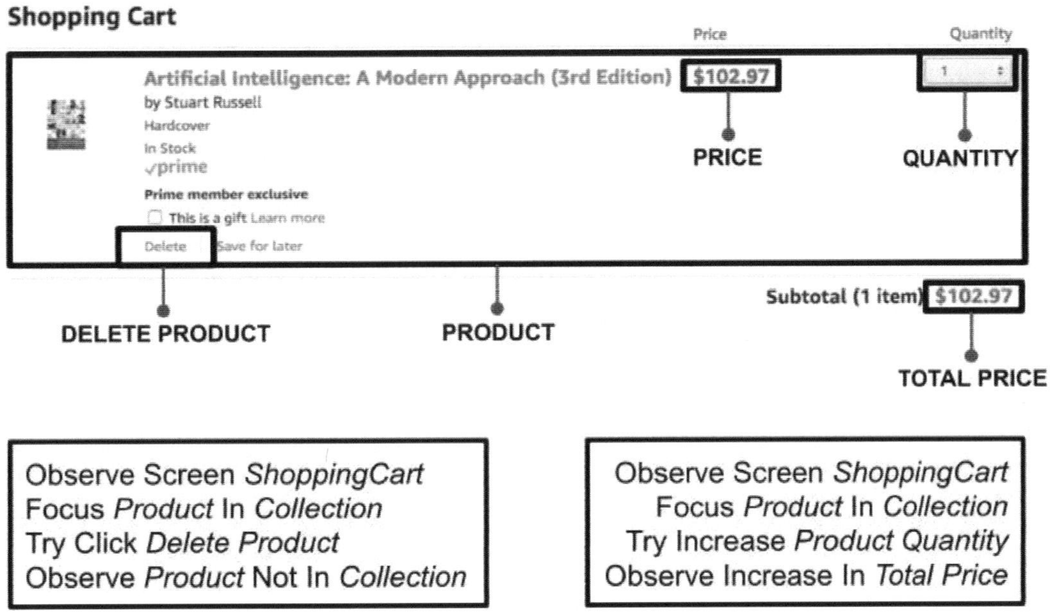

It is important to note that the test flows are described at a higher level of abstraction than the specific underlying SUT that motivated their creation. For example, the equivalence class "VALID" is used in place of any specific First Name. Additionally, the "Commit" element class is used instead of referencing a specific "Save" button. This allows learning generalized test flows that may be used to generate test cases across various SUTs. As an example, the test flows presented in the shopping cart example are reusable across different e-commerce web apps.

Having defined a language capable of expressing test flows, we can now use the techniques we learned about in **Section 3.3**. Since we now have a mechanism of expressing test flows using strings belonging to a language, we map the problem of text generation to that of generating strings that belong to the language that we have defined.

Using the **word encoding** technique for representing text sequences, below is an example of an ML-based training and prediction approach to test flow generation:

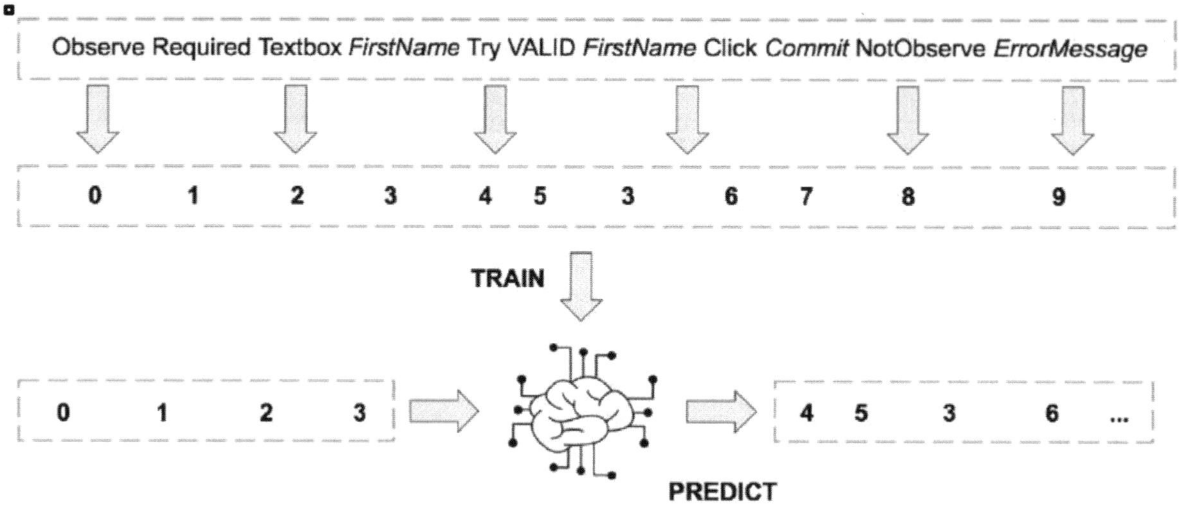

To use test flows as training data, a **sliding window** data augmentation technique is used to expand the training data. We frame the test flow learning problem as a supervised learning problem by taking each test flow from the training set and expanding it one word at a time, creating a new training example with a more complete sentence at each iteration. For each generated training example, the next step of the sentence is the correct assigned label.

Being able to train an ML system to generate test flows means we can now leverage humans not just to train a system to detect objects on a web page, but also to train a system on how those objects should interact in ways that are meaningful to testing.

4. State of the Art in AI for Testing

Companies such as test.ai (http://test.ai/) are making a significant impact in the field of AI for Testing. Built on top of AI-based approaches to mobile object recognition, reinforcement learning, and an abstract intent test language for expressing high-level test cases, the test.ai system is capable of automatically crawling through many mobile apps and is capable of reusing general test cases across concrete apps. In addition to test.ai, other products are leveraging ML to increase the efficiency of software testing.

For example, mabl (https://www.mabl.com/) can self-heal test cases by relying on ML approaches to detecting web page objects at runtime. Applitools (https://applitools.com/) uses an AI-powered visual testing approach capable of detecting rendering issues and visual differences between app builds. Eggplant AI (https://eggplant.io/) is able to intelligently navigate applications and predict where quality issues are most likely to manifest themselves.

At Ultimate Software, quality research and development teams have worked on building tools that leverage AI for software testing. One such effort involved creating a system discovery and testing platform capable of leveraging ML to explore a SUT and discover states and interactions automatically. Reinforcement learning is used to seek interactions that yield high reward (discovering a new state, discovering a significant state variant). Image recognition and natural language processing techniques are also used to extract information encountered on web pages, such as error messages.

The platform enables the creation of agents that are tailored to perform specialized testing tasks. For example, an agent may be created that automatically explores a SUT looking for exceptions, stack traces, etc. A separate agent may explore a SUT while actively resizing the web browser, looking for rendering defects along the way. Using the techniques described in **Section 3.2**, a system may be trained to classify web pages as being improperly rendered under different screen sizes.

A significant problem that AI for Testing systems encounter is the domain knowledge gap problem. The knowledge gap problem stands in the way of being able to achieve tasks such as filling out complicated forms and being able to understand the expected behavior of applications with complex workflows. Without knowledge of expected system behavior, appropriate test oracles cannot be constructed. At Ultimate Software, ongoing research is being expended towards the creation of an AI-based Domain Expert (AIDE). Leveraging existing research on expert systems, we have been able to start building knowledge bases that aim to reduce the domain knowledge gap problem encountered by AI for Testing systems.

The Artificial Intelligence for Software Testing Association (https://www.aitesting.org/) defines three important problems in the space of AI and testing. *AI for Testing* focuses on applying AI in order to identify software quality issues, apply test inputs, validate outputs, and emulate users or other conditions. *Testing AI* focuses on methods for testing software where AI is a major component of functionality or purpose. *Self-testing* in the context of AI is a new area of research focused on how to enable systems to test themselves. While this paper focuses on exploring the *AI for Testing* problem, it is important to be aware of the ongoing work in each of the aforementioned areas.

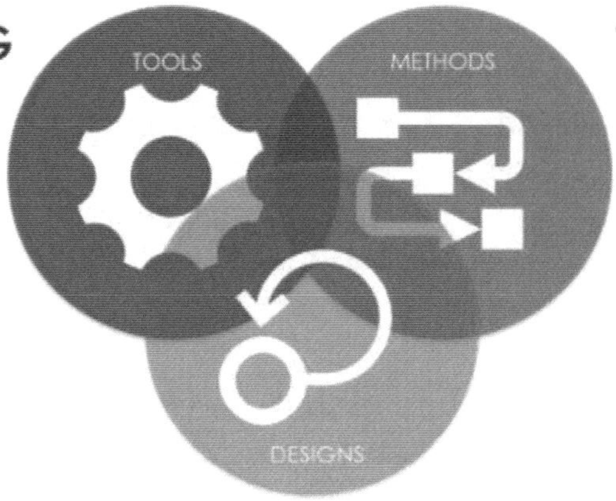

5. Breaking into AI

If you are ready to take the next step and start learning more about AI to start contributing towards the true automation of software testing, there are many excellent resources to start from.

Several tutorials and massive open online courses (MOOCs) are available that range from covering foundational material to covering deeper domain-specific AI problems. Blogs such as Jason Brownlee's machine learning mastery blog can also be good resources for finding many applied ML examples.

The AISTA is another resource for learning more about this exciting space, and for getting involved. AISTA is focused on applying, and extending AI to the world of software quality in all forms, and hopefully obviating the need for human testing activities. Genuinely automating software testing is not just a fundamental problem, but also a challenging problem. AISTA serves as an open community that fosters collaboration towards the common goal of achieving more intelligent automated software testing. One of the goals of AISTA is to provide a way for the community to contribute towards building datasets that may be used for training ML systems. Also, AISTA strives to provide a platform for sharing knowledge on different AI approaches to various testing problems.

The following presentations/tutorials also provide insightful information into the world of AI and testing:

- Jason Arbon, "AI and Machine Learning for Testers", PNSQC 2017
- Tariq King, Keynote "Rise of the Machines: Can Artificial Intelligence Terminate Manual Testing?", StarWest 2017
- Paul Merrill, "Machine Learning & How It Affects Testers", Quality Jam 2017
- Geoff Meyer, Keynote "What's Our Job When the Machines Do Testing?", StarEast 2018

- Angie Jones, Keynote "The Next Big Things: Testing AI and Machine Learning Applications", StarEast 2018
- Jason Arbon and Tariq King, "Artificial Intelligence and Machine Learning Skills for the Testing World", StarEast 2018

The following books cover many topics in great detail for readers that desire to attain a deep understanding of AI and ML:

- "Artificial Intelligence: A Modern Approach", Peter Norvig and Stuart J. Russell
- "Python Machine Learning", Sebastian Raschka
- "Deep Learning with Python", François Chollet
- "Deep Learning", Ian Goodfellow, Yoshua Bengio, Aaron Courville

The following resources are freely available online:

- Book: "Neural Networks and Deep Learning", Michael Nielsen, http://neuralnetworksanddeeplearning.com/
- YouTube: A full Stanford course on Machine Learning, taught by Andrew Ng

The following resources cover topics specifically surrounding AI and testing:

- AI Summit Guild (https://aisummitguild.com) has presentations from many of the leaders in the field
- Jason Arbon provides many additional resources on AI and testing (https://www.linkedin.com/pulse/links-ai-curious-jason-arbon/)

6. Closing Remarks

This paper aimed to stimulate research and innovation in software testing through the use of AI and ML. We presented an example of our journey and experiences of applying existing AI research to testing. We have also provided critical takeaways for how quality professionals can get the necessary foundation to break into the AI world and start contributing to this ripe emerging field of intelligent automated software testing. We have also highlighted a few practical applications of AI research, as well as related work being done by several companies. Along the way, we have also raised several important and challenging outstanding problems.

Current web test automation approaches rely heavily on the construction of page objects that are coupled to the implementation details of the SUT. The research and practical applications presented in this paper show that it is possible to raise the level of abstraction for working with webpage components. We also defined test flows and a well-defined language capable of expressing test flows. Also, we leveraged ML-based text generation techniques to learn how to recall and generate strings that belong to the language. It follows that it may be possible to use a combined learning approach to automatically generate and execute test cases against a SUT.

The application of AI and ML to testing is not going to happen in the future. It is already happening right now. As we discussed in **Sections 4 and 5**, more and more companies are starting to pay closer attention to this problem. As research and development continues and more data is collected to be able to train smart AI-driven testing bots, we will get closer to reaching a new level of test automation. As we shift closer to "true automation", human testers will need to adjust, and our roles will certainly be redefined. Within the next 5-10 years, it is quite possible that we will be experiencing a shift in testing culture and in testing responsibilities. Instead of spending time manually crafting automated scripts, we will be spending that time collecting and annotating more training data to make the bots even smarter. With thousands and thousands of these bots at our command doing the work we've taught them to do, it will help free us from the burdens of test automation scripting and maintenance, and allow us to focus on more important aspects of testing, such as exploratory testing and finding defects.

If nothing else, we hope that after reading this paper, the reader has increased awareness of how significant these problems are, and how important it is to start getting involved. We hope that by sharing our experiences in the fashion by which it was presented, it establishes a framework for others to follow and start contributing to these problems.

Appendix

This section presents our research and preliminary results for an *AI for Testing* approach that combines a trainable classifier that perceives application state, a language for describing test flows, and a trainable test flow generation model to create test cases learned from human testers.

In **Section 3.2**, we discussed the application of image-based classification to the problem of perceiving web application state. Aside from collecting and labeling images, as part of our research we collected and labeled structural information from web pages. To leverage structural information from a web page, we start by collecting a render tree. A render tree contains information on the DOM structure and about styling. A Computed Render Tree (CRT) representation of the webpage is then constructed. In contrast to a standard render tree, a CRT extends browser render trees by collecting the render tree only once the web browser has finalized rendering, and by calculating additional information such as: (1) element positions; and (2) element sizes.

Using the CRT representation, a feature synthesis step is then performed. An element-wise pass is done through all of the elements in the CRT, synthesizing several features for each element. Although the synthesis is done at the local level for each element, the full global context (information on the entire set of elements) is used to compute several features. The feature synthesis results in the generation of training data that can be annotated for the purpose of training ML models. A set of example synthesized features is described in the following table:

Feature	Description
HTML Tag	The tag for the given element.
Parent HTML Tag	The tag for the given element's parent.
"For" Attribute	The existence of a value for the HTML "For" attribute.
Num. Children	The number of HTML nodes that are children of the given element's node.
Num. Siblings	The number of HTML nodes that are siblings of the given element's node.
Depth	The depth of the given element's node within the ADOM tree.
Horizontal Percent	The relative horizontal position (in percentage) of the given element.
Vertical Percent	The relative vertical position (in percentage) of the given element.
Font Size	The relative (normalized against the full set of elements) font size of the given element.
Font Weight	The relative (normalized against the full set of elements) font weight of the given element.
Is Text	Describes whether a given element is a text node.
Nearest Color	The closest color computed using CIEDE2000 algorithm.
Nearest Background Color	The closest background color computed using CIEDE2000 algorithm.
Distance from Input	The relative (normalized against the full set of elements) distance to the closest input widget from the given element.
Text	The actual text associated with the given element.

In order to evaluate the web classification approach, CRTs were collected and hand-labeled for 7 different SUTs, comprised of 95 web pages and 17,360 web elements. Among the labeled data were 122 elements labeled as page titles, 384 elements labeled as widget labels, 91 labeled as error messages, and 16,762 noise data points. For each of the three component classes analyzed, an experiment was done to compare the performance of the following ML classifiers: (1) random forests, (2) J48 decision trees; (3) k-nearest neighbor; (4) support vector machines; and (5) Bayesian networks.

The evaluations were done using percentage split and cross-validation. Performance was measured using accuracy, precision, recall, and F1 score (Goutte 2005). For the problem of classifying widget labels, the results show that the random forest algorithm performed best with an F1-Score of **96.3%**. When classifying error messages, the random forest technique also performed the best, resulting in an F1-Score of **99.4%**. The data suggests page title classification to be the most difficult of the classification problems that were investigated. The K-Nearest Neighbor algorithm performed the best with an F1-Score of **71.6%**.

	Label Candidates				Error Messages			
Classifier	**Accuracy**	**Precision**	**Recall**	**F1-Score**	**Accuracy**	**Precision**	**Recall**	**F1-Score**
Random Forest (100 Estimators)	**99.83%**	**98.9%**	**93.8%**	**96.3%**	**99.99%**	**100.0%**	**98.9%**	**99.4%**
J48 Decision Tree	99.64%	95.0%	88.8%	91.8%	99.94%	91.8%	98.9%	95.2%
K-Nearest Neighbor (K=3)	99.61%	92.7%	89.6%	91.1%	99.98%	97.8%	98.9%	98.4%
SVM	99.29%	99.2%	68.8%	81.2%	99.97%	95.7%	98.9%	97.3%
Bayesian Network	99.13%	78.2%	84.1%	81.1%	99.88%	83.2%	97.8%	89.9%

	Page Titles			
Classifier	**Accuracy**	**Precision**	**Recall**	**F1-Score**
Random Forest (100 Estimators)	99.52%	67.3%	62.3%	64.7%
J48 Decision Tree	99.56%	79.5%	50.8%	62.0%
K-Nearest Neighbor (K=3)	**99.64%**	**82.8%**	**63.1%**	**71.6%**
SVM	99.41%	85.7%	19.7%	32.0%
Bayesian Network	97.32%	17.0%	72.1%	27.5%

In **Section 3.4**, we mentioned the creation of a **language** that could be used to express test flows. In order to validate both the designed language, as well as test flow generation, a prototype was constructed. An Extended Backus-Naur Form (EBNF) (McCracken 2003) language parser implementation was developed using the Lark library available in Python (Lark 2018). A total of 250 test flows utilizing all of the features of the language were crafted and parsed successfully using the custom Lark parser. Each of the 250 crafted test flows captured real test cases that could feasibly be performed by a human tester against a web application. Using the sliding window data augmentation technique, a dataset containing a total of 2610 labeled examples for the purposes of using ML for test flow generation was created. The Keras framework was used to build the neural networks for the prototype.

The performance of the LSTMs were measured using the built-in categorical cross-entropy loss function available in the Keras neural network programming framework. Training set accuracy was based on whether or not a predicted test flow was a valid test flow sub-sequence in the training data. In addition, the output predictions were only considered valid if the resulting test flow was able to be parsed by the custom Lark parser. Different network topologies, optimization algorithms, and regularization technique settings were compared. The following table shows a detailed breakdown of the performance of each configuration that was evaluated:

Epochs	Layers	Units	Dropout	Optimizer	Accuracy	Epochs	Layers	Units	Dropout	Optimizer	Accuracy
50	1	32	No	Adam	63.62%	**500**	**1**	**256**	**No**	**RMSProp**	**93.85%**
50	1	32	Yes	Adam	39.86%	**500**	**1**	**256**	**Yes**	**RMSProp**	**93.85%**
50	1	64	No	RMSProp	84.17%	50	2	64+64	No	RMSProp	88.17%
50	1	64	Yes	RMSProp	82.63%	50	2	64+64	Yes	RMSProp	89.03%
50	1	64	No	Adam	81.57%	50	2	64+64	No	Adam	73.06%
50	1	64	Yes	Adam	84.92%	50	2	64+64	Yes	Adam	81.06%
50	1	128	No	RMSProp	88.55%	50	2	128+128	No	Adam	86.67%
50	1	128	Yes	RMSProp	82.63%	50	2	128+128	Yes	Adam	86.67%
50	1	128	No	Adam	88.68%	50	2	128+128	No	RMSProp	89.98%
50	1	128	Yes	Adam	85.64%	50	2	128+128	Yes	RMSProp	85.57%
50	1	256	No	RMSProp	59.59%	50	3	128*3	No	RMSProp	91.49%
50	1	256	Yes	RMSProp	87.15%	50	3	128*3	Yes	RMSProp	86.50%
50	1	256	No	Adam	91.52%	**500**	**3**	**128*3**	**No**	**Adam**	**93.74%**
50	1	256	Yes	Adam	86.19%	**500**	**3**	**128*3**	**Yes**	**Adam**	**93.85%**

Each trained LSTM model was used for generating a total of 2925 test flows. When evaluating each LSTM configuration, accuracy was measured by dividing the number of generated test flows that were valid strings in our language by the total number of generated test flows. Experiments included varying the number of training iterations (epochs), the number of LSTM layers, and the number of LSTM units per layer. The Adam and RMSProp optimizers were also evaluated, as well as dropout regularization. Based on the results, the highest accuracy (**93.85%**) was achieved when training a single LSTM layer network for 500 epochs, using the RMSProp optimization algorithm. Equivalent accuracy was observed when using multiple stacked LSTM layers. Generally, increasing the number of layers and units improved accuracy; however, training time was also observed to increase. Stacking LSTM layers appears to be a viable option for increasing accuracy as more training data is added. While dropout regularization generally reduced training set accuracy, it did not greatly affect accuracy when training for longer durations or when using larger networks.

References

Abadi, Martín, Paul Barham, Jianmin Chen, Zhifeng Chen, Andy Davis, Je rey Dean, Matthieu Devin, et al. 2016. "TensorFlow: A System for Large-scale Machine Learning." In *Proceedings of the 12th USENIX Conference on Operating Systems Design and Implementation*, 265-283. OSDI'16. Savannah, GA, USA: USENIX Association. https://www.usenix.org/system/files/conference/osdi16/osdi16-abadi.pdf.

AIST. 2018. *IEEE International Workshop on Automated and Intelligent Software Testing.* Http://paris.utdallas.edu/AIST18/ (Accessed March 18, 2018).

AISTA. 2018. *AI for Software Testing Association.* Https://www.aitesting.org/ (Accessed March 18, 2018).

Arbon, Jason. 2017. *AI for Software Testing.* In *Pacific NW Software Quality Conference. PNSQC, 2017.* Http://uploads.pnsqc.org/2017/papers/AI-and-Machine-Learning-for-Testers-Jason-Arbon.pdf (Accessed July 18, 2018).

Bojarski, Mariusz, Davide Del Testa, Daniel Dworakowski, Bernhard Firner, Beat Flepp, Prasoon Goyal, Lawrence D. Jackel, et al. 2016. "End to End Learning for SelfDriving Cars." *CoRR* abs/1604.07316. arXiv: 1604.07316. http://arxiv.org/ abs/1604.07316.

Brownlee, Jason. 2016. *Text Generation With LSTM Recurrent Neural Networks in Python with Keras.* Https://machinelearningmastery.com/text-generation-lstm-recurrent-neuralnetworks-python-keras/ (Accessed April 4, 2018).

Goutte, Cyril, and Eric Gaussier. "A probabilistic interpretation of precision, recall and F-score, with implication for evaluation." In *European Conference on Information Retrieval*, pp. 345-359. Springer, Berlin, Heidelberg, 2005.

Graves, Alex. 2013. "Generating Sequences With Recurrent Neural Networks." *CoRR* abs/1308.0850. arXiv: 1308.0850. http://arxiv.org/abs/1308.0850.

LabelImg. 2018. *A graphical image annotation tool.* https://github.com/tzutalin/labelImg (Accessed August 10, 2018).

Lark. 2018. *A modern parsing library for Python.* https://github.com/lark-parser/lark (Accessed August 10, 2018).

McCracken, Daniel D., and Edwin D. Reilly. "Backus-naur form (bnf)." (2003): 129-131.

Moyer, Christopher. 2016. *How Google's AlphaGo Beat a Go World Champion Inside a man-versus-machine showdown.* Https://www.theatlantic.com/technology/archive/2016/03/theinvisible-opponent/475611/ (Accessed April 4, 2018).

Ng, Andrew. 2018. *Machine Learning (free online course on Coursera).* Http://www.andrewng.org/courses/ (Accessed March 10, 2018).

Stanford. 2018. *Machine Learning.* Https://online.stanford.edu/course/machine-learning1/ (Accessed March 18, 2018).

Xiong, Wayne, Jasha Droppo, Xuedong Huang, Frank Seide, Mike Seltzer, Andreas Stolcke, Dong Yu, and Geoffrey Zweig. 2017. "The Microsoft 2017 Conversational Speech Recognition System." In *2017 IEEE International Conference on Acoustics, Speech and Signal Processing (ICASSP),* 5255-5259. doi:10.1109/ICASSP.2017.7953159.

Thanks to the following people for their help editing this paper: Rick D. Anderson, Keith Stobie, and Keith Briggs. Thanks to the following people for their contributions to AI for testing efforts at Ultimate Software: John Maliani, Robert Vanderwall, Michael Mattera, Brian Muras, Keith Briggs, David Adamo, Justin Phillips, Philip Daye, and Patrick Alt.

Gating Code Commits, Approaches Taken by Two Large Scale

Authors

Clark Boylan (Intel)
Jack Morgan (OpenStack)

Abstract

An effective method for increasing software quality is by preventing defects from entering the code base in the first place. Pre-merge gating tests, that must pass before code changes are allowed to merge, help prevent defects from ever entering a code base. This code gating process increases project velocity allowing you to merge hundreds of changes each week while ensuring a high degree of code quality.

Blatant bugs are caught outright. Code reviewers are given as much information as possible on the functionality of the software under examination, and when things do break, logs provide additional information to determine when behavior changed.

This paper discusses the methods and tools developed by OpenStack[1] and the Open Platform for Network Function Virtualization (OPNFV)[2] to make this software approach practical. Both projects perform pre-merge testing on every change and require that they pass testing before they can merge. This paper will give other organizations a place to start should they choose to implement similar code gating practices to increase the quality of their code as well.

Biography

Clark Boylan is part of the infrastructure team that runs OpenStack's developer tooling. This includes code review and continuous integration services as well as mailing lists and other communication and collaboration tools. When not helping others merge code, Clark can often be found on an Oregon river fishing for Salmon and Steelhead.

-

1 https://www.openstack.org/software/

2 https://www.opnfv.org/software/technical-overview

Jack Morgan is a Network Software Engineer at the Intel Corporation. Jack is a former Project Technical Lead and current committer for the OPNFV Pharos project. Previously, Jack served as a committer-at-large member for the Technical Steering Committee and managed the Intel OPNFV Pharos lab. Jack has a passion for software automation within Open Source communities.

1. Gating

Ideally we would never write broken code. Unfortunately, all software has bugs and the next best thing is to not commit broken code. Gating code merges by requiring certain tests pass, helps get to this ideal state: an unbroken code base. A reliable working base allows continuous delivery and deployment. This idea may seem obvious and while not new (Hoare 2014), it is not a very common practice to find within organizations or software projects. The availability of free and easy to use services like Travis CI[3] have made pre-merge testing more common, but it is less common for projects to require that *everything* pass for code to merge. There are a number of challenges that one is faced with when attempting to gate all code commits on test passing. Following are challenges we encountered and the approaches we have taken to make code commit gating work within OpenStack and OPNFV.

2. Challenges

Understanding the challenges that gating poses is important for anyone implementing gating as it will shape the approach taken. This has definitely been true for OpenStack and OPNFV and there are some specific challenges we faced that have had a major impact on our approaches.

2.1. Resources

If every single commit needs to be tested prior to merging, you now need enough test job resources to run the tests at least once for each commit. If you have more than one developer, you will likely need enough resources to run several test jobs in parallel so that one developer does not block the others.

2.1. Execution Time

Your test suite has the demand of running within a reasonable amount of time. The time it takes to merge code is directly related to how quickly you are able to run the test suite that gates merging.

-

3 https://travis-ci.org/

The coupling between test resources and test suite runtime is even more apparent when you realize that to avoid races between multiple commits that conflict with each other you need to serialize your testing and merging of commits. If you do not, it is possible for commit A, which breaks commit B but both pass testing independently, to merge and result in a broken base. The test runtime effectively determines the maximum number of commits that can merge per day unless, you find some way to safely run tests in parallel for commits A and B.

2.3. Reliability

Unfortunately, no matter how hard you try software will still have bugs. If left unmanaged, these bugs can quickly have major consequences for your gating system. Assume you have twenty unrelated bugs in your software and each of them cause an independent test failure 1% of the time. In aggregate, your test suite will now fail 18.2% of the time (almost one in five runs). This leads to not being able to construct good code in a timely fashion, as well as developer frustration.

A gating system incentivizes keeping the tests that gate a project working. Generally, this is desirable unless it pulls developers away from larger scale testing that, due to time constraints, is not part of the gate. We have seen that this is a particular issue within OpenStack; few developers will care about tests unless they are gate tests. Google has written about their struggles with this problem too. According to Google 1.5% of their test runs exhibit flaky results (Micco 2016). Unfortunately, mitigation strategies, like rerunning failed tests, tend to encourage developers to ignore flaky tests even though they may expose real bugs in the software (Micco 2016).

While you can run periodic "bit rot" test jobs outside of the gate, if your project developers start to care only for the testing that allows their code to merge, then any lower activity code bases tend to "bit rot" or erode and their test suites stop functioning. If developers do not push code to these code bases, the gate tests do not run, and the "bit rot" tests are ignored leading to a broken base after all.

Another aspect to consider is that your tests are only as reliable as the infrastructure they run on. Even if the software being tested has no bugs, your operating system and hardware do have bugs. You must care for the infrastructure you rely on just as much as the software you are developing, and do your best to make them as reliable as possible.

2.4. Security

Pre-merge testing implies running tests before trusted developers have verified the changes themselves. This comes with security concerns, particularly for Open Source projects that accept code changes from individuals on the Internet. You should assume your contributors are well meaning, but you must still protect against the possibility that malicious code could be contributed. Typically, you would address this by reviewing code and not merging anything that looks suspicious, but when gating you are explicitly running tests before merging the code making these test environments vulnerable to this sort of attack.

2.5. Perceptions

Developers that have not used a gating system before (or used a poorly implemented system) there tends to be a reasonable amount of skepticism that you have to overcome. Developers do not like being told that some mechanical agent is responsible for merging their code.

3. OpenStack

Within the OpenStack project, we require all commits to be reviewed prior to merging and all commits to be gated by their test respective suites. This provides a consistent process to all contributors, but we faced many of the challenges detailed above that were worth addressing in order to maintain a functional base and allow for continuous delivery of our software.

All of our continuous integration systems and test job resources run on donated cloud instances from interested parties. This reduces much of the initial concern over finding and allocating (and funding) test resources, but we do still want to be good stewards of the resources we have. In order to ensure we only use what we need, we have built a demand based resource allocator, Nodepool[4]. This creates test nodes as needed and deletes them when completed. If the project is idle, we use near zero resources, but can ramp up in a very short period of time to meet demand (OpenStack Graphite 2018).

-

[4] https://zuul-ci.org/docs/nodepool/

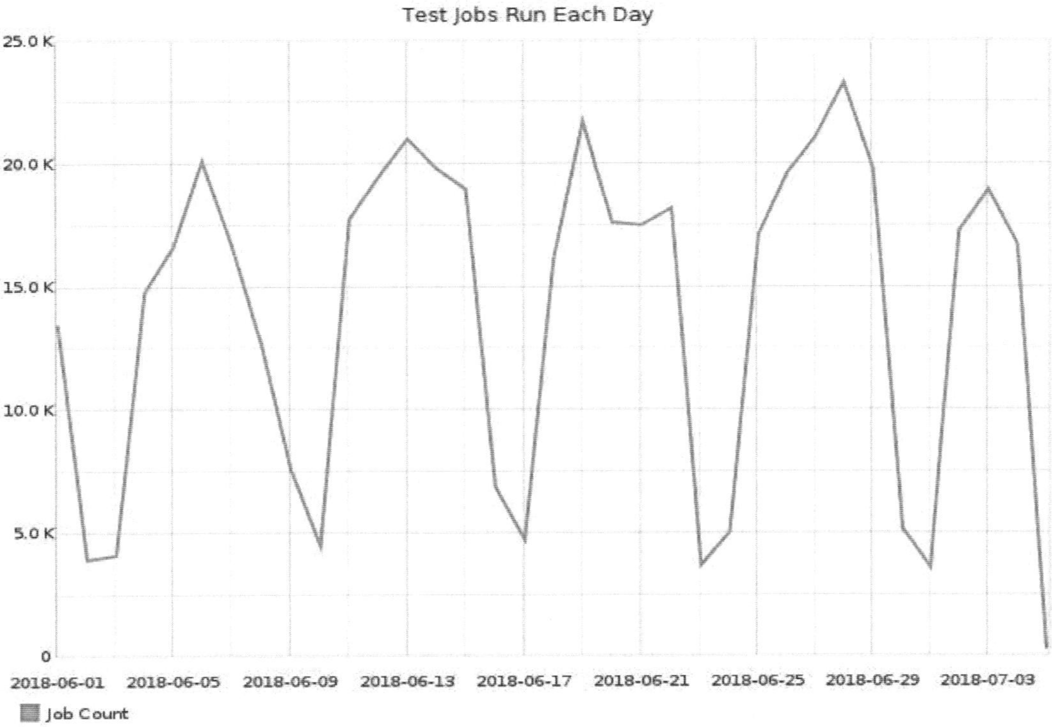

Another benefit to the Nodepool system is every test environment is used once then deleted. This behavior, combined with using virtual machines, largely mitigates the security concern created by running tests for code commits before they are reviewed and merged. In fact, we explicitly give our users administrative super user access within the test environments to make this point clear. A developer could do something malicious but only up to the test job timeout, then everything is deleted and the system is available again for testing, in a clean state.

Every test job instance we boot has a daily snapshot of our code repositories. We use Git[5] for revision control allowing us to have a complete copy of every code repository distributed to every test node. Every cloud region we run in has a region local host which mirrors Linux distribution packages and Python Package Index packages. Our software is predominantly written to run on Linux and is written in Python, consequently many of the dependencies we need are found in Linux package mirrors and the public Python package index. These mirror nodes also act as caching proxies for external resources like Docker Hub. This highly reduces the external costs of running tests. It also minimizes the runtime cost of copying and installing test dependencies.

5 http://www.git-scm.com/

Very early on we were serializing gate testing of projects. At that time, the test suite would take about an hour to run. This meant that the best case scenario was merging twenty-four commits a day, quickly becoming a bottleneck we had to address. The fix for this problem is to run the gate tests for commits in parallel using a speculative future state. This assumes that once changes get to the gate, the chances they will fail in the gate are low. This assumption is necessary because failures require building new global states, and discarding all previous test results, which is not cheap. In order to ensure this assumption is a good one, we run the test suite on a commit proposal before anyone reviews the commits. Then reviewers only "approve" the commits for the gate if this "check" testing has passed.

In order to make this possible with our tool set at the time, we had to build a new continuous integration service called Zuul[6]. Since that time, Zuul has become far more general purpose and should be usable by anyone with projects hosted on Gerrit[7] or Github[8].

-

6 https://zuul-ci.org/docs/zuul/

7 https://www.gerritcodereview.com/

8 https://github.com/

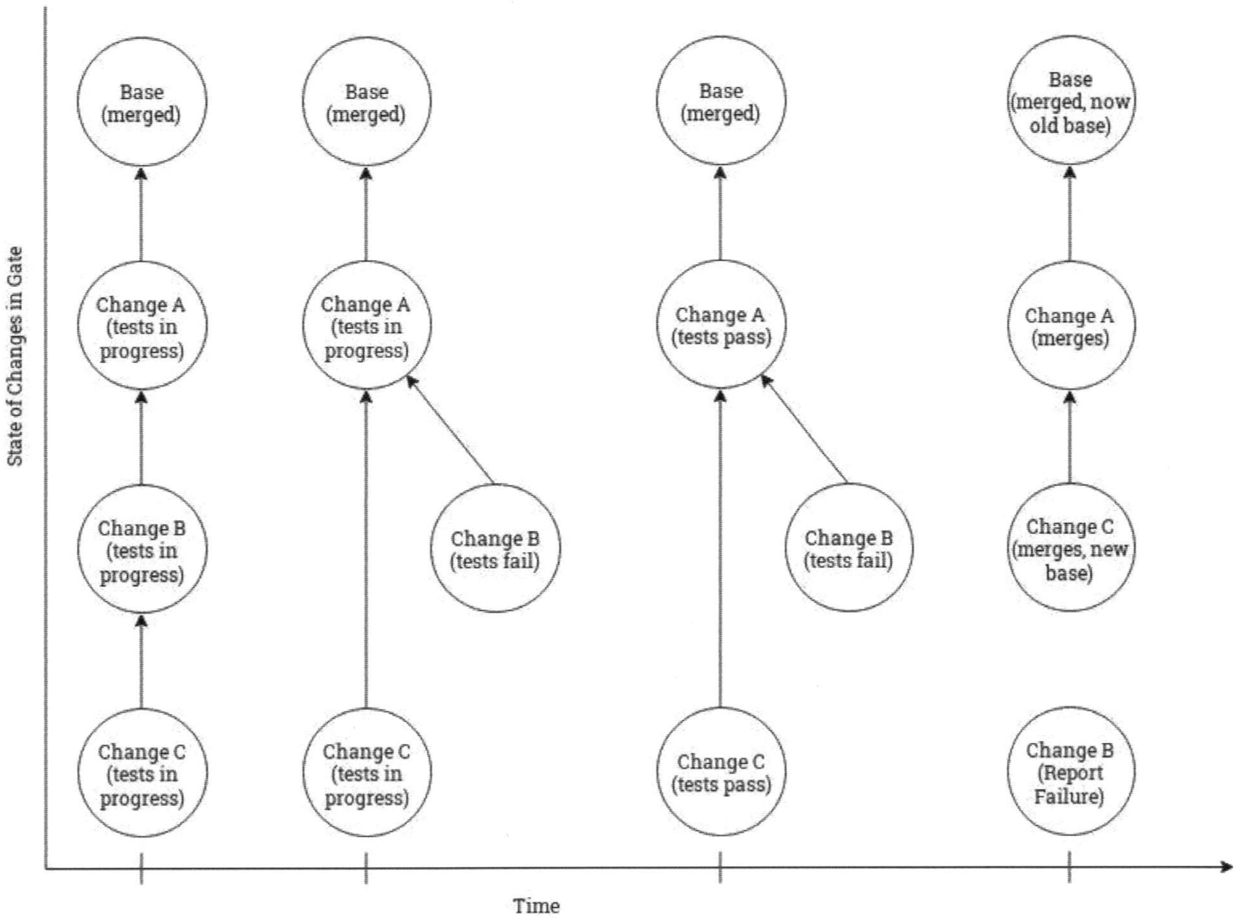

To keep track and manage the "small" bugs that cause big problems in aggregate, we indexed all of our test job logs and built a set of bug fingerprints to identify when specific bugs hit our tests. This allows us to track the cost of specific bugs as it relates to gate reliability and to know with a high degree of accuracy when specific bugs are fixed. All of this data is presented to our developers with a top level dashboard[9]. If we can identify the cause of a failure quickly, we report back to the code review itself with that data. This allows our developers to prioritize bug fixes with the greatest impact and provides understanding at a high level what sort of problems we are currently facing.

-

9 http://status.openstack.org/elastic-recheck/gate.html

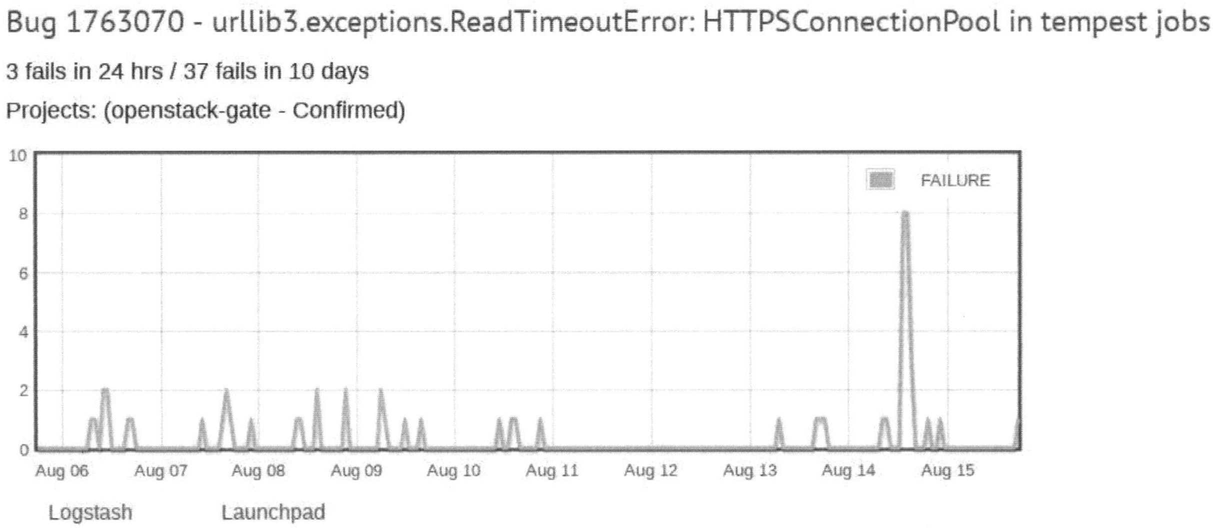

Managing "bit rot" has also required providing information back to our developers. We have built a more detailed status dashboard[10]. that allows people to easily consume information on jobs that run periodically outside of the gate. Developers can subscribe to web feeds using the Rich Site Summary protocol and automatically get notified when there are new test results. Additionally, they may manually access the page and search for test results that interest them. Making it easy to find this information, when it is not directly affecting the ability to merge code, has resulted in healthier periodic "bit rot" jobs.

Putting all of this together largely addresses the developer behavior concerns that contributors have. Providing the tools that make this possible allows them to use the continuous integration and gating systems as an extension of their workflow, getting more work done than they would otherwise. Many of our contributors end up using the continuous integration systems as an extension of their local workstations for running tests. They can also approve commits for merging without worrying about ordering things themselves or whether or not everything will break when they are done. Release managers can release when necessary to get bug fixes out quickly, including addressing security concerns. In 2016 this required we run more than 6 million test jobs (OpenStack Foundation 2016). In 2017 we enabled 2,344 developers to approve, gate, and merge 65,823 commits (OpenStack Foundation 2017). All this was done while requiring every commit to pass testing before merging.

-

10 http://status.openstack.org/openstack-health/ - /g/build_queue/periodic

4. OPNFV

Open Platform for Network Function Virtualization is a collaborative project under the Linux Foundation which provides an ecosystem for development, integration, deployment, and testing. It incorporates many "upstream" projects like OpenStack and supports the needs of its various target audiences. These include OPNFV developers who work with upstream projects, end users wanting to try specific use cases and network function virtualization (NFV) developers who use OPNFV as a reference platform for compliance verification.

Developers who work with one or more upstream projects can easily deploy and test their work. They can automatically verify their code in a realistic use case. It usually takes days to pull together each of the components that are relevant to their use case and when things break, it's easy to throw away their code and re-deploy. OPNFV provides a way to include the latest working version, current stable release or development version.

End users want to run one of the supported OPNFV use cases. They are interested in a stable environment and the ability to use the deployment for prolonged periods of time or multiple times without having to re-deploy. They value stability over having the latest upstream versions.

Companies that offer commercial carrier-grade open source NFV solutions use OPNFV. They want their products to have good interoperability with 3rd party MANO systems, virtualized network function (VNF) hardware, and key customer requirements. OPNFV provides a compliance verification program[11] which confirms that the reference implementation has been verified according to transparent and well defined criteria.

OPNFV has a number of community labs[12] to do development, testing and to support OPNFV releases. These are provided by member organizations and vary by size and function. These community labs are located throughout the globe to ensure the community needs can be met. Some of the challenges of these labs is that the number of hardware resources is fixed. This can cause resource contention during critical testing done before the release. To solve this problem, a lab was built to dynamically create OPNFV testing environments that could easily scale as needed.

-

11 http://www.opnfv.org/verified

12 https://wiki.opnfv.org/display/pharos/Community+Labs

OPNFV gating strategies work similarly to OpenStack's in that code gets checked and tested before it is accepted. OPNFV confidence gate includes several levels of testing including a health check, smoke test and long duration test cases. The first level of gating is done in a virtual environment. It includes minimal functional testing for specific requirements for the project.

Additional testing can be done if needed. The next level of gating is done in a lab on bare metal and includes additional feature testing. Specific testing to support a release is also performed. These include high availability (HA) testing for redundancy and some longer running testing. The last gating includes long duration testing and tests that support the compliance verification program.

OPNFV has several challenges due to having to meet the requirements of different stakeholders. These different stakeholders require trade-offs between recent versus stable components. The maturity of each installed version can vary, though the goal is to be able to deploy a reproducible stack every time.

5. Working Together

Starting in 2018, Open Source projects like OpenStack, OPNFV, OpenDaylight, and Ansible have begun collaborating on continuous integration concerns through the OpenCI[13] initiative. To date we have had two face-to-face meetups and intend to continue meeting quarterly.

The two initial meetings were mainly spent learning about who we are and what we do, building common vocabulary to establish shared understanding around items like code gating, and planning specific areas where we can work together to improve the continuous integration and code quality within and across our open source projects. Topics included designing a system to send notifications from one continuous integration system to another, and documenting the ways in which we ensure our test environments remain secure.

OpenStack is one of OPNFV's many "upstreams", meaning OPNFV pulls in changes to OpenStack and integrates them with other software to provide a complete platform for network function virtualization.

Being able to automatically negotiate between OpenStack's Zuul and OPNFV's Jenkins when new software is tested, merged, and published would drastically simplify the accounting process for OPNFV to pull in new artifacts. Today, this is a largely manual process managed by humans, but much of the data is already machine readable, we just need to move it from point A to point B. One potential outcome of this would be to have OpenStack Zuul act as a contributor to OPNFV via proposals to update dependencies which would then be run through OPNFV's gate. The results of OPNFV's gate could then be fed back into OpenStack's gate.

13 https://www.openci.io/

6. Run Your Own

Specialized tools help, but are not critical to successfully running a gating system. In most cases the ideal would be to start with a small active project and rather than replace existing tools build upon them. This reduces the number of variables involved and should be easier for development teams to buy into. At the same time an active project is the perfect proving ground for a gating system as you know developers will be using it.

If new tools are of interest, a revision control system, a code review system, and automated continuous integration tooling are all highly recommended. OpenStack uses a combination of Git for revision control, Gerrit for code review, and Zuul for continuous integration. This combination has been proven to work well over half a decade of gating commits and is entirely free and open source software.

Assuming that goes well, the likely next step is expanding to other code bases. Ideally you would do this one project at a time. Increasing load and demand on testing infrastructure has a tendency to find problems in that infrastructure. These problems are easier to debug and fix if the system undergoes small changes. This is important because the reliability of the infrastructure is now directly tied to developers' ability to merge code.

There are several straightforward mechanisms that can be employed to ensure reliability over the long term. Many organizations tend to build software using a common set of languages and packaging tools. Standardizing your method for running unit tests against a particular language makes it easy to spin up testing for new projects. It also ensures that new projects end up using proven test tooling, leading to better reliability. When things do go wrong, fixing the standard quickly fixes it for all projects and you do not need to track down multiple cases of the same issue. You can extend this to code "linting", functional testing, integration testing, package builds, and even deployment of your software.

With a reasonable set of standardized tests and jobs in place, you can build your infrastructure to further accommodate these standards and improve reliability. Base images with a common set of necessary tools as well as caching proxies or mirrors for external resources improve reliability by keeping network accesses to a minimum.

At the same time, you do want to accommodate differences among projects. An inflexible system is not likely to make its users happy. Technology moves at such a rapid pace that you will likely need to change your standards at some point. Happy users acting as beta testers are a great way to discover what does and does not work. All projects may not be held to the same standard of testing in their gates. The higher the standards, the more developers of a project will get out of it, but that may not be practical for all cases. A code base used in the short term may rely on static linting to catch the most obvious of bugs, while other more important code bases will perform a variety of testing including linting, unit testing, and integration testing.

Finally, you will want a safety valve of some sort. There is a non-zero chance that at some point it will be impractical to force a change to go through gating. One common situation that calls for bypassing the gate is when you have multiple issues affecting your code base at once, preventing fixes for any one issue from merging. You can either squash the fixes for all of the issues together into a single logical change or disable gating and merge the fixes separately. From the gate's perspective squashing, the fixes together is the correct solution, but that may not be desirable if it results in hard to follow change history. From a human perspective it tends to make developers happy if they know there is an out if things go wrong in unexpected ways.

You should avoid relying on this safety valve. In our experience, changes that are merged bypassing the gate tend to be followed up with a change to fix whatever the ungated change broke. When you do use it, be sure to record the who and why associated with that change. This means using your code review system as you would otherwise, so as to not completely bypassing your tooling. This helps avoid unintentional mistakes by individuals that rarely have to do this themselves as the tooling typically handles it. It also gives you history to refer back to when you have to follow up an ungated change with a fix to that change.

While we call this process "gating", the intent is to enable developers to merge reliable code changes quickly with minimal overhead. Every organization will have to find their own balance between the work machines are required to perform, how much of that work must be successful before humans can override it, and the quality they desire in their code base. There is no single setup that will work for everyone and it will change over time. As long as you continue to accommodate these changing needs, you should end up with a successful gating system.

6.1. Implementation Ideas

These implementation ideas are opinionated and likely will not fit every project. The intent is to give concrete examples with specific tools and documentation starting points that individuals can get started with quickly.

6.1.1. Quickstart a Small Project

One of the easiest ways to start gating code commits is to host your project on Github and test it with Travis CI. Once hosted on Github the first step is to get reliable test jobs running with Travis CI. Travis CI supports a number of programming languages and tools and comes with extensive documentation to get you started[14]. At this point nothing prevents you from merging Github Pull Requests when the tests are failing.

14 http://www.docs.travis-ci.com/user/getting-started/

To start gating on tests you will need to enable branch protection[15] on your project and require the Travis CI status checks pass[16] before Pull Requests can merge. This will prevent force pushes to your repository and require all Pull Requests have passing tests before Github will let you merge them.

This is a quick and easy way to get started because both Github and Travis CI are free to Open Source projects and have extensive documentation as well as many users to help you get set up. You do not need to run any of your own infrastructure which keeps the barrier to entry low. The drawbacks to this system are that your tests are limited by the constraints that Travis CI puts in place and the software has to be publicly available.

6.1.2. Retrofit Existing Jenkins Installations

Many organizations use Jenkins[17] as the engine to manage their existing continuous integration efforts. Typically Jenkins is configured to pull code repositories on a periodic cycle and run jobs against the code in its post merge state. Developers can check the Jenkins status dashboard to see if these builds are passing or failing. Assuming you have a code review system we can configure Jenkins to run these builds when code changes are proposed then report results back to the code review system pre merge.

The Jenkins Github plugin has documentation[18] on setting Jenkins up with Github similar to Travis CI in the previous example. You will want to protect your branches and require the Jenkins status results to enforce that Pull Requests have passing tests before they merge. This requires you run your own Jenkins, but many already do and this allows you to avoid the constraints put in place by Travis CI.

6.1.3. Large Scale Project with Many Repositories and Developers

Zuul presents many advantages to large scale projects. It can test speculative future states across many code repositories in parallel allowing large projects to move quickly without blocking for every change to be gated serially. It is able to scale up horizontally to handle a large number of changes and the required test jobs to gate them.

-

15 https://help.github.com/articles/about-protected-branches/
16 https://help.github.com/articles/about-required-status-checks/
17 https://jenkins.io/
18 https://www.cloudbees.com/blog/better-integration-between-jenkins-and-github-github-jenkins-plugin

Zuul publishes an administrator guide[19] (as well as user docs[20]) which includes a "Zuul From Scratch" document to get you started[21]. This document guides you through the process of installing Zuul and Nodepool on a number of Linux distributions and has info for pointing Zuul at Github and Gerrit. This process is a bit more involved than the previous two as you will be starting from scratch, but you should end up with a robust system capable of scaling to the demands you throw at it.

References

Hoare, Graydon. 2014. "Technicalities: 'Not Rocket Science' (the Story of Monotone and Bors)." *Frog Hop*, February 2, 2014,
http://www.graydon2.dreamwidth.org/1597.html
(accessed July 20, 2018).

Micco, John. 2016. "Flaky Tests at Google and How We Mitigate Them." *Google Testing Blog*, May 27, 2016,
https://testing.googleblog.com/2016/05/flaky-tests-at-google-and-how-we.html
(accessed August 15, 2018).

OpenStack Foundation. 2016. *OpenStack Foundation 2016 Annual Report,* 2016,
https://www.openstack.org/assets/reports/OpenStack-2016-Annual-Report-final-draft.pdf
(accessed July 20, 2018).

OpenStack Foundation. 2017. *OpenStack Foundation 2017 Annual Report*, 2017,
https://www.openstack.org/assets/reports/OpenStack-AnnualReport2017.pdf
(accessed July 20, 2018).

OpenStack Graphite. 2018. *Test Jobs Run Each Day*, 2018,
http://graphite.openstack.org/render/?title=Test%20Jobs%20Run%20Each%20Day&from=20180601&until=20180705&target=alias(summarize(sumSeries(stats_counts.zuul.tenant.openstack.pipeline.*.all_jobs),%20%271d%27),%20%27Job%20Count%27)&height=480&width=640&xFormat=%Y-%m-%d&lineWidth=2
(accessed July 20, 2018).

19 https://zuul-ci.org/docs/zuul/admin/index.html

20 https://zuul-ci.org/docs/zuul/user/index.html

21 https://zuul-ci.org/docs/zuul/admin/zuul-from-scratch.html

Notes

To determine the chance that a test suite will fail we determine the chance the suite will succeed then subtract from 100%.

Probability of Test Suite Failure $= 1 - \prod_{k=1}^{n} \textit{Test Success Probability}_k$

For example we get $1 - 0.99^{20} =$ .1821 or 18.2%

Talking About Quality: How to Define Quality Targets in an Agile World

Author

Kathy Iberle, Iberle Consulting Group, Inc. (kiberle@kiberle.com)

Abstract

Have you been tripped up by unspoken requirements? Product owners who can't articulate or simply don't talk about their expectations for usability, reliability, understandability, and all those other "ilities"? Do you know some of your "nonfunctional" requirements, but worry that you've missed some? Or perhaps your project has gotten those expectations on the table, but you're unsure whether to handle them as a user story, or in your Definition of Done, or in some other way.

This paper demonstrates how to solve these quandaries by combining traditional tools for defining quality targets with modern agile methods. We'll present a checklist of nonfunctional requirements, a set of agile tools for incorporating those attributes into your project, and some criteria for deciding which tool to use in which circumstances. As a bonus, we'll also explore how to surface hidden quality requirements by developing a defect severity chart.

Biography

Kathy Iberle is the Principal Consultant at Iberle Consulting Group, Inc., where she helps clients improve their productivity and quality. Her extensive background in process improvement and quality methods enable her to blend classic quality control with the best of current Lean thinking. Kathy Iberle has been working with software quality and development process improvement in both agile and traditional teams for many years. After a long career at Hewlett-Packard as a programmer, quality engineer, and process improvement expert, she is now the principal consultant and owner of the Iberle Consulting Group. She has published regularly since 1997, served as co-chair of the Program Committee of the Pacific Northwest Software Quality Conference (PNSQC) in 2009, and participated in the invitation-only Software Test Managers Roundtable for five years.

Kathy has an M.S. in Computer Science from the University of Washington, and an excessive collection of degrees in Chemistry from the University of Washington and the University of Michigan. Visit her website at www.kiberle.com

1. Introduction

Customers and developers spend most of their time talking about features and functionality – in other words, what the system will do. After all, that's why people buy your system, right? If your agile team uses good testing practices and a solid Definition of Done, your system should also have all those other characteristics such as availability, reliability, installability, usability, and so forth, as if by magic.

Ah, but often the magic doesn't quite happen. After a few weeks or months of building individually delightful user stories which pass all their acceptance tests, the team discovers that the performance has degraded. Or the users can't find their way through the numerous screens. Or the system starts hanging sporadically. What's gone wrong?

Usually the problem traces back to a lack of awareness regarding the nonfunctional requirements for this product. *Nonfunctional requirements* define not **what** a system does, but how **well** it does it. Nonfunctional requirements describe expectations for system-level characteristics or *quality attributes* such as availability, usability, reliability, security, performance, and so forth. A nonfunctional requirement states how much of a particular attribute is desired. How fast should the system respond? How comfortable should a particular type of user feel?

Products fall short of meeting expectations regarding quality attributes for two main reasons:

1) Nobody ever nailed down the nonfunctional requirements – the goals for the quality attributes. The team didn't have a clear definition of what the stakeholders and users expected, so they didn't drive the design and the code to meet the users' expectations.

2) The team understood the expectations, but didn't successfully capture them in any structure or process, so the expectations were overlooked or forgotten.

The first problem involves talking about *quality* – clearly stating the expected behavior. The second problem involves talking about your *quality process* – how your team will make the expected behavior happen. In this paper, we'll talk about both.

2. Talking About Quality

If you simply ask your product owner for their nonfunctional requirements, you'll probably get a blank stare. And if you ask about quality expectations, most likely you'll hear a discussion of either defect counts or test coverage. None of these are an effective way to discover what the users actually want.

We need to understand what quality means to the users for this product. How would the users recognize quality? What level of performance, or scalability, or reliability, or usability should the product have? And how can we tell whether the product has that?

2.1. Establish a Common Language for Quality Attributes

Having a conversation with your stakeholders about their expectations for quality attributes is much easier if you have some common language. The team can provide the stakeholders with some language by using a quality attributes list.

The following list is adapted from chapter 14 of Karl Wiegers' excellent book *Software Requirements, Third Edition* [WIEG2013].

Accessibility	How easily people with a range of physical abilities can use the system.
Availability	The extent to which the system's services are available when and where they are needed.
Installability	How easy it is to correctly install, uninstall, and re-install the application.
Manufacturability	How easy it is to correctly produce copies of the software on intended media.
Integrity	How well the system prevents information loss and preserves data entered into the system
Correctness	For systems which analyze data or make predictions, how accurate is the answer provided
Performance	How quickly and predictably the system responds to user inputs or other events
Reliability	How long the system will run before experiencing a failure
Robustness	How well the system responds to unexpected operating conditions
Safety	How well the system protects against injury or damage
Security	How well the system protects against unauthorized access to the application or data
Usability	How easy it is for people to learn, remember, and use the system.
Interoperability	How easily the system can interconnect and exchange data with other systems or components.
Efficiency	How efficiently the system uses computer resources.
Scalability	How easily the system can grow to handle more users, transactions, servers, or other extensions

You can find similar lists many places, organized in various ways. You might see lists called *nonfunctional requirement types*, *quality characteristics*, *quality attributes*, *capabilities*, or even *the -ilities*. The most complex collection is the ISO/IEC standard 205010 [ISO2010], which organizes quality attributes into eight quality characteristics and thirty-one subcharacteristics.

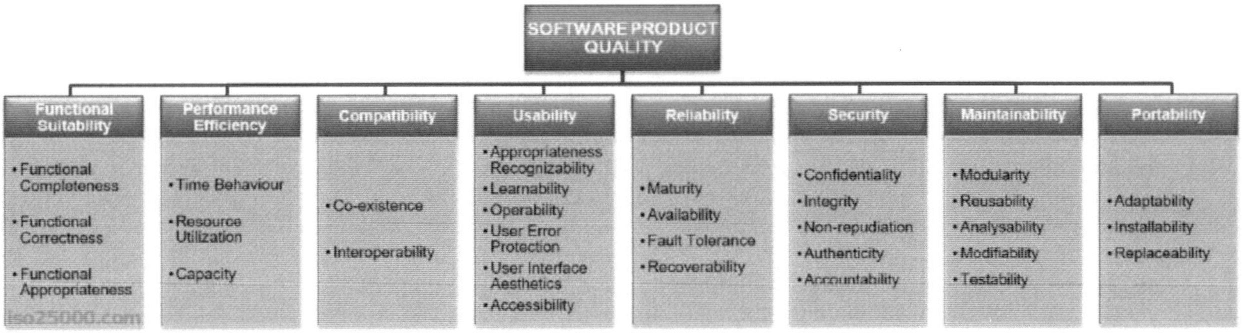

Since the early 1980s, system test strategists have used a similar list of *system test types* to structure test coverage and brainstorm system tests.

All these different lists are heuristics or shortcuts for finding overlooked nonfunctional requirements. Most are not intended to be exhaustive or complete. They are tools to trigger thinking about important requirements which might have been missed. The definitions are part of the trigger, to help ask "how well does our product do this?"

2.2. Skip Attributes Which Aren't Relevant

The quality attributes list is meant to trigger conversations. For your product or business, there are probably some quality attributes you don't need to discuss. Either they aren't relevant, or they are so central to your product that they've been extensively discussed already. On the other hand, if your organization usually overlooks particular attributes (and is sorry later), add those attributes to your list.

Sue's team is developing the electronic brake control module (EBCM) for a major auto manufacturer. As part of their initial project startup, they sit down to review a list of quality attributes looking for things they've missed.

> Sue: "How about scalability?"
> Bitra: "The ability to handle more users, transactions, or whatever? That's not relevant – our firmware has to do its job, but the job isn't going to grow."

The rest of the team agrees, so they drop "scalability" from their quality attributes list. They won't ask their stakeholders for expectations in that area. But if Sue's team was working on an Internet service, they would definitely ask about scalability.

Before removing an attribute from your list, consider all your stakeholders, not just the end users. Some of your other stakeholders might include buyers, operations staff, or maintenance staff. For instance, the operations staff of a utility company is usually quite interested in the installability of customer-facing applications, because they have to install them onto the company's servers. The utility's customers aren't even aware of the installation, so they aren't going to have useful opinions on how much installability is needed.

A list of quality attributes forces the team to look at the system from different perspectives. For instance, one might think that the attribute "availability" is only relevant to Internet services. But if one component in an app is unavailable to another component because the first component is off doing garbage collection, that can cause a huge quality problem. Asking about "availability" might surface this simply because you're looking at the system from a different angle.

2.3. Ask the Customers What Matters to Them

A quality attributes list helps you have productive conversations with your stakeholders.
Sit down with a stakeholder and walk through your quality attributes list, asking them which attributes matter to them. When the stakeholder identifies an attribute, ask for specific goals in that area. You might find these questions useful:

- "What do you want?"
- "How will you know when you have it?" These lead to acceptance tests.
- "What will that do for you?" Understanding the relative value of different attributes helps when there are trade-offs to make.

2.4. Get Specific

In agile projects, goals for quality attributes are usually captured as acceptance criteria, tests, or release criteria. In waterfall projects, the goals are captured as written requirements. In either case, vague statements such as "the system must be fast" or "the system must be user-friendly" aren't very helpful. The development team needs measurable, testable specifics, so they can tell when a story is "done" or when the software is "good enough" to release.

Johanna Rothman shares some examples of "good enough to release" in her book *Create Your Successful Agile Project* [ROTH2017]. These "Release Criteria" are high-level goals which were set by stakeholders.

- *"Performance*: For a given scenario (Describe it in some way), the query returns results in a maximum of two seconds.
- *Reliability:* The system maintains uptime under these conditions (describe the conditions).
- *Scalability*: The system is able to build up to 20,000 simultaneous connections and scale down to under 1,000 connections."

Notice that these are measurable, testable statements of expectations. The scenarios and conditions are critical parts of the requirements. There are plenty of examples of such specifics in any standard requirements text. It's worth being familiar with some of these even if you never write a formal requirements document, because they help you ask interesting questions.

For instance, Karl Wiegers points out that it can be helpful to explore the attribute from multiple perspectives [WIEG2013]:

- What would users consider an unacceptable response time for this query?
- What times of the day, week, or month have much heavier usage than usual?
- How many simultaneous users do you have on average?

Expected performance attributes for the EBCM look somewhat different than performance attributes for an Internet application, but they follow the same principles. The EBCM firmware responds to "events", which are triggered either by end user actions such as applying the brakes or by measurements delivered on a regular basis from other system components, such as sensors measuring speed. Sue's team might put together a chart of performance requirements such as the one below.

Event	**Must respond to event within...**	**Must not respond in less than...**	**Notes**
BRAKE01	2 msec	0 msec	
BRAKE02	3 msec	0 msec	
SRM01	2 msec	0 msec	
SRM02	4 msec	0.5 msec	Too fast a response can cause mechanical stutter

2.5. Landing Zones

In some cases, there is a degree of flexibility in the requirements. Often this is a tradeoff situation, such as smartphone weight versus battery life. If the battery life is significantly better, it may be ok for the phone to be a bit heavier. In these cases, the stakeholders may want to delineate a "landing zone", such as in this example from Rebecca Wirfs-Brock [WIRF2011].

Landing Zone for Smart Phone

ATTRIBUTE	MINIMUM	TARGET	OUTSTANDING
Battery life – standby	300 hours	320 hours	420 hours
Battery life – in use	270 minutes	300 minutes	380 minutes
Footprint in inches	2.5 x 4.8 x .57	2.4 x 4.6 x .4	2.31 x 4.5 x .37
Screen size (pixels)	600 x 400	600 x 400	960 x 640
Digital camera resolution	8 MP	8 MP	9 MP
Weight	5 oz.	4.8 oz.	4.4 oz.

The team is expected to aim for the target values, but has the option to accept a minimum value in one attribute in order to achieve outstanding in another.

This method was pioneered by Tom Gilb in the 1980s [GILB1988] using the terms "Goal, Stretch, Wish", and has since appeared in other places using terms such as "Must, High Want, Want", or "Must, Want, Wish". These older sets of terms are sometimes misinterpreted, resulting in the team aiming for the lowest value rather than the middle value. In contrast, "Minimum, Target, Outstanding" clearly says: "You should aim for the target, and accept minimum only if you have to. And a gold star if you reach outstanding!" The terms themselves contribute to a productive conversation with stakeholders.

In addition to the usual pass/fail results, the team will probably be expected to report the observed value for each landing-zone attribute. This tells the organization exactly where the system has landed within the defined landing zone. If the economic return on each attribute is known, trade-off decisions can be made. See Wiegers for a systematic method to make such quality attribute trade-offs. [WIEG2013]

2.6. Ask the Business What Else Matters

Quality attributes which matter mainly to the development and maintenance teams are sometimes called *Internal Quality Attributes*. A shortfall in internal quality attributes is often considered to be technical debt rather than a defect per se.

Some Typical Internal Quality Attributes	
Modifiability	How easy it is to maintain, change, enhance, and restructure the system
Portability	How easily the system can be made to work in other operating environments
Reusability	To what extent components can be used in other systems
Verifiability or Testability	How readily developers and testers can confirm that the software was implemented correctly.

Expectations around internal quality attributes can affect how you choose to do your development, so it's important to understand those expectations early in the project. Let's see what these four internal quality attributes mean to Sue and her team.

After a lively discussion, Sue's team writes down list of attributes, associated requirements, and their action items to meet those requirements.

Quality Attribute	Our Requirements for this Attribute	What we will do
Modifiability Requirements	We want to refactor easily and safely, so we want: • Clear, complete documentation of API contracts. • Compliance with our company's "Future Maintenance Standard" (which covers revision control, storage of tests, coding style standards). • Enough low-level tests to quickly detect whether we've broken a module • Enough documented, repeatable tests to detect whether system is staying stable.	Include in our Definition of Done: • API documentation review. • Review of compliance with our "Future Maintenance Standards" • Has documented unit tests (coverage TBD) Create some automated end-to-end regression tests
Portability Requirements	We don't see any beyond the "Future Maintenance Standard"	n/a
Reusability Requirements	None that we know of.	n/a
Verifiability or Testability Requirements	Testability requirements from other subsystems. Verifiability regarding correct ABS responses.	Go ask the other teams. Already covered in stories.

A project may also have other miscellaneous nonfunctional requirements or constraints. Perhaps the head of the Information Technology department has forbidden use of Gnu GPL (General Public License) open source code. Or required that any use of open-source code must include capturing the exact origin and license. These types of requirements must also be taken into account in a similar fashion.

3. Quality Process: Capture and Implement the Expectations

So now you have a bunch of nonfunctional requirements. What do you do with them? In a Waterfall project, you'll capture them in a Software Requirements Specification (SRS), and then start writing acceptance tests to verify that the system meets these requirements.

In an agile project, you won't write an SRS. But user stories aren't necessarily the answer either. In agile, we have more than one way to capture expectations and make sure they happen. User stories are the primary method, particularly for functionality, but we also capture expectations through story acceptance criteria, tests, Definition of Done, and Release Criteria.

Let's look at how to decide which method to use for a particular requirement.

3.1. Why Not User Stories?

User stories do two things for us:

1) Capture the user's point of view, ensuring we understand the purpose and value of a feature

2) Split the work into small, independent sections so we can get immediate feedback from users on each section

Many nonfunctional requirements can be written in user story format, such as "As an admin, I want to receive a response to any input in less than a second, so I can get on with my day." That captures the user's point of view nicely. But it doesn't split the work into small, independent sections. This story will affect many, many other user stories, and the story isn't implementable on its own. A story which affects many other stories is known as a *crosscutting story*.

Behavior related to a quality attribute very often results in a crosscutting story. Crosscutting stories don't help you manage your work, but instead create confusion.

3.2. Capture Expectations as Acceptance Criteria or Definition of Done

Since crosscutting user stories aren't a good idea, what else can we do? One answer is a *quality gate*. A quality gate checks whether a story, or group of stories, or the entire product meet expectations.

All of these are quality gates:

- Acceptance Criteria for specific stories. These are often captured in the form of an acceptance test. For instance, "One-month sales data can be displayed within 1 second."

- Definition of Done, which applies to a group of stories. This is often captured as a regression test run during every sprint. For instance, "Every story related to data display must pass Test B which demonstrates that screen response time is still 1 second."

- Team Operating Agreement. "Everyone shall abide by our security coding standard."

- Release Criteria. Release criteria are acceptance criteria for the entire product. While many release criteria are quality-related measurements such as "zero open high-priority defects", some projects capture system-wide behavior specifications as release criteria, as in the example in section 2.4.

Quality gates support the experimental, iterative approach which is central to agile. Literally, we "Do the simplest possible thing that could possibly work." [JEFF1998] and then test to see whether it passes the quality gate.

Back to Sue's team. They're looking at some more quality attributes. Let's see how they apply these ideas.

> Bitra: "'Integrity: How well the system prevents information loss'. Isn't integrity mostly a capability of databases? Maybe it doesn't apply to our module."
>
> Sue: "Does the EBCM firmware capture and store any data at all?"
>
> Bitra: "Well, there's some logging. The logs are used when something goes wrong. We've got user stories about the logging already. The diagnostic codes go into nonvolatile memory, of course."
>
> Tom: "Remember that space probe which failed because its logs overflowed? Maybe we should have some acceptance criteria for the logging stories which test the failure modes. We could just put a note in the user story now and add the criteria when we work on the story."

In this case, the expectations for the attribute "Integrity" led to acceptance criteria for just a handful of stories. Sometimes that happens. Other times, a great many stories are affected. For example, performance is almost always crosscutting. Sue's team has defined performance requirements for each individual user story in the acceptance criteria, but will that be enough?

Bitra: "I know each user story already has acceptance criteria to ensure adequate response time, but what happens if implementing a later story makes an earlier story's response time longer? Do we have enough regression testing to notice this?"

Sam: "What if we pulled together all the tests for response times and put them in one big test? We could put that in our Definition of Done so we run it every sprint."

Tom: "Wow, that would be a big test. We'd have to automate it for sure. But then the test itself would define the acceptable performance, right? That'd be good. We could review the test with the communication harness team, to make sure they agree with us on the response times."

When it would make more sense to run the test once per sprint instead of once per user story, the test is often put into the Definition of Done rather than into acceptance criteria for individual stories. This can be appropriate for regression tests which haven't been finding many problems, or tests which require an expensive or time-consuming setup. Sue's team has used both acceptance criteria and a Definition of Done as quality gates.

For more discussion of a Definition of Done, see: http://www.jamesshore.com/Agile-Book/done_done.html

3.3. Use Standard Practices When Appropriate

Standards such as architecture, design guidelines, and coding standards take a more prescriptive approach than quality gates. Standards say: "Do the work *this* way so the end product *will* be good enough".

In a traditional waterfall project, quality gates are much more widely spaced than in an agile project. Problems accumulate between these quality gates. The organization tries to prevent the issues with layer upon layer of standards.

Agile methods depend on their frequent quality gates, but there is still a place for standards. Sometimes it is obvious that you will have to do certain things in certain ways. For instance, your security requires protecting against SQL injection. That in turn requires following certain coding practices. If you know this up front, it would be rather wasteful to **not** follow those practices in multiples stories and then go back and refactor. Necessary standards are usually captured in either the Definition of Done or the Team Operating Agreement.

Whether you are doing agile or waterfall, your decisions on whether a standard is necessary should be based on data, not "everybody knows it should be done this way". In Sue's company, the maintenance teams created their Maintainability Standard to prevent specific problems they'd encountered in the past when code was "thrown over the wall". If no one can remember why a particular standard is necessary, it may be time to question it. An experiment or spike can sort out which design guidelines, coding standards, or architecture decisions are actually necessary.

For more details on the use of standards versus quality gates, see Neal Herman's 2016 paper "Implementing Agile in an FDA Regulated Environment" [NEAL2016]. It's an interesting tale of their transition from a standards-based process to an agile process.

3.4. Not Sure? Use a Spike

Sometimes it's not clear what "good enough" would look like. Or it's not obvious what type of test would detect "not good enough", so you can't write the acceptance criteria. Or you suspect that a particular design choice isn't going to meet your stakeholder's expectations, but you're not sure.

In these cases, a spike or experiment is very helpful. A spike is a time-boxed bit of programming which is intended to answer a particular question. Once the question is answered, the spike stops. Sometimes the code is thrown away, sometimes it is integrated into the product, but the end goal of the spike isn't code. The end goal is knowledge – the answer to the question.

James Shore presents an example of a technical spike here:
http://www.jamesshore.com/Agile-Book/spike_solutions.html. [SHOR2010].

3.5. If It Is a Feature, Create a User Story

Sometimes a quality attribute review turns up something which **can** be captured as an independently implementable user story.

Sue's team continues through their quality attributes list, looking for more things they might have missed. They find two features.

> Sue: "Let's take a look at what else we might have forgotten. Let's see, how about installability?"
>
> Bitra: "The car comes with the firmware already loaded into the module. So installability isn't relevant."
>
> Tom: "What about the original installation of the firmware into the module?"
>
> Bitra: "That sounds like manufacturability, not installability. I think the manufacturing engineers will want the firmware installation to be automated."
>
> Sue: "It doesn't matter what we call it, as long as we capture it. Do we have a new epic here?"

Tom writes: *"As a manufacturing engineer, I can automate installation of the firmware onto the chip."*

Joe: "Wait – don't we issue updates sometimes? Which would be installed by service techs?"
Tom: "The EBCM isn't supposed to be serviceable, it just gets replaced."

Sue: "Hmm, if there was a warranty issue, would the company ever want to do a firmware update rather than a replacement? Let's put it in the backlog and ask our product owner."
Tom writes a new epic: *"As a service tech, I can install a firmware update, so the car is fixed under warranty."*

Notice that the two user stories just written by this team are quite ordinary. There's a specific action, and a specific result. The story doesn't cross-cut other stories. The question "How much installability do you want?" doesn't even make sense. That's how we know they are valid user stories.

A quality attribute list is a good place to keep track of aspects of the system which are often overlooked in a particular organization, whether or not those are literally "system-level characteristics". Installability, manufacturability, configurability, and interoperability are often found on quality attribute lists yet can usually be captured in garden-variety user stories.

4. Nobody Wants to Play? Try a Defect Severity Chart

Sometimes, you're at the other end of the spectrum. Not only is no one interested in a systematic and thorough approach, but you can't even get the stakeholders to sit down and look at a quality attribute list, or discuss how good is good enough.

This lack of engagement can be addressed by starting at the opposite end of development, with test failures. Assume you will have defects, and ask which types of defects are serious and which aren't. Sometimes this approach is easier for stakeholders who have little development experience.

Their answers can be captured in a "Defect Severity Chart", which is an objective way to decide on the severity of a defect.

A defect severity chart is specific to the product and project for which it was written, because it defines what is considered a "serious" problem for this type of product and this group of users. That means the chart is a form of requirement. For instance, while potential injury to a user will probably be treated as a critical defect in all fields, the tolerance for intermittent failures or screen layout problems varies quite a bit depending on what type of product you are making and for whom.

Creating a defect severity chart of your own may help your team understand "how bad is bad?". For example, this severity chart has a row for intermittent failures. That's a reliability specification, albeit a rather fuzzy one. Stakeholders who have no experience with formally stated reliability targets will usually understand and be able to respond to a target stated in this fashion.

Sample Rubric for Grading Defects by Severity				
Type of Problem	**Critical**	**High**	**Medium**	**Low**
Safety	Can injure user	--	--	--
Functionality used by 80% of users	Fail with no workaround, OR causes damage to data or system OR report incorrect data.	Fail with workaround, requires support call	Fails with obvious workaround	--
Functionality used by 20% or fewer of users	Causes damage to data or system OR report incorrect data.	Fail with no workaround	Fail with workaround, requires support call	Fails with obvious workaround
Intermittent Failure	Causes damage, or fails more often than 1/day	Happens 1/day	Happens 1/week	Happens 1/month
Internation - alization	Screen is unreadable. Language considered insulting in a major market or preventing importation	Screen is readable but looks very sloppy Translated text is wrong, correct meaning is not obvious to user	Text is cut off in minor ways Translated text is wrong but meaning is obvious	Minor messiness

The severity chart sometimes surfaces interesting implied requirements. For instance, if all safety problems are considered critical, has anybody thought about the various ways in which the software could injure the user? That might yield some new requirements which are intended to prevent failures. Severity charts can also reveal negative requirements. In this example, the internationalization row suggests that there is probably a list of phrases which should not appear in the user interface.

5. Conclusion

Quality problems often trace back to overlooking or shortchanging some of the system's nonfunctional requirements. Quality can be improved, and development made easier by using some simple tools and methods aimed specifically at surfacing and implementing nonfunctional requirements.

First, enable more productive conversations with stakeholders around nonfunctional requirements by using a quality attributes list. A quality attributes list provides:

1) language with which you can ask specific questions that will trigger useful feedback, and
2) a structure to prevent forgetting some area entirely

A quality attributes review at the start of a project may take only a few hours when the team is proficient with both the list and their subject area. If the risks, technologies, or customer expectations are quite new to the team, there is considerable disagreement concerning the expectations, or the project is quite large, the process may take as much as a few days.

If your organization has a system test team which is separate from the development team, it is definitely worth asking your system test team what they are doing regarding nonfunctional requirements. Frequently they are also asking stakeholders about quality attributes in order to develop a system test strategy. Combining efforts will likely save both groups some time. The overlap is more obvious on traditional waterfall projects using the V-model, because one of the early steps in the V-model is writing high-level acceptance tests based on the functional and nonfunctional requirements, which means the test team is out looking for those requirements even if they are not written down.

Second, systematically consider how you will ensure your product meets the nonfunctional requirements. Agile projects have more tools to employ than the team may realize. Different tools are more effective for different requirements, so you will probably use more than one.

- For non-crosscutting requirements, user stories and their acceptance criteria.
- For crosscutting requirements, quality gates at various levels:
  - Story acceptance criteria.
  - Definition of Done at either story or sprint level
  - Release criteria.
- Standard operating procedures captured in a Team Operating Agreement.

Waterfall projects use quality gates as well, albeit much more widely spaced, and usually make heavy use of standard operating procedures. The relationship between tests and requirements is less obvious on a waterfall project than it is in an agile project, so a requirements traceability matrix might be used to keep track of all the details.

Lastly, a defect severity matrix can help surface hidden requirements, especially when the organization is not enthused about a systematic review.

These methods are fairly simple to implement and can dramatically reduce unpleasant surprises late in a project. I hope you have seen at least one method which will help you talk about quality more effectively with your stakeholders and your teammates.

References

Gilb, Tom. *Principles of Software Engineering Management*. Addison-Wesley. 1988.

Herman, Neal. 2016. "Implementing Agile in an FDA Regulated Environment". Agile Dev/Better Software DevOps West 2016. https://www.stickyminds.com/presentation/implementing-agile-fda-regulated-environment-0 (accessed 7/14/2017).

ISO 2500 Standards -> ISO 25010. http://iso25000.com/index.php/en/iso-25000-standards/iso-25010 . downloaded July 1, 2018.

Jeffries, Ron. 1998. https://ronjeffries.com/xprog/articles/practices/pracsimplest// (accessed 6/12/2018).

Rothman, Johanna. 2002. "Release Criteria: Is This Software Done?" *STQE Magazine*, March/April 2002. https://www.jrothman.com/articles/2002/03/release-criteria-is-this-software-done/

Rothman, Johanna. 2017. *Create Your Successful Agile Project*. The Pragmatic Programmers.

Shore, James. "The Art of Agile Development: Spike Solutions". http://www.jamesshore.com/Agile-Book/spike_solutions.html. Dated 6/04/2010, (accessed 7/24/2018)

Wiegers, Karl and Beatty, Joy. 2013. *Software Requirements, Third Edition*. Microsoft Press.

Wirfs-Brock: http://wirfs-brock.com/blog/2011/07/20/introducing-landing-zones/ (accessed 6/15/2018).

And if you'd like to know more about electronic brake control modules, here's a glimpse: https://www.autozone.com/repairguides/GM-Century-Lumina-Grand-Prix-Intrigue-1997-2000/ANTI-LOCK-BRAKE-SYSTEM/Electronic-Brake-Control-Module-EBCM/_/P-0900c152802180a3 (accessed 6/15/2018).

The "Do Nots" of Software Testing

Author

Melissa Tondi (melissa.tondi@gmail.com)

Abstract

In this talk, we will discuss some of the lessons learned in software testing – otherwise known as the "Do Nots". Melissa will present the top five items that are practiced by and within QA teams where, at some time may have added value, but have now become stale or, in some cases, impactful to both the industry and project team. She will suggest different approaches and recommendations to help you either remove those items and replace them with more meaningful approaches or modernize them to ensure innovation is a driving force within your testing team.

Biography

Melissa Tondi has spent most of her career working within software testing teams. She is the founder of Denver Mobile and Quality (DMAQ), past president and board member of Software Quality Association of Denver (SQuAD), and Professional Services Manager/Consultant at Rainforest QA, where she assists companies to continuously improve the pursuit of quality software—from design to delivery and everything in between. In her software test and quality engineering careers, Melissa has focused on building and organizing teams around three major tenets—efficiency, innovation, and culture – and uses the Greatest Common Denominator (GCD) approach for determining ways in which team members can assess, implement and report on day to day activities so the gap between need and value is as small as possible.

1. Introduction

In this talk, we introduce the five "do nots" of software testing. These "do nots" serve as a reminder that innovation should be at the forefront of our industry and even best-laid plans and ideas that make it in to our QA playbook should be re-visited to ensure they are applicable, align with the industry, and are collaboratively discussed within our agile teams in order to support the highest efficiency and productivity on our quest to deliver quicker and with high quality. Here are the top "do nots" I've gathered in hopes that our community can continue to continuously improve and broaden our information sharing.

2. On-Boarding for New Hires Only

When we invest in on-boarding activities for new hires, we are making a statement that it's important to provide consistent information at the onset of a team member's career with the company. Far too often, we don't invest that same thought process to the rest of the team or re-visit processes put in place months (or, sometimes, years) ago to ensure they are still valid and supportive of what actually takes place.

We implemented a playbook titled Definition of Done. The playbook allows us to level-set all the services our team provides and present those to our agile teams.

2.1. Definition of Done Playbook Sample Sections

- What QA Does and How
    - Test Planning
    - Test Management
    - Test Execution both scripted and un-scripted
    - Reporting
- QA's Expectations from Development, Design, Product Management, and Scrum Master

3. Automate Everything

Fundamentally, we all know that not all tests should or can be automated, but I'm still surprised when I hear teams are being measured on the number or percentage of tests automated versus weighing the overall value the automation is bringing to the team. A better way to approach this is to have an intuitive selection process to quickly determine when something should be considered for automation. Notice how I used the word "considered" instead of giving instruction to automate a test. When you are held to a meaningless metric like "everything" your creative license is essentially removed and how fun is it to be told what to do rather than doing what you know is more valuable?

3.1. The Automated of Automatable (AofA) Metric

Because we did away with the "traditional percentage of test cases that are automated" metric that tends to be an inaccurate measure of software quality, we focused deeper on a metric that showed value, not only to the QA team, but to the agile project team as well. The AofA is determined by a selection process that succinctly shows the percentage of automated valuable tests given the following sample criteria:

- Its severity to the business in terms of:
    - Revenue Loss
    - Security Vulnerability
    - Customer Loss
- Its importance to customer happiness
- Compliance

Given these, during refinement sessions, we indicate which user story and/or acceptance criteria meets any of the above criteria and consider it for automation. Once the initial sorting happens, we size the work according to the project team's norms and plan the work accordingly.

For reporting purposes (either daily or recurring throughout the sprint), we can report on the number of items that met our criteria and could be automated versus what was actually automated. We increased our percentages of AofA to the mid 90th percentile to 100% in most cases.

Using the guidelines in section 5, we worked in serial order of priorities. For example, if any test in our Priority 1 suite was not green, we swarmed to fix and did not expand any other automation until all higher prioritized automation was green.

4. Assume You Have an Equal Seat

Many times when I've provided SDLC assessments for companies, I observe their team dynamics and any agile ceremonies that are followed. When I chat with QA and their management, there is a pattern of exclusion during key meetings where Development may have received more information than what was represented in the user story or its acceptance criteria. This usually results in QA not being able to size the work correctly or to assume behavior on "light" acceptance criteria. This then causes more triage by Product for bugs reported, mis-interpretation of intended behavior by QA and general tension between QA and other team members because they were not privy to adhoc or informal conversations that have taken place without them.

One option we've used to counteract that is smaller working refinement sessions. We do this by setting outcomes for refinement and have Product provide a list of prioritized stories ready to be refined at least 48 hours before the refinement session. We provide expectations for a story ready to be refined and have any one with responsibility on the story attend and contribute by providing a high-level summary of how they will approach the work. If any of those items are not complete during refinement, the story is not refined, and, therefore, cannot and should not be planned and committed to for an upcoming sprint or for Kanban, work should not be started. By holding smaller working sessions with those who have tasks, this creates a much more efficient, collaborative session where contextual information is being shared and heard, and implicit information becomes explicit and used for higher quality activities. It also ensures that each person and their practice are equally collaborative and represented for true sizing and estimates.

5. Assume QA/QE Owns All Testing

In addition to the above, we know the Development team does their own testing, but sometimes we don't know what that is. By defining who does what and creating a playbook of each agile pillar's consistent practices at the individual contributor level, it removes ambiguity and take the guesswork out of what actually happens when that card or ticket moves to the "ready for QA" column. We advocate a collaborative discussion and refinement of work across the agile team to ensure test activities performed by QA are not only not redundant, but that are highly valuable and done at the right time during that phase.

5.1. Sample Automation Definition Across Teams

We have 1-3 Priority criteria that aligns with the success of the agile team; not just QA/QE. This feeds in to each team's Definition of Done playbook and allows for more consistency, less ambiguity, and greater predictability to ensure teams are operating at the highest efficiency as possible.

- Development: P1 Intake Test
    - The ISTQB Definition
        - A special instance of a smoke test to decide if the component or system is ready for detailed and further testing. An intake test is typically carried out at the start of the test execution phase.
    - Intake tests are executed upon every code check-in and merge.
- Quality Assurance/Engineering: P2 Smoke Test
    - ISTQB Definition
        - A subset of all defined/planned test cases that cover the main functionality of a component or system, to ascertaining that the most crucial functions of a program work, but not bothering with finer details.
    - Smoke tests are executed upon merge and deployments and failures of these tests are designated as critical and would cause a HotFix if released in to Production. These tests are the baseline of the regression suite.
- Quality Assurance/Engineering and Product Management: P3 = User Advocacy
    - User Advocacy tests are tied to key customers or end-to-end flows and – anything that would cause a Priority 1 issue classification from Product Management or the Business.

6. Stagnant Missions and Offerings

A while ago, we changed the name and mission of QA in our organization. We determined that Quality Engineering and how we defined it most matched what we were currently doing, where we eventually wanted to do, and, perhaps most importantly, where we knew our value would be emphasized the most within the organization. When given the opportunity, sometimes it's good to disrupt with a name change when a company or its leadership has misperceptions of what QA's role is versus what it should be.

This quote "Influence the Building of the Software before the Software is Built" drives our daily activities. We do this by:

- Balancing technical acumen with user advocacy and ensure we emphasize both.
- Using context-driven techniques. Given the information we have, we determine if it's enough and if not, we find more by:
    - More collaboration within Development, Product, other QE teams, Customer Support, and Customers.
    - Reaching out to the community. We both consume from and contribute to the community whenever we can.

In our QE playbook, we highlight the following traits and characteristics of the "Engineer" in Quality Engineer.

6.1. Breakdown of Engineering Traits

- Define success, outcome and measurements. Using context-driven approaches to gather the right data and information. Usually, the easiest information to gather is the that which is explicit (user stories, requirements, acceptance criteria, etc.). QE adds value when we uncover valuable information that is implicit at first.
- Design a comprehensive strategy.
- Build the solution. Write the tests, write the charters/sessions for unscripted testing.
- Execute the solution.
- Measure the results. Prove it!
- Report the outcome throughout.

By re-visiting and addressing any or all of these "do nots" you'll be operating at higher efficiency and productivity and can continue to innovate and continuously improve.

Finding and Fixing Your Organization's Agile Potholes

Author
Les Grove (lgrove@catalyte.io)

Abstract
On the road to agility there are organizational impediments ("potholes") that teams could run into if not removed. An agile coach could be brought in to help the organization identify and resolve those potholes. But where should a coach look to find the potholes? They could attend and observe countless ceremonies and interview dozens of team members. But it is time consuming and difficult to discover organizational impediments. A better approach is to use an agility assessment tool that easily and quickly captures data about multiple teams and guides coaching strategies.

This paper describes Catalyte's Agile Coaching Center of Excellence process to build a simple agile assessment methodology and tool that can assess teams and their organizations. The assessment tool started as a document-based worksheet that teams incorporate as part of its retrospectives. It evolved into a spreadsheet that added scoring and measured changes over time. Then a survey form was used to better capture individual responses. The coach collects and analyzes the results from multiple teams and visually compiles the data providing pictures into each team and the organization simultaneously; helping teams at the enterprise level by identifying team and organizational impediments.

Biography
Les Grove is a Principal Agile Project Manager at Catalyte. Les has a Master's degree in Software Engineering and holds certifications as a Certified Scrum Professional (CSP), SAFe Advance Scrum Master (SASM), and Project Management Professional (PMP).

Les has over 30 years of experience in project management, software development, and agile. He was involved with the Pacific Northwest Software Quality Conference (PNSQC) from 2002-15 as an author, reviewer, volunteer, chairperson, and board member.

This work is the result of many people who have participated in the Catalyte Agile Coaching Center of Excellence and without them the assessment tool, and this paper, would not be possible. I want to thank Eric Landes, Abby Edwards, Garrett Vonk, Adam Curtis, TJ Trujillo, Mike Gicking, Paige Hines, Rob Winkler, Torin Tierney, Temitope Olonisakin, Miguel Buddle, Danielle Schell, Sam Landesberg, Natalie Barroga, Meghan Arthur, Theo Levine, David Kaus, and David Bernal.

1. Introduction
Agile, from learning to adoption to practice, isn't a one-and-done exercise. It is a journey rather than a destination. With that metaphor we can equate a team with driving and navigating a

car, where it needs fuel (requirements) and mechanical problems need to be discovered and repaired (inspect and adapt). Extending the metaphor further, the organization can be considered "the road" – multiple teams travel on it and any organizational impediments are the potholes that all teams end up needing to navigate around or running into. But organizations often do not see the potholes they have created for its teams. This is where an agile coach comes in. A coach can reinforce agile values and key practices while working at both the team level and organizational level.

Most agile frameworks are aimed at the team level.

- Daily standups help identify team impediments so that they can be quickly removed
- Retrospectives are vital for improving team performance and product quality
- Sprint reviews ensure the team is moving the product in the right direction

As the number of teams increase, the complexity of resolving issues at the organizational level increases exponentially because it's difficult for an organization to identify and prioritize issues at this level.

Organizational "potholes" include

- Lack of knowledge/training
- Inadequate tools
- Not using or incorrectly leveraging an agile framework
- No cross-team learning
- Non-transparency
- Poor estimation
- Over-management preventing self-direction
- Lack of business analysis capabilities
- Non-involvement of stakeholders

It becomes a situation where the loudest team or the most recent complaint gets prioritized for help from the organization.

Scaled agile frameworks have some mechanisms in place to help identify and remove organizational impediments. But these frameworks are primarily for multiple teams working on a single large product. These mechanisms don't help much for organizations that have multiple teams working for multiple products, in different domains, and for multiple clients.

Agile coaches are often brought in at the organizational level to help multiple teams. They identify organizational impediments by observing and interviewing multiple teams for several sprints and look for anti-patterns that repeatedly occur that individual teams cannot resolve on their own. This would take months.

Fortunately, there is a way for a coach to quickly gather the information they need to identify common anti-patterns: an assessment. By assessing each team, analyzing the findings and looking for opportunities that could improve multiple teams simultaneously, an organization can save time and money.

2. Background

The most common stumbling block to adopting and practicing agile is organizational culture and its resistance to change. To succeed in agile adoption, IT leaders need to train their organizations and reinforce agile values and key practices, create communities of practice, and deliver business outcomes. To effectively institute cultural change, companies need to develop comprehensive hands-on agile coaching programs to assist real-world projects.

Catalyte has an Agile Coaching Center of Excellence (CoE) that provides coaching services to its teams and its clients. This group is made up of agile coaches, project managers, analysts, developers – anyone within the company who is interested in agile and coaching. The CoE was created to centralize all previous work regarding agile coaching, create coaching collateral for training and reporting, and drive initiatives to improve agile within Catalyte and its clients.

Much of Catalyte's coaching practice was based on directly observing teams, which is time-consuming and hides organizational impediments. The Agile Coaching CoE thought that a low-impact assessment would provide a quicker "lay of the land" and create opportunities for immediate recommendations.

There were several business reasons for creating a common agile assessment solution. First, Catalyte provides software development teams that work in a variety of domains: healthcare, finance, hospitality, retail, logistics, etc. Some teams are stand-alone and are managed internally; some are blended with client teams and managed by either us or the client; and others are managed by the client. The challenge is to identify teams that need coaching or expose issues that require cooperation with our clients.

Second, Catalyte provides agile coaching services for both new agile transformations and teams that are already on their agile journey. For novice organizations, assessments are like test-driven development. The initial assessment is expected to fail but improvements are expected in subsequent assessments. For mid-journey teams, assessments provide the initial snapshot of the strengths and opportunities that a coach can use to advise teams and organizations.

Lastly, Catalyte teams often need to work within a client's established agile framework. Assessments would be great to identify any organizational impediments prior to Sprint 1 and help Catalyte work with the client to mitigate risks.

2.1. Requirements for Assessments

Once the CoE decided to try assessments, the next task was to come up with some initial requirements for an assessment method.

Assessments need to be quick - People are less willing to participate in an assessment if it interferes with their sprint commitments. The longer the assessment, the less accurate the responses. We determined that an assessment shouldn't take more than 15-20 minutes to complete.

Results need to reflect the team and not individuals – Agility is about the team. Any assessment needs to focus on improving the team. This means keeping individual responses confidential in anything that is shared outside the team as well as not assessing individuals. Since the Scrum Master and Product Owner are individuals caution must be exercised when assessing the performance of those roles.

Participants need no other instructions or guidance than what's provided – Participants shouldn't have to figure out what's expected of them when completing the assessment. Observational trials can help, but always expect opportunities for assessment improvements based on feedback.

Results identify opportunities for team improvement – A team will be more likely to participate if they get something for their efforts. The team results can be something they can use towards their own excellence.

Aggregate results to identify organizational impediments – Aggregated results can show patterns that may indicate tools, process, or training issues that affect many or all teams. Teams may not even be aware as they are more focused internally.

Participants need to be able to provide details on their responses – To make assessments quick, simple responses are required, but at the cost of understanding why best practices aren't used. A more detailed feedback mechanism needs to be in place during or after the assessment. This, in turn, feeds back into the assessment.

Identify improvements or regressions over time – Follow-up assessments provide additional snapshots to see whether teams are improving, staying stagnate, or getting worse.
Accommodate any flavor of agile, not just Scrum – Even though most teams practice Scrum, it's not a guarantee. An assessment needs to be applicable to many flavors of agile, including Kanban.

2.2. Building the Assessment Tool

In building an assessment tool, we wanted to focus on getting the tool right before covering all agile topics. We decided on five initial assessment topics to be covered in Version 1 of the tool. We felt that these were a good initial sampling of topics covering issues that we have seen in our projects at Catalyte. The five topics were:

- Team Integrity (ability to get its work done without external interference)
- Retrospectives
- Requirements
- Backlog Management
- Refactoring

Next, we determined a method for the assessment. We chose to have five-to-seven statements for each topic, where each statement represented an intended practice or outcome. To make the assessment easy to take and to generate comparative results, we chose a Likert scale: "Always", "Mostly", "Sometimes", and "Never" where "Always" would be the most positive response.

For each topic, most of five-to-seven statements were written from scratch then reviewed and revised in the CoE several times. Others were pulled from other existing assessments [0] and revised to fit our goals and format.

2.3. Version 1 – Word Document

For the first iteration, we were more interested in piloting the topics, method, and statements than making the tool a great user experience. So, for executing the assessment we created a simple Word document that teams would use during one of their retrospectives. The document included instructions and places for feedback on the assessment itself.

Refactoring	Always	Mostly	Sometimes	Never
There is a business justification when refactoring is performed				
Refactoring is performed with a goal in mind (maintainability, portability, etc.)				
There are "safeguards" against introducing defects when code is refactored (e.g., regression testing, unit tests, and acceptance tests)				
Defects are not introduced when code is refactored				
Refactored code follows the same quality controls that new code goes through (e.g., peer review, pull request, QA)				
Refactoring work is tracked and managed with full visibility of stakeholders				

Figure 1: Early survey items for refactoring topic

Error! Reference source not found. shows the survey section for the Refactoring topic. Teams would fill it out together, usually during the Gather Data part of their retrospective [0], giving them an opportunity to discuss areas where they were not responding with "Always" or "Mostly". This version of the assessment tool was piloted with six teams.

From an organizational perspective, **Error! Reference source not found.** shows an agile practice that is usually being done across the organization.

Team Integrity	Always	Mostly	Sometimes	Never
Estimates are only made by the team	XXXXX	X		

Figure 2: Successful Agile Results

From a team coaching opportunity perspective, **Error! Reference source not found.** shows that one team is not having full participation in retrospectives. A team coach or scrum master can investigate where this team is taking any actions to help improve this.

Retrospectives	Always	Mostly	Sometimes	Never
Every member of team participates (including PO and SM)	XXX	XX		X

Figure 3: Single Team Opportunity Identified

When looking at **Error! Reference source not found.**, only one team stated that they were freezing story cards, but the other five teams were indicating that in-sprint story cards are often being changed during sprints. A coach working at the organizational level, would want to dig into this a little deeper to see if there are any organizational impediments that teams are working against. In this example, one team stated that they were always preventing card changes, but it might be worth the effort to check with that team to see if that's truly the case – they could have misunderstood the statement or found a way to overcome the organizational impediment that other teams could leverage.

Team Integrity	Always	Mostly	Sometimes	Never
Cards are not changed after they're pulled from the Product Backlog	X		XXXX	X

Figure 4: Organizational Pothole Discovered?

There were two main drawbacks to this Word-based version of the tool. First, it was time-consuming to compile the results by hand – and therefore error-prone and not very scalable. Second, there was a challenge to show team and organizational improvements or regressions after repeating the assessments.

2.4. Version 2 – Spreadsheet

One of the CoE members took a Scaled Agile Framework (SAFe) course and discovered the SAFe Team Self-Assessment [0]. The similarities surprised us as both our home-grown assessment and the SAFe Team Self-Assessment covered five topics and had a similar number of statements per topic.
The CoE also liked these additional features:

- More refined choices of responses that allowed for more precise measurement
- A scored response for each statement
- A combined percentage score for the topic providing indications of change in subsequent assessments
- A comment section for each statement that provided details at the statement response level rather than at a topic level

The CoE decided not to use the SAFe spreadsheet statements because it covered some topics, like PI Health, not relevant in non-scaled situations. Also, its terminology was very SAFe-specific and something not necessarily familiar to most participants. However, some statements from the SAFe assessment form were added to Version 2 of Catalyte's assessment (see **Error! Reference source not found.**).

1	catalyte			
2	Agile Coaching CoE			
3	Team Assessment			
4	**Team Name:** xxxxxxxxxxxxxxxx **Date**: xx/x/20xx			
5	**Scoring:** 0 - Never, 1 - Rarely 2 - Occasionally, 3 - Often, 4 - Very Often, 5 - Always			
6	**Area / Question**	**Score**		**Comments**
7	**Team Integrity**			
8	The Product Owner provides a clear vision of the product	3.0		
9	Someone is responsible for removing impediments so the team can get work done	3.0		
10	Estimates and commitments are only made by those doing the work	3.0		
11	Cards brought into a sprint remain unchanged and unblocked until completed	3.0		
12	Team members are fully dedicated to the project	3.0		
13	Team members are self-organized, respect each other, help each other complete cards/tasks, manage interdependencies and stay in-sync with each other	3.0		
14	***Team Integrity Score***	**18.0**	**60%**	
15	**Retrospectives**			
16	Retrospectives are held at regular intervals	3.0		
17	Every member of team participates (including PO and SM)	3.0		
18	Ways to improve team performance are identified	3.0		
19	Ways to improve product quality are identified	3.0		
20	Generate improvement action items that the team commits to completing	3.0		
21	It can be determined whether action items are completed	3.0		
22	***Retrospectives Score***	**18.0**	**60%**	

Figure 5: Assessment Spreadsheet Derived from SAFe

Unlike Version 1's table format, Version 2's spider chart (see **Error! Reference source not found.**) now shows all team scores in all topics in one place.

There are three key learnings from the chart in **Error! Reference source not found.**:

- Team 3 did well with requirements. Need to find out what the other teams can learn
- Team 2 needed to improve their retrospectives.
- Teams 5 and 6 scored relatively low overall

As an agile coach, there is plenty of data to help individual teams and to find some areas to improve at the organizational level:

- Why were Requirements so inconsistent?
- Why weren't there any teams that scored at the highest levels for Team Integrity and Refactoring?
- What was going wrong with Teams 5 and 6?
- Why were half the teams underperforming in Retrospectives?

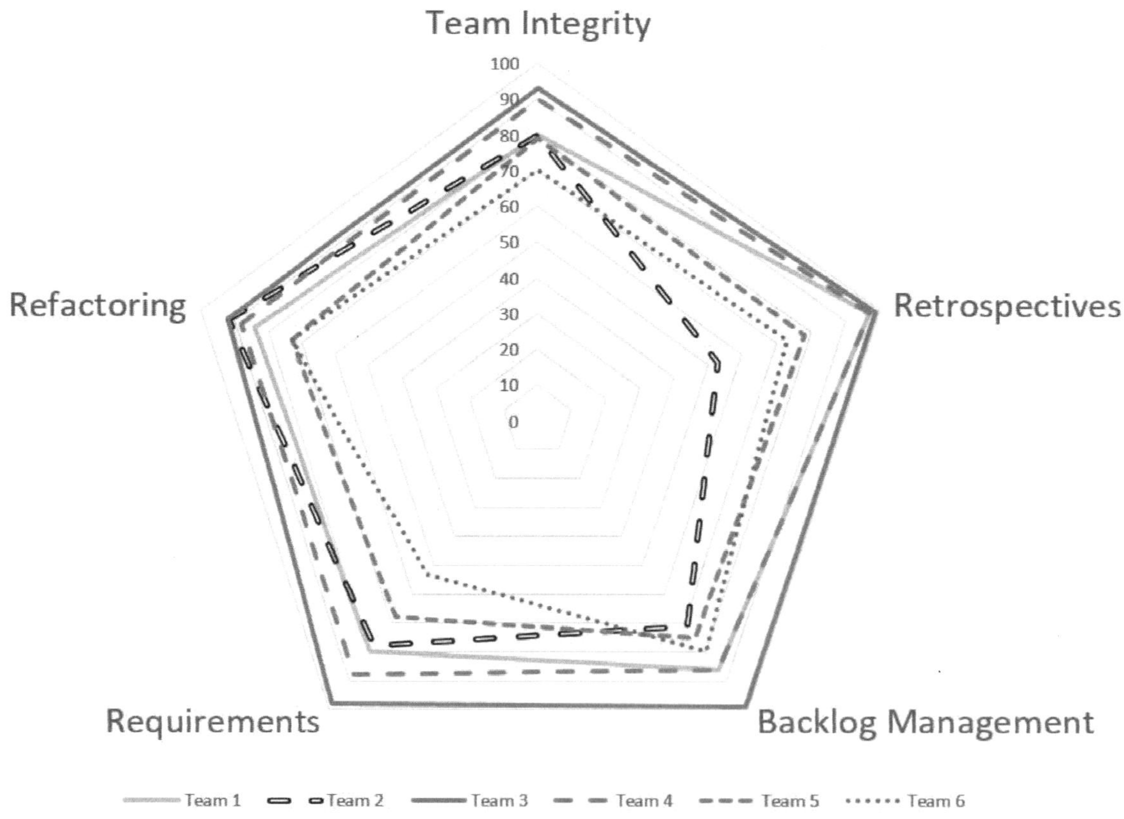

Figure 6: Spider Chart for Version 2 Assessment

2.5. Version 3 – Google Form

One of the teams took the Version 2 spreadsheet and created a Google Form and had each team member fill out the survey individually then they met as a team, reviewed the results, and formed a consensus response on the spreadsheet. The CoE liked that concept and used the form for the next round of assessments. The thinking was that responding to surveys might minimize the effect of strong, dominating voices pushing the responses higher in a group setting.

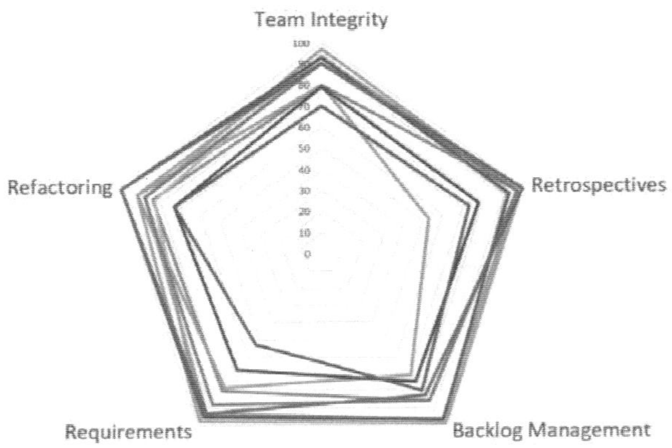

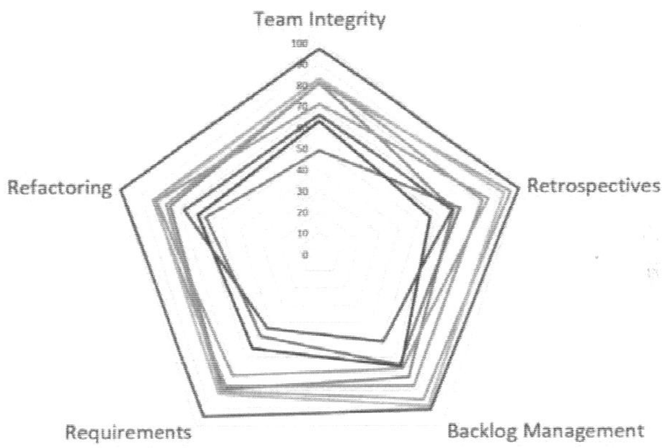

Figure 7: Comparison of single team response vs averaging individual responses

We found that when we compare the results using this method with the previous results the data points were generally lower and more spread out (see **Error! Reference source not found.**). There are two key advantages to surveying individuals. First, it's easier to identify the organizational potholes. For example, Backlog Management looks to be an area that is inconsistently performed. Second, a large spread of responses within a team to the same statement could be a signal a lack of common understanding, a practice that is not consistently done within the team, or an ambiguously written assessment statement.

2.6. Version 4 – Expanded Topics

For the next iteration of the assessment tool, our intent was to increase the number of topics covered. We went to some of Catalyte's other CoEs (Architecture, DevOps, and Quality) and asked them for a set of assessment statements to include in the tool. Any results from these topics would be shared directly with the respective CoE for their own analysis and follow-up. For the Quality topic, the following statements were included in the survey:

- Our test coverage satisfies our test quality goals

- Critical defects are prevented from reaching Production
- Our product is stable
- The tests are automated where possible
- Test results are used as the basis of code integration and deployment

Error! Reference source not found. shows an analysis of teams that have potential coaching needs with respect to quality.

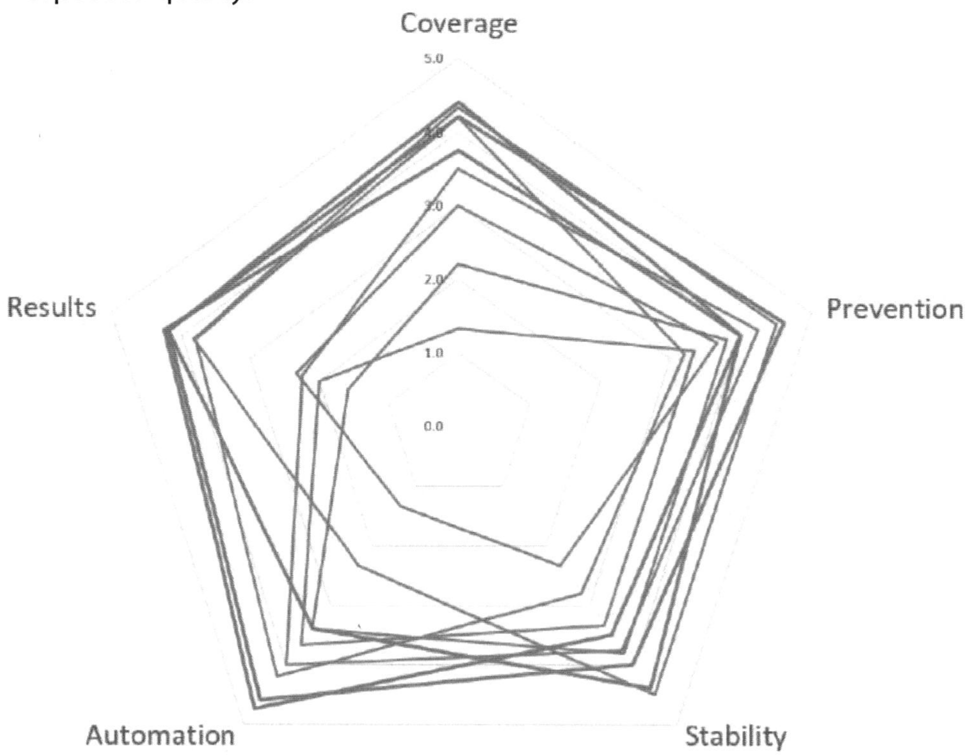

Figure 8: Analysis of Quality Topic (Team Subset)

There are some key coaching opportunities when look at the survey results:

- There are some teams doing well with test automation but there are some other teams that are doing poorly. This would be a great time for knowledge sharing between the strong teams and the struggling teams.
- In looking for organizational improvements, there seems to be some barriers preventing any teams from scoring well in test code coverage and using test results in integration and deployment.

3. Next Steps

One of the challenges of an internally developed, custom tool is that a lot of extra effort is required to administer assessments, analyze the data, and share results with the teams. This is fine for a handful of teams, but this will not scale and may not be as professional when we assess client teams. The Agile Coaching CoE is piloting the Comparative Agility tool (comparativeagility.com). Although it has its own topics and statements, and it doesn't meet some of the original requirements, the CoE feels it is worth it to see if the added value is greater than the requirements not met.

Valuable features include:

- Easily compare team results with its previous results, with the organization, or with a world index of all teams that have taken the assessment
- Quick and easy reports that are also interactive
- Visual representation of the distribution characteristics for each statement to show where there are large disagreements within the team

Comparative Agility covers the quality topic with these statements:

- Product owners actively participate in the creation of the acceptance criteria for each feature.
- All bugs are fixed during the iteration in which they are found.
- At the end of each iteration there is little or no manual testing required.
- The team performs a variety of types of testing including functional, performance, integration, and scalability each iteration.
- Team members who perform testing are involved and productive right from the start of each iteration.
- At the end of each iteration, the team has high-quality working software that it is comfortable being tested by people outside of the team.
- The team has pre-defined and agreed-upon criteria for considering a feature done.

4. Summary

Our journey in building our Agile Assessment Tool, just like our teams' journeys to agility, it's never ending. Catalyte's Agile Coaching Center of Excellence has learned as much about assessments as has been learned about the teams. We've learned

- The faster and more accurate we can process assessment data, the better we, as coaches, can help teams and organizations
- Visual representation of data helps identify coaching opportunities
- Multiple individual survey responses are often better than single team responses in identifying areas for deeper investigation

With better visibility of the organizational road we can find and fix the organizational potholes and help teams go faster in their journey to agility.

References

Ben Linders Consulting, "How Agile Are You?" https://www.benlinders.com/tools/agile-self-assessments/ (accessed July 6, 2018).

Derby, Ester, Larsen, Diana, 2006 *Agile Retrospectives: Making Good Teams Great*, Pragmatic Bookshelf

Gartner Research, Market Guide for Agile and DevOps Services, Oct 2017

Grove, Les. 2002. "Charting the Course through Software Process Improvement." PNSQC Proceedings (2002).

Scaled Agile Framework, "SAFe Team Self-Assessment", https://www.scaledagileframework.com/metrics/#T4 (accessed July 20, 2018)

Virtual Platforms Driving Software Quality in Pre-Silicon

Author

Amith David Pulla (amith.pulla@intel.com)

Abstract

Over the last two decades, tech industry has seen increasing pressure on software-development schedules and quality, this is true even for electronics design, device software, BIOS, firmware, device drivers, operating systems, hypervisors and end-user application development. Today in the semiconductor industry, majority of companies are adopting some type of system prototyping strategy, mainly in the form of simulators and emulators. The system level simulation and emulation tools available to software development teams can accelerate software development, testing, debugging and end-to-end validation in a virtual lab setting, driving the overall quality of the hardware and software platforms. Simulation tools are often referred to as virtual platforms because they are a fully software based solution running on operating systems. Virtual platforms or virtual prototyping platforms are the new class of tools based on high-level of design abstraction, can enable software development teams to start development and validation way ahead of actual hardware or silicon availability. Pre-silicon software enabling and validation is becoming the standard in compute platform development lifecycle in the semiconductor industry. Enabling the software stack in pre-silicon has a huge impact on quality of the software stack, reducing the number of hardware software integration issues in post-silicon and improving the time-to-market for end-to-end compute platforms. This paper explores the use of software based simulators and emulators for software/firmware development and validation, including industry leading simulation and emulation platforms, common virtual prototyping approaches, advantages and constraints. The paper will also cover how these tools and platforms help software teams to be more agile, responding to the changing business needs and quality expectations by continuous feedback mechanisms in software testing and validation processes.

Biography

Amith Pulla is a Technical Program Manager at Intel Corp, currently working at the Intel site in Hillsboro, Oregon. Amith works with engineering teams developing virtual platforms in the pre-silicon software space. Amith works with platform software enabling plans in pre-silicon to scope virtual platform features and capabilities. Over the last 18 years, Amith has been involved in software testing strategies and processes for applications from sales, marketing to data analytics and system software. Amith also worked in market research and intelligence space for data center and server market. Amith has worked extensively on projects involving multiple platforms and complex architectures. Amith worked on developing test methodologies and techniques to meet the business needs and schedules. As part of his QA lead role for the first 8 years of his career, Amith focused on improving and refining QA processes and standards for efficient software testing in agile environment. Amith also took on ScrumMaster roles working with agile development teams.

Amith has an M.S. in CIS from the New Jersey Institute of Technology; Amith got his CSTE and PMP certifications in 2006, CSM certification in 2012.

1. Introduction

With the increasing pressure on software-development schedules, the cost of software has become the undisputed leading factor in electronics design. Software development has been changing the electronics industry, semiconductor companies are constantly looking for product differentiation through software. To increase the software development windows and shorten the time to market (TTM), hardware platform development teams have started looking towards simulation and prototyping tools to begin the software stack development and validation before the real hardware is available. This new category of tools are sometimes referred to as virtual prototyping platforms or simply virtual platforms.

Virtual platforms are based on a high-level of design abstraction. Software development on virtual platforms is mainly focused on embedded software like BIOS/UEFI, firmware, device drivers, operating system enabling and diagnostics tools, but it's increasingly getting used for application development and workload optimization in Pre-silicon. Embedded software development teams need an accurate model of the hardware to test and validate software components, on the other hand hardware designers need complete software stack to fully validate the hardware. A hardware platform may contain a combination of CPUs, memory, storage, application specific integrated circuit (ASIC), SoC etc.

Software development has fundamentally changed the shape of the electronics industry, from large integrated device manufacturers (IDMs) to a complex disaggregated design chain of heavily interacting companies. Hardware intellectual property (IP) providers deliver blocks and subsystems to semiconductor companies, who in turn deliver chips and board subsystems to system houses who increasingly seek differentiation through software. All of the hardware-related players interact with software providers who create everything from low level drivers to complex end-user applications. Virtual platforms footprint in pre-silicon software development is growing steadily.

There are two types of models used in Pre-Silicon software development the cycle accurate models and functionally or register accurate models. The cycle accurate models or prototypes are built from real hardware with number of field programmable gate arrays (FPGAs) or pre-built solution like hardware emulator. These hardware-based solutions are ideal for silicon logic validation but typically very expensive and not very flexible for software development and validation. Virtual platforms close this gap by offering software designers early access to a development platform. A Virtual Platform is a software based system that simulates your full target System-on-Chip or board. Virtual platforms shift the software development earlier in the product development lifecycle and are cost effective compared to hardware equivalents.

lifecycle and are cost effective compared to hardware equivalents.

Simics SYSTEMC

Virtual Platforms
Architectural Level Accuracy
SW/FW Development and Testing

2. Physical Hardware and Software Stack

A compute system will consist of physical hardware and layers of software running on it. Let's focus on some of the key components of physical hardware that make up a compute platform.

2.1.1. CPU/Processor

A central processing unit (CPU) is the key component of the computer responsible for carrying out the instructions of a computer program. A CPU performs basic arithmetic, logical, control and input/output (I/O) operations that the computer programs instructs. A typical CPU consists of arithmetic logic unit (ALU) that performs arithmetic and logic operations, processor registers that holds data that is being processed and a control unit that coordinates the fetching of data from memory. CPUs have now become microprocessors where all components are integrated as a single integrated circuit (IC) chip. When an integrated circuit contains a CPU plus other components such as memory, peripheral interfaces, it's called a systems on a chip (SoC). In a multi-core processor where single chip contains multiple CPUs also known as cores, the chip is considered as a socket.

2.1.2. Memory

Memory in computing refers to the integrated circuits that store data for immediate use by a CPU; memory should operate at a high speed and this is the reason it's mostly referred to as random-access memory (RAM). Memory in computers are primarily silicon-based transistors on a chip. This semiconductor memory can be further classified as volatile and non-volatile memory. Flash memory, ROM, EPROM and EEPROM that is used for storing system firmware like BIOS or UEFI can be considered as non-volatile memory. Whereas dynamic random-access memory (DRAM), static random-access memory (SRAM) are considered as volatile memory.

2.1.3. I/O

Input/output or I/O is the communication between a computing platform and other computing platform or a human. Inputs are the data received and outputs are the data sent out from a computing platform. Transfer of data to CPU and memory and back to a storage device like a disk drive is considered I/O, for example by reading data from a disk drive, is considered I/O. Memory-mapped I/O (MMIO) and port-mapped I/O (PMIO) are methods that can be used for carrying out input/output (I/O) between the peripheral devices and computing platform like the CPU. I/O can also be performed by dedicated I/O processors that can execute their own instructions.

2.1.4. Storage

A storage device is a piece of computing hardware for storing and extracting data, it can be stored permanently or temporarily. Storage devices are part of the compute platforms and can be connected using several different options.

2.1.5. Board

Board connects the central processing unit (CPU) memory and other devices on the platform, the board also provides connectors to peripherals that connect to the main compute platform. This is the main printed circuit board (PCB) found in microcomputers, it's also referred to as mainboard, system board or logic board.

2.1.6. Platform

A platform is the overall computing system where software applications are executed. It can include the hardware and all the software/firmware ingredients including BIOS/UEFI, IP specific firmware, device drivers. Sometimes Operating system (OS), application programming interfaces (APIs) and applications are considered as part of the platform.

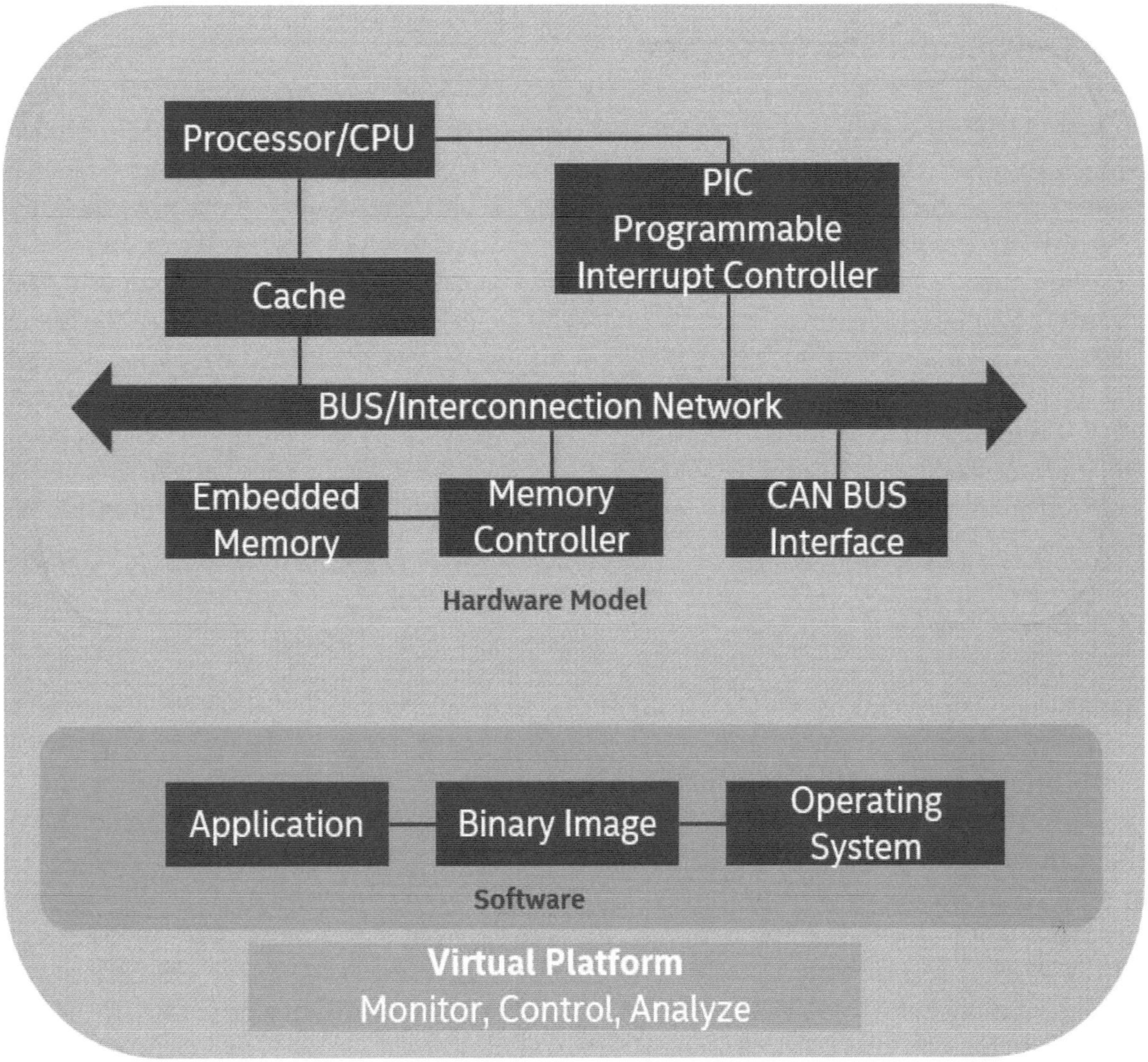

2.2. Software Stack

2.2.1. BIOS/UEFI

BIOS is the Basic Input/Output System (BIOS) firmware traditionally used to define the interface between the platform hardware and the operating system. Unified Extensible Firmware Interface (UEFI) replaced the BIOS in most of the modern computing platforms. UEFI covers the legacy support for BIOS enabled services. UEFI can have advanced features like remote diagnostics and maintenance that can be accessed independent of the operating system (OS), even without the OS being installed. Features like Reliability, availability and serviceability (RAS) are enabled in UEFI. RAS can protect data integrity, increase uptime making the platform more resilient and fault-tolerant.

2.2.2. Firmware and Device Divers

Firmware is a specific class of software often embedded in the hardware. Firmware is designed and developed for specific hardware to provide low-level control of the devices hardware capabilities and features. Firmware is typically installed in the non-volatile memory devices on the platform like the flash memory, ROM or EPROM. Each device or hardware capability on the platform may run its own firmware. All platform firmware needs to be developed and tested before the completed platform can be released. Device drivers enable a specific devices connected to the platform, the drivers installed on the platform controls that specific device. The driver is the software interface to underlying hardware enabling the OS to access hardware features. Drivers are specific to hardware and operating systems that allow connected devices to work with multiple versions of hardware OS combinations. Like the firmware, devices drivers are also software that needs to be developed and tested as part of the overall platform validation plan.

2.2.3. Operating System (OS)

An operating system (OS) manages the hardware and all the other software resources in a computer. The OS is initially loaded onto the platform by a boot program. The OS manages all the applications, the applications make requests for services with compute, network and storage resources using APIs defined in the OS. Users can also interact with OS using the user interface. As the new hardware features and capabilities, including new instruction set architecture (ISAs) added to the compute platforms, OS needs to be updated to take advantage of the new features and enhancements. In addition to OSs, there are hypervisors for virtualization that run directly on compute platform without on OS. The OS changes and updates are mostly done in parallel with the hardware design and development. The changes to OS needs to be tested as part of the platform validation plan.

2.2.4. Applications and Workloads

Software applications sometimes categorized as workloads is software that's designed to perform a set of functions for user needs and applications. These end-user applications or workloads can be optimized to specific hardware platform or OS, this is generally referred to as workload optimization. Any code additions or changes in applications or the middleware needs to be validated and optimized with the hardware platform.

3. Hardware/Software Co-Development

Traditionally hardware and software design and development was treated as two parallel development efforts. The software is run on hardware first time when the silicon is ready and any integration issues found would require design updates in the hardware. In the past, this process worked fairly well since the software was simple to change to work around hardware issues or defects, as the software is becoming more complex and platform delivery schedules were becoming more aggressive, this model of disconnected parallel hardware and software development was becoming more challenging.

Hardware and software collaborative co-development has become a new reality as hardware and software integration was becoming the crux of building high quality end to end solutions for customer needs. For hardware and software development teams, the collaborating should start from requirements to the overall development lifecycle including design, development and validation. With this quality management in this integrated development environment has become more important than ever. Integrated hardware and software testing, collaborative quality management platforms that enable co-debugging are playing a vital role. Centralized quality management tooling and metrics would help teams work on issues with end to end mindset with cross-discipline collaboration.

4. Pre-Silicon Enabling Vehicles

Pre-silicon enabling vehicles encompasses all the hardware simulation, emulation and prototyping tools used by hardware design teams and software development teams to develop and test software before the actual hardware or silicon is available. There are variety of pre-silicon enabling vehicles in the industry today that are developed using software that serve this purpose. For example, some emulators provide rich debugging environment and virtual platforms that provide a design or register accurate models that mimic hardware.

4.1. Register Accurate Simulators

Any model or tool that creates virtual software environment that simulates hardware system exactly from registers to specs is considered as register accurate models. These simulators are architecturally accurate and simulates the system so accurately that the full software stacks can run on them with no changes. Most virtual platforms are register accurate models that mimic the hardware. Virtual platforms are designed for fast execution of code in a virtual environment, they can reach up to few hundred millions of simulated instructions per second. This allows the users to complete hours of simulated time to be run in minutes or seconds of actual time. This high-speed execution in simulation is only possible by abstracting and approximating the timing of the real hardware. This also allows register accurate models like virtual platforms to be run on user's desktops and workstations. Virtual platforms are ideal for validation of software functionality and feature set as they are not representative of cycle times of real hardware.

4.1.1. Virtual Platforms

Virtual Platforms are design accurate functional models of the hardware mainly targeted for software development, integration and validation. They are also known as virtual prototyping tools or full system simulators. Several leading Electronic Design Automation (EDA) vendors offer virtual platform tools and solutions for the semiconductor industry today. Some of the examples are Vista Virtual Prototyping by Mentor Graphics, Certitude, Platform Architect MCO and Virtualizer by Synopsys, Virtual System Platform, and Palladium Hybrid by Cadence and Simics full system simulator by Windriver. All of these tools at a minimum provide the benefits such as early availability of hardware model in pre-silicon for software development and integration, provide debug capabilities, visibility into software execution, simulation capabilities for OS enabling for application/workload optimization and validation.

Vista virtual prototype by Mentor Graphics is a stand-alone simulation engine that can run on either Windows or Linux desktops. It's based on a transaction-level modeling (TLM) platform. With the integrated IDE, software engineers can gain debug visibility into the hardware and power analysis. Vista can run in two modes, functional and performance. Functional mode is ideal for software integration, validation and debugging and performance mode can be used for analyzing and optimizing the software stack for power and performance tuning. SystemC is also widely used in simulation models, SystemC is system-level modeling language that contain libraries and frameworks for hardware simulation that can be used by hardware modelling teams.

Simics is a full system simulator that can simulate any target hardware, with Simics software teams can experiment with different hardware setups, test the software behavior with different configurations of memory size, core counts, processor speeds, etc. Simics is based on the fast instruction-set simulators (ISS) which can execute several compute architectures like x86, ARM, DSP, MIPS, Power Architecture and SPARC. "Simics is designed for fast execution of code on the virtual system, typically reaching several hundred millions of simulated instructions per second, allowing full workloads to be executed." (Jakob Engblom and Dan Ekblom 2006). To run operating system on the model Simics needs other simulation models like memory-management units (MMU) to be included in the simulator. Simics can execute the system in forward and reverse direction, this capability of reverse debugging, in addition to start stop execution, checkpointing can help software teams to root cause bugs and issues faster.

4.1.2. Key Capabilities of Virtual Platforms

- Flexible and configurable, no restrictions of physical hardware for developers/architects
- Non-intrusively debug and inspect complex systems, can execute a system in forward and reverse direction for easy debugging
- Provides an abstract, executable representation of the hardware to SW/FW developers
- Runs unmodified target software from the physical target system (BIOS, FW, OS, BSP, middleware, applications)

4.1.3. Key Advantages of Virtual Platforms for Software

- Early software development on pre-RTL models, before silicon, RTL simulation, FPGA prototype is available
- Enables SW testing, debugging, find and fix SW/FW bugs in Pre-Silicon
- Improves collaboration between hardware and software design teams
- Platform SW/FW Completeness and Validation before PO (Power On)
- Path Clearing for SLE (System Level Emulation) Models
- Enables external hardware OEMs and ODMs to start SW/FW development early
- Replicable on compute platforms and shared across distributed teams
- Applications and Workloads qualification in pre-silicon

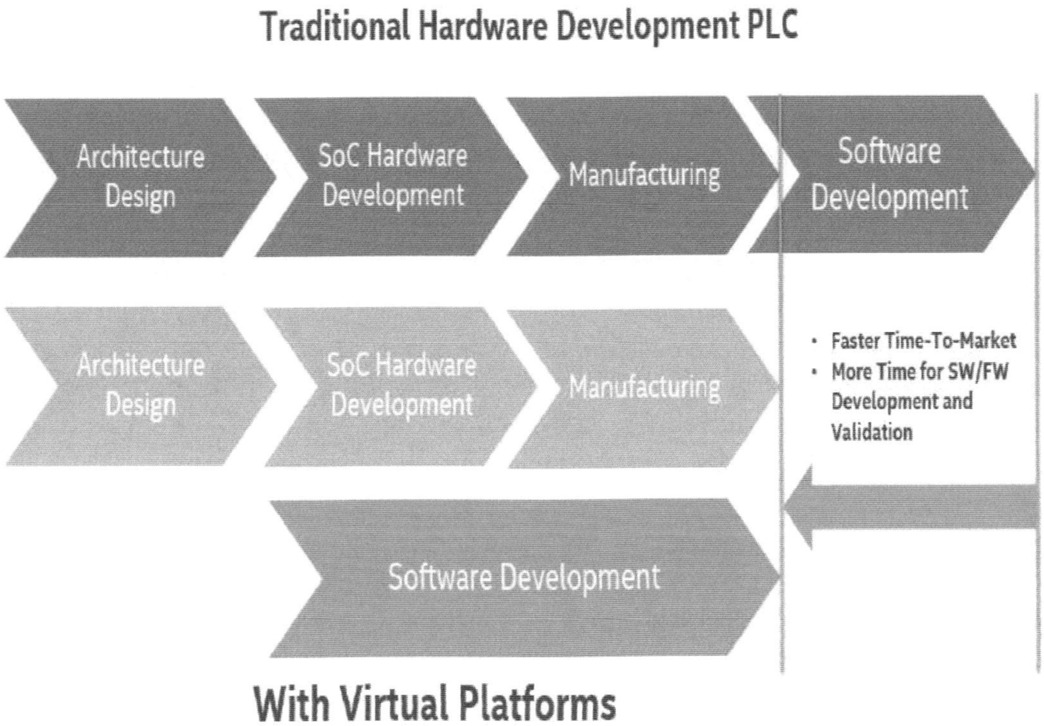

4.2. Cycle Accurate Simulators

Cycle-accurate models or simulators simulates the microarchitecture of the system based on cycle-by-cycle execution. Cycle-accurate models are dependent on specific implementation of architecture and can mimic the time precisions. For new microprocessors and microarchitecture designs, cycle-accurate simulators can help with testing and accurately benchmarking software execution in a virtual environment. All operations executed in a cycle-accurate model need to take into account architectural aspects of microprocessors like cache misses, data fetches, pipeline stalls, thread switching, branch prediction etc. A purely software based cycle accurate simulator is cost prohibitive to build. "a software-based cycle-accurate simulator would require tens to hundreds of thousands of processors which is currently infeasible and would be very costly." (Derek Chiou et al. 2006). This is the reason cycle accurate simulators use specialized hardware configurations using FPGAs.

4.2.1. System Level Emulation (SLE)

Hardware emulation mimics the behavior of the target hardware with other hardware like a special purpose-built emulation system. The emulation models are based on hardware description language (HDL), the primary purpose of emulation system is functional verification and debugging of the system that's being designed. Functional errors and bugs at RTL (Register transfer layer) stage of the design process can be identified and fixed using the emulation models, this will reduce the number of silicon respins and steppings saving big costs for semiconductor designers and manufactures. Functional verification using emulation also reduces overall product cost and time to market.

Major EDA vendors like Cadence, Mentor Graphics and Synopsis offer industry leading emulation platforms like Palladium Z1, Veloce Emulation Platform and ZeBu Fast Emulation. Emulation platforms take advantage of FPGAs (Field programmable gate arrays) and FPGA-based emulation software to design emulation systems. Emulation models help design and verification teams verify and debug functional and logic flows, make changes to designs as needed with a realistic cycle and architecturally accurate hardware model.

4.3. FPGA-Based Prototyping

FPGA-Based Prototyping is separate class of hardware models based on fast FPGAs for hardware verification and early software development and validation. Unlike virtual platforms which are purely a software based solution, FPGA-Based prototyping cannot be scaled to hundreds of software developers in the organization due to cost constraints. These prototyping models are used for SoC and ASIC design and verification. There is also hybrid prototyping approach that connects virtual platform with FPGA-based prototypes for software validation and hardware/software integration in early design cycles. Unlike virtual platforms, FPGA prototyping systems have almost zero debug capabilities, but are used to make stable design copies of target hardware for software development teams to use.

5. Enabling SW Stack in Pre-Silicon

5.1. BIOS/UEFI Development

BIOS or Basic Input/Output System is firmware typically stored in non-volatile memory is used for hardware initialization for booting process, BIOS also provides runtime services for operating systems and applications. Unified Extensible Firmware Interface (UEFI) has replaced BIOS, UEFI defines interface between OS and other platform firmware. BIOS is designed and developed for specific computing platform and development activities can start in pre-silicon using virtual platforms. Starting the BIOS development in pre-silicon gives the team additional time to implement features, improve quality and stability of the code. UEFI code can run on a virtual platform and can achieve basic and secure OS boot to multiple operating systems in pre-silicon. Starting this development and validation activity sooner in the overall platform development lifecycle will help the team find and fix integration issues and bugs in pre-silicon. The rich debug environment provided by virtual platforms offer the right tools for the BIOS developers to root cause bugs in software and can help the teams execute end-to-end functional and system level testing on virtual platform in pre-silicon. Most of the issues and bugs are already fixed improving the quality of the final BIOS release. Once the real silicon is available, the BIOS code is already tested and ready to be run on the silicon. The overall quality of the BIOS code is already improved at the silicon power on (PO), integration and PO time is reduced from months to days.

5.2. SW and FW Stack Development

Once the BIOS is enabled on the virtual platform, other software and firmware ingredients on the platforms can execute their set of use cases in the form of end-to-end functional and system level test cases. A typical server or client compute platform will have a 10 plus software or firmware ingredients that go with the platform. All these ingredient SW/FW releases can be validated on virtual platforms. In addition to SW/FW ingredients, there are multiple device drivers and other tools for systems diagnosis and management that can be validated in pre-silicon on virtual platforms. For power-on, the individual SW/FW ingredients will be already matured and well tested on virtual platform, improving the overall quality of the platform.

5.3. OS Enabling

Every hardware platform in the market follows a specific instruction set architecture for the processer like x86, ARM, MIPS, Power Architecture, and RISC-V to name a few. Instruction set architecture (ISA) abstracts the hardware for software programs to run on them. The ISA is the key interface between hardware and software. All software programs are written for a specific ISA and that software can run on diverse implementations of the same ISA. This allows binary compatibility among multiple generations of hardware. There are several different classifications of ISAs today, one of them is by architectural complexity, complex instruction set computer (CISC) and reduced instruction set computer (RISC) architectures are the two major categories. CISC has many specialized instructions while RISC simplifies the CPU by implementing only a subset of instructions commonly used by software applications. In RISC, the rarely used ISA operations are implemented as subroutines.

As hardware manufactures are adding new instruction sets to their CPU's or processors to meet the compute demand and improve efficiency of existing, new and emerging workloads and applications, operating systems need to take advantage of these new instructions sets and enable them in the OS. Traditionally lot of this OS feature set enabling happens in post-silicon that is after the hardware silicon samples are available, with the virtual platform all the OS enabling can move early into pre-silicon phase, giving OS enabling teams' additional time to develop and test new code. In addition to new instruction sets, any new devices that goes into an in development hardware platform like new memory technology, accelerators, I/O technology, hardware based security features, hardware based diagnostics and telemetry technologies need to be enabled in operating systems for software and applications to take advantage of these new hardware enabled enhancements. Major operating system families like Microsoft Windows, Apple iOS, Android, Linux, Chrome OS and Hypervisors, both native (bare metal) and hosted need to be enabled and optimized for new instruction sets and hardware features. OS enabling in pre-silicon on a hardware simulator like virtual platform moves the development and validation activities early in the development lifecycle giving software developers and testers ability to complete the quality processes and quality exit criteria before the silicon is ready. This means faster time to market with higher quality of the platforms ready for consumers.

5.4. Workloads Optimization

Going up the software stack, the opportunity to optimize the entire software stack for a specific middle ware framework, workload or application can be explored starting from pre-silicon, virtual platform tools offer capabilities to start the optimization and performance tuning in pre-silicon.

5.5. Workload Characterization

With the growing demand of new and emerging workloads like AI (Machine Learning/Deep Learning), Big Data Analytics, Blockchain, media streaming, web search, natural language processing and image recognition/computer vision, IoT etc. on compute platforms, workload characterization becomes a critical part of building and configuring scalable compute platforms and solutions. Measuring response times, CPU utilization, disk I/Os, memory access, network and storage latency in pre-silicon gives software developers key insights on software stack performance and power management tuning for target workloads and applications.

6. Software Development and Testing on Virtual Platforms

Leading industry standard software development and release practices like agile development, scaled agile frameworks, continuous integration and DevOps can be used for hardware software stack development and validation on virtual platforms in pre-silicon.

6.1. Continuous Integration

Automated regression testing of functional and system level test cases within a CI framework has now become an industry standard in software development. Expanding these capabilities and tools to hardware simulation platforms or virtual platforms can bring agility and efficiency to hardware software stack ingredient development teams, with seamless visibility and tracking of all integration issues and bugs in one CI framework can improve the collaboration and bug fix turnaround times. The CI environment enables faster feedback loops on bugs and fixes for all software ingredients within one framework. "Simulation can also bring other benefits, such as better feedback loops to developers for issues discovered in testing, and expansion of testing to handle faults and difficult-to-setup configurations" (Jakob Engblom. 2015).

6.2. Software Quality Qualification and Software Stack Readiness in Pre-Silicon

With Virtual Platforms and other pre-silicon software enabling vehicles, the entire platform software stack from BIOS/firmware to workloads/ applications can be run, integrated and validated to meet the expected software quality goals. This level of software integration and validation was only possible on real silicon few years ago, but with virtual platforms and other virtual prototyping tools, and with the convergence of agile development frameworks, this can be achieved in pre-silicon. Software development and integration teams can target executing 100% of system and functional test cases in pre-silicon, setting the goals of 90 to 100% test execution and test pass rates. With this level of software quality and readiness at pre-silicon exit or power on, compute platforms and solutions can be ready for market in matter of months, significantly reducing the number of post-production software bugs and issues. Application and workloads can run to their fullest efficiency and potential, taking advantage of latest hardware innovations as soon as the hardware platform is available to the consumer.

References

Derek Chiou, Huzefa Sunjeliwala, Dam Sunwoo, John Xu and Nikhil Patil, 2006 FPGA-based Fast, Cycle-Accurate, Full-System Simulators. https://pdfs.semanticscholar.org/3909/2c04278c375c1343e4ed0d2a24c616e4eb43.pdf

Jakob Engblom and Dan Ekblom 2006 SIMICS: A COMMERCIALLY PROVEN FULL-SYSTEM SIMULATION FRAMEWORK http://www.engbloms.se/publications/engblom-sesp2006.pdf

Jakob Engblom. 2015. Continuous Integration for Embedded Systems using Simulation, Embedded World 2015

Testing All the World's Apps

Author

Jason Arbon (jarbon@gmail.com)

Abstract

How do you test all of the world's apps? Over 10 million mobile apps and 5 billion web pages are updated and need testing. Today test automation efforts aim to test just one or a small subset of applications. Most of these apps and test cases are similar, yet each app team reinvents and re-implements the same test cases from scratch. Testing even a single app is difficult, slow and expensive, non-deterministic and often unreliable. Building test automation that executes reliably on all the world's apps requires rethinking all aspects of test automation. Three major problems needed to be solved to test at this scale:

- Reuse of test artifacts and logic
- Reliable test execution
- Contextualization of test results

This paper will help app teams and software testers understand the significant implications of testing at this scale, what testing at full scale looks like, and apply those lessons to your own test automation and infrastructure.

Biography

Jason Arbon is the CEO of test.ai, which has raised over $17 million in investments, and is delivering an AI-first approach to software testing. Jason previously held test and engineering leadership roles at Google (Search and Chrome) and Microsoft (Bing, Windows, SQL) where he tested large-scale neural network training systems. He was also director of engineering and product at Applause.com/uTest.com. Jason is a co-author of How Google Tests Software and App Quality: Secrets for Agile App Teams.

1. Introduction

Modern software test automation efforts target a single application, and teams often rewrite the same test case for each platform (iOS, Android, Web). This approach hasn't scaled well as most apps have no regression automation, and those that do have tests struggle to maintain a small amount of coverage. Engineering and organizational changes such as agile, continuous integration, DevOps, and better development tooling add additional pressures to test automation development. There is a different approach, and that is developing test automation at the scale of all apps.

Together, a few insights show that testing at this scale is now possible:

- AI / Machine learning enable test cases independent of the application's implementation.
- Apps share many common user interactions and flows.
- Reliable test execution infrastructure is now possible because of decreased compute costs.
- Test results are more insightful when compared to similar applications.

This paper details the implementation of a reference system that can test at the scale of all the world's applications, outlines the benefits of testing at this scale, and considers the impact this will have on the test automation profession and software quality. There are many implementations of such a scalable testing system. This paper describes the design, implementation, and lessons learned building test infrastructure that scales to test the world's apps at test.ai.

This paper also addresses UI-based functional regression testing. There are, of course, unit tests, integration tests, monitoring, etc. but at the end of the day the most important thing is that the software works for the human being controlling it via a user interface. This type of testing is also traditionally the most difficult and expensive to create, maintain, and scale, which is why it was chosen as a reference system. It is an exercise for the reader, or a later paper, to describe how these very same methods can be adapted to other aspects of testing.

describe how these very same methods can be adapted to other aspects of testing.

2. Testing Apps Individually

The state of the art in automated testing focuses on one app at a time. Modern app test teams don't have the budget to thoroughly test their own app, let alone develop automation for other applications.

Testing apps one at a time is often a brutal experience, fraught with peril and full of anti-patterns. Test automation often breaks exactly at the moment when the team needs it--right after minor changes in the application. App teams find themselves in a cycle where they start manual testing that doesn't scale, build out automation that ends up in a boondoggle of maintenance, close down their automation efforts, return to manual testing, and inevitably automate again with new leadership, new tools, and the same dreams. Even the smartest teams at Google, Apple, Microsoft, and Facebook all have the same issues, but they can afford to keep trying to test their apps over and over again with little wins here and there. The tragedy is that the vast majority of apps today have no testing. Most app teams cannot afford a tester, or even know how to get started. The realization that so few apps have any testing at all motivated much of the work below.

There have been attempts at larger, cash-rich, companies that make 10's or 100's of applications to re-use some test automation code across their fleet of apps. But that reuse is often scarce, limited to shared components, in the form of code, and creates its own new set of problems to maintain single code bases for multiple apps in different stages of shipping. The most mature testing efforts in the world often turn to test frameworks to scale the problem and share them with other engineers. These test frameworks don't have the test logic in them--they only speed up the ability to generate more test code or add new capabilities for test authoring for verifications. These test frameworks make it better to generate test coverage for a single app, not for all apps.

Testing applications one at a time is the current state because of the nature of testing. Software testers are often risk-averse--introducing a new test framework or methodology distracts from testing itself and is often seen as a risk in itself. What tester would have the audacity to pitch the idea of testing apps other than their own? Testers are often working in silos within their own companies, let alone collaborating cross-company. Testers are also late adopters when it comes to changes in technology--very few testers are playing with machine learning these days. Strangely, test automation vendors who should be motivated to build reusable components are also motivated to build tests for individual apps because that is their business model--one app at a time, and billing for human labor increases the top line. Lastly, the most ambitious engineers are usually focused on product, not testing, so that energy and ambition have been lacking in the testing space. Testing has been viewed as a necessary evil and cost center--not a place to truly innovate. Ultimately, it is not surprising test automation has been trapped in a linear, app-by-app mode considering some of these uncomfortable observations.

3. Scaling with AI

The application of AI to the test automation challenges makes all this solvable. AI is a set of Machine Learning techniques, to teach a machine to replicate human behavior. Here, the human behaviors to mimic are recognizing elements in an application and knowing how to interact with them in sequences that represent test cases. Just like humans, machines can be taught to execute test cases.

Traditional software test automation requires a developer to discover a unique way to find an element in the application. Elements are defined via custom identifiers, CSS selectors, XPATH expressions, simple image recognition, or hard-coded into the testing logic. This takes time, has to be repeated for each application, and when the application changes slightly the code needs to be updated to reflect the new implementation. Additionally, the sequencing of test steps is often hard-coded in a procedural programming language, so if the flow of the application changes, the code also will break and must be updated. Test automation today is expensive, slow, and laborious. With tens of millions of apps, billions of web pages, there isn't enough money or engineers in the world to test all this software with the traditional approach.

AI-based test automation doesn't suffer from these issues. Most importantly, the AI-based approach enables reuse of test automation artifacts.

3.1. Element Identification via AI

AI-based element identification is as simple as training a system to recognize cats versus dogs in photos. Here the machine is shown images of a login button, search boxes, password fields, etc. until the machine, like a human, and can readily recognize a new element in an application it has never seen before. The machine looks at the screen, just like a human tester and can recognize all the interesting parts of the application. No need for magic IDs, CSS Selectors, or XPATHs.

The robustness of this form of element identification derives from the fact that the 'AI' processes many different attributes of the element, and it has been trained on many different variations of that element. Training a network to recognize say a search_box is done by passing hundreds of element attributes such as height, width, position, ID, average color, CSS, number of edges, text, etc. into a neural network and telling the network 'this is a search_box'. Much like a human unconsciously sees many of these attributes, not just one, to identify it as a search_box. Also like a human, the neural network has seen hundreds, even thousands of different search boxes and learns what range of values search boxes typically have, and what values are often correlated with each other. So, if the search box moves from the bottom of the screen to the top, or changes color, or gets wider, the neural net will still recognize it as a search_box if the new value seem to still be consistent with a 'search box'. Traditional element identification breaks if only a single feature of the search box changes (e.g. its ID, x/y, CSS, or HTML hierarchy). The AI approach to element identification is far more robust to changes in the element, meaning lower maintenance costs as the application is redesign or re-implemented.

Most notable is that this AI method of element identification means that for common elements, this training need only happen once. This means there is no need for the test developer to identify the CSS or XPATH for each element in an application--the AI already knows that it is a search button in a new application it has never seen. So, speed of element identification drops to near zero, and the identification is far more robust to changes, reducing maintenance costs to near-zero.

3.2. Step Sequencing via AI

AI-based test sequencing is a bit more complicated implementation of machine learning, but it still behaves much like a human executing a test case. When a human is executing a test case manually, they have several subgoals. An example test case for a search engine might be:

- Find the search text box
- Enter in the word "Gradient"
- Click the search button
- Verify that there is a search result item with the word "Gradient"', in it.

It is worth noting that humans also intuitively check for things like usability, look and feel, and sanity checking behavior based on a larger context of human experience. AI can approximate much of this aspect of human testing as well, but is not the focus of this paper, which is scaling UI functional regression automation.

Each of these individual steps is a simple goal. The reference AI-based system leverages a mechanism called reinforcement learning, where the machine attempts to walk around in the application, and it is given a reward when it 'accidentally', but correctly, clicks the search button for example. After thousands of learning attempts, the machine builds up heuristics of what to do to accomplish each test case step. The machine can now take an application it has never seen, and execute the same test logic against that new application. This approach requires no cod and is re-usable across applications and platform. This approach also requires no prior knowledge of the application design or implementation, so it is robust to changes in application design. Just like a human tester, the AI is flexible and learns over time.

Not only does an AI-based approach mean faster test development and less maintenance, it means a test case need only be written once, and the test can be executed on another app where that test case should be relevant.

4. Scaling Test Case Definitions

With an AI-based approach to execute test cases, we need to design the tests for the automation to execute. For example, we need a way to tell the machine to 'search for "Gradient". Work is underway to teach AI-based systems how to create test cases themselves, but the human mind is still far better at test design. The humans need a quick way to compose these tests.

The AIT (Abstract Intent Test) schema is designed to be a human and AI/machine-readable test case format. The format deliberately doesn't support or need, the complexity of magic IDs, CSS, XPath, etc. The format also only captures the 'Intent' of the test case and contains as little information as necessary to execute such a test case. AITs only deal with sequences of interactions defined at the 'label' level. Where a label is something like 'search_button', which is understandable to a human and readable by the AI-powered automation system. AITs are easy to construct in a text editor in a simple Gherkin-like language or an equivalent JSON format. The reference implementation also has a simple drag and drop User interface to compose test cases using pictures of components of the application. AITs can also be programmatically generated. Regardless, all the test case logic is embedded in the simple, human and machine readable AIT file.

Designing scalable test cases requires a different mindset than traditional test case definitions. Traditional test case design typically has a few 'setup' steps, to get to the part of the application where functional behavior or user-interface characteristics checked. Traditional test cases not only have to contain the steps needed to execute a test case, but they are also specific to the application's current implementation.

4.1. Test Design for Reusability

Designing tests that can be reused across many apps take into consideration. An approach taken in the reference system is to group applications with similar functionality and implementation. For each cluster of applications, define the standard test cases as AIT tests, paying particular attention to ensure the underlying logic and flow of the test case is as general as possible, so those steps are logically similar across all the apps. With the 'search for "Gradient' test case example, the AIT test logic is general enough to be executed on all top search applications. The AIT doesn't contain any app-specific nuances of how to navigate to the search text input box--e.g., In applications, the search box is on the initial loading page, in other apps it only appears after other dialogs or screens. The key to writing scalable AIT test cases is to ensure they are app-agnostic and look for as much 'reuse' across as many applications as possible.

4.2. App-Specific Test Data

During test execution, the AITs are parameterized with app-relevant test data input. AITs can contain a specific string such as "LeBron James", but they can also contain test input or validations on the output of the form "<basketball_player>". The system maintains a mapping of these category names, to specific instances such as "Stephen Curry", or "Kevin Durant", or "LeBron James". The test execution system identifies the type of application at run-time, looks at parametrizable values in the AIT, and replaces those values with domain and application-specific values. The human editorial goes a long way toward ensuring test data is relevant at the individual app level.

This test input can impact later steps and the validation to be performed. So, later steps that also refer to <basketball_player> are all set to the same value. Meaning you can search for <basketball_player> then verify <basketball_player> appears somewhere on the search results page. Both input and output values will have the same value. Also test input may be labeled with a 'scenario' tag. This means that particular test data is relevant for a given 'scenario'. When parameterizing later test step values, only values that are also relevant in that given scenario are used. This is a quick, declarative way to ensure coherency in the test execution.

These tests are called the 'Standard Tests'. These are tests to be executed on all similar apps. Not only do we get a high return on the effort of designing test tests as they are executed on many apps, but this also has the benefit of relative quality assessments. More on that in the reporting section below.

4.3. Scaling Exploratory Testing

Having a list of reusable standard tests across large numbers of apps is great and reproduces rote, scripted testing. Another common form of testing is 'exploratory' testing. Essentially the human tester manually walks through the application and 'plays' with the application and observes basic behavior for correctness. The reference system not only executes the Standard

Tests, but it also tests the application in an automated, and exploratory way. This is called "AIT Chaining'. The process is:

1. Identify the current app screen and elements
2. Search through a database of common, small AIT test definitions that match the label of the screen or element on the page.
3. Execute that general test case
4. Report Pass/Fail for that test
5. GOTO 1

This AIT-chaining allows for reuse of test cases for common subsections of applications. For example, many applications have similar sign-in flows where an invalid email address should block sign in flow. If you try to use the malformed email address of '@foo.com', the flow can be expected to stop. The AIT for a test case definition for this would be:

1. When on login_page,
2. Enter '@foo.com' into the email_address field',
3. Click 'login_button'
4. Verify still on 'login page' (we should be stuck here)

Many apps have similar sub-flows within them. AITs like this can be easily authored, and then when executing in an AI-Chaining mode, relevant test cases can be pulled from the repository and executed. The humans here still provide the test case logic, but the machine can intelligently and automatically select and execute them at scale on any application.

4.4. Scaling Automation

How to test parts of applications that require a signed in user? Again, just a little human editorial work goes a long way. Functionally, the 'username' and 'password' values are passed into the application and executed like other AIT tests which use those values on things in the app that match the labels 'username' and 'password.' How do we the usernames and passwords for the words top apps? Two highly technical approaches to getting this login information in the reference implementation:

1. The team editorially goes down the top app lists--creating test accounts for all apps.
2. A quick email or ping on LinkedIn can often get a company to share a test account with us as we are adding to their testing coverage as a byproduct and are interested in seeing the results.

Interestingly, an engineer would assume that testing at this scale would get our infrastructure flagged as bots with so many login attempts. In practice, this hasn't been a problem. When apps flag the bot account, it is just an excuse to reach out to the team and share our findings--and get the test account blessed as a testing bot.

4.5. Scaling Test Design Summary

The key to defining human-intelligent test case definitions that can scale to the world's apps is re-use. Even if it takes a little bit of time to curate and manually define great test cases in a format such as AIT, the fact that they are quick to define, and there is no need to worry about the automated execution and reporting means testers can focus on what they do best--design great tests. With that efficiency, and the above test design approaches, a basic set of intelligent test cases for the top 10,000 applications is doable with the effort of just a few human testers.

At this point, the astute test or engineering mind will be thinking of all the corner cases AITs cannot support yet, or realize that you cannot write a test case that checks with a database to verify the stock price in the application is the correct value. This is all true! Scaling has its tradeoffs and benefits.

As an aside, it is worth noting that the feeling of writing a test case that can be run on hundreds of apps, even apps you've never seen, is a great feeling as a tester.

5. Scaling Infrastructure

Many teams might have a lab of between 5 and maybe hundreds of test devices. When you are testing at the scale of all the world's apps, all the problems normally associated with test labs grow as well.

Most test labs, whether machines laid out on a conference table, or in a modern, remote cloud-based test environment suffer from a few common challenges: flaky tests and limited capacity. Much of these problems come from engineering optimizing for the cost of computing, not person hours or reliability. When testing at large scale, these issues are too numerous to investigate. We turned the most common test lab design assumptions upside down in what is called 'SuperScaling' in the reference system

5.1. One-to-One

Most test labs are configured to have a single 'controller' machine drive as many test devices as possible. This costs money as controller machines can cost $1-$2 thousand dollars each. Labs can get up to 16 test devices or emulators per single controller machine. This configuration, however, leads to contention for network, CPU, and memory across all the devices. This contention leads to test steps or page loads timing out as the test logic or network is shared with the other devices. The scaling infrastructure instead uses only one controller per test device. This ensures there isn't any contention for the controller, resulting in many, many fewer test step timeouts. This does cost about 15 times as much money to deploy, but that is still less than the cost of a single engineer to debug the infrastructure or deal with false positives across thousands of applications. The fundamental rule discovered to scale test infrastructure is that machines are cheaper than humans today. Modern test labs don't realize how much human cost is associated with cheap infrastructure.

5.2. Networking

Most test labs share networking capacity across multiple devices, often tunneling through the controller's single network connection. This means unpredictable networking which can cause false positives and also means that performance metrics won't be consistent run over run. To SuperScale, we have a dedicated, guaranteed 10MB connection for each controller and each test device. Yes, this wastes a lot of network capacity, but at scale, this is far less expensive than having false positive test results and paying humans to investigate issues.

5.3. Local Procedure Calls

Many of the more popular test frameworks have the test code executing at a remote machine, and test case steps make a remote call over HTTP to the test lab where the test machines live. The internet is surprisingly unreliable, especially at scale. The time spent waiting for each remote call over HTTP, and the occasional lost request leads to test execution timeouts, invalid object (e.g., the object referenced in test step can change state while the command is traversing the web). With SuperScaling the solution is to write our communication layer to the application and put the test driving logic local, on the same computer as the simulator to device.

5.4. Pristine Machine State

Lastly, most lab machines are re-used across test cases, sometimes even test runs. This can lead to silly issues like running out of disk space, accumulated memory leaks, software state 'cruft' accumulation, all leading to unreliable test execution and the need for human intervention. The SuperScaling model again does the inverse: controller machines (e.g., MacMini's) are re-imaged at the ROM level between each single test execution. The machine images are stored on nearby storage area networks (SANs) with dedicated network lines to not interfere with any application network traffic. Yes, this costs money as the machine cannot process work while they are re-imaging. But, the SuperScaling key to scaling and reliability is having these systems reliable without human intervention and minimize any complexity due to machine state.

Essentially, the SuperScaling test infrastructure design turns each device into its own isolated mini-lab. This lab design philosophy results in >.998 reliability in test execution, which enables an engineer (no DevOps) team to support the test execution of tens of thousands of applications.

6. Scaling Test Reporting

To scale test case reporting to millions of apps, and billions of web pages, the reference system has built a non-traditional reporting infrastructure. Most importantly, testing at this scale also enables a whole new way to view and judge application quality.

6.1. Delayed SQL

Traditional test reporting post results of test cases to a SQL server, and at run-time, the reporting UI runs SQL queries to report on the data Test case pass-fail results are also often just that, a little bit of text. Traditional reporting also only has one or perhaps ten users querying the data at any given time. The AI-driven testing bots, however, produce a GigaByte or more of results data per test run. Generally with scalable reporting design, things are kept as long as necessary in flat JSON files. These JSON results are then post-processed and saved in cloud storage. A separate process parses all these JSON files and pushes that data into ready-to-serve schemas in a SQL data store to enable real-time complex querying to support engineering, internal reporting. Keeping the data in JSON formats as long as possible, and preprocessing the data into standard report formats before pushing it into a datastore helps avoid any data store contention and dramatically reduces the compute time and latency of traditional dynamic test report generation.

6.2. Search

Traditional test reporting post results of test cases to a SQL server, and at run-time, the reporting UI runs SQL queries to report on the data Test case pass-fail results are also often just that, a little bit of text. Traditional reporting also only has one or perhaps ten users querying the data at any given time. The AI-driven testing bots, however, produce a GigaByte or more of results data per test run. Generally with scalable reporting design, things are kept as long as necessary in flat JSON files. These JSON results are then post-processed and saved in cloud storage. A separate process parses all these JSON files and pushes that data into ready-to-serve schemas in a SQL data store to enable real-time complex querying to support engineering, internal reporting. Keeping the data in JSON formats as long as possible, and preprocessing the data into standard report formats before pushing it into a datastore helps avoid any data store contention and dramatically reduces the compute time and latency of traditional dynamic test report generation.

To navigate this mass amount of data, where engineers aren't even sure which apps are tested, or when, the reference system also has a search engine, indexing all test cases, apps, and test results.

6.3. Benchmarking and Competitive

The most exciting aspect of reporting on testing at this scale is the cross-application analytics. Most app teams can barely keep up with testing their own application--they don't have time even to imagine testing their competitor's apps. When testing at this scale, with standard and common test cases, it is to pivot the reporting in a few ways:

- Competitive Performance: The performance of clicking a 'search_button' across the top web search apps can now be compared against each other. For example, we can easily tell that Walmart's app is slower to log in, but has a faster search experience compared to Amazon's app.

- Flow Comparisons: Since AITs describe a user intent, it is possible to see how other applications accomplish the same intent. One app may have extra steps due to better design or may have features that another app doesn't have.

- Feature-Level Benchmarks: If an application's performance for facebook OAuth login is slow, but they know it is also slow in another app, they can prioritize their time on other performance issues in the application since they likely don't have control over it. The performance of common actions in apps can now be compared to the 'average' in all apps.

6.4. Device, OS, App Store Testing

Individual app teams find it difficult to automate the testing of their app. But there are also test teams out there with almost impossibly large testing problems:

- App stores: App stores strive to 'test' every app that is submitted from developers to protect their users and brand from low-quality applications. App stores today, generally have a mix of human manual testing and random monkey tests to look for basic crashes and other issues. Now App stores can test and verify the functionality of 'all' apps at scale.

- Operating Systems/ Browsers: The makers of OS's and browsers have the accountability to make sure applications work great on their platform. Today's approach to test automation means only a few apps can be tested to catch reliability, performance, and functional regressions when the operating system updates. With scaled testing, more intelligent quality reporting can be made to compare OS vs. OS, or Browser vs. Browser.

- Hardware Manufactures: Hardware also has an impact on application performance and sometimes functionality and reliability. Testing at scale means it is now feasible to verify how hardware changes impact applications. Finding issues, or just verifying that things still work, would be significant progress.

- Carriers: Cell phone carriers have to verify that now hardware, operating system versions, and applications won't adversely impact their network and services. Scaled testing can help verify the fully deployed system will behave from the app-level down.

The reporting on massive amounts of application test results can reveal the test results for lots of individual applications. This reporting also gives insights into:

- The relative quality between applications, can measure quality across all apps

- Regress new operating system versions

- Verify the correctness of fully deployed end-to-end carrier tech stacks

AI-driven testing at this scale enables new measures of quality not possible before. Performance, crash rates, even user flows can now be compared across applications and benchmarked. Most importantly, this approach to scaled testing means every team, even teams that cannot afford dedicated testing resources for automation, can benefit from the value of test automation.

7. Team Structure

Interestingly, when developing the reference system, the structure of the team was the most surprising aspect. The original thinking was was to bring the best test automation engineers on the planet together and just build it. It turned out that most test automation engineers were the very ones who had honed their skills on testing one or at most just a few apps, and they came with all their inherent biases. We also found that most of the problems were classical AI / Machine Learning problems that just happened to be in the service of a testing problem. Mid way we realized that what we had really build was a hybrid of a search engine and machine learning platform. The system is a search engine in the fact that it is crawling large numbers of apps, indexing all their content, scoring the results, and measuring quality in statistically and in aggregate. It is also a machine learning platform in that it has specialized tooling for labeling data, expressing rewards for the reinforcement learning, and a data pipeline that mass produces global and per-app classifiers. If we knew how hard it would be, we may not have started :)

The team construction that ended up being important:

- Machine Learning and Statistics PhDs focused on the ML

- Engineers with Experience in Search Crawling, Indexing, and Serving

- Test Automation Engineers experienced in testing at scale (e.g. Chrome, Search)

- Test Design Engineers well-versed in the breadth of testing problems, platforms, familiar with all the great test designs, and can recognize the anti-patterns of test design.

- Experienced Designer for Data Driven UX

- Senior Front End Engineers to build data-heavy, complex, performant UI

- Experienced Infrastructure engineers to design robust, distributed and scaling data pipelines, execution and reporting.

Interestingly, most of the team members aren't testers or automation engineers. Testing at this scale is really a combination of two product teams: Search and Machine Learning Infrastructure.

8. Summary

This paper has walked through the challenges of testing applications at scale, explored solutions, and discussed new benefits that this approach can bring to software quality. Testing at scale, with test case reuse, isn't just 'better, faster, cheaper', it impacts the role of testing, the overall quality of software, and given that apps power much of our daily lives, it might just make this a better world.

References

Special thanks to Jeff Nyman, Wayne Roseberry, Michelle Petersen, Joe Mikhail, Kevin Pyles, David Morgan, and Carlos Kidman for their insightful edits and suggestions.

Abstract Intent Test (AIT) Specification. https://goo.gl/3YMNcG (accessed Aug 29, 2018).

Using Open Source MEAN Stack Tools to Develop Web Applications and Maintain Big Data

Authors

Kavitha Naveen (kavin@tektronix.com)
Rishikanta Mohanty (rishikanta.mohanty@tektronix.com)

Abstract

Presenting data to upper management and maintaining it is a challenge in any organization. Moreover, updating the data on a day-to-day basis and keeping the stakeholders informed about the progress is an added overhead. The data is often from different teams. For example, the testing team needs to present data with respect to the number of test cases added, number of test cases that passed/failed, and traceability of the test cases to the requirements. The development team needs to present data on the features implemented, estimation to implement the features, defects fixed and so on. After the product is released to the market, you will have customer found defects. This data also needs to be collected, resolved and maintained.

To maintain all the data from different teams working on various projects requires a lot of development effort and time in finding the right storage system with low maintainability. Challenges include analysis, storage, search, and query operations. Hence, we need a good database, which helps us store the information and retrieve it when required. The industry offers several open source tools stack. The most popular, LAMP (LINUX, Appache, MySQL, PHP), is a stack tool that uses MYSQL, a traditional database introduced in 1995, and has performance issues handling huge data that the technology demands. In addition, you require specialists for front end and back end development. To solve some of the existing problems in LAMP stack, the latest MEAN stack tool is a solution. MEAN stack is a free and open source Javascript tool stack for both front end and backend in web applications. MEAN stands for MongoDB, ExpressJS, AngularJS and NodeJS.

This paper presents an introduction to the MEAN stack tools' advantages over another open source web app tool, LAMP stack. As an example, the paper would also cover the Dashboard web application we developed in our organization using the MEAN stack tools to collect and present various types of data from different teams for different products. Due to the ease of use of MEAN stack tools, with short ramp up time we were able to create and maintain our database and web application quickly.

Biography

Kavitha Naveen is a senior lead engineer in Tektronix. She works in the wide band solutions team and has experience in working with signal generators and oscilloscopes. She has wide experience in working with test automation tools. Her interests include reading more about test automation tools and coming up with innovative ideas to automate the manual test case execution cycles. In her spare time, she likes to listen to music.

Rishikanta Mohanty is a software engineer working in Tektronix. He works in signal generator projects and particularly on software test automation. He is very passionate about software coding, especially web application development. In his free time, he likes playing cricket and cooking.

1. Introduction

In any organization where, multiple products are developed and released year after year there will be huge collection of data. The data includes the requirements capture, test cases development and traceability coverage, release cycle testing, defects submission and maintenance, schedule estimation, number of products released, automated test cases' coverage etc. Due to the numerous types of data collections, there is a need to use different tools to collect and maintain the data.

In our organization, we have defect tracking tools to submit, track and maintain the defects. For requirements and test cases management, there again is a separate tool to capture the requirements, track their status, traceability coverage and maintain it release after release. After the product release to the customers, we have another tool that is used to submit and maintain customer found defects.

The management finds it difficult to access all the data, as you need to login to each tool and access the data for various products developed. To make the data available and easily accessible, displaying all the data in one place using a Dashboard web application would be a huge advantage. At the click of a mouse button on the Dashboard webpage, the data is available. When product development occurs in multiple locations, internal communication within the teams and keeping the stakeholders updated also becomes very easy.

To develop the Dashboard web application and maintain the data we selected MEAN stack tool due to the various advantages it offers compared to the other web application development tools like LAMP present in the industry. In the following sections, you will see the advantages of MEAN stack tools over the traditional tools available.

MEAN stack is the latest technology in the industry. MEAN stack is an open source tool solution and uses Javascript as a single language both from the client side and server side to develop web applications. Hence, developers have the flexibility of using Javascript for both the front-end and back-end.

MEAN stack stands for MongoDB, ExpressJS, AngularJS and NodeJS (Figure 1)

- MongoDB is a NoSQL (Non-Structured Query Language) Javascript database and is document based. It stores data as a document in BSON (Binary JSON), which is like JSON (JavaScript Object Notation format).
- ExpressJS is a web application framework for NodeJS. It provides a flexible and wide variety of features for developing web and mobile applications easily using Javascript.
- AngularJS is an open source web application framework for front-end development using Javascript.
- NodeJS is an open source Javascript run time environment. It allows you to run Javascript on the server side.

MEAN stack can be used for maintaining big data and it is gaining importance in mobile application development, web applications, social media and health care industry where large amounts of data are used for analysis and storage. The flexibility and ease of use is one of the primary reasons why the industry is switching over to MEAN stack to develop web applications. The data transfer from server to client is done using JSON data format and along with it comes performance improvements. For developing cloud applications MongoDB is the right choice as it provides many flexible features to develop, test and host applications in the cloud.

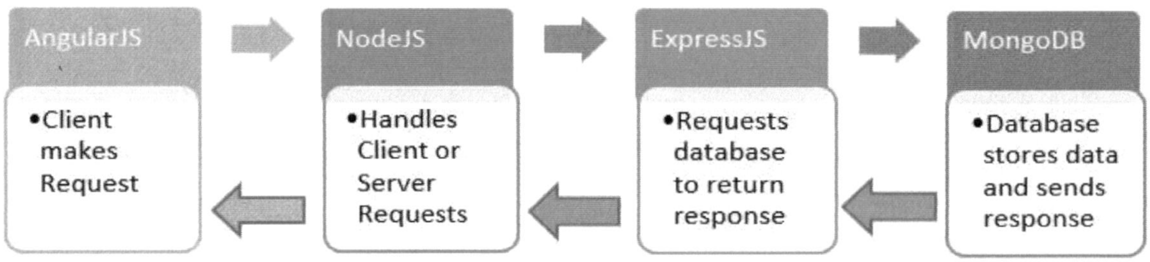

Figure 1: MEAN STACK Tool Set

2. Why MEAN Stack Tool?

For developing web applications, industry offers many open source tools. MEAN stack is a stack of tools bundled together, while LAMP is also an open source stack of tools bundled together as shown in Figure 2a. Let us look at the advantages of MEAN stack tools over LAMP (LINUX, Apache, MySQL, PHP) which has been a widely used tool since its introduction in 1995. MEAN stack, introduced in 2009, is gaining its importance, as it is easy to use and deploy cloud applications, which is the recent trend in web development.

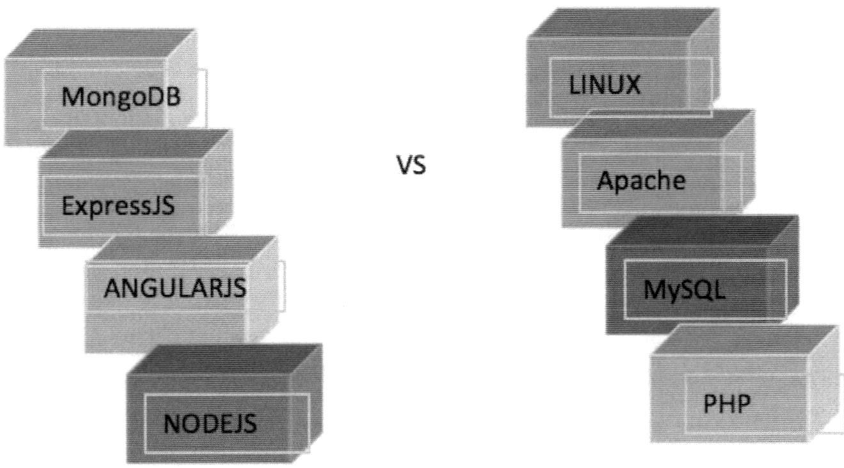

Figure 2A: MEAN and LAMP Stack

The different elements of the stack is as shown in Figure 2b.

MongoDB (database)	MySQL (database)
ExpressJS (server side Framework)	PHP (programming language)
AngularJS (client side app Framework)	Linux (Operating system)
NodeJS (web server)	Apache (web server)

Figure 2B: MEAN and LAMP stack components

Comparison of MEAN stack with LAMP stack

LAMP	MEAN
LINUX (OS)	MongoDB(Database)
Apache(web server)	ExpressJS (server side application Framework)
MySQL (Database)	AngularJS(client side application Framework)
PHP	NodeJS (Server side Language)
It has been around for decades and is a proven method of web app development	Relatively new and is gaining popularity
Not built originally for cloud applications	MEAN is designed with cloud in mind. It supports JSON, the document format which is flexible for cloud applications
Several experts needed, for MySQL, PHP	Both front end and back end are built on Javascript. You Only need Javascript expert to develop web applications
Different languages for front and back ends	Since both font and back ends work on Javascript, command execution is quicker
Slower due to its blocking structure	Easily scalable as code can be easily added and removed
Supported by - Google, IBM, Samsung	Supported by - Oracle and Linux Foundation

The primary reason for selecting MEAN stack for our dashboard web app development is due to the advantage of developing front end and back end using Javascript and we did not need an expert who knows different languages as required by Lamp stack. In addition, the performance to host the web server is very easy in MEAN stack and this gave us an added benefit.

3. Brief Introduction to the MEAN Stack Tools

MEAN stack as shown in Figure 3 is a stack of components that uses JavaScript-based technologies used to develop dynamic web applications and mobile applications. MEAN denotes MongoDB, ExpressJS, AngularJS, and NodeJS, the technologies used in the stack. It has gained importance because it allows developers to use the same language for both front and back end development.

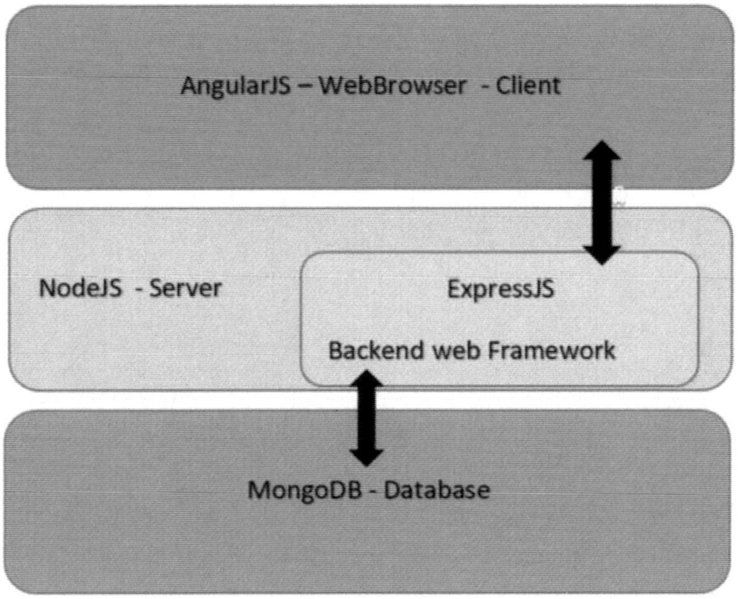

Figure 3: MEAN Stack Components

3.1. MongoDB

MongoDB is the database in the MEAN stack tool. This is a NoSQL database with lots of flexibility and high performance. Traditional relational databases are being used for enterprise applications for decades. However, these days the industry is moving to an agile method of development, faster time to market to beat competition and innovative ways to quickly productize the design and maintain data easily with lots of scalability.

Maintaining huge data and connecting all of it together for the end-user with high accuracy requires faster and efficient ways to store the data and retrieve it as quickly as possible. Social media, online shopping and web portals are examples where large amounts of data need to be connected and accessible from any device anywhere in the world with a common login ID. Changes and improvements in such huge development projects cannot follow the traditional model where the features are tested at the end of the development cycle. Development and testing need to happen in parallel. To address the rapidly growing data, the industry is embracing the MongoDB database to help solve these issues.

The key features of MongoDB include:

1. Storing data in a document format called BSON (which is like JSON)
2. If any field in the document needs to be added, a change can be made to that particular document without having to take the system off-line.
3. Similar fields are grouped together in documents and this helps to query the data quite easily.

4. Data represented as documents are similar to data types in programming languages and this helps developers easily map the data in the application to the database.
5. Companies who have shifted to MongoDB have seen 2X to 3X improvement in their product lifecycle.
6. Schema rigidity is not present in MongoDB; this again helps developers save time compared to MySQL where the schema needs to be well defined.
7. MongoDB helps to build cloud applications with the best security practices. It provides features to operate and deploy the database in the cloud using the industry's cloud platforms.
8. Supports Indexing on any attribute in the database, rich queries, replication and fast, in place updates.
9. Provides cost effective way to store and maintain data.

Documents in MongoDB

MongoDB is an open source document database that provides high performance, reliability and scalability. In MongoDB, a record is a document represented as Key value pairs. The documents are similar to JSON objects. The values of the keys can be arrays or other documents.

Example:

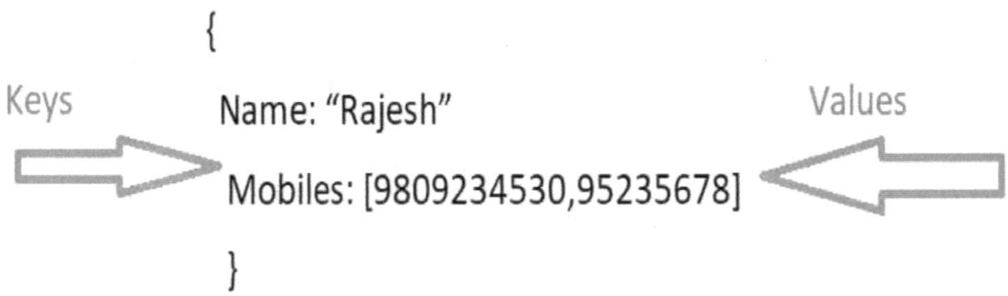

3.2. NodeJS:

- NodeJS is a server side JavaScript based open source webserver, which is built on Chrome's V8 JavaScript engine
- It supports event driven and non-blocking I/O API where the commands execute in parallel
- We can build interactive web applications by using only JavaScript
- NodeJS latest LTS Version: 8.11.3 (includes npm 5.6.0)

3.3. ExpressJS:

- Express is a NodeJS based open source web application framework released under an MIT license to develop web and mobile applications
- Express uses MVC model (Model-View-Controller)
- Express 4.16.3 is the latest release version

3.4. Angular JS:

- AngularJS is an open source Javascript based front-end web development framework. It is maintained by Google
- AngularJS has a simple architecture, extends HTML with new attributes and is easy to learn
- The data binding capability eliminates much of the code that otherwise needs to be written and hence helps in faster development of web apps

4. Dashboard Web Application for Requirements/Tests/Defects Data Using MEAN Stack

The block diagram of the Dashboard application is as given below in Figure 4. The purpose of the Dashboard app is to collect data for requirements, test cases, and defects of all the products developed and display it in the webpage

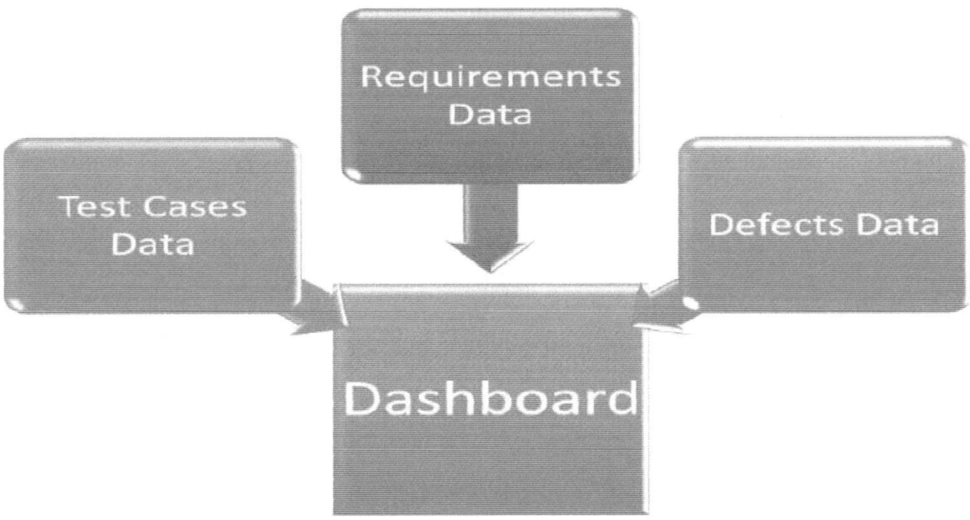

Figure 4: Dashboard Block Diagram

4.1. Requirements Data

All the requirements for the various projects are captured and maintained in the requirement management tool. For any of the products developed, the requirement tool is used to capture the following data

1. Newly added requirements
2. Existing requirements
3. Priority of the requirements
4. Status of the requirements
5. Traceability from requirements to test cases
6. Target release
7. Platform supported

For 'n' number of products there would exist 'n' number of projects. The data that are of primary importance to the management or stakeholders are the number of requirements that have been developed, the number of new requirements that have been captured along with priority and status. To present this data in the web application, the data existing in the requirement management tool are automatically exported to a spreadsheet for all the products developed. The data present in the spreadsheet are used as input in the web application and stored in the database MongoDB.

Example data for requirements gathering for 'n' number of projects is given below. Data are collected for all the projects and displayed in our Dashboard web application. Hence, at any point of time the data are available by accessing the web app for any of the projects desired.

Requirements Data	**Project A**	**Project B**	**Project C**	**Project D**	**Project E**
Total Requirements	**1000**	**2000**	**5000**	**10000**	**7000**
Newly Added Requirements	**200**	**500**	**700**	**1000**	**3000**
Existing Requirements	**800**	**1500**	**4300**	**9000**	**4000**
High Priority Requirements	**700**	**1500**	**4000**	**8000**	**6000**
Status	**Done**	**In Progress**	**In Progress**	**In Progress**	**Done**
Target Release	**Jan 2018**	**Jan-20**	**Mar-20**	**Jun-19**	**March-18**
Platform supported	**Windows**	**Linux**	**Windows**	**Windows**	**Linux**

Table 1: Requirements Data

4.2. Test Cases Data

The test cases written against the requirements are collected from the requirement management tool and exported automatically to a spreadsheet. The details collected for test cases are included in the list below. The data collected in the spreadsheet serve as the test case data input to the web application and the database MongoDB

1. Total test cases
2. Test case traceability to requirements
3. Test case priority
4. Test case status
5. Total number of automated test cases
6. Total number of manual test cases

4.3. Defect Tracking Data

The defects for the software application developed are of two types:

1. Defects found during testing phase
2. Customer found defects after the software is released to the market.

The details of the defects are collected from the defect management tool, including the list below, are exported to a spreadsheet. The data present in the spreadsheet serves as the input to the database MongoDB.

1. Total defects count for each product
2. Total defects in open state
3. Total number of defects of each priority level
4. State of the defects
5. Resolution rate of the defects

5. Procedure to Develop Dashboard Web Applications Using MEAN Stack Tools

First, you need to set up the environment by installing the MEAN stack tools in a development system used to develop web applications. You need to install MongoDB, ExpressJS, AngularJS and NodeJS. As shown in Figure 1.2, AngularJS is used as the Web Browser, ExpressJS is the framework that supports NodeJS, NodeJS is a webserver and MongoDB is the database. For details on installation of the various components of MEAN stack, please refer to the Appendix. Section 5.1 explains the steps to create the Dashboard application for customer submitted defects. Similar steps need to be followed for adding requirements data and test case data to the Dashboard application.

5.1. Example Dashboard Application for Customer Submitted Defects

After following the instructions in the Appendix, the required Mean stack tool is installed. In this section, we will create a sample web application for collecting data and displaying the data. In the example, we will consider around 14 teams (i.e. TEAMA, TEAMB, TEAMC, TEAMD, TEAME, TEAMF.... Etc.)

We collect the customer found defects after the software is released to the market. Since there are several teams in our organization, each team having "n" number of projects, data from all these teams and all their projects are collected and presented to upper management.

The projects include the new active projects and projects already released and in maintenance phase, with newly added requirements.

The defects submitted by customers are analyzed and appropriate action takes place as per the diagram in Figure 5. The inflow of defects is counted and the state of defects is to be presented to the management team. The state of the defects changes on a daily basis as per the resolution rate or analysis rate by the development team. Hence, the changes in state also needs reporting on a daily basis. Towards this end, we required a good tool to store the data, analyze the data and present it to the management team. MEAN stack tool helped us store the data effectively, and easily query for the required results and display it on a daily basis.

The process followed for any customer submitted defect is as follows:

- The defect is submitted by the customer
- The product team analyzes the defect and plans for further action
- If further information is required, then the customer is contacted and information is gathered accordingly
- The defect is assigned to the respective team

- The team works on the defect
- The software with the defect fix is shared with the customer
- The customer works on the new software and acknowledge the defect as resolved
- The team verifies the state of the defect and then closes it.

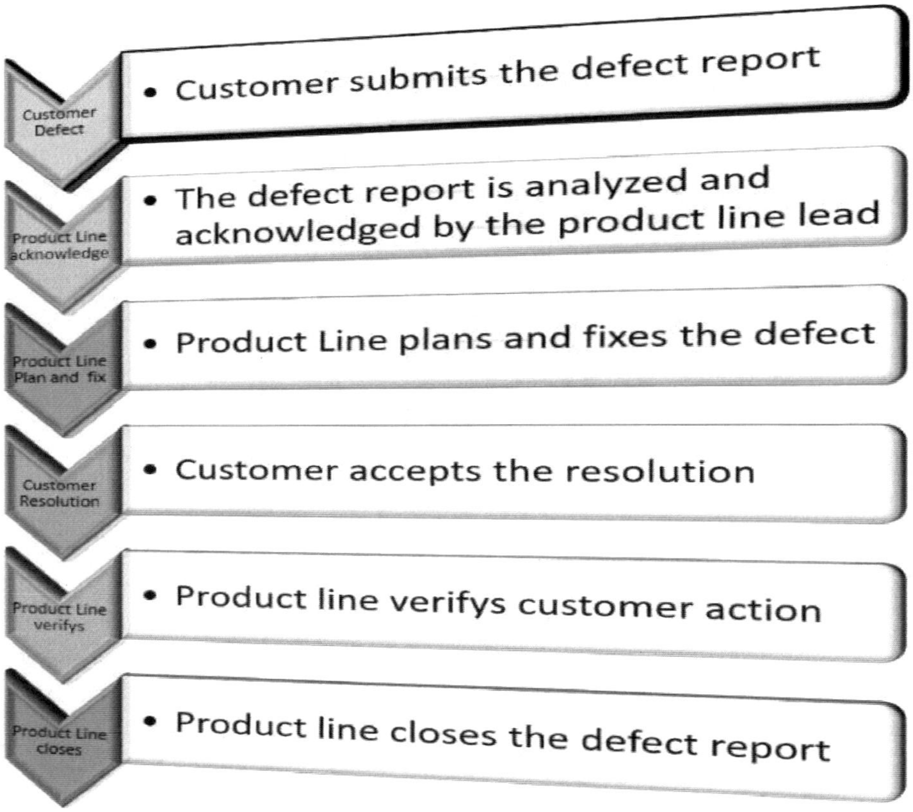

Figure 5: Customer Submitted Defects State Flow Diagram

The data presented include the following:

1. The total number of defects for each product line
2. Defects in state: open
3. Defects in state: in progress
4. Defects that has been fixed.

The below block diagram (Figure 6) explains the software design.

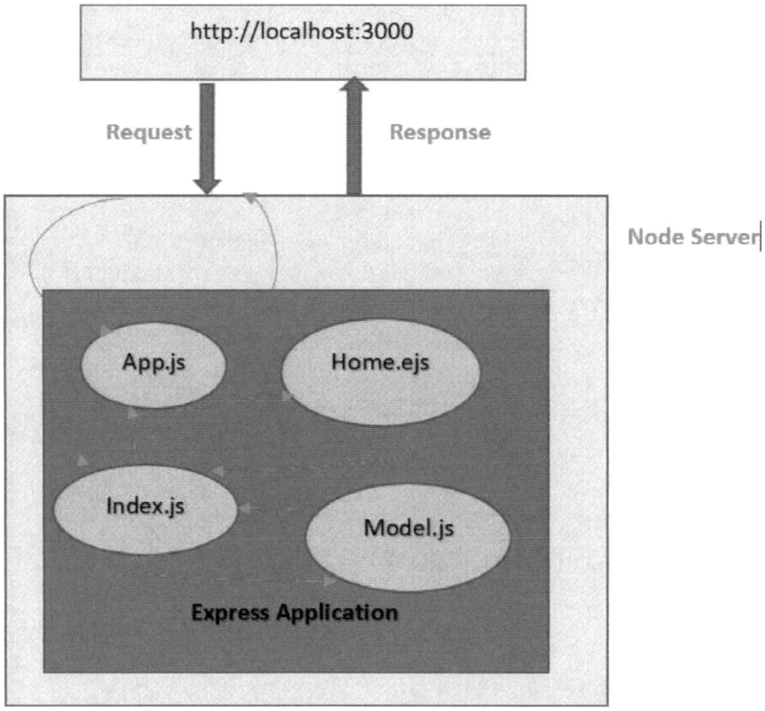

Figure 6: Block Diagram – Software Design

➢ To create a project with folder structure, use the following command: 'express express-demo-app --view=ejs'.

```
:\Users\rmohant1>express express-demo-proj --view=ejs

   create : express-demo-proj\
   create : express-demo-proj\public\
   create : express-demo-proj\public\javascripts\
   create : express-demo-proj\public\images\
   create : express-demo-proj\public\stylesheets\
   create : express-demo-proj\public\stylesheets\style.css
   create : express-demo-proj\routes\
   create : express-demo-proj\routes\index.js
   create : express-demo-proj\routes\users.js
   create : express-demo-proj\views\
   create : express-demo-proj\views\error.ejs
   create : express-demo-proj\views\index.ejs
   create : express-demo-proj\app.js
   create : express-demo-proj\package.json
   create : express-demo-proj\bin\
   create : express-demo-proj\bin\www

   change directory:
     > cd express-demo-proj

   install dependencies:
     > npm install

   run the app:
     > SET DEBUG=express-demo-proj:* & npm start
```

➢ Open the project using VS Code, project structure will look like this:

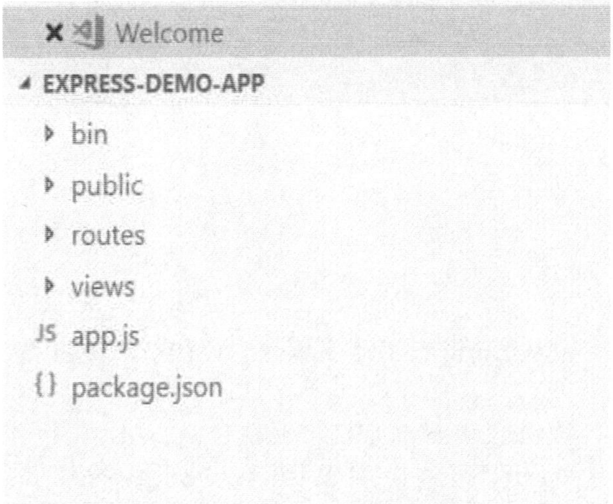

➢ Here app.js is the entry point to the application.

➢ In bin folder there will be a file with name 'www', which will contain the port number needed to run the application. We can specify the host name here as localhost.

```
var port = normalizePort(process.env.PORT || '3000');
app.set('port', port);

/**
 * Create HTTP server.
 */

var server = http.createServer(app);

/**
 * Listen on provided port, on all network interfaces.
 */

server.listen(port,"localhost");
server.on('error', onError);
server.on('listening', onListening);
```

➢ Public folder will contain all the UI related stuff, like image files, js files and css files.

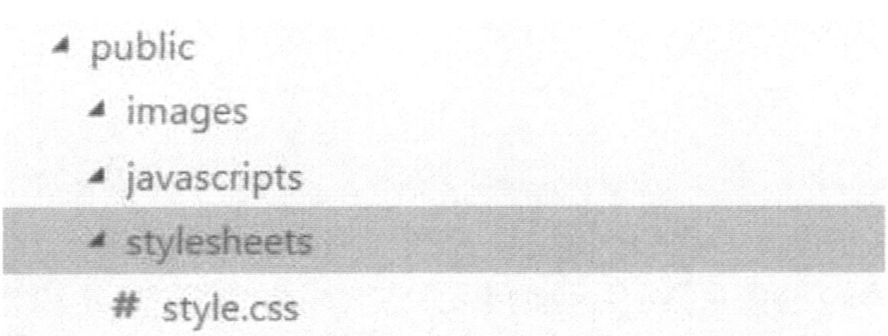

- View folder will contain all the .ejs files to create the web page UI.

```
▲ views
  <> error.ejs
  <> index.ejs
```

- Routes folder will contain all route .js files.

```
▲ routes
  JS index.js
  JS users.js
```

- Route files are the .js files, which will execute according to the request from the user.

Example:
If the URL is http://www.tek.com/ and if we need to display user controls and some other specific task, we need to redirect the request to 'index.js', as specified in the following code:

```
var index = require('./routes/index');
app.use('/', index);
```

If url is http://www.tek.com/user, we can redirect the request to 'user.js'.

```
var users = require('./routes/users');
app.use('/users', users);
```

- In route .js file we can specify different functions like this:

This function will execute for get request with '/' like http://www.tek.com/

```
router.get('/', function(req,res) {

  res.render('arts_home.ejs');
});
```

- Use 'nodemon' module, which will always watch the files of the application, if any file changes, it will automatically reload and restart the server. To install nodemon use the following command:
  'npm install -g nodemon'

➢ To start the application only, type 'nodemon'.
➢ To see the application, open the brower and type the URL accordingly, specify in 'www' file which is present in bin folder like http://localhost:3000 and you can see the application.
➢ The screenshot shown in Figure 7 displays the different states of customer submitted defects

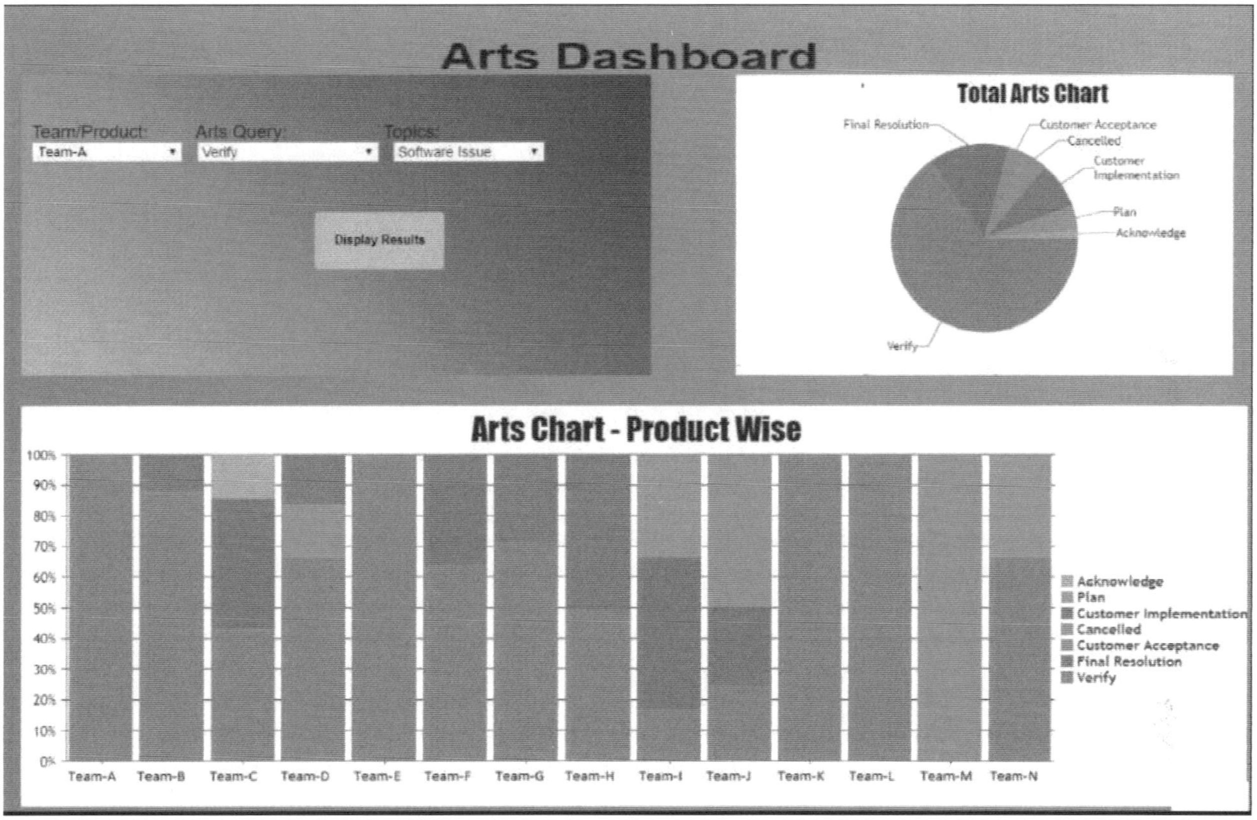

Figure 7: Defect Chart

6. Return on Investment (ROI) for Defects Data

In the time before the webpage was developed, when a new defect is submitted, the team would spend a day or two to download the defect list from the defect management tool for each of the products and then analyze the data and decide on a further course of action.
Once our tool was developed, it helped the team members to quickly get the data for their respective projects, analyze the defects and take appropriate action. There was steady progress in the saving time for analyzing the defects as shown in Figure 8.

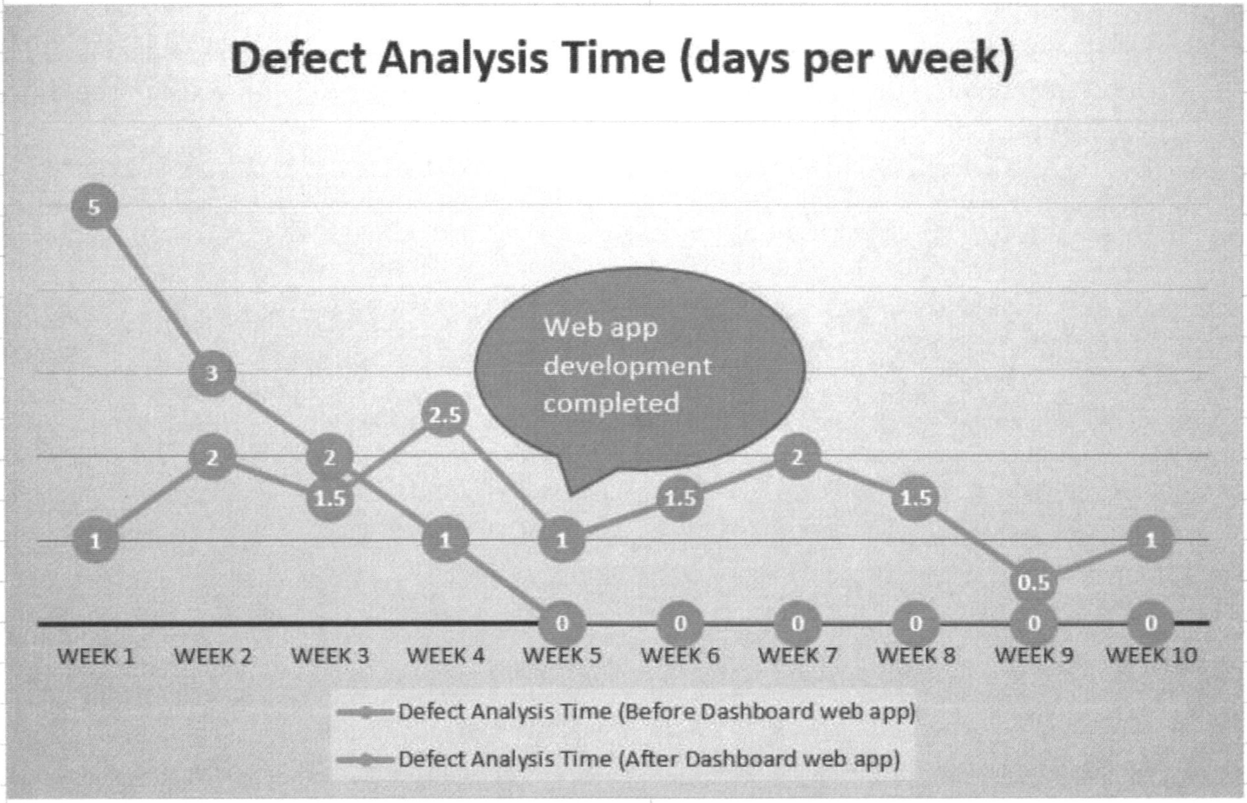

Figure 8: ROI

7. Conclusion

Before the development of the Dashboard web application, the data were scattered over various tools and it was difficult for the management to get overall statistics of the requirements, test cases coverage, and defect trends of the various products being developed. For each of the products the specific tools needed to be accessed, to extract the required data. Selecting MEAN stack tool for development helped us to build the application quickly, and we required only one resource who is good in a single language, i.e. Javascript, for both the front and back end. The MEAN stack components, being an open source tool, saves cost. Updates are available on a regular basis. MongoDB the database has several functionalities, which help to get query results faster and increase the performance in accessing the desired data.

This Dashboard web application helps us display the data for the requirements coverage, test cases coverage and defect trend at a single location for multiple products in the company.

The requirements coverage data provides a quick glance of the number of requirements implemented and not implemented in the products. The details enable better schedule prediction and release plans for the products.

The test cases coverage data help us understand how well we have tested the product against the requirements. The number of manual test cases vs automated test cases data help us better understand the test and release cycle time for any products that are being developed. In addition it serves as data for estimating the release date for future products.

Collecting data and analyzing the failures help us fix customer problems as quickly as possible. The teams are notified on a daily basis on the total defects open and the state of those defects. Since the data are available in a web site page, multiple teams can access it easily and work on the defects for which they are responsible. Accessing data from a common location help the team members to be coordinated with each other. Transparency is maintained at all levels i.e. from the developer to the manager on the defect fix rate, issues faced and how soon we can deliver a solution to the customer.

The dashboard application thus brought huge benefits in our organization and better communication with our team members who work in multiple locations. Single point of access helps all the team members, to access the data at any point of time and updated with the latest information.

For continuous improvement and exploring new ways to use MEAN stack, we are excited about the opportunities we have, to bring in more such applications like this to our organization.

8. Appendix

8.1. Installation of MongoDB on Windows System

MongoDB version 3.6 is the current stable released version available. The open source version of MongoDB is licensed under free software foundation, GNU AGPL (The Affero General Public license). We will use the open source license for developing our web application.

1. **Interactive Installation:**
   - Download the MongoDB.msi from this url:

https://www.mongodb.com/lp/download/mongodb-enterprise?jmp=nav

   - Double click the .msi file, follow the instructions, and complete the process.
   - If you don't change the installation path, then the default path will be: C:\Program Files\MongoDB\Server\<Version Of mongo dB>
   - During the installation, there will be an option to install MongoDB Compass, which is the user interface (UI) for MongoDB server. If you require to see or create the database through a UI, you need to use MongoDB Compass.

2. **Unattended Installation:**
- Open the Command Prompt with Administrator privilege.
- Go to the directory which contains the .msi file and use this command:
  msiexec.exe /q /i mongodb-win32-x86_64-2008plus-ssl-3.6.0-signed.msi ^
  INSTALLLOCATION="C:\Program Files\MongoDB\Server\3.6.0\" ^ADDLOCAL="all"

8.2. Running MongoDB on Windows System

1. **Set up the MongoDB environment:**
   - MongoDB requires Data Directory to store all data. Create the directory by running this command:
     EX: - "C:\Program Files\MongoDB\Server\3.6\bin\mongod.exe" --dbpath d:\test\mongodb\data
   - If the path contains any white space, enclose the entire path with double quotes.

2. **Start MongoDB:**
   - To start MongoDB, run mongod.exe from the command prompt:
     "C:\Program Files\MongoDB\Server\3.6\bin\mongod.exe"
   - This starts the MongoDB database process.

3. **Connect to MongoDB:**
   - To connect to MongoDB, open another command prompt and run the mongo.exe:
     "C:\Program Files\MongoDB\Server\3.6\bin\mongo.exe"

4. **Begin using MongoDB:**
   - MongoDB provides Getting Started Guides in various driver editions.

8.3. Configure a Windows Service for MongoDB

- Open the command prompt with Administrator privilege.
- To create directories for DB and log file enter the following commands:

  Mkdir c:\data\db

  Mkdir c:\data\log

- Create configuration file in the following path:

  C:\Program Files\MongoDB\Server\3.6\mongod.cfg

- Edit the config file using the following commands:

  SystemLog: destination: filepath: c:\data\log\mongod.log

  Storage: dbPath: c:\data\db

- To install the MongoDB service, open the command prompt with Administrator privilege and enter the following command:
  "C:\Program Files\MongoDB\Server\3.6\bin\mongod.exe" --config "C:\Program Files\MongoDB\Server\3.6\mongod.cfg" –install
- To start the MongoDB service type enter the following command:
  Net start MongoDB
- If you want to stop the MongoDB service use the following command:
  Net stop MongoDB
- To remove the MongoDB service, use the following command:
  "C:\Program Files\MongoDB\Server\3.6\bin\mongod.exe" --remove

8.4. Installation of NodeJS on Windows System

Download NodeJS

- From the official site, download Node.js according to OS Type:
  https://nodejs.org/en/download/

About NPM

- NPM (Node Package Manager) is automatically installed when you install Node.js.
- NPM is used to download the modules and packages, which you need to use to develop different applications.
- To check the NPM version, open the Node.js Command Prompt and type the following command:
  Npm -version

8.5. Installation of ExpressJS on Windows System

Express Installation

- Before installing Express make sure that NodeJS and NPM are installed on the machine.
- To start writing the code for creating the web application, you can use different types of editors like Visual Studio Code, Sublime Text, etc.
- You can download and install the Visual Studio Code (VS Code) from the given link: https://code.visualstudio.com/download
- To install ExpressJS, you can use the Command prompt or the terminal given by VS Code.

- To open the terminal in VS Code, view option in the tool bar of the editor and then click Integrated Terminal option.
- Now type the following command "**npm install express --save**", it will create node_module directory and package-lock.json file.
  Node_module directory will contain all packages required for Express

```
c:\project>cd ExpressDemo

c:\project\ExpressDemo>npm init
This utility will walk you through creating a package.json file.
It only covers the most common items, and tries to guess sensible defaults.

See `npm help json` for definitive documentation on these fields
and exactly what they do.

Use `npm install <pkg>` afterwards to install a package and
save it as a dependency in the package.json file.

Press ^C at any time to quit.
package name: (expressdemo) expressdemo
version: (1.0.0) 0.0.0.1
Invalid version: "0.0.0.1"
version: (1.0.0) 1.0.1
description: EXpress Demo Application
entry point: (index.js)
test command:
git repository:
keywords:
author: Rishikanta Mohanty
license: (ISC)
About to write to c:\project\ExpressDemo\package.json:

{
  "name": "expressdemo",
  "version": "1.0.1",
  "description": "EXpress Demo Application",
  "main": "index.js",
  "scripts": {
    "test": "echo \"Error: no test specified\" && exit 1"
  },
  "author": "Rishikanta Mohanty",
  "license": "ISC"
}


Is this ok? (yes) yes
```

- It will create the package.json; it will contain all the package information, which you install for the application.
- Create the entry point of your application that is index.js specified in package.json file.
- In index.js, you will write the code.
- To start the application, use the command (node index).
- To access the application, open the browser and type http://localhost:3000 (3000 is the port number specified in index.js file, you can assign a different port number also).
- To develop the UI, there are different templates available like EJS, Pug, etc.

- For this project, use EJS (Embedded JavaScript Template).
- By using EJS, you can generate the HTML page by using plain JavaScript.
- To install EJS in your application, type the following command: **npm install ejs**
- For more information on EJS, you can visit the link: http://ejs.co/

8.6. Installation of Angular JS

- Angular CLI is a command line tool by using this we can create projects and perform different tasks like testing, building and deployment.
- Before installing Angular make sure Node.js and npm is installed in your development environment.
- To work with latest Angular JS, make sure you are using Node.js version 8.x or greater and npm version 5.x or greater.
- To install Angular CLI globally open a command prompt and enter the below command

npm install -g @angular/cli

```
C:\Users\rmohant1>npm install -g @angular/cli
C:\Users\rmohant1\AppData\Roaming\npm\ng -> C:\Users\rmohant1\AppData\Roaming\npm\node_modules\@angular\cli\bin\ng
npm WARN optional SKIPPING OPTIONAL DEPENDENCY: fsevents@1.2.4 (node_modules\@angular\cli\node_modules\fsevents):
npm WARN notsup SKIPPING OPTIONAL DEPENDENCY: Unsupported platform for fsevents@1.2.4: wanted {"os":"darwin","arch":"any"} (current: {"os":"win32","arch":"x64"})

+ @angular/cli@6.1.2
added 26 packages, removed 720 packages, updated 68 packages and moved 11 packages in 72.115s
```

It will take some time to install all related files.

- To create a new project, open a command prompt and go to the directory where you want to create the project and enter the below command

ng new angular-demo-app

It will create the project with name "angular-demo-app" with all the required files.

- To run the application open a command prompt and go to the project folder and type the below command

ng serve –open

It will open the application in the browser.

```
C:\Users\rmohant1\my-anglaur>ng serve --open
Your global Angular CLI version (6.1.2) is greater than your local
version (1.7.4). The local Angular CLI version is used.

To disable this warning use "ng config -g cli.warnings.versionMismatch false".
** NG Live Development Server is listening on localhost:4200, open your browser on http://localhost:4200/ **
 16% building modules 52/55 modules 3 active ...r\node_modules\html-entities\index.jswebpack: wait until bundle finished: /
te: 2018-08-08T10:07:47.394Z
Hash: d0f522f5888b504b7d24
Time: 6095ms
chunk {inline} inline.bundle.js (inline) 3.85 kB [entry] [rendered]
chunk {main} main.bundle.js (main) 18.1 kB [initial] [rendered]
chunk {polyfills} polyfills.bundle.js (polyfills) 555 kB [initial] [rendered]
chunk {styles} styles.bundle.js (styles) 41.5 kB [initial] [rendered]
chunk {vendor} vendor.bundle.js (vendor) 7.43 MB [initial] [rendered]

webpack: Compiled successfully.
```

References

http://mean.io/
https://www.mongodb.com/
http://expressjs.com/
https://angularjs.org/
https://nodejs.org/en/
https://resources.mongodb.com/migrating-to-mongodb/mongodb-quantifying-business-advantage
https://en.wikipedia.org/wiki/JSON

Changing Engineering Culture with SDETs

Authors

Sheetal Hulloli (sheetal_hulloli@mcafee.com)
Santosh Sahu (Santosh_sahu@mcafee.com)
Mayur Premi (mayor_premi@mcafee.com)

Abstract

Often, the silos of Development and Blackbox Testing groups within an Engineering team result from issues that are more than mere skill differences. There is a much larger cultural aspect that usually needs addressing for an engineering team that has clear cut Development and Blackbox Testing roles but struggles to deliver quality software. While an all-round engineering team must have various skills, we want to highlight the importance and the role of "Software Development Engineers in Test" (SDET) in bringing about a culture change in engineering paradigm. When our own team at McAfee made the conscious decision to arm the team with SDETs, little was known as to what they would do and how their role would be different than the clear-cut demarcations that already existed. As we found out, it was a journey that resulted in greater collaboration, testing of areas unheard of in the team, increased operational efficiencies and a mature engineering team. In this paper we want to share our experience of how SDETs were change agents in the evolution of our engineering team, what challenges we faced along the way and how we were able to overcome barriers as a team. We hope to highlight the following:

1. What a model testing team should be comprised of in skill sets (SDET, Automation, and Product Experts)
2. How the role of SDETs differ from Blackbox/System testing roles
3. Why SDETs are important in fast paced engineering environments (with our own example of a complex product platform)
4. How to hire, train and engage successful SDETs
5. What metrics to introduce to measure success
6. Making role models out of SDETs
7. Seeing measurable improvements in product quality by using SDETs
8. Using SDETs to take the team to the next level

Our paper will cite real examples and we hope that our experience will give engineering leaders an insight into how they can bring about change in their teams but more importantly that we will encourage young engineering professionals to look at becoming future SDETs.

Biography

Sheetal Hulloli is a Senior SDET in McAfee with twelve years of industry experience in software testing and quality assurance.
Santosh Sahu is a Senior Software QA Engineer in McAfee with around nine years of industry experience in software development, testing and quality assurance.
Mayur Premi is a Senior Software Engineer in McAfee with around ten years of industry experience in software development.

1. Introduction

Nowadays, performance and scalability requirements have drastically increased to cater modern business information systems. It is often seen that the performance validation is pushed to the end of the release cycle this could result in uncovering problems that can jeopardize the original project goals and deadlines. Hence, it is essential to focus on performance at the early stages of development.

Software is always evolving and growing in complexity. In a typical environment where multiple security software co-exist depending on a single platform product, the software quality and early availability of the dependent software becomes paramount.

Being a platform product, multiple security solutions (products) had to be integrated with us to make them extremely powerful to fight cyber-attacks. To cater newer business and security needs, we decided to revamp our product architecture and design. As we embraced the new design, technology and implementation, we felt it was also time to re-think on the process that we had been following for our sustenance projects - traditional approach of Dev team and QA (Quality Assurance) team. The process followed being Agile, which required a parallel code and test development.

2. Thinking Beyond the Traditional Approach

The new design and implementation gave us an opportunity to try out our new idea - test the code before the build with the core modules integrated was ready, so that this could be consumed by our internal security software products. This demanded the team have engineers adopting the new role of software test developers a.k.a. SDET (Software Development Engineer in Test) s.

Being a team that followed the traditional software procedure having virtually two groups - software development and Testing group (QA) despite working for the same product, the first thought was to look outside for engineers to fit this new role in the team. After hiring a few SDETs, we came to realize this was an uphill task as there aren't many who could effectively satisfy our need.

The thought crossed our minds – Why shouldn't we look for our own teammates who could fit this role by following a few transitioning steps to become SDETs? But there were a few storms that had to be weathered – How to change the engineering culture? What are the transition steps? How do we measure and appreciate success?

3. Challenges – Weather the Storm

We also knew this transition could not be done overnight because it involves

1. Addressing the cultural change in the team.
2. Removing Engineers' stigma to adopting the new role, as they were not sure about the expectation for this role.
3. Coming onboard the required skills and meeting the expectations.

Considering a team such as the one mentioned under modern approach - having an SDET engineer, who could be a developer willing to test software or a black box QA engineer who could write tools to test the software, will help in early identification of defects. With automation engineers available, automating end-to-end scenarios during early phase of software development would drastically bring down the manual regression time and increases the team's confidence in the software.

Traditional Approach
1. Developers
2. Black Box QA
3. Process - Water Fall/Agile

Modern Approach
1. Developers
2. Software Development Test Engineers (Dev/QA)
3. QA Engineers as Product Champions (PCs)
4. Automation Engineers (Develop the automation frame work)
5. Process – Agile

4. SDETS are Change Agents – How?

The team's composition being this – Developers, SDET, PC (Product Champion) s, and Automation Engineers to bring in early defects and confidence, greater collaboration amongst them was needed.

1. As the product design discussion started, the SDETs and PCs (aspiring to become SDETs) were very much part of the discussion to understand and provide constructive feedback on the design.

2. SDETs worked collaboratively with developers to come up with UT (Unit Test) and WB (White Box) Framework and to add test cases incrementally.

3. After the Design Commit phase, in parallel to the development activity, SDETs were made available with a prototype of the module (in the form of header files) to start test preparation.

4. SDETs also worked with the PCs to help them understand the test frameworks (UT and White Box Testing), provide training on development and testing tools (Visual Studio, WinDbg, Valgrind, BullsEye, Coverity)

5. SDETs and PCs came up with test plan and test cases for modules under development and seek early feedback from developers.

6. Module development was done in phased manner where, upon every module phase completion, the library was available for SDETs to work on the following checks: Unit Testing, Error Conditions, Test for buffer overflow error, Memory Leak errors, Design deviation, False Positive behavior tests, Boundary Value Checks.

7. Being a product that will be integrated by multiple internal security products, conscious decision to test modules used by them was taken as part of SDK (Software Development Kit) testing. As part of this activity, exposed APIs for integration would be tested in a WB framework. The focus was on Argument errors, functional behavior, and scenario-based testing.

8. Based on the results of above tests, the module was either re-worked or made available as part of nightly builds.

The other area of focus was Automation where, automation engineers came up with an automation framework to test E2E scenarios.

1. They worked closely with PCs on the end-to-end scenario identification and get early feedback from the developers.
2. PCs (aspiring to become automation experts) where given training on scripting language, working and execution of automation framework.

Finally, with all the collaborative work, on the nightly build with incrementally developed modules, following validations are done in parallel - UT suite, static Analysis check and automation would be run.

Additionally, these builds were used to measure the code coverage against the available UTs. This code coverage results also facilitated the SDETs to add more UT cases to identify negative scenarios and dead-code. This activity ensured that "the code" is tested to the maximum using WB methodology.

Now comes the million-dollar question – How QA engineers were transformed to SDETs and Automation Experts? What are transition steps? Our long journey on product development provided the answer - in order to adopt the above said new approach we came across the following transition phases in our team.

5. The Transformation Approach

Based on the current role an engineer plays in the software industry, we would like to propose different approaches for transformation to SDET considering the current role of team member.

5.1. Approach 1 – Transition of Black Box QA Engineer to SDET

The first approach is for an engineer who currently performs quality assurance and testing using typical black box methodology and aspires to be a SDET

1. Identify a black box QA engineer willing to transform into a SDET.
2. Provide the language training related to software, if required.
3. Undergo training from developers on product implementation and design.
4. Participate on code reviews and design discussions.
5. Start developing UT and tools that tests software modules

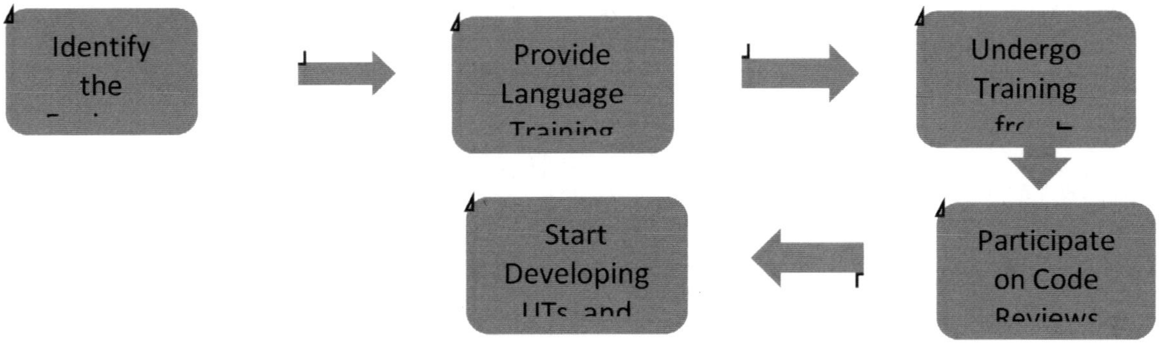

5.2. Approach 2 – Transition of Black Box QA Engineer to Automation Engineer

The second approach is for an engineer who currently performs quality assurance and testing using typical black box methodology and aspires to be an automation engineer who basically writes code to test the commonly used functionality of the software to provide quick confidence on the software builds.

1. Identify a black box QA engineer willing to transform into an automation engineer.
2. Provide the language training related to automation, if required.
3. Undergo training from product champions on software from end-to-end user perspective.
4. Identify features or test cases that could be automated.
5. Design frameworks and start automating feature test cases.

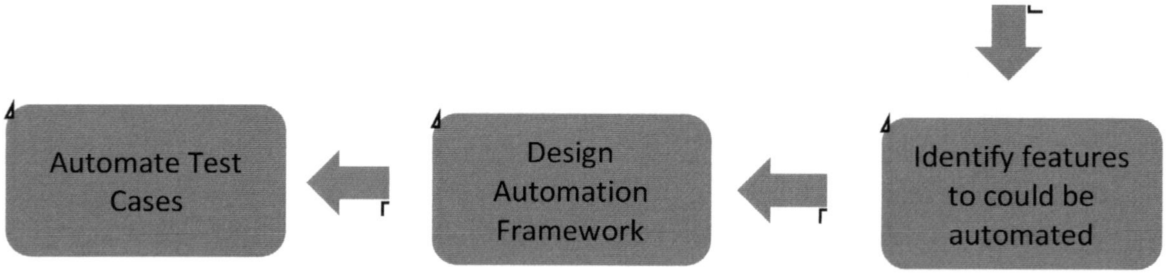

5.3. Approach 3 – Transition of a Developer to SDET

The third approach is for an engineer who currently develops software is aspiring to perform the role of an SDET.

1. Undergo training from PC understand the software from end-to-end user perspective.
2. Identify the features that could be tested using test tools.
3. Start developing test tools on the features.
4. Integrate with automation framework for daily run.

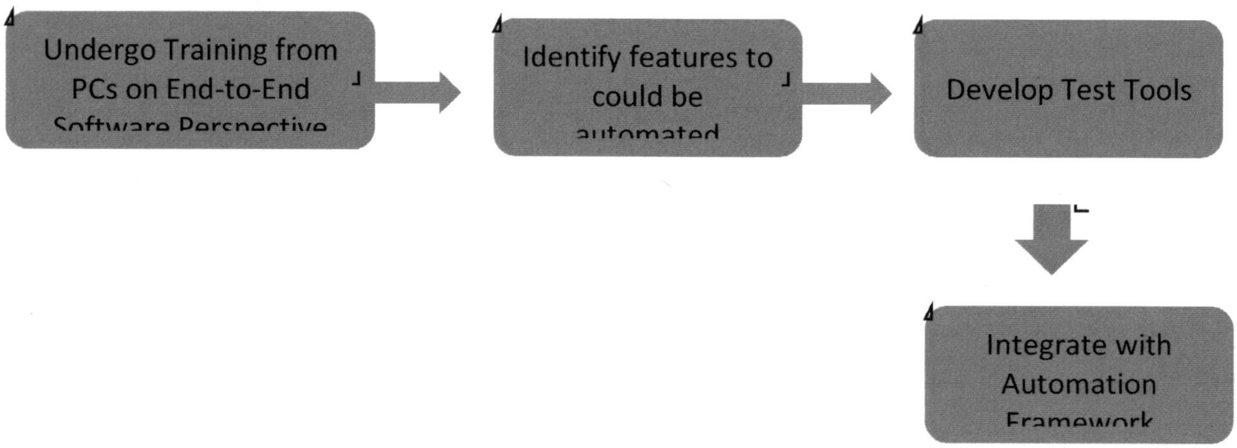

6. Results

Traditionally team's release check-list would e – BVT (Basic Verification Test), FVT (Functional Verification Test), Soak, Regression, Open Defects etc.

With the new approach the check-list was modified as – Unit Test, Memory Leak check, Scenario based white box testing, Static Analysis, FVT, BVT, Soak, Automation Results, Number of high severity open defects.

Advantage of a PC (one who is aware of the end-to-end functionality of the product) transitioning as an automation engineer would ensure the presence of better automation framework that suits the product and yield better test coverage.

Defect Removal Method	Minimum Efficiency	Maximum Efficiency	Average Efficiency
Formal design inspection	65%	97%	87%
Formal code inspection	60%	96%	85%
Static analysis	65%	95%	85%
Pair Programming	40%	65%	55%
Informal Peer Review	35%	60%	50%
Risk-based Testing	55%	80%	70%
System Testing	27%	55%	42%
Unit Testing	20%	50%	40%
Regression Testing	35%	45%	35%
Acceptance Testing	15%	40%	35%

Source: The Economics of Software Quality by Capers Jones, Olivier Bonsignour

How gaps in the Testing life cycle were filled by SDET activity's and their early feedback right from design discussion phase to actual end to end scenario testing. This will help to get quality product at the end of the life cycle.

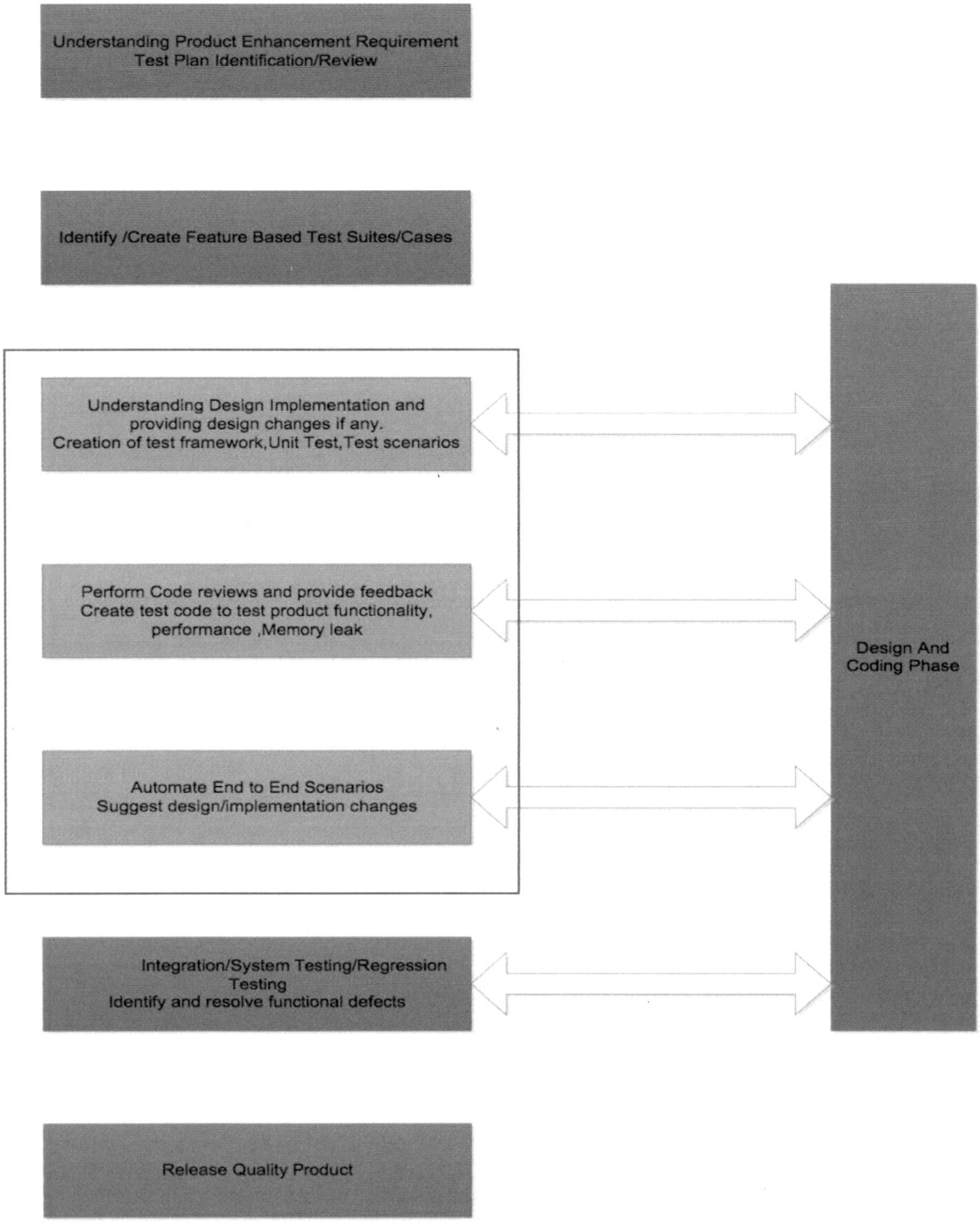
Understanding Product Enhancement Requirement
Test Plan Identification/Review
Identify /Create Feature Based Test Suites/Cases
Understanding Design Implementation and
providing design changes if any.
Creation of test framework,Unit Test,Test scenarios
Perform Code reviews and provide feedback
Create test code to test product functionality,
performance ,Memory leak
Automate End to End Scenarios
Suggest design/implementation changes
Integration/System Testing/Regression
Testing
Identify and resolve functional defects
Release Quality Product
Design And
Coding Phase

Resources.

The Economics of Software Quality by Capers Jones, Olivier Bonsignour

Acronyms

QA	-	Quality Assurance
SDET	-	Software Development Engineer in Test
PC	-	Product Champion
UT	-	Unit Test
WBT	-	White Box Testing
VS	-	Visual Studio
SDK	-	Software Development Kit
FVT	-	Functional Verification Test
BVT	-	Basic Verification Test

PNSQC/Pacific Agenda
PO Box 10733
Portland, OR 97296-0733
USA

ISBN 978-1-5108-7042-0

CURRAN ASSOCIATES INC.
proceedings.com